Structured Equity Derivatives

Wiley Finance Series

Structured Equity Derivatives

The Definitive Guide to Exotic
Options and Structured Notes

Harry M. Kat

JOHN WILEY & SONS, LTD

Chichester • New York • Weinheim • Brisbane • Singapore • Toronto

Other Wiley Editorial Offices

John Wiley & Sons Inc., 111 River Street, Hoboken, NJ 07030, USA

Jossey-Bass, 989 Market Street, San Francisco, CA 94103-1741, USA

Wiley-VCH Verlag GmbH, Boschstr. 12, D-69469 Weinheim, Germany

John Wiley & Sons Australia Ltd, 33 Park Road, Milton, Queensland 4064, Australia

John Wiley & Sons (Asia) Pte Ltd, 2 Clementi Loop #02-01, Jin Xing Distripark,
Singapore 129809

John Wiley & Sons (Canada) Ltd, 22 Worcester Road, Etobicoke, Ontario M9W 1L1

Wiley also publishes its books in a variety of electronic formats. Some content that
appears in print may not be available in electronic books.

Library of Congress Cataloging-in-Publication Data

Kat, Harry M.
  Structured equity derivatives : the definitive guide to exotic options and structured
notes / Harry M. Kat
  p. cm.–(Wiley finance series)
Includes bibliographical references and index.
ISBN-10: 0–471–48652–3
ISBN-13: 978–0471–48652–7
  1. Derivative securities. 2. Exotic options (Finance) 3. Structured notes (Securities)
I.Title. II. Series
HG6024.A3 K385 2001
332.63′2-dc21   2001023390

British Library Cataloguing in Publication Data

A catalogue record for this book is available from the British Library

ISBN-10: 0 471 48652 3 (HBK)   ISBN-13: 978 0471 48652 7 (HBK)

Typeset in 10/12pt Times by Laser Words, Chennai, India
Printed and bound in Great Britain by Biddles Ltd, King's Lynn, Norfolk
This book is printed on acid-free paper responsibly manufactured from sustainable
forestry, in which at least two trees are planted for each one used for paper production.

Contents

Preface

Derivatives structuring is about designing financial instruments to solve financial economic problems. The problems that derivatives may solve are virtually unlimited. Derivatives can be used to manage exposure to a large variety of risks, enhance yield or reduce funding costs. In addition, derivatives can also be used to exploit the tax, accounting and regulatory environment. Although the theoretical pricing and hedging of derivatives has been dealt with in a large number of working papers, articles and books, surprisingly little has been written about the structuring and practical applications of derivatives. Whenever so, the discussion tends to be restricted to the applications of a given type of instruments, like index futures, interest rate swaps or currency options for example. The same product orientation is also found in day-to-day practice, where derivatives structurers[1] spend most of their time on the question of which of a given set of products or combination of products provides the best solution to the problem at hand.

When the addition of a new product to the existing product range is very time-consuming, this so-called 'building block' or 'LEGO' approach seems justified. Over the last 10 years, however, both our understanding of derivatives pricing and risk management, as well as the speed with which the required calculations can be performed, have increased tremendously. Today, the availability of a general and efficient pricing and risk management framework makes it possible for derivatives structurers to leave the product-based LEGO approach to derivatives structuring behind and adopt a more natural and flexible approach. One of the main goals of this book is to introduce derivatives structurers to such an approach.

Since our approach assumes that everything is possible, it allows derivatives structurers to creatively structure solutions to a large variety of problems in a very natural way. As in the traditional approach, the starting point of all discussions is a specific problem to be solved. Instead of (a combination of) ready-made products, however, the solutions to these problems consist of tailor-made packages of cash flows. Whether these packages already exist as a product or not is only of secondary importance. What is important is that they provide the best solution to the problem in question. We fit solutions to problems instead of problems to solutions. The reader will see the most complex derivatives contracts arise as the obvious solutions to common real-life problems. The approach is an extremely natural one. The only limit is the structurer's own creativity.

---

[1] We use the term 'derivatives structurer' for any person involved in derivatives structuring. As such it not only entails end-users and their consultants, but also derivatives marketers, derivatives traders, etc.

Throughout the book we approach matters from the **end-user's perspective**. This contrasts with most other books which tend to take the point of view of the derivatives firm instead of that of the end-user. This concentration on production technology is quite surprising if one realizes that the number of people within a derivatives firm responsible for the actual pricing and hedging of derivatives contracts is very small. In other words, the bulk of the derivatives literature seems to be aimed at only a handful of people. Given its unique orientation, this book complements virtually any other book on derivatives published so far. Even in the one chapter on derivatives pricing the reader will hardly find any overlap with other books. Basically, this is the book that everybody should read before picking up any other more technical book on the pricing and hedging of derivatives.

Apart from the well-known Black–Scholes–Merton formula there are **no complex pricing formulas or numerical procedures** to be found in this book as we concentrate on derivative product design and not pricing. Prices are thought to come from a derivatives firm's trading desk, calculated using a pricing framework more or less typical of those used by the major derivatives firms. This emphasizes that derivatives structuring is first and foremost '**financial architecture**' and not 'financial engineering'. The financial engineer only comes in when the structuring process yields products that the derivatives firm has not traded before. Given the enormous progress which financial engineers have made over the last decade, however, most structuring nowadays can be done without having to fall back on a financial engineer. The emphasis on intuition and common sense rather than complex formal results makes this book accessible to people with a large variety of backgrounds. Despite the fact that there are 414 equations in the book, highschool math will prove to be more than sufficient.

Because there is very little written on the actual structuring of derivatives this book is not an overview of the available literature nor is it a collection of previously published articles. Instead of teaching the reader a little bit of everything but not enough of anything, the aim of this book is to teach the reader a profession. The book can be used as a reference guide on a multitude of issues long after reading it for the first time. Moreover, although we restrict ourselves to equity derivatives, the approach advocated works for any type of derivative irrespective of the reference index used. Exactly the same approach we use here to structure equity derivatives can be used to structure interest rate, FX, commodity, credit, energy, catastrophe derivatives, etc.

Contrary to popular belief, derivatives are not a recent phenomenon. Early references can be found in the writings of Aristotle, who tells us about the philosopher Thales of Miletus (625–547 B.C.) who made a fortune from buying options on the use of olive presses. A bit closer to the present, American investors have had access to an OTC equity options market (then termed 'privileges' instead of options) for more than a century. Following the Civil War, an active market in put and call options developed in New York with numerous brokers quoting bid and ask prices for options on a dozen stocks. These brokers also provided advice as to how options might be used as part of an investment strategy. Things in those days were not too different from what goes on in today's derivatives markets. This underlines the fact that in terms of ideas and applications finance practitioners are often way ahead of academics.

The book is made up of two parts. In the first part, which covers Chapters 1–5, we introduce **the general philosophy and the derivatives structurer's toolbox**. In Chapter 1 we present our cash flow-based approach to derivatives structuring. The approach is extremely general. It is not restricted to equity derivatives but can be used to structure any kind of financial product. In Chapter 2 we discuss stock market indices, the most common reference indices for equity derivatives. We discuss how they are calculated as well as how they have behaved over the last 10 years. Chapter 3 deals with the various rights and restrictions that can be found in derivatives contracts. We discuss so-called knock-in and knock-out features in quite some detail as they have become one of the most popular extras in derivatives contracts. In Chapter 4 we discuss index-linked cash flows. This chapter provides an overview of most of the cash flow structures that are around nowadays. In Chapter 5 we discuss how derivatives firms price derivatives contracts. A detailed treatment of this subject would fill a book by itself. There are, however, too many of them around already, so we keep the discussion quite general.

In the second part of the book, which covers Chapters 6–13, we use the approach and tools developed in Chapters 1–5 to solve a large variety of real-life problems. In these chapters it will become clear that for a derivatives firm there are two ways to sell derivatives. First, it can structure derivatives as cheaper, more efficient alternatives to traditional cash market transactions. Second, it can structure derivatives contracts which allow end-users to do things that would not have been possible otherwise. Of course, to do this successfully one must thoroughly understand the relevant goals and restrictions. In Chapters 6–8 we investigate how equity derivatives can help **institutional investors** like mutual funds, hedge funds, pension funds and life insurance companies. In Chapter 6 we investigate how equity derivatives can help institutional investors to improve efficiency by reducing operational and transaction costs as well as by avoiding undesirable regulatory and fiscal effects. In Chapters 7 and 8 we study how equity derivatives can be used to tailor the payoff of an investment portfolio to the specific views and preferences of its manager. We look at general asset allocation strategies as well as the timing of market entry and market exit.

Over the last five years stock market investing has gained substantially in popularity among **retail investors**. Apart from stocks or mutual funds, many retail investors have bought specially designed products. Most of these products, which have become extremely popular with retail investors in Europe, can be classified as so-called equity-linked notes. In Chapters 9–12 we discuss the structuring and pricing of equity-linked notes in great detail. There are two reasons why we spend four chapters on this subject. First, it allows the reader to see a large number of worked out examples. This provides not only a valuable overview of the different types of notes and options around, but also what might be called 'synthetic experience'. Second, equity-linked notes are the ideal platform to justify the existence of exotic equity derivatives. Although derivatives firms would like us to believe otherwise, the bulk of the more exotic contracts traded in the market end up in equity-linked notes and similar products. In Chapter 13 we turn to products designed for investors who want equity exposure but do not have enough money available to actually buy stocks or equity-linked notes. We discuss in detail how such equity-linked savings products are structured, as well as their pricing and marketing. Following Chapter 13, the reader will find a brief overview of the major stock market indices in the world, a glossary of the option contracts discussed in the book, as well as a very extensive bibliography.

The idea to write a book on derivatives structuring which is accessible to the non-mathematical reader resulted partly from a desire to write down and pass on what I found out over the years, and partly from dissatisfaction with the sometimes very high level of abstraction in modern finance theory. Until the 1960s finance was a very practical subject, concentrating on financial statement analysis, taxation, regulation, etc. In the late sixties and seventies, however, finance turned into a special branch of neo-classical price theory. Instead of accounting and law, modern finance concentrates on the abstract formalization and analysis of products and decision-making problems. By itself there is nothing wrong with this. As a matter of fact, it is exactly what we will be doing in this book. The problem, however, is that an increasing number of finance researchers appear to get caught up in their abstract theoretical models and elaborate econometric techniques. Many of them know a lot about a variety of theoretical models and methods, but appear to know little about the actual structure and extreme complexity of the world they are supposedly modeling. As a result, it can sometimes be very hard to find a satisfactory academic answer to a perfectly sound practical question. In this context it is also interesting to note that a well-known academic publisher declined to publish this book because it was thought to be 'too practical to appeal to the academic market'.

Over the years, the number of individuals who took the time to answer my questions has become too numerous to mention. Some, however, deserve special acknowledgement. First of all, I would like to thank many of my former colleagues at the University of Amsterdam, MeesPierson (Amsterdam), First Chicago (Tokyo), TMG Financial Products (London) and Bank of America (London) for a very interesting time in many more areas than just finance. Brian Scott-Quinn, my boss at the ISMA Centre at the University of Reading, created the perfect environment to finish the book as planned. Jaap van Dijk (UBS Warburg) provided the data used in Chapter 2. Jaime Cuevas Dermody (Adams, Viner and Mosler) gave me one of his computers because he was fed up not being able to correspond with me by e-mail. Michael Bull (Dresdner Kleinwort Benson) kept me informed about developments in the OTC index options market. Alexander Ineichen (UBS Warburg) provided general information on the market for guaranteed structured products in Europe and supplied Figures 5.10–5.12. Jan Meulenbelt (ING Investment Management) hired me as a consultant to his structured investment products group, which has resulted in many valuable discussions and ideas.

Although we do not go into technical details, much of the book is about what happens to the prices of options and structured notes if one or more parameters are changed. To efficiently produce these insights a large number of complex option and structured note pricing routines had to be programmed. I could not have completed the book in time without the help of the following former ISMA Centre students: Alistair Fox, Dimitris Gkoutzioupas, Michalis Ioannides and Stefania Serato. The book has also benefitted from the comments and suggestions of Peter Carr (Banc of America Securities), Don Chance (Virginia Tech), Tony Herbst (University of Texas, El Paso), Ira Kawaller (Kawaller & Co.), Jack Marshall (Marshall, Tucker & Associates), Anthony Neuberger (London Business School), Mark Rubinstein (University of California, Berkeley), and Ali Yigit-basioglu (ISMA Centre). Of course, all remaining errors are my own. I wish to devote special thanks to my wife Marion for her unlimited support and encouragement. Since it must be difficult to be married to a man who spends his time reading, writing, watching TV and working in the garden, I hope that the proceeds of this book will at least be sufficient to buy her that new Range Rover I promised her some time ago.

Finally, I accept that a work of this size will never be complete or perfect. Therefore, if you have any comments or suggestions that could improve the book, please do not hesitate to contact me at Comments@harrykat.com.

1
The General Framework

1.1 INTRODUCTION

Derivatives structuring is about solving problems. These problems may take many different forms. Corporate treasurers for example will always be on the lookout for ways to reduce their company's funding costs, or to enhance the yield on short-term investments. In addition, they may want to hedge or speculate on movements in interest rates, exchange rates and commodity prices, credit exposure, etc. Investment managers will be interested in reducing the costs of exposure adjustments, hedging against or speculating on expected market movements, and all forms of yield enhancement. Banks and life insurance companies are always looking for new products to offer to their client base; new types of loans and mortgages as well as new investment, life insurance and pension products. Of course, all these problems have to be solved within the relevant institutional framework, i.e. taking into account the relevant tax, accounting and regulatory environment. What looks like a good idea at first sight may be a lot less interesting from a tax, accounting or regulatory point of view. In this chapter we introduce the general framework to solve problems like these. The discussion in this chapter is kept very general. It simply sets the stage for a much more detailed discussion in Chapters 2–5.

1.2 CASH FLOWS

The natural building blocks of the derivatives structurer are **cash flows**, i.e. payments from one counterparty to another. Generally speaking, a cash flow is characterized by two parameters:

- The **amount** to be exchanged.
- The **date** on which the exchange takes place.

With respect to the amount we can distinguish between two types of cash flows: fixed and index-linked. A **fixed cash flow** concerns the exchange of a prefixed amount. For example, the payment of USD 100 million three months from now. With an **index-linked cash flow** the amount to be exchanged is not fixed in advance but depends on the future value(s) of one or more variables; the so-called **reference indices**. Since the future values of these reference indices are unknown in the present, index-linked cash flows are inherently uncertain.

The goal of the derivatives structurer is to package fixed and/or index-linked cash flows together in such a way that the particular problem at hand is solved. Since money is a valuable commodity, both counterparties will typically end up paying each other; sometimes on the same dates, sometimes on different dates. The payment dates are not the biggest worry though, nor are the fixed cash flows. The real challenge for the derivatives structurer lies in the index-linked cash flows.

1.3   REFERENCE INDICES

When structuring derivatives the first question to ask is what the relevant reference indices are. In other words, what are the relevant risk factors for the problem at hand? New problems introduce new reference indices. This means that there is no complete list of possible reference indices. However, many problems dealt with by derivatives structurers involve some kind of market risk. The most popular reference indices to link cash flows to are therefore **market prices**, such as

• Stock prices
• Bond prices
• Interest rates
• Exchange rates
• Commodity prices

Apart from taking the price level itself as the relevant reference index, one may also **derive new indices** from these price levels, for example by taking a moving average. Note that the above indices are either expressed in money terms or as a percentage.

Apart from market prices, derivatives structurers may sometimes also use **other economic variables** as reference indices, such as

• Stock market indices
• Macro-economic price indices
• Credit ratings
• The occurrence of a default or a takeover
• The total of claims made to one or more insurance companies during some period and attributable to some catastrophe

A third group of reference indices consists of **non-economic variables**, such as

• The outcome of a lottery
• The occurrence of an earthquake, hurricane or other disaster of a certain magnitude
• Rainfall or temperature

Events like defaults, takeovers and catastrophes are not real indices in the sense that they take on all kinds of values over time. We can, however, treat them as such by assigning them a value of 0 if the relevant event does not occur and a value of 1 if it does. This means that there are basically two types of indices: indices which can take a whole range of possible values and indices which can take only two values. We refer to the latter as **digital indices**.

It is typically not possible to say exactly when a reference index will realize its next value. However, when structuring a derivatives contract the times and dates on which the reference index is to be monitored are fixed in advance. What is being monitored though is not the index value precisely at these monitoring points, but the **last realized value**.

1.4   VANILLA INDEX-LINKED CASH FLOWS

Having identified the relevant payment dates and reference indices, the next step is to link the cash flows on these dates with these indices. The easiest way to create an index-linked cash flow is to simply make the cash flow equal to the value of the reference index on the payment date. In doing so, there are three potential problems that may need to be solved. We discuss these below.

1.4.1   Monetization

The first problem is that the reference index may not be expressed in money terms. Stock, bond or commodity prices do not present a problem, but this is not true for indices such as interest rates, which are expressed as a percentage, or stock market indices, which are just numbers without unit. To solve this problem, we implicitly multiply non-money indices by a **monetizer**. In other words, if we think of the reference index, we think of it as an amount of money. For example, when the S&P 500 index is at 1400 we interpret that as USD 1400. Likewise, when 6-month USD LIBOR is at 5% we interpret that as USD 0.05. Although a non-money index can be monetized into any currency we like, most non-money indices do have a **natural currency of denomination**. If so, they are monetized into that currency. This means for example that the S&P 500 is always monetized in US dollars and not in euros or yen.

   Apart from not being expressed in money terms, some indices are not even numbers. Credit ratings for example take on values like AAA, AA, A, etc. To use them as indices we must first determine what values are possible and in what order they occur. Subsequently, we can then assign money values to these values. Another awkward type of indices are digital indices. Defaults and takeovers do not take on several values, they just occur or do not occur. Of course, these can also be monetized by assigning them a money value, but a more logical thing is to look at these as knock-in or knock-out trigger variables added to a fixed cash flow. We will discuss this in detail in Chapters 3 and 4.

1.4.2   Currency Translation

A second problem which may need to be addressed is the fact that the reference index may not be denominated in the currency in which we want to get paid. In other words, the **payment currency** may not be the same as the **index currency**. For example, we might want to link our cash flow to the S&P 500 index but get paid in euros instead of US dollars. The solution is the introduction of an explicit **currency translator** which converts the index currency into the payment currency. The most obvious translator is of course the **spot rate** on the payment date. This is not the only alternative though. Instead of the spot rate, we could convert the observed value of the reference index using for example

- A prefixed exchange rate
- The average exchange rate over some period
- The highest or lowest exchange rate over some period
- The highest or lowest of a prefixed rate and the spot rate on the payment date

   It is important to remember that **reference indices are monetized before they are currency translated**. One might be inclined to monetize directly into the payment currency. Doing so, however, sacrifices the flexibility that comes with a separate currency translator. Monetizing directly into the payment currency is different from first monetizing into the index currency and then converting the index currency into the payment currency using an explicit currency translator. The first approach produces a cash flow solely dependent on the reference index, while the second approach generates a cash flow which depends on the reference index as well as the exchange rate. For example, monetizing the S&P 500 index directly into euros produces a euro amount equal to the S&P 500. On the other hand, monetizing the S&P 500 first into US dollars and then converting into euros produces a euro amount equal to the S&P 500 times the currency translator used. This example shows that **monetizing directly into the payment currency is the same as converting at a prefixed exchange rate**.

1.4.3 Scaling

A third problem concerns the size of the cash flow. A cash flow equal to the (monetized and currency translated) value of the reference index will typically only be small, especially when the index is expressed as a percentage. Fortunately, increasing the size of an index-linked cash flow is easy. We can simply multiply the index value by a fixed **multiplier**. For example, instead of a cash flow equal to the value of the S&P 500 one year from now, we could talk about a cash flow equal to 100,000 or 250,000 times the index value.

Multiplying the index by a multiplier generally works well, except with cash flows linked to interest rates. Because interest rates tend to be expressed on an annual basis, cash flows linked to interest rates are typically expressed as the product of (1) a multiplier, (2) a so-called **day count fraction** and (3) an annualized interest rate. The day count fraction equals the fraction of a year during which interest is actually being paid. To make things more confusing, **different markets tend to work with different day count conventions**. Some take the actual number of days passed and divide this by 365 (denoted as actual/365). In the UK this is referred to as 'money market basis'. In the US on the other hand this is known as 'bond basis'. Money market basis in the US means dividing the actual number of days by 360 (denoted as actual/360). Others calculate on a so-called 30/360 basis by assuming that every month has 30 days. A fourth way to calculate the day count fraction is on an equal coupon basis. This means counting every month as 1/12 of a year, every quarter as 1/4 of a year, etc. With so much variation around it is important to always keep an eye on **the only thing that really matters: the size of the cash flow**.

Generally, the multiplier will be a prefixed number. There are some exceptions though.

- In special cases the multiplier may be a **complex function**. One might, for example, structure a cash flow equal to the price of a bond with predefined characteristics (existing or imaginary) but a yield equal to that of another bond. In that case the multiplier (the function translating the yield figure into a cash flow) is the complex function implicit in the terms of the bond to be priced.
- Sometimes things become more transparent if, instead of a fixed multiplier, we think in terms of an **index-linked multiplier**. Examples can be found in cases where people want to hedge positions the size of which is not known at present. An investment manager for example might want to hedge the 6-month foreign exchange exposure on a portfolio of international stocks. Since he does not know what his portfolio will be worth six months from now, he will have to link the size of his hedge to the value of his portfolio in six months.

1.5 STRUCTURED INDEX-LINKED CASH FLOWS

So far we have looked at cash flows which equal the value of the reference index at some future date. But there is more. Vanilla cash flows can be combined into more complex cash flows using a number of operations **in any combination one sees fit**. First, we can structure cash flows which are equal to the **sum** of two or more cash flows. An investor might, for example, be interested not so much in a cash flow equal to the value of a single stock as in a cash flow equal to the value of a portfolio of 10 different stocks. We can also structure cash flows which are equal to the **difference** between two cash flows. An oil company for example might be very interested in a cash flow equal to the difference between the price of crude oil and the price of unleaded gasoline. Similarly, an investor might have good use for a cash flow equal to the difference between the yield on a 7-year corporate bond and the yield on a 7-year Treasury bond. We can also structure cash flows equal to the **product** or **ratio** of two cash flows. Another possibility is to structure cash flows that equal the **highest** or **lowest** of two or more cash flows. Many investors might, for example, be very interested in a cash flow equal to 100m times the highest of zero and the 1-year return on the S&P 500.

With structured cash flows it is important to note that when it comes to multiplication and currency translation **every component cash flow in the package comes with its own multiplier and currency translator**. In practice, one single multiplier and currency translator are often backed out. By itself this is not a problem as long as one realizes that every component cash flow does bring its own multiplier and currency translator, and that the multiplier and currency translator which are backed out are there for notational convenience. If one does not, then part of the available flexibility is lost as some cash flows simply cannot be obtained without specifying different multipliers and currency translators for the different component cash flows.

1.6 ZEROS AND FORWARDS

Knowing how to link cash flows to reference indices, we are ready to take on the world. Confronted with a problem, we first identify the relevant reference indices and payment dates. Subsequently, we hook up the cash flows on those payment dates with the reference indices, and package all cash flows into a single contract. Although there is a huge variety in the problems that derivatives structurers are confronted with, the resulting solutions can be classified into two different groups: (1) index-linked notes and (2) forwards and swaps. Anticipating what is to come in the remainder of the book, in this section we briefly discuss the general structure of each type of contract. For clarity, we concentrate on cash flows to be exchanged in the future and ignore possible cash flows in the present.

A very common problem is what to do with a temporary (maybe long-term) cash surplus. One solution is to pay the cash to some counterparty in return for a single payment by that counterparty in the future. This is known as buying a **zero-coupon note**, or **zero** for short. With a traditional zero one counterparty pays the other an amount the size of which is fixed in the present. However, there is no reason why this cash flow needs to be fixed in advance. It may well be index-linked, in which case we speak of an **index-linked zero**. An index-linked zero is a claim to an index-linked cash flow just like an ordinary zero is a claim to a fixed cash flow. There is another similarity. Index-linked zeros with different maturities can be packaged together to form a **note with index-linked**

coupons in exactly the same way as ordinary zeros of different maturities can be packaged together to form a note with fixed coupons.

The coupons paid on a note are traditionally seen as compensation for the use of capital, while the redemption payment constitutes the return of that capital to the lender. From a derivatives structuring point of view this distinction between **coupons** and **redemption** is irrelevant, however. By buying a note an investor acquires the right to a stream of cash flows. These cash flows perform both the task of compensating the investor for making his capital available to the issuer of the note as well as repaying that capital. Repayment and compensation may be done separately but also in conjunction.

With index-linked zeros and notes with index-linked coupons all future cash flows go one way, i.e. one counterparty always pays the other. In many cases, however, things are not that simple. Often the best solution to a problem is to trade in one cash flow for another, i.e. to take away an unwanted or less desirable cash flow and replace it with a more attractive one. This gives rise to contracts where both counterparties pay each other. Such contracts are known as **forwards**. The payoff of a forward contract consists of two future cash flows, one from each counterparty to the other. Under a traditional forward the payment dates of both cash flows are the same, one cash flow is fixed and the other is index-linked. There is no reason why this should always be the case though. Depending on the problem at hand, the cash flows may occur at different dates and both payments may be index-linked.

Sometimes one needs to replace not just one but a whole series of future cash flows. Consider for example a corporate treasurer who funds at a floating rate. If he thought that interest rates were on their way up he might want to replace his floating interest payments over the next couple of years by fixed payments. Fortunately, this does not present a problem as the idea behind forwards can easily be extended into a multi-period setting. This gives rise to contracts which are known as **swaps**. A swap is a strip of forwards, i.e. a contract which obliges the counterparties involved to exchange cash flows on two or more future payment dates. Traditionally, as with forwards, swap payment dates are equal for both 'legs'; the cash flows in one leg are fixed and the cash flows in the other leg are index-linked. There is no reason why this should always be the case though. Again depending on the problem at hand, cash flows may occur at different times and both legs of the swap may have index-linked cash flows.

Looking at forwards and swaps as financial assets, a question which might arise is which counterparty is the buyer and which is the seller. The buyer of an asset is typically defined as the counterparty that pays the price of the asset to the seller. With forwards and swaps, however, contract parameters are often chosen such that no money is exchanged upon entering the contract. Without a price it is hard to determine who is buying and who is selling. With standard forwards and swaps people usually look at who benefits if the reference index goes up to determine the buyer. This makes the counterparty paying the fixed cash flow(s) the **buyer** and the one paying the index-linked cash flow(s) the **seller**. The buyer is said to be **long** the forward or swap contract and the seller is said to be **short** the contract. All this is just semantics though. In the end the only thing that really matters is who pays what and when.

1.7   CONTRACT EXTENSIONS

The above procedure allows us to create solutions to a wide array of problems. Sometimes, however, one can do even better by including one or more additional **rights** or

restrictions. Here are a few of the possibilities. We will discuss these extensions as well as some others in greater detail in Chapter 3.

- The process of replacing one cash flow by another is often hindered by the fact that on the payment date the new cash flow may turn out to be less attractive than the old one. A common way to solve this problem is to give one of the counterparties the right to cancel the contract at maturity, i.e. to decide on the maturity date whether the exchange will actually take place or not.
- Instead of the right to cancel a contract we may give a counterparty the right to require the other counterparty to exchange the existing contract for another contract. An example can be found in convertible bonds, where the convertible bondholder has the right to require the issuer of the bond to exchange the bond for a number of shares.
- We may also introduce a feature which specifies that a contract only pays off under a restricted number of scenarios with respect to one or more reference indices. The contract may pay off only if a certain scenario realizes or it may be that the contract always pays off unless a certain scenario realizes.

1.8 TAX, ACCOUNTING AND REGULATION

Every financial economic problem has a tax, accounting and regulatory angle. Sometimes the problem may even result from the particular tax, accounting or regulatory environment. Since the goal of the derivatives structurer is to provide a solution which deals with these matters in the most efficient way for all counterparties involved, insight into these matters is of great importance. The tax, accounting and regulatory treatment of derivatives is very much product-based. This has some far-reaching consequences. First, since legislation takes time, it means that the rules are behind on the latest developments in the market. The question 'how will this be taxed?' is typically not an easy one to answer. Second, calling the same cash flow schedule by a different name or structuring things slightly differently may result in significant differences in tax, accounting or regulatory treatment. One can, for example, structure one contract to solve a problem but sometimes it is possible to split that contract into two or more other contracts which, when combined, yield exactly the same cash flow schedule but which will be taxed differently. Another example can be found in Chapter 13. This shows how important it is for a derivatives structurer to have access to a deep knowledge base on tax, accounting and regulatory issues.

Despite the obvious importance of tax, accounting and regulation for the ultimate outcome of the structuring process, we will largely ignore these issues. There are three good reasons for this. First, as mentioned, taxation, accounting and regulation are still very much in their infancy when it comes to derivatives. Second, keeping up to date with developments in these areas is a job in itself. Derivatives structurers should have sufficient basic knowledge to be able to communicate with the experts but should not attempt to do these people's jobs as well. Third, the tax, accounting and regulatory environment depends very much on where you are and who you are. Including tax, accounting and regulatory considerations in the discussion would mean making strong assumptions about the nature and whereabouts of the parties involved, which would make the discussion less interesting for all those readers who do not fit the bill. Readers interested in the taxation of derivatives might consult the work of Conlon and Aquilino.[1] The sheer size of this publication and the fact that it is regularly updated and expanded gives an indication of the complexity and timeliness of these matters.

1.9 CONCLUSION

Derivatives structuring is about packaging fixed and index-linked cash flows into financial contracts to solve financial economic problems. Conceptually **the procedure** is as follows.

- **Step 1.** Identify the relevant payment dates and reference indices.
- **Step 2.** Link the cash flows on the payment dates to the reference indices in such a way that the problem at hand is solved.
- **Step 3.** Add additional rights and/or restrictions if required.
- **Step 4.** Package everything into a single contract.
- **Step 5.** Ask a derivatives firm to quote a price for the contract.

Although these five steps sound very straightforward, in practice things do not always work out that way. Most problems arise with steps 2 and 3. In Chapters 3 and 4 we therefore discuss a variety of index-linked cash flows and extensions in greater detail. These are the true building blocks of the derivatives structurer.

When it comes to the **documentation** of deals, it is common for end-users to leave the paperwork to the derivatives firm that is taking the other side of the contract in question. Typically, the derivatives firm also acts as the **calculation agent**, i.e. it calculates the index-linked payments to be made by both counterparties and checks for the occurrence of special events. During the structuring process and the negotiations that follow, derivatives firms provide their clients with so-called **indicative term sheets** which briefly summarize the proposed contract at every stage. When all contract details are agreed upon, the derivatives firm sends the client a **final term sheet**, followed a little later by a **confirmation** which embodies the formal contract. The confirmation details not only the cash flows and payment dates but also contains lots of 'small print' concerning things such as what happens if the reference index cannot be observed or traded, etc.

Derivatives firms tend to write their confirmations along the lines suggested by the International Swap and Derivatives Association (ISDA). Typically, there will already be a so-called **ISDA master agreement** in place between the derivatives firm and its client which details their business relationship in general. When the client and the firm enter into a specific deal, the confirmation for that deal will refer to and act as a supplement to the master agreement. Writing a confirmation for an equity derivatives transaction, the derivatives firm will make use of the so-called **ISDA equity derivatives definitions** that were specially developed for that purpose. Although very important, for brevity we will not go into these matters. For details the reader is referred to the various ISDA publications.[2]

Finding a derivatives firm willing to quote a price is easy. Finding a good quote can be a lot more difficult however. When it comes to finding a price three points have to be kept in mind.

---

[1] S. Conlon and V. Aquilino, *Principles of Financial Derivatives: US and International Taxation*, Warren, Gorham & Lamont, 1999.

[2] See the ISDA website at www.isda.org.

- It is in the end-user's best interest to **ask at least a couple of derivatives firms for a quote**. The knowledge that they are in competition is often enough for derivatives firms to sharpen their pencils. Only when a trade is to be kept confidential does it pay to call on only one firm. This is for example the case if a trade is very large, if it is something that has not been done before, or if the trade is explicitly designed to arbitrage the tax, accounting or regulatory environment.
- Derivatives marketers are under high pressure to perform. At the end of the month they need to show their boss that they have made a worthwhile contribution to the firm. As a result, a marketer who has spent a significant amount of time with one particular client would rather do a deal with that client that brings in little or even no money than not do a deal at all. Within reason, end-users should therefore aim to **consume a fair amount of a marketer's time before asking for a quote**.
- During negotiations end-users typically do not discuss matters such as what happens when the reference index cannot be observed or traded, etc. This is surprising as different firms may use different conventions which may have significantly different consequences. It may well turn out that one quote is slightly better than the other just because the small print of the derivatives firm in question takes many more liberties, i.e. transfers more risks to its counterparty. End-users should always **check the small print before comparing quotes**.

We end this chapter on a philosophical note. Often it looks as if, with the exception of trading on inside information, nepotism and the like, making money is first and foremost a matter of being in the right place at the right time, taking risk and being lucky. Fortunately, there is more to it than that. **To make money we must simply ask ourselves how we can help people**. Only if we help people can we expect them to pay us willingly and come back for more. Looking at things from this perspective there is nothing complicated about making money, and ideas will pop up wherever we go. This should also be the mindset of the derivatives structurer. A derivatives structurer's goal should be to structure contracts which allow people to make money, save money or better manage the risks to which they are exposed. When done correctly, the money will come by itself.

2
Stocks and Stock Market Indices

2.1 INTRODUCTION

The first step in our approach to derivatives structuring is the identification of the relevant reference indices. In this chapter we discuss stocks and especially stock market indices in more detail, concentrating on their composition, calculation and behavior.

Traditionally, stock market indices were designed and published to give the investing public a general idea of how the market was doing. The number of stocks was typically limited because data collection and index calculation had to be done manually. Over time investors started to look for reliable benchmarks against which to measure the performance of their portfolios. Combined with increasing computing power this led to the introduction of more broad ranging indices. The publishers of these indices, often newspapers, exchanges or securities firms, did not make money from these indices directly. This changed when exchanges started to trade derivatives on these indices, and indexation (see Chapter 6) and equity-linked investment products (see Chapters 9–13) became more popular. Since index publishers hold recognized intellectual property rights to their indices, nowadays **one has to obtain a license** from the publisher of an index before one is allowed to use that index as a reference index.

There are various types of licenses depending on who you are. Licenses for mutual funds give the fund the right to use the index in question as the basis of an investment portfolio and use the index name in promotional material. The typical fee consists of a minimum amount plus a variable amount depending on the average net asset value of the fund. Unlike licenses for mutual funds, licenses for financial exchanges are generally exclusive, meaning that for a period of 5 or 10 years the exchange is the only one allowed to trade products linked to the index in question. The exact terms can vary, however. A license sometimes provides worldwide exclusivity but it may also be limited to certain time zones or geographical areas. License fees for exchanges are typically based on trading volume. Financial institutions dealing in OTC derivatives and issuers of equity-linked notes are also required to acquire licenses. These licenses can be taken out one at a time or can be structured to cover any product issued during a certain period of time. Since there is often little to hook up with, the license fee is typically a prefixed amount. Since selling licenses can be quite lucrative, it is not surprising that the number of stock market indices keeps growing at a fast pace.

2.2 COMMON STOCKS

In this section we briefly discuss the basics of common stocks. Since it is the largest stock market in the world, we concentrate on the US. It should be kept in mind that, although similar, things may be somewhat different in other parts of the world.

Generally speaking, stocks represent an ownership interest in a business entity. This is a so-called **residual interest** because it is subordinate to all other claims, i.e. stockholders receive whatever is left after all debts are paid off. As there are different types of business entities around, we can distinguish between different types of stock. The simplest type of business entity is the **sole proprietorship**. The sole proprietor has full control over his business and answers to no one but himself. When a number of people start a business together this is often done in the form of a **partnership**. This is very similar to a sole proprietorship except that there are now multiple owners. With a sole proprietorship as well as a partnership, the business and its owner(s) are one and the same. This means that in case of a sole proprietorship the sole proprietor, and in case of a partnership each individual partner, is liable for the obligations of the whole business entity. This is not the case when a business is structured as a **corporation**. A corporation is a legal entity by itself and is therefore clearly distinguishable from its owners. Management of the firm is in the hands of professional managers and the stockholders have limited liability.

Stocks issued by a corporation are known as **common stock**. Common stockholders are therefore the owners of a corporation. Although in theory common stockholders have ultimate control over the company's affairs, in practice this is limited to a right to vote on appointments to the board of directors and several other issues, such as a merger for example. Voting can be done either in person or by transferring the voting right to a second party by means of a so-called **proxy**. Corporations hold a periodic election of directors, with votes being taken at the annual meeting. Typically, each year one-third of the directors are voted for, for a 3-year term. There are different voting systems in use. With so-called **majority voting** each director is voted upon separately with one share representing one vote. With **cumulative voting** the directors are voted upon jointly and shareholders can allot all their votes to just one candidate. Suppose an investor held 1000 shares and there were six directors. In that case he could, if he wanted, cast 6000 votes for his favorite candidate instead of just 1000 as with majority voting.

Companies typically only issue one class of common stock. Sometimes, however, there may be two classes of common stock outstanding, usually referred to as class A and B, with different voting and/or dividend rights. The class of shares with limited voting privileges typically trades at a discount of 2–4%. Especially in large corporations, the issues on which shareholders are asked to vote are hardly ever contested. Sometimes, however, the existing management ends up having to compete with a group of outsiders for control of the corporation. In that case management will compete with the outsiders for the available proxies, which is known as a **proxy fight**. These fights are hardly ever successful though, as the existing management has the luxury of being able to make the corporation pay for the costs involved.

The total number of shares issued and the number of shares outstanding need not necessarily be the same, as a company may own some of its own shares. If so, the number of **shares outstanding** is smaller than the number of **shares issued**. The number of shares outstanding is sometimes used as a measure of liquidity. However, if a large number of the shares outstanding are closely held, i.e. owned by investors who are not active traders, this may give a distorted picture of the actual liquidity situation. The market value of the shares outstanding is known as the company's **market capitalization**. Like bonds, most stocks do have a **par value** but, unlike bonds, this is just a formality with very little economic significance. Par value is typically low, as it is not possible to sell stocks below par.

Although investors outside the US have been investing in (for them) foreign stocks for a very long time, in the US this is a more recent development. To make foreign stocks more easily accessible to US investors, special trusts have been created which buy a large number of a particular foreign stock and finance this by the issuance of so-called **American Depository Receipts (ADRs)** which pass on (almost) all distributions made by the stock in question. ADRs are US securities that trade in the US in the usual way and should therefore take away fears over foreign settlement procedures, language problems, excessive commissions, currency controls, local taxes, etc. Ownership of an ADR is not exactly the same as owning the stock though. The owner of an ADR has a share in a trust and not in the company.

The ADR structure has become quite popular in the US, not least because international diversification itself has become more popular with US institutional investors. The liquidity of ADRs depends on the level of investor interest and varies strongly among issues. Telephonos de Mexico (Telmex) for example is more actively traded in the US as an ADR than in Mexico as a local issue. Transaction costs for ADRs are not always lower than in the local market, but custody costs generally are. Non-US firms that want to raise capital in the US can do so by issuing shares in ADR form. The advantage of doing so is that it allows these firms to avoid the strict financial disclosure requirements in the US as well as the cost of producing US-style financial statements.

2.3 CORPORATE ACTIONS

Apart from the usual ups and downs of stock prices, common stockholders' wealth is also affected by a number of so-called **corporate actions**. We briefly discuss the most important ones below.

2.3.1 Dividends

A share of stock has value because the owner of the stock is entitled to receive dividends. Mostly, dividends are paid in **cash**, quarterly, semi-annually or annually. Because investors tend to expect dividends not to go down, companies sometimes distinguish between **regular dividends**, which the company expects to be able to maintain, and **extra dividends**, which it does not. A company may also declare a so-called **stock dividend**. In that case the dividend comes in the form of newly issued stocks. A cash dividend is typically taken out of the company's current earnings. The earnings not paid out as dividends are retained by the company. With a stock dividend on the other hand the company retains all earnings and simply increases the number of shares outstanding.

Dividends are set by the board of directors. The latter are not completely free in doing so, however. Bondholders will place a limit on dividends, as the higher the dividend the higher the risk that there will not be enough money left to pay off the company's debt. Regulation is aimed at the same goal. In most jurisdictions a company is prohibited from paying dividends that would make the company insolvent.

When it comes to dividends there are two important dates. First, there is the **announcement date**. On this date the company declares how much dividend it will pay and in what form. Dividend announcements typically state that the dividend will be paid to all shareholders registered on a particular **record date**. The latter is usually one week after the dividend is declared. Two weeks after that dividend checks are mailed out. One would not expect the stock price to change as a result of the announcement of either a cash or a stock dividend. However, in practice stock prices often do. Stock dividends for example tend to raise stock prices significantly. There are at least two possible explanations for this.

First, at the time of the dividend announcement a company may issue other information as well. Even if it does not, investors may interpret a dividend increase or decrease as a signal that the company is doing better or worse than they thought. Second, one could argue that a company will only decide on a stock dividend if it thinks its stock price is likely to rise in the future. In that case the announcement of a stock dividend implicitly tells investors that the company might be in better shape than they think it is. Stocks are normally trading **cum dividend**, i.e. with the right to the next dividend, up to a few days before the record date. After that the stock is traded **ex dividend**. If one buys a stock cum dividend but too late for registration, the seller has to pass the dividend on to the buyer when received.

A second date that is important is the **ex date**, i.e. the date that the stock starts trading ex dividend. In case of a cash dividend one would expect the stock price to simply drop by the amount of the dividend. In case of a stock dividend all the firm does is increase the number of shares outstanding. One would therefore expect the stock price to drop in accordance with the increase in the number of shares. In practice, however, things tend to be more complicated. In case of a cash dividend the stock price often drops by substantially less, say 20–30%, than the dividend. The oldest explanation is based on the idea that investors value dividends on an after-tax instead of a pre-tax basis. An investor paying 25% taxes will value a 1.00 dividend at 0.75 instead of 1.00. When the stock goes ex dividend it therefore only loses 0.75 of its value. In case of a stock dividend stock prices often drop by less than expected as well. The reasons for this are still somewhat of a mystery, although we know that it cannot be taxes as stock dividends are typically tax neutral.

2.3.2 New Issues

When companies need money they nowadays can choose from a whole range of securities to issue. We will not go into the details of this choice here, but let's simply assume a company had decided to issue common stock. The first choice to be made then is whether it is going to be a private placement or a public issue. With a **private placement** the firm simply sells new shares to not more than a dozen or so investors by separate negotiation. Since it is a private transaction the issuer is not obliged to register the issue with the Securities and Exchange Commission (SEC). With a **public issue** on the other hand anybody can participate in the primary offering. Because it is public, there is strict regulation, most of which derives from the Securities Act of 1933. First, a company prepares a **registration statement** for the SEC, presenting information about the firm and the proposed financing. When approved, part of the latter statement is then distributed to the public in the form of a **prospectus**.

The SEC allows the filing of a single registration statement covering financing plans for up to two years. This is known as **shelf registration**. With a registration statement on the shelf, a company can issue whenever it needs money without much additional paperwork. Having a registration statement on the shelf not only reduces costs, but also allows for greater flexibility. Since the firm can issue on short notice it can time the issue to take advantage of perceived favorable market conditions. It also makes it easier for the firm to shop around for the cheapest underwriter (see below).

With a public issue one can distinguish between two methods. The most popular is a **general cash offer** where new stocks are sold to anybody who wants to buy them.

There is one little twist though. Companies do not sell their shares directly to the public, but sell them to a so-called **underwriter** instead. The underwriter is typically a major investment bank. The underwriter buys the whole issue from the company and then resells it to the public. This relieves the company of the burden of marketing the issue as well as the risk of not being able to sell at the offering price. The underwriter is paid by the company in the form of a **spread**, i.e. the underwriter is allowed to buy the shares for less than the offering price at which they are sold to the investing public. Sometimes the underwriter also receives warrants as part of its compensation package. If the issue is large the company may, instead of one, decide to deal with a **syndicate** of underwriters, led by a so-called **syndicate manager**, that takes care of the structuring of the issue, the registration statement, etc.

With a syndicated issue the syndicate manager tends to take about 20% of the spread, the other syndicate members 30%, with the remainder going to the other firms involved in the actual selling of the issue. This is not money for nothing though. Underwriters are not allowed to sell at a price higher than the agreed offering price, but bear the risk that the stock price drops below the offering price before the closing date of the offer. On October 15th, 1987 the UK Government agreed to sell its holdings of BP shares at GBP 3.30 per share to a syndicate of underwriters for a total of more than GBP 12b. On October 19th, 1987 the stock market crashed. BP's stock price fell to GBP 2.96 by the closing date of the offer, leaving the underwriters with a huge loss. It is therefore not surprising that underwriters aim to minimize the time between the final pricing and the actual offering, as well as steer towards a relatively low offering price. Research has shown that this is especially true for initial public offerings (IPOs), i.e. the first public issue made by a company.

A public issue can also be structured as a **rights issue**. In case of a rights issue shareholders are given so-called **rights**. A certain number of rights, say 5 or 10, allows a shareholder to buy one new share at the **subscription price**. Of course, shareholders who do not want to participate in the issue may always sell the rights they receive. Likewise, shareholders who want a larger share of the issue can always buy more in the market. Rights issues do not require the involvement of an underwriter. The subscription price is usually set well below the market price of the stock in question, making the issue unlikely to fail. However, to protect itself against the risk that the issue is not sold, a firm can arrange for the issue to be underwritten. In that case the underwriter does not buy the issue, but is paid a **standby fee** in return for buying all unsubscribed shares at the subscription price.

As with dividends, with new issues we can identify two important dates. First, there is the **announcement date**. Assuming the firm issues at a price not significantly below the prevailing stock price and that it has good use for the proceeds of the issue, one would not expect the stock price to change. In practice, however, the announcement of a stock offering is often accompanied by a small drop in the stock price. This is generally thought to be an information effect. Since a company is more likely to issue new stock if its management thinks the company's stock is overvalued, investors interpret the announcement of a new issue as bad news. With rights issues a second key date is the date that the stock starts trading ex right, i.e. the **rights ex date**. One would expect the stock price to drop by the value of the right at that date. Unfortunately, we do not know of any research that confirms or rejects this hypothesis.

2.3.3 Stock Splits

When a company's stock price rises to a relatively high level it may decide to split its stock into two or more new stocks to make it easier for small investors to invest in it. In a 3-for-1 split, for example, each old share is replaced by three new shares. In theory a stock split is not a very exiting event as, similar to a stock dividend, the number of shares outstanding increases but without anything else changing. One would therefore expect the stock price not to change on the **announcement date**. In practice, however, the announcement of a stock split tends to raise the price of the stock in question. This can be explained in the same way as with a stock dividend. First, at the time of the split announcement companies may issue additional information. Second, over the years investors have learned that a company will only decide on a stock split if it thinks its stock price is likely to rise further. The majority of splitting companies announce above-average increases in dividends during the year following the split. On the **split date** one would expect the stock price to drop in line with the increase in the number of shares on the date of the split. Often, however, this is not the case and the stock price drops by less. The exact reasons for this are still to be discovered.

2.4   INDEX CALCULATION

Generally speaking, an index number is a number which expresses the ratio between the level of a given variable at one moment and that at an earlier moment. The latter is referred to as the index's **base value**. The base value can be set more or less arbitrarily, for example at 80 or 100. This then is the starting value of the index. Comparison of the variable's current value with its base value automatically gives the current value of the index. For example, suppose on January 3rd, 2000 the price of stock X was 130, on May 12th, 2000 it was 90, and by October 6th, 2000 it had again risen to 150. If we were to choose January 3rd as our basis with a base value of 80, then the index would be equal to $90/130 \times 80 = 55.38$ on May 12th and $150/130 \times 80 = 92.31$ on October 6th. In other words, to calculate the current index value we have to divide the stock's current price by its price on January 3rd and subsequently multiply by the chosen base value. The stock return from May 12th to October 6th can be calculated from the index values on those dates as $(92.31 - 55.38)/55.38 = 67\%$. This figure is independent of the base value chosen.

If we want to keep track of the development of the stock market as a whole, we can use the same principle. Instead of a single stock price, however, we will have to use a variable which provides a good summary of the price level on the market being studied. In other words, we will have to average stock prices in some way. When choosing such an average we have to decide on two important issues. First, we have to choose the stocks which are to be included in the average. Second, we must decide on the weights given to these stocks. There are considerable differences in the number and nature of the stocks included in well-known indices. Some are restricted to just a handful of stocks, while others are meant to provide a more general picture of the market. Some indices concentrate on stocks with very high market capitalizations, while others go for low market capitalizations instead. Furthermore, one has to keep in mind that the composition of stock market indices is by no means constant. Sometimes the composition of the index is determined by a special committee, while in other cases the stocks to be included are selected in accordance with some mechanical rule.

Calculating the average of a number of stock prices, we have to decide on the relative importance of every individual stock within the average. There are two different weighting schemes in use. The simplest scheme is to purchase one share of stock for every company selected. In this case price movements are weighted by the prices of the stocks themselves. The higher a stock's price, the greater its influence on the behavior of the index. Such an index is called **price-weighted**. The second scheme is based on the market capitalizations of the stocks included. Indices using this scheme are known as **value-weighted** indices. In these indices the influence of a given stock on the behavior of the index is determined by the market capitalization of the stock in relation to the total market capitalization of all stocks included. The higher a company's market capitalization, the higher the weight given in the calculation of the index.

Let's look at a simple example. Suppose we wanted to create an index containing the stocks of three companies called X, Y and Z. These stocks' prices are currently at 30, 20 and 40, respectively. Company X has 50 shares outstanding, company Y 100 shares and company Z 200 shares. Starting with a base value of 100, Table 2.1 then provides us with the index values on three arbitrary future dates $t = 1, 2, 3$ for both weighting schemes. The entries in Table 2.1 are calculated as follows. At $t = 0$ the sum of the prices of X, Y and Z is equal to 90. At $t = 1$, however, this has risen to 102. Starting with a base value of 100, this means that at $t = 1$ the price-weighted index will be $102/90 \times 100 = 113.3$. The value of the value-weighted index can be calculated by comparing the total market value of the three stocks at times $t = 0$ and $t = 1$. At the base moment the latter is equal to 11,500, rising to 12,550 at $t = 1$. The value-weighted index at $t = 1$ is therefore $12,550/11,500 \times 100 = 109.1$. The other entries are calculated in the same way.

From Table 2.1 we clearly see the difference between both weighting schemes. Because the market capitalization of company Z is several times larger than that of the other two stocks, Z's stock price is given a lot of weight in the calculation of the value-weighted index. Since Z's stock price rises the least, the rise in the index therefore remains limited. The price-weighted index presents another picture. Despite the fact that company Z still has the largest weight, the other two stocks now also strongly influence the behavior of the index. Because the stock prices of X and Y show a larger increase than the price of Z, the price-weighted index rises significantly more than the value-weighted index.

Looking at the above example, it is clear that we can calculate the value of the price-weighted index at any time t as

$$I_t = \frac{P_t^1 + P_t^2 + P_t^3}{D_t}, \tag{2.1}$$

Table 2.1   Weighting schemes and index values

	$t = 0$		$t = 1$		$t = 2$		$t = 3$	
	Price	Index	Price	Index	Price	Index	Price	Index
X	30.00		35.00		37.00		30.00	
Y	20.00		26.00		25.00		20.00	
Z	40.00		41.00		44.00		40.00	
Value-weighted		100		109.1		114.3		100
Price-weighted		100		113.3		117.8		100

where P_t^i is the price of stock i, $i = 1, 2, 3$, at time t and D_t is the index's **divisor**. In the above example the divisor is equal to $90/100 = 0.9$ since the sum of the stock prices on the base date was 90, but we wanted the index to start at a value of 100. The divisor has a time subscript, i.e. it may change over time, because it is used to ensure the continuity of the index in the face of changes. Suppose that in our example stock Y split 2:1 at $t = 1$. As a result, the sum of the stock prices would drop from 102 to 89. If we did not change the divisor the index would drop from 113.3 to 98.9 just as a result of the split. Because we do not want this to happen we adjust the divisor so that the new sum of the stock prices produces the same index value as before. This means the new divisor has to drop from 0.9 to 0.7855. Split-ups make the divisor go down, but the opposite may also happen, for example when a high priced stock is substituted for a low priced stock. Suppose at $t = 1$ we dropped company Y and replaced it by company W with a stock price of 60. Without adjustment of the divisor the new index value would jump from 113.3 to 151.1. Since we want the index to stay at 113.3, however, this means we have to increase the divisor from 0.9 to 1.2.

The value-weighted index is slightly more difficult to calculate. If we denote the number of shares outstanding of company i at time t as N_t^i, the value of the value-weighted index at time t is calculated as

$$I_t = \frac{N_t^1 \times P_t^1 + N_t^2 \times P_t^2 + N_t^3 \times P_t^3}{D_t}, \tag{2.2}$$

where D_t again denotes the index's divisor. In the above example the divisor was equal to $11{,}500/100 = 115$ because the sum of the market capitalizations on the base date was 11,500 and we wanted the index to start at a value of 100. For a value-weighted index a split-up has no direct consequences, since it does not affect the market capitalization of the relevant stock. This is not true for new issues, however. Suppose at $t = 1$ company X issued 50 more stocks. Accompanied by a well-organized road show and good news about the company's next year's results, the company's stock price remains unchanged despite a doubling of the number of stocks outstanding. Its new market capitalization is therefore 3500, bringing the total at $t = 1$ to 14,300 instead of 12,550. Without adjusting the divisor this would bring the index to 124.3. Since we want to keep it at 109.1, however, we have to increase the divisor to 131.1.

Another way to understand the difference between both weighting schemes is to link the percentage change of both indices to the returns on the individual stocks over the same period. In doing so, we see that in both cases **the percentage change in the index value equals the weighted sum of the returns on the component stocks**. The difference between both indices lies in the weighting scheme used. For the price-weighted index the weights are equal to the relative prices of the stocks included in the index. At $t = 0$ the sum of the stock prices of X, Y and Z is equal to 90, while over the period up to $t = 1$ the individual stock returns are 16.7%, 30.0% and 2.5%, respectively. For the price-weighted index the percentage change from $t = 0$ to $t = 1$ therefore equals $30/90 \times 16.7 + 20/90 \times 30.0 + 40/90 \times 2.5 = 13.3\%$. The same figure would be obtained if we calculated the percentage change of the index directly as $113.3 - 100 = 13.3\%$. For the value-weighted index the weights are equal to the relative market capitalizations. The percentage change of the value-weighted index can be calculated as $1500/11{,}500 \times 16.7 + 2000/11{,}500 \times 30.0 + 8000/11{,}500 \times 2.5 = 9.1\%$, since the market capitalizations of the individual stocks are equal to 1500, 2000 and 8000, summing to 11,500 in total. Direct calculation of this figure from the index values at $t = 0$ and $t = 1$ yields the same result: $109.1 - 100 = 9.1\%$.

So far we have concentrated on indices that focus exclusively on price fluctuations. Such indices are known as **price indices**. If we were to replicate these indices by actual portfolios of stocks, the portfolios would show higher returns than the indices themselves because their owner would also earn the dividends paid on these stocks. As a measure of investment performance price indices are therefore biased downwards. To solve this, some indices take dividends into account as well. These are referred to as **total return indices**. The distinction between price indices and total return indices is not only relevant for investors. As we will see in Chapter 8, whether an index takes dividends into account has a significant influence on the pricing of derivatives contracts which use that index as reference index.

2.5 SOME WELL-KNOWN STOCK MARKET INDICES

Most well-known stock market indices were not constructed to act as reference indices for derivatives contracts but are simply meant to give investors a rough indication of how the market is doing. Some indices therefore give a relatively high weight to low grade stocks, while others tend to overweigh particular industry sectors. Even indices that concentrate on large capitalization stocks may present a problem, as many such stocks are typically held by long-term investors. Sometimes only 25% or less of the number of shares outstanding is available for trading, while the full 100% is reflected in the index.

Given that stock market indices are very popular reference indices for derivatives contracts, it is of obvious importance to know more about the composition and construction of the most popular stock market indices. **Appendix A** provides some useful information on a number of major stock market indices. Although there are marked differences in the number of stocks included in these indices, there are quite a number of similarities as well.

- **Market capitalization** and **liquidity** are important (and sometimes even the only) criteria for stock selection.
- With the exception of the Dow Jones and the Nikkei 225, all these indices are **value-weighted**.
- Except for the DAX, all these indices are **price indices**.
- Major **changes in composition** occur quite frequently.
- All these indices function as reference indices for listed **futures and options**.

It is important to note that, although the name stays the same, due to composition changes and autonomous weight shifts, the risk and correlation structure of stock market indices may change substantially over time. The investment consulting firm BARRA has estimated the S&P 500's sensitivity to a number of so-called risk indices since January 1977. The results can be found on BARRA's website (www.barra.com). From the charts provided it is clear that even over a relatively short period of time the S&P 500's sensitivity to BARRA's risk indices is capable of significant change.

2.6 THE BEHAVIOR OF EQUITY INDICES

Knowing how the various indices are calculated is important but not enough. We also need to have an idea of these indices' behavior over time. There is a vast literature on this subject. Many scholars will tell us that market prices correctly reflect all available information at all times. This **efficient markets hypothesis** is a direct consequence of the assumption of rational investor behavior that dominates modern finance theory. Over the last 30 years a wealth of empirical research has shown that stock prices change randomly, that professional investors are unable to consistently beat the index, etc. This is exactly what one would expect if the efficient markets hypothesis was true.

There is one problem, however. The efficient markets hypothesis is not the only theory that supports these findings. If we said that markets were purely driven by mass hysteria, the same results would make sense as well. As always, the truth lies somewhere in the middle. There is no doubt that stock prices react to information. On the other hand, contrary to what the efficient markets hypothesis predicts, stock prices seem to be too volatile to always be equal to the present value of rationally predicted future dividends.[1] From psychological studies we know that when making forecasts people tend to overweigh recent information. We also know that once a threat, in this case losing money or missing out on a profit, is perceived people tend to become more vigilant and a lot faster to react. This suggests that, in no insignificant part, changes in stock prices could well originate within the market itself. From our perspective though the question of whether the stock market is rational or not is not the most interesting. Whatever the case, we will not be able to predict stock prices more accurately, i.e. we will not be able to develop a trading strategy that promises superior results. In a way this means we can still refer to markets as being informationally efficient, because the available information does not allow us to consistently outperform the average. We just do not know exactly why this is.

We start with a simple visual inspection of the daily return behavior of the S&P 500, the DAX and the Nikkei 225, and then move on to the more formal modeling of daily index return behavior. Those readers with a strong aversion to econometrics will be happy to learn that the material in this section is not essential for the understanding of the remainder of the book.

2.6.1 Visual Inspection

Figures 2.1–2.3 show the frequency distribution of daily returns on the S&P 500, the DAX and the Nikkei 225 over the period from January 1995 until August 1999. The graphs also depict a normal distribution with a mean and variance equal to those calculated from the data used to construct the frequency distributions. From the figures we see that compared to the normal distribution the frequency distributions of daily index returns assign a **higher probability to returns around zero as well as very high positive and negative returns**. This phenomenon is known as **leptokurtosis**.

Figures 2.4–2.6 show the daily returns of the S&P 500, the DAX and the Nikkei 225 over the period from January 1995 until August 1999 over time. We see that world equity markets have clearly become more volatile during the second half of the 1990s. Several events stand out. In 1997 Asian currencies and equity markets showed extreme drops. What started as a currency crisis in the Thai baht spread quickly through the whole region as foreign investors and local speculators jumped ship. From July 1997 to July 1998 the Thai and Malaysian stock markets dropped by almost 60%. The Russian debt crisis of 1998 was another main event. On August 17th the Russian Government announced that

---

[1] See for example R. Shiller, *Market Volatility*, MIT Press, 1989.

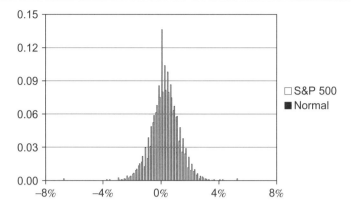

Figure 2.1   Frequency distribution of daily returns on the S&P 500, January 1995–August 1999

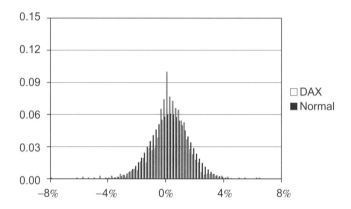

Figure 2.2   Frequency distribution of daily returns on the DAX, January 1995–August 1999

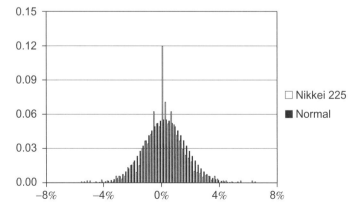

Figure 2.3   Frequency distribution of daily returns on the Nikkei 225, January 1995–August 1999

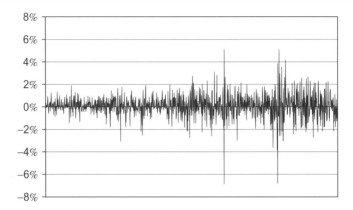

Figure 2.4   Daily returns on the S&P 500, January 1995–August 1999

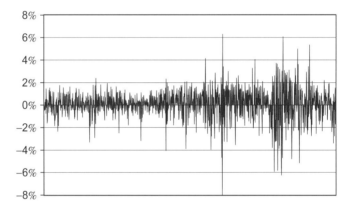

Figure 2.5   Daily returns on the DAX, January 1995–August 1999

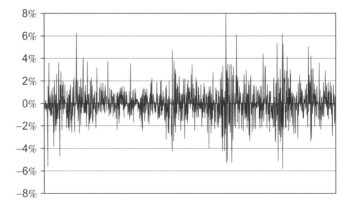

Figure 2.6   Daily returns on the Nikkei 225, January 1995–August 1999

it would reschedule payments on GKOs (short-term rouble denominated debt) and that it was imposing a moratorium on payments by Russian banks on their obligations under certain forward contracts (estimated at about USD 50 billion). Russian bonds lost most of their value and global equity markets dropped substantially. Many major hedge funds and banks had to report large losses.

The graphs in Figures 2.4–2.6 also show that **the predictability of daily returns is very low**. Returns seem to wander randomly. The fact that an index goes up or down one day does not seem to provide information about what will happen the next day. We also see that there are periods during which index volatility is relatively low and periods during which index volatility is relatively high. This is known as **volatility clustering**. It means that although we may not be able to predict future returns from past returns, we are able to say something about future volatility. If volatility is high (low) it will probably be high (low) the next couple of days as well.

2.6.2 The GARCH (1,1) Model

A realistic model of the statistical behavior of index returns needs to capture the above phenomena. One such model is the so-called **GARCH (1,1) model**. Formally, this model looks like

$$R_t|\{R_{t-i}, i > 0\} \sim \text{Normal}(\mu + \beta R_{t-1}, \sigma_t^2), \tag{2.3}$$

where

$$\sigma_t^2 = \alpha_0 + \alpha_1 \varepsilon_{t-1}^2 + \alpha_2 \sigma_{t-1}^2,$$

$$\varepsilon_t = R_t - (\mu + \beta R_{t-1}).$$

The above may look quite intimidating, but it is not. It simply says that subsequent returns R_t are normally distributed with a mean return equal to $\mu + \beta R_{t-1}$ and a volatility equal to σ_t. We refer to the latter distribution as the **conditional return distribution** because it is the distribution given, i.e. conditional on, the sequence of past returns. The so-called **unconditional return distribution** is the distribution we would be confronted with if we did not know the sequence of past returns. The frequency distributions we discussed before can be seen as estimates of this unconditional distribution, since they were constructed by simply lumping together all observed index returns without paying any attention to the sequence in which they were observed.

The mean of the conditional return distribution in (2.3) is not constant, but allows for the return over period t to depend on the return over the previous period $t - 1$. Although this is probably not the case, we include this feature to formally test the hypothesis that past returns say nothing about future returns. If we estimate the model from index return data and find that β is not significantly different from zero, this confirms the hypothesis. The conditional return distribution's variance is not constant either. This period's volatility depends on last period's volatility as well as on how much last period's index return deviated from its expected value. High (low) volatilities will tend to persist and unexpected upward or downward moves in the index will tend to increase future volatility. Since the residual return ε is squared, upward and downward moves have identical implications. It has been suggested that this is not correct. Because negative stock returns increase the financial and operating leverage of a company, negative returns should have a stronger effect on volatility than positive returns. Recent research has shown, however, that the economic importance of this so-called leverage effect is very small.[2]

What exactly does the GARCH (1,1) model say about future volatility? Let's look at the unconditional distribution first. It can be shown that, as should be the case, compared to the normal distribution the unconditional return distribution is leptokurtic. The model's unconditional variance is given by

$$\sigma_u^2 = \frac{\alpha_0}{1 - (\alpha_1 + \alpha_2)}. \tag{2.4}$$

Contrary to the unconditional distribution, the conditional return distribution is normal by assumption. Conditional one-day ahead volatility forecasts can be calculated directly from the explicit specification of the model's conditional variance. More-than-one-day ahead forecasts can be generated by repeated substitution. A time t volatility forecast over the next N periods can be obtained from

$$E_t[\sigma^2(N)] = N \times \left(\sigma_u^2 + (\sigma_{t+1}^2 - \sigma_u^2) \times \frac{1 - \gamma^N}{N(1 - \gamma)} \right), \tag{2.5}$$

where $\gamma = \alpha_1 + \alpha_2$. The above expression shows clear **mean-reversion**, with the volatility forecast tending towards the model's unconditional variance as the number of periods increases. For small values of N, on the other hand, the forecast tends towards σ_{t+1}^2. We can interpret γ as a measure of the speed with which volatility shocks decay. When γ approaches 1, the effect of past shocks increases and may cause volatility to deviate from its long-term mean for a long period of time. From a practical point of view the GARCH (1,1) model is very well suited for real-time application. Forecast updates are easy to produce, either based on old parameter estimates or re-estimations partly based on new observations.

2.6.3　Parameter Estimation

The estimation of the GARCH (1,1) model is a technical subject that we will not go into. For every index in Appendix A we estimated the GARCH (1,1) model on daily returns data over the period from January 1995 until August 1999. The results can be found in Table 2.2. As expected, the estimated values for β are close to zero, meaning that **past returns provide little or no information about future returns**. The parameters of the conditional variance, however, are significantly different from zero. Looking at the value of $\alpha_1 + \alpha_2$ it is clear that in all the major equity markets **volatility shocks tend to decay only slowly**.

2.6.4　Did Return Behavior Change During the Nineties?

Visual inspection of the data shows that the world's equity markets became more volatile during the nineties. The question is whether this was due to a structural change in the return generating process, or simply the result of an intensification of shocks to the system.

---

[2] See T. Andersen, T. Bollerslev, F. Diebold and H. Ebens, The Distribution of Stock Return Volatility, Working Paper, Northwestern University, December 1999.

Table 2.2 GARCH (1,1) parameter estimates from daily returns January 1995–August 1999

Index	μ $(\times 10^{-4})$	β	α_0 $(\times 10^{-5})$	α_1	α_2	$\alpha_1 + \alpha_2$	σ_u (%)
S&P 500	9.2217	−0.0079	0.0789	0.0687	0.9207	0.9894	13.93
DJIA	8.9536	0.0137	0.1240	0.0771	0.9085	0.9856	15.00
Eurotop 100	7.6823	0.0813	0.1075	0.0798	0.9079	0.9877	15.14
Eurostoxx 50	8.2504	0.0769	0.0910	0.0669	0.9236	0.9905	15.74
FTSE 100	5.4619	0.0990	0.0377	0.0412	0.9533	0.9945	13.37
DAX	8.0681	0.0174	0.2967	0.1041	0.8766	0.9807	20.02
AEX	9.0398	0.0519	0.1452	0.0925	0.8940	0.9865	16.73
SMI	8.0220	0.0516	0.2975	0.0919	0.8823	0.9742	17.29
CAC 40	7.3126	0.0382	0.1143	0.0447	0.9474	0.9921	19.44
IBEX 35	9.0379	0.1054	0.2858	0.0837	0.8982	0.9819	20.27
MIB 30	8.0641	0.0270	1.3421	0.1368	0.8049	0.9417	24.47
Nikkei 225	−0.0982	−0.0686	0.4111	0.0573	0.9237	0.9810	23.76
Hang Seng	5.4029	0.0018	0.3192	0.0981	0.8968	0.9949	40.32
ASX All Ord.	3.8203	0.0201	0.9066	0.1214	0.7335	0.8549	12.75

To investigate this we estimated the GARCH (1,1) model on daily returns over the period 1990–1994 and compared the parameter estimates with those obtained previously for the period 1995–1999. The estimates for both periods were not significantly different. In terms of the GARCH (1,1) model little has therefore changed over the decennium. In other words, **the observed increase in index return volatility appears to be the result of more and bigger shocks to the system** and not of a structural change in the return generating process.

2.6.5 Forecasting Volatility with the GARCH (1,1) Model

Having estimated the parameters of the GARCH (1,1) model, we can easily calculate volatility forecasts. In this section we evaluate the volatility forecasts produced by the GARCH (1,1) model. We do this by comparing the performance of the GARCH (1,1) volatility forecasts with the performance of a forecast taken from a random walk model with constant volatility. The methodology is identical to that followed by Heynen and Kat in their article on volatility forecasting.[3] The period from January 1990 until December 1995 is used for estimation purposes, and the period from January 1996 until August 1999 for out-of-sample forecasting and evaluation. Forecasting over horizons ranging from 2 to 100 days, the forecast performance of both predictors is measured by the median absolute percentage forecast error. When evaluating the outcomes it is important to make a distinction between short-term and long-term forecast performance. Short-term performance depends on the ability of the predictor to take into account information about actual volatility behavior, whereas long-term volatility forecasts depend on the predictor's ability to correctly specify the long-term volatility level. The results can be found in Table 2.3. Looking at the forecast errors of the GARCH (1,1) model and the random walk model we see that for both predictors the forecast error tends to decrease if the forecast horizon increases. This is due to the variability of realized volatility, which decreases if the horizon increases. Table 2.3 shows that **for most indices the**

---

[3] R. Heynen and H. Kat, Volatility Prediction: A Comparison of the Stochastic Volatility, GARCH(1,1) and EGARCH(1,1) Models, *Journal of Derivatives*, Winter, 1994, pp. 50–65.

Table 2.3 Median absolute percentage forecast error in volatility forecasts

Index	Model	Forecast horizon							
		2	5	10	20	30	50	75	100
S&P 500	GARCH	60.44	29.46	24.16	19.43	17.72	17.31	20.33	27.66
	Const.	54.94	32.34	32.15	28.04	27.66	27.48	29.66	26.22
DJIA	GARCH	62.13	27.88	22.31	25.59	22.74	19.02	20.29	29.43
	Const.	58.61	29.14	25.55	24.14	26.13	25.61	26.16	23.56
Eurotop 100	GARCH	59.56	28.08	21.92	24.59	26.99	28.58	26.94	27.80
	Const.	60.34	38.72	32.10	28.99	28.65	32.58	31.48	30.19
Eurostoxx 50	GARCH	59.65	31.81	23.35	16.86	21.33	25.11	29.18	30.76
	Const.	60.44	40.78	39.13	34.61	33.99	37.01	39.60	34.89
FTSE 100	GARCH	56.14	27.21	23.65	19.20	20.41	22.12	29.43	26.70
	Const.	61.71	35.25	31.58	31.89	35.26	33.63	34.43	33.62
DAX	GARCH	59.30	32.32	28.01	25.61	26.45	26.79	30.25	27.93
	Const.	62.20	36.54	35.35	30.83	28.16	30.27	27.98	35.61
AEX	GARCH	54.84	30.22	21.46	18.24	19.55	24.60	23.92	29.38
	Const.	51.98	37.08	31.46	30.16	29.41	31.15	31.16	33.75
SMI	GARCH	59.77	33.86	28.01	21.84	28.06	22.64	25.49	24.32
	Const.	61.26	37.28	25.66	25.29	22.39	19.13	25.62	25.74
CAC 40	GARCH	69.24	30.11	20.83	22.10	22.00	16.01	17.75	20.14
	Const.	69.36	33.68	25.51	22.82	24.02	17.36	16.72	20.77
IBEX 35	GARCH	68.84	30.50	21.63	21.62	17.23	20.85	26.04	28.21
	Const.	70.73	34.28	30.99	24.89	24.60	27.41	29.81	28.04
MIB 30	GARCH	59.12	36.88	31.38	25.49	22.29	24.34	20.78	19.38
	Const.	63.01	37.76	32.66	24.98	24.87	25.13	22.07	20.35
Nikkei 225	GARCH	58.55	33.60	28.37	28.37	24.86	31.36	31.11	30.24
	Const.	73.72	44.31	40.11	35.88	33.93	33.16	30.24	29.30
Hang Seng	GARCH	60.93	36.48	25.58	34.17	37.44	30.80	29.76	28.15
	Const.	65.95	43.96	41.12	44.42	49.11	40.11	40.63	34.83
ASX All Ord.	GARCH	63.43	28.60	22.60	19.27	20.66	18.64	18.70	12.71
	Const.	65.21	34.03	26.33	20.73	23.08	19.67	18.00	10.77

GARCH(1,1) predictor outperforms the random walk predictor for short-term as well as longer term horizons.

We conclude with a **word of caution**. Although the GARCH (1,1) model's volatility forecasts tend to be more accurate than those of the random walk model, they are still far from perfect. The same is true for forecasts generated by other more complex statistical models. In this context it is helpful to distinguish between statistical and economic significance. Statistically, the forecasts produced by the GARCH (1,1) model and other models are better than those obtained from simpler models. However, in practice this may not make much difference. It has been shown elsewhere for example that in the hedging of derivatives (see Chapter 5), the attainable improvement in overall hedging performance is only small.[4] The same is true for models forecasting correlation. This suggests that **research aimed at improving the quality of volatility and correlation forecasts will not necessarily pay off commercially**.

---

[4] See H. Kat, *The Efficiency of Dynamic Trading Strategies in Imperfect Markets*, Ph.D. Thesis, University of Amsterdam, 1992.

2.7   CONCLUSION

Almost all stock market indices are value-weighted and do not take dividends into account. Well-known exceptions are the DJIA, which is a price-weighted index, and the DAX, which is a total return index. Many exchanges nowadays trade derivatives on these indices. As we will discuss in Chapter 5, this offers derivatives firms better opportunities to hedge themselves. During the nineties stock markets around the world experienced an increase in volatility. Preliminary analysis, however, suggests that the return generating process has not really changed. The observed increase in volatility is primarily the result of an increase in the number and extent of shocks to the system. This is especially true for the period 1997–1998, when the market was confronted with severe crises in Asia and Russia.

3
Special Contract Features

3.1 INTRODUCTION

In Chapter 1 we briefly mentioned special rights and restrictions in derivatives contracts. Such special contract features can be added to a contract as a whole, i.e. to all the cash flows in the contract, but also to specific individual cash flows and even to other special contract features. The latter possibility allows us to place restrictions on special rights or on other restrictions. In this chapter we discuss some of the possibilities in more detail, starting with the restrictions. For simplicity, we assume that all rights and restrictions are added to a contract as a whole.

Reading this chapter it should be kept in mind that it is not a complete overview of everything that is possible. Much more modestly, we simply aim to introduce the reader to the restrictions and rights most commonly used in derivatives contracts as well as the accompanying terminology. Terminology is nothing to fear. It is part of a language, i.e. a set of signs and sounds designed to efficiently describe certain matters.

3.2 KNOCK-IN AND KNOCK-OUT FEATURES

The most popular restriction to add to a derivatives contract is a so-called **knock-in** or **knock-out** feature which specifies that the contract only pays off under a restricted number of scenarios. With a knock-in feature the contract pays off **only if** a certain event occurs, in which case the contract is said to 'knock in'. Similarly, with a knock-out feature the contract pays off **unless** a certain event occurs. If it does, the contract is said to 'knock out'.

Logically, the distinction between knock-in and knock-out is not a very strict one. We may say about a contract that the relevant exchange takes place unless some event occurs, but in that case it is equally true that the exchange takes place only if that event does not occur. In the first case we might speak of a knock-out feature, while in the second case we might call it a knock-in feature. This means that whether we are dealing with a knock-in or a knock-out feature depends very much on how we tell the story. In practice, however, we always choose for the version that explains what happens when the relevant event occurs. This makes the above contract a knock-out contract.

All of this sounds very abstract. Time therefore to look at some specific examples of knock-in and knock-out features.

- One obvious example can be found in **life insurance**. Consider a policy which pays a fixed amount if a certain person dies during some period. Such a contract can be broken up into (a) a contract paying off a fixed amount under all scenarios, i.e. a zero, and (b) an additional knock-in feature saying that the zero will pay off only if the person in question dies.

- A very early example of a knock-out feature can be found in Hammurabi's Code. About 4000 years ago Hammurabi, then King of Babylon, stipulated that in the event of a

failed harvest farmers owing money did not have to pay any interest for one year. In other words, in case of a crop failure that year's interest payment knocked out.

- Hammurabi's Code also mentions another example of a knock-out feature. So-called sea loans were used to finance maritime commerce and were repayable only upon safe arrival of a ship or cargo. If the **ship or cargo was lost**, the loan knocked out.

- Instead of paying a small coupon to every bondholder, so-called premium bonds pay one very large coupon to only one bondholder. The bondholder to be paid is determined by means of a lottery. In other words, instead of paying regular coupons a premium bond lets bondholders participate in a series of **lottery draws**. Because a bondholder only gets paid if his number comes up, the coupons on a premium bond can be seen as fixed cash flows that knock in when the right number comes up.

- Suppose a manufacturing company wanted to protect itself against a specific client not being able to pay its bills. To do so the company could enter into a contract where its counterparty paid for all bills not paid by the client in case the latter defaulted. In this case the knock-in event is the occurrence of a specific **default**.

- Many companies are in some way exposed to **catastrophes**. It therefore sometimes makes sense to structure contracts that knock in or out when some catastrophe occurs. Such a feature allows us to closely tailor derivatives contracts to the needs of specific clients. This saves money as the client gets exactly what he needs and nothing more. For example, because in case of a major earthquake in Japan many Japanese firms will have to withdraw their investments in the US, they might be interested in purchasing a hedge against a drop of the US dollar versus the yen which is exercisable only in the event of a major earthquake in Japan.

- Another interesting category of knock-in and knock-out events are **takeovers**. A company could for example protect itself against an unfriendly takeover by entering into a contract that allowed it to sell additional shares to a friendly investor whenever an unfriendly takeover bid was made.

The above examples are only the tip of the iceberg. If we look at derivatives markets worldwide, by far **the most popular knock-in or knock-out event is the reaching of some prefixed level by some reference index during some monitoring period**. For example, a contract could have a knock-in feature that said it would pay off only if the S&P 500 index reached a level of 1500 during the life of the contract. If during the contract's life the S&P 500 did not reach 1500, the contract would be void. Likewise, a contract might be structured to knock out if 3-month USD LIBOR fell below 4.5%. The level of the reference index at which a knock-in or knock-out occurs is generally referred to as the **barrier**, and the reference index in question as the **barrier variable**.

It is important to note that, more generally speaking, a barrier defines a level of some variable where some action is triggered. That action may be the knocking in or knocking out of a contract as discussed here, but also, as we will see later, the locking in of intermediate profits, the adjustment of some contract parameter, the (de)activation of another barrier, the loss or receipt of a specific right, the (de)activation of a cap and/or floor, etc. In this section we concentrate on knock-ins and knock-outs, but most of the discussion is equally valid for these other cases.

3.3 BARRIERS

When adding a knock-in or knock-out feature it is important that all the relevant parameters are fully specified. If this is not the case, the contract may be open to dispute in the future.

With barriers there are a number of decisions to be made. We need to select the barrier variable(s), the monitoring point(s), the barrier level(s) at those monitoring points, and the exact nature of the barrier(s). We discuss these choices, as well as the accompanying terminology, in the subsections that follow.

3.3.1 The Barrier Variable

Most barrier features rely on a single barrier variable. Sometimes, however, it may be necessary to work with two or even more barrier variables. A barrier condition may for example state that the contract in question knocks out if the S&P 500 is higher than 1500 and at the same time the FTSE 100 is lower than 4000. Adding such a **multivariate barrier** feature is not the same as adding two separate **univariate barrier** features. In the latter case the barrier condition would state that the contract knocked out if either the S&P 500 was higher than 1500 or the FTSE 100 was lower than 4000. With a bivariate barrier feature both conditions need to be satisfied at the same time. In what follows we concentrate on univariate barriers.

Another important distinction concerns the question of whether the barrier variable is a new index or an index that was already present in the contract, although in another function. Typically, the reference index of the contract to which a barrier feature is added also acts as the barrier variable. In that case we speak of an **inside barrier**. Sometimes, however, the barrier variable is chosen differently. We might, for example, take a contract linked to the S&P 500 index and add a knock-out feature which says that the contract knocks out if the 10-year Treasury rate rises above 8%. Because in that case the barrier variable comes from outside the original contract, we refer to this as an **outside barrier**. In the case of an outside barrier we have to distinguish between the **payoff variable**, i.e. the reference index used in the original contract, and the barrier variable. This includes cases where the barrier variable is derived from the payoff variable, for example by taking a moving average. With an inside barrier the payoff and the barrier variable are identical.

3.3.2 The Monitoring Points

Having selected a barrier variable we need to decide on the dates and times that variable will be monitored. When barriers were first introduced the **monitoring period**, i.e. the period between the first and last monitoring point, covered the full life of the contract the feature was added to. This is referred to as **full monitoring**. However, there is no reason why we should always stick to full monitoring. With **partial monitoring** the barrier variable is monitored only during the first, middle or last part of a contract's life.

The monitoring points within the monitoring period can be distributed over time in any way we see fit. With so-called **continuous monitoring** we look at every successive index value within the monitoring period. In other cases, however, the barrier variable may only be monitored at fixed points in time, like every trading day at 14.00 hours or every Wednesday at 11.30 hours. In that case we speak of **discrete monitoring**. Although they typically are, with discrete monitoring the monitoring points need not necessarily be equally spaced. When they are we can identify an explicit **monitoring frequency** such as daily, weekly, monthly, etc.

A special type of barrier feature arises when there is only one monitoring point, either somewhere during the life of the contract or at maturity. To distinguish between this type of barrier feature and the type where the barrier variable is monitored more than once, market participants refer to the former as a **European barrier** and to the latter as an **American barrier**. With a European knock-out barrier at maturity, for example, the barrier condition states that the contract will pay off unless at maturity the barrier variable is higher or lower than some specific value.

3.3.3 The Barrier Level

Having decided on the barrier variable and the monitoring points, we need to decide on the barrier level at every monitoring point, i.e. the value to compare the observed value of the barrier variable with to decide whether a knock-in or knock-out has occurred. Traditionally, the barrier is set at the same level for every monitoring point. Over time, however, several types of non-constant barriers have been introduced. Nowadays the barrier level may evolve like a step function, i.e. change at fixed points in time but remain constant in between, or grow like an exponential function for example. One can even go one step further and instead of a **deterministic barrier** use a **stochastic barrier**. In that case the barrier level is not set in advance but made to depend on another reference index known as the **barrier determinant**. Any index can be used as a barrier determinant, but the most popular choice is to use the barrier variable itself. Doing so creates a barrier condition where one and the same index determines the barrier level at each monitoring point as well as the occurrence of a knock-in or knock-out event. One way to make the barrier level a function of the barrier variable is by letting the barrier level follow the barrier variable if it goes up (down) but not if it goes down (up). This is sometimes referred to as a **ratchet barrier**. Likewise, with partially monitored barriers that only become active at a later date, the barrier level at the first monitoring point may be fixed from inception but can also be fixed later as a function of the barrier determinant. In that case we speak of a **forward-starting barrier**.

3.3.4 The Nature of the Barrier

It may look as if we have thought of everything, but that is not the case. With all barriers one has to specify what happens if the barrier variable ends up exactly at the barrier. If in that case the contract knocks in or out, we speak of an **including barrier**; if not, we speak of an **excluding barrier**. But there is more. With a barrier that does not become active immediately, one has to specify whether the barrier variable actually has to hit the barrier to trigger a knock-in or knock-out or not. Suppose we had a 6-month contract with a constant knock-out barrier located 10% above the spot value of the barrier variable. The barrier variable is only monitored during the last two months of the contract's lifetime. The question then is what would happen if after four months the barrier variable had risen by, for example, 12%. Some might say that since the barrier variable has not hit the barrier yet, the contract is still alive. Others, however, might argue that since it is above the barrier it knocked out as soon as the barrier condition became active. In the first case we speak of a **hit barrier** and in the second case of a **dividing barrier**.

The distinction between dividing barriers and hit barriers is unique for partial barriers. With a full barrier, the barrier variable necessarily has to hit the barrier to get to the other side of it. Essentially, what we are talking about here is the question of what the relevant trigger event is. Is it the barrier's function to divide the outcome space into an 'in' and 'out' range, or does the barrier actually need to be hit? In the first case, the trigger event consists of finding the barrier variable at one particular side of the barrier. In the second case it is an actual barrier hit. With hit barriers one can go even further and distinguish between barriers where it makes no difference whether the barrier is hit from above or below, and barriers where it does. The former are referred to as **two-way hit barriers** and the latter as **one-way hit barriers**. Throughout the book we will concentrate on dividing barriers, as these are by far the most common in practice.

3.3.5 Lazy Barriers and Tranching

The barriers discussed so far define a level for the barrier variable which immediately triggers a knock-in or knock-out of the whole contract. Often this is considered too rigorous. Over the years, the market has seen a number of structures that try to solve this problem. One alternative is to take a **moving average** of the original barrier variable and use that as the relevant barrier variable. Since the moving average of an index moves more slowly than the index itself, this will only trigger a knock-in or knock-out if the original barrier variable stays at the other side of the barrier long enough to also pull its moving average to the other side.

An alternative is to use a so-called **lazy barrier**. Lazy barriers come in two types. Let N denote a prefixed number. In that case a **strong lazy barrier** requires that the last consecutive N observations on the barrier variable are all at the other side of the barrier before a knock-in or knock-out is triggered. We can think of this type of barrier as having an internal clock which measures what might be referred to as **barrier time**, i.e. the time spent at the other side of the barrier. As soon as the barrier variable crosses the barrier, the clock starts ticking. However, if the barrier variable moves back, the clock is reset to zero and everything starts all over again. A second type of lazy barrier is a so-called **loose lazy barrier**, which is similar to a strong lazy barrier except that it does not require the N observations to be consecutive. In other words, with a loose lazy barrier the clock measuring barrier time is not reset. For some reason, strong lazy barriers are sometimes referred to as **Parisian barriers** and loose lazy barriers as **ParAsian barriers**.

Barriers based on moving averages and lazy barriers also provide **protection against market manipulation**. Suppose the barrier variable came very close to the barrier. In that case the counterparty in whose interest it would be if the contract knocked in or out might be tempted to try to go out in the market and push the barrier variable across the barrier. In the case of a moving average or a lazy barrier such a strategy would be prohibitively costly, however, as it would not be enough to shift the barrier variable just momentarily. To make these barriers trigger a knock-in or knock-out the barrier variable not only has to be moved to the other side of the barrier, it also has to be kept there for a long enough period of time.

With a moving average barrier as well as with a lazy barrier the contract in question still knocks in or out as a whole. The knocking in or out does not occur gradually, there is just more time to see it coming. If we wanted to create a truly gradual knock-in or knock-out feature, we could split the contract in question into several **tranches** and give every tranche its own barrier. This will make the contract knock in or knock out tranche by tranche, thereby creating the gradual effect we are after. Suppose we divided a contract into three tranches of equal size and added a full knock-out barrier to every tranche at a level of 110%, 115% and 120% of the spot value of the barrier variable. If the barrier variable hit 110% the contract size would shrink by one-third. If it hit 115% it would again shrink by one-third, etc. An even smoother knock-in or knock-out pattern could be created by splitting the contract into a larger number of tranches and changing each tranche's barrier level by only a small step.

Apart from equipping different tranches with different barrier levels, lazy barriers offer another interesting possibility. Instead of giving each tranche a different barrier level, we could give every tranche the same barrier level but a different value of N, the number of times the barrier variable has to be seen at the other side of the barrier to trigger a knock-in or knock-out. Suppose that we divided a contract into three tranches of equal size and added a loose lazy knock-out barrier to each tranche; the first one with $N = 5$, the second one with $N = 10$, and the third one with $N = 15$. If the barrier variable spent a total of 5 observations on the other side of the barrier, one-third of the contract would knock out. If it spent a total of 10 observations on the other side, another one-third would knock out, etc. Again, we could create a smooth effect by splitting a contract into a large number of tranches, each with a slightly higher value for N. Suppose there were P monitoring points and we split a contract into P tranches and gave each tranche its own loose lazy knock-in barrier; the first one with $N = 1$, the second one with $N = 2$, etc. If the barrier variable spent 1 observation on the other side of the barrier the first tranche would knock in. If it spent 2 observations on the other side the second tranche would knock in, etc. If in total $P - 10$ observations were on the other side of the barrier, then the first $P - 10$ tranches would have knocked in and the last 10 would not.

It is important to realize that the above is not the same as giving each tranche a European barrier. Suppose again there were P monitoring points and the contract was split into P tranches. Each tranche is given a European knock-in barrier monitored only once at times $t = 1, 2, 3, \ldots, P$, respectively. If the barrier variable at the first monitoring point was on the other side, the first tranche would knock in. If it was on the other side at the second monitoring point, the second tranche would knock in, etc. If in total $P - 10$ observations were on the other side of the barrier, $P - 10$ tranches will have knocked in and 10 will not. Unlike with lazy barriers, however, we cannot say in advance which tranches will have knocked in and which not. If we wanted to make the knock-in or knock-out phenomenon more time dependent we should work with European barriers. On the other hand, if we wanted to control the sequence in which tranches knocked in or out we should work with lazy barriers.

3.3.6 Index-Linked Multipliers

Knock-in and knock-out features can also be interpreted in terms of index-linked multipliers, i.e. multipliers that are a function of some reference index. Without a barrier feature, the contract multiplier is a prefixed number. Let's call it M. If we add a barrier feature to the contract, the multiplier becomes a digital variable: M if the contract knocks in or does not knock out and 0 otherwise. Splitting the contract into a number of tranches, each with its own barrier condition, allows the multiplier to take on even more values. In the above example where a contract was split into three equal tranches, the multiplier can be interpreted as taking on the value M if no knock-out occurs, $2/3 \times M$ if only the first tranche knocks out, $1/3 \times M$ if the first two tranches knock out, and 0 if all three knock out.

3.4 DOUBLE BARRIERS

After the first barrier-driven knock-in and knock-out features were introduced it did not take long before derivatives structurers realized they could add more than one barrier to a contract and the **double barrier feature** was born. There are a very large variety of double barrier features that can be added to a contract. Theoretically, there is no limit to what one can come up with. As things get more complicated, however, they also become more difficult to justify and explain, and thereby more difficult to sell. We will therefore only briefly discuss the most popular double barriers and then move on to the various rights that may be given to the counterparties in derivatives contracts.

The simplest version of a double barrier is the case where there are either two knock-in or two knock-out barriers. We refer to these as **vanilla double barriers**. Within the family of vanilla double barriers we can distinguish between three groups.

- **One-hit vanilla double barrier:** a knock-in or knock-out is triggered if either one of the two barriers is hit.
- **Arbitrary-order two-hit vanilla double barrier:** a knock-in or knock-out is triggered only after both barriers have been hit, but there is no requirement as to which barrier must be hit first.
- **Fixed-order two-hit vanilla double barrier:** a knock-in or knock-out is only triggered when both barriers are hit in a fixed order.

We can vary double barriers in the same way as single barriers. We can vary the monitoring points, the barrier level, and we can also split a contract into a number of tranches and give each tranche its own double barrier. Suppose there were P daily monitoring points. We could then split a contract into P tranches and give each tranche a European one-hit vanilla double knock-out barrier monitored only once on day $1, 2, 3, \ldots, P$, respectively. If at the first monitoring point the barrier variable was on the other side of either barrier, the first tranche would knock out. If it was on the other side of either barrier at the second monitoring point, the second tranche would knock out, etc. If in total $P - 10$ observations were outside the range created by both barriers, then $P - 10$ tranches will have knocked out and 10 will not.

We do not need to have as many tranches as there are monitoring points. We might for example make $P/5$ tranches and give each tranche an American one-hit vanilla double knock-out barrier monitored five days in a row. The first tranche's barrier would be monitored on day 1, 2, 3, 4, 5, the second tranche's barrier on day 6, 7, 8, 9, 10, etc. This would turn the daily knock-out process we had before into a weekly process. Each tranche would pay off unless on any of the five monitoring points the barrier variable was outside the range defined by both barriers. As before, we can also interpret this in terms of an index-linked multiplier. Without the barrier restriction the contract multiplier would be a constant. With a barrier feature in place, however, the multiplier can take on more values depending on how many tranches can knock in or out.

3.5 THE RIGHT TO CANCEL A CONTRACT

So far we have only discussed restrictions, but adding restrictions is not the only addition that can be made to a derivatives contract. There are a number of rights that can be added as well. A right which allows one to significantly change a contract's payoff can be a valuable asset. If so, the counterparty that obtains this right will have to compensate the other counterparty for granting it. This can be done in a variety of ways. In this section we do not go into this, but concentrate on the various rights per se.

One of the most worthwhile rights we can give to one of the two counterparties in a contract is the right to cancel that contract. There are at least two parameters to this right.

- **The point(s) in time the right can be exercised**. We can distinguish between (a) contracts that can only be cancelled at one specific point in time, (b) contracts that can be cancelled at two or more specific points in time, and (c) contracts that can be cancelled at any time during some period.
- **The extra payment to be made when exercised**.

The simplest and at the same time most powerful case arises if we give a counterparty the right to cancel a contract at maturity without any extra payment. We look at this case first.

3.5.1 The Option Right

Under a forward contract two counterparties commit themselves to exchange two cash flows. This commitment is legally binding. Whatever the future holds, the exchange specified in the contract will have to be made. In many applications this is considered too rigid though. Often one counterparty is therefore given the exclusive right to cancel the contract at maturity without any extra payment. We call this the **option right**. The result is straightforward. Whenever the holder of the option right has to pay more than he is to receive, he will cancel the contract. This means that we can compare the option right with an **insurance policy**. Since the holder of the option right can cancel the contract if it works out to his disadvantage, he knows in advance he is fully protected against a loss. The reverse goes for his counterparty. Knowing in advance that the holder of the option right will cancel if he has to pay more than he is to receive, his counterparty knows he is never going to make money on the contract. This is equivalent to selling insurance.

Suppose that two counterparties agreed to exchange a fixed cash flow of USD 1600 and an index-linked cash flow equal to the value of the S&P 500 index one year from now. Now suppose the fixed cash flow payer was given the right to cancel the contract at maturity. Since he will exercise his option right if the S&P 500 ends below 1600, his counterparty knows in advance that on balance he will never receive anything. He may end up paying though. If the index ends at or below 1600 the deal is effectively off, but if the S&P ends above 1600 he on balance pays the difference between the value of the index and 1600. Alternatively, suppose the index-linked cash flow payer was given the right to cancel the contract at maturity. Since he will exercise his option right if the S&P 500 ends above 1600, his counterparty again knows in advance that on balance he will never receive anything. If the S&P 500 ends at or above 1600 the deal is off, but if it ends below 1600 he on balance pays the difference between 1600 and the value of the index.

The introduction of the option right significantly changes a forward contract's payoff profile. Initially both counterparties have a more or less equal chance to make money. After the introduction of the option right, however, the holder of the option right knows that he is never going to lose and his counterparty knows he is never going to win. **The right to cancel a contract at maturity is an extremely valuable asset**. The counterparty acquiring the option right will therefore have to compensate the other party in some way. This is typically done by means of an upfront payment, referred to as the **option premium**.

What is typically referred to as an option is nothing more than a forward where one counterparty has the right to cancel the contract at maturity. This definition is a lot more general than the one commonly used in derivatives textbooks. Traditionally, an option is defined as the right to buy or sell some underlying asset by a certain date for a certain price. Our definition deviates substantially from this. The traditional definition assumes that at maturity some underlying asset is physically exchanged for cash. In our definition, however, it is not the underlying asset but a cash amount equal to that asset's price that is exchanged. Furthermore, since we exchange cash flows we do not need to limit ourselves to using asset prices as reference indices. As discussed in Chapter 1, we are free to use any variable we want as reference index.

With forwards there are only two alternative positions one can take, depending on which cash flow is paid and which one is received. If party A pays a fixed amount and party B an index-linked cash flow, then A is said to be **long** and B to be **short** the forward. In terms of buying and selling, A is said to be the **buyer** and B the **seller** of the forward. With options there are not two but four alternative positions since, apart from the side one is on with respect to the cash flows involved, it also depends who has the right to decide whether payments are actually going to be made or not. Suppose we had a forward between two counterparties; A and B. If we give counterparty A the right to cancel the contract, party A would be **long** the option and B would be **short** the option. In terms of buying and selling, A would be the **buyer** of the option and B would be the **seller** or **writer** of the option. In practice, the latter term is the most common.

With options who is the buyer and who is the seller depends on who has the option right and not on who pays what. With options this is nevertheless important, but now to decide what kind of option we are talking about. If the buyer of the option pays an index-linked amount and the writer pays a fixed amount we speak of a **put option**. If on the other hand the buyer pays the fixed amount and the writer pays the index-linked amount we speak of a **call option**. In both cases the fixed amount to be paid is referred to as the option's **strike price** or simply as its **strike**. If both counterparties pay an index-linked amount the distinction between put and call options becomes less clear. The obvious thing to do in those cases is to interpret the least volatile cash flow as the option's so-called **floating strike**.

Another important distinction is the distinction between out-of-the-money, at-the-money and in-the-money options. An option is called **out-of-the-money (OTM)** when the buyer of the option would make no money if the option contract matured immediately. If the option matured immediately and the buyer would make money the option is said to be **in-the-money (ITM)**. If the buyer would neither win nor lose the option is referred to as being **at-the-money (ATM)**. A call option is ITM when the index is higher than the strike. It is OTM when the index is lower than the strike, and ATM when the index equals the strike. For put options things are of course exactly the other way around. A put option is ITM when the index is lower than the strike. It is OTM when the index is higher than the strike, and ATM when the index equals the strike.

3.5.2 The Right to Exchange a Contract for Cash

With the option right the option holder can cancel the contract without making any payment to his counterparty. There is no particular reason, however, why cancellation should not be accompanied by an extra payment to compensate the other counterparty for losing the contract. We can give a counterparty the right to cancel a contract by paying the other counterparty a prefixed amount, but we can also do things the other way around and give a counterparty the right to cancel a contract by requiring the other counterparty to pay him a prefixed amount. In the first case we speak of a **callable** contract and in the second case we speak of a **puttable** contract. Of course, **the difference between a**

callable and a puttable contract lies in the cancellation payment. In the case of a callable contract this payment is positive, while in the case of a puttable contract it is negative.

3.5.3 The Right to Exchange One Contract for Another

With a callable or puttable contract one counterparty has the right to exchange the relevant contract for cash or require the other counterparty to do so. Instead of cash, we could also exchange the contract for another contract. As with callable and puttable contracts, there are two versions. If a counterparty has the right to replace the relevant contract by another contract we speak of an **exchangeable** contract. Alternatively, if one counterparty has the right to require the other counterparty to replace the relevant contract by another contract we speak of a **convertible** contract.

Of course, in both cases certain rules need to be specified in advance regarding the set of alternative contracts to choose from. The new contract which replaces the old one need not necessarily be a derivatives contract though. With a typical convertible bond for example the holder of the bond has the right to require the issuer of the bond to replace the bond by a certain number of shares of stock. Similarly, the new contract need not necessarily be with the same counterparty. Some convertibles do not deliver the bond issuer's own stocks, but deliver the stocks of another company. Convertibles that deliver another company's stocks are becoming more and more popular. In Europe about 60% of recent issuance has been of this type. One of the attractions of this type of convertible for the buyer lies in the fact that the credit spread of the issuer is less correlated with the equity that the bond converts into. For the issuer there can also be clear advantages. For example, when used as a way to sell off existing equity holdings, the issuer can delay paying capital gains tax.

3.6 THE RIGHT TO CHANGE A CONTRACT PARAMETER

In the majority of cases contract parameters will be fixed in advance. Sometimes, however, we need to allow a counterparty to change a parameter at a later point in time. Of course, doing so one will need to specify certain rules in advance regarding

- **The set of possible parameter values to choose from**
- **The point(s) in time this right can be exercised**
- **The extra payment to be made when exercised**

One interesting right we can give to one of the counterparties in a contract is the right to shorten or lengthen the maturity of a contract. When the time to maturity can be increased the contract is said to be **extendible**, while when the time to maturity can be decreased the contract is referred to as **time retractible**. A special case of a time retractible contract arises when one of the counterparties has the right to let the contract mature immediately, i.e. to reset the contract's remaining time to maturity to zero, without making an extra payment. This is known as the right of **early exercise**. The right of early exercise allows a counterparty to pinpoint the time the underlying exchange of cash flows is to occur (given the values of the reference index or indices up to that point in time). If the holder of the right of early exercise can make the contract mature at any time before the original maturity date, the contract is said to be **American**, while if he can do so only at specific times, the contract is called **Bermudan** or **Mid-Atlantic**. To distinguish them from American and Bermudan contracts, contracts without an early exercise feature are called **European**.

Apart from time to maturity, another parameter that may need resetting is the multiplier of a contract. When the contract multiplier can be increased the contract is said to be **expandible**, while when the multiplier can be decreased the contract is referred to as **size retractible**. A third example of the right of parameter reset is the right to switch to another reference index. We call this the **right of index reset**.

Sometimes it may be necessary to combine two parameter reset rights to allow for the possibility to change a contract in such a way that its overall value stays more or less unchanged. Suppose we sold a call option, i.e. we entered into a contract where we paid the index value, our counterparty paid a fixed amount and also had the right to cancel the contract at maturity. If for some reason we wanted to make sure that the option matured ITM we could ask for the right to lower the fixed amount payable by our counterparty. If we did, this would raise the value of the contract for our counterparty as he would have to pay less to receive the same. However, if we also had the right to change the contract's time to maturity we could do so in such a way as to prevent the contract's value from changing significantly.

3.7   RIGHTS AND AUTOMATIC FEATURES

Every right can be turned into an **automatic feature**, which says that if a certain event occurs that right is exercised automatically. Of course, we can also turn automatic features into rights. For example, instead of automatically adjusting a contract parameter we could give a counterparty the right to do so.

Turning a right into an automatic feature means we have to select a **trigger event** to guide the exercise of the right in question. If we wanted to automate the right of early exercise, for example, we could say that the contract would mature the moment a prespecified takeover or default occurred. Alternatively, we could say that the contract would mature the moment some reference index reached a prefixed barrier level. Of course, we do not always have to let the contract mature immediately. We could also say that the contract would mature a given number of days, weeks or months after the occurrence of the trigger event. Note that sometimes the holder of a right may also have to make a choice between two or more alternatives. In that case we not only need to decide on a trigger event, but also on an explicit **decision rule** for choosing between these alternatives.

It is important to realize that **if we assume rational behavior of the holder of a right, that right becomes an automatic feature**. Let's look at the option right for example. Although the option holder is free to decide whatever he wants, a rational person will only cancel a contract if he has to pay more than he will receive. We can therefore also interpret the option right as a European knock-in feature that says the contract will pay off only if the deal ends such that the option holder pays less than he receives. In other words, assuming rational behavior of the option holder, the option right is an automatic feature. In practice, relatively simple rights are treated as automatic features instead of as rights. Some of the structured cash flows we will discuss in the next chapter are in fact nothing more than the rational automatic version of rights that at first sight seem rather far-fetched. A cash flow equal to the highest of the values of two different reference indices for example is really nothing more than the rational automatic version of the right of index reset.

Let's look at a practical example. Suppose we were called in by an insurance company to structure a contract that protected its equity portfolio against losses. One solution is to structure a forward contract where the insurance company pays the value of its equity portfolio one year from now and receives the current value of the portfolio. Unfortunately, this not only eliminates the downside but also the upside. To solve this we could grant the insurer the right to cancel the forward at maturity, thereby turning the forward into a put option, but this would require the insurer to make a substantial upfront payment. Thinking about the problem a little bit further, it becomes clear that the only time the insurer really needs protection is if he has so many claims coming in that he has to start liquidating his assets. The obvious thing to do therefore is to offer the insurance company a put option which pays off only if a major catastrophe occurs. Because this is unlikely to happen, this will reduce the price of the protection. We can do even better though. Suppose the knock-in put had an initial maturity of one year but knocked in after a month. In that case the insurer would acquire a put option with 11 months to maturity. He has no need for an 11-month put option, however, as he needs the money to pay off the incoming claims much sooner. This means we can save more money by letting the option mature automatically a couple of weeks after it knocks in. A contract like this would provide the insurance company with exactly what it needs but nothing more, which keeps the price down.

3.8   CONCLUSION

Part of the reason why there is such a great variety of derivatives contracts around in today's markets is the possibility of introducing special restrictions and/or rights into contracts. This allows derivatives structurers to tailor a contract more closely to the specific problem at hand. By far the most popular right to be added to a derivatives contract is the option right. It allows its holder to cancel the contract in question at maturity at zero cost. Knock-in and knock-out features, especially in the form of a barrier condition, are the most popular restrictions. Special features are typically added to a contract as a whole, but there is no reason why they cannot be added to specific individual cash flows or even to other special features. Adding a knock-out feature to the option right for example will turn the option in question into a forward when a knock-out is triggered. Likewise, adding a knock-out feature to the right of early exercise will turn the American option in question into a European option.

4

Index-Linked Cash Flows

4.1 INTRODUCTION

Much of the secret of derivatives structuring lies in the construction of the index-linked cash flows. This chapter therefore provides an overview of the most popular index-linked cash flows used in derivatives structuring. As with the special features discussed in Chapter 3, it is not a complete overview. It is meant to give the reader a general flavor of some of the more popular possibilities. Apart from discussing many index-linked cash flows qualitatively, we will also discuss one or more formal expressions for each cash flow. Formalization is a very important stage in the structuring process for two reasons.

- An idea can only be analyzed satisfactorily if it can be formalized. Therefore, if an idea cannot be formalized it has little chance of succeeding.
- In the term sheet and confirmation that will eventually embody a contract we have to specify how that contract's payoff will be calculated. A formal expression does so much more precisely and efficiently than written text.

There is no need to fear the formalization process as it is nothing more than the translation from one language (English) into another (mathematics). Formalization does not add anything new. It simply allows us to express our ideas in a language which is better suited for analysis than plain English. The goal of this book is to provide the reader with enough intuition and understanding to allow him to structure equity derivatives contracts without having to resort to ready-made lists of products. Read this chapter carefully. However, do not try to memorize it as that will spoil most of the fun.

ASSUMPTIONS & NOTATION

Unless stated otherwise, we will assume that all cash flows are settled immediately after the amount to be exchanged has been determined. Note, however, that due to operational constraints **in practice the size of an index-linked cash flow will have to be determined at least a few days before the payment date**. In other words, in practice there will always be at least a few days between the moment the size of an index-linked cash flow is determined and the actual exchange. Time will be measured in years. The present is denoted as $t = 0$, one year from now as $t = 1$, two years from now as $t = 2$, etc. When speaking more generally, the cash flow payment date is denoted as time T. The time t value of the reference index is denoted as I_t. In case there is more than one reference index we differentiate between them using superscripts 1, 2, etc. In case we need to convert currencies, the number of units of payment currency one has to pay for one unit of non-payment currency is denoted as E_t.

4.2 FIXED CASH FLOWS

A fixed cash flow is a given amount of money to be exchanged at some future date. USD 100 million payable in five years is a fixed cash flow because, despite the fact that the cash flow will not occur for five years, there is no uncertainty about the size of the cash flow (ignoring credit risk). One may not be used to looking at fixed cash flows this way, but fixed cash flows do have multipliers. The basic fixed cash flow is an amount of 1.00. Any other amount can be thought of as the product of a multiplier and 1.00. Denoting the cash flow as CF_T and the multiplier as M, this means that a fixed cash flow can formally be expressed as

$$CF_T = M \times 1.00. \tag{4.1}$$

It may seem a little far-fetched to think about fixed cash flows this way, but sometimes this level of detail comes in handy. We will leave the 1.00 out from now.

Now suppose the fixed amount M was denominated in another currency than the currency in which we wanted to get paid, and we decided to convert it into the desired payment currency at the time T exchange rate E_T. In that case the cash flow would be equal to

$$CF_T = M \times E_T. \tag{4.2}$$

Since we convert at the time T exchange rate, our fixed cash flow is not really fixed any more as it now depends on the exchange rate at time T. If we did not want this, for example because we expected the payment currency to appreciate, we could convert at a prefixed rate. An obvious choice would be the present exchange rate E_0. In that case we could simply substitute E_0 for E_T to give us a so-called **quantoed fixed cash flow** equal to

$$CF_T = M \times E_0. \tag{4.3}$$

If we thought the exchange rate was going down, the quantoed cash flow is a good solution as it eliminates all exchange risk. However, we would do even better if we made the cash flow an inverse function of the exchange rate. We could for example structure a cash flow equal to

$$CF_T = M \times \frac{E_0^2}{E_T}. \tag{4.4}$$

Of course, such a cash flow can also be seen as a quantoed cash flow with an exchange rate-linked multiplier equal to $M \times E_0/E_T$. Other currency conversion alternatives can be handled in the same way.

4.3   DIGITALS

Suppose we had a fixed cash flow equal to M. Now suppose we added a knock-out barrier to this cash flow. Suddenly it would no longer be a fixed cash flow, as we now have a barrier variable determining whether the exchange actually takes place or not. The index-linked nature of the new cash flow is very special since there are only two possible outcomes. Either the exchange occurs or it does not, which is why cash flows like this are referred to as **digitals**. Digitals are also known under a variety of other names, such as **binaries**, **cash-or-nothings** or **flip-flops**. We can equip fixed cash flows with any type of barrier feature we see fit. When doing so there are a number of decisions to be made, including

- The **barrier variable(s)**
- The **monitoring point(s)**

- The **barrier level(s)** at each of the monitoring points
- The **exact nature** of the barrier(s)

We discussed this in detail in Chapter 3, so we will not go into this again here.

Suppose we combined a fixed cash flow with a knock-out condition that said the exchange occurs **unless** at one or more of the monitoring points the barrier variable is equal to or higher than a fixed barrier level H. Formally, this would give us a cash flow equal to

$$CF_T = D \times M, \tag{4.5}$$

where

$$D = 0, \quad \text{if } \exists j \; I_j \geqslant H,$$
$$= 1, \quad \text{if } \forall j \; I_j < H.$$

In the above expression the subscript j counts the monitoring points, $\exists j$ means 'there exists a j for which' and $\forall j$ means 'for all j'. Note the digital nature of D. It takes on either of two values: 0 in case the barrier variable is seen at or above the barrier and 1 if not. Every knock-in or knock-out condition can be expressed in this way. To turn the above knock-out condition into a knock-in condition which lets the cash flow occur **only if** at one or more monitoring points the barrier variable is equal to or higher than H, we only have to switch the 0 and the 1, i.e. we would have

$$D = 1, \quad \text{if } \exists j \; I_j \geqslant H,$$
$$= 0, \quad \text{if } \forall j \; I_j < H.$$

From the above it is clear that a knock-out digital and an equivalent knock-in digital always sum to the fixed cash flow to which the knock-out and knock-in conditions were added. When the knock-out digital knocks out, the knock-in digital knocks in and the other way around. On balance, we therefore always get paid.

Over time fixed cash flows with certain types of knock-in or knock-out features have earned their own names in the market, such as the following.

- **European digital:** fixed cash flow with a European barrier. European digitals only pay off if at the monitoring point the barrier variable is above or below a certain value. In the first case we speak of a **digital call** and in the second case of a **digital put**.
- **American digital:** fixed cash flow with an American barrier. These are sometimes also referred to as **one-touch binaries** or simply **barriers**.
- **Digital spread:** fixed cash flow with a double European knock-out barrier. A digital spread only pays off if at the monitoring point the barrier variable is within some prefixed range.
- **BRICK:** fixed cash flow with a double European bivariate knock-out barrier. BRICKs only pay off if at the monitoring point both barrier variables are within some prefixed range.
- **Mixed digital:** European digital with an additional American barrier. When the American barrier is hit (for a knock-in) or not hit (for a knock-out) the cash flow still only occurs if at the monitoring point the barrier variable is above or below a certain value.

It is interesting to note that **digital spreads can be packaged from digital calls or digital puts**. A digital call pays off if the index is above a certain value. A digital spread pays off if the index is between H^1 and H^2 ($H^1 < H^2$). This means that the payoff of a digital spread can be obtained by buying a digital call which pays off above H^1, while simultaneously selling a digital call which pays off above H^2. Alternatively, one could of course buy a digital put that pays off below H^2 and sell a digital put that pays off below H^1.

4.4 VANILLA INDEX-LINKED CASH FLOWS

As discussed in Chapter 1, a vanilla index-linked cash flow is a cash flow equal to the value of the reference index on the payment date. For example, a cash flow equal to the USD value of the S&P 500 index one year from now. Formally, this means we now have a cash flow equal to

$$CF_T = M \times I_T. \tag{4.6}$$

This cash flow depends linearly on the index value. A higher (lower) value of the reference index will produce a proportionally higher (lower) cash flow.

If the reference index's natural currency of denomination was not the currency in which we wanted to get paid, and we converted the index currency at the exchange rate on the payment date, the cash flow would become equal to

$$CF_T = M \times E_T \times I_T, \tag{4.7}$$

which shows that the cash flow now varies with the reference index as well as the exchange rate. The cash flow is higher the higher the index and the higher the exchange rate. This is known as a **composite cash flow**. If we did not want the cash flow to depend on the exchange rate we could convert the index currency at a prefixed rate, yielding a **quantoed index-linked cash flow**. If we used the $t = 0$ exchange rate to do so, we would end up with a cash flow equal to

$$CF_T = M \times E_0 \times I_T. \tag{4.8}$$

In the above expressions time T plays a double role. It not only denotes the cash flow payment date but also the date the amount to be paid is determined. In other words, with a standard vanilla index-linked cash flow the exchange takes place as soon as the amount to be exchanged has been determined. It is also possible to delay the payment for a while, i.e. to fix the amount to be exchanged some time before the actual payment date. In that case we speak of an index-linked cash flow with **delayed settlement**. Formally, this means we now have a cash flow equal to

$$CF_T = M \times I_{t^*}, \quad t^* < T, \tag{4.9}$$

where now T denotes the payment date and t^* denotes the date the reference index is monitored to determine the amount to be exchanged at time T. Note that delayed settlement does not concern the settlement delay that usually occurs between the index monitoring date and the actual payment date. We are talking here about a delay on top of the usual settlement delay.

Delayed settlement is not a concept that is limited to vanilla cash flows. **We can delay the settlement of any index-linked cash flow**. In equity derivatives delayed settlement cash flows are not very common. In the interest rate area, however, delayed settlement is the rule and immediate settlement the exception as the interest to be paid over some period of time is typically fixed at the beginning of that period based on the interest rate at that point in time.

Adding a knock-in or knock-out feature to a vanilla index-linked cash flow is no different from adding one to a fixed cash flow. If we combined our index-linked cash flow with a knock-out condition that said the cash flow would occur unless at one of the monitoring points the barrier variable was equal to or higher than a fixed barrier level H, we would get a cash flow equal to

$$CF_T = M \times D \times I_T, \tag{4.10}$$

where

$$D = 0, \quad \text{if } \exists j \, I_j \geqslant H,$$
$$= 1, \quad \text{if } \forall j \, I_j < H.$$

This is sometimes referred to as an **asset-or-nothing**. As with fixed cash flows, a knock-out and an equivalent knock-in index-linked cash flow always sum to an ordinary index-linked cash flow.

4.5 BASKETS AND SPREADS

In many cases the problem to be solved does not depend on one single stock price or one single stock market index, but on a number of them. Not many investors for example invest all their money in one single stock or even in one single market. A common thing therefore is to work with cash flows equal to sums of stock prices or stock market indices. These are referred to as **baskets**. With a total of N reference indices this creates cash flows such as

$$CF_T = M^1 \times I_T^1 + M^2 \times I_T^2 + \cdots + M^N \times I_T^N, \tag{4.11}$$

where I_T^i denotes the time T value of reference index $i = 1, 2, \ldots, N$ and the M^i terms are the multipliers that come with each index in the basket. The above cash flow equals the sum of N vanilla index-linked cash flows. Again, the size of the cash flow depends linearly on the values of the reference indices. Higher (lower) index values produce a higher (lower) cash flow.

Since we are simply talking about a sum of vanilla index-linked cash flows, currency conversion is easily incorporated. Suppose the second and the Nth reference index were denominated in a currency different from the payment currency. In that case we would first convert them into the payment currency and then sum the resulting cash flows with the others just as before. Converting at the time T exchange rate, this would yield a cash flow of

$$CF_T = M^1 \times I_T^1 + M^2 \times E_T^2 \times I_T^2 + \cdots + M^N \times E_T^N \times I_T^N, \tag{4.12}$$

where E_T^2 is the exchange rate between the currency of index 2 and the payment currency and E_T^N is the exchange rate of the currency of index N. To eliminate the dependence on these exchange rates we can quanto both foreign indices in the same way as before or use any other form of currency translation.

We are completely free in our choice of cash flows to add. Instead of vanilla cash flows we could work with cash flows with delayed settlement or any of the more complex cash flows we will discuss in the sections that follow. Instead of only index-linked cash flows we could also include a fixed cash flow in the sum. With a fixed amount plus an index-linked cash flow it is important, however, to note that by itself the fixed cash flow does not imply a minimum value for the total cash flow. In some cases, however, the index-linked part of the cash flow cannot be negative by its very nature, which produces the illusion of a minimum value where in more general terms there is none.

Instead of the sum we sometimes need a cash flow equal to the difference between two reference indices. Such cash flows are referred to as **spreads** and can be formally expressed as

$$CF_T = M^1 \times I_T^1 - M^2 \times I_T^2. \tag{4.13}$$

For example, I^1 could be the price of a share of Microsoft and I^2 the S&P 500 index, and the multipliers could be set such that $M^1 \times I_0^1 = M^2 \times I_0^2$. In that case the above cash flow would give us the outperformance of Microsoft relative to the S&P 500 index over the period from $t = 0$ to $t = T$.

As with sums, we do not need to restrict ourselves to vanilla cash flows. We can use any cash flow we want, including fixed cash flows. When working with a fixed and a vanilla index-linked cash flow a special case arises when the fixed cash flow is set equal to the present value of the reference index of the vanilla cash flow. In that case we speak of a long change and a short change, respectively. The **long change** can be expressed as

$$CF_T = M \times (I_T - I_0) \tag{4.14}$$

and the **short change** as

$$CF_T = M \times (I_0 - I_T). \tag{4.15}$$

Instead of calculating the change from the present value of the reference index one may also use the index value on a later date. This means replacing I_0 by the delayed settlement cash flow I_{t^*}, in which case we speak of a **forward-starting change**.

4.6   RATIOS AND PRODUCTS

Sometimes we need a cash flow that expresses the magnitude of one reference index relative to another. This means we have to divide two cash flows. Assuming both cash flows are vanilla index-linked cash flows, this means we have a cash flow equal to

$$CF_T = \frac{M^1 \times I_T^1}{M^2 \times I_T^2}. \tag{4.16}$$

When calculating this cash flow we first monetize, currency translate (if necessary) and multiply the values of both reference indices. Dividing money amounts, however, produces a number without unit and also takes the biggest part of the multipliers out. We therefore need to **re-monetize** and **re-multiply** the resulting ratio. This re-monetization is just a formality, however, as all the relevant monetization and currency translation will have been done before the calculation of the ratio. We therefore **always monetize ratios into the payment currency**.

Instead of both component cash flows being index-linked, one of them could be fixed. We could for example create a cash flow equal to the value of the reference index at time T divided by the value of the same index at $t = 0$. We could use this as a measure for the change in the reference index over the period from $t = 0$ to $t = T$. A ratio higher than one would indicate the index had gone up and a ratio lower than one that it had gone down. This is known as a **wealth ratio**. This also shows that when both component cash flows are index-linked they need not necessarily be linked to different reference indices.

At other times we may need a cash flow equal to the product of two other cash flows. This would produce a cash flow equal to

$$CF_T = (M^1 \times I_T^1) \times (M^2 \times I_T^2). \tag{4.17}$$

Note that with a cash flow equal to the product of two other cash flows both cash flows have to be index-linked, because if one was fixed it would just be a change of multiplier.

4.7 HIGHEST AND LOWEST

The attraction of derivatives structuring is in large part due to the possibility of creating cash flows equal to the highest or lowest of two or more other cash flows. The highest and lowest are often referred to as '**the best**' and '**the worst**'. Although this terminology is very common, it can be somewhat confusing at times since what is best (worst) for one counterparty is worst (best) for the other. Suppose we had two cash flows; a fixed amount K and a vanilla index-linked cash flow. Taking the **highest** of these two can formally be written as

$$CF_T = \text{Max}\,[K, M \times I_T]. \tag{4.18}$$

If the index on the payment date is such that it yields an index-linked cash flow larger than K this cash flow is identical to a vanilla index-linked cash flow. However, for index values that produce an index-linked cash flow smaller than K this cash flow is identical to a fixed cash flow equal to K. Taking the **lowest** of the two cash flows can be expressed as

$$CF_T = \text{Min}\,[K, M \times I_T]. \tag{4.19}$$

If the index-linked cash flow is larger than K this cash flow is identical to a fixed cash flow of K and equal to the vanilla index-linked cash flow otherwise.

There are no restrictions on the nature and number of component cash flows we can use. If we had three vanilla index-linked cash flows and we wanted a cash flow equal to the highest of these three, this could be denoted as

$$CF_T = \text{Max}\,[M^1 \times I_T^1, M^2 \times I_T^2, M^3 \times I_T^3]. \tag{4.20}$$

As before, every cash flow brings its own multiplier. When structuring a cash flow like this we need to take care that the multipliers are chosen in such a way that the three component cash flows are comparable in size. Suppose the first reference index was currently at 100, the second at 200 and the third at 400, and that they were equally volatile. Using the same multiplier for all three indices would in that case probably lead to a cash flow equal to $M^3 \times I_T^3$, i.e. the Max operator would be trivial.

Cash flows equal to the highest or lowest of a number of other cash flows can be interpreted and presented in two other ways.

- We can see them as rational automatic versions of the right of index reset which we mentioned in Chapter 3. If we allow the receiver or payer of a cash flow to choose which of two or more cash flows he wants to exchange, the receiver will choose the highest and the payer the lowest.
- We can see them as **floored** (in case of the highest) or **capped** (in case of the lowest) cash flows where the floor or cap level is equal to another cash flow.

We can also use a fixed or index-linked cash flow with a knock-in or knock-out barrier to set the cap or floor level. This would mean that the cap or floor would apply only if or unless the barrier variable reached a certain level. Putting a fixed floor on an index-linked cash flow means taking the highest of a fixed cash flow and the relevant index-linked cash flow. If we make the fixed cash flow knock out when the index is equal to or higher than H, we end up with a cash flow equal to

$$CF_T = \text{Max}\,[D \times K, M \times I_T], \tag{4.21}$$

with

$$D = 0, \quad \text{if } \exists j\ I_j \geqslant H,$$
$$= 1, \quad \text{if } \forall j\ I_j < H.$$

If the floor does not knock out, the cash flow would be identical to that in (4.18). On the other hand, if the floor knocks out the cash flow would simply be equal to a vanilla index-linked cash flow.

4.8   VANILLA RETURNS

When it comes to investment applications, people typically think in terms of return on investment. A cash flow equal to the return on some reference index over some period is obtained by dividing a cash flow equal to the difference between the index value at the end of the period and the index value at the beginning, i.e. the long change, by a cash flow equal to the index value at the beginning. As mentioned before, dividing money amounts creates the need for re-monetization and re-multiplication. This re-monetization is just a formality, however, as all the relevant monetization and currency translation will have been done before the calculation of the return figure. We therefore **always monetize returns into the payment currency**.

Investors often work with cash flows that are multiples of the return on a basket of reference indices instead of a single index. They may for example work with the return on a basket of 20 different telecommunications stocks or a basket of five different stock market indices. When some of these reference indices are denominated in different currencies we are at the same time also confronted with currency translation. Adding to the confusion is the fact that the same cash flow can often be formalized in different ways, with some derivatives structurers preferring one way and others preferring another. Insight into the different ways a given cash flow may be expressed and knowledge of the least intimidating way to do so is of great importance for derivatives structurers. We will therefore spend quite some time on this subject. We start the discussion with the case of a single reference index and proceed with the case of a basket of indices. Especially in the latter case things may easily become messy. For clarity, we set all multipliers equal to 1.

4.8.1   Single Index Returns

Suppose the natural currency of denomination of the reference index was the same as the payment currency, so there was no need for currency translation. The **vanilla return on a domestic index** over the period from $t = 0$ to $t = T$ could in that case be calculated as

$$R^{\mathrm{d}}_{0,T} = \frac{I_T - I_0}{I_0} = \frac{I_T}{I_0} - 1. \tag{4.22}$$

How would this change if the index was denominated in another currency and we had to implement some form of currency conversion? Obviously, it would depend on the chosen conversion method. If we were to quanto the index value using the $t = 0$ exchange rate nothing would change, since the **vanilla return on a quantoed index** can be calculated as

$$R^{\mathrm{q}}_{0,T} = \frac{E_0 \times I_T - E_0 \times I_0}{E_0 \times I_0} = \frac{I_T}{I_0} - 1. \tag{4.23}$$

If we converted the index value using the exchange rate at the same time the index was observed we would get a different result, as the **vanilla return on a composite index** is given by

$$R^{\mathrm{c}}_{0,T} = \frac{E_T \times I_T - E_0 \times I_0}{E_0 \times I_0} = \frac{E_T \times I_T}{E_0 \times I_0} - 1. \tag{4.24}$$

4.8.2   Basket Returns

If instead of a single reference index we hooked up our cash flow with a basket of indices, we would have to deal with a number of indices at the same time. As a result, the expressions become more complicated, especially when currency translation is involved. In these cases it is of even greater importance to know how to express the cash flow to be exchanged in the form of a simple formula. Suppose there were two reference indices, both denominated in the payment currency, with time t values I^1_t and I^2_t. From these two indices we construct a **basket** with value B_t as follows

$$B_t = a \times I^1_t + b \times I^2_t. \tag{4.25}$$

The multipliers a and b can be interpreted as the number of shares of index 1 and index 2 that go into the basket. For example, if I^1 and I^2 were stock prices we could see a and b as the number of stocks making up a portfolio with total value B_t. The vanilla return on the basket is defined as

$$BR^{\mathrm{d}}_{0,T} = \frac{B_T - B_0}{B_0}, \tag{4.26}$$

which can be rewritten as

$$BR^{\mathrm{d}}_{0,T} = \frac{a \times I^1_T + b \times I^2_T - a \times I^1_0 - b \times I^2_0}{B_0}. \tag{4.27}$$

Now let us define the **basket weights** x_1 and x_2 as follows

$$x_1 = \frac{a \times I^1_0}{B_0}, \quad x_2 = \frac{b \times I^2_0}{B_0}. \tag{4.28}$$

Since $x_1 + x_2 = 1$ these basket weights tell us how the basket's initial value B_0 was divided over the two reference indices. Again thinking of both indices as stock prices, the basket weights tell us what part of the total amount initially invested is invested in stock 1 and what part in stock 2. We can now rewrite the expression for the **vanilla return on a basket of domestic indices** as

$$BR_{0,T}^{\mathrm{d}} = \left[x_1 \times \left(\frac{I_T^1}{I_0^1} \right) + x_2 \times \left(\frac{I_T^2}{I_0^2} \right) \right] - 1 \tag{4.29}$$

$$= x_1 \times R_{0,T}^{\mathrm{d},1} + x_2 \times R_{0,T}^{\mathrm{d},2}, \tag{4.30}$$

where $R_{0,T}^{\mathrm{d},i}$ denotes the vanilla return on domestic index i, $i = 1, 2$. Expression (4.30) shows us that the vanilla return on the basket can be expressed as the weighted sum of the vanilla returns on the component indices where the weights are the basket weights x_1 and x_2. The advantage of (4.30) is that **we do not have to know the exact number of units of both indices**. It is enough to know the basket weights x_1 and x_2, i.e. it is enough to know how the initial value of the basket is spread over its components.

Now assume that both indices are denominated in a currency different than the payment currency. Quantoing the indices in the basket again makes no difference for the return expression, but if we translate them into the payment currency using the exchange rate at the time of observation we do obtain different results. The basket value can in this case be written as

$$B_t = a \times E_t^1 \times I_t^1 + b \times E_t^2 \times I_t^2, \tag{4.31}$$

where E_t^i denotes the time t exchange rate between the payment currency and the currency of index i. This means that the **vanilla return on a basket of composite indices** is equal to

$$BR_{0,T}^{\mathrm{c}} = \left[x_1 \times \left(\frac{E_T^1 \times I_T^1}{E_0^1 \times I_0^1} \right) + x_2 \times \left(\frac{E_T^2 \times I_T^2}{E_0^2 \times I_0^2} \right) \right] - 1 \tag{4.32}$$

$$= x_1 \times R_{0,T}^{\mathrm{c},1} + x_2 \times R_{0,T}^{\mathrm{c},2}, \tag{4.33}$$

where $R_{0,T}^{\mathrm{c},i}$ denotes the vanilla return on composite index i, $i = 1, 2$. The vanilla return on a composite basket can thus be expressed as the weighted sum of the vanilla returns on the component composite indices where the weights are equal to the basket weights x_1 and x_2.

4.8.3 The Basket as Reference Index

So far we have split each basket up into the component reference indices and expressed the basket return as the weighted sum of the returns on these indices. This is not the only (or best) way to denote the basket return. An alternative is to **treat the basket value as an index number**. In case of a **basket of domestic indices** this means defining

$$V_0 = 100, \tag{4.34}$$

$$V_t = 100 \times \left[x_1 \times \left(\frac{I_t^1}{I_0^1} \right) + x_2 \times \left(\frac{I_t^2}{I_0^2} \right) \right]. \tag{4.35}$$

This makes the basket value an index number with a $t = 0$ value of 100 and a $t = t$ value equal to $100 \times (1$ plus the vanilla return on the basket). With the above definition the vanilla return on the basket can simply be expressed as

$$BR_{0,T}^{\mathrm{d}} = \frac{V_T - V_0}{V_0}, \tag{4.36}$$

since the individual reference index values are already captured in the definition of the index number. In case of a **basket of composite indices** we could do the same and define the new index number as

$$V_0 = 100, \tag{4.37}$$

$$V_t = 100 \times \left[x_1 \times \left(\frac{E_t^1 \times I_t^1}{E_0^1 \times I_0^1} \right) + x_2 \times \left(\frac{E_t^2 \times I_t^2}{E_0^2 \times I_0^2} \right) \right]. \tag{4.38}$$

With the latter definition the vanilla return on the basket can be expressed as in (4.36).

4.9   ARITHMETIC AVERAGES

A popular type of cash flow is a cash flow equal to the average of a number of index values over some period of time. Such a cash flow is equal to the sum of a number of vanilla index-linked cash flows with delayed settlement. Suppose that over some period of time we monitored the reference index N times. A cash flow equal to the average of these N observations could in that case formally be described as

$$CF_T = \frac{1}{N} \times (M_1 \times I_1 + M_2 \times I_2 + \cdots + M_N \times I_N), \tag{4.39}$$

where I_i denotes the value of the reference index at the ith monitoring point, $i = 1, 2, \ldots, N$, and M_i is the accompanying multiplier. Although every component cash flow can have a different multiplier, in which case we speak of a **weighted average**, in most cases all multipliers are the same. This means we can rewrite (4.39) as

$$CF_T = M \times \frac{1}{N} \times (I_1 + I_2 + \cdots + I_N) = M \times \frac{\sum_{i=1}^{N} I_i}{N}, \tag{4.40}$$

in which case we speak of an **unweighted average**.

Even with an unweighted average we still need to set the monitoring points. We can determine the average over the full lifetime of the relevant contract, but this is not always desired. The so-called **averaging period**, i.e. the period between the first and the last monitoring point, may only cover the first part of the life of the contract, the middle part of the contract's life, or only the last part. In between the first and last monitoring point we can scatter monitoring points any way we want. Usually monitoring is done on a daily, weekly or monthly basis, but there is no reason why monitoring points should always be equally spaced.

Note that the number and location of the monitoring points is an important determinant of the **volatility of the average**. When the number of monitoring points is increased the average becomes less volatile. If over a period of a month the reference index moved from

100 to 120, a monthly one-year average would add $120/12 = 10$ to the sum from which the average is calculated. A weekly average on the other hand, assuming the index climbed gradually from 100 to 120, would add only $105/52 + 110/52 + 115/52 + 120/52 = 8.65$, while a daily average would add even less.

Thanks to the presence of a large number of component cash flows, if we wanted to floor or cap a cash flow equal to the average there are various alternatives available. Apart from flooring or capping the average as a whole, we can floor or cap every component cash flow separately. With every component capped at the same fixed level K this yields a cash flow equal to

$$CF_T = M \times \frac{\sum_{i=1}^{N} \text{Min}\,[K, I_i]}{N}. \tag{4.41}$$

This is only one of the possibilities though. We could cap different component cash flows at different fixed levels, or instead of fixed caps we could introduce index-linked cap levels. An interesting variation occurs if we cap every component at a factor times the value of the average to date. In that case we would end up with a cash flow equal to

$$CF_T = M \times \frac{\sum_{i=1}^{N} \text{Min}\,[\alpha A_i, I_i]}{N}, \tag{4.42}$$

where A_i denotes the average index value over the first i monitoring points and α is a constant. In a way the average is restricting its own behavior here.

4.10   AVERAGE RETURNS

We can create a whole range of new types of returns by substituting other cash flows for the value of the reference index on the payment date I_T. Let's see what we would get if we calculated the return not from the index value at time T, but from the average value of the index over some period.

4.10.1   Single Index Average Returns

Suppose we wanted to create a return cash flow at time T based on the average of the index values at $t = 1$, $t = 2$ and $t = 3$. In that case the **average return on a domestic index** can be expressed as

$$AR^d_{0,T} = \frac{A_T - I_0}{I_0}, \tag{4.43}$$

with

$$A_T = 1/3 \times (I_1 + I_2 + I_3).$$

Substitution produces the following result

$$AR^d_{0,T} = 1/3 \times \left(\frac{I_1}{I_0} + \frac{I_2}{I_0} + \frac{I_3}{I_0} \right) - 1 \tag{4.44}$$

$$= 1/3 \times \left(R^d_{0,1} + R^d_{0,2} + R^d_{0,3} \right), \tag{4.45}$$

which shows that the average return on a domestic index can be expressed as an average of domestic vanilla returns. Note, however, that **all these vanilla returns have the same base value**, i.e. they all measure the change in the reference index since $t = 0$.

Matters become somewhat more complicated when we introduce currency translation. As before, compared to the domestic case quantoing does not make any difference as we are multiplying every index value by the same number. For the **average return on a composite index**, however, we have the following expression

$$AR_{0,T}^{c} = \frac{A_T - E_0 \times I_0}{E_0 \times I_0}, \tag{4.46}$$

with

$$A_T = 1/3 \times (E_1 \times I_1 + E_2 \times I_2 + E_3 \times I_3).$$

Substitution shows that

$$AR_{0,T}^{c} = 1/3 \times \left(\frac{E_1 \times I_1}{E_0 \times I_0} + \frac{E_2 \times I_2}{E_0 \times I_0} + \frac{E_3 \times I_3}{E_0 \times I_0} \right) - 1 \tag{4.47}$$

$$= 1/3 \times (R_{0,1}^{c} + R_{0,2}^{c} + R_{0,3}^{c}). \tag{4.48}$$

In other words, the average return on a composite index can be written as an average of composite vanilla returns. Again, all the latter share the same base value: $E_0 \times I_0$.

4.10.2 Basket Average Returns

We now turn to returns calculated from the average of a number of basket values over time. We start with the domestic case. Again there are two indices I_t^1 and I_t^2 making up a basket with time t value B_t defined by (4.25). However, the return will this time not be calculated from the time T value of the basket, but from the average of the basket values at $t = 1$, $t = 2$ and $t = 3$. In that case the **average return on a basket of domestic indices** is equal to

$$ABR_{0,T}^{d} = \frac{AB_T - B_0}{B_0}, \tag{4.49}$$

with

$$AB_T = 1/3 \times (B_1 + B_2 + B_3).$$

Substitution then yields the following result

$$ABR_{0,T}^{d} = 1/3 \times \left[x_1 \times \left(\frac{I_1^1}{I_0^1} + \frac{I_2^1}{I_0^1} + \frac{I_3^1}{I_0^1} \right) + x_2 \times \left(\frac{I_1^2}{I_0^2} + \frac{I_2^2}{I_0^2} + \frac{I_3^2}{I_0^2} \right) \right] - 1 \tag{4.50}$$

$$= x_1 \times AR_{0,T}^{d,1} + x_2 \times AR_{0,T}^{d,2}, \tag{4.51}$$

where $AR_{0,T}^{d,i}$ is the average return on domestic index i, $i = 1, 2$. From (4.51) we see that the average return on a basket of domestic indices can be expressed as the weighted sum of the average returns on the component domestic indices.

When both indices are denominated in another currency than the payment currency but quantoed into the payment currency nothing would change again. If we translated using the exchange rate at the time of observation, however, things would. With the time t value of the basket given by (4.31), it is easy to show that the **average return on a basket of composite indices** could in that case be calculated as

$$ABR^c_{0,T} = x_1 \times AR^{c,1}_{0,T} + x_2 \times AR^{c,2}_{0,T}, \tag{4.52}$$

where $AR^{c,i}_{0,T}$ is the average return on composite index i, $i = 1, 2$. Put another way, the average return on a basket of composite indices can be expressed as the weighted sum of the average returns on the component composite indices.

4.10.3   The Basket as Reference Index

With average returns we can also treat the basket value as an index number. As before this means defining

$$V_0 = 100, \tag{4.53}$$

$$V_t = 100 \times \left[x_1 \times \left(\frac{I^1_t}{I^1_0} \right) + x_2 \times \left(\frac{I^2_t}{I^2_0} \right) \right]. \tag{4.54}$$

With this definition the average return on the basket can simply be expressed as

$$ABR^d_{0,T} = \frac{AB_T - V_0}{V_0}, \tag{4.55}$$

with

$$AB_T = 1/3 \times (V_1 + V_2 + V_3).$$

No further elaboration is necessary as all the reference index values are captured in the definition of the index number. A basket of composite indices can be handled in the same way. We could define a new index number as

$$V_0 = 100, \tag{4.56}$$

$$V_t = 100 \times \left[x_1 \times \left(\frac{E^1_t \times I^1_t}{E^1_0 \times I^1_0} \right) + x_2 \times \left(\frac{E^2_t \times I^2_t}{E^2_0 \times I^2_0} \right) \right], \tag{4.57}$$

and calculate the average return on the basket as in (4.55).

4.11   VANILLA EXTREMA

Cash flows equal to the highest or lowest of a number of reference index values over some period of time can also be very useful in derivatives structuring. Like averages, cash flows like these are made up of a number of vanilla index-linked cash flows with delayed settlement. Instead of taking the average, however, this time we take the highest or the lowest. Assuming all component cash flows have the same multiplier, a cash flow equal to the highest of N subsequent index values can formally be written as

$$CF_T = M \times \text{Max}\,[I_1, I_2, \ldots, I_N] = M \times M^+_{1,N}, \tag{4.58}$$

where $M^{+}_{1,N}$ is the **highest** or **maximum** index value in the set. The expression for the lowest index value is similar and is given by

$$CF_T = M \times \text{Min}\,[I_1, I_2, \ldots, I_N] = M \times M^{-}_{1,N},\qquad(4.59)$$

where $M^{-}_{1,N}$ is the **lowest** or **minimum** index value in the set. Cash flows equal to these extrema can be interpreted in the same way as the highest or lowest in general: at maturity the receiver or payer chooses one cash flow from a set of vanilla index-linked cash flows which equal the reference index values at a number of points in time.

The variations found in extrema are similar to those found in averages. The so-called **lookback period**, i.e. the period of time between the first and the last monitoring point, may span the full lifetime of the relevant contract or just the first, middle or last part. Of course, the longer the lookback period, the more opportunity we have to observe an extremely high (low) index value. Within the lookback period monitoring can be done daily, weekly, monthly or anything else, with the monitoring points equally or not equally spaced. The more often we monitor the index, the more likely we are to find an extremely high (low) index value.

If we used the highest of N subsequent index values to calculate a **return** figure, the resulting cash flow would be equal to

$$CF_T = \frac{M^{+}_{1,N} - I_0}{I_0} = \text{Max}\left[R^{\text{d}}_{0,1}, R^{\text{d}}_{0,2}, \ldots, R^{\text{d}}_{0,N}\right].\qquad(4.60)$$

This shows that calculating a return from the highest of a sequence of N index values produces the same cash flow as choosing the highest of N vanilla returns, each corresponding to the N observed values of the reference index. All these vanilla returns have different ending levels but share the same base level I_0. We can also use the lowest index value as the base for a return calculation. In that case we would have a cash flow equal to

$$CF_T = \frac{I_T - M^{-}_{1,N}}{I_0} = \text{Max}\left[R^{\text{d}}_{1,T}, R^{\text{d}}_{2,T}, \ldots, R^{\text{d}}_{N,T}\right].\qquad(4.61)$$

This shows that using the lowest of N subsequent index values as the base for the return calculation produces a cash flow equal to the highest of N vanilla returns with base levels equal to the observed index values and common ending level I_T.

4.12   STEPWISE EXTREMA

Determining vanilla extrema is a two-step procedure. Given the monitoring points we first gather a set of index values from which we then choose the highest or the lowest. We can expand on this principle by changing the way the set of index values to choose from is being put together. One popular alternative is to compare every observed index value with a prefixed set of reference values and, instead of the observed index value itself, include the reference value which is the least below or the least above the value actually observed. Suppose we were looking for the highest value over some period of time. With the index at 100 we fix our reference set at 110 and 120. Suppose the first observed index value after the initial 100 was 112. Since this is above 110 but below 120 we would add 110 to the set of values to choose from. The next index value is 118, which is above 110 but still below 120. We therefore register 110 again. The next index value we observe is 123. Since this is above 120 we add 120 to the set of values to choose from. We can do the same thing looking for the lowest value of the reference index. Suppose we fixed our reference values at 90 and 80. If the first observation was 89 we would add 90 to the set of values to choose from. If the next index value was 77 we would add 80.

Two things are worth noting about the above procedure. First, we only register the reference values. We therefore have a problem if the index does not reach the first reference value as in that case we do not know what the cash flow is going to be. We can solve this problem by starting the set we choose from with one additional value; typically the value of the reference index at inception. This means that if none of the reference values is reached the cash flow equals I_0. Second, what we are really doing is rounding our observations downwards when looking for the highest or upwards when looking for the lowest. Looking for the highest for example, every observation between 100 and 110 becomes 100, every observation between 110 and 120 becomes 110, and every observation above 120 becomes 120.

How do we express the stepwise maximum or minimum formally? One way is as follows. Suppose we wanted the **stepwise maximum** over N monitoring points with reference values H^1 and H^2 ($I_0 < H^1 < H^2$). In that case our cash flow would be equal to

$$CF_T = M \times \text{Max} \left[I_0, D_1 \times H^1, D_2 \times H^2 \right] = M \times S_{1,N}^+, \qquad (4.62)$$

where $S_{1,N}^+$ denotes the stepwise maximum

$$D_1 = 1, \quad \text{if } \exists j \ I_j \geqslant H^1,$$
$$= 0, \quad \text{if } \forall j \ I_j < H^1,$$

and

$$D_2 = 1, \quad \text{if } \exists j \ I_j \geqslant H^2,$$
$$= 0, \quad \text{if } \forall j \ I_j < H^2.$$

In the above expressions the subscript j counts the monitoring points. What we have done is express the stepwise maximum as the highest of three fixed cash flows; two with knock-in conditions attached. The cash flow is equal to the highest of I_0, H^1 and H^2. H^1, however, only comes into play if at one or more monitoring points the reference index is higher than H^1. The same goes for H^2. H^2 becomes a viable alternative only if the reference index is higher than H^2 at one or more monitoring points.

We can write down a similar expression for the **stepwise minimum** over N monitoring points. With $I_0 > H^1 > H^2$ our cash flow would be equal to

$$CF_T = M \times \text{Min} \left[I_0, D_1 \times H^1, D_2 \times H^2 \right] = M \times S_{1,N}^-, \qquad (4.63)$$

where $S_{1,N}^-$ is the stepwise minimum

$$D_1 = 1, \quad \text{if } \exists j \ I_j \leqslant H^1,$$
$$= \infty, \quad \text{if } \forall j \ I_j > H^1,$$

and

$$D_2 = 1, \quad \text{if } \exists j \; I_j \leqslant H^2,$$
$$= \infty, \quad \text{if } \forall j \; I_j > H^2.$$

The above cash flow is equal to the lowest of I_0, H^1 and H^2. Both H^1 and H^2, however, are only viable alternatives if at one or more monitoring points the reference index is equal to or lower than H^1 and H^2, respectively. If not, D equals infinity, which effectively takes the reference value in question out of the equation.

In practice, the above story is told with a little bit more commercial appeal. The set of reference values is generally referred to as the **ladder** and the individual reference values as the ladder's **rungs**. Likewise, the monitoring period is often referred to as the **ladder period**. Whenever the reference index hits a rung that index value is said to be **locked in**. Note that with stepwise extrema we not only have to choose the monitoring points, but also the number and level of the ladder rungs involved. In doing so, we have exactly the same choices to make as when adding a knock-in or knock-out barrier feature, since technically the stepwise extremum's ladder rungs are not different from knock-in or knock-out barriers. **The event that is triggered is different but the barriers themselves are not**.

An interesting variation on the above is to lock in only a fraction of the rung value instead of its full value. Suppose we had three rungs at 130, 160 and 190. If the index reached 130 we could lock in 130 as before. At 160, however, we could only add 0.7 times the index value over 130. If the index reached 160 we would lock in an amount of $130 + 0.7 \times 30 = 151$ instead of 160. At 190 we could only add 0.5 times the index value over 160, meaning that if the index reached 190 we would lock in an amount of $151 + 0.5 \times 30 = 166$ instead of 190.

The above example makes it clear that when looking at stepwise extrema we have to distinguish between (a) the ladder rungs, i.e. the index levels where a lock-in takes place, and (b) the index values that are locked in when a rung is hit. With the standard stepwise extremum the index value that is locked in is the same as the rung that is hit. Looking at the above example, however, we see that this is not always the case. If the index hits 160, an index level of 151 is locked in. Likewise, if the index hits 190 an index value of 166 is locked in. Abstracting from the first rung, this means we now have the following cash flow

$$CF_T = M \times \text{Max} \, [I_0, D_1 \times 151, D_2 \times 166], \tag{4.64}$$

where

$$D_1 = 1, \quad \text{if } \exists j \; I_j \geqslant 160,$$
$$= 0, \quad \text{if } \forall j \; I_j < 160,$$

and

$$D_2 = 1, \quad \text{if } \exists j \; I_j \geqslant 190,$$
$$= 0, \quad \text{if } \forall j \; I_j < 190.$$

If we used the standard stepwise maximum to calculate a return figure, the resulting cash flow would be equal to (assuming multipliers equal to 1 and two rungs at H^1 and H^2)

$$CF_T = \frac{S_{1,N}^+ - I_0}{I_0} = \text{Max}\left[0, D_1 \times \left(\frac{H^1 - I_0}{I_0}\right), D_2 \times \left(\frac{H^2 - I_0}{I_0}\right)\right], \qquad (4.65)$$

where D_1 and D_2 have the same meaning as in (4.62). In other words, calculating a return from the stepwise maximum produces the same cash flow as choosing the highest of zero and the two vanilla returns implied by both rung values. Both the latter, however, only become relevant when for at least one of the monitoring points the index is equal to or higher than the rung. The above expression clearly shows that a return calculated from the stepwise maximum has a natural floor at zero due to the fact that the stepwise maximum as we defined it is at least equal to I_0. If this is not desired one can simply redefine the stepwise highest with another floor.

A cash flow equal to the stepwise extremum is nothing more than the highest or lowest of two or more fixed cash flows; one without and the rest with a knock-in condition. The fact that the latter cash flows are already equipped with a knock-in feature does not mean that we cannot add more knock-in or knock-out features though. Suppose we added a knock-out condition to the rungs in the stepwise maximum which says that the rungs will knock out if at any of the monitoring points the index is equal to or lower than a level $H^0 < I_0$. With two rungs H^1 and H^2 this would produce a cash flow equal to

$$CF_T = M \times \text{Max}\left[I_0, D_1 \times H^1, D_2 \times H^2\right], \qquad (4.66)$$

where D_1 and D_2 are given by

$$D_i = 1, \quad \text{if } \exists j \; I_j \geqslant H^i \text{ and } \forall j \; I_j > H^0,$$
$$= 0, \quad \text{if } \forall j \; I_j < H^i \text{ or } \exists j \; I_j \leqslant H^0.$$

If the knock-out barrier is hit both rungs disappear and the cash flow becomes a fixed cash flow equal to $M \times I_0$. If the knock-out barrier is not hit the cash flow is the same as the ordinary stepwise maximum.

4.13   EXTENDED STEPWISE EXTREMA

Since we only register the rungs, the stepwise maximum cannot be higher than the highest rung reached during the monitoring period. Suppose we had a ladder with rungs at 120, 140 and 160. If during the monitoring period the index reached a level of 120 we would know that the cash flow on the payment date would at least be equal to 120. The same happens at 140 and 160. However, if the index ended at 158 without ever touching 160 the cash flow would be 140, not 158. The same would happen if the index ended higher than 160, say at 176. In that case the cash flow would be 160, not 176. Sometimes the above is considered too rigid. We can solve this by making a small adjustment. Instead of paying the highest rung hit we could pay the highest of the highest rung hit and the index value at maturity. This means we use the stepwise maximum as a floor on the index value (or the other way around). An **extended stepwise maximum** like this can be denoted as

$$CF_T = M \times \text{Max}\left[I_0, D_1 \times H^1, D_2 \times H^2, I_T\right] = M \times ES_{1,N}^+, \qquad (4.67)$$

where $ES_{1,N}^+$ denotes the extended stepwise maximum and D_1 and D_2 have the same meaning as in (4.62). We can do the same with the stepwise minimum. This yields an

extended stepwise minimum equal to

$$CF_T = M \times \text{Min} \left[I_0, D_1 \times H^1, D_2 \times H^2, I_T \right] = M \times ES^-_{1,N}, \tag{4.68}$$

where $ES^-_{1,N}$ is the extended stepwise minimum and D_1 and D_2 have the same meaning as in (4.63).

4.14 PIECEWISE LINEAR CASH FLOWS

A vanilla index-linked cash flow has a linear relationship with the value of the reference index on the payment date. We can also structure cash flows which have other functional relationships with the index value at maturity. A very popular alternative is **piecewise linear** functions. With a piecewise linear cash flow the size of the cash flow is a **kinky** function of the index value.

Suppose that instead of a linear function of I_T we wanted a cash flow profile with two kinks. For example, something like

$$CF_T = M \times (\text{Min}\,[I_T, I_0] + 1.4 \times \text{Min}\,[\text{Max}\,[0, I_T - I_0], 0.2I_0]$$
$$+ 0.8 \times \text{Max}\,[0, I_T - 1.2I_0]). \tag{4.69}$$

This cash flow exhibits two kinks. The first one at $I_T = I_0$ and the second one at $I_T = 1.2I_0$. Suppose that $I_0 = 100$. Now let's move I_T upwards starting from zero. From 0 to 100 the cash flow rises proportionally with I_T just as with a vanilla index-linked cash flow. At $I_T = 100$, however, this changes and the cash flow starts rising more than proportionally with I_T. Suppose $I_T = 110$, in that case the cash flow would be $100 + 1.4 \times 10 = 114$. This more than proportional rise ends when $I_T = 120$. From that point onwards the rise becomes less than proportional. With $I_T = 150$ we would have a cash flow equal to $100 + 1.4 \times 20 + 0.8 \times 30 = 152$.

We can do the same with returns. We could for example structure a piecewise linear return equal to

$$CF_T = M \times \left(\text{Min} \left[0, \frac{I_T - I_0}{I_0} \right] + 1.4 \times \text{Min} \left[\text{Max} \left[0, \frac{I_T - I_0}{I_0} \right], 0.2 \right] \right.$$
$$\left. + 0.8 \times \text{Max} \left[0, \frac{I_T - 1.2I_0}{I_0} \right] \right). \tag{4.70}$$

This one has two kinks; one at 0% and another at 20%. For an index return below 0% the so-called **participation rate** is 1.0. Between 0% and 20% it is 1.4, and above 20% it is 0.8. This means that as long as the index shows a return lower than 0% we get 100% of the index return. However, if the index shows a positive return the participation rate goes up. With an index return of 10% for example we receive 14%, while if the index at maturity yields a return of 30% we get $1.4 \times 0.2 + 0.8 \times 0.1 = 36\%$. From the above example it is clear that with piecewise linear cash flows we have to decide on issues like

- The number and location of the kinks, i.e. the values of I_T where the level of participation changes.
- The levels of participation between kinks.

Clearly, this allows for quite a lot of variation.

4.15 CLIQUETS

Sometimes it is advantageous to see the change in the reference index over a longer period of time as the sum of the index changes over a number of subsequent shorter periods. So-called **cliquet** or **ratchet** cash flows are equal to the sum of the floored, capped or collared, i.e. simultaneously capped and floored, index changes over a number of subperiods. Assuming all component cash flows have the same multiplier, a 5-year **floored cliquet cash flow** which accumulates the index changes on a yearly basis can be expressed as

$$CF_T = M \times \sum_{i=1}^{5} \text{Max}\,[f, I_i - I_{i-1}], \tag{4.71}$$

where i counts the years from inception and f denotes the floor level. This cash flow is made up of five parts corresponding to the five years until the payment date. Each year contributes an amount equal to the change in the reference index over that year, floored at f.

We can do the same for the index return. If instead of the yearly changes we sum the yearly returns on the index, we obtain a cash flow equal to

$$CF_T = M \times \sum_{i=1}^{5} \text{Max}\left[F, \frac{I_i - I_{i-1}}{I_{i-1}}\right], \tag{4.72}$$

where F denotes the yearly **floor rate**. This cash flow equals the sum of the floored index returns over the five individual years until the payment date. If we also cap the yearly returns we get a cash flow equal to

$$CF_T = M \times \sum_{i=1}^{5} \text{Min}\left[\text{Max}\left[F, \frac{I_i - I_{i-1}}{I_{i-1}}\right], C\right], \tag{4.73}$$

where C is the yearly **cap rate**. In this case every year's contribution is equal to the index return over that year but never less than F nor more than C.

Looking at the above formulas, we see that with cliquet cash flows we have to decide on

- The number of subperiods
- The level of the floors
- The level of the caps

The more subperiods we introduce the higher the cash flow can become as there is more opportunity to collect contributions. With respect to the floor and/or cap it is important to note that flooring and/or capping the contributions of the individual years is different from flooring and/or capping the whole cash flow at once. Suppose that individual years produced index returns of 10%, 12%, −5%, −8% and 14%. If we simply place a floor of 0% under the sum of these returns this would make no difference, as we would still get 23%. Flooring every single year at 0%, however, would produce a return equal to 36%.

4.16 HAMSTERS

Adding a number of digitals together may produce very interesting cash flows. For example, it allows us to create cash flows the size of which depend on the number of days, weeks or months the reference index spent within some particular range. For every period that the index did not get out of the range we would add something to the size of the cash flow. Since cash flows like these grow bigger the more time the index spends within the range, they are called **hamsters**. They are sometimes also referred to as **corridor options**, **time trades** or **range accruals**. Apart from the reference index, a typical hamster has the following four characteristics.

- The **range**. Inside the range the hamster grows, i.e. the cash flow accumulates, but outside the range it does not. The range can be fixed in advance but it can also be made to move over time and/or with the index.
- The **elementary period**. The hamster grows stepwise. Every elementary period during which the index does not venture outside the range makes a contribution to the cash flow. If the elementary period is a week we say that the hamster grows on a weekly basis.
- The **contribution** per elementary period. This is by how much the hamster grows (if it does). The contribution may be a prefixed amount but it could also be made to move over time and/or with the index.
- The **monitoring points** within the elementary periods. This determines how stringent the range condition really is.

Note that it is possible to have only one monitoring point per elementary period. We could for example let the cash flow grow on a daily basis and each day monitor the index only at the close of trading.

Suppose we set the lower range boundary at H^1 and the upper range boundary at H^2 to create a one-year hamster with weekly contributions of K. This means we would get a cash flow equal to

$$CF_T = \sum_{i=1}^{52} D_i \times K, \tag{4.74}$$

where

$$D_i = 0, \quad \text{if } \exists j \ I_j \leqslant H^1 \text{ or } I_j \geqslant H^2,$$
$$= 1, \quad \text{if } \forall j \ H^1 < I_j < H^2,$$

i counts the number of weeks and j counts the monitoring points within week i. With the above hamster there are 52 elementary periods of one week. With daily monitoring the index would be monitored five times per week. If at all five monitoring points the index was inside the range, the relevant week would contribute an amount K to the cash flow on the payment date T. However, if during the week the index was seen outside the range at least once, that week would make no contribution.

The above description makes it clear that the hamster is nothing more than the sum of 52 digitals. Every one of these digitals has an American double knock-out barrier feature which covers a one-week period and, if alive, pays an amount K at time T. The first digital's barrier covers the first week, the second digital's barrier covers the second week, etc. Note that each digital has the same multiplier, i.e. each digital contributes the same amount. Hamsters are usually structured this way, but in principle different components can have different multipliers, i.e. different weeks may contribute different amounts to the final cash flow.

Since there are so many different types of digitals there are also a lot of different types of hamsters. One distinction is between **in-range hamsters** and **out-range hamsters**. Contrary to the hamsters discussed so far, the latter only pay when the index is outside the range. In-range and out-range hamsters are each other's mirror image in exactly the same way as knock-in and knock-out digitals are. In-range hamsters are sums of knock-out digitals, while out-range hamsters are sums of equivalent knock-in digitals. We will concentrate on in-range hamsters.

Another distinction is between **straight hamsters** and **reverse hamsters**. The former build up the cash flow over time, while the latter build down the cash flow over time. Reverse hamsters start off with a fixed amount and make deductions for every elementary period the index is outside the range. In other words, a reverse hamster is a fixed amount minus a straight out-range hamster. Note that the amount at the start need not necessarily be equal to the total number of elementary periods times the contribution. If it is lower, however, the cash flow may become negative.

So far the contribution outside the range has been equal to zero. We can, however, also create a hamster where the contribution outside the range is negative instead of zero. Such a **give-and-take hamster** would pay a positive **give amount** for every elementary period the index was in the range and a negative **take amount** for every period it was outside the range. Basically, this is a combination of an in-range hamster with a positive elementary contribution and an out-range hamster with a negative elementary contribution. Again this structure allows for a negative cash flow as the hamster may take more than it gives. The index may spend more time outside the range than inside, and even if not the elementary take amount may have been set higher than the elementary give amount.

Another possible variation is the so-called **multiple range hamster**. Instead of a binary payment structure these hamsters have a more detailed range structure where different amounts are paid in different ranges. A layered payout structure means choosing a narrow range and a less narrow range (containing the narrow range). When the reference index stays within the narrow range the highest contribution is paid. If the index gets out of the narrow range but stays within the less narrow range a lower contribution is paid. If the index comes outside the less narrow range there is no contribution. This is sometimes also referred to as a **wedding cake structure**.

Normally the range boundaries will be chosen not too far apart. If the range is very wide the probability that the index escapes from the range will be very small, which defeats the purpose of constructing a hamster. What can be done, however, is set the upper range boundary equal to infinity or the lower range boundary equal to zero. In the first case the relevant range is the outcome space above the lower range boundary, and in the second case it is the space between the upper range boundary and zero. We call this a **one-sided hamster**.

One problem with the above hamsters is that the range is fixed in advance. It therefore only takes one jump of the reference index to essentially kill the hamster even if the index stabilizes again afterwards. One solution is to periodically revise the location of range boundaries. We could for example maintain the same range width but relocate the range such that the reference index started in the middle of the range again. In that case the range would more or less follow the reference index. If the index suddenly jumped upwards or downwards this would be corrected in the next range revision. Such a **cliquet hamster** is the same as an ordinary hamster, but this time the knock-out barriers are forward-starting instead of fixed in advance. Instead of making the range adjustments according to an automatic rule we could also give the investor the explicit right to revise the range himself. In that case we would fix the range width while the investor periodically decides on its location. This is sometimes referred to as a **range rover**.

Another possibility is to create a hamster which is permanently stripped from the possibility of receiving more contributions as soon as the reference index gets outside the range. Until now this only cost us the contribution of one elementary period. With this extended knock-out feature, however, we would lose the contributions of all months to come as well. This is sometimes referred to as an **exploding hamster**. To create an exploding hamster all we have to do is to let all barriers become active from day one, i.e. extend them backwards to time $t = 0$. Originally, the 50th week's barriers for example were only active from the beginning of week 50 until the end of week 50. In the case of an exploding hamster, however, they are active from the beginning of week 1. If at any time between the beginning of the first week and the end of the 50th week the index gets outside the range, the 50th week's contribution is lost. We could of course also extend the barriers forward, but this would mean that we could never be sure of any contribution until the payment date.

Using digitals with bivariate barriers we can extend the hamster concept to the case of two reference indices and create **bivariate hamsters**. These pay a fixed amount for every elementary period the two indices are within their boundaries. The variations for bivariate hamsters are similar as for univariate hamsters, but there are more of them. For example, we can now also structure combined in-range and out-range hamsters, i.e. hamsters which only grow when one index stays inside its range and the other gets outside its range. There are also many more one-sided hamsters since we now have two more range boundaries that we can set to infinity or zero.

From a derivatives structuring point of view hamsters are just one of many types of index-linked cash flows. We can therefore expose them to the same trickery as other cash flows. We can add them or subtract them, cap them or floor them just as any other index-linked cash flow. We can also add knock-out or knock-in features to hamsters. We could for example create a hamster which knocks out when the accumulated contributions reach a certain maximum. Reverse and give-and-take hamsters may also be structured to knock out when the remaining contribution reaches a certain minimum.

Finally, it is important to note that **hamsters are often expressed in terms of an index-linked multiplier**. We can for example rewrite the hamster in (4.74) as

$$CF_T = WIR \times K, \tag{4.75}$$

where *WIR* (weeks in range) is the number of weeks the index did not get out of the range. We now have a cash flow equal to a fixed amount times a multiplier which depends on the number of weeks the index is in the range.

4.17   VANILLA FORWARDS AND ORDINARY OPTIONS

Having established how to denote individual cash flows we can now turn to the formal notation of the payments under some common derivatives contracts. Since they only involve one cash flow, we need not spend much time on zeros. Basically, we have been talking about zeros all along. When it comes to forwards it is important to note that although technically both counterparties pay each other, they will of course **only exchange the balance** of both cash flows. This is also the way in which things are typically notated.

We simply say that one counterparty will pay the other an amount equal to the balance of the two cash flows in question. A similar reasoning goes for the option right. In Chapter 3 we discussed the fact that if we assume rational behavior of the holder, the option right is an automatic feature. This means that instead of saying that the option holder has the right to cancel, we can simply say that the writer of the option will pay the buyer an amount equal to the highest of zero (corresponding to cancellation by the buyer) and the balance of the relevant cash flows. Let's see how this works out formally.

Earlier we defined a forward as a contract which calls for two counterparties to exchange two cash flows in the future. Suppose an investor and a derivatives firm entered into a **vanilla forward** where one year from now the investor was to pay a fixed amount K and the derivatives firm was to pay an amount equal to the then prevailing value of the reference index I_1. In that case the investor would be **long** the forward and would on balance receive a payoff of

$$X_1 = I_1 - K. \tag{4.76}$$

The derivatives firm would be **short** the forward and would on balance receive an amount equal to

$$X_1 = -(I_1 - K) = K - I_1. \tag{4.77}$$

If the index at maturity was higher than K the derivatives firm would (on balance) pay the investor and if it was lower than K the investor would end up paying the derivatives firm. The fixed amount K is referred to as the **forward price**. Note, however, that **the forward price is not the price of the forward but the price mentioned in the forward contract**, i.e. the price to be paid in the future in return for the index value.

Now suppose we gave the investor the right to cancel the above forward at maturity. Since the investor pays the fixed amount this would turn the vanilla forward into an **ordinary call option**. The investor would be **long** the option and would on balance receive an amount equal to

$$X_1 = \text{Max}\,[0, I_1 - K]. \tag{4.78}$$

If the index ended below K the investor would cancel the deal and the payoff would be zero. If on the other hand it ended higher than K he would leave things as they were and collect $I_1 - K$. The payoff to the investor is therefore equal to the highest of zero and the forward payoff. The mirror image of the investor's payoff is the payoff which the derivatives firm receives that is **short** the option. The latter is given by

$$X_1 = -\,\text{Max}\,[0, I_1 - K] = \text{Min}\,[0, K - I_1]. \tag{4.79}$$

The derivatives firm either receives nothing when the index at maturity is lower than K and the investor cancels the deal or it has to pay the investor $I_1 - K$ if the index is higher than K. The payoff is therefore equal to the lowest of zero and the forward payoff.

Note that after the introduction of the option right the fixed amount K is no longer referred to as the forward price but as the option's **strike price** or simply as the option's **strike**. If the index value is below the strike, the option is said to be **out-of-the-money (OTM)**. If the option matured immediately, the payoff would be zero. If the index is higher than the strike, the option is said to be **in-the-money (ITM)**. If the option matured immediately, the payoff would be positive. Finally, if the strike and the index value are equal, the option is said to be **at-the-money (ATM)**.

If we gave the derivatives firm the right to cancel the deal the vanilla forward would become an **ordinary put option** since the derivatives firm is paying the index-linked cash flow. The investor would be **short** the option and on balance receive an amount equal to

$$X_1 = -\,\text{Max}\,[0, K - I_1] = \text{Min}\,[0, I_1 - K]. \tag{4.80}$$

The derivatives firm would be **long** the option and receive a payoff equal to

$$X_1 = \text{Max}\,[0, K - I_1]. \tag{4.81}$$

If the index ended below the strike the derivatives firm would proceed with the deal and on balance receive $K - I_1$. If the index ended higher than the strike, however, the firm would cancel the deal and the payoff to both counterparties would be zero. The payoff to the derivatives firm is therefore equal to the highest of zero and the forward payoff, while the payoff to the investor equals the lowest of zero and the forward payoff. Whether the put option is referred to as ITM, OTM or ATM depends again on what the payoff would be in case the contract matured immediately. If the index is below the strike the option is ITM, if it is above the strike it is OTM, and if the strike and the index value are equal the option is said to be ATM. The above payoff functions are the most common, which explains the 'ordinary'. When things get more complicated, however, **it is typically not the general form of the payoff that changes but only the cash flows involved**. We will encounter many examples in the chapters that follow.

4.18   CONCLUSION

Much of the art of derivatives structuring lies in the specification of the index-linked cash flows involved. Structured index-linked cash flows allow derivatives structurers to link cash flows to reference indices in very specific ways. As such they are the most important tools in the derivatives structurer's toolbox. It is important to keep in mind that **there is no fixed set of structured cash flows** from which one has to make a choice. Derivatives structuring is all about understanding the problem at hand and being creative. The fact that something has not been done before does not necessarily mean that it does not make sense or cannot be done. You cannot discover new land until you have the courage to lose sight of the shore.[1]

An important quality for a derivatives structurer is to be able to formalize his ideas. This is required to allow further analysis as well as to produce the term sheet and confirmation that will eventually embody the contract. This chapter supplies a large number of examples of structured cash flows and the way in which they can be formalized. We suggest that the reader uses them to practice translating them from English to math and back again.

---

[1] Quote taken from a coffee mug in Las Vegas.

5
Pricing and Hedging

5.1 INTRODUCTION

After identifying the relevant reference indices and linking them with cash flows in more general terms we have to decide on the precise values of all contract parameters. Of course, we have to make sure the contract in question is structured in such a way that both counterparties are happy to proceed. Typically, counterparties fix all but one parameter and leave the latter for negotiation. This unknown variable is not always a price in the usual sense of the word, i.e. a cash flow in the present. Often we will have to solve for a fixed future cash flow, a payment date, or a barrier level. 'Solving for the unknown contract parameter' would therefore be a more accurate description than 'pricing'. In practice, however, we always speak of pricing. For simplicity, we will assume in this chapter that we are dealing with contracts where the only parameter left to be determined is the amount both counterparties exchange in the present.

We concentrate on the pricing and hedging of individual options. One might object that derivatives firms do not hedge every individual option separately, but only the exposure that remains after allowing individual positions to (partially) cancel each other out. Although this is certainly true, the degree of diversification that derivatives firms are able to achieve in their books is typically substantially less than for market makers in listed options. The managing director of OTC options at Union Bank of Switzerland, for example, once remarked in an interview that 'If I do a structured transaction, I'm 95% certain I'll be living with that position until it matures'.[1]

5.2 PRICING AND HEDGING IN GENERAL

The price at which a deal gets done is the outcome of a negotiation process where both counterparties will try to achieve the most favorable terms. In this chapter **we concentrate on the pricing of derivatives from the point of view of a large derivatives firm**. There are two reasons for this.

- Although, credit considerations aside, end-users are free to deal with any counterparty, they will typically deal with a derivatives firm as they may not be able to find another end-user willing to take the other side, may require expert advice concerning the exact structure of the deal, may require periodic revaluations for accounting purposes, etc.
- Derivatives firms do not enter into derivatives contracts for any other reason than securing a profit. Because they will try to hedge themselves as well as possible, derivatives firms have a **cost price** for every contract. Competition amongst them will subsequently ensure that transaction prices do not wander too far from this cost price.

---

[1] Sheldon Epstein in *Global Finance* (March 1993, p. 49).

Derivatives firms will try to hedge out all the risks embedded in the derivatives contracts they enter into. The price quoted on a contract must therefore first and foremost depend on the **expected hedging cost**, i.e. the amount that the derivatives firm thinks it needs to invest in the present to generate the relevant contract's payoff in the future with zero expected hedging error. We can only speak about the expected error and the expected costs because, as we will see later, in practice derivatives hedges generally do not provide an exact hedge under all circumstances. To get to the actual price that a derivatives firm will quote we have to raise (when the firm is selling) or lower (when the firm is buying) the expected hedging costs with the desired **profit margin**. With respect to the latter one has to distinguish between the minimum required margin and everything over that. The minimum required margin depends on the hedging risk, the amount of capital required to cover this risk, and the firm's desired minimum return on capital. The riskier the hedge, the more capital is required and therefore the higher the minimum required margin. Whether the firm is able to make anything on top of that depends on the competitive situation. If competition is fierce, there will be little opportunity to make something extra.

Apart from obvious factors such as the exact nature of the contract to be hedged, the size of the deal and the hedging strategy followed, the expected hedging costs also depend on the composition of a firm's books at the time the deal comes in and the expected changes in the future. The same contract may fit in very well at one point in time but very badly at another. In the first case the expected hedging costs will be lower and in the latter case they will be higher than normal. This means we are more than anything else interested in the **marginal** expected hedging costs of a contract.

Not all derivatives firms are the same. There are differences in the level of experience in structuring, pricing and hedging certain types of derivatives, funding rates, hedging strategies used, model inputs, transaction costs, outstanding positions, return on capital requirements, eagerness to do business, etc. On the other hand, differences are often not as large as one might think. All derivatives firms employ people with the same educational background who get many of their ideas from the same journals, magazines, newspapers, conferences and workshops. Moreover, since loyalty is an unknown concept in the derivatives industry, these people will work for one firm one year and for another firm the next. As a result, most firms share the same ideas and methods.

We already mentioned it in Chapter 1, but **end-users should always call around for the best price**. Not only will different firms tend to show different quotes because of the factors we just mentioned, but calling around will also signal to the firms in question that they are in competition. The only exception to this rule arises when confidentiality is an issue, for example because the proposed trade is very large, the trade was developed by one particular firm, or because it has a very strong tax, accounting or regulatory angle. Instead of going through a broker, it is best to **do the calling around oneself**. There are two reasons for this. First, even large brokers tend to have little experience with more complicated derivatives structures. Second, it allows one to choose the firms to be approached oneself. Calling on firms that will call the deal around themselves is likely to spoil the market.

Since every structuring effort eventually boils down to a pricing exercise, knowledge of how a professional derivatives firm prices derivatives contracts is of great importance for derivatives structurers. Although pricing derivatives often involves quite complex mathematics, in this book we concentrate on qualitative results. We stick to the truth as closely as possible, but for pedagogical reasons we may simplify things just a little bit now and then. For more details on the mathematics of derivatives pricing the reader is referred to the many books, articles and papers that are available on this subject. An extensive bibliography can be found in the back of the book. Also, our discussion will mainly focus on how things are currently done and not on how things could be done better. Although there is always room for improvement, a book on derivatives structuring is not the best platform to introduce and discuss such ideas.

ASSUMPTIONS & NOTATION

We will stick to the notation introduced in Chapter 4. Most importantly, time will be measured in years. The present is denoted as $t = 0$, one year from now as $t = 1$, two years from now as $t = 2$, etc. When speaking more generally, the payment date is denoted as time T. The time t value of the reference index is denoted as I_t and the continuously compounded interest rate as r.

5.3   THE EXPECTED HEDGING COSTS

When it comes to hedging, the first thing to do is to check whether the payoff of the contract to be hedged is a linear or a non-linear function of the value of the reference index. Vanilla forwards and swaps have payoffs that move up and down with the index value in a **linear** fashion. This means that these contracts can be hedged by simply buying or selling the reference index. Ordinary calls and puts on the other hand have payoffs that move with the index value in a **non-linear** fashion. If the index goes up an ordinary call pays off like a forward. However, if the index goes down the owner will cancel the contract and the payoff will be zero wherever the index goes. The reverse goes for an ordinary put. This means that ordinary calls and puts provide their owners with **convex** payoffs. Obviously, the writer of an ordinary put or call is therefore confronted with a **concave** payoff. Although the framework applies to any payoff whether linear or not, in this chapter we concentrate on the hedging and pricing of derivatives contracts with arbitrary convex and concave payoffs. The discussion of the hedging and pricing of contracts with linear payoffs is left until Chapter 6.

One might expect that to determine the expected hedging costs of a contract derivatives firms carefully study a number of possible hedging strategies over a large number of possible scenarios and from there draw conclusions on the actual hedging strategy to be followed, the expected hedging error and the expected hedging costs. This is hardly ever the case though. **The determination of the expected hedging costs is primarily a theoretical exercise**. First, the firm puts together an abstract model of the world it is assumed to be living in. The most important part of this is the specification of the behavior of the prices of the available hedging instruments over time and the trading possibilities. Typically, assumptions are made such that it is possible to hedge the contract in question perfectly. Although far from the truth, it is assumed that market prices move smoothly over time without jumps and that derivatives firms can rebalance their hedge portfolio continuously without transaction costs. Given this model of the world the next step is to derive the particulars of the hedging strategy that hedges the contract perfectly. Given this hedging strategy the amount of money required to start the strategy can easily be calculated. The latter amount is generally referred to as the **theoretical price** of the contract and the formula used to calculate it as the **pricing formula**.[2]

Let's look at an example. Suppose a derivatives firm entered into a contract where at some future date T it paid an index-linked cash flow equal to the prevailing value of the reference index I_T and received a fixed amount K in return. Suppose also that the counterparty paying the fixed amount had the right to cancel the contract at maturity. More compactly: the derivatives firm **sells an ordinary call**. In doing so, the derivatives firm is confronted with a payoff at maturity equal to

$$V_T = -\text{Max}\,[0, I_T - K] = \text{Min}\,[0, K - I_T]. \tag{5.1}$$

The firm will either pay nothing when the contract is cancelled or will on balance have to pay $I_T - K$. It will never receive anything though.

Note that the payoff which the firm sells is a **convex** function of the index value at maturity. As a result, the firm itself is confronted with a payoff that is a **concave** function of the index. To hedge a concave payoff it must be combined with a convex payoff. The firm's hedging strategy therefore has to generate a convex payoff. Of course, if the derivatives firm had been long a convex payoff its hedging strategy would have had to generate a concave payoff. Generally speaking, there are two ways in which a derivatives firm can end up with a long position in a concave payoff. It can either buy one or it can sell a convex payoff. Likewise, a long position in a convex payoff can either result from the purchase of a convex payoff or the sale of a concave payoff. The distinction between convex and concave payoffs will prove to be very important in what follows.

To determine what its counterparty has to pay, the derivatives firm will first construct a model of the world it is living in. It will assume that there are two hedging instruments that it can trade: the reference index with time t value I_t and a zero-coupon bond paying 1.00 at time T. If we assume the term structure of interest rates to be flat and constant, the latter has a time t value of $e^{-r(T-t)}$, where r denotes the continuously compounded interest rate. The behavior of the reference index over time is assumed to be described by a model known as **geometric Brownian motion**. Mathematically it looks like

$$dI_t = \mu I_t \, dt + \sigma I_t \, dW_t, \quad I_0 > 0, \tag{5.2}$$

where W_t is an uncertain factor known as **Brownian motion** and μ and σ are positive constants. The process of Brownian motion is named after the Scottish botanist Robert Brown, who in 1827 used it to describe the behavior of pollen particles suspended in water. Some 80 years later Albert Einstein, in the context of diffusion phenomena, rediscovered the model and further investigated its mathematical properties.

Expression (5.2) tells us that changes in the index (dI_t) are made up of two parts. The first part represents the index's trend or **drift**. It says that over a period of time (dt) the index will tend to move upwards at a rate μ. The second part tells us that on top of this upward trend there is an uncertain part that has the potential to pull the index away from its trend both upwards and downwards. The rate at which this effect operates is given by σ; the index's **volatility**. The model for the behavior of the bond price is a lot simpler than that for the index, as it is assumed that over the life of the contract interest rates

---

[2] Often it is not possible to derive an analytical pricing formula. In that case one has to revert to one of various numerical methods. For simplicity, however, we will refer to these numerical routines as 'formulas' as well.

do not change. With respect to trading possibilities and transaction costs it is assumed that we can rebalance the hedge portfolio continuously over time without incurring any transaction costs.

Given this model of the world, the derivatives firm will determine a hedging strategy that (at least within the model) perfectly hedges the payoff of the contract to be priced. In other words, it will create a strategy trading the index and bonds that generates a payoff at maturity equal to $\text{Max}[I_T - K, 0]$. This is the amount the firm will have to pay to its counterparty. Although mathematically this is quite a complicated operation, the resulting strategy is straightforward. For the number of shares of the index to hold at any time t, Θ_t^I, we obtain

$$\Theta_t^I = N \left[\frac{\ln (I_t/K) + (r + \frac{1}{2}\sigma^2)\tau}{\sigma\sqrt{\tau}} \right] = N[d_1] \qquad (5.3)$$

and for the number of bonds to hold at any time t, Θ_t^B, we get

$$\Theta_t^B = -KN \left[\frac{\ln (I_t/K) + (r - \frac{1}{2}\sigma^2)\tau}{\sigma\sqrt{\tau}} \right] = -KN[d_2], \qquad (5.4)$$

where $N[x]$ denotes the standard normal cumulative density function evaluated at x and τ denotes the time remaining until the contract's maturity date, i.e. $\tau = T - t$.

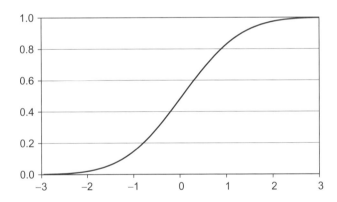

Figure 5.1   Standard normal cumulative density function

Figure 5.1 shows the value of $N[x]$ as a function of x. The graph shows that $N[x]$ is always equal to or larger than zero. Therefore, the **hedging strategy controls** given by (5.3) and (5.4) tell us that to hedge this contract the derivatives firm always has to be long in the index and short in bonds, i.e. hold stocks and borrow. If the index goes up the firm has to increase its index holdings as well as its short bond position. If the index drops it does the reverse. Since $N[d_1]$ and $N[d_2]$ will never be larger than one, the firm never has to hold more than one share in the index, nor does it have to short more than K bonds. On the contract's maturity date, i.e. when $\tau = 0$, both cumulative probabilities approach either 0 or 1. If I_T exceeds K the derivatives firm ends up holding one share of the index and K bonds short. If K exceeds I_T it ends with no position at all. The above hedging strategy tells the firm at any time t how many shares of the index to hold and how many bonds to short. Since at time t a share of the index is worth I_t and a bond is worth $e^{-r\tau}$, this implies that at any time t the value of the hedge is given by

$$V_t = I_t \Theta_t^{\text{I}} + e^{-r\tau} \Theta_t^{\text{B}} = I_t N[d_1] - e^{-r\tau} K N[d_2], \tag{5.5}$$

which is the ordinary call option pricing formula first published by Fischer Black, Myron Scholes and Robert Merton in 1973.[3] The derivatives firm will use this formula to calculate the expected hedging costs at $t = 0$. Note that the pricing formula provides the derivatives firm with an estimate of the expected hedging costs but it does not take the desired profit margin into account. **Profit has to be added separately.**

5.4 TIME VALUE

The above pricing formula requires a value for the volatility of the index σ but does not require a value for the index's drift μ. This is not only the case with the Black–Scholes–Merton formula but with all option pricing formulas derived along the above lines. The expected index return is not in the formula because the index value is already there. If the option price was related to the level of the Brownian motion W_t rather than the index value I_t, then the drift parameter would show up again. One could of course argue that therefore the index volatility should not be there either. The latter is there for a very special reason though. The part of the initial investment in the strategy, i.e. the theoretical option price, that is due to volatility can be calculated as the difference between the total investment required and the investment that would be required if volatility was zero. This component is referred to as the strategy's or the option's **time value** and the remainder as its **intrinsic value.**

If we look more closely at hedging strategies that aim to generate a convex payoff, we see that the higher the volatility and the longer the time to maturity, the higher the strategies' time value. In other words, **when generating a convex payoff we are penalized by volatility**, with the penalty being higher the longer the time to maturity. The reverse goes for hedging strategies generating concave payoffs. **When generating a concave payoff we are rewarded by volatility**, with the reward increasing with time to maturity. But there is more. Irrespective of whether it was meant to generate a convex or a concave payoff, if we relate a strategy's time value to its time to maturity we see that the time value per unit of time becomes higher the shorter the time to maturity. In other words, **strategies with relatively short maturities tend to have relatively high time values.**

The explanation of these phenomena lies in the mathematics of the process used to model the behavior of the reference index. Consider the particulars of a hedging strategy aiming to generate a convex payoff, for example to hedge the sale of an ordinary call. As we saw, if the index goes up, the derivatives firm buys more shares of the index and sells additional bonds. If the index goes down it does the reverse. Now suppose the index rose first but returned to its starting level soon afterwards. Following the above hedging strategy would mean buying at the high and selling at the low, which obviously would generate a loss. The same would happen if the index dropped first and rose afterwards.

---

[3] See F. Black and M. Scholes, The Pricing of Options and Corporate Liabilities, *Journal of Political Economy*, Vol. 3, 1973, pp. 637–654 and R. Merton, Theory of Rational Option Pricing, *Bell Journal of Economics and Management Science*, Spring, 1973, pp. 141–183.

The firm would sell low and buy high and therefore again lose money. Now consider the process used to model the behavior of the index. The process of Brownian motion has several unique characteristics. One of them is the fact that a variable following a Brownian motion cannot stand still, even for the slightest moment. Put another way, over any interval of time the index will go up and down infinitely many times. This is known as Brownian motion's **infinite crossing property**. If we combine this with the above hedging strategy which buys high and sells low, it becomes clear why the hedging strategy loses money just by the passage of time alone.

The same reasoning explains why the passage of time generates money in strategies that aim to generate concave payoffs. Suppose that the derivatives firm purchased an ordinary call. In that case the derivatives firm's hedging strategy would have to generate a concave payoff. Since convex and concave payoffs are each other's mirror image, to generate a concave payoff the derivatives firm must do exactly the opposite of what it does to generate a convex payoff, i.e. sell stocks if the index goes up and buy stocks if the index goes down. If the index were to go up and down, the firm would sell at the high and buy at the low. The same would happen if the index first went down and then up again. In both cases the firm would make money.

Since volatility determines the magnitude of the fluctuations in the index, the more volatile the index, the more the hedging strategy will lose or win. In this way, volatility can be compared to the concept of **friction** in physics, which tells us that in terms of energy expended a given movement is more costly the higher the degree of friction that has to be overcome.

The above also explains why contracts with relatively short maturities have relatively high time values. Let's go back to the sale of an ordinary call. The hedging strategy would tell the derivatives firm to buy more equity if the index goes up and sell if it goes down. If we look at the effect of time to maturity on these controls, we see that the strategy tends to make bigger adjustments in the hedge portfolio the closer we get to maturity. This is most obvious close to maturity. At the contract's maturity date the firm either holds one share of the index and K bonds short when $K < I_T$, or it keeps no position at all when $K > I_T$. This means that if we are very close to maturity and the index moves from one side of K to the other the derivatives firm has to buy or sell a whole share of the index. Because the hedge adjustments tend to increase, the costs of infinite crossing increase as well.

In real life indices do not exhibit infinite crossing. Einstein noted already in 1906 that the mathematical model of Brownian motion 'nicht für beliebig kleine Zeiten gültig sein kann'.[4] This means that the **theoretical prices of options with a convex (concave) payoff contain a mark-up (mark-down) for something which does not exist in reality**. In other words, when selling (buying) a convex payoff at the theoretical price the derivatives firm will be asking (paying) too much. Likewise, when selling (buying) a concave payoff at the theoretical price the derivatives firm will be asking (paying) too little. The reason why this phenomenon is hardly ever discussed in the literature[5] is that time value has a very plausible interpretation. Consider an ordinary call option. The longer the time to maturity

---

[4] A. Einstein, Zur Theorie der Brownschen Bewegung, *Annalen der Physik*, Vol. 19, 1906, p. 380. Translation: 'cannot be valid for arbitrarily small time intervals'.

[5] The most noteworthy exception being P. Carr and R. Jarrow, The Stop-Loss Start-Gain Paradox and Option Valuation: A New Decomposition into Intrinsic and Time Value, *Review of Financial Studies*, Vol. 3, 1990, pp. 469–492.

and the higher the volatility of the index, the higher the probability that the option yields a substantial payoff. Since people prefer more money to less, the option price is higher. This sounds very plausible, but it should always be remembered that in the theoretical model there is no need for preference-based considerations because options can be hedged perfectly. In the theoretical model it is purely a mathematical idiosyncrasy that causes options to have time value.

5.5   A SHORTCUT FOR THE EXPECTED HEDGING COSTS

Although it does not show from the Black–Scholes–Merton formula, calculating the expected hedging costs for a contract can be a very time-consuming process as we first have to derive the appropriate hedging strategy. The more complicated the contract payoff, the more difficult it will be to derive that strategy. It would be a lot easier if we could somehow calculate the expected hedging costs directly. Fortunately, there is such a shortcut.

The expected hedging costs for a derivatives contract are equal to the present value of the amount the derivatives firm expects to pay in the future.

This may sound a bit too straightforward and indeed it is. **For this shortcut to work we must make two additional assumptions**.

- All stock prices and stock market indices in a country tend to rise at a rate equal to the interest rate of that country's currency.
- The exchange rate between any two currencies tends to change at a rate equal to the interest rate differential between both currencies.

Under the first assumption all stocks, irrespective of their risk characteristics, offer the same expected return as a savings account. In terms of the geometric Brownian motion given by (5.2) this means that the drift μ is equal to the interest rate, which simply reflects the cost of carrying money through time. This new stock price process is referred to as the **risk neutral** price process because it is the price process we would observe if all investors were risk neutral, i.e. if they only cared about the expected payoff of assets and not about the risks involved. It is important to understand, however, that this similarity is purely coincidental. At no point do we really assume investors to be risk neutral.

The second assumption implies that if the foreign interest rate is higher than the domestic interest rate, the foreign currency will tend to depreciate relative to the domestic currency. If the foreign rate is lower than the domestic rate, the foreign currency will tend to appreciate. There is a simple trick to remember this link between the interest rate differential and the drift of the exchange rate. If a currency has a relatively high interest rate, the world must expect that currency to depreciate. If not, money would have flown in and interest rates would have dropped. Likewise, if a currency has a relatively low interest rate the world must expect that currency to appreciate. If not, money would have flown out and interest rates would have risen.

The above shortcut turns the problem of calculating the expected hedging costs into an exercise in probability theory. Because of this, **a little probabilistic intuition can go a long way in understanding (changes in) derivatives prices**. The shortcut has become a very important tool for financial engineers and derivatives structurers alike. Financial engineers use it to derive formal pricing results for new types of contracts. Structurers use it to gain intuition about how the price of a contract will change if one or more parameters are changed, or if new rights or restrictions are added. We will see many examples of this in later chapters.

The above shortcut tells us that to find the expected hedging costs of a derivatives contract we have to calculate its expected future payoff under the assumption that over time the reference index drifts upwards at a rate equal to the prevailing interest rate and discount that back to the present. To be able to calculate a contract's expected payoff we need to know the probability distribution of the contract's payoff. The latter can be derived by combining (a) the payoff function which defines the contract in question, and (b) the distribution of the reference index. Knowing the possible payoffs and the accompanying probabilities we can then calculate the expected payoff by multiplying every possible payoff value by its probability and adding them together.

Let's look at a simple example. Suppose we had to price a **forward** where at maturity the end-user pays a fixed amount of 100 and the derivatives firm pays an index-linked amount I_1. The interest rate is 5%. On balance, the derivatives firm will have to pay an amount equal to $I_1 - 100$. Since we do not know in advance what I_1 is going to be, we do not know what the derivatives firm will have to pay the end-user. However, we can derive a distribution for the payoff of the contract by combining the above payoff formula with the probability distribution of the index. Taking into account that to make the shortcut work we have to assume that the index tends to rise by 5%, research has led the derivatives firm to believe that there is a 25% probability that $I_1 = 95$, a 50% probability that $I_1 = 105$, and a 25% probability that $I_1 = 115$. This means that there is a 25% probability that the firm will receive 5.00, a 50% probability that it will have to pay 5.00, and a 25% probability that it will have to pay 15.00. Knowing the distribution of the payoff we can then calculate the expected payment as $0.25 \times -5.00 + 0.5 \times 5.00 + 0.25 \times 15.00 = 5.00$. Discounting back at 5%, this means the expected hedging costs of the forward are 4.76.

The above example is rather simple in the sense that the contract does not have any additional restrictions or rights. The introduction of the latter may significantly change the probability distribution of the contract's payoff. Suppose we gave the end-user the right to cancel the contract at maturity, i.e. we turned the forward into an **ordinary call**. In that case the payment by the derivatives firm is equal to Max[0, $I_1 - 100$]. Using the same distribution for the index as before, this means there is a 25% probability that the firm will pay nothing, a 50% probability that it will pay 5.00, and a 25% probability that it will have to pay 15.00. The derivatives firm can therefore be expected to pay an amount at maturity equal to $0.25 \times 0 + 0.5 \times 5.00 + 0.25 \times 15.00 = 6.25$. Discounting back to the present, this means that the expected hedging costs for the option are 5.95. The difference from the 4.76 we found for the forward is due to the cost of the option right.

To be able to say more about derivatives prices without having to go through complex mathematical calculations we need to have a thorough understanding of the values the contract payoff may take and the accompanying probabilities. With respect to the latter it is important to keep in mind that as a working hypothesis **stock and stock market index returns are best thought of as being normally distributed**. This means that the distribution of stock and stock market index returns is fully described by only two parameters.

- **Expected return.** For the shortcut to work we have to assume that stock prices tend to rise at a rate equal to the interest rate. In expected terms stocks therefore offer the same

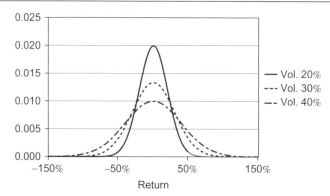

Figure 5.2   Normal distribution for volatilities of 20%, 30% and 40%

return as cash. This is clearly at odds with reality. However, we need this assumption to make the shortcut work.

- **Volatility.** The more volatile a stock or index the higher the probability that the actual return on that stock or index ends up substantially different from the expected return.

Figure 5.2 shows the normal distribution for an expected return of 5% and volatilities of 20%, 30% and 40%. From the graph we clearly see that if volatility is low, the distribution has a high dominating peak. Returns are most likely to fall around the expected return. If volatility is high, the distribution is dominated by the tails. In that case there is a high probability of an extreme return.

The next question is how the return distribution changes if we move out further into the future. This means we need to know more about the relationship between returns calculated over different subsequent periods. Again as a working hypothesis, **subsequent stock and stock market index returns are best thought of as being independent**. This means that last month's return does not say anything about next month's return. What does this mean for the return distribution? It means that if we calculate a return over a longer period, the expected value grows linearly with time. Over a horizon twice as long we can expect to make a return twice as high. Unlike the expected return, volatility does not grow linearly with time. Denoting the volatility over a period of a year as σ_1, the volatility over a period of N years σ_N can be calculated as

$$\sigma_N = \sqrt{N} \times \sigma_1. \qquad (5.6)$$

This means that given a one-year volatility of 20%, the volatility over a period of two years will be 28% and over four years 40%. In other words, instead of two it takes four years to double the volatility.

5.6   PUTTING THEORY INTO PRACTICE: HEDGING ERRORS

Obviously, the world that underlies option pricing models has very little in common with the world that we live in. The next question to answer is therefore what happens if we take our theoretical hedging strategies into the real world. To answer this question we have to take a look at the differences between the real world and the world from which theoretical hedging strategies are derived. There are quite a number of them, such as the following.

- **Jumps:** instead of moving smoothly, stock prices may sometimes jump from one level to the next.
- **Discrete trading:** instead of continuously, the hedge portfolio can only be adjusted discretely.
- **Transaction costs:** every trade we make is accompanied by commissions, market impact, etc.
- **Volatility misprediction:** the model assumes we know future volatility, while, as discussed in Chapter 2, in practice future stock market volatility is extremely hard to predict.

Given the above, theoretical hedging strategies can be expected to be far from perfect when executed in practice. Of course, the theoretical model gives us no indication how large the risks are, as in its own abstract world it produces a perfect hedge. This raises an important question: **are the expected hedging costs calculated from theoretical pricing formulas a good estimate of the actual hedging costs** we can expect when executing theoretical hedging strategies in the real world? Do the differences between the theoretical world and the real world only create uncertainty about the outcome of the hedging strategy, or do they systematically pull the expected hedging costs away in one direction? In this section we will provide some qualitative answers to these questions.

5.6.1 Jumps

Stock prices do not move smoothly over time but may jump from one level to the next without there being an opportunity to trade in between. Whenever this happens the derivatives firm is confronted with a hedging error. Figures 5.3 and 5.4 show this graphically. In Figure 5.3 the curve depicts the theoretical value of the hedge portfolio which the derivatives firm will hold when generating a convex payoff. We refer to this as **case 1**. The curve in Figure 5.4 depicts the theoretical value of the hedge portfolio the derivatives firm will hold when generating a concave payoff. We will call this **case 2**.

The above theoretical values are curves rather than straight lines because in the model the index simply cannot jump from one value to the other. It will always move smoothly and during that move the derivatives firm will adjust its hedge. As discussed, in case 1 the firm buys if the index goes up and sells if it goes down. In case 2 it buys if the index goes down and sells if the index goes up. Suppose the index was at I_0. The theoretical and the actual value of the hedge are both equal to V_0. Now suppose the index jumped to I_1 without the derivatives firm rebalancing its hedge. Since it is holding a fixed number of shares in the index the actual value of the hedge would move linearly to V_1^A. The theoretical value, however, would move to V_1^T, leaving a hedging error of $V_1^A - V_1^T$. In case 1 the firm loses and in case 2 it wins. The same happens if the index drops to I_2. The hedge's theoretical value changes to V_2^T, while its actual value moves to V_2^A. Again, case 1 shows a negative error and case 2 a positive error. In sum, **in case 1 jumps cost the firm money, while in case 2 they make it money**.

5.6.2 Discrete Trading

In theory, the hedge portfolio is adjusted continuously. In practice, the derivatives firm cannot do so if only because of the transaction costs involved. It will therefore rebalance

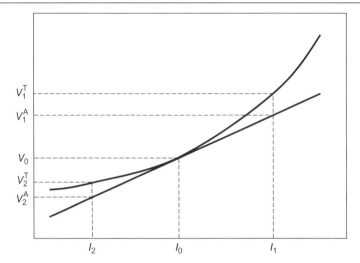

Figure 5.3   Hedging errors for convex payoff after jump

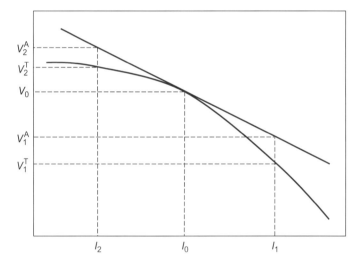

Figure 5.4   Hedging errors for concave payoff after jump

the hedge portfolio **discretely**, for example every other day or only if the index moves by 2% or more since the last rebalancing. This has serious consequences. When the index shows an upward or downward move, the value of the hedge will not be able to follow as planned and a hedging error will result in very much the same way as when the index jumps. Let's look at the sale of a convex payoff. From Figure 5.3 it is clear that in such a case discrete rebalancing can turn out to be quite costly. Fortunately, the derivatives firm has some money to burn in the form of the time value that it charged when the strategy was started. The firm overcharged because it calculated the expected hedging costs using a pricing formula based on the implicit assumption that the index exhibits infinite crossing, while it does not. A similar argument goes for the sale of a concave payoff where discrete rebalancing will compensate for the fact that the firm undercharged.

It can be shown that a strategy's **time value equals the expected costs or savings from discrete rebalancing**. On average, therefore, discrete rebalancing corrects the error made by implicitly assuming the presence of infinite crossing in the theoretical model. The emphasis, however, is on the 'on average'. On average the derivatives firm will be fine, but in individual cases there may be quite a large difference between time value and the actual costs or benefits from discrete trading. This becomes clear if we look at the process by which time value and discrete rebalancing tend to compensate each other. Consider case 1 again. Over time the actual value of the hedge portfolio will drop due to discrete rebalancing. The theoretical value, however, will also drop because it loses time value. If the change in the index is small, the loss from discrete trading will be smaller than the amount of time value lost, and a positive hedging error will result. On the other hand, if the change in the index is relatively large the loss from discrete trading will exceed the loss in time value, causing a hedging loss. This is illustrated in Figure 5.5.

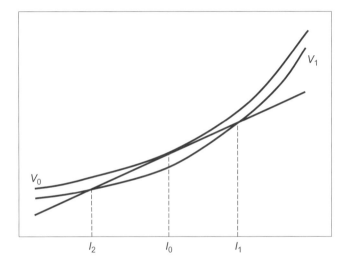

Figure 5.5 Hedging errors for discrete hedge rebalancing convex payoff

Figure 5.5 is similar to Figure 5.3 except that this time we look at the change in the index over the relevant hedge rebalancing interval instead of an immediate change in the index value. V_0 depicts the theoretical value of the hedge on one rebalancing date and V_1 depicts the theoretical value on the next rebalancing date. The drop represents the time value running out over time. The straight line represents the value of the hedge. Initially the index is at I_0. From the figure we see that as long as the index does not rise above I_1 or fall below I_2 the strategy will show a positive error. Outside this range, however, the strategy shows a negative hedging error.

Discrete rebalancing may not change the expected hedging costs but it does introduce uncertainty about the outcome of the hedging process. One way to obtain insight into the resulting degree of uncertainty is to analyze this mathematically. Since this yields quite complicated results, we will not do so in detail. When hedging the **sale of an ordinary call**, however, there is a simple approximation for the standard deviation of the cumulative hedging error, i.e. the difference between the time T value of the hedge portfolio and the amount required to pay off the option contract. The latter is given by

$$\sigma_{\text{error}} = \frac{1}{\sqrt{N}} \times (0.354 \times I_0 \times \sigma\sqrt{T} \times e^{-d_1^2}), \tag{5.7}$$

where N is the number of times between $t = 0$ and maturity that the hedge portfolio will be rebalanced and d_1 is defined in (5.3). The above expression clearly shows how the choice of the rebalancing frequency influences the uncertainty about the outcome of the hedging process. For example, if we rebalance four times as frequently we halve the standard deviation of the hedging error. Note that the standard deviation of the cumulative hedging error increases with the volatility of the index.

The magnitude of the hedging error standard deviation is best interpreted in the light of the initial option price. For ATM ordinary calls there is a very simple formula to express the standard deviation of the hedging error as a multiple of the theoretical option price. As a rough approximation it is given by

$$\frac{\sigma_{\text{error}}}{V_0} = \frac{0.886}{\sqrt{N}}. \tag{5.8}$$

Surprisingly, the outcome only depends on the number of times we rebalance the hedge portfolio. If we look at an option with one year to maturity we see that the hedging error risk as a percentage of the initial option price will be about 25.6% when rebalancing monthly ($N = 12$) and 5.6% when rebalancing daily ($N = 250$).

5.6.3 Transaction Costs

Discrete rebalancing creates uncertainty about the outcome of the hedging process but it does not change the expected hedging costs. This is not true for transaction costs. Transaction costs are always positive and therefore systematically affect the expected hedging costs. In addition, they contribute to the uncertainty with respect to the ultimate outcome of the hedging process, as sometimes the hedge will require relatively little adjustment and therefore generate low transaction costs, while at other times it will require major adjustments and generate high transaction costs.

Unlike what is assumed in the theoretical model, in practice trading does not have a negligible impact on prices, neither are trading decisions always executed immediately after they are taken. The transaction costs of a trade can therefore be divided into four major cost components.

1. **Commissions.** The fee paid to a broker to execute the order.
2. **Market impact.** The displacement of prices resulting from order arrival.
3. **Opportunity costs.** The costs (which may be negative) of market price movements due to forces other than the particular trade during the time elapsed from the moment the decision to trade was made until the actual completion of the trade.
4. **Miscellaneous other costs.** This includes items such as transfer taxes and execution errors.

In less developed markets opportunity costs may significantly outweigh the direct observable costs. In that case the transaction costs structure looks very much like an iceberg, with commissions and market impact visible above the surface but the much

larger costs of delayed and missed trades hidden below the surface. The cost components 1–3 are generally interrelated as well. A reduction of one of them may have an
adverse impact on the others. Forcing commissions down, for example, may result in
increased market impact and increased opportunity costs, while minimizing market impact
by trading slowly through the market increases opportunity risk and the other way around.
It should be noted that the above cost components are not fixed, but may change over
time. It is generally thought for example that after the Asian, Russian and LTCM crises
in the late nineties liquidity in most equity markets deteriorated significantly, leading to
a corresponding rise in market impact costs.

Apart from marginal supply and demand conditions, transaction costs also depend on
the trading style used in the execution of a trade. Traders can be classified into two groups
according to their eagerness to trade. So-called **passive traders** wait for the other side
of the market to come to them, i.e. they supply liquidity in the form of limit orders.
Because the price may move away from the order price, execution is uncertain. **Active
traders** are the ones to initiate transactions, i.e. to demand liquidity. By placing market
orders rather than limit orders, they tend to pay a premium for immediate execution as
they need to move the price to find liquidity. Execution is near certain, but the execution
price is not. Trying to stick to the recommendations of the models used as closely as
possible, most hedge trading is active in nature.

For common levels of transaction costs and rebalancing frequencies, the present value
of the transaction costs the derivatives firm can expect to incur is easily calculated.[6]
When generating a **convex payoff**, for example to hedge the sale of an ordinary call,
the expected transaction costs can be calculated as the difference between the theoretical
price one would obtain with a volatility input equal to σ^*_{cx} given by

$$\sigma^*_{cx} = \sqrt{\sigma^2 \left(1 + \sqrt{2/\pi} \frac{c}{\sigma\sqrt{\Delta t}} \right)} \tag{5.9}$$

and the price with a volatility input equal to the actual index volatility σ. In the above
expression c denotes round-trip transaction costs as a fraction of the value of the stocks
traded and Δt represents the length of the rebalancing interval. Because transaction costs
are positive, modified volatility will exceed the actual volatility of the index.

In case the derivatives firm has to generate a **concave payoff**, for example to hedge
the purchase of an ordinary call, it can calculate the expected transaction costs as the
difference between the theoretical price one would obtain with a volatility input σ^*_{cc}
equal to

$$\sigma^*_{cc} = \sqrt{\sigma^2 \left(1 - \sqrt{2/\pi} \frac{c}{\sigma\sqrt{\Delta t}} \right)} \tag{5.10}$$

and the price with a volatility input equal to the actual index volatility σ. In this case
modified volatility will be lower than the actual index volatility. Because the desired
payoff is concave, however, the theoretical price goes up if volatility drops.

Concentrating on strategies generating convex payoffs, we see from (5.9) that the
expected transaction costs will be higher the higher the costs of trading, the shorter the

---

[6] See H. Leland, Option Pricing and Replication with Transaction Costs, *Journal of Finance*, Vol. 40, 1985,
pp. 1283–1301.

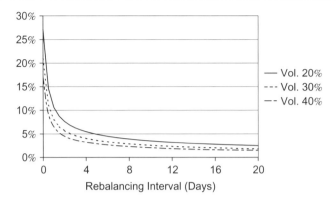

Figure 5.6 Expected transaction costs for a 1-year ATM ordinary call as a function of rebalancing interval

rebalancing interval, and the more volatile the index. For volatilities of 20%, 30% and 40%, and assuming interest rates are at 5%, Figure 5.6 shows the expected transaction costs as a percentage of the theoretical option price for the hedging strategy for a 1-year ATM ordinary call as a function of the rebalancing interval. Round-trip costs are equal to 0.5%. From the graph we clearly see the influence of the rebalancing interval. Frequent rebalancing can be expected to be extremely costly. With a volatility of 20% and daily revision of the hedge portfolio the expected transaction costs are equal to 10.5% of the theoretical option price. Put another way, **if the derivatives firm plans to rebalance its hedge on a daily basis it should ask at least 110.5% of the price which the theoretical model tells it to ask**. Note that Figure 5.6 also shows that when expressed as a percentage of the theoretical option price the expected transaction costs drop when the index becomes more volatile.

The expected transaction costs also depend heavily on the contract to be hedged. A longer **time to maturity** means a longer hedging effort, which translates into higher expected transaction costs. It is easy to show, however, that every extra year of maturity adds less than the previous year. Figure 5.7 shows the expected transaction costs as a percentage of the theoretical option price for the hedging strategy of an ATM ordinary call as a function of the option's time to maturity with either daily or weekly rebalancing. Although the expected transaction costs rise in absolute terms, they drop when expressed as a percentage of the theoretical option price. With daily rebalancing the expected transaction costs, expressed as a percentage of the index, rise from 1.10% for a 1-year option to 1.95% for a 5-year option. Expressed as a percentage of the theoretical option price, however, the expected transaction costs drop from 10.5% to 6.7%. Despite the drop, this still means that if it wants to keep the expected hedging error at zero, the derivatives firm should ask at least 106.7% of the theoretical price for the 5-year option.

When it comes to the influence of the **strike** we again have to go back to the hedging strategy given by (5.3) and (5.4). With ITM options the hedging strategy starts out heavily invested in equity. If the index goes up there is little further trading required. The hedging strategy for OTM options starts out heavily invested in cash. Therefore, if the index goes down there is hardly any equity to sell. ATM options start out somewhere in between ITM and OTM options. This means that wherever the index goes, the hedging strategy will

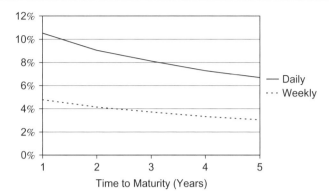

Figure 5.7 Expected transaction costs for an ATM ordinary call as a function of time to maturity

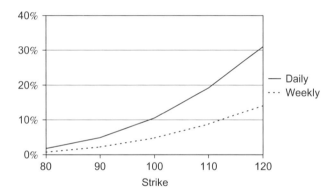

Figure 5.8 Expected transaction costs for a 1-year ordinary call as a function of strike

require the derivatives firm to do quite a lot of trading. In other words, when an option is ATM transaction costs can be expected to be at their highest. Starting with a relatively low strike the expected transaction costs will rise first but drop again later. This of course does not mean that the expected transaction costs expressed as a percentage of the theoretical option price show the same behavior. Although in absolute terms the expected costs rise first and drop later, they simply increase when expressed as a percentage of the theoretical option price. This is illustrated in Figure 5.8, which shows the expected transaction costs as a percentage of the theoretical option price for the hedging strategy of a 1-year ordinary call as a function of the option's strike.

5.6.4 Volatility Misprediction

To be able to use the Black–Scholes–Merton pricing formula, or any other option pricing formula for that matter, the derivatives firm will need to say something about the volatility of the index. The theoretical model assumes that the latter is known, but in reality this is not the case. If the firm put in the wrong volatility, i.e. if the index turned out to be more or less volatile than expected, three problems would arise.

- **Strategy controls.** The hedging strategy's controls require a volatility input. If actual volatility turns out to be different from the volatility input used, the derivatives firm will be holding the wrong number of shares and bonds. Sometimes it will hold too many and sometimes too few. As a result, the accuracy of the hedge deteriorates.
- **Market moves.** If volatility turns out higher than expected there are more large moves in the index than the firm thought there would be. If we look at the case of a convex payoff in Figure 5.5, this means that the firm will lose more money than it thought it would. If volatility turns out lower than expected there will be fewer large moves, meaning the derivatives firm will lose less money than expected.
- **Transaction costs.** As can be seen in (5.9) and (5.10), if volatility is higher (lower) than expected there may be more (less) trading required than expected, which in turn means that transaction costs will be higher (lower) than expected.

Sometimes the derivatives firm's volatility forecast will be too high and at other times it will be too low, but as long as the firm is able to come up with an unbiased forecast this will not really affect the expected hedging costs. It does create additional uncertainty, however.

Before the derivatives firm can use the pricing formula to calculate the expected hedging costs it needs to decide on a volatility input. There are basically two ways to go about this.

- **Historical volatility.** The most obvious route is to study the volatility of the index in the past and use that to predict future volatility. Apart from the GARCH (1,1) model which we discussed in Chapter 2, there is nowadays a whole range of statistical models one can choose from.
- **Implied volatility.** When there is a liquid market for other options on the same reference index the firm can ask itself what volatility the market must be using to arrive at the prices at which these contracts are trading. Having answered this question it can then use the same volatility to price the contract in question.

The latter route is known as **calibrating the pricing model to the market**. The volatility parameters which require calibration, i.e. what is really meant by implied volatility, depend on the specific model chosen. If the derivatives firm used the geometric Brownian motion given by (5.2) it would only have one single volatility parameter to work with. According to this model all contracts based on the same reference index share the same volatility. If we take this model out into the marketplace, however, we find that **different contracts produce significantly different implied volatility values**. Figure 5.9 shows the implied volatilities as seen on January 5th, 2000 in the market for ordinary calls on the S&P 500, using the Black–Scholes–Merton formula for calculation. From the figure we see clearly how implied volatilities vary with the options' time to maturity. This is referred to as the **term structure of implied volatility**. For a given time to maturity, implied volatilities for different strikes are not the same either. This is known as the **implied volatility skew**. Sometimes this skew is referred to as the 'volatility smile'. We prefer the term 'skew' to 'smile', however, as intuitively 'smile' implies a very particular type of relationship that might not always be correct. From Figure 5.9 we also see that **short maturities tend to display a more pronounced skew than long maturities**.

Although implied volatility can intuitively be thought of as the 'market's view' on the future evolution of the index, realistically speaking implied volatility is nothing more than a transformation of an option price or a set of option prices where the influence

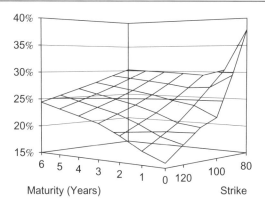

Figure 5.9 Implied volatilities of S&P 500 calls as a function of time to maturity and strike on January 5th, 2000

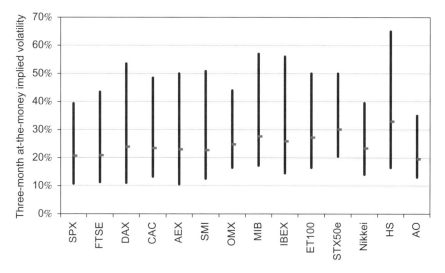

Figure 5.10 Implied volatilities from 1996 to 1999 for 3-month ATM ordinary calls. Source: UBS Warburg

of all the theoretical determinants of the option price (according to some model) except volatility is filtered out. This means that implied volatility collects everything which is not, or not correctly, reflected in the theoretical model. Given this, it is not surprising that **implied volatility is not constant**. Substantial changes may occur over short periods of time. For various major indices Figures 5.10 and 5.11 show the Black–Scholes–Merton implied volatilities observed over the four year period from 1996 to 1999 in the market for 3-month and 5-year ATM ordinary calls. The vertical line shows the trading range observed over the four year period and the horizontal line the mean. From these graphs it is clear that implied index volatility can vary a lot. Over the period studied, 3-month S&P 500 implieds for example have been as low as 10% and as high as 40%. Longer dated implieds are less volatile, but even 5-year S&P 500 implieds have been seen as low as 15% and as high as 35%.

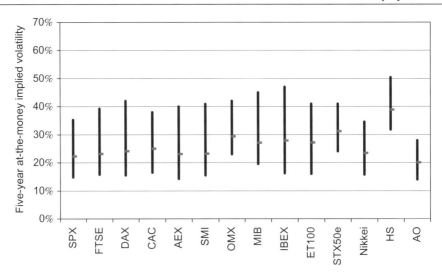

Figure 5.11 Implied volatilities from 1996 to 1999 for 5-year ATM ordinary calls. Source: UBS Warburg

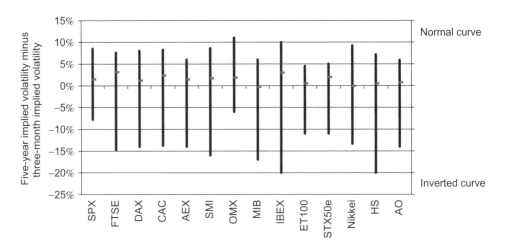

Figure 5.12 Difference between implied volatility on 5-year and 3-month ATM ordinary calls from 1996 to 1999. Source: UBS Warburg

When implied volatilities move, they do not move all together, i.e. **the shape of the term structure and skew changes over time**. To get an idea of the possible changes in the term structure of volatility for a number of indices, Figure 5.12 shows the difference between the implied volatilities on a 5-year and a 3-month ATM ordinary call as seen over the period from 1996 to 1999. Again, the vertical line shows the observed trading range and the horizontal line the mean. From this graph we see that on average the term structures studied have been fairly flat, but also that there has been a lot of variation over the period studied. On occasion long-dated volatility has been substantially higher than short-dated volatility, but the reverse has also been observed.

With every option essentially having its own implied volatility the systematic pricing of options for which there is no liquid, observable market becomes problematic. Practitioners have come up with various ways to solve this problem. One way to capture the variety of implied volatilities produced by models with a single volatility parameter is to extend these models somewhat and explicitly allow for the volatility of the index to vary with time. The calibration of such a model of course requires the use of prices of contracts with different maturities, as we need to unravel how volatility changes with time. Although the new model would catch the dependence of implied volatility on time to maturity, it still does not explain why ordinary options with different strike prices produce different implieds. To incorporate this phenomenon we could extend the model even further and make volatility a function of the index value as well. Derivatives researchers all over the world are working on models like these. References to their results so far can be found in the bibliography under the heading 'Model Calibration and Implied Volatility'.

5.7   PUTTING THEORY INTO PRACTICE: SIMULATION

It is one thing to qualitatively guess what the effect of certain 'imperfections' is going to be, but it is better to have some quantitative insights as well. To obtain these we revert to the stochastic simulation techniques used in earlier research to study hedging error behavior.[7] The use of stochastic simulation allows us to investigate the performance of a hedging strategy under many different circumstances, which gives a good approximation of the distribution of the hedging errors which that strategy may generate. Historical simulation cannot provide this kind of information because there exists only one limited set of historical data. Manipulation of these data cannot change this without interfering with the dependencies between successive observations.

5.7.1   The Model

In the simulations we look at the hedging of three different types of call options with an initial time to maturity of one year, trading the S&P 500 as the reference index and a zero coupon bond as the riskless asset. We construct 1000 alternative 1-year series of hourly mid-quote S&P 500 index values and daily interest rates using statistical models that produce data that are (virtually) indistinguishable from real-life S&P 500 and short-term interest rate data. All these 1-year series start at the same point. The index starts at 100 and the interest rate at 5%.

Because the S&P 500 is well diversified and the absolute amounts involved in the strategies to be studied will be relatively limited, the displacement of prices resulting from our trading activity will be limited as well. Market impact in the stock market is therefore assumed to be constant at 0.25% per share of the index. Identifying ourselves with a member firm, commission costs are assumed to be zero. Instead of perfect divisibility of all assets, we assume a minimum order size of 500 shares of the index. We assume no costs or indivisibilities in the trading of the reserve asset since this substitutes for borrowing and lending, the form of which is left unspecified.

We will study the outcomes of the hedging strategies for three different types of derivatives contracts, in all three cases assuming the derivatives firm is the writer of the relevant

---

[7] See H. Kat, Delta Hedging of S&P 500 Options: Cash versus Futures Market Execution, *Journal of Derivatives*, Spring, 1996, pp. 6–25.

contract. The first is an **ordinary call** with a payoff to the buyer equal to

$$\text{Max}\,[0, I_T - K].\tag{5.11}$$

The second is a contract similar to an ordinary call except that instead of I_T the derivatives firm now pays its counterparty an amount equal to the daily average of the index values over the contract's life. A contract like this is known as a **fixed-strike Asian call**. Denoting the average as $A_{0,T}$, the payoff to be generated by the hedging strategy is now

$$\text{Max}\,[0, A_{0,T} - K].\tag{5.12}$$

The third contract is also similar to an ordinary call but instead of a fixed amount K the derivatives firm's counterparty now pays an amount equal to the lowest index value reached during the life of the contract. With $M_{0,T}^-$ denoting the lowest index value observed, the payoff to be produced by the hedging strategy is therefore

$$\text{Max}\,[0, I_T - M_{0,T}^-].\tag{5.13}$$

If the index goes up there is little difference with an ordinary option. However, if the index goes down the derivatives firm's counterparty's final payment goes down as well, meaning that the contract can never be OTM. A contract like this is known as a **floating-strike lookback call**.

We selected the Asian call and the lookback call for a special reason. The hedging strategy for the Asian call is similar to that for an ordinary call. Since the strategy payoff is convex in the average, the derivatives firm buys the average when it goes up and sells the average when it goes down. Unfortunately, the firm cannot simply buy or sell the average, so it needs to combine the former hedging strategy with a second strategy that generates the average. To generate an amount of money equal to the average the firm starts off fully invested in stocks. As time passes by, the stocks are sold off and the proceeds are invested in bonds. At maturity, the value of the bond holdings will have grown to an amount equal to the average, and the stock holdings will be depleted. The strategy the derivatives firm will follow is a combination of this strategy and the ordinary call strategy. This means that we now have a strategy where the number of shares of the index to hold falls to zero at maturity.

Although initially very much like an ordinary option, the Asian call strategy's trading becomes less aggressive when maturity approaches. The lookback option was chosen for the opposite reason. If the index goes up there is little difference with an ordinary option. However, if the index goes down the derivatives firm's counterparty's final payment goes down as well. Since this is permanent, it represents an additional risk to the derivatives firm, requiring a more aggressive hedging effort. This relatively aggressive profile can be expected to make lookbacks more difficult to hedge than ordinary and especially Asian options.

Before we can simulate the above strategies we have to decide on the volatility input used. In this study we will use the GARCH (1,1) predictor which we discussed earlier in Chapter 2. This model's forecasting performance is representative for the large variety of volatility predictors that are around nowadays. The hedge portfolio is rebalanced discretely every 0, 1, 2, 3, 4, 5, 8, 11, 14, 17, 20 days, where 0 stands for hourly rebalancing. In total we therefore have 11 different operationalizations of the three hedging strategies to be studied. For every one of these we calculate the average, the standard deviation and the skewness of the frequency distribution of the time T hedging errors, i.e. the differences between the time T value of the hedge portfolio and the actual option payoff, assuming we start off with an investment equal to the options' theoretical value. In all three cases we assume we are hedging 250,000 options. All hedging errors, however, are expressed per option. Starting with a volatility of 16%, the initial investment required by the ordinary call hedging strategy is 8.96. For the Asian call strategy and the lookback strategy the initial investments are 4.93 and 14.48, respectively.

5.7.2 Simulation Results

The simulation results are presented graphically in Figures 5.13–5.15 with the time between rebalancings on the horizontal axis and the average, standard deviation and skewness, respectively, of the 1000 time T hedging errors for the ordinary, Asian and lookback call hedging strategies on the vertical axis. The **average error is consistently negative**, indicating that on average the initial investment in the strategies was too low. Reducing the rebalancing frequency improves the average error as transaction costs tend to decline. After our discussion of transaction costs, none of this comes as a surprise. Irrespective of the rebalancing frequency, all three strategies are unable to deliver the desired payoff with a high degree of accuracy. The hedging error distributions exhibit **substantial standard deviation** and are **unfavorably skewed**. The high standard deviations for high rebalancing frequencies emphasize the **path dependence** of the strategies, with some paths requiring much more trading over the year than others, and therefore generating much higher transaction costs. Skewness on the other hand seems to be largely unaffected by the rebalancing frequency.

There are **significant differences between the three strategies**. The Asian call strategy produces average errors, standard deviations and skewness values that behave similarly to those for the ordinary call strategy. Quantitatively, however, the average errors are higher, i.e. more favorable, than those for the ordinary call strategy, and the standard deviations and skewness values are lower and higher, respectively. This reflects the less aggressive trading required to hedge the Asian call. For the lookback call strategy we see that qualitatively the results have a lot in common with the ordinary call strategy as well. Quantitatively, however, the average errors tend to be significantly lower and the standard deviations substantially higher than for the ordinary call strategy. This reflects the fact that for the lookback strategy the number of shares of the index to hold tends to be more sensitive to the index than for the ordinary call strategy.

The observed hedging errors are the combined result of (a) transaction costs, (b) volatility misprediction, (c) discrete hedge rebalancing, and (d) the fact that actual stock prices and interest rates behave differently than assumed when deriving the hedging strategy. Using the simulation model we can investigate what causes what. To single out the influence of **transaction costs** we repeated the above simulations assuming zero transaction costs. The outcomes can be found in Figures 5.16–5.18. The results show that with zero transaction costs, the average errors are all close to zero and the standard deviations rise more or less linearly with the time between rebalancings. Transaction costs appear to be a relatively unimportant source of skewness though. Note that the behavior of the average errors and the standard deviations is very much in line with what we discussed before.

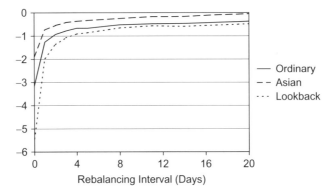

Figure 5.13   Average hedging errors for ordinary, Asian and lookback calls

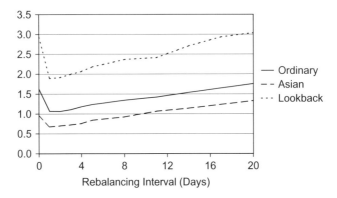

Figure 5.14   Standard deviation hedging error distributions for ordinary, Asian and lookback calls

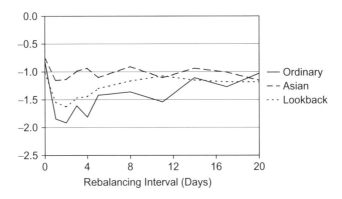

Figure 5.15   Skewness hedging error distributions for ordinary, Asian and lookback calls

To study the influence of **volatility misprediction**, we investigated how the strategies would have performed if we had known the actual level of volatility in advance. Keeping transaction costs at zero, the results are shown in Figures 5.19–5.21. The average errors do not change much. The standard deviations, however, are well below those generated before, while the difference is more or less independent of the rebalancing frequency.

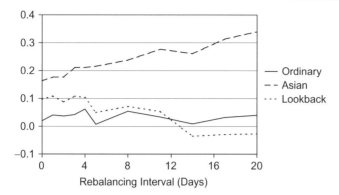

Figure 5.16 Average hedging errors for ordinary, Asian and lookback calls with zero transaction costs

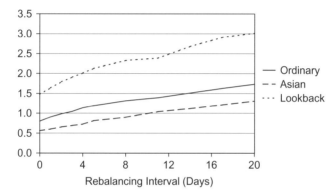

Figure 5.17 Standard deviation hedging error distributions for ordinary, Asian and lookback calls with zero transaction costs

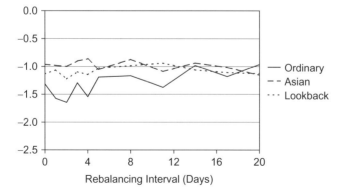

Figure 5.18 Skewness hedging error distributions for ordinary, Asian and lookback calls with zero transaction costs

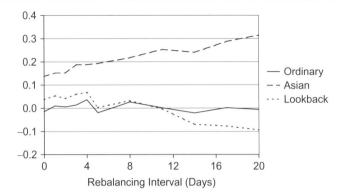

Figure 5.19   Average hedging errors for ordinary, Asian and lookback calls with zero transaction costs and perfect volatility forecasts

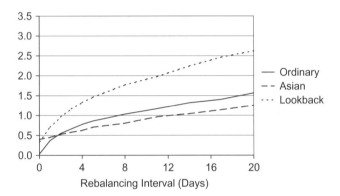

Figure 5.20   Standard deviation hedging error distributions for ordinary, Asian and lookback calls with zero transaction costs and perfect volatility forecasts

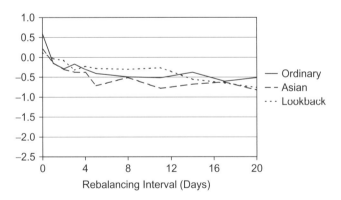

Figure 5.21   Skewness hedging error distributions for ordinary, Asian and lookback calls with zero transaction costs and perfect volatility forecasts

The skewness values are much closer to zero now. This means that volatility misprediction is an important source of hedging error standard deviation and skewness. With the errors from transaction costs and volatility misprediction eliminated, the results also provide information on the importance of **discrete hedge rebalancing**. For low rebalancing frequencies discrete trading is an important source of hedging error standard deviation. As predicted, it has no significant influence on the average error or the skewness of the error distribution however.

This leaves the error from using hedging strategies that were derived from **abstract models** of the behavior of the index and the interest rate. If we look at hourly rebalancing we see that the standard deviation of the hedging error of the ordinary call strategy is almost equal to zero, i.e. **the hedge is virtually perfect**. This means that the lack of realism of the assumed price processes has no significant implications for the outcome of the hedging process for the ordinary call. For the Asian call and the lookback call things are different though. Even with hourly rebalancing there is substantial uncertainty about the outcome of the strategies. This means that, unlike for the ordinary call, the lack of realism of the assumed price processes has a significant impact. This is not surprising if one realizes that the payoff of the Asian and the lookback call depends on the whole path taken by the index to reach its time T value. The payoff of an ordinary call only depends on the index value at maturity. A correct specification of the behavior of the reference index is therefore much more important for Asian or lookback calls than it is for ordinary calls.

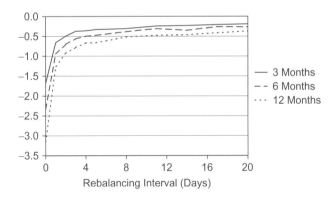

Figure 5.22 Average hedging errors for 3-month, 6-month and 12-month ordinary ATM calls

We can also use the simulation model to study how the average hedging error varies with options' time to maturity and strike. Figure 5.22 shows the average hedging errors for ordinary ATM calls with **times to maturity** of 3, 6 and 12 months. The theoretical prices for these options are 3.82, 5.77 and 8.96. From the graphs we see that the average hedging error is higher the longer the time to maturity. Looking at the vertical distances between the three lines, however, it is clear that the average hedging error does not grow linearly. On a per month basis the 3-month option exhibits a much higher average error than the 6-month and especially the 12-month option. This is in line with what we discussed earlier.

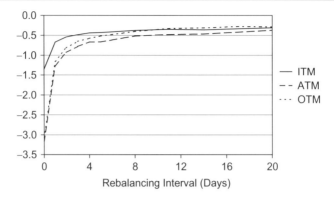

Figure 5.23   Average hedging errors for ordinary 15% OTM, ATM and 15% ITM calls

Figure 5.23 shows the average hedging errors for ordinary calls with one year to maturity and **strikes** 15% OTM, ATM and 15% ITM. The theoretical prices for these options are 3.00, 8.96 and 19.76, respectively. From the graphs we see that on average ATM options show lower errors than OTM and especially ITM options. As discussed earlier this can be explained by the composition of the hedge portfolio at initiation. ITM options require little further trading if the index goes up and OTM options require little further trading if the index goes down. ITM options do slightly better than OTM options because over time the index trends upwards. ATM options start in between ITM and OTM options. Wherever the index goes, the hedging strategy will require the derivatives firm to do quite a lot of trading. The average error for the ATM option is therefore the largest of the three.

We repeated the above simulations for a large number of different volatility predictors, rebalancing rules and also different contracts. Unfortunately, this did not result in more impressive outcomes. It therefore seems safe to conclude that **theoretical hedging strategies are unable to hedge options accurately**. Transaction costs will lead a derivatives firm to mis-estimate the expected hedging costs, and are a significant source of uncertainty when rebalancing relatively frequently. Volatility misprediction and discrete rebalancing do not seem to affect the expected hedging costs, but are main sources of uncertainty. The extent of these effects depends heavily on the nature of the hedging strategy's recommendations. The more the prescribed composition of the hedge changes after a move in the index, the higher the expected hedging costs and the higher the hedging risk. In addition, the more an option's payoff depends on the path followed by the index to reach its value at maturity, the more important the assumptions about the behavior of the relevant prices made to derive the option's hedging strategy become. Again, this may not add to the expected hedging error but it does cause additional uncertainty.

5.8   FUTURES MARKET EXECUTION

The above simulations showed that the only 'imperfection' which systematically pulls the hedging error away from zero is transaction costs. In other words, **if transaction costs were zero, the theoretical price would be a good estimate of the actual expected hedging costs**. Because transaction costs have such a strong impact, derivatives firms are always searching for ways to reduce transaction costs, i.e. cheaper ways to adjust exposure. Many exchanges nowadays list forwards on stock market indices (which are in that case no longer called forwards but **index futures**). As we will discuss in Chapter 6, buying or selling futures can be seen as a substitute for cash market trading. Adjusting exposure with futures, however, tends to be many times cheaper than cash market trading in terms of commissions as well as market impact. For example, the transaction costs of buying or selling a USD 25m S&P 500 index portfolio in the cash market will be about 0.21%. In the futures market, however, the costs will be only 0.03%. Outside the US differences are even more significant. Trading the FTSE 100 in the cash market will cost 0.70%, while in the futures market the costs will only be 0.06%. This difference in transaction costs makes index futures an extremely attractive vehicle for strategies whose frequent trading in and out of the market would otherwise excessively erode results.

From a transaction costs perspective futures market execution is to be preferred to cash market execution. There are also some things to be said against the use of futures, however.

- Since futures markets thin out with longer maturities, it may not be possible to find a liquid futures contract with a maturity date equal to the relevant hedging strategy's terminal date. Relying on futures with short maturities means the firm will have to **roll over** to the next nearby contract four to six times a year. Each rollover imposes additional transaction costs as well as additional uncertainty.

- Actual future prices may deviate significantly from their correct, arbitrage-free price; a phenomenon known as **mispricing**. Research has shown that large price moves in the S&P 500 cash market, for example, tend to be accompanied by changes in S&P 500 futures mispricing in the same direction as the cash price move. This is especially damaging to strategies that buy after prices have risen and sell after a fall. Another consequence of this overshooting phenomenon is that it increases the hedging capacity of a futures contract. It effectively makes the contract larger than it is. When not explicitly accounting for overshooting, the firm may end up buying or selling more exposure than desired.

Elsewhere we used stochastic simulation methods to investigate whether the transaction costs advantage weighs up against the above disadvantages.[8] The futures market simulation results showed that the transaction costs advantage heavily outweighs the rollover and mispricings disadvantage. Due to the much lower transaction costs, the average errors were close to zero for all three options considered. The standard deviations were somewhat higher than with cash market execution, however, which can partly be attributed to mispricings and partly to changes in interest rates (which, as we will see in Chapter 6, are a major determinant of futures prices). The strong U-shaped relationship with the rebalancing interval was absent because of the much lower transaction costs. Skewness was less negative but still significant. In sum, these results confirm that, at least for the options and index studied, futures market execution is to be preferred over cash market execution. It also means that **with futures market execution the theoretical option price is a much better estimate of the expected hedging costs than with cash market execution**.

When futures are mispriced the derivatives firm faces a problem. Suppose the firm sells an ordinary call option. To hedge the resulting short position it will have to buy equity exposure, i.e. buy futures. However, if the futures price is too high, the firm will pay too

---

[8] See H. Kat, Delta Hedging of S&P 500 Options: Cash versus Futures Market Execution, *Journal of Derivatives*, Spring, 1996, pp. 6–25. We will restrict ourselves to a brief summary of the results. Readers interested in more details should consult the article.

much, resulting in a negative hedging error. The same problem occurs at maturity when the hedge has to be sold off (assuming the option matures ITM). To solve the mispricings problem derivatives firms often try to slip in mispricings in the price quoted for an option as well as the payoff at maturity. They do this using the concept of **implied spot**. Implied spot is the index value at which the prevailing futures price would be correct. If the futures price is too high, implied spot is higher than the cash index and the other way around. To incorporate the initial mispricing the trader will price the option assuming the index is at its implied spot level instead of its actual value. He may do the same to calculate the option payoff. Effectively this means that the firm is using implied spot as the reference index for the contract in question. Some derivatives firms are so accustomed to this that they do not even mention it any more when they give out quotes. The end-user, however, should always check as there can be a significant difference between a payoff based on the value of the cash index and a payoff based on implied spot.

5.9   ALTERNATIVE HEDGING STRATEGIES

Knowing where hedging errors come from does not mean that hedging accuracy can easily be improved upon. From a practical point of view there are two major problems with theoretical hedging strategies.

- **Too much trading.** Every time we trade, we incur transaction costs. The latter eat away a significant chunk of the money initially invested while still leaving substantial hedging error risk.
- **Too much knowledge.** Theoretical models assume detailed insight into the behavior of stock prices and interest rates. Apart from the functional form we are also assumed to know all the model's parameters, like volatility for example.

Derivatives firms are painfully aware of this and put a lot of research effort into developing hedges which require less trading and which are less dependent on specific assumptions regarding the behavior of stock prices and interest rates. In what follows we will discuss these approaches in general terms. As always, technical details can be found in the many papers and articles listed in the bibliography.

5.9.1   Common Sense Hedging

Sometimes one can think of a good hedge by simply using old-fashioned common sense instead of reverting to complex mathematics. Many remarkable deals and even whole businesses have been built on this approach.

Back-to-Back Dealing

The simplest example of a common sense hedge is the so-called **back-to-back deal**. In this case the derivatives firm simply sets out to find a counterparty that is willing to enter into exactly the same contract as the firm is about to enter into, but at a better price. Having found somebody, the firm buys from one counterparty and at the same time sells to the other. Since both contracts are identical, the price difference is the derivatives firm's profit. Two points about back-to-back hedges are worth noting. First, both contracts need to be absolutely identical in every detail. If not, the hedge is not perfect. Especially with path-dependent options, like lookback or Asian options, it pays to take a very close look at all the details before signing anything. Second, the profit locked in with a back-to-back deal is of very high quality. With the contract details matching exactly, all the derivatives firm has to worry about is credit risk.

Parity Relationships

Going one step further than the back-to-back hedge we find hedges based on parity considerations. Sometimes the payoff of a contract can be decomposed into the payoffs of two or more other contracts. If this is the case, the derivatives firm can create a perfect hedge by entering into the component contracts at the same time it closes on the original contract. Instead of combining two or more contracts into a new one it can also reverse this process and create a perfect hedge by entering into a non-matching contract, splitting the latter up into two or more component contracts and selling the unwanted components off in the market.

Let's look at a simple example. Suppose a derivatives firm was asked to enter into a vanilla forward where the firm paid the value of the index I_T and its counterparty paid a fixed amount K. On balance the payoff to the derivatives firm would be equal to

$$V_T = K - I_T. \tag{5.14}$$

If the index at maturity was lower than K the firm would win and if it was higher it would lose. To hedge itself the derivatives firm's hedging strategy will need to generate an amount $I_T - K$. To do so, the firm could make use of the following equality

$$I_T - K = \text{Max}\,[I_T - K, 0] - \text{Max}\,[K - I_T, 0]. \tag{5.15}$$

The first term on the right-hand side is the payoff of an ordinary call. The second term is the payoff of an ordinary put. The above expression therefore tells us that the firm can hedge itself by buying an ordinary call while at the same time writing an ordinary put, both with strike K. If the index at maturity was lower than K the firm would cancel the call and the put would require the firm to pay $K - I_T$, which is the same amount it receives on the forward. If the index was higher than K the opposite would happen. The put would be cancelled and the derivatives firm would receive $I_T - K$ on the call, which it would pass on to its forward counterparty. This shows that forwards can be hedged with ordinary puts and calls. It also implies that ordinary calls can be hedged with forwards and ordinary puts and that ordinary puts can be hedged with forwards and ordinary calls. Applying this so-called **put–call parity** relationship one has to be careful, however. All contract details must match exactly. If not, the hedge will not be perfect.

Parity relationships can also be used as a **shortcut for the derivation of pricing formulas**. Above we saw that the payoff of an ordinary put is equal to the payoff of an equivalent ordinary call minus the maturity value of the index plus a fixed amount equal to the options' strike. From this it follows that the current value of an ordinary put must be equal to the current value of an equivalent call minus the current value of the index plus the present value of a fixed amount equal to the options' strike. In other words

$$P_0[K, \tau] = C_0[K, \tau] - I_0 + e^{-r\tau}K, \tag{5.16}$$

where $P_0[K, \tau]$ and $C_0[K, \tau]$ denote the prices of a put and a call, respectively with strike K and time to maturity τ. The theoretical price of an ordinary call is given by (5.5).

Combining this with the above expression we can write down the Black–Scholes–Merton formula for the theoretical price of an ordinary put as

$$V_t = -I_t N[-d_1] + e^{-r\tau} K N[-d_2].\qquad(5.17)$$

Note the similarity between this expression and that for an ordinary call.

5.9.2 Taylor Series Hedging

Nowadays all major exchanges in the world not only trade index futures, but also short-term ordinary call and put options on stock market indices as well as selected individual stocks. This greatly enhances the set of hedging vehicles available. In this subsection we briefly discuss the most popular way to incorporate listed options in a hedging strategy.

Let's denote the price of an arbitrary option as V and assume that it is determined by two other variables; the reference index I and implied volatility σ. In general terms, we say there are two **risk factors**. We can link the change in the option price over any period of time to the change in both risk factors by means of a formula known as a **Taylor series expansion**. This formula is given by

$$\Delta V = \frac{\partial V}{\partial I}\Delta I + \frac{1}{2}\frac{\partial^2 V}{\partial I^2}(\Delta I)^2 + \frac{1}{6}\frac{\partial^3 V}{\partial I^3}(\Delta I)^3 + \cdots$$

$$+ \frac{\partial V}{\partial \sigma}\Delta\sigma + \frac{1}{2}\frac{\partial^2 V}{\partial\sigma_2}(\Delta\sigma)^2 + \frac{1}{6}\frac{\partial^3 V}{\partial\sigma^3}(\Delta\sigma)^3 + \cdots,\qquad(5.18)$$

where ΔX denotes a change in variable X. Although (5.18) looks complicated, it simply says that the change in the option price can be decomposed into a number of terms. The first term reflects the sensitivity of the option price to changes in the index. However, this is only a rough approximation because as the option price changes, so will its sensitivity to the index. $\partial V/\partial I$ is only a good sensitivity measure when the change in the index is small. We therefore say it is only good **locally**. This shortcoming is corrected by the second term which reflects the sensitivity of $\partial V/\partial I$ to changes in the index. The first two terms give a much better approximation of the change in the option price than the first term alone, because we now also capture the change in the option's sensitivity to the index that will occur when the index changes. Of course, there is no end to this reasoning as the sensitivity of the option's sensitivity to the index may also change when the index changes. This is captured by the third term. A similar story can be told for implied volatility, which explains the second part of (5.18).

For simplicity the sensitivities in the Taylor series are given their own names. The sensitivity of the option price to the index is referred to as the option's **delta**. Delta's sensitivity to the index is known as **gamma**, and gamma's sensitivity to the index as **omega**. Likewise, the sensitivity of the option price to volatility is generally referred to as **vega** (which sounds Greek but is not), and its sensitivity to the interest rate as **rho**. Since most of these names are taken from the Greek alphabet they are collectively known as **the greeks**. The option to be hedged is in a way defined by its greeks. Therefore, if we could combine the available hedging instruments in such a way that the resulting portfolio had exactly the same greeks as the option to be hedged, we would have found the perfect hedge. We would have recreated the option.

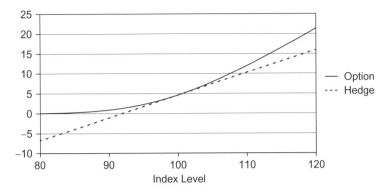

Figure 5.24   Price of an ordinary call as a function of index level

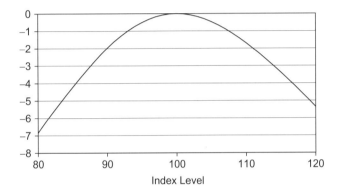

Figure 5.25   Delta hedging error for an ordinary call as a function of index level

Suppose we were hedging the sale of a 6-month ATM ordinary call. The index is at 100, interest rates are at 5% and volatility is 20%. In Figure 5.24 the curve depicts the theoretical price of the call as a function of the index level. Now suppose we build a hedge portfolio with the same value and delta as the option to be hedged, i.e. a portfolio with the same **local sensitivity** to the index. This is known as a **delta hedge**. Since the option's delta at this point is 0.60, the option price will tend to change by 0.60 for every 1.00 move in the index. We can imitate this by buying 0.60 shares of the index. The costs of doing so will of course exceed the option price. The option is worth 6.86 while the shares cost 60.00. We therefore have to borrow 53.14. The value of this hedge position is depicted by the straight line. How very local delta is as a sensitivity measure becomes clear if we compare the option value and the value of the hedge. If the index moves up or down by just a little bit, the hedge falls short significantly. This is emphasized by Figure 5.25, which shows the difference between the option value and the hedge value.

Figure 5.25 is not really different from Figure 5.3 because there is a one-to-one link between theoretical hedging strategies and delta hedging strategies. From the Black–Scholes–Merton formula it can be derived that the delta of an ordinary call is equal to

$$\frac{\partial V}{\partial I} = N[d_1]. \tag{5.19}$$

If the index moves by 1.00 the option price moves approximately by $N[d_1]$. To match this we have to buy $N[d_1]$ shares of the index. If we look back at (5.3) we see that this is exactly what the theoretical hedging strategy tells us to do. The same is true for other types of option contracts. In terms of the Taylor series approach therefore **theoretical hedging strategies are delta hedging strategies**.

Now suppose that next to the cash market there was also an options market where ordinary calls and puts on the index were trading in sufficiently large volumes. We could use these options to match the delta as well as the gamma of the option to be hedged. This is known as a **delta–gamma hedge**. We could pick an option, calculate its gamma, and buy enough of that option to match the gamma of the option to be hedged. Because the options bought will bring in some delta as well, we will have to correct our cash market holdings to make sure that we maintain the same delta as before. Our 6-month call has a gamma of 0.03. This is how much this option's delta changes when the index changes. A 3-month ATM call on the other hand has a gamma of 0.04. This means we can match the 6-month call's gamma if we buy 0.75 3-month calls. The 3-month call's delta is 0.57. This means that to match the 6-month call's delta and gamma at the same time we not only have to buy 0.75 3-month calls but also $0.60 - 0.75 \times 0.57 = 0.17$ shares of the index. If for simplicity we assumed that all the 3-month call's higher sensitivities were equal to zero, the difference between the value of the resulting hedge portfolio and the 6-month call's theoretical value would look as in Figure 5.26. The graph clearly shows that we are now well hedged against quite large swings in the index.

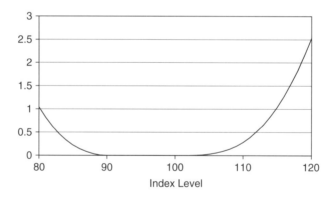

Figure 5.26   Delta–gamma hedging error for an ordinary call as a function of index level

We could continue the above process and also match higher sensitivities like omega for example, and do the same for implied volatility and interest rates. **The more sensitivities we can match, the better the hedge and the less hedge rebalancing will be required during the life of the contract**. In doing so, however, the construction of the hedge portfolio may become more and more cumbersome as relatively large long and short positions may be required. Not being able to match all sensitivities in the Taylor series, we have to decide what sensitivities to match and how to do it. Since it is nothing more than an ad hoc tool, the Taylor series itself does not tell us. Practitioners have developed a number of different approaches to solve this problem. Many are based on some form of optimization which also allows one to impose other restrictions, like a maximum or minimum order size, take account of the composition of the existing hedge portfolio and the fact that, unlike what we assumed, the hedge will typically have non-zero values for sensitivities which are not explicitly matched.

The Taylor series approaches the hedging problem top down by taking the pricing formula of the contract to be hedged as given and deriving a hedge from there. This makes the outcome very sensitive to the actual model and the input parameters used. We now return to the traditional bottom up approach, where we first construct a hedge, before we talk about pricing in the hope of finding a hedge which not only economizes on trading but also depends less on specific model assumptions and inputs.

5.9.3 (Semi-)Static Hedging

Back-to-back hedges and hedges based on parity relationships are forms of arbitrage. The derivatives firm simultaneously buys and sells the same payoff. The resulting hedge is perfect. Unfortunately, there are severe limitations to this process as not many derivatives contracts allow for a strict parity relationship with simpler, more liquid options. To solve this we can weaken the parity idea a little and ask ourselves whether it is possible to combine the available ordinary calls and puts in such a way that the resulting package at least provides an accurate hedge. If so, we will have found the next best thing to strict parity: a static but nevertheless accurate hedge. Of course, there will be cases where it is not possible to find an acceptable static hedge either. In those cases we can weaken the parity concept a little bit further and allow for a limited number of hedge revisions. In other words, in those cases we could investigate whether it is at least possible to create an accurate semi-static hedge.

Even a good static or semi-static hedge will not be perfect. Sometimes, however, it is possible to improve these hedges by combining them with a bit of delta or more advanced Taylor series hedging at the side. In that case we speak of a **static core hedge** or, looking at it from the other side, an **enhanced delta hedge**. Basically, this means that after the (semi-)static hedge is put in place we investigate the differences with the contract to be hedged and plug the gaps with a more dynamic (delta) hedging strategy. In this context it is interesting to interpret static hedges in the light of the Taylor series approach. Doing so makes it clear that **a good static hedge is a hedge portfolio which accurately matches (many of) the greeks of the contract to be hedged**.

The search for (semi-)static hedges has attracted a lot of attention from practitioners as well as academics. One could easily fill a whole book on this subject alone. However, since the exact workings of these methods and their pros and cons are secondary to what we are trying to accomplish in this book, we end the discussion here. Readers interested in further details are referred to the many papers and articles listed in the bibliography under the heading '(Semi-)Static Hedging'.

5.10 THE EXPECTED HEDGING COSTS AGAIN

In the previous section we saw that, next to delta hedging, the availability of a listed options market opens up at least two other hedging alternatives:

- Taylor series hedging
- (Semi-)static hedging

This brings us to the expected hedging costs of these strategies. One way to estimate the latter is to simply look at the initial investment required to set up the hedge, just as we do in the theoretical model. How good this estimate is depends primarily on whether transaction costs systematically pull the outcome away from the desired result. Since the above strategies are specifically designed to reduce turnover, the initial investment can be expected to be a fairly accurate estimate of the expected hedging costs of these strategies.

This leaves one very important question: what error do we make if, instead of first figuring out the details of the hedging strategy that we are going to follow, we price a contract using a properly calibrated theoretical pricing formula? This is an important question as derivatives firms show their clients (as well as each other) many quotes each day. Most of these are for indicative purposes only, but even indications need to be accurate. It is therefore important that quotes can be generated quickly. Generally speaking, **a price calculated from a properly calibrated pricing model will provide a fairly accurate estimate of the expected hedging costs of the above hedging strategies**. To see this, remember that the implied price process is nothing more than a convenient summary of the option prices it was derived from. A pricing model which is calibrated to a set of option prices will therefore not only closely reproduce the prices of the options used in the calibration procedure, but will price any other contract as if it were possible to construct a perfect static hedge from these options.

5.11   CONCLUSION

Conceptually there is little difference between derivatives firms on the one hand and life insurance companies and defined benefit pension plans on the other. All of them offer one or more index-linked future cash flows, and doing so leaves them with a hedging problem. When it comes to solving this problem, however, derivatives firms are clearly ahead. The typical defined benefit pension product is offered without there being a preconceived hedging scheme to support it. Also, the global drop in interest rates has made it clear that many life insurance companies have been selling embedded interest rate guarantees without (even thinking of) hedging them. This contrasts sharply with the derivatives industry. The latter only came to development after the appropriate hedging technology was created. A derivatives firm will not enter into a sizeable deal without having obtained a view on the hedging procedures to follow, the costs involved and the residual risks.

There are a large number of pricing formulas around. Despite the name, however, all these formulas produce numbers, not prices. **A number only becomes a price if a trader is willing to quote that number to the market**. Apart from the absence of a profit margin, traders will often be reluctant to quote the theoretical price as it will not be considered an accurate estimate of the actual expected hedging costs. Our simulations show that the cash market hedging strategies on which theoretical option pricing formulas are based do not work very well in practice. Transaction costs, discrete hedge rebalancing, volatility misprediction and modeling error create substantial hedging risk. Moreover, because transaction costs pull the outcome of the hedging process systematically away in one direction, theoretical option prices are biased estimates of the actual expected hedging costs. To bring the expected hedging error back to zero, derivatives firms at least need to add the expected transaction costs to the theoretical price when selling, or deduct the expected transaction costs when buying. Assuming the index is at 100, 20% volatility, 5% interest rate, 0.5% round-trip transaction costs and weekly hedge rebalancing, this means for example that the expected hedging costs of selling a 5-year ATM ordinary call are 30.08, and not 29.14 as the theoretical model will tell us. If we add a profit margin of 2.00 on top of that, this means the derivatives firm should quote an ask price of at least 32.08, which is 10% higher than the theoretical price.

Exchanges all over the world trade futures and ordinary options on a variety of stock market indices. This has opened up new ways for derivatives firms to hedge themselves. When executing a hedging strategy in the futures market, one can expect dramatic savings in transaction costs. Due to the transaction costs advantage, with futures market execution theoretical prices are much better estimates of the actual expected hedging costs than with cash market execution. The hedging risk, however, will still be there. When a liquid market in ordinary options is also available, various alternative hedging strategies can be developed that yield improved hedging accuracy. Since these strategies generate lower transaction costs as well, the expected hedging costs of these strategies can be estimated by calculating prices from properly calibrated theoretical models.

The actual price that a derivatives firm will quote to its client depends not only on the expected hedging costs, but also on the desired profit margin. Whether a firm is able to make anything on top of the minimum required margin depends very much on the competitive situation. In this context it is important to remember that over time every product and every industry goes through a number of distinct phases.

- **Invention phase:** the product is invented and brought to the market by one or a limited number of initial suppliers. The latter make substantial profits which compensates them for the effort and risk taken.
- **Entry phase:** attracted by the high margins, more suppliers enter the market. Demand and supply grow hand in hand, however, and everybody on the supply side makes good money. The product still evolves.
- **Elimination phase:** supply outgrows demand and competition intensifies. Margins come under extreme pressure and the least efficient suppliers are forced to exit the industry. Product innovation slows down.
- **Maturity phase:** after elimination of the least efficient producers, margins improve to a level where the remaining firms can make a living. It is no longer product innovation but efficiency which drives revenues on the supply side.

Dealing derivatives used to be a highly profitable activity. Over the last couple of years things have changed, however, as **most of the derivatives business has moved into the elimination phase**. In today's markets there is less and less opportunity to make excess profits. This explains the current popularity of mergers, acquisitions, strategic alliances and joint ventures. The above does not mean that product innovation has completely come to a halt, but it has changed direction. Initially, market participants aimed to create new payoff profiles. This process has largely come to an end, however, as (a) the most useful payoffs have been invented by now, and (b) nowadays every major derivatives firm is able to copy a new payoff within days. The focus of innovation in the derivatives industry has therefore shifted towards new reference indices. Rather than create complex derivatives on simple indices, the game is now to create simple contracts on complex reference indices, such as credit and weather for example.

A priori there is no reason why an end-user could not execute the hedging strategy that a derivatives firm will use to hedge a particular derivatives contract himself. This may lead one to think of derivatives firms as nothing more than hired helps. However, this does not do justice to what derivatives firms really do. The end-user may be able to execute the hedging strategy himself, but if he does he is also liable for all the hedging errors that will arise. Derivatives firms not only execute hedging strategies, they also add value by guaranteeing the outcome of these strategies to their counterparties. **Derivatives firms' profit margins are in part compensation for absorbing the hedging risk**.

The above remark brings us to the true nature of the derivatives business. Derivatives cannot be hedged perfectly. Over time derivatives firms are therefore confronted with hedging errors. However, as long as the prices on which deals are done are based on an accurate assessment of the expected hedging costs, on average they can expect to make money. The emphasis here is on the 'on average' though. It is unrealistic to expect every individual deal to make money, but as long as derivatives firms continue to do business, the law of large numbers will ensure that on average they do. This is comparable to a gambler who has developed a system that gives him slightly better odds at roulette. He is not going to win every game, but as long as he continues to play, does not vary the size of his bets too much and, as anybody who worked for LTCM in 1998 can tell you, does not default in the meantime, he will eventually walk out a wealthy man.

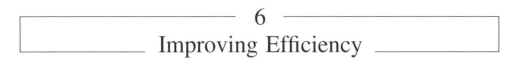

6

Improving Efficiency

6.1 INTRODUCTION

There are three areas where the derivatives structurer may be able to add value. The first area is **efficiency**. If people and organizations are able to achieve the same result at lower cost, it will allow them to make more money. Second, there is the area of **risk management**. Every person and every organization is, willingly or unwillingly, exposed to a multitude of risks. Thoughtful management of these risks allows them to concentrate on the things that really matter instead of having sleepless nights. Finally, there is the quest for **new products**. Success in business depends on a lot of things, but one of the most important is the ability to come up with new product ideas before the old ones go out of fashion. In this chapter we will concentrate on efficiency. We discuss risk management in Chapters 7 and 8 and new product design in Chapters 9–13.

Reduction of transaction costs will be one of the main themes in this chapter. Although for a long time transaction costs and their impact on investment performance have been an almost forgotten subject, research into the implementation process revived as a result of an increasing awareness that investment performance can be improved not only by better decision making, but also by controlling transaction costs. In an environment where 0.5% is the difference between outperformance and underperformance, careful management of costs can yield tremendous dividends. Some even go as far as to claim that superior trading is the only way in which large institutions can realize superior performance. Finding cheaper ways to adjust exposure is therefore of the utmost importance.

In this chapter we will discuss how investors can use equity derivatives to obtain the same exposure and make the same exposure adjustments in a more efficient way. We will look at ways to reduce operational and transaction costs as well as index tracking error. In this chapter we will also say more about the hedging and pricing of forwards and swaps. We deliberately keep the cases studied simple. This allows us to concentrate on the actual structuring routine without becoming too distracted by the specific details of the problem in question.

ASSUMPTIONS & NOTATION

As before, time will be measured in years. The present is denoted as $t = 0$, one year from now as $t = 1$, two years from now as $t = 2$, etc. When speaking more generally, the cash flow payment date is denoted as time T. The time t value of the reference index is denoted as I_t, and the interest rate for a maturity of i years as r_i. The compounding frequency will be clear from the context.

6.2 INDEXATION

Over the last 30 years many investors have come to the conclusion that stock picking is not really worth the effort. Many studies have shown that when the average investment manager is asked to select a number of stocks that he thinks will outperform the market, this portfolio tends to do no better than a portfolio of randomly selected stocks, especially if management fees are taken into account. More and more institutional as well as retail investors are therefore turning to **indexation**, i.e. instead of aiming to outperform the market they simply aim to replicate the market. Over the last 20 years indexation has become extremely popular, with total worldwide explicitly indexed assets currently estimated to exceed USD 1 trillion. As of April 5th, 2000 the largest US index fund alone (the Vanguard 500 Index fund, which tracks the S&P 500) had USD 107.2b in assets. The rationale behind indexing becomes painfully clear if one realizes that over the past 10 years, out of the 4402 US equity funds tracked by Lipper, only 152 managed to beat the Vanguard 500 Index fund. For a large part this is due to management cost differences. The Vanguard 500 Index fund only charges 0.18% of assets per year, while the average equity fund in the US charges 1.4%.

6.2.1 DIY Indexation

As we saw in Chapter 2, the percentage change of a price-weighted as well as a value-weighted index equals the weighted sum of the returns on the stocks included. In this respect an index is no different from an investment portfolio, since the return on any investment portfolio equals the weighted sum of the returns on the individual stocks in that portfolio, with every return weighted by the fraction of total wealth invested in each individual stock. This means that, at least in theory, it is easy to construct a portfolio which provides returns identical to those on the index. The behavior of a price-weighted index can be replicated by buying all the stocks included in the index in equal numbers. The resulting portfolio is known as the **tracking portfolio** of the relevant index. The same goes for a value-weighted index, which can be replicated with a portfolio of all stocks included in the index, where total wealth is divided over these stocks in line with their share in the total market value of all these stocks taken together.

The above approach to replicating the behavior of the index is known as **full replication**, because all stocks included in the index are also included in the tracking portfolio. Especially when the index contains a large number of different stocks, full replication may present some serious problems.

- **Transaction costs.** As shown in Table 6.1, which gives the explicit round-trip costs of trading a USD 25m index portfolio, buying and selling an index can be quite an expensive operation, especially when dealing with a non-US index. The table shows that even in an extremely liquid stock market like the US round-trip transaction costs may easily amount to 40bp or more.

Table 6.1 Estimated round-trip transaction costs (%)

Index	Commissions	Market impact	Taxes	Total
S&P 500	0.12	0.30	0.00	0.42
CAC 40	0.25	0.50	0.00	0.75
DAX	0.25	0.50	0.00	0.75
Nikkei 225	0.20	0.70	0.21	1.11
Hang Seng	0.50	0.50	0.34	1.34
FTSE 100	0.20	0.70	0.50	1.40

- **Custody fees.** Buying and selling stocks is costly, but so is holding them. In developed markets custodians charge about 0.05% per annum, but in less developed markets it is more likely to be 0.10–0.15%. In some emerging markets only participants in the domestic settlement system can hold the relevant assets. Foreign investors must in that case use the services of local nominees or custodians, the costs of which can be quite substantial.

In addition to transaction and custodian costs one also has to deal with other facts of life, such as odd-lot constraints and changes in the composition of the index over time. Odd-lot constraints are only problematic for small portfolios, but this is not true for the many composition changes that may occur. Over the period 1987–1998 there were more than 250 changes in the composition of the S&P 500 for example. Apart from generating additional transaction costs, these changes may cause serious problems when new stocks are added to the index at prices which are unattainable for investors. Given these problems, even replicating a popular liquid market index may not always work out as planned. This is known as **tracking error**.

The above problems could be reduced somewhat if we were able to replicate the index with a substantially lower number of shares than actually included in the index. The true art of index replication is to limit the tracking errors and at the same time avoid the disadvantages of full replication. It is this trade-off that ultimately determines the choice of replication method. One alternative for full replication is known as **stratified sampling**. This technique categorizes the available stocks into a number of different groups according to their market capitalization and main sector of activity. Subsequently, a number of stocks are chosen from every group such that the importance of every group for the resulting portfolio is the same as in the index. The main disadvantage of this approach is the fact that the choice of which stocks are to be included is made by the investor himself, instead of being the result of some objective rule. This means there is not much we can say about tracking error.

A second alternative is known as **optimized sampling**, which is the more academic version of stratified sampling. The idea is that price movements and thereby returns are caused by a number of different factors. However, not all stocks are equally sensitive to every one of these factors. For example, the results of an airline company will be much more sensitive to changes in fuel prices than those of a publishing company. The sensitivity of the index for these factors is determined by the stocks that it contains. Including more airlines and fewer publishers will raise the index's sensitivity to fuel price changes, and the other way around. Optimized sampling first studies the sensitivities of the index to the factors selected and subsequently constructs a portfolio with identical factor sensitivities as the index. Because the latter sensitivities are generally estimated from historical data, we obtain, under the assumption that these sensitivities do not change too much, direct insight into the tracking error which may be expected. Through the use of an optimization routine the technique selects those stocks which minimize the expected tracking error. Generally speaking, the results that are being obtained by optimized sampling are very satisfactory. Even with 30% of the number of shares included in the index in the tracking portfolio, tracking error is usually limited.

6.2.2 Index Participations

The above shows that accurate indexation is a thing that is easier said than done. If an investor wanted to make sure that he obtained exactly the same performance as the index without any hassle, we could structure a derivatives contract for him which at maturity paid a multiple of the value of the index on that date, i.e. a vanilla index-linked cash flow equal to

$$V_T = M \times I_T. \tag{6.1}$$

A contract with a payoff like this is known as an **index participation**. It allows the investor to fully participate in the ups and downs of the relevant index. It does not offer exactly the same payoff profile as buying the index itself, however, as it does not pay any dividends. There might be a good reason for this, but if not we can expand the contract by paying the investor the same dividends as paid by the stocks in the index. We could do so as soon as a dividend was paid, but we could also accumulate the dividends and pay them out periodically, such as monthly or quarterly. A third alternative would be to reinvest the dividends in index participations. This would mean that the multiplier in (6.1) would increase slightly whenever a stock in the index paid a dividend.

6.2.3 Pricing Index Participations

What would the derivatives firm's offer price for the above index participation be? To answer this question we have to look at how the derivatives firm prices derivatives. As discussed in Chapter 5, the starting point of any pricing exercise is the determination of the expected hedging costs. On top of that the derivatives firm will put a profit margin which depends on the hedging risk and the degree of competition encountered. More hedging risk means the firm has to reserve more capital, implying a higher margin. In addition, when there is less competition the firm will try to take out a little extra for itself. Given the strong price competition in most segments of the equity derivatives business nowadays, however, end-users can eliminate most of the excess profit margin by **calling the deal around**, i.e. by asking a number of derivatives firms for a quote instead of only one. This leaves us with the expected hedging costs and the minimum required profit margin.

We start with the expected hedging costs of the index participation. Because the contract payoff is a linear function of the index value at maturity, index participations do not require a dynamically rebalanced hedge as used to hedge options. To hedge the sale of index participations, the derivatives firm can simply buy the index. The expected hedging costs of the index participation are in that case equal to the index value plus the costs of establishing and maintaining the relevant tracking portfolio. Given that the hedging strategy is so simple, the hedging risk will be small. This means that the capital required for a contract like this, and thereby the minimum required profit margin, will not be very high either. In sum, this means that **the index participation will be slightly more expensive than the index**.

One important reason for us to structure the index participation was to solve the problem of transaction and custodian costs. However, if the derivatives firm hedges itself by doing exactly what the investor would have done himself, and in addition looks to make a profit as well, it is difficult to see what makes the index participation such a good solution. Fortunately, there are several reasons why the derivatives firm may be able to hedge itself at lower costs than the investor.

- **Cash market cost advantage.** The derivatives firm can be expected to trade at lower costs and better prices than the average investor. The firm may be a member firm and have its own people on the exchange floor.
- **Futures hedging.** Instead of in the cash market, the firm could go out into the futures market to create a hedging strategy. Using futures is more involved and slightly more risky than cash market hedging. However, transaction costs in the futures markets are only a fraction of what they are in the cash market.
- **Warehousing.** The derivatives firm enters into derivatives contracts with many different counterparties. Not just index participations but all kinds of contracts. Some of these contracts will (partially) cancel each other out. In that case the firm does not need to hedge every contract separately, but only the residual exposure that is left. The costs of doing so have to be paid by the collective of counterparties, but because of the firm's so-called **warehousing** activity these costs are lower than they would have been if every deal was hedged separately.

Dividends and Dividend Risk

The above assumes that the index does not pay dividends or that the derivatives firm simply passes the dividends which it receives on to the investor, i.e. that the index participation pays the same dividends as the index. In case the index participation does not pay dividends while the index does, things are different. In that case the derivatives firm can keep the dividends which it receives. As a consequence, **the expected hedging costs drop by an amount equal to the present value of the expected dividends over the contract's life**. The derivatives firm will in that case determine the price of the index participation such that, when combined with a loan equal to the present value of the expected dividends, it can buy the index tracking portfolio. Note that when we speak about 'the present value of the expected dividends' what we are referring to is 'the present value of the expected dividends to the derivatives firm'. It is the derivatives firm's dividend expectation and the derivatives firm's funding rate that are used to calculate the present value of the expected dividends.

Although it is well appreciated that most companies are reluctant to reduce dividends, future dividends are not known in advance. Especially with longer maturities this introduces a risk for the derivatives firm. To compensate for this the derivatives firm will do its pricing using fairly conservative dividend estimates. When it is receiving the dividends it will tend to underestimate and when it is paying it will tend to overestimate future dividends. The derivatives firm can also let the investor absorb the dividend risk. Derivatives structurers in Australia and New Zealand have come up with long-dated index participations where the investor takes the full dividend risk. Listed on the stock exchange, these are known as **endowment warrants**. Depending on the relevant stocks' expected dividend yields and interest rates, the investor pays an upfront amount. The difference between this amount and the actual index value is referred to as the initial **outstanding amount**. This is the amount the derivatives firm needs to borrow to be able to purchase the tracking portfolio. During the life of the index participation the outstanding amount grows at the interest rate and shrinks with the dividends paid by the index. At maturity there are two possible outcomes. Either the dividends received have been sufficient to reduce the outstanding amount to zero or not. In the first case the investor receives the index value. In the second case the investor receives an amount equal to the difference between the index value and what is left of the outstanding amount. In other words, the investor pays what is left of the outstanding amount and the derivatives firm pays the value of the index.

6.3   LEVERAGED BUYING AND SHORT-SELLING

Sometimes an investment manager may want to buy equity with money he does not (yet) have or sell stocks he does not own. This is known as leveraged buying and short-selling, respectively. Leveraged buying requires the investment manager to borrow money, while short-selling requires him to borrow stocks. Both can be problematic at times. In this section we discuss how derivatives can solve this problem.

6.3.1   Leveraged Buying

Suppose an investment manager was convinced the equity market was ready for a serious rally over the next year. To capitalize on his view he spent all his money purchasing equity as represented by the index. He would like to buy even more but he is not allowed to borrow. Frustrated about missing out on what he considers to be a unique opportunity, he approaches a derivatives firm to see if they are able to come up with an alternative.

The starting point is to carefully investigate what the investment manager is really after. In this case he wants a contract that replicates the leveraged buying of the index. If he could do this for real he would borrow I_0, buy the index, and at the end of the year sell the index again and pay off the loan plus interest. Formally, from selling the index he would receive an amount equal to

$$CIF_1 = M \times I_1. \tag{6.2}$$

The loan on the other hand would cost him a total amount of

$$COF_1 = M \times I_0(1 + r_1), \tag{6.3}$$

where r_1 denotes the 1-year interest rate (annual compounding) at $t = 0$. To replicate this we must structure a contract under which the investment manager pays and receives exactly these amounts. This means that the investment manager requires a contract that on balance provides him with a payoff equal to

$$V_1 = CIF_1 - COF_1 = M \times (I_1 - I_0(1 + r_1)). \tag{6.4}$$

This is the payoff of a **vanilla forward**. In other words, to replicate the leveraged purchase of the index the investment manager should buy vanilla forwards with a forward price equal to $I_0(1 + r_1)$. If at maturity the index is higher than the forward price the investment manager receives more than he pays and makes a profit. On the other hand, if the index ends below the forward price he will show a loss as he will have to pay more than he receives. Just as with real leveraged buying.

The payoff of the above forward can be rewritten in various ways, each allowing us to view the contract payoff from a slightly different angle. We can for example write the above payoff as

$$V_1 = M \times ((I_1 - I_0) - r_1 \times I_0). \tag{6.5}$$

This shows that at maturity the investment manager pays the derivatives firm the interest he would have paid if he had actually borrowed money, and the derivatives firm pays the change in the value of the index over the life of the contract. If the investment manager is correct and stock prices do indeed rise over the year the equity-linked component of the payoff is positive. In that case the investment manager receives an amount equal to the rise in the value of the index minus the interest component. If the investment manager is wrong, however, and stock prices fall the investment manager pays interest plus the drop in the value of the index.

A third way to express the payoff to the investment manager is in relative terms. This yields

$$V_1 = N \times \left(\frac{I_1 - I_0}{I_0} - r_1 \right),$$

(6.6)

where $N = M \times I_0$. When expressing a contract's payoff in this way, N is typically referred to as the contract's **notional amount** or **notional** for short. The notional combines the monetizer and the multiplier (see Chapter 1) of both cash flows into one, i.e. it turns non-money indices into money and scales them up at the same time. Expression (6.6) shows that on a notional amount equal to N the investment manager makes a return equal to the difference between the return on the index and the 1-year interest rate.

6.3.2   Short-Selling

Now consider the opposite case of an investment manager who was convinced that the equity market was ready for a major correction over the next year. To capitalize on his view he has sold all his stocks and put his money in the bank. He would like to sell even more but **short-selling is not as simple as it sounds**. Before one can sell a stock short, one has to find someone willing to lend it, agree on a borrowing fee, and put up the appropriate collateral. Apart from a borrowing fee, the borrower also has to pay the lender all dividends and other distributions paid by the stock as they arise. In case of a rights issue, for example, the borrower will have to go out into the market to buy the rights and deliver them to the lender. In addition, when the investment manager is not able to borrow the stock for a fixed term he runs the risk that the stocks are recalled by the lender prematurely. In that case the investment manager either has to see if he can borrow the stock somewhere else or close his short position by buying the stock in the market. All this can make short-selling quite costly, operationally intensive as well as risky. It would simplify things a lot if we could structure a derivatives contract that at maturity paid the investment manager an amount equal to the result he would have obtained with a real short sale, but without all the hassle.

To structure the desired contract we first need to investigate what cash flow the investment manager wants to trade in and what cash flow he wants to receive in return. With a real short sale the investment manager borrows and sells stocks and invests the proceeds. At maturity he buys back the stocks and delivers them to the stock lender. This means that at maturity he receives an amount equal to

$$CIF_1 = M \times I_0(1 + r_1)$$

(6.7)

and pays an amount equal to

$$COF_1 = M \times I_1.$$

(6.8)

A derivatives contract which replicates a short sale should therefore on balance provide the investment manager with a payoff equal to

$$V_1 = CIF_1 - COF_1 = M \times (I_0(1 + r_1) - I_1).   \tag{6.9}$$

This is the same payoff as for the case of leveraged buying but with a minus sign in front of it. This means that to replicate a short sale the investment manager should sell **vanilla forwards** with a forward price equal to $I_0(1 + r_1)$. If at maturity the index is lower than the forward price the investment manager receives more than he pays and makes a profit. On the other hand, if the index rises above the forward price he pays more than he receives and loses.

In exactly the same way as before, we can also write the payoff to the investment manager as

$$V_1 = M \times (r_1 \times I_0 - (I_1 - I_0)).   \tag{6.10}$$

Alternatively, we can express the payoff in relative terms as

$$V_1 = N \times \left(r_1 - \frac{I_1 - I_0}{I_0}\right),   \tag{6.11}$$

where $N = M \times I_0$. Expression (6.10) shows that at maturity the derivatives firm pays the investment manager the interest he would have received if he really had sold the index short, and the investment manager pays the change in the value of the index. If the investment manager is correct and stock prices fall then the equity-linked component of the payoff is negative. In that case the investment manager not only receives interest but also an amount equal to the drop in the value of the index. If the investment manager is wrong and stock prices do not fall he still receives his interest but has to pay away the rise in the value of the index. From (6.11) we see that on a notional amount N the contract pays the investment manager a return equal to the difference between the 1-year interest rate and the return on the index.

6.3.3 Pricing Vanilla Forwards

The question that arises next is whether the forward contract has any present value. In other words, will the investment manager have to pay the derivatives firm for entering into a contract like this or will the derivatives firm have to pay the investment manager?

Let's look at the case of **synthetic leveraged buying**, where the investment manager buys a vanilla forward with forward price $I_0(1 + r_1)$. In that case the payoff to the derivatives firm is equal to

$$V_1 = M \times (I_0(1 + r_1) - I_1).   \tag{6.12}$$

If for simplicity we put $M = 1$, then (6.12) tells us that at maturity the derivatives firm will receive a fixed amount of $I_0(1 + r_1)$ for paying the value of the index. The first part can be hedged by taking out a loan in the amount of I_0. This will produce a debt at maturity equal to the amount to be received. The second part of the payoff equals the payoff of a short index participation. This can be hedged by buying the index tracking portfolio at initiation and holding it until the maturity date. The investment required to do so is equal to I_0.

Since the proceeds of the loan are exactly enough to fund the purchase of the equity, the expected hedging costs of the contract are equal to just the costs associated with purchasing and maintaining the tracking portfolio. With the resulting hedge being of very high quality, there will not be much hedging risk. As a result, the derivatives firm's minimum required profit margin will not be very high either. **The investment manager can therefore expect to buy the forward at a price slightly above zero**. The investment manager can pay the derivatives firm upfront, but it is customary to postpone payment until the contract's maturity date. This can be formalized as a mark-up on the fixed amount payable by the investment manager under the forward contract. In other words, in that case the investment manager pays the derivatives firm in the form of a **slightly higher forward price**.

A similar reasoning goes of course for the case of **synthetic short-selling**, where the investment manager sells a vanilla forward with forward price $I_0(1 + r_1)$. In that case the payoff to the derivatives firm is equal to

$$V_1 = M \times (I_1 - I_0(1 + r_1)). \qquad (6.13)$$

At maturity the derivatives firm receives the index value in return for paying a fixed amount. The first part of the above payoff is the payoff of a long index participation which can be hedged by selling the index tracking portfolio short until the contract's maturity date. The second part of the above payoff can be hedged by investing an amount I_0 at initiation. This will produce an amount at maturity equal to the amount to be paid.

Since the proceeds of the short sale are exactly enough to cover the required investment, the derivatives firm will not require any funds to set up and run the hedge apart from the costs associated with short-selling the index. The expected hedging costs of the contract will therefore be very low, as will the derivatives firm's minimum required profit margin. This means that **the investment manager can expect to sell the forward at a price slightly below zero**. Again, the investment manager can pay upfront, but it is more common to postpone payment until the contract's maturity date, in the form of a **slightly lower forward price**.

So far we have assumed that the derivatives firm hedges itself in the cash market and basically does what the investment manager was planning on doing himself. As with index participations, however, the derivatives firm is free to hedge itself in whatever way it sees fit. It can hedge itself in the cash market, but it can also do so in the futures market for example. The expected hedging costs of doing so may be lower than the costs of cash market hedging. In addition, the firm may be able to offset the risk with one or more other deals which again may lead to a reduction in price.

Dividends and Dividend Risk

The conclusion that the price of the above forward contract will not be far from zero implicitly assumes that the stocks in the index do not pay any dividends during the contract's lifetime. If the index does pay dividends, things depend on the way dividends and other distributions are handled under the forward contract. Let's look at **synthetic leveraged buying** again. To hedge the forward the derivatives firm will buy stocks and will therefore receive the dividends. With the forward paying off an amount purely depending on the index value at maturity, this means the firm is better off now. The expected hedging costs will drop by the present value of the dividends the derivatives firm expects to receive over the life of the contract. The derivatives firm will have to pay this amount to the investment manager to make him enter into the contract, which is typically done in the form of a **reduction of the forward price** to be paid by the investment manager.

In the case of **synthetic short-selling**, where the derivatives firm shorts the index, the derivatives firm does not receive the dividends but needs to pay them to the stock lender. This means the derivatives firm will have to generate its own dividends by putting enough money in the bank now to produce future payoff amounts equal to the required dividends. This in turn means that the expected hedging costs of the forward will increase by an amount equal to the present value of the dividends the derivatives firm expects to pay over the contract's lifetime. The investment manager will have to pay this amount to the derivatives firm to make it enter into the forward; either upfront or in the form of a **reduction of the forward price** to be paid by the derivatives firm.

To compensate for the fact that future dividends are not known with certainty, the derivatives firm will tend to do its pricing using fairly conservative dividend estimates. An alternative way to deal with dividends is to adjust the payoff of the forward. For example, the derivatives firm could simply pass all dividends on to the investment manager as soon as it received them. In that case the investment manager would end up with exactly the same payoff as he would have had from actually buying the index himself. With the derivatives firm passing all dividends on to the investment manager, the expected hedging costs would be back to zero again. Another alternative is to let the investment manager absorb the dividend risk. We discussed this earlier in the context of index participations.

Different Forward Prices

In the above we set the forward price equal to $I_0(1 + r_1)$ because we wanted to replicate a bank account. This is known as **at-market pricing**. As a result, the price of the forward contract was (almost) zero. Sometimes it may happen that the forward price needs to be set higher or lower than this, which is known as **off-market pricing**. Whenever this happens it is not difficult to figure out what will happen to the price of the forward contract. All we need to do is see what happens to the derivatives firm's expected hedging costs. Suppose the derivatives firm sold a 1-year off-market vanilla forward with a forward price higher than $I_0(1 + r_1)$. To hedge the equity exposure on the resulting position the firm will borrow an amount I_0 and buy the index. At maturity this yields a debt of $I_0(1 + r_1)$. Since the forward price is higher than this, however, the firm receives more than it needs to pay off this debt. As a result, the price of the forward can come down by an amount equal to the present value of the difference between the actual forward price and $I_0(1 + r_1)$. The derivatives firm now has to pay the investment manager an amount upfront.

A similar thing would happen if the derivatives firm sold a 1-year off-market vanilla forward with a forward price lower than $I_0(1 + r_1)$. As before, to hedge itself the firm will borrow I_0 and buy the index, yielding a debt at maturity of $I_0(1 + r_1)$. However, since the forward price is lower than this, the firm will not be able to pay off this debt with the amount it receives from its counterparty. Therefore, the price of the forward has to go up by an amount equal to the present value of the difference between $I_0(1 + r_1)$ and the actual forward price. The investment manager will in this case have to pay the derivatives firm.

A Check of the Pricing Shortcut

In Chapter 5 we discussed the fact that the expected hedging costs of any derivatives contract can be calculated as the present value of the expected payoff of that contract, assuming all stock prices drift upwards at a rate equal to the interest rate. Given that we now know the expected hedging costs of a number of forward contracts, we can put this shortcut to the test. Suppose that the derivatives firm sold a 1-year vanilla forward with a forward price of $I_0(1 + r_1)$. This means that one year from now the derivatives firm will have to pay $I_1 - I_0(1 + r_1)$. With an interest rate of r_1 the expected index value one year from now is $I_0(1 + r_1)$. The expected payment by the derivatives firm is therefore equal to 0, implying the expected hedging costs are 0 as well; exactly what we found earlier. If the forward price was higher, the expected payment by the firm would be equal to the difference between $I_0(1 + r_1)$ and that forward price. According to our pricing shortcut the expected hedging costs of the forward contract would in that case be equal to the present value of this difference. Again, this is exactly what we found.

6.4   SWITCHING FROM EQUITY TO CASH

The decision process leading up to the purchase of a particular investment portfolio is typically seen as being made up of three subsequent decisions. The first is the so-called **strategic asset allocation** decision. This decision is concerned with the question of how the portfolio should be invested across each of several asset classes assuming neutral market conditions exist. The strategic asset allocation is therefore best interpreted as the average long-term asset allocation. The next decision to be made is how far the actual asset allocation must deviate from the strategic asset allocation given present market conditions. This is the so-called **tactical asset allocation** decision. Having determined the tactical asset allocation the next question is how each asset class portfolio should be invested in each of the securities making up that asset class. This is known as the **security selection** decision. Led by a now well-known article by Brinson, Hood and Beebower[1] on the determinants of portfolio performance, it has become generally accepted that for the typical investor, i.e. an investor who is not in the habit of taking large bets on individual securities, the asset allocation decision is far more important than the security selection decision. In other words, for a portfolio's overall performance it is much more important how the portfolio's net asset value is spread over the various asset classes than how it is divided over the securities within each asset class. Given this, we concentrate on the asset allocation decision.

6.4.1   The Basic Case

Over time the tactical asset allocation will change as market conditions and expectations change. Investment managers will (partially) switch asset classes when one is perceived to offer better opportunities than the other. So-called tactical asset allocation funds may even do so on a monthly or quarterly basis. Given the size of many institutional portfolios, changing the asset allocation by selling the relevant assets in the cash market and buying them back shortly afterwards can be a very costly operation. In this section we therefore

---

[1] G. Brinson, L. Hood and G. Beebower, Determinants of Portfolio Performance, *Financial Analysts Journal*, July–August, 1986, pp. 39–44.

discuss how equity derivatives can be used to make the desired exposure adjustments at lower costs.

Let's assume we were dealing with an investment manager who, if he holds equity, simply holds all the stocks in the index. Now suppose that for the next 12 months this investment manager wanted to shift his asset allocation from equity to cash because he thought the stock market was ready for a major correction. Traditionally, he would sell (part of) his equity holdings and take the proceeds to the bank. After a year he would receive an amount equal to

$$CIF_1 = M \times I_0(1 + r_1). \tag{6.14}$$

Buying back the stocks which he sold would on the other hand cost him an amount equal to

$$COF_1 = M \times I_1. \tag{6.15}$$

To replicate this we can structure a derivatives contract under which he trades in one for the other, i.e. a contract that on balance pays the investment manager an amount equal to

$$V_1 = CIF_1 - COF_1 = M \times (I_0(1 + r_1) - I_1). \tag{6.16}$$

We encountered the exact same payoff before when we discussed synthetic short-selling. It is the payoff of a short **vanilla forward** with a forward price equal to $I_0(1 + r_1)$. This is not too surprising if we realize that what the investment manager is trying to accomplish here is not really different from short-selling. In both cases his goal is to trade in the change in the value of the index for a fixed interest payment.

6.4.2 Non-Index Portfolios

Would the above result change much if the investment manager was not an index investor, i.e. if his portfolio was significantly different from the index? If that was the case we could do several things. First, instead of the index, we could structure a contract payoff based on a **basket of stocks** equal to the investment manager's portfolio. This solution provides a perfect fit of the derivatives contract to the investment manager's portfolio, but often works out to be more expensive as it means more work and higher hedging costs for the derivatives firm. An alternative solution is to split the investment manager's portfolio into an index part and a residual part and only hedge the index part. Apart from the fact that a hedge based on the index may be cheaper, there is a second reason why this makes sense. As discussed in Section 6.2, in the absence of superior insights the investment manager should best hold the index. The fact that he does not suggests that the investment manager thinks he knows something the market does not yet know. In that case it does not make sense to hedge the portfolio exactly, because it would eliminate the possibility of capitalizing on this knowledge.

A stock's price change can be split into a part that is shared with other stocks and a part that is specific to that particular stock. The first component can be seen as the result of changes in market sentiment, a changed outlook for the economy as a whole, etc. The second component results from changes in the outlook for the particular sector the company operates in, or from even more specific influences. In line with this observation, a stock's return is often seen as the sum of a so-called **market component** and a **specific**

component. The market component reflects that part of the stock's return which is being generated by factors which are of interest to all stocks, while the specific component reflects influences which are more specific to the company in question. Of course, not all companies are equally sensitive to economy-wide factors. A changing fuel price for example will have a much more profound influence on the profitability of a transporting company than on that of a software company (assuming it does not work for a transporting company). The sensitivity of a given stock to all such general factors is often summarized in one single number, known as the stock's **beta** (β).

Beta is a relative measure of a stock's sensitivity for economy-wide disturbances. It is a relative measure because it is assumed that the average beta is equal to 1. With a beta of 0.8 a stock is less, and with a beta of 1.2 a stock is more sensitive to economy-wide factors than the average stock. Because beta is a relative measure, a stock's beta is not only determined by the nature of the stock itself but also by the average chosen. The choice of the average is very important. **A different average may produce a different beta for a given stock**. In practice, the average used will typically be a well-known market index which in this context is often referred to as the **market portfolio**. As there are significant differences between the various market indices around, however, one should always make sure on which market index a given beta is based and only compare betas when they are based on the same index.

With beta being a relative measure of a stock's sensitivity to economy-wide influences, we can obtain the market component of a stock's return by multiplying that stock's beta by the return on the index used to calculate that beta. The difference between the true return and this market component then, by definition, equals the stock return's specific component. Since a portfolio is just a basket of individual stocks, the same reasoning applies of course to portfolios of stocks. Given the betas of all individual stocks, the beta of a portfolio can be calculated as the weighted sum of the betas of the stocks that make up the portfolio, where these betas are weighted in line with the way in which the total amount invested is divided over these stocks. For example, suppose we had a portfolio of two stocks, one with a beta of 1.1 and another with a beta of 1.3, and we divided our money over both stocks 50–50. In that case the portfolio's beta would be $0.5 \times 1.1 + 0.5 \times 1.3 = 1.2$.

If we wrote all of this down more formally, we would end up with the following expression

$$R_t^{\mathrm{P}} = \alpha_{\mathrm{P}} + \beta_{\mathrm{P}} R_t^{\mathrm{I}} + \varepsilon_t^{\mathrm{P}}, \tag{6.17}$$

where R_t^{I} denotes the index return and R_t^{P} the portfolio return. This equation tells us that the return on a stock portfolio equals (1) a constant α_{P} plus (2) the product of the portfolio's beta and the index return plus (3) a residual $\varepsilon_t^{\mathrm{P}}$. The parameters α_{P} and β_{P} are specific to the portfolio, as is the variable $\varepsilon_t^{\mathrm{P}}$. The latter is nothing else than a residual term which makes sure that (6.17) is always valid. It follows automatically given values for α_{P}, β_{P}, R_t^{P} and R_t^{I}. **In a well-diversified portfolio the residual return is typically small**.

Expression (6.17) tells us that the portfolio return is made up of two components. The term $\beta_{\mathrm{P}} R_t^{\mathrm{I}}$ equals the **market component** of the portfolio's return and is, as discussed earlier, determined as the product of the portfolio's beta and the index return. The term $\alpha_{\mathrm{P}} + \varepsilon_t^{\mathrm{P}}$ equals the **specific component** of the portfolio's return. If the residual return was equal to zero then alpha would be the return we would realize with a zero market return.

If we choose the index as our portfolio, the portfolio's beta would be equal to one and alpha would be zero. This is not surprising as we are also using the index as our idea of the average stock.

In practice, alpha and beta will have to be estimated in some way. There is a whole body of literature on how to do this best. The easiest (and probably not even a bad) solution is to do so from historical return data by means of OLS regression. Suppose we had portfolio return data available over N periods $j = 1, 2, \ldots, N$ of given length, say one month. In that case we can use the following estimator for the portfolio's beta

$$\beta_{\mathrm{P}} = \frac{\sum_{j=1}^{N}[R_j^{\mathrm{I}} - \mathrm{Avg}\,(R^{\mathrm{I}})][R_j^{\mathrm{P}} - \mathrm{Avg}\,(R^{\mathrm{P}})]}{\sum_{j=1}^{N}[R_j^{\mathrm{I}} - \mathrm{Avg}\,(R^{\mathrm{I}})]^2}, \qquad (6.18)$$

where $\mathrm{Avg}\,(R)$ equals the average return. The accompanying portfolio alpha then follows automatically from

$$\alpha_{\mathrm{P}} = \mathrm{Avg}\,(R^{\mathrm{P}}) - \beta_{\mathrm{P}} \times \mathrm{Avg}\,(R^{\mathrm{I}}). \qquad (6.19)$$

Suppose we had the returns on an index and five well-diversified portfolios A, B, C, D, E over five consecutive periods $j = 1, 2, 3, 4, 5$. The data and the alphas and betas that can be calculated from them using the above expressions are given in Table 6.2. The table shows that portfolio A has a beta of 1.2 and an alpha of -0.4%. This means that, given the return on the index, the return on portfolio A can be calculated as $R^{\mathrm{A}} = -0.4 + 1.2R^{\mathrm{I}}$. In other words, if the index remains unchanged we will realize a return of -0.4%, while this increases by 1.2 times the return on the index when the index does change.

We can use this framework to determine how an investment manager who holds a portfolio which is significantly different from the market index can hedge himself using a derivatives contract based on the index. The **procedure** is as follows. First, we determine the portfolio beta. This tells us how the portfolio return and the index return move together. With a beta of 0.9 the portfolio return picks up 90% of the index return while with a beta of 1.2 it picks up 120% of the index return. Roughly speaking, in the first case we can say that the portfolio is equivalent to 0.9 times the index and in the second case that it is equivalent to 1.2 times the index. Knowing this, all we need to do is raise the relevant contract multiplier in line with the portfolio's beta. The contract payoff required

Table 6.2 Betas and alphas

		Return				
j	Index	A	B	C	D	E
1	−20.0	−24.4	−28.0	−31.8	−36.6	−40.0
2	−10.0	−12.4	−14.0	−15.8	−18.6	−20.0
3	0.0	−0.4	0.0	0.2	−0.6	0.0
4	10.0	11.6	14.0	16.2	17.4	20.0
5	20.0	23.6	28.0	32.2	35.4	40.0
Beta	1.0	1.2	1.4	1.6	1.8	2.0
Alpha	0.0	−0.4	0.0	0.2	−0.6	0.0

to synthetically switch the investment manager's equity portfolio to cash is therefore given by

$$V_1 = \beta \times M \times (I_0(1 + r_1) - I_1). \tag{6.20}$$

Entering into a contract with the above payoff will bring the investment manager's overall beta, i.e. the beta of his equity portfolio combined with the above forward, down to zero, but it does not eliminate any portfolio-specific risk. This is not necessarily a bad thing though. The investment manager holds a portfolio that is different from the index because he thinks the stocks he is holding will do better than the index. If we eliminate all specific risk as well, we would essentially be taking away his potential to outperform the index. For simplicity, in the remainder of the book we will assume that we are dealing with the index portfolio.

6.4.3 Multi-Period Contracting

There is an important reason why buying or selling a forward may be just a little too simple in real-life applications. Sticking with the above example, if the stock market indeed comes down over the year the derivatives firm may end up owing the investment manager a very large sum of money. This means that the investment manager's credit exposure to the derivatives firm may become very substantial over the year.

One way to solve the above problem is to replace the vanilla forward by a **swap contract** where both counterparties settle profits and losses not just at maturity but also at one or more intermediate dates. We could for example structure a contract which at the end of every quarter required the investment manager to pay the derivatives firm the return on the index over that quarter and the derivatives firm to pay the investment manager interest. This would mean that at the end of each quarter i, $i = 1, 2, \ldots, 4$, the investment manager would receive a payoff equal to

$$V_{i/4} = N \times \left(\frac{r_1}{4} - \frac{I_{i/4} - I_{i/4-1/4}}{I_{i/4-1/4}} \right), \tag{6.21}$$

where $N = M \times I_0$ and r_1 denotes the 1-year quarterly compounded interest rate at $t = 0$. As mentioned before, N is known as the swap's **notional amount** or **notional** for short. In the above swap the notional is equal to the investment manager's initial asset value $M \times I_0$. Expression (6.21) therefore simply tells us that over every quarter the investment manager makes a return on his initial asset value equal to the difference between the interest rate and the return on the index over that quarter.

The above expression is very similar to (6.11). This means that **the four-period swap can be seen as a package of four different forwards** with maturities of 3, 6, 9 and 12 months. Note that only the first of these four forwards is a vanilla forward. Like a vanilla forward, the other three contracts call for the derivatives firm to pay a fixed amount. Unlike a vanilla forward, however, they require the investment manager to pay an index-linked amount that depends not only on the index value at maturity, but also on the index value three months before maturity.

Suppose the index was at 100 and did not pay dividends, the investment manager's initial asset value was 100m and the term structure of (quarterly compounded) interest rates was flat and constant at 5%. Under these assumptions, Table 6.3 gives the payments the investment manager and the derivatives firm would have to make when the index

Table 6.3   Fixed rate equity-for-cash swap with fixed notional

t	I_t	Derivatives firm	Investment manager	Balance to investment manager
0	100.0			
1/4	90.0	1.25	−10	11.25
1/2	99.0	1.25	10	−8.75
3/4	89.1	1.25	−10	11.25
1	80.19	1.25	−10	11.25

fell by 10% in the first quarter, rose by 10% in the second quarter, fell by 10% in the third quarter, and fell by another 10% in the fourth quarter. Over the first quarter the derivatives firm pays the investment manager 1.25m interest plus the 10% drop of the index, i.e. 11.25m in total. Over the second quarter the derivatives firm again pays interest of 1.25m but this time the investment manager has to pay 10m since the index has gone up instead of down. The third and fourth quarters are identical to the first: the derivatives firm pays the investment manager 1.25m interest plus the drop of the index.

The above looks straightforward: at the end of each quarter the derivatives firm pays the investment manager or the other way around. However, to make the structure work there is a lot more to be done than just making the specified payments. Let's take a closer look at the practicalities of the above swap, assuming the derivatives firm hedges itself in the cash market.

- **Initiation.** The derivatives firm shorts 100m in equity and invests the proceeds at a rate of 5%. This generates the required interest payments over the year and also serves as collateral for the stocks borrowed. On balance the derivatives firm's position is worth zero. The investment manager holds 100m in equity.
- **First quarter.** The derivatives firm has to pay the investment manager 11.25m. The firm shorts an additional 10m in equity to maintain the size of its hedge at 100m. The proceeds of the short sale are paid to the investment manager together with the 1.25m interest which the firm receives on its collateral. The firm's position is worth zero. The investment manager receives 11.25m but because the swap notional is fixed at 100m he needs 10m of that to buy more equity. He puts 1.25m in the bank. Together with his equity portfolio he is now worth 101.25m.
- **Second quarter.** The value of the investment manager's equity portfolio goes up to 110m and he sells 10m to pay the derivatives firm. This brings his equity holdings back to 100m. The derivatives firm uses the 10m which it receives to buy stocks and reduce its short position to 100m again. In addition, the derivatives firm pays the investment manager 1.25m interest. On balance its position is worth zero again. The investment manager now owns 100m in equity, 2.50m in the bank plus 15,625 interest on the 1.25m he took to the bank at the end of the first quarter; 102.52m in total.
- **Third quarter.** Similar to the first quarter. The derivatives firm shorts an additional 10m in equity and pays the investment manager 11.25m. The firm's position is still worth zero. The investment manager receives 11.25m and spends 10m of it to buy more equity. He puts 1.25m in the bank. Together with the 31,445 in interest which he receives the investment manager is worth 103.80m now.
- **Fourth quarter.** The derivatives firm sells off its collateral and covers its short position at a 10m profit which it pays to the investment manager together with the last

interest payment of 1.25m. Its position is worth zero. The investment manager receives 11.25m from the derivatives firm and 47,463 interest from the bank. Together with his 90m equity portfolio and the 3.80m already in the bank, this means he is now worth 105.09m.

When it comes to pricing the above swap we have to go back to the derivatives firm's expected hedging costs. Going over the above example we see that the derivatives firm is able to hedge itself perfectly without asking the investment manager for an upfront payment. In practice, the derivatives firm will of course be confronted with various costs and risks that we did not take into account, including those resulting from the necessity to short stocks for a long period of time. In addition, it will want to make a profit on the deal. This means that, as with forwards, the investment manager will have to pay the derivatives firm something. Instead of doing so upfront, this payment is typically divided equally over the swap payment dates and formalized as a slight **discount on the fixed rate** to be paid by the derivatives firm.

Towards a More Efficient Contract

With the above swap the investment manager gets exactly what he bargained for as he ends the year with $100m \times (1.0125)^4 = 105.09m$. Also, the derivatives firm was right not to charge the investment manager for entering into the contract as the hedging strategy does not show any loose ends. The investment manager adds/takes the equity-linked payments to/from his equity portfolio and takes the interest he receives to the bank. The derivatives firm does essentially the same.

Although the above result is encouraging, it requires quite a lot of work from both counterparties. The reason for this is that the notional amount of the swap is fixed at $M \times I_0$. Suppose we applied the quarterly index return and the interest rate to a notional equal to M times the index value at the beginning of each quarter, instead of a notional equal to the investment manager's initial asset value $M \times I_0$. This would produce a quarterly swap payoff to the investment manager equal to

$$V_{i/4} = M \times I_{i/4-1/4} \times \left(\frac{r_1}{4} - \frac{I_{i/4} - I_{i/4-1/4}}{I_{i/4-1/4}} \right). \tag{6.22}$$

As before, this swap is nothing more than a package of four forwards with maturities of 3, 6, 9 and 12 months. The 3-month forward is again a vanilla forward. The other three forwards, however, are not. The latter now call for the exchange of two index-linked cash flows instead of a fixed and an index-linked cash flow.

Because the quarterly equity return is now applied to a notional of $M \times I_{i/4-1/4}$, there is no more need for the investment manager to buy or sell equity every quarter. When the value of the investment manager's equity portfolio falls he does not have to buy more, as next quarter's return will be applied to this lower value. Similarly, when the value of the equity portfolio rises he does not need to sell equity as next quarter's return will be applied to this higher value. The same goes for the derivatives firm, that no longer needs to increase its short position after a market drop or cover part of it after a market rise. The above swap is said to have a **variable notional** equal to $M \times I_{i/4-1/4}$, while the first swap is said to have a **fixed notional** of $M \times I_0$. A fixed notional swap hedges an investment where the amount of the investment is kept constant, while a variable notional swap hedges an investment where the amount invested varies with the market.

Table 6.4 Fixed rate equity-for-cash swap with variable notional

t	I_t	Derivatives firm	Investment manager	Balance to investment manager
0	100.0			
1/4	90.0	1.25000	−10.00	11.25000
1/2	99.0	1.12500	9.00	−7.87500
3/4	89.1	1.23750	−9.90	11.13750
1	80.19	1.11375	−8.91	10.02375

An example of the cash flows under a variable notional swap can be found in Table 6.4. The assumptions are the same as those underlying Table 6.3. The mechanics of the structure are as follows.

- **Initiation.** As before, the derivatives firm shorts 100m in equity, invests the proceeds at a rate of 5%, and puts it up as collateral. The investment manager holds 100m in equity.
- **First quarter.** At the end of the first quarter the derivatives firm has to pay the investment manager 11.25m. The firm receives 1.25m in interest, liquidates 10m of surplus collateral and pays the investment manager. The investment manager takes the 11.25m which he receives to the bank. He is now worth 101.25m.
- **Second quarter.** The derivatives firm pays the investment manager 1.125m, which is the interest the derivatives firm receives on its 90m collateral. The investment manager pays the firm 9m out of his bank account which the firm invests and puts up as additional collateral for its short position. Neither party needs to do anything more. The investment manager receives 140,625 interest which means that on balance he now has 3.52m in the bank. With his 99m portfolio this brings his net worth to 102.52m.
- **Third quarter.** Because the index has gone down again, the derivatives firm owes the investment manager 9.9m plus 1.2375m interest. The interest equals the interest the firm receives on its collateral. The additional 9.9m is obtained by selling surplus collateral. The investment manager now has 14.65m in the bank and also receives 43,945 in interest, which brings his total net worth to 103.80m.
- **Fourth quarter.** This is similar to the third quarter. The derivatives firm owes the investment manager 8.91m plus 1.11375m interest. It sells off its collateral, covers its short position and pays the investment manager. The investment manager receives 183,713 in interest. With his 80.19m in equity this leaves him with a total net worth of 105.09m.

The mechanics of the variable notional swap are much more economical than those of the fixed notional swap because there is no more buying and selling of equity. Despite the fact that the notional for the interest payments by the derivatives firm changes over time, the investment manager gets paid interest on the full initial value of his portfolio. The difference with the previous case, however, is that not all interest comes from the derivatives firm. If the portfolio value drops, the investment manager receives a payment from the derivatives firm which he puts into the bank. The next quarter's interest payment which he receives from the derivatives firm will be smaller due to the lower notional, but this is supplemented by the interest he receives from the bank.

A Floating Interest Rate

So far we have assumed that interest rates do not change during the life of the swap. However, interest rates do move over time, meaning that especially with the variable notional swap the investment manager and the derivatives firm are confronted with **interest rate risk**. We can eliminate the risk for the derivatives firm by, instead of at a prefixed rate, paying interest on a **floating rate** basis. In that case we would have a quarterly swap payoff to the investment manager equal to

$$V_{i/4} = M \times I_{i/4-1/4} \times \left(\frac{r_{1/4}}{4} - \frac{I_{i/4} - I_{i/4-1/4}}{I_{i/4-1/4}} \right), \qquad (6.23)$$

where $r_{1/4}$ denotes the 3-month interest rate at $t = i/4 - 1/4$. In practice, most equity-for-cash swaps use LIBOR to calculate the interest payments to be made by the derivatives firm, with the tenor of the rate set equal to the time between settlements. In our case this means calculating the interest payments using 3-month LIBOR.

Table 6.5 gives an example of how such a floating rate swap would work out assuming 3-month LIBOR started at 5%, went up to 6%, down to 5.5%, and up again to 6%. The practicalities would be as follows.

- **Initiation.** The derivatives firm shorts 100m in equity, invests the proceeds for three months at 5%, and puts that up as collateral. The position's net worth is zero. The investment manager has 100m which is all invested in equity.
- **First quarter.** The derivatives firm pays the investment manager 1.25m interest plus 10m of surplus collateral. The firm lends the remaining 90m at 6% for another three months. The investment manager receives 11.25m. He lends this at 6% for three months. The derivatives firm's net worth is zero. The investment manager now has 90m in equity plus 11.25m in cash; 101.25m in total.
- **Second quarter.** The derivatives firm pays the 1.35m interest which it receives on its collateral to the investment manager. The investment manager pays the derivatives firm 9m. The derivatives firm therefore has 99m to invest for another three months at 5.5%. Its net worth is zero. The investment manager receives 168,750 in interest. He now has 99m in equity plus 3.77m in cash; a total of 102.77m.
- **Third quarter.** The derivatives firm pays the investment manager the interest it receives plus 9.9m. It invests 89.1m for another three months at 6% and its net worth is zero again. Together with the 51,820 interest he receives from the bank, the investment manager now has 89.1m in equity and 15.08m in cash; a net worth of 104.18m in total.
- **Fourth quarter.** The derivatives firm covers its short position and pays the investment manager the interest it receives plus an additional 8.91m. Its net worth is again zero.

Table 6.5 Floating rate equity-for-cash swap with variable notional

t	I_t	3-Month LIBOR (%)	Derivatives firm	Investment manager	Balance to investment manager
0	100.0	5.0			
1/4	90.0	6.0	1.25000	−10.00	11.25000
1/2	99.0	5.5	1.35000	9.00	−7.65000
3/4	89.1	6.0	1.36125	−9.90	11.26125
1	80.19		1.33650	−8.91	10.24650

The investment manager now has 80.19m in equity and 25.55m in cash, and therefore ends the year with a net worth of 105.74m.

The derivatives firm is again able to hedge itself without asking the investment manager for an additional payment. However, if we take account of the various costs and risks the derivatives firm will have to deal with, as well as its desired profit margin, the investment manager will have to pay the derivatives firm something to get it to enter into the swap. This payment is typically structured as a **spread** applied to the floating rate paid by the derivatives firm. Instead of 3-month LIBOR flat, the derivatives firm may therefore end up paying the investment manager 3-month LIBOR minus 0.2% for example.

The above structure eliminates the interest rate risk for the derivatives firm but not for the investment manager. If the investment manager really wanted to fix the rate that he was going to receive over the life of the swap, he could combine the floating rate equity-for-cash swap with a so-called **floating-for-fixed interest rate swap** under which every quarter he paid away 3-month LIBOR on a notional amount of 100m in return for a prefixed rate. This does not fix the interest which the investment manager earns on the interest that he receives during the life of the swap, but that should not cause him any sleepless nights.

6.5   SWITCHING FROM EQUITY TO BONDS

Suppose that instead of switching his asset allocation from equity to cash our investment manager wanted to switch from equity to government bonds. In that case we could offer him the opportunity to enter into a forward or swap where he paid the equity return to the derivatives firm and received the return on a specific bond or bond portfolio. Choosing a swap with variable notional, this would produce a quarterly payoff to the investment manager equal to

$$V_{i/4} = M \times \left(B_{i/4-1/4} \times \left(\frac{B_{i/4} - B_{i/4-1/4}}{B_{i/4-1/4}} \right) - I_{i/4-1/4} \times \left(\frac{I_{i/4} - I_{i/4-1/4}}{I_{i/4-1/4}} \right) \right), \quad (6.24)$$

where B_t denotes the value of the relevant bond portfolio at time t and $I_0 = B_0$. Starting with an equally valued equity and bond portfolio, at the end of each quarter the investment manager pays the derivatives firm the change in the value of his equity portfolio and the derivatives firm pays the change in the value of the bond portfolio. With respect to the dividends paid on the stocks and the coupons paid on the bonds there are again various possibilities, the most obvious being a full exchange. This means the investment manager passes all dividends through to the derivatives firm and receives all coupons paid on the relevant bond or bond portfolio.

The message will be clear by now. For once thinking in terms of products instead of problems, **forwards and swaps offer the investment manager an efficient way to switch from one asset or asset class into the other**. The investment manager may switch from equity to cash and back, from equity to bonds and back, and even from one equity index to another equity index if so desired.

6.6   SYNTHETIC INDEXATION AND ALPHA EXTRACTION

An investor who wanted to replicate the performance of a specific market index could either (a) run his own index tracking strategy in the cash market (or hire an outside manager to do that for him) or (b) buy index participations. Since we now know how easy it is to swap less desirable cash flows into more desirable ones, these are no longer the only alternatives available. Suppose a fund manager wanted to create an index fund without tracking error. Could he do so without buying index participations? The answer is yes. He could make his own index participations by investing the fund's assets in floating rate notes and then use a swap contract to trade in the note coupons which he receives for index returns. Doing so would require a **cash-for-equity** swap, where the fund manager paid away the interest payments which he received in return for the return on the relevant market index. The result is known as a **synthetic index fund**.

Although constructed in a completely different way, to the outside world the synthetic index fund would look exactly like a cash market index fund. Actually, it would be better. First, the swap creates an easy but at the same time strict formal link with the index and therefore eliminates tracking error. For fund managers whose compensation is based on how well the fund tracks the index this can be an important point. Second, when it comes to the question of whether an investor should take the synthetic route, the tax, accounting and regulatory environment is also an important factor. A synthetic index fund's profit is made up of interest plus the gains under the swap. A cash index fund's profit on the other hand consists of dividends and gains on the stocks which are held. There may be significant differences in the way these different sources of income are taxed, leading to significant differences in after-tax returns.

6.6.1 Enhancing Index Returns

Using swaps to create a synthetic index fund also offers the potential for the fund to outperform the index. First, the fund manager might be able to find a counterparty that offers him extremely good conditions on the swap. Apart from pricing errors, this might be the result of the derivatives firm having found an efficient way to hedge the swap and passing part of the efficiency gains on to the fund manager. A second possibility to outperform the index lies in **taking on extra credit risk** on the notes which the fund buys. Suppose that the derivatives firm was willing to provide the fund manager with the required index return if in return the fund paid LIBOR flat. This means that the fund manager will obtain the index return if he buys floating rate notes paying LIBOR flat. However, he could also buy notes issued by lower rated issuers which pay a spread over LIBOR, such as LIBOR + 0.3% or even LIBOR + 0.5%. Since he can obtain the index return by paying the derivatives firm LIBOR, this guarantees him an outperformance of the index by 0.3% or 0.5%.

Managers of so-called **enhanced index funds** try to generate excess returns while at the same time maintaining a low tracking error with the index. Apart from taking on extra credit risk, such managers also use more risky tactics in their attempts to outperform the index. Instead of buying floating rate notes, a fund manager might for example take on some bond market risk in an attempt to raise the expected return of his portfolio above LIBOR. It might also happen that the manager of an equity index fund thought he had superior bond picking skills. Such a manager could use a **bonds-for-equity** swap to transfer his bond picking skills into the index fund. The mechanics would be similar to what we discussed earlier. Instead of the stocks in the index, the fund manager would buy a portfolio of bonds which he thought would outperform the market. At the same time he would enter into a swap with a derivatives firm where he paid away the return on some standard bond portfolio and received the return on the relevant equity index. If the fund manager indeed had superior bond picking skills his bond portfolio would outperform the bond portfolio used in the swap and he could add the difference in performance to that of the index fund.

An index fund manager who had substantial expertise in some foreign equity market could use an **equity-for-equity** swap to transfer his specific expertise into the fund. The index fund manager could buy the foreign stocks that he thought were going to outperform the foreign market index and swap the return on the foreign index for the return on the domestic index. Using the equity-for-equity swap in this way the fund manager would be able to supplement the index fund return with the outperformance of his foreign stocks.

6.6.2 Enhancing Money Market Returns

A money market fund that wanted to boost its performance could use the reverse of the strategies used by the index fund manager. The fund could buy the index and use an **equity-for-cash** swap to turn the index returns into cash returns, thereby creating a **synthetic money market fund**. If the fund could find a counterparty willing to take the other side of the swap at favorable conditions, this would add to the fund's performance. But there is more. Suppose the manager of a money market fund thought that there was a lot more money to be made in stock picking than in trading money market instruments. Simply buying the stocks that he expected to outperform the index would take the risk–return profile of the fund too far away from where it was supposed to be. However, he could buy the undervalued stocks and at the same time enter into an **equity-for-cash** swap where he paid away the equity index return and received LIBOR. On balance this would leave him with LIBOR plus the outperformance of the stocks that he bought relative to the index. Combined with the interest received under the swap, this could make for an outstanding money market fund performance. Likewise, if the fund manager was into bond picking he could consider buying the bonds he thought were especially interesting while using a **bond-for-cash** swap to exchange the regular bond return for LIBOR.

6.6.3 Pure Alpha Extraction

Enhancing index fund or money market fund returns means adding the outperformance of a stock (portfolio) or bond (portfolio) relative to another stock (portfolio) or bond (portfolio) to the standard fund return. Going back to the market model discussed earlier, this outperformance is typically referred to as the relevant asset's or portfolio's **alpha**. Buying promising stocks and swapping the market risk out of them to extract these stocks' alpha is not limited to money market funds, since one does not need to own the money used to buy the stocks with. One could simply borrow to fund the purchase of the stocks. Suppose we borrowed at LIBOR flat, bought the stocks we wanted and entered into an **equity-for-cash** swap where we paid the return on the index and received LIBOR flat. The LIBOR flow received under the swap agreement would pay for the interest on our borrowings and our equity holdings would generate the equity-linked payments. The end result would be that we were left with the stocks' alpha. Any investment manager who is able to buy stocks with borrowed funds could use this strategy to capitalize on his stock picking skills.

Investment managers who are not allowed, or prefer not, to borrow money can take things one step further and enter into a derivatives contract that combines the borrowing of money, the buying of stocks and the equity-for-cash swap all into one. A contract like this simply pays its holder what he is interested in: the relevant stocks' alpha. Suppose an investment manager thought that a particular company was certain to outperform the market over the next year. With a stock's alpha being equal to the difference between the stock return and the (beta-adjusted) index return the obvious solution for the investment manager is to enter into a contract where he pays the return on the index and receives the return on the relevant stock. This way of extracting alphas combines two swap contracts into one. The first is a contract where the investment manager receives the return on the stock and pays interest in return. This replicates the leveraged purchase of the stock. The second is a contract where the investment manager pays away the index return and receives interest. This contract replicates the short sale of the index and the investment of the proceeds in cash. With the interest simply flowing through, **the end result of simultaneously entering into both contracts is the stock's alpha**.

The above contract is an extremely efficient tool to extract alphas, since implicitly it takes care of a large number of cash market transactions. To achieve the same result in the cash market the investment manager would initially have to (1) buy the stock he thought was going to outperform the market and (2) borrow the stocks in the index and sell them short. Likewise, at maturity he would have to (3) sell the stocks that he purchased and (4) buy back and deliver the stocks that he sold short. Because the stock which he buys may not make suitable collateral for the stocks which he borrows, the investment manager may also have to find collateral for his short sale. In addition, during the time the trade was put on he would also have to deal with the various operational complications that come with holding and short-selling stocks. The above forward allows the investment manager to accomplish all of this in one simple transaction. This emphasizes that all the above applications are nothing more than efficient alternatives for exposure adjustments, which in theory could also have been made through a combination of buying and (short-)selling in the cash markets. In practice, however, these trades will often be considered too complicated and too costly to really happen. With the right derivatives contract on the other hand all of this can be accomplished in one single transaction.

6.7 DIFFERENT PROBLEMS, SAME SOLUTION

We have introduced index participations, forwards and swaps concentrating on transaction costs, convenience and replication precision. We did so because these are common problems which do not require detailed knowledge of tax, accounting and regulation. However, we could have introduced these contracts starting off with any of a large number of problems, many of which do derive from specific tax, accounting and/or regulatory issues. In this section we briefly discuss two of them.

6.7.1 Expansion of the Investment Universe

Investors are typically constrained by a large number of internal and external constraints. They may not be allowed to invest in certain assets or asset classes, or they may not have access to certain markets. Direct investment in emerging markets for example often proves problematic for a number of reasons. First, the purchase and/or sale of a currency for investment purposes may sometimes require central bank approval or be regulated in some other way. In Chile, for example, securities gains have to remain in the country for at least one year prior to repatriation. Second, foreign ownership of local securities may be restricted in one or more ways. In some countries the total amount of a company's equity that can be held by foreign investors is limited as well. If that limit is reached, foreign investors can only buy their equities from other foreign investors. As a result of constraints like these, actual performance may deviate substantially from the results that would have been obtained had these constraints not been in place. Index participations, forwards and swaps offer investors a way to circumvent these constraints by buying the desired exposure indirectly instead of directly.

6.7.2 Management of Concentrated Equity Risk

Some investors find themselves with an excessively large position in one single stock. This is known as a **concentrated equity** position. Apart from belonging to the founder(s) of a company or its senior executives, such positions can be the result of a successful LBO or venture capital investment for example. Investors holding concentrated equity positions may want to diversify their exposure. Doing so, however, requires them to sell off part of their position, which may not be feasible due to a variety of reasons, including tax and regulation. If that is the case, investors can use forwards or swaps to switch exposure from the stocks in which they are invested to something else. Hedging themselves in this way retains all dividend and voting rights and allows investors to extract some cash from their position as the hedged position, i.e. stocks plus forward or swap, may be used to secure a loan.

Let's look at an interesting real-life example. Autotote Corporation is a New York company which provides computerized wagering equipment to the racing industry, offering its products for on-track, off-track and inter-track wagering, lotteries and legalized sports betting in the US, Canada, Mexico, Latin America, New Zealand and the Far East. On March 18th, 1994, three days before the announcement of the company's quarterly earnings, Autotote's chairman and CEO Allen Lorne Weil entered into an equity-for-cash swap with Bankers Trust, maturing on March 25th, 1999. The swap covered 500,000 of Weil's shares in Autotote priced at $26.78, i.e. a notional amount of $13.4m. On March 21st, Autotote announced quarterly earnings below analysts' expectations and the stock price dropped by 8.29%. On March 24th the stock fell by 14.28% and on March 25th it dropped another 10%. Since then Autotote's stock price has dropped a lot further. On March 25th, 1999, the swap's maturity date, the stock was trading at only $1.625. If we look at the swap payments, it is obvious that Weil did a very good deal. Not only did Bankers Trust have to pay him the depreciation of the stock, amounting to $12.6m, but it also had to pay him interest on $13.4m over five years.

Entering into an equity swap is not the only way to hedge and monetize a concentrated equity position. Zero-cost collars and trust structures are two other possibilities. We will discuss collars in Chapter 7.

6.8 CONCLUSION

In this chapter we applied the structuring toolbox which we developed in Chapters 1–5 to solve some simple investment problems. **The routine** so far has proven to be very straightforward.

- Find out what cash flows the investor wants and what cash flows he wants to give up in return.
- Structure a contract where he pays away the unwanted and receives the desired cash flows.
- Ask one or more derivatives firms for a price.

The analysis confirms that for contracts with linear payoffs, like index participations, vanilla forwards and swaps, the expected hedging costs can be calculated using either old-fashioned common sense or the pricing shortcut introduced in Chapter 5. The hedging strategies are straightforward and the hedging risk is small, which in turn translates into a low minimum required profit margin. Given the fierce competition in this area, which largely results from the simplicity of the hedging strategies, it is unlikely that a derivatives firm will be able to make an excess profit over the minimum required margin on this type of product. Of course, this excludes cases where confidentiality or size is an issue.

7
Risk Management

7.1 INTRODUCTION

In the previous chapter we concentrated on the structuring of derivatives contracts that allow investors to manage their exposure with less effort and/or at lower costs. Since the resulting contracts were explicitly designed as substitutes for buying and selling in the cash market, it is not surprising that their payoffs turned out to involve only vanilla index-linked cash flows. Using what we discussed in Chapters 1–5, however, we can structure solutions to a much wider range of problems. As many of these problems are substantially more complicated than the ones discussed in Chapter 6, the resulting contracts are likely to involve one or more structured index-linked cash flows that are a non-linear function of the index value. Suppose for example that we were asked by an investor to structure a contract that, when combined with his existing portfolio, eliminated the probability of a return lower than 0% with minimal effect on the upside. This can only be accomplished by a contract with a payoff that varies non-linearly with the index. In this chapter we discuss how to structure such contracts.

7.2 DERIVATIVES IN INVESTMENT MANAGEMENT

As we will see in this chapter, derivatives offer investment managers the possibility to closely tailor the payoff profile of their portfolio to their own specific views. Investment managers are therefore often thought of as the natural users of derivatives. Unfortunately, it does not always work out that way. To evaluate an investment manager his performance is typically compared to that of some **benchmark**. This can be a specific stock market index, but also a portfolio that was specially constructed to reflect the special nature of the strategy in question. A second more implicit benchmark is formed by the performance of the competition. Beating the competition is even more important than beating the benchmark, because doing so offers new marketing opportunities, leading to an increase in assets under management and thereby to increased management fees. There is an old story on Wall Street about two investment managers who go camping together. After setting up camp, one says to the other 'Do you know there are bears around here?'. His friend answers, 'Well, I'm not too worried; I am a pretty good runner'. 'I know', says the first guy, 'but you can't outrun a bear'. 'I know that', responds the other guy, 'but I only need to outrun you, don't I!?'.

Using derivatives to tailor the payoff profile of an investment portfolio to a specific view may create a payoff profile which differs very significantly from that of the relevant benchmark index and the competition. Since investment managers also have a job to protect, however, most investment managers will not be willing to do so. If the investment manager's view proves correct he will outperform his benchmark. However, if he is wrong he may seriously underperform his benchmark which will cost him part of his business and maybe even his job. Clearly, one has to be extremely convinced of oneself to take a risk like that. **Running a portfolio with a payoff profile which is very different from**

that of the relevant benchmark is a dangerous strategy. Generally, it is considered better to fail conventionally than to succeed unconventionally. An article in *The Wall Street Journal* quoted the manager of a large US pension fund as follows: 'If you made the right call and used derivatives, you might get a small additional return. But if you make the wrong call, you could wind up unemployed, with a big dent in your credibility as an investor'.[1]

A 1998 survey carried out by the New York University School of Business, CIBC World Markets and the KPMG Investment Consulting Group showed that only 27% of the institutional investors surveyed used derivatives, with the average derivatives position only covering 6.7% of assets. Academic support for professional investment managers' lack of interest in derivatives can be found in the work of Koski and Pontiff.[2] The latter found that out of 675 US equity mutual funds only 21% used derivatives. Moreover, the authors were unable to find systematic differences between the risk–return characteristics of funds that did and did not use derivatives. In other words, the funds that do use derivatives do so in a way that does not significantly affect the payoff profile of their portfolios.

Apart from the fact that most rational investment managers will simply not be interested, there are other problems with the use of derivatives in investment management as well.

- The **mandate** may be such that the investment manager is simply not allowed to use derivatives. Also, regulation may prohibit the use of (certain types of) derivatives. If this is the case then all ends there. The survey mentioned before showed that in the US only 46% of institutions allow their asset managers to use derivatives.
- Many institutional investors have become so large that if they want to do a trade that really has an impact on their portfolio the sheer **size of the trade** will be outside most derivatives firms' league. Derivatives firms will only venture into this type of trade if they can (partially) hedge them back-to-back, i.e. find another investor to take the other side of the trade.
- Active investment managers can be expected to make regular **changes in the composition of the portfolio**. This means that it is not exactly clear what the portfolio will look like six months or a year from now. Since derivatives are typically based on a prefixed reference index or set of indices this may create basis risk as the actual portfolio may turn out to be significantly different from the index used in the derivatives contract in question.

ASSUMPTIONS & NOTATION (CHAPTERS 7 AND 8)

In what follows we will assume we are consultants to an investment manager who is not hindered by any of the above considerations and who can and will do whatever is necessary to outperform his benchmark. We provide a large number of examples. All these examples are based on the assumption that our investment manager manages a portfolio initially worth 100 million. All reference indices are assumed to be at 100 initially and pay no dividends. To avoid unnecessary complication, we work with continuously compounded interest rates throughout, assuming the term structure of interest rates is flat and constant

---

[1] *The Wall Street Journal*, August 24th, 1995.

[2] J. Koski and J. Pontiff, How Are Derivatives Used? Evidence from the Mutual Fund Industry, *Journal of Finance*, Vol. 54, 1999, pp. 791–816.

at 5%. The interest rate for a maturity of i years is denoted as r_i. The total amount to be invested is denoted as N. The number of shares in the reference index that an amount N buys is denoted as M, i.e. $M = N/I_0$. Under the above assumptions $N = 100m$ and $M = 1m$.

As discussed in Chapter 5, when pricing derivatives contracts derivatives firms will first calculate the expected hedging costs and then put a profit margin on top of that. Amongst others, the expected hedging costs depend on the model inputs used and on whether the firm is buying or selling. The profit margin also depends on a number of different factors, including the size and complexity of the deal. Since we are more interested in structures than in prices, however, we will simplify things somewhat. First, we will assume that the term structure of implied volatility is flat and constant at 20% without any skew. Second, calibrating on the above, we will assume that the expected hedging costs are equal to the theoretical price, irrespective of whether the firm is buying or selling. Third, we will ignore the derivatives firm's profit margin. These are strong assumptions. For our purpose, however, they suffice. Although for pricing purposes we assume the derivatives firm's bid and offer are the same, we do differentiate between them in the text. Offers are indicated by the superscript 'a' (for ask) and bids by the superscript 'b' (for bid).

7.3 PROTECTED LEVERAGED BUYING AND SHORT-SELLING

In the previous chapter we discussed how investment managers can synthetically borrow money and buy equity or synthetically sell stocks short by entering into a forward or swap contract. Of course, such contracts are quite risky. An investment manager who buys a forward will lose if the index at maturity is lower than the forward price. Likewise, an investment manager who sells a forward will lose if the index at maturity is higher than the forward price which he agreed upon. The most straightforward way to eliminate this risk is to give the investment manager the right to cancel the forward contract at maturity. With the **option right** in hand, the investment manager knows he will never lose. If he has to pay more than he is to receive he simply cancels the contract.

7.3.1 Protected Leveraged Buying

In the case of synthetic leveraged buying the investment manager pays a fixed amount of $e^{r_1}I_0$ to receive the index value at maturity. Now suppose we gave him the right to cancel this contract at maturity. In that case he is no longer long a forward but the proud owner of an **ordinary call option**. After the introduction of the option right the payoff to the investment manager can be expressed as

$$V_1 = M \times \text{Max}\,[0, I_1 - e^{r_1}I_0]. \tag{7.1}$$

The non-zero term within the square brackets is the payoff of the long vanilla forward given by (6.4). With the option right, however, the investment manager will only accept this payoff if it is positive. This is formalized by the Max operator, which states that on balance the investment manager will receive a payoff equal to the highest of zero and the payoff of a long vanilla forward. Remember from Chapter 4 that after the introduction of the option right $e^{r_1}I_0$ is no longer referred to as the forward price but as the option's **strike**. If the index value is below the strike the call is said to be out-of-the-money (OTM).

If the index is higher than the strike it is said to be in-the-money (ITM), and if the strike and the index value are equal the call is said to be at-the-money (ATM).

7.3.2   Protected Short-Selling

Something similar goes for the case of synthetic short-selling where the investment manager pays the index value at maturity in return for a fixed amount of $e^{r_1}I_0$. If we gave him the right to cancel this contract at maturity he would no longer be short a forward but long an **ordinary put option**. The payoff at maturity to the investment manager could in this case be expressed as

$$V_1 = M \times \text{Max}\,[0, e^{r_1}I_0 - I_1]. \tag{7.2}$$

The term within the square brackets is the payoff of a short vanilla forward given by (6.9). The investment manager will only accept this payoff if it is positive. The above expression therefore says that on balance the investment manager will receive a payoff equal to the highest of zero and the payoff of a short vanilla forward. Again, we no longer refer to $e^{r_1}I_0$ as the forward price but now call it the put option's strike. Whether the put is referred to as ITM, OTM or ATM depends on what the payoff would be in case the contract matured immediately. If the index is below the strike the put is ITM, if it is above the strike it is OTM, and if the strike and the index value are equal the put is said to be ATM.

7.3.3   The Option Premium

The introduction of the option right has far-reaching consequences for the payoff of a contract. With a forward the investment manager and the derivatives firm have a more or less equal chance to make money. After the introduction of the option right, however, the investment manager knows that he is never going to lose and the derivatives firm knows it is never going to win. It therefore makes sense that the investment manager will have to compensate the derivatives firm in some way. This is typically done in the form of an upfront payment, referred to as the **option premium** or the **option price**.

How derivatives firms determine the option premiums they show to their customers was discussed in Chapter 5. Under the assumptions made, the investment manager will have to pay the derivatives firm a premium of 8.02m for payoff (7.1) and 7.90m for payoff (7.2). Although there is nothing against it, this is not how option prices are generally expressed though. The multiplier is usually set equal to 1, after which **the option premium is expressed as a percentage of the index value**. This allows the investment manager to see immediately how buying or selling the relevant option will affect his performance. In this case the investment manager's strategy will have to produce a return of at least 8.02% and 7.90% to make up for the option premium he will have to pay.

The premium quoted by the derivatives firm depends on the contract's expected hedging costs. This means that, if we want to say something about how prices will change if we change one or more contract parameters, we have to go back to the hedging strategy. However, it is typically a lot easier to use the pricing shortcut we discussed in Chapter 5. The latter says that if we assume all stock prices drift upwards at a rate equal to the prevailing interest rate, derivatives prices are nothing more than discounted expected payoffs. Suppose we raised the **strike** of the above ordinary call. In that case the expected payoff to the investment manager would drop because he would have to pay more to receive the same index value. This means the option premium will drop. If we raised the strike of the ordinary put the opposite would happen, as the investment manager would receive more for paying the same index value. The premium of 1-year calls and puts as a function of the strike is shown in Figure 7.1.

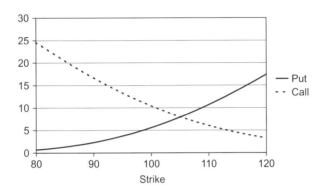

Figure 7.1 Ordinary call and put premiums as a function of strike

We can use the same reasoning to predict how option prices will react to changes in **time to maturity**. If we increase the time to maturity, we see two effects. First, the longer the maturity, the further the index can move away from the strike. This raises the expected payoff of both the call and the put because the option holder can always cancel the contract if the index moves the wrong way. Second, the longer the time to maturity the more the index can drift upwards. This raises the expected payoff of the call but reduces the expected payoff of the put. The call price can therefore be expected to rise faster than the put price. This is exactly what we see in Figure 7.2 for ATM calls and puts. Put prices rise with time to maturity but at a strongly decreasing rate. For longer maturities the put price hardly reacts to a change in maturity.

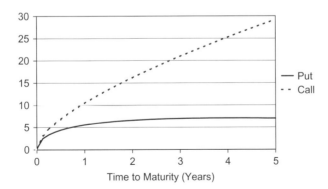

Figure 7.2 ATM ordinary call and put premiums as a function of time to maturity

When it comes to the question of how option prices respond to changes in the pricing environment, i.e. interest rates, implied volatilities and dividends, we can look at what happens to the expected hedging costs or the expected payoff. If **volatility** went up both call and put prices would go up because, as discussed in Chapter 5, the expected hedging costs would increase. Alternatively, one might say that a higher volatility makes the index more likely to deviate significantly from the strike, which makes the expected payoff of both options go up. For 1-year ATM calls and puts this is illustrated in Figure 7.3.

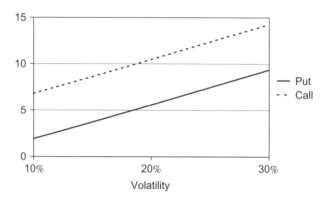

Figure 7.3 ATM ordinary call and put premiums as a function of volatility reference index

If **interest rates** went up call prices would go up and put prices would go down. As discussed in Chapter 5, to hedge a call the derivatives firm borrows money and buys stocks. The higher the interest rate the higher the cost of borrowing and therefore the higher the expected hedging costs. The opposite goes for puts. To hedge a put the firm shorts stocks and banks the proceeds. The higher the interest rate, the higher the interest received and therefore the lower the expected hedging costs. Alternatively, we could of course say that the higher the interest rate, the stronger the upward drift of the index will be. This makes it more likely for calls and less likely for puts to pay off. Figure 7.4 illustrates this graphically for 1-year ATM calls and puts. In the graph we also see that when interest rates are zero, ATM call and put prices are equal. This makes sense as without any drift in the index both have the same expected payoff.

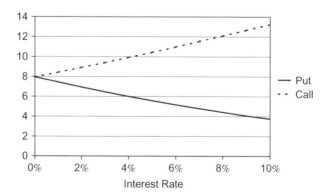

Figure 7.4 ATM ordinary call and put premiums as a function of interest rate

Finally, we turn to the impact of **dividends**. When hedging calls the derivatives firm buys stocks. This means that if a stock pays a dividend the firm receives it, which reduces the expected hedging costs. With puts the opposite happens. Since the firm shorts stocks it needs to pay the dividend away to the party it borrowed the stocks from. This increases the expected hedging costs. We come to the same conclusion if we look at the expected payoffs. As discussed in Chapter 2, the payment of dividends puts a brake on the upward trend in stock prices. This means that dividends reduce the expected payoff of calls and increase the expected payoff of puts. Figure 7.5 gives an example of how the prices of 1-year ATM calls and puts change with dividend yield. The graph clearly shows that **it does not take a large change in dividend yield to significantly change option prices**. We will put this observation to good use in later chapters.

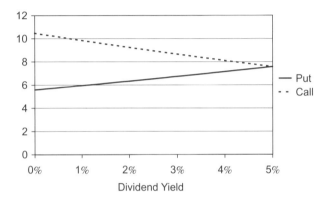

Figure 7.5   ATM ordinary call and put premiums as a function of dividend yield reference index

In the remainder of this chapter, as well as the chapters that follow, we will encounter a large number of different types of options. Although they provide different payoffs, many of these options' prices respond to changes in strike, time to maturity, interest rates, volatility and dividends in ways similar to ordinary calls and puts. This is not a rule without exceptions though.

7.4   OPTIMAL ASSET ALLOCATION

In Chapter 6 we mentioned that for a typical institutional investor the asset allocation decision is far more important than the security selection decision. In this section we will therefore discuss some applications of cquity derivatives aimed at providing investors with a payoff equal to the best performing of two or more different asset classes.

7.4.1   The Best of Equity and Cash (Portfolio Insurance)

Suppose an investment manager had two asset classes to invest in: (a) cash and (b) equity, with the latter represented by some stock market index. His goal is to invest the money available in both asset classes to maximize the portfolio's performance over the 1-year evaluation horizon. The idea is to be invested in equity when the market goes up and to be in cash when the market goes down. If the investment manager thinks equity is going to outperform cash he will therefore tilt his asset allocation towards equity and the other way around. Although this sounds straightforward, there is one major problem: it assumes the investment manager can actually predict where the equity market is going. An overwhelming body of academic research has shown that this is highly unlikely.

One alternative is for the investment manager to invest all his money in equity and enter into a contract with a derivatives firm that, when combined with his equity position, produces a result that makes it look as if he really had superior asset allocation skills. To structure such a contract we first have to decide on the desired overall payoff. Suppose we wanted to end the year with a net asset value equal to the highest of some **floor value** f and the value of the index. Formally, this means an end-of-year payoff to the investment manager equal to

$$X_1 = M \times \text{Max}\,[I_1, f]. \tag{7.3}$$

The multiplier M is equal to the portfolio's initial value divided by the initial index value, i.e. the number of shares in the index the portfolio value initially buys. The floor value can be expressed as

$$f = I_0(1 - d), \tag{7.4}$$

where d is the **deductible**. The latter can be equal to, higher or lower than zero. The use of some insurance terminology stems from the fact that the floor value's function is to provide the portfolio with a minimum value at the end of the year. In other words, it provides insurance against a loss in portfolio value exceeding the deductible chosen. This is why the above payoff is generally referred to as **portfolio insurance**.

With the above payoff we set our goals for the investment manager's end-of-year payoff in absolute terms. We can also do so in relative terms. We could for example aim for a return on investment equal to the highest of some prefixed **floor rate** F and the return on the index. In that case we would be looking at an overall payoff equal to

$$X_1 = N \times \left(1 + \text{Max}\left[F, \frac{I_1 - I_0}{I_0}\right]\right), \tag{7.5}$$

where $F = -d$ and the notional amount N equals the initial value of the portfolio, i.e. $N = M \times I_0$. This means that at the end of the year this payoff gives the investment manager his money back plus a return on investment equal to the highest of the floor rate and the index return. Although this payoff looks different from (7.3) it is not. This is easily checked given that $f = (1 + F)I_0$ and $M = N/I_0$. Since ultimately it is the return on his investment that the investment manager is interested in, **throughout we will denote the overall payoff to the investor in relative terms**.

Although the above payoff is what the investment manager would like to receive, this is not what the derivatives firm will have to pay him since he has his own money to invest as well. For simplicity, assuming that the investment manager is able to track the index without error, investing all his money in the index will give him an end-of-year payoff equal to

$$H_1 = M \times I_1 = N \times \left(1 + \frac{I_1 - I_0}{I_0}\right). \tag{7.6}$$

This means that to provide him with the desired payoff the derivatives firm needs to pay him an amount equal to

$$V_1 = X_1 - H_1 = M \times \text{Max}\,[0, I_0(1 + F) - I_1]. \tag{7.7}$$

This is not a new payoff. It is the payoff of M **ordinary puts** with a strike equal to $I_0(1 + F)$. In other words, the investment manager can obtain the desired payoff by investing in equity and buying ordinary puts. If the market goes up he cancels the option contract and is left with the equity portfolio. If on the other hand the market goes down, he pays the value of his equity portfolio to the derivatives firm in exchange for a prefixed amount equal to $M \times I_0(1 + F)$.

The above structure allows the investment manager a riskless investment in equity. If the market goes up he shows the same performance as if he was fully invested in equity, and if it goes down he is protected by the floor. This sounds too good to be true and indeed it is. As the following trades make clear, it allows for **arbitrage**.

- Consider payoff (7.3) with a zero deductable. If we could obtain this payoff at a price equal to the initial value of the portfolio, we could short the index and use the proceeds to buy the payoff. The latter would pay us the highest of the value of the index at maturity and its initial value. If the index went up we would neither win nor lose. If the index went down, however, we would win since we would be able to cancel our short position at a price lower than the payoff we received.
- Consider payoff (7.5) with a floor rate equal to the interest rate. If we could obtain this payoff at a price equal to the initial value of the portfolio, we could borrow money and buy the payoff. If the index went up less than the interest rate we would receive a return equal to the interest rate. Since this is exactly what we would have to pay on the loan, our profit would be zero. If the index rose by more than the interest rate, however, we would get a return higher than the interest rate and therefore make a profit.

A second indication that there might be something wrong comes from the expected return of the structure. The pricing shortcut we discussed in Chapter 5 tells us to assume that all stock prices drift upwards at a rate equal to the interest rate. This means that the expected return on any investment, whether it be cash, equity or a mix of the two, is equal to the interest rate. Now let's look at the payoff given by (7.5). Without the floor this payoff is identical to that of a straightforward equity investment. According to the pricing shortcut, such an investment offers an expected return equal to the interest rate. This means, however, that with a floor, which eliminates (most of) the negative outcomes, the expected return must be higher than the interest rate.

The existence of arbitrage opportunities is due to the fact that we have ignored the investment manager having to pay the derivatives firm to enter into the option contract. The option right which the investment manager obtains is extremely valuable as it allows him to cancel the contract in case he has to pay more than he receives. Since the puts in question do not come for free, **the amount required to obtain the payoff given by (7.5) will exceed the amount available**. To bring the expected return down to thc interest rate we either have to raise the amount we put in or settle for a less ambitious payoff. With the amount available being fixed, the first alternative is not an option. We therefore have to cut back on the payoff.

Internal Funding

The investment manager needs money to buy the puts which are required to provide the downside protection he is after. One alternative is to simply take the money from the portfolio itself. This means we split the investment manager's money into two parts. An amount $(1 - \alpha)N$ is paid to the derivatives firm to buy the desired downside protection. The remainder αN is invested in equity to supply upside potential. We call this **internal funding**. This means we are now aiming for a payoff equal to

$$X_1 = N \times \left(1 + \text{Max} \left[F, \alpha \left(\frac{I_1 - I_0}{I_0} \right) \right] \right). \tag{7.8}$$

Because he only invests αN in the index, the investment manager only receives a fraction α of the index return. In exchange he knows that the value of his portfolio will never fall below a floor value of $N \times (1 + F)$. In practice, α is referred to as the structure's **participation rate**. If we lower the participation rate the expected payoff comes down, which in turn means that the payoff will become cheaper. The trick is to find the value of α that balances the budget, i.e. that matches the value of the payoff with the initial portfolio value.

The investment manager invests a fraction α of his money in the equity market himself. After a year this investment will yield a payoff equal to

$$H_1 = \alpha M \times I_1 = \alpha N \times \left(1 + \frac{I_1 - I_0}{I_0} \right). \tag{7.9}$$

This means that to provide the investment manager with the desired payoff at maturity the derivatives firm needs to pay him an amount equal to

$$V_1 = X_1 - H_1 = (1 - \alpha)N + \alpha M \times \text{Max} \left[0, I_0 \left(1 + \frac{F}{\alpha} \right) - I_1 \right]. \tag{7.10}$$

The first part of the above expression is a fixed amount equal to the difference between the initial portfolio value and the amount which the investment manager invests in equity himself. Since the participation rate will be smaller than 1, we can think of this as the redemption of a loan which the investment manager provides to the derivatives firm. The second part equals the payoff of αM **ordinary puts** with strike $I_0(1 + F/\alpha)$. Comparing the above result with (7.7) we see that three things have changed.

- The **number of options** has dropped. Instead of M options the investment manager now buys αM options. This makes sense as he only buys αM shares of the index as well.
- The **strike** of these puts has gone up (assuming F is positive) from $I_0(1 + F)$ to $I_0(1 + F/\alpha)$. This results from the fact that the same floor value now has to be provided by fewer options.
- We now have a **fixed amount** in the contract payoff. It is there because, despite the higher strike, the combination of equity plus puts is not enough to provide the desired floor. In case of a market drop the latter combination only generates $(\alpha + F)N$. It is only with the fixed amount that the investment manager ends up with the desired $(1 + F)N$.

From this point there are two ways to proceed. First, the investment manager can ask the derivatives firm to show a quote on a contract with a payoff equal to (7.10). Implicitly, this means the investment manager not only buys puts from the derivatives firm but also provides the derivatives firm with a loan. If the investment manager can easily take the derivatives firm's credit this is no problem. However, this need not always be the case. The investment manager may already have done a lot of business with the firm in question in the past, which may have consumed most of the available credit line. Alternatively, the investment manager may plan to do more business with the same firm in the future and therefore wish to keep his lines open. If this is the case he could consider splitting the above derivatives contract into an explicit loan and a block of puts and do the loan with another counterparty. This minimizes his credit exposure to the derivatives firm. For simplicity, we assume the whole deal is done with the derivatives firm.

The remaining question then is: **what is the value of α?** To calculate the attainable participation rate we have to realize that since the investment manager invests αN in equity, he only has $(1 - \alpha)N$ to spend on the derivatives contract. This means we have the following budget equation to deal with

$$(1 - \alpha)N = e^{-r_1}(1 - \alpha)N + \alpha M \times P_0^a \left[I_0 \left(1 + \frac{F}{\alpha} \right), 1 \right], \qquad (7.11)$$

where r_1 is the 1-year bid rate which the derivatives firm uses to calculate the present value of a cash outflow of $(1 - \alpha)N$ in one year and $P_0^a[K, T]$ is the derivatives firm's offer for an ordinary put with strike K and maturity date T. The right-hand side of (7.11) is the present value of the derivatives contract which we structured. The first part is the implicit loan which the investment manager provides to the derivatives firm. The second part is the derivatives firm's offer for the required puts.

By paying $(1 - \alpha)N$ now the investment manager obtains a future payoff of $(1 - \alpha)N$ plus the payoff of αM ordinary puts. This means that the investment manager provides the derivatives firm with a loan, the interest on which equals the value of the puts. What the budget equation therefore does is simply equate the present value of the interest the derivatives firm would normally have paid with the present value of the puts the investment manager is buying. This becomes clear if we rewrite (7.11) as

$$(1 - e^{-r_1}) \times (1 - \alpha)N = \alpha M \times P_0^a \left[I_0 \left(1 + \frac{F}{\alpha} \right) \right]. \qquad (7.12)$$

The term on the left-hand side equals the present value of the interest the derivatives firm would normally have paid on a loan in the amount of $(1 - \alpha)N$.

In trying to solve the attainable participation rate from (7.11) a problem arises. Because the participation rate appears in the puts' strike we cannot simply calculate what the upside capture will be, but have to revert to some numerical method to find the value of the participation rate that fits the equation. There are various methods to solve this problem. The simplest one is known as the **bisection method**, which is nothing more than a systematic way of guessing. First, we make a high guess h and a low guess l and check how well they fit the equation. When indeed one is too low and the other is too high we now guess the correct value to be right in between, i.e. our next guess is $(h + l)/2$. When after checking this guess is too low our next guess is in between $(h + l)/2$ and h, i.e. $(3h + l)/4$. When this is too high our next guess is in between $(h + l)/2$ and $(3h + l)/4$. We keep doing this until we arrive at the correct value.

Under the assumption of a -5% floor rate the participation rate will be equal to 0.63. A graph of the resulting portfolio return to the investment manager can be found in Figure 7.6. The straight line represents the return if the portfolio had been fully invested in equity. The kinked line is the return profile which we structured. The graph clearly shows that if the index goes down the investment manager is protected against a loss

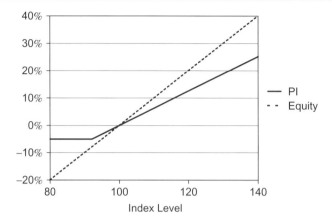

Figure 7.6 Return profile for portfolio insurance with internal funding

higher than 5%. On the other hand, if the index goes up the portfolio insurance payoff will be lower than the payoff of a straight equity investment. The difference can be interpreted as the cost of the portfolio insurance.

When it comes to derivatives structures, it is fashionable to look at the effect that the inclusion of derivatives has on the **probability distribution of the overall portfolio return**. All this takes is to combine the overall payoff profile with the return distribution of the index. There is one problem though. Probabilities are nothing more than numbers (summing to 1) that people assign to events. The occurrence of an index return higher than 10% does not have a certain probability by its very nature. It only gets a probability if we assign one. Different people assign different probabilities to the same event. Some people derive their probabilities from history. If the index went up by more than 10% in 30 out of 50 years they will say that the probability of the index going up by more than 10% next year is 60%. This suggests an objectivity that from a purely logical perspective is not there. Different people use different methods to arrive at the probabilities they attribute to events. Whatever method is followed, however, information is the key element. Suppose somebody was about to throw a dice. A person who thought there was nothing wrong with the dice might say that the probability of a six was one in six. Somebody who knew that the dice was fixed, however, would tell you that the probability of a six was in fact one in five. Somebody who knew that the dice was fixed and who also knew that the person throwing the dice would throw it in a very specific way aimed at throwing a six might even claim that it was one in four. Going back to our return distribution, this means that there are many return distributions we can come up with, depending on whose index return distribution we use to start with. **Since derivatives structuring is concerned with designing products that fit sometimes very specific views and preferences it does not make sense to evaluate all these products in the same way using the same index return distribution**. We therefore leave this to the reader.

Having found the value of the participation rate implied by the budget equation we can calculate the index value where the investment manager will start to participate in the market, i.e. the highest index value which still generates a payoff equal to the chosen floor value. The latter can be calculated as

$$I_1^* = I_0 \left(1 + \frac{F}{\alpha}\right),$$ (7.13)

which is of course equal to the puts' strike. As can be seen from the graph in Figure 7.6, in the above example I_1^* would be equal to 92. In other words, the index will have to end above a level of 92 for the investment manager to show a return higher than -5%.

The attainable upside capture depends heavily on the floor rate chosen. Figure 7.7 provides insight into the trade-off between the floor rate and the participation rate. It shows that **the higher the floor rate, the lower the participation rate** and therefore the higher the price level where the investment manager starts to participate in the market.

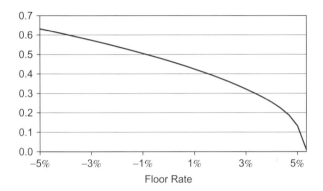

Figure 7.7 Trade-off between floor rate and participation rate for portfolio insurance with internal funding

There are two ways to interpret this result; either via the budget equation or via the expected payoff of the structure.

- Buying puts prevents the investment manager from investing his total net asset value in equity. The higher the floor rate, the more expensive the puts, the lower the number of shares that can be bought, the longer it takes to match the floor value, and the less is gained afterwards. With a high floor rate the remaining profit potential will be very limited. Actually, with a floor rate equal to the interest rate the participation rate will be zero to prevent the possibility of arbitrage.
- Our pricing shortcut says that for pricing purposes the expected return on any financial asset should be taken to be equal to the interest rate. The higher the floor rate, the higher the expected payoff on the above structure. However, since the initial investment is fixed, the expected payoff is fixed as well. The participation rate will therefore have to come down to compensate.

Given budget equation (7.11) it is easy to see how the participation rate depends on the pricing environment. If **interest rates** go up, the left-hand side of the equation does not change. On the right-hand side, however, the present value of $(1 - \alpha)N$ drops and so does the price of puts. To balance the budget equation, the participation rate will therefore have to increase. If **implied volatility** increases, puts get more expensive. This means the right-hand side of (7.11) becomes bigger than the left-hand side. To make both sides equal again, the participation rate will have to come down. If we introduce **dividends** the price of puts goes up. However, since the investment manager is holding αM shares of the index he will have the present value of the dividend on those shares available to spend on the derivatives contract. On balance, the right-hand side will therefore come to outweigh the left-hand side, which allows the participation rate to increase. Of course, we can reach the same conclusions by looking at the expected payoff.

External Funding

Instead of paying for the desired downside protection out of the investment portfolio, the investment manager could invest all his money in equity and simply take out a loan to buy the desired protection with. We refer to this as **external funding**. External funding yields the following payoff to the investment manager

$$X_1 = N \times \left(1 + \text{Max}\left[F, \frac{I_1 - I_0}{I_0} - \beta\right]\right),\tag{7.14}$$

where β denotes the **cost of the strategy** attributed to the index return. This payoff differs significantly from the one we had before. Instead of proportionately, the index return is now reduced by a fixed percentage.

To solve for the cost of the strategy we can follow the same procedure as before. First, we determine the exact nature of the derivatives contract required and then we solve the cost of the strategy from the resulting budget equation. The investment manager invests the initial value of his portfolio fully in equity. This yields a payoff at maturity equal to

$$H_1 = M \times I_1 = N \times \left(1 + \frac{I_1 - I_0}{I_0}\right).\tag{7.15}$$

To provide the investment manager with the payoff given by (7.14) the derivatives firm will therefore need to pay him at maturity

$$V_1 = X_1 - H_1 = M \times \text{Max}\,[0, I_0(1 + F + \beta) - I_1] - \beta N.\tag{7.16}$$

The first part of the above expression is the payoff of M **ordinary puts** with a strike of $I_0(1 + F + \beta)$. The second part is a fixed amount which we can interpret as the result of a loan which the derivatives firm provides to the investment manager.

Knowing what the payoff of the required derivatives contract looks like, and given that the investment manager invests all his money in equity and therefore has no money left to spend on the derivatives contract, the budget equation for this case is given by

$$0 = M \times P_0^a[I_0(1 + F + \beta), 1] - e^{-r_1}\beta N,\tag{7.17}$$

where r_1 is the 1-year offer rate which the derivatives firm uses to calculate the present value of a cash inflow of βN one year from now. Taking a closer look at this expression we see that **the derivatives firm not only sells the investment manager the required puts but at the same time lends him the money to buy them**. The size of the loan is given by the second term on the right-hand side, meaning that β is nothing more than the price of the puts involved (expressed as a percentage of the index value) plus one year's interest. This becomes clear if we rewrite the budget equation as

$$\beta = e^{r_1} \times \frac{P_0^a[I_0(1 + F + \beta), 1]}{I_0}.\tag{7.18}$$

Solving for the cost of the strategy under the assumption of a -5% floor rate yields a cost percentage of 6.58%. This consists of 6.26% for the put plus 0.32% interest.

The highest index value for which the payoff still equals the floor value can in this case be calculated as

$$I_1^* = I_0 \left(1 + F + \beta\right), \tag{7.19}$$

which, as before, is equal to the puts' strike. In the above example I_1^* is equal to 101.58. In other words, the index will have to rise above a level of 101.58 for the investment manager to show a return higher than -5%. A graph of the return to the investment manager can be found in Figure 7.8. The graph clearly shows that with external funding the investment manager retains the same participation rate as with straight equity investment, but that the index level where he actually starts to participate is higher.

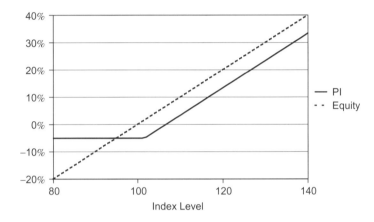

Figure 7.8   Return profile for portfolio insurance with external funding

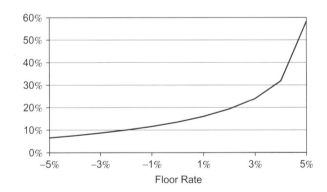

Figure 7.9   Trade-off between floor rate and cost percentage for portfolio insurance with external funding

Figure 7.9 shows the trade-off between the floor rate and the cost of the strategy. It shows that **the cost of the strategy increases with the floor rate**, especially when the floor rate gets above 0%. As with internal funding, there are two ways to interpret this result. First, we can look at the budget equation. If the floor rate goes up, the puts required in the structure become more expensive. This raises the cost of the strategy since the latter are equal to the put price plus one year's interest. Second, we can use our pricing shortcut. Since the initial investment is given and the expected return should be equal to the interest rate, the expected payoff of the structure is fixed in advance. This means that to compensate for the rise in the expected payoff caused by a higher floor rate the cost of the strategy will have to go up.

Turning back to the budget equation to see how the cost of the strategy depends on the pricing environment, we see that if **volatility** goes up, puts become more expensive and the cost of the strategy goes up as well. If **interest rates** rise, put prices drop and so does the cost of the strategy. Finally, if we introduce **dividends**, puts become more expensive but the investment manager will now have the present value of the dividends on M shares in the index available to spend on the derivatives contract. On balance this means that the cost of the strategy can come down.

It is interesting to compare internal and external funding in terms of (a) the index level where the investment manager starts to benefit from a higher index value and (b) how much is gained if the index at maturity exceeds that level. With external funding the investment manager gains 1% for every per cent the index return exceeds $1 + F + \beta$, while with internal funding the investment manager gains α% for every per cent the index return exceeds $1 + F/\alpha$. Since the gain is higher for external funding, the index level at which the investment manager starts to benefit from a higher index value must be higher as well. If not, external funding would offer a higher expected return than internal funding, which is not allowed. Figure 7.10 shows the index values below which internal funding provides a more advantageous payoff than external funding. The latter are easily calculated as $I_0(1 - \beta/(\alpha - 1))$. As is clear from the graph, these break-even levels depend heavily on the floor rate chosen. The higher the floor rate, the higher the break-even price. Given that buyers of portfolio insurance will do so out of fear for a bear market, **internal funding will typically be the most sensible choice**.

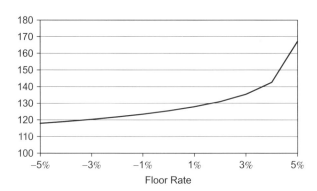

Figure 7.10   Break-even prices for internal and external funding as a function of floor rate

7.4.2   The Best of Equity and Bonds

So far we have concentrated on providing the investment manager with the best of equity and cash. We can use the same approach to provide him with the best of equity and another asset class, like bonds for example. Suppose we had two asset classes: equity as represented by some equity index with time t value I_t^1 and bonds as represented by some bond index with time t value I_t^2. We could set out to structure the investment manager a derivatives contract which, when combined with his own investments, paid him the highest of the returns on both indices, i.e. a payoff equal to

$$X_1 = N \times \left(1 + \text{Max} \left[\frac{I_1^1 - I_0^1}{I_0^1}, \frac{I_1^2 - I_0^2}{I_0^2} \right] \right). \tag{7.20}$$

It will not come as a shock that the above payoff is not attainable. If this was not the case we could sell one index short and use the proceeds to purchase the above payoff, thereby obtaining the possibility of a profit without the countervailing possibility of a loss at a zero investment. If the index that was shorted turned out to be the best performing one, we would lose nothing, while in the other case we would gain the difference between both returns.

Internal Funding

To match the present value of the above payoff with the available net asset value we will have to reduce the payoff. We can do this in the same way as before. Using **internal funding** to match the value of the payoff to the investment manager with the initial value of his portfolio yields the payoff function

$$X_1 = N \times \left(1 + \text{Max} \left[\alpha_1 \left(\frac{I_1^1 - I_0^1}{I_0^1} \right), \alpha_2 \left(\frac{I_1^2 - I_0^2}{I_0^2} \right) \right] \right). \tag{7.21}$$

Note that both indices have their own participation rate. Suppose the investment manager invested a fraction α_1 of his money in the equity market. This would yield a payoff at maturity of

$$H_1 = \alpha_1 M \times I_1^1 = \alpha_1 N \times \left(1 + \frac{I_1^1 - I_0^1}{I_0^1} \right). \tag{7.22}$$

Assuming that $I_0^1 = I_0^2 = I_0$, to provide the investment manager with the desired payoff the derivatives firm therefore needs to pay him an amount equal to

$$V_1 = X_1 - H_1 = (1 - \alpha_1)N + M \times \text{Max} \left[0, \alpha_2 \left(I_1^2 - I_0 \right) - \alpha_1 \left(I_1^1 - I_0 \right) \right]. \tag{7.23}$$

The first part is a fixed amount which we can again think of as a loan which the investment manager provides to the derivatives firm. The second part is a payoff we have not encountered before. We can see it as the payoff of a contract which allows the investment manager to trade in the change in value of his equity portfolio for the change in value of the bond portfolio if one turned out higher than the other.

Although the above expression shows clearly what goes on, it is often rewritten as

$$V_1 = (1 - \alpha_1)N + M \times \text{Max} \left[0, \left(\alpha_2 I_1^2 - \alpha_1 I_1^1 \right) - I_0 (\alpha_2 - \alpha_1) \right]. \tag{7.24}$$

The second part of this expression equals the payoff of a contract where at maturity the derivatives firm pays the difference between α_2 times the value of the bond index and α_1

times the equity index, the investment manager pays a fixed amount and the investment manager has the right to cancel the contract. A contract like this is known as a **spread call option** because it is like an ordinary call where the reference index is the (weighted) spread between both indices.

Note that if we set $\alpha_1 = \alpha_2 = \alpha$ things would simplify considerably. In that case the payoff of the required derivatives contract would become equal to

$$V_1 = (1 - \alpha)N + \alpha M \times \text{Max}\left[0, I_1^2 - I_1^1\right]. \tag{7.25}$$

Again this introduces a new payoff. The second part of the above payoff is equal to the payoff of a contract where at maturity the investment manager pays the derivatives firm the value of the equity index, the derivatives firm pays the value of the bond index, and the investment manager has the right to cancel the contract. A contract like this is known as an **exchange option** because in a way it offers the investment manager the opportunity to exchange the equity index for the bond index.

Knowing that the investment manager has $(1 - \alpha_1)N$ to spend on the derivatives contract, the budget equation is given by

$$(1 - \alpha_1)N = e^{-r_1}(1 - \alpha_1)N + M \times SPC_0^a[I_0(\alpha_2 - \alpha_1), \alpha_1, \alpha_2, 1], \tag{7.26}$$

where $SPC_0^a[K, a, b, T]$ denotes the derivatives firm's offer for a spread call with strike K, weights a and b, and time to maturity T. The above expression says that the present value of the derivatives contract which we structured must be equal to the loan which the investment manager implicitly provides to the derivatives firm. The derivatives firm obtains a loan from the investment manager, but instead of interest it pays the latter the payoff of M spread options. The budget equation therefore equates the present value of the interest the derivatives firm would normally have paid on a loan in the amount of $(1 - \alpha_1)N$ with the value of the spread options.

Since there are now two participation rates instead of one we have some freedom in setting these parameters. We can freely choose one and the budget equation will then tell us what the other has to be. This is comparable to what we did before when we studied portfolio insurance: we selected the floor rate and the budget equation subsequently told us what that choice implied for the participation rate. To get an idea of the trade-off between α_1 and α_2 we have to price the spread option. There is nothing unusual about this except that, since there are now two indices, we need to say something about the correlation between them. Figure 7.11 shows the trade-off between α_1 and α_2 for implied correlation coefficients of -0.5, 0 and 0.5. We assume that bonds have half the volatility of equity, i.e. 10%. The straight line depicts the values where both participation rates are equal.

Figure 7.11 shows that choosing a relatively high participation rate on one index reduces the participation rate on the other index. If one participation rate goes up the other goes down at an increasing rate, which makes it clear that **one needs a good reason not to set α_1 and α_2 equal to each other**. The trade-off between both participation rates is not symmetrical around the 45° line. For example, suppose we had zero correlation and we set $\alpha_2 = 0.4$. In that case $\alpha_1 = 0.33$. If we set $\alpha_1 = 0.4$, however, the highest possible value for α_2 would only be 0.28. **Bond participation comes cheaper than equity participation** because bonds are less volatile. This can be understood if we realize that in the extreme case where the participation rate on one index is zero the participation rate on the other index will be equal to that in the case of portfolio insurance with a zero floor rate. Because

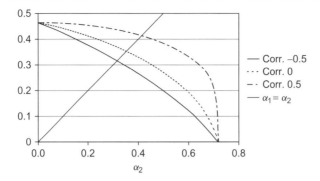

Figure 7.11   Trade-off between α_1 and α_2 for best-of-equity-and-bonds with internal funding

portfolio insurance boils down to buying ordinary puts and, as we saw in Figure 7.4, put prices rise with volatility, the portfolio insurance participation rate drops when volatility increases. If we choose a low participation rate on equity, we are left with portfolio insurance on a bond index. Given that the bond volatility is relatively low, this allows for a relatively high participation rate on the bond index. On the other hand, if we choose a low participation rate on bonds we end up with portfolio insurance on an equity index. Because equity has a relatively high volatility, this yields a relatively low participation rate on the equity index.

Another point concerns the **correlation** between both indices. From the graph we see that the way in which one participation rate drops if the other is raised depends heavily on the degree of correlation between both index returns. The same goes for the value at which α_1 and α_2 are equal, which is 0.32 when the correlation coefficient between both indices is -0.5, 0.35 with zero correlation, and 0.41 with a correlation of 0.5. This reflects the fact that the less correlated both indices are, the more likely it is that they will move away from each other over the year. This raises the expected payoff, which in turn needs to be compensated by lower participation rates. The budget equation tells a similar story. The lower the correlation, the more expensive the spread option which the investment manager obtains.

Looking at the participation rates again, the result is not very encouraging. When both indices are uncorrelated and both participation rates are equal, the investment manager gets paid only 0.35 times the highest index return. To find a way to improve the participation rate we have to take another look at the budget equation. This makes it clear that we can improve the level of participation by increasing the structure's time to maturity. If we increase the time to maturity, the present value of $(1 - \alpha_1)N$ will drop. Similar to what we saw before in the case of an ordinary call, the spread option's price will increase but at a decreasing rate. On balance therefore, the left-hand side of (7.26) will come to exceed the right-hand side, meaning that given α_1 we can raise α_2.

Figure 7.12 shows the trade-off between α_1 and α_2 for times to maturity of one, two and three years assuming zero correlation between both indices. From the graph we see that the longer the maturity the higher the participation rates can be. With one year to maturity both participation rates are equal at 0.35. With two years to maturity this happens at 0.43, while with three years to maturity it happens at 0.48. With five years to maturity both participation rates would be equal at 0.53. This implies that the best-of-equity-and-bonds structure is better suited for long investment horizons.

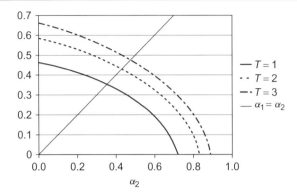

Figure 7.12 Trade-off between α_1 and α_2 for best-of-equity-and-bonds with internal funding for three times to maturity

External Funding

We continue with a best-of-equity-and-bonds payoff with **external funding**. The total payoff would in that case be equal to

$$X_1 = N \times \left(1 + \text{Max} \left[\frac{I_1^1 - I_0^1}{I_0^1} - \beta_1, \frac{I_1^2 - I_0^2}{I_0^2} - \beta_2 \right] \right), \tag{7.27}$$

where β_i denotes the cost of the strategy attributed to index i. When the investment manager invests all his money in the equity market this yields a payoff at maturity of

$$H_1 = M \times I_1^1 = N \times \left(1 + \frac{I_1^1 - I_0^1}{I_0^1} \right). \tag{7.28}$$

Assuming that $I_0^1 = I_0^2 = I_0$ this means the derivatives firm needs to pay him an amount equal to

$$V_1 = X_1 - H_1 = M \times \text{Max} \left[0, \left(I_1^2 - I_1^1 \right) - I_0(\beta_2 - \beta_1) \right] - \beta_1 N. \tag{7.29}$$

The first part of this payoff is the payoff of M **spread call options** with strike $I_0(\beta_2 - \beta_1)$. The second part is a fixed amount. As we saw earlier in the case of portfolio insurance, the derivatives firm sells the investment manager options but because the latter invests all his money in equity the derivatives firm has to lend him the money to purchase these options. Note that if we set $\beta_1 = \beta_2 = \beta$ the payoff of the derivatives contract simplifies to

$$V_1 = M \times \text{Max} \left[0, I_1^2 - I_1^1 \right] - \beta N, \tag{7.30}$$

which takes us back to the **exchange option** again.

With all the investment manager's money invested in the equity market the relevant budget equation is given by

$$0 = M \times SPC_0^a[I_0(\beta_2 - \beta_1), 1, 1, 1] - e^{-r_1}\beta_1 N, \tag{7.31}$$

which means that, similar to what we saw in the case of portfolio insurance,

$$\beta_1 = e^{r_1} \times \frac{SPC_0^a[I_0(\beta_2 - \beta_1), 1, 1, 1]}{I_0}. \tag{7.32}$$

Figure 7.13 shows the trade-off between β_1 and β_2 for correlation coefficients of -0.5, 0 and 0.5. The straight line depicts the values where both are equal. From the figure we see that if we attribute relatively high costs to one index we can get away with attributing relatively low costs to the other index. Although it seems to be a good working approximation, the trade-off is not completely symmetrical around the 45° line. For example, if with zero correlation we set $\beta_2 = 15\%$ we see that $\beta_1 = 5\%$, while if we set $\beta_1 = 15\%$ we get $\beta_2 = 5.7\%$.

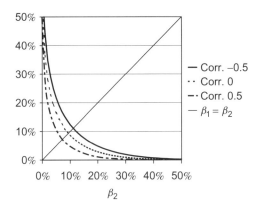

Figure 7.13   Trade-off between β_1 and β_2 for best-of-equity-and-bonds with external funding

The above shows that **bonds are better in absorbing costs than equity**. This reflects their relatively low volatility. The higher the costs attributed to an index, the less likely it is that the index's part of the payoff will actually pay off. The overall payoff therefore becomes very much like that of a straight investment in the other index, which does not carry any costs. The lower an index's volatility the earlier this effect kicks in. With respect to the correlation between both indices we see a similar response as in the case of internal funding. The lower the correlation, the more expensive the spread option which the investment manager obtains, and therefore the higher the costs of the strategy and the higher the value at which β_1 and β_2 are equal. With a correlation coefficient of -0.5 β_1 and β_2 are equal at 11.1%, with zero correlation at 9.4%, and with a correlation of 0.5 at 7.2%.

Taking another look at Figure 7.13 we are confronted with the same problem as with internal funding: the costs of the strategy are extremely high. As before, we can remedy this by increasing the time to maturity. The price of the spread option will increase, but less than proportionately. This means that on a per annum basis the costs will come down. Assuming zero correlation, Figure 7.14 shows the trade-off between the per annum costs of the strategy for one, two and three years to maturity. The graph clearly shows the drop in per annum costs as time to maturity increases. With one year to maturity both cost percentages are equal at 9.4%. With two years to maturity this drops to 7%, while for three years it drops further to 6%. For five years it would only be 5%. This confirms that **the best-of-equity-and-bonds payoff is primarily a longer dated structure**.

Before we move on, it should be noted that internal and external funding can also be combined in a single payoff. We could, for example, structure a contract that provided

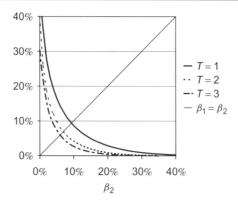

Figure 7.14 Trade-off between β_1 and β_2 for best-of-equity-and-bonds with external funding for three times to maturity

the investment manager with a payoff equal to

$$X_1 = N \times \left(1 + \text{Max} \left[\alpha_1 \left(\frac{I_1^1 - I_0^1}{I_0^1} \right) - \beta_1, \alpha_2 \left(\frac{I_1^2 - I_0^2}{I_0^2} \right) - \beta_2 \right] \right). \qquad (7.33)$$

With the investment manager investing a fraction α_1 of his money in the equity market this would require a derivatives contract with a payoff equal to

$$V_1 = ((1 - \alpha_1) - \beta_1)N + M \times \text{Max} \left[0, \left(\alpha_2 I_1^2 - \alpha_1 I_1^1 \right) - I_0((\alpha_2 - \alpha_1) - (\beta_2 - \beta_1)) \right]. \qquad (7.34)$$

This payoff is a combination of the internal funding and the external funding payoffs we encountered earlier. The first part is a fixed amount and the second part equals the payoff of M **spread call options**. As before, things simplify considerably if we set $\alpha_1 = \alpha_2$ and $\beta_1 = \beta_2$.

The best-of-equity-and-bonds payoff provides the investment manager with the same performance he would have obtained if he had known at the beginning of the year which index was going to show the best performance, minus a cost factor. Intuitively, we can see these costs as the fee of a clairvoyant which the investment manager consulted at the beginning of the year. A priori there is no way to escape these costs. As is clear from Figure 7.13, if we attributed no costs to the first index, we would be forced to raise the costs attributed to the second index. In other words, the payoff will not outperform the payoff of a buy-and-hold strategy under all circumstances. When the returns on both indices are more or less equal, the portfolio return is depressed by the costs of the strategy. This makes the portfolio perform worse than a buy-and-hold strategy, which is costless. The essence of this remark is that derivatives do not provide a free lunch. **Although derivatives allow for sophisticated exposure management, they cannot and do not guarantee superior results under all scenarios**.

7.4.3 The Best of Equity, Bonds and Cash

There is no reason why we should limit ourselves to payoffs that provide the best of two asset classes. We could for example combine both the previous cases into one and structure a best-of-equity, bonds-and-cash payoff equal to

$$X_1 = N \times \left(1 + \text{Max} \left[F, \frac{I_1^1 - I_0^1}{I_0^1}, \frac{I_1^2 - I_0^2}{I_0^2} \right] \right), \tag{7.35}$$

where as before I_t^1 denotes the time t value of some equity index and I_t^2 the time t value of some bond index. The above payoff provides the investment manager with the best of both worlds. The cash asset provides a floor value while both risky assets offer the investment manager upside potential. As before, this payoff is not attainable since it offers too much upside and not enough downside. This means we have to revert to internal or external funding techniques again. We will only discuss internal funding. The case of external funding is left to the reader as an exercise.

Using internal funding to match the value of the payoff to the investment manager with the initial value of his portfolio yields the following payoff function

$$X_1 = N \times \left(1 + \text{Max} \left[F, \alpha_1 \left(\frac{I_1^1 - I_0^1}{I_0^1} \right), \alpha_2 \left(\frac{I_1^2 - I_0^2}{I_0^2} \right) \right] \right). \tag{7.36}$$

Suppose the investment manager invested a fraction α_1 of his money in the equity market. To provide him with the above payoff the derivatives firm would in that case have to pay him an amount equal to (assuming that $I_0^1 = I_0^2 = I_0$)

$$V_1 = (1 - \alpha_1)N + M \times \text{Max} \left[0, (\alpha_2 I_1^2 - \alpha_1 I_1^1) - I_0(\alpha_2 - \alpha_1), \alpha_1 \left(I_0 \left(1 + \frac{F}{\alpha_1} \right) - I_1^1 \right) \right]. \tag{7.37}$$

If we compare this expression with (7.10) and (7.24) we see that it contains elements of both. Apart from the usual fixed amount we now have a second term which looks like a spread call and an ordinary put at the same time. The spread option part allows the investment manager to trade in the result on his equity portfolio for that on bonds, and the put option part allows him to trade in his equity for cash. A contract with a payoff like this is known as an **alternative option**. This name stems from the fact that it provides the buyer with a payoff equal to the best of the payoffs of two alternative options; a spread call and an ordinary put.

Knowing that the investment manager has $(1 - \alpha_1)N$ to spend on the derivatives contract, the budget equation is given by

$$(1 - \alpha_1)N = e^{-r_1}(1 - \alpha_1)N + M \times AO_0^a[A, B, 1], \tag{7.38}$$

where

$$A = \text{Max} \left[0, (\alpha_2 I_1^2 - \alpha_1 I_1^1) - I_0(\alpha_2 - \alpha_1) \right],$$

$$B = \text{Max} \left[0, \alpha_1 \left(I_0 \left(1 + \frac{F}{\alpha_1} \right) - I_1^1 \right) \right],$$

with $AO_0^a[A, B, T]$ denoting the derivatives firm's offer for an alternative option which at time T pays the best of the payoffs A and B. The mechanics of the budget equation are the same as before. The derivatives firm obtains a loan from the investment manager, but instead of interest it pays the latter the payoff of M alternative options. The budget equation therefore equates the present value of the interest the derivatives firm would normally have paid on a loan in the amount of $(1 - \alpha_1)N$ with the value of the alternative options.

We now have a floor rate and two participation rates to choose. Figure 7.15 provides an indication of the trade-off between both participation rates for a floor rate of either -3% or $+3\%$, assuming an implied correlation coefficient of 0. Similar to what we saw before in the case of portfolio insurance and the best of equity and bonds, choosing a high participation rate on one index reduces the participation rate on the other index, and the higher the floor rate the lower the participation. The important thing, however, is that for a floor rate of -3% the trade-off between both participation rates is no different from that in the case of the best of equity and bonds. Contrary to single index portfolio insurance, **even relatively high floor rates do not significantly reduce the upside participation**. This is even more clear from Figure 7.16, which shows the values where both participation rates are equal as a function of the floor rate. The reason why the presence of the floor is only felt with high floor rates is that since the structure pays off the best of two indices it is unlikely that the floor will come into play. From a marketing perspective this is an important observation as it allows one to offer the investment manager solid downside protection at (almost) no extra cost.

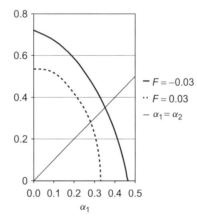

Figure 7.15   Trade-off between α_1 and α_2 for best-of-equity-bonds-and-cash with internal funding

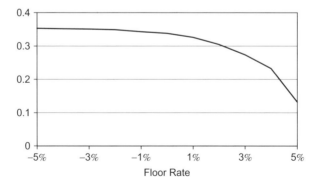

Figure 7.16   Values where α_1 and α_2 are equal as a function of floor rate

Before we move on it is important to emphasize **the power of the approach advocated here**. An alternative option paying the best of an ordinary put and a spread option is a very unusual contract. As far as we know, the pricing of an option like this has not been discussed anywhere in the literature. Traditional building block-based structurers would not have come up with the above solution because the option is not in their toolbox. This is no hurdle for the cash flow-based structurer, however. Thinking in terms of cash flows instead of a fixed set of products led us directly to the alternative option.

7.5 YIELD ENHANCEMENT

An investment manager who thinks that the market is going down can take a number of actions. As discussed in Chapter 6, he can sell a forward where he pays the index value at maturity in return for the index value at initiation. Entering into a contract like this eliminates both the downside risk on his portfolio as well as the portfolio's upside potential. After all, selling a forward is like selling the index and banking the proceeds. The investment manager could ask the derivatives firm for the right to cancel the contract at maturity, but this would mean paying a hefty premium. We discussed this before. If we compare these two alternatives it becomes clear why the protection offered by the forward comes for free: it takes away the upside potential to finance the downside protection. This points us to a third course of action: the investment manager could sell off his upside potential and use the proceeds as a buffer against a drop in the value of his portfolio.

Suppose the investment manager thought that the market was in for a correction over the next 12 months. In other words, he considers it likely for the market to fall and quite unlikely for it to rise. As he thinks the market will not go up, selling off the portfolio's upside potential in return for a fixed amount of money makes a lot of sense. The investment manager gets paid for giving up something that is of little or no value to him. Formally, this means we are now looking at an overall payoff to the investment manager equal to

$$X_1 = N \times \left(1 + \text{Min} \left[0, \frac{I_1 - I_0}{I_0} \right] + B_1 \right), \tag{7.39}$$

where the **buffer rate** B_1 is fixed in advance. The first part of this expression does not look very encouraging. The investment manager fully participates if the market drops but he does not participate if the market rises. Whatever happens, however, he will receive a payment equal to $N \times B_1$ from the derivatives firm which he can use as a buffer. This means that, compared to doing nothing, **the investment manager will be better off under all scenarios except those where the market rises by more than the buffer rate**.

Given that the investment manager invests in equity himself, the derivatives contract for him to enter into is a contract with a payoff equal to

$$V_1 = M \times (\text{Min} \, [0, I_0 - I_1] + B_1 \times I_0), \tag{7.40}$$

where, as always, the multiplier M equals the number of shares in the index which the investment manager's portfolio will buy. The first part says that if the index goes up the investment manager will have to pay away his gains to the derivatives firm. If the index goes down the investment manager need not pay anything but neither does he receive anything. It is this last twitch that makes this contract different from selling a forward. On top of this the investment manager receives an unconditional amount equal to $N \times B_1$.

To determine the buffer rate which the investment manager will be able to obtain we only need to rewrite the contract payoff to the investor as

$$V_1 = M \times (B_1 \times I_0 - \text{Max}\,[0, I_1 - I_0]). \tag{7.41}$$

This shows that the payoff to the investor is nothing more than a fixed amount plus the payoff of a short position in M **ordinary calls** with strike I_0. Since the investment manager will not want to pay for the above payoff, the budget equation from which we have to solve the buffer rate is equal to

$$0 = M \times (e^{-r_1}(B_1 \times I_0) - C_0^b[I_0, 1]), \tag{7.42}$$

where $C_0^b[K, T]$ denotes the derivatives firm's bid for an ordinary call with strike K and time to maturity T. If we rewrite this budget equation as

$$B_1 = e^{r_1} \times \frac{C_0^b[I_0, 1]}{I_0}, \tag{7.43}$$

it becomes clear what is really going on here. The investment manager sells M ATM calls to the derivatives firm and in return the latter pays him a fixed amount of $N \times B_1$ at maturity. Since the derivatives firm pays nothing else, this fixed amount must be the call premium plus one year's interest on that premium. Under the assumptions made, selling ATM calls will yield the investment manager 10.45% upfront premium income. With 5% interest on top of that this means that by selling ATM calls he will be able to create a buffer against a downturn of the market over the next year of 10.97%. Figure 7.17 shows the resulting overall return to the investment manager.

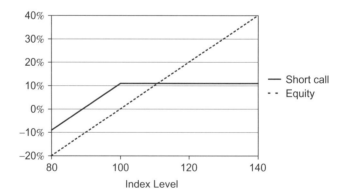

Figure 7.17   Return profile after writing ATM call

Although much less common, there is no reason why the investment manager could not write more complex derivatives. We will discuss a large number of them throughout the remainder of the book. The proceeds from doing so could be substantially higher than the proceeds from writing ordinary call options. However, one should always be aware of the fact that, apart from imbalances in demand and supply, if an option can be sold dearer it is because it offers its buyer a higher expected payoff. Since derivatives is a **zero-sum game**, where the buyer's gain is the seller's loss, this means that unless the buyer and the seller differ significantly in their expectations, the option offers its seller a higher expected loss.

7.6   REDUCING THE RISK OF WRITING CALLS

Writing ATM calls introduces two kinds of risk. First, the drop in the index may exceed the buffer rate. In that case the investment manager will still lose. For our investment manager this is not a serious problem as he is not so much interested in absolute performance as in **relative performance**, i.e. performance relative to some benchmark. As long as he does better than the benchmark he is fine. The second problem is more serious. If the index goes up instead of down the investment manager might end up far behind on his benchmark. In this section we discuss some alternatives that reduce this risk.

7.6.1   Raising the Strike

One way to reduce the risk of relative underperformance is to sell off only part of the upside potential. For example, the investment manager could decide to sell only the upside above a specific index value $I^1 > I_0$. To structure a contract that accomplishes this we do not have to go through the above procedure again as it is obvious that we only have to raise the strike of the calls which the investment manager sells from I_0 to I^1. Instead of ATM calls he should now write OTM calls. Doing so would yield an overall payoff to the investment manager of

$$X_1 = N \times \left(1 + \text{Min} \left[\left(\frac{I^1 - I_0}{I_0} \right), \left(\frac{I_1 - I_0}{I_0} \right) \right] + e^{r_1} \times \frac{C_0^b[I^1, 1]}{I_0} \right). \qquad (7.44)$$

Since $I^1 > I_0$ this payoff can be higher than the previous one. However, since the expected payoff is not allowed to change, this implies that the investment manager must receive less premium for the calls that he sells. An example of how the buffer rate can be expected to react to a higher strike can be found in Figure 7.1, which shows that ordinary call prices fall when the strike goes up. Figure 7.18 shows the overall return to the investment manager, assuming the investment manager sells calls that are 10% OTM at a premium of 6.04%.

7.6.2   Writing Less

Another variation is not to sell the upside on the whole portfolio but only on part of it. Another way to look at this is to say that instead of the full upside we only sell a fraction of it. The investment manager can accomplish this by simply selling less than M options. Suppose that instead of M he sold $M^* < M$ OTM calls with strike $I^1 > I_0$. This would produce an overall payoff equal to

$$X_1 = (N - N^*) \times \left(1 + \left(\frac{I_1 - I_0}{I_0} \right) \right)$$

$$+ N^* \times \left(1 + \text{Min} \left[\left(\frac{I^1 - I_0}{I_0} \right), \left(\frac{I_1 - I_0}{I_0} \right) \right] + e^{r_1} \times \frac{C_0^b[I^1, 1]}{I_0} \right), \qquad (7.45)$$

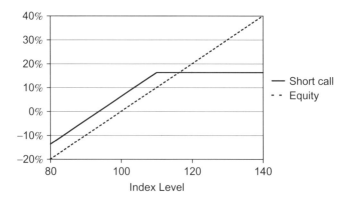

Figure 7.18   Return profile after writing OTM call

where $N^* = M^* \times I_0$. The first part is the payoff of the equity on which the upside was not sold off, while the second part covers the equity that was stripped of its upside. If the index was higher than I^1 the investment manager would end the year with

$$X_1 = (M - M^*) \times I_1 + M^* \times (I^1 + e^{r_1} \times C_0^b[I^1, 1]), \qquad (7.46)$$

and therefore still have some participation in the rise of the market. If we set $M^* = 0.5m$ and $I^1 = 110$ this structure would still generate the investment manager 3.02% upfront premium income. A graph of the resulting overall return to the investment manager can be found in Figure 7.19.

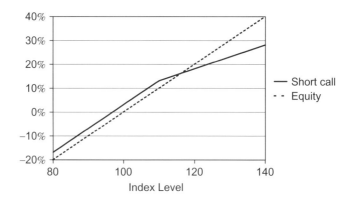

Figure 7.19   Return profile after writing partial OTM call

7.6.3   Piecewise Linear Segmentation

So far we have sold the upside above an index level of I^1. We can, however, also introduce a second index level $I^2 > I^1 > I_0$ and only sell off the profit potential between I^1 and I^2. Suppose the investment manager wanted to sell his profit potential between these two index levels but not above. In that case he would have to go after an overall payoff of

$$X_1 = N \times \left(1 + \text{Max}\left[\left(\frac{I_1 - I_0}{I_0}\right) - \left(\frac{I^2 - I^1}{I_0}\right),\right.\right.$$

$$\left.\left.\text{Min}\left[\left(\frac{I^1 - I_0}{I_0}\right), \left(\frac{I_1 - I_0}{I_0}\right)\right]\right] + B_1\right). \tag{7.47}$$

With this structure the investment manager participates in a market rise up to I^1 and then again from I^2 onwards. The derivatives contract required to provide this payoff is a contract with a payoff equal to

$$V_1 = M \times (\text{Min}\,[0, I^1 - I_1] + \text{Max}\,[0, I_1 - I^2] + B_1 \times I_0), \tag{7.48}$$

which can be rewritten as

$$V_1 = M \times \left(-\,\text{Max}\,[0, I_1 - I^1] + \text{Max}\,[0, I_1 - I^2] + B_1 \times I_0\right). \tag{7.49}$$

A package of a long call with one strike plus a short call with a higher strike is generally referred to as an **ordinary call spread**. The first part, which equals the payoff of a short call with strike I^1 plus a long call with strike I^2, is therefore nothing more than the payoff of a short call spread. If the index at maturity was below I^1 the payoff of the latter would be zero. If the index finished above I^1, however, the investment manager would have to pay the derivatives firm an amount equal to $M \times (I_1 - I^1)$, capped at $M \times (I^2 - I^1)$.

The next step is the budget equation. Since the above payoff has to have zero value the latter is given by

$$0 = M \times (e^{-r_1}(B_1 \times I_0) - CS_0^b[I^1, I^2, 1]), \tag{7.50}$$

where $CS_0^b[K^1, K^2, T]$ denotes the derivatives firm's bid for an ordinary call spread with lower strike K^1, upper strike K^2, and time to maturity T. Again, this yields a very easy expression for the buffer rate

$$B_1 = e^{r_1} \times \frac{CS_0^b[I^1, I^2, 1]}{I_0}. \tag{7.51}$$

If we set $I^1 = 105$ and $I^2 = 115$ this would generate 3.55% upfront premium income from the call spread and therefore a buffer rate of 3.73%. The resulting return profile is shown in Figure 7.20.

Since the payoff of the short call spread can be split into the payoff of a short call with strike I^1 and a long call with strike I^2, one might be inclined to calculate the amount of premium the investment manager can expect to receive from the derivatives firm as the difference between the derivatives firm's bid price for M calls with strike I^1 and the derivatives firm's offer price for M calls with strike I^2. Asking for quotes, however, one should always **ask for a bid on the call spread** and not for quotes on the component options. It is important to let the derivatives firm know that one intends to trade both options simultaneously, because the expected hedging costs and hedging risk of the call spread may differ significantly from the sum of the expected hedging costs and hedging

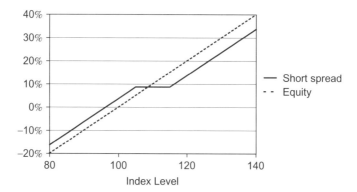

Figure 7.20 Return profile after writing call spread

risk of both options separately. As a result, the bid price for the call spread may not be equal to the difference between the bid price for a call with strike I^1 and the offer price for a call with strike I^2. Figure 7.21 gives an example of the prices one can expect for a call spread with lower strike $I^1 = 105$ as a function of the upper strike I^2.

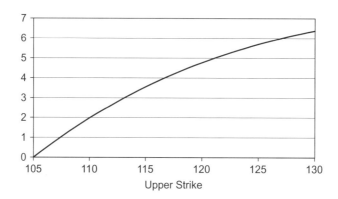

Figure 7.21 Price of call spread with lower strike 105 as a function of upper strike

We can take the above idea a lot further. Instead of one, we could introduce two or even more additional strikes and only sell the upside between some of them. We can also combine this with partial call writing as discussed before. This would mean that instead of selling all the upside potential between two strikes the investment manager would only sell a fraction. Because this does not add anything new, we will not go into this any further. The reader is encouraged to try out a few of the possibilities for himself.

7.6.4 Knock-In and Knock-Out Features

Another way to control the risk of an opportunity loss on a written call option is to introduce a knock-in or knock-out condition in the contract. As discussed in Chapter 3, with a knock-in condition the contract pays off **only if** some predefined event occurs. If it does not occur, the contract is cancelled. A knock-out condition is the mirror image and makes the contract pay **unless** some prespecified event occurs. If it does, the contract is cancelled. Although the event triggering a knock-in or knock-out can be anything, the most popular is the reaching of some barrier level by some barrier variable. When adding a barrier condition to an option contract, it is important that the relevant variables and parameters are all fully specified. **When the relevant variables and parameters are not fully specified, the contract is open to dispute** which may cause serious problems.

Suppose that instead of ordinary calls the investment manager wrote **knock-out calls**. We could say that the options that he wrote would knock out if at maturity the index had risen by 20% or more. In that case the contract payoff to the investment manager would be equal to

$$V_1 = M \times (B_1 \times I_0 - D \times \text{Max}\,[0, I_1 - I_0]), \tag{7.52}$$

where

$$D = 1, \quad \text{if } I_1 < 1.2I_0,$$
$$= 0, \quad \text{if } I_1 \geqslant 1.2I_0.$$

This is a **European knock-out barrier**. D takes on two values: 0 in case a knock-out is triggered and 1 if not. Without the knock-out feature D equals 1, which brings us back to the ordinary call. This looks very similar to writing a call spread with an upper strike of $1.2I_0$, but it is not. If the index ends above the upper strike a call spread will require the writer to pay the maximum amount. With the knock-out call, however, the whole option contract nullifies and the writer does not need to pay anything. **The knock-out call therefore offers more protection than the call spread**.

Because it offers more protection than a call spread the European knock-out call will yield a lower buffer rate. Figure 7.22 shows the price of a call spread with lower strike 105 and the price of an equivalent European knock-out call with a barrier equal to the call spread's upper strike. From the graph we see that due to the fact that the knock-out call does not just limit the loss but cancels the whole contract, there is a very significant price difference.

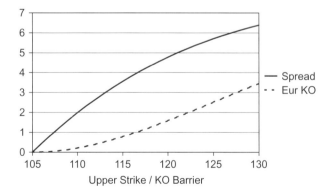

Figure 7.22   Price of call spread and equivalent European knock-out call

Although the European barrier already provides more protection than needed, we could take the concept one step further and say that the option will knock out whenever during its life the index hits the barrier. This means we are now working with an **American knock-out barrier**. The contract payoff to the investment manager would not really change, except that we would now have

$$D = 1, \quad \text{if } \forall j \, I_j < 1.2I_0,$$
$$= 0, \quad \text{if } \exists j \, I_j \geqslant 1.2I_0.$$

The problem with the American barrier is that the premium which the writer of the option will receive will be even lower than with a European barrier. There are two reasons for this. First, since the barrier is American there is a higher probability of knocking out. This translates into a lower expected payoff and therefore a lower price for the option. Second, the barrier is in the wrong location. With the knock-out barrier located above the option's strike, the option knocks out when it is most likely to pay off. That the option is not very valuable can also be seen in Figure 7.23. The latter compares the price of a call spread with lower strike 105 with the price of an equivalent American knock-out call, assuming daily monitoring of the index.

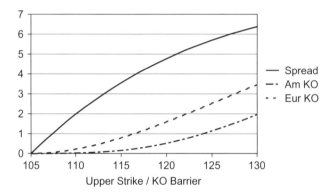

Figure 7.23 Price of call spread and equivalent American knock-out call

Although it does not show from Figure 7.23, another important feature of barrier options is that **when an option is OTM it is no use placing the barrier between the index value and the strike**. With a knock-out barrier this means that the option will knock out before it comes ITM, while with a knock-in barrier the option will knock in before it comes ITM. In the first case the barrier option will be worthless. In the second case the barrier option is identical to an ordinary option. We will say a lot more about barrier options in Chapter 8.

7.7 COLLARS

The investment manager now has two (non-linear) ways to protect himself against a drop of the market using options. He can either buy put options or he can write call options. Buying puts will cost money; writing calls will generate money. This points at a third alternative. Instead of using the premium income he receives when writing calls as a buffer against a possible loss, the investment manager could use the money to buy puts. He does not have to do so separately. He can combine the selling of calls and the purchase of puts in a single contract. Suppose the investment manager was after an overall payoff of

$$X_1 = N \times \left(1 + \text{Max} \left[\left(\frac{I^1 - I_0}{I_0} \right), \text{Min} \left[\left(\frac{I^2 - I_0}{I_0} \right), \left(\frac{I_1 - I_0}{I_0} \right) \right] \right] + B_1 \right), \quad (7.53)$$

with $I^2 > I^1$. Ignoring B_1, with the above payoff the overall portfolio return will never be lower than $(I^1 - I_0)/I_0$ and never higher than $(I^2 - I_0)/I_0$. The index values I^1 and I^2 are therefore the index values below and above which the investment manager is out of the market.

Knowing what the investment manager has as well as what he wants, we can capture the selling off of upside potential and the purchase of protection in one single contract with a payoff equal to

$$V_1 = M \times (\text{Max}\,[0, I^1 - I_1] - \text{Max}\,[0, I_1 - I^2] + B_1 \times I_0). \quad (7.54)$$

The first part of this payoff is the payoff of a long position in **ordinary puts** with strike I^1. The second part is the payoff of a short position in **ordinary calls** with strike I^2. The third term is the usual fixed amount. Ignoring the latter, if the index rose above I^2, the investment manager would have to pay the derivatives firm $M \times (I_1 - I^2)$. If it ended between I^1 and I^2 he would pay nothing and if it ended below I^1 he would receive $M \times (I^1 - I_1)$. Because it keeps the overall portfolio return between two extremes, a contract with a payoff like this is known as a **collar**.

To find the value of B_1 we have to look at the budget equation again, which this time is given by

$$0 = M \times (e^{-r_1}(B_1 \times I_0) + CL_0^a[I^1, I^2, 1]), \quad (7.55)$$

where $CL_0^a[K^1, K^2, T]$ denotes the derivatives firm's offer for a collar with lower (put) strike K^1, upper (call) strike K^2, and time to maturity T. This yields the following expression for the buffer rate

$$B_1 = e^{r_1} \times \frac{-CL_0^a[I^1, I^2, 1]}{I_0}. \quad (7.56)$$

Because we can split the payoff of a collar into the payoff of a long put with strike I^1 and a short call with strike I^2, one might be tempted to calculate the price of the collar as the difference between the derivatives firm's bid for a call with strike I^2 and the firm's offer for a put with strike I^1. As before, however, we should let the derivatives firm know that we intend to trade both options simultaneously, i.e. **what we are after is a price for the collar** and not a price for both options separately. If we set $I^1 = 90$ and $I^2 = 105$ the collar would yield the investment manager 5.71% upfront premium income and therefore a buffer rate of 6%. The overall return to the investment manager is depicted in Figure 7.24. From the figure we see that the collar prevents the overall return from falling below -4% or rising above 11%.

The price of the collar depends heavily of course on the strikes chosen. Figure 7.25 provides an indication of the prices one can expect for different strikes. From the graph we see that collar prices, and therefore buffer rates, can be positive as well as negative. When the collar price is negative, the investment manager gets paid to enter into the contract. This implies that the value of the downside protection which he buys is less

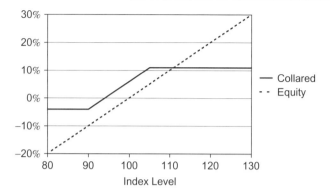

Figure 7.24 Return profile after buying collar

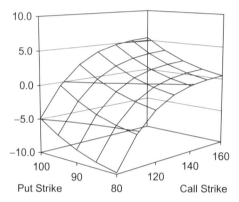

Figure 7.25 Collar prices as a function of strikes

than the value of the upside potential that he is giving up. The price is at its lowest if both the put strike and the call strike are low. In that case the investment manager buys little downside protection, but still sells off a lot of upside potential.

From the graph we see that for every put strike there is a call strike which produces a **zero-cost collar** and vice versa. At these zero-cost strikes the premium received from selling off upside potential equals the premium paid for downside protection. These strikes are easily found by setting $B_1 = 0$ in the budget equation. It almost goes without saying that zero-cost collars are quite popular among investment managers. However, when deciding what kind of structure to trade, one should not look at price alone. A zero-cost structure may not cost anything, but it does not bring much either. Finally, note that when $I^1 = I^2 = I$ the contract payoff to the investment manager is equal to

$$V_1 = M \times ((I - I_1) + B_1 \times I_0). \tag{7.57}$$

This means that here we are simply looking at prices for forward contracts.

Zero-cost collars with relatively low put strikes have become quite popular with investors, including corporate insiders, holding **concentrated equity positions** that for some reason cannot be sold. The value of many such positions has ballooned during the bull market to such a level that it makes up an inordinate portion of these investors' net worth. Many investors would like to protect themselves against a possible drop in the market, and maybe extract some cash as well, but this has to be accomplished without selling the stocks in question. One alternative is to enter into an equity-for-cash swap. We discussed this in Chapter 6. The disadvantage of the swap structure, however, is that putting it on may lead to a taxable event, i.e. it will be seen as a constructive sale and be taxed accordingly. As long as the put strike is not too high, zero-cost collars do not have this problem because the investor is still at risk. The collared position retains dividend and voting rights and some of the upside potential and can also be used to secure a bank loan, in which case we sometimes speak of a **monetizing collar**. The loan will typically be provided by the same party that provides the collar, and amount to 70–80% of the market value of the collared stocks.

7.8   SYNTHETICS

In Chapter 6 we saw how an index fund manager can eliminate tracking error by buying floating rate notes and at the same time entering into a forward where he pays away the note coupons and receives the index return. Our investment manager could of course do the same. Instead of holding stocks he could obtain the desired equity exposure by combining cash with a vanilla forward. Suppose he wanted a payoff like the one given in (7.8) or (7.39). In that case he could do what we discussed earlier, i.e. buy puts or sell calls, but he could also combine the buying of puts or the selling of calls with the purchase of a vanilla forward into one single contract. This is what we discuss next.

7.8.1   Portfolio Insurance

Suppose that our synthetic index fund manager decided to go for the portfolio insurance payoff given by (7.8). What kind of derivatives contract should he enter into, given that he has all his money invested in cash? To acquire the desired payoff the investment manager will have to exchange the interest which he receives for the protected equity return given by

$$V_1 = N \times \text{Max}\left[F, \alpha\left(\frac{I_1 - I_0}{I_0}\right)\right]. \tag{7.58}$$

We can rewrite this payoff as

$$V_1 = N \times F + \alpha M \times \text{Max}\left[0, I_1 - I_0\left(1 + \frac{F}{\alpha}\right)\right]. \tag{7.59}$$

The first term is a fixed amount. The second term is equal to the payoff of αM **ordinary calls** with a strike equal to $I_0(1 + F/\alpha)$. With the present value of the interest which the investment manager will pay to the derivatives firm being equal to $e^{-r_1} \times (e^{r_1} - 1)N = (1 - e^{-r_1})N$, we can solve the participation rate which the investment manager will be able to obtain from the budget equation given by

$$(1 - e^{-r_1})N = e^{-r_1}(N \times F) + \alpha M \times C_0^a\left[I_0\left(1 + \frac{F}{\alpha}\right), 1\right], \tag{7.60}$$

where the right-hand side is the value of the payment to be made by the derivatives firm. Assuming a floor rate of -5% this yields a participation rate of 0.63. Exactly as before.

So to obtain portfolio insurance an investment manager who invests in equity should buy ordinary puts and an investment manager who invests in cash should buy ordinary calls. This points to a **second version of put–call parity**. In Chapter 5 we discussed that buying an ordinary call while at the same time writing an ordinary put yields the same payoff as buying a vanilla forward. The above, however, implies that a stock plus an ordinary put is the same as cash plus an ordinary call. In other words, it tells us that buying a call while writing a put is the same as buying a stock and borrowing money. If we think back to our discussion of forwards in Chapter 6, this does not really come as a surprise. We saw there that buying a forward is simply an efficient alternative for the leveraged buying of stocks.

7.8.2   Yield Enhancement

Suppose that instead of buying portfolio insurance the investment manager wanted to sell off his upside potential over the next year and use the proceeds as a buffer against a drop in the value of his portfolio. What kind of derivatives contract would accomplish that for him? Again, we have to start with the overall payoff the investment manager is looking for. The latter is given by (7.39). Since he generates an amount N himself, the investment manager will have to trade his interest income in for a payment equal to

$$V_1 = B_1 \times N - M \times \text{Max}\,[0, I_0 - I_1].\tag{7.61}$$

The first term is a fixed amount. The second term is equal to the payoff of a short position in M **ordinary puts** with strike I_0.

The next step is to determine the value of the buffer rate that the investor will be able to obtain. We can solve the buffer rate from the budget equation given by

$$(1 - e^{-r_1})N = e^{-r_1}(B_1 \times N) - M \times P_0^{\text{b}}[I_0, 1].\tag{7.62}$$

Rewriting yields

$$B_1 = (e^{r_1} - 1) + e^{r_1} \times \frac{P_0^{\text{b}}[I_0, 1]}{I_0}.\tag{7.63}$$

In line with earlier results this yields a value for the buffer rate of 10.97%. It also shows that cash plus a written ordinary put yields the same payoff as equity combined with a written ordinary call, which leads us to the same put–call parity relationship we discovered earlier.

7.9   SEPARATING FX RISK FROM EQUITY RISK

When diversifying his portfolio internationally our investment manager takes on two risks at the same time. First, he takes on **local stock market risk**. If he bought equity in Thailand for example he would become exposed to the ups and downs of the Thai stock market. In addition, he also takes on **exchange rate risk**, i.e. exposure to the ups and downs of the Thai baht. If his stocks go up but at the same time the Thai baht comes down, he may have been right about the equity market but he still does not make anything off it. It would therefore be very interesting to see if we can structure a contract that allows the investment manager to separate the local stock market risk and the exchange rate risk on his foreign investments. This would create a whole new asset class: **currency hedged foreign equity**.

7.9.1 The FX Lock

Suppose the investment manager followed an indexation strategy and simply bought all the stocks in some foreign stock market index. After a year this would yield a payoff equal to

$$H_1 = M \times E_1 \times I_1 = N \times \left(1 + \frac{E_1 \times I_1 - E_0 \times I_0}{E_0 \times I_0}\right), \qquad (7.64)$$

where I_t denotes the value of the foreign index in foreign currency and E_t denotes the value of a unit of foreign currency in terms of the investment manager's domestic currency. The multiplier M is equal to the number of shares in the foreign index his initial net asset value buys at the $t = 0$ exchange rate E_0, i.e. $M = N/E_0 I_0$. Expression (7.64) clearly shows the payoff's dependence on both the index and the exchange rate. If the investment manager was bullish on both this would be an ideal payoff. But suppose his goal was only to invest in the equity market. In that case the exchange rate could easily get in the way. It might even be the case that the investment manager expected the stock market to go up because he expected the currency to come down. In that case he would be a lot happier with a payoff like

$$X_1 = M \times E_0 \times I_1 = N \times \left(1 + \frac{E_0 \times I_1 - E_0 \times I_0}{E_0 \times I_0}\right). \qquad (7.65)$$

The difference between this payoff and the previous one is that now the exchange rate at which the index value at maturity is converted into the investment manager's domestic currency is fixed in advance. We set it equal to E_0, but it could of course be any number.

Knowing what payoff the investment manager can achieve by himself and what he would prefer to get paid, we are ready to structure a derivatives contract that solves his problem. The most obvious is a forward under which he pays away the result on his own investment and receives the desired payoff in return. This means that at the end of the year he receives a contract payoff equal to

$$V_1 = X_1 - H_1 = N \times \left(\left(\frac{I_1 - I_0}{I_0}\right) - \left(\frac{E_1 \times I_1 - E_0 \times I_0}{E_0 \times I_0}\right)\right), \qquad (7.66)$$

which can of course be expressed more compactly as

$$V_1 = M \times (E_0 - E_1) \times I_1. \qquad (7.67)$$

This shows that what this forward does is fix the currency conversion rate at E_0. If the foreign currency depreciates, i.e. if E_1 is lower than E_0, the forward provides the investment manager with a positive payoff and the other way around. A contract like this is therefore referred to as an **FX lock**.

Note that instead of as an equity derivatives contract, we can also interpret the FX lock as a currency derivative. This is due to the fact that the middle part of (7.67), i.e.

the $E_0 - E_1$ part, equals the payoff of an exchange rate forward where the investment manager pays the exchange rate at maturity in return for the initial exchange rate. In this interpretation all the investment manager does is purchase $M \times I_1$ exchange rate forwards. The remarkable thing is that with the FX lock he is able to buy as many forwards as he needs to hedge the maturity value of his equity portfolio. **Instead of at inception, the number of contracts is fixed at maturity**. In other words, the multiplier is index-linked.

The price of the FX lock will be set by the derivatives firm based on its expected hedging costs. Based on our discussion of forwards in Chapter 6 one might be inclined to expect that the investment manager could enter into an FX lock without an upfront payment to the derivatives firm. However, the pricing and hedging of an FX lock is different from a vanilla forward because there are now two risk factors: the foreign index and the exchange rate. On the maturity date the FX lock pays the derivatives firm an amount equal to

$$V_1 = M \times E_1 \times I_1 - M \times E_0 \times I_1. \tag{7.68}$$

The first term is the payoff of an index participation that pays (in domestic currency) the value of the foreign index at maturity. The derivatives firm can hedge this cash inflow by simply shorting M shares of the index. So far this is similar to a vanilla forward. The second term is more complicated though. It is the payoff of an index participation that pays the value of the foreign index at maturity converted at the exchange rate at initiation. The latter **can only be hedged by dynamically trading the foreign index and the foreign currency**.

Although we will not go into the details of this,[3] the hedging strategy for the second term in (7.68) uses the foreign index to hedge changes in the exchange rate and the foreign currency to hedge movements in the foreign index. At initiation the derivatives firm borrows foreign currency and invests the proceeds in foreign stocks. If the exchange rate goes up the firm sells foreign stocks and reduces its foreign borrowings with the proceeds. Intuitively, this makes sense. When the actual exchange rate is higher than E_0 the firm can do with less foreign stock and still generate the required payoff. Something similar happens when the foreign index changes. If the index goes up the firm will borrow in foreign currency and invest the proceeds in domestic currency. Again, this makes sense. With the index eventually being converted at E_0 any gains should be repatriated before the exchange rate changes.

The question then is whether the derivatives firm can start the above hedging strategy without an upfront payment by the investment manager. Unless the interest rate differential is zero, the answer is no. This is due to the fact that the hedging strategy requires the firm to borrow in foreign currency and invest domestically. If the foreign interest rate is higher than the domestic rate the derivatives firm will require compensation for the loss of interest. In that case the investment manager will have to pay the derivatives firm. On the other hand, if the foreign rate is lower than the domestic rate the reverse is true and the derivatives firm will have to pay the investment manager.

We arrive at the same conclusion if we look at the FX lock's discounted expected payoff. As discussed in Chapter 5, the latter equals the contract's expected hedging costs under the assumption that the index goes up by the interest rate and the exchange rate changes at a rate equal to the interest rate differential. If the foreign and domestic interest rates are equal, the FX lock's expected payoff is zero. If the foreign interest rate is lower

---

[3] See bibliography under the heading 'Quanto and Composite Options'.

than the domestic rate we must assume that the foreign currency is about to appreciate relative to the domestic currency. If that indeed happened, E_1 would exceed E_0 and the FX lock would provide the investment manager with a negative payoff. If the foreign rate was higher than the domestic rate the reverse would happen. We would have to assume that the foreign currency was about to depreciate, which would produce a positive expected payoff for the investment manager.

There is another reason why the FX lock is an interesting contract. In Chapter 5 we discussed that the prices of contracts with payoffs that are a linear function of the reference index do not depend on volatility. However, this is not true for the FX lock. Because in the payoff function the exchange rate and the index are multiplied with each other, the price of the FX lock depends on the degree of correlation between the index and the exchange rate and their respective volatilities. If the exchange rate goes up (down) the hedging strategy will sell (buy) foreign stocks. If the exchange rate and the stock market are positively correlated this will lead to a profit. If they are negatively correlated it will produce a loss. Likewise, if the index goes up, the strategy will convert foreign currency into domestic currency and the other way around. Again, with positive correlation this implies a profit and with negative correlation a loss. How large these profits and losses will be depends on the size of the index and exchange rate movements, i.e. the index and exchange rate volatility. This means that the higher the volatility, the stronger the correlation effect will be. This in turn means that with positive (negative) correlation the FX lock becomes less (more) expensive when volatility rises.

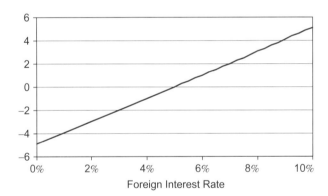

Figure 7.26   Price of an FX lock as a function of foreign interest rate

The correlation between equity markets and exchange rates is typically fairly weak. This means that in most cases we can more or less ignore the above effect. What we cannot ignore, however, is the influence of the interest rate differential. An example of the prices one may expect for a 1-year FX lock as a function of the foreign interest rate can be found in Figure 7.26. For simplicity we assumed zero correlation between the exchange rate and the foreign index. The graph shows that roughly speaking the price of an FX lock equals the interest rate differential. This means that **when the foreign interest rate is lower than the domestic rate the investment manager gets paid to hedge his exchange rate risk**. Of course, this is not necessarily a free lunch. If the foreign currency appreciates, the investment manager misses out on the appreciation. On the other hand, the interest rate differential is by no means a perfect forecast of future exchange rate behavior. If the exchange rate drops, the investment manager will not only get paid at inception but again at maturity.

7.9.2 The FX Lock Option

If the exchange rate at maturity exceeds the initial exchange rate the FX lock will make the investment manager pay the derivatives firm. We can prevent this by giving the investment manager the right to cancel the contract at maturity. This would allow the investment manager to convert against the best rate. If $E_1 < E_0$ he would stick to the contract and if $E_1 > E_0$ he would cancel. He would therefore obtain a contract payoff equal to

$$V_1 = M \times \text{Max}\,[0, E_0 - E_1] \times I_1. \tag{7.69}$$

The payoff of this **FX lock option** is very interesting as it is the same payoff that the investment manager would obtain if he purchased $M \times I_1$ ordinary puts on the foreign exchange rate. Actually doing so, however, would be impossible as the number of options to buy would not be known at inception. Given this, the above option is sometimes also referred to as an **equity-linked foreign exchange option**, or **ELF-X**.

Giving the investment manager the right to cancel the contract at maturity changes a lot about the pricing of the structure. Let's look at the payoff to the derivatives firm again. The latter is given by

$$V_1 = M \times E_1 \times I_1 - M \times \text{Max}\,[E_0, E_1] \times I_1. \tag{7.70}$$

As with the FX lock, the first term can be hedged by simply shorting the foreign index. The second term is more troublesome. It is the payoff of an index participation that pays the maturity value of the foreign index converted at the best of the exchange rate at inception and the exchange rate at maturity. The latter can be hedged with a dynamic trading strategy that is similar to the FX lock hedging strategy, except that this time a change in the exchange rate or the index will trigger trading in both foreign equity and foreign currency. If the exchange rate rises, for example, the strategy will not only sell foreign stocks but will also move further into foreign currency.

Because the payoff to the derivatives firm will never be positive, the investment manager will now have to pay the derivatives firm to enter into the contract, irrespective of the interest rate differential. The amount payable will of course still depend heavily on the interest rate differential. However, because the contract payoff is now a convex function of the exchange rate, we are also confronted with a much more important role for the volatility of the exchange rate. We discussed this phenomenon in Chapter 5. This means that the price of the FX lock option will rise with the foreign interest rate as well as the volatility of the exchange rate.

7.10 IMPROVING THE TIMING OF MARKET ENTRY AND EXIT

The life of an investment manager is far from easy. If he thinks that a stock or even the whole market is undervalued, when should he buy? Likewise, if he thinks a stock or market has become overvalued, when should he sell? These are without doubt the most difficult problems in investment management, especially since most money in equity seems to be made during so-called **speculative bubbles** when market prices move away from fundamental values. To solve these timing problems we first have to get a clear idea of what it is that the investment manager in question is really after. Ideally, he wants to buy at the lowest and sell at the highest price without having to forecast when that is exactly. As we will see, structured equity derivatives can provide him with exactly that.

7.10.1 Market Entry

We start with the problem of market entry. Irrespective of when the investment manager enters the market, he always runs the risk that prices will fall after he has bought his stocks. The investment manager's view could be correct over a longer period of time, but because he went in too early he may not benefit as much as he could have.

Lookbacks

Suppose the investment manager simply bought the index. This means that his actual profit over the next six months would be equal to

$$AP_{0,1/2} = M \times (I_{1/2} - I_0). \tag{7.71}$$

If the index went up from the moment the investment manager entered the market this would be fine, but if it went down first he could have made more by entering the market at a later date. Ideally, he therefore wants his profit after six months to be equal to

$$DP_{0,1/2} = M \times (I_{1/2} - M_{0,1/2}^-), \tag{7.72}$$

where $M_{0,1/2}^-$ denotes the lowest index value recorded during the six month period.

Knowing what he has and what he wants we can structure a contract where the investment manager trades in one for the other, i.e. a forward contract under which the investment manager pays away his actual profit in exchange for his ideal profit. Such a contract would on balance provide him with a payoff equal to

$$V_{1/2} = DP_{0,1/2} - AP_{0,1/2} = M \times \left(I_0 - M_{0,1/2}^- \right). \tag{7.73}$$

A contract with a payoff like this is known as a **fixed-strike lookback put**. Referring to (7.73) as the payoff of an option instead of a forward may seem somewhat strange. However, one should realize that the payoff which the investment manager receives will never be negative. In that sense the payoff has much more in common with an option than with a forward.

Assuming he can obtain it for free, buying the above lookback put provides the investment manager with an overall payoff equal to

$$X_{1/2} = M \times (I_{1/2} + I_0 - M_{0,1/2}^-). \tag{7.74}$$

If the initial index value was also the lowest index value over the six month period the lookback put payoff would be zero and the investment manager would be left with the value of his equity portfolio. If, however, the initial index value was not the lowest index value, the lookback put would subsidize his portfolio in such a way as to make it look as though he bought at the lowest point. We can also interpret this in terms of an increased multiplier if we rewrite (7.74) as

$$X_{1/2} = \left(M \times \left(1 + \frac{I_0 - M_{0,1/2}^-}{I_{1/2}} \right) \right) \times I_{1/2}. \tag{7.75}$$

This expression shows that the lookback feature raises the multiplier in case an index value lower than the initial index value is registered.

Should the investment manager pay the derivatives firm to enter into such a contract? Of course he should. The payoff of the lookback put cannot be negative, so the derivatives firm knows in advance it will never win. Assuming the index is monitored once a day for a new minimum, a 6-month lookback put will cost the investment manager 8.85%. Funding at an interest rate of 5%, the overall payoff to the investment manager is therefore equal to

$$X_{1/2} = M \times (I_{1/2} + I_0 - M_{0,1/2}^- - 9.074). \tag{7.76}$$

Insurance against entering the market too early does not seem to come cheap. There are many ways to reduce the price of options, including lookback puts. We will discuss a variety of them in Chapter 8. In this section, however, we will restrict ourselves to two alternatives that apply specifically to this case.

Ladders

We can reduce the price of the lookback put by changing the way in which the lowest index value is determined. As discussed in Chapter 4, there are various alternatives for the vanilla extremum. Instead of the actual minimum we could use the extended stepwise minimum. This will produce a cheaper contract, because the set of index values from which we choose the minimum will be constructed differently. How this is done was discussed in Chapter 4. Suppose we replaced the actual minimum by the extended stepwise minimum. In that case we would be looking at a contract payoff to the investment manager equal to

$$V_{1/2} = M \times (I_0 - ES_{0,1/2}^-), \tag{7.77}$$

where $ES_{0,1/2}^-$ is the extended stepwise minimum index value over the period from $t = 0$ to $t = 1/2$. A contract with a payoff like this is known as a **fixed-strike ladder put**. It is important to remember that the rungs in a ladder are not different from the barriers in a knock-in or knock-out feature. This means that we have to make sure to specify (1) the monitoring points, (2) the rung levels at every monitoring point, and (3) the exact nature of the rungs. If not fully specified, the contract will be open to dispute.

Before we can look at some prices, we have to decide on the number and level of the rungs. The more rungs, the more expensive the ladder put will be. Intuitively, this makes sense since as the **number of rungs** increases, the ladder put becomes more and more like a lookback put. In practice, therefore, the number of rungs is typically kept limited. Figure 7.27 shows the price difference (as a percentage of the price of the ordinary put) between a 6-month ATM ladder put and a 6-month ATM ordinary put. The ladder put has one, two or three rungs at 99, 98 and 97, respectively. The index is monitored daily. For comparison, the price difference between a lookback put and an ordinary put is almost

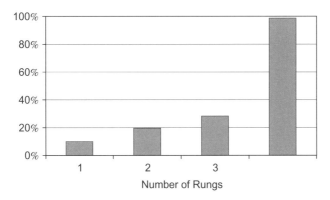

Figure 7.27 Value of ladder feature added to an ATM ordinary put as a function of number of rungs

100% (last column in graph). If the number of rungs increases, the ladder feature becomes more valuable. With the above three rungs, however, the ladder put is still significantly cheaper than the lookback put.

Apart from the number of rungs, the **location of the rungs** is also very important for the price of the ladder put. There are two opposite forces at work here. The further away from the initial index level, the lower the probability that the rung will be hit, the lower the expected payoff, and therefore the cheaper the contract. On the other hand, as the rung is further away from the initial index value, the payoff locked in when the rung is hit becomes more drastic, making the contract more expensive. So we have a **probability effect** and a **locking-in effect**.

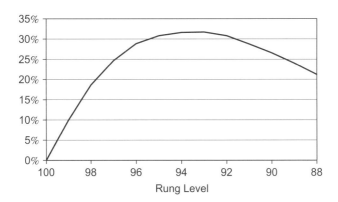

Figure 7.28 Value of single rung ladder added to an ATM ordinary put as a function of rung level

Figure 7.28 gives, for different rung levels, the difference (as a percentage of the price of the ordinary put) between the price of a 6-month ATM ladder put with one rung and a 6-month ATM ordinary put. Note that Figure 7.28 does not show the marginal value of a rung, i.e. the increase in the value of a ladder when the rung in question is added to an existing ladder. When added to a ladder which already has a 99 rung and a 98 rung, the value of a rung at 97 is only 0.389%. By itself, however, the 97 rung is worth 1.092%.

The graph in Figure 7.28 shows that if the rung level is lowered, the price rises first only to drop again later. This means that initially the locking-in effect is stronger than the probability effect, but this changes when the rung level is lowered further. Of course, all this depends heavily on the index volatility. The higher the volatility, the longer it takes before the drop sets in, i.e. the longer it takes before the probability effect becomes stronger than the locking-in effect.

A Second Look

Insurance against entering the market too early in the form of a fixed-strike lookback or ladder put seems to be very expensive. It is therefore worthwhile to take a second look at these contracts to make sure that the investment manager is not buying more protection than he really needs. If so, we can structure a cheaper solution by stripping away whatever it is that he does not need.

The overall payoff that results after buying a fixed-strike lookback put is given by (7.74). If we look what happens if the index goes down first and up later, it appears to be exactly what the investment manager wants. However, if we look at a scenario where the index goes down but does not go up again, it becomes clear that the lookback put does a lot more than just improve the investment manager's timing. If the index at maturity was also the lowest index value recorded, the overall payoff would be equal to $M \times I_0$. In other words, apart from improved timing **the lookback put also provides the investment manager with portfolio insurance** with a 0% floor rate. This explains why the option is so expensive.

Starting with equity, portfolio insurance is obtained by buying ordinary puts. This implies that we can strip the fixed-strike lookback put from its portfolio insurance services by combining its purchase with the sale of an ATM ordinary put. The resulting contract would have a payoff equal to

$$V_{1/2} = M \times (I_0 - M_{0,1/2}^- - \text{Max}\,[0, I_0 - I_{1/2}]), \tag{7.78}$$

which yields an overall payoff of

$$X_{1/2} = M \times (I_{1/2} + I_0 - M_{0,1/2}^- - \text{Max}\,[0, I_0 - I_{1/2}]). \tag{7.79}$$

Just as before, if at maturity the index was higher than at inception the investment manager would be paid

$$X_{1/2} = M \times (I_{1/2} + I_0 - M_{0,1/2}^-). \tag{7.80}$$

However, if the index ended lower than where it started the overall payoff would be equal to

$$X_{1/2} = M \times (I_{1/2} + I_0 - M_{0,1/2}^- - [I_0 - I_{1/2}]) = M \times (2I_{1/2} - M_{0,1/2}^-). \tag{7.81}$$

If the index value at maturity was also the lowest index value recorded, the payoff would simply be equal to $I_{1/2}$. If the lowest index value was lower than the index value at maturity the payoff would be higher, which represents the timing feature. The derivatives firm offers the above contract at 4.43%, which certainly looks a lot better than the 8.85% which it quoted for the fixed-strike lookback put. Of course, we can do the same with the ladder put.

7.10.2 Market Exit

We can apply the same principles to solve the problem of market exit. Human psychology is often thought to cause the issue of market exit to be surrounded by one of two problems.

- **Problem 1.** Investors who are at a loss often sell too quickly, thereby turning a paper loss into a real loss. Fear takes over from common sense.
- **Problem 2.** Investors sitting on a substantial profit often wait too long before selling. As a result, they run the risk of losing out on a substantial part of their profits. Greed takes over from common sense.

We look at problem 1 first.

Problem 1

The investment manager wants to make sure that if during some period after he sells his stocks the index reaches a higher level he gets paid as if he sold at this higher level. In other words, at the time of selling he wants to enter into a contract which, if the index goes up after the sale, gives him the right to exchange his sales proceeds for a higher amount. To see what this contract's payoff should be we first have to write down the payoff that he would normally get as well as the payoff that he would like to receive if the index went up. Referring to the time of selling as $t = 0$, the former is equal to

$$H_0 = M \times I_0. \tag{7.82}$$

However, if after three months the index is higher than at $t = 0$ he wants to receive

$$X_{1/4} = M \times I_{1/4}. \tag{7.83}$$

A forward will not do in this case as the investment manager only wants (7.83) if it is higher than (7.82). We therefore need to give the investment manager the right to cancel the contract. On balance, the derivatives firm therefore has to provide the investment manager with a payoff equal to

$$V_{1/4} = M \times \text{Max}\,[0, I_{1/4} - I_0], \tag{7.84}$$

which is nothing more than the payoff of M **ordinary calls** with strike I_0. If the index rises, the investment manager exchanges the proceeds of the sale of his portfolio for what his portfolio would have been worth at $t = 1/4$. If the index falls, he cancels the contract and sticks with what he has got. The price of a 3-month ATM call is 4.64%.

   Although buying ordinary calls provides one solution to the problem of market exit, it is not a very effective one. The payoff of the calls depends solely on the index value at $t = 1/4$. This means that under a scenario where the index rises first but drops later, the investment manager will not get paid. Ideally, what the investment manager wants is to sell his portfolio at the best possible price. This means that what he is really after is a payoff of

$$X_{1/4} = M \times M_{0,1/4}^{+}, \tag{7.85}$$

where $M_{0,1/4}^{+}$ denotes the highest index value recorded during the quarter. Combining this with what he gets from selling his portfolio at I_0, the required payoff to the investment manager would in that case be equal to

$$V_{1/4} = X_{1/4} - H_0 = M \times (M^+_{0,1/4} - I_0). \tag{7.86}$$

We do not need the option right in this case. If the price at which he sold at $t = 0$ is also the highest price of the quarter, the contract payoff is zero. If during the quarter following the sale a higher price is observed, the investment manager gets paid the difference. A contract like this is known as a **fixed-strike lookback call**. Under the assumptions made and monitoring the index daily, the price of a 3-month ATM lookback call is 8.10%, which shows that insurance against selling too late does not come cheap.

One way to reduce the cost of insurance is to revert to the concept of a ladder again. This means replacing the actual maximum recorded during the quarter by the extended stepwise maximum to create a so-called **fixed-strike ladder call**. The price of an ATM ladder call with three rungs at 102, 104 and 106 will be equal to 6.21%. The way the price of the ladder call reacts to a change in the number and level of the rungs is very similar to what we have seen before with the fixed-strike ladder put. The more rungs, the more expensive the ladder call will be. When it comes to the level of the rungs we again see two effects. The further away the rung, the lower the probability that it will be hit and therefore the lower the price of the option. On the other hand, with the rung further away, it locks in a higher payoff when it is hit. This makes the contract more expensive. Typically, if the rung level is raised, the option price rises first but drops again later.

Problem 2

We now turn to problem 2. The problem here is that instead of too early, the investment manager sells too late. It is not an uncommon scenario. After a sustained market rally the market comes to look seriously overvalued. Inspired by recent success, however, the investment manager decides not to sell. Not long afterwards the market indeed comes down while the investment manager is still fully invested in equity. He sells eventually, but only after having lost a sizeable portion of his earlier profits. Staying fully invested in equity, the investment manager would like to enter into a contract that a few months down the road gave him the right to exchange the prevailing value of his equity portfolio for the portfolio value at the time of entering the contract if the latter was higher. In other words, he wants the right to give up

$$H_{1/4} = M \times I_{1/4} \tag{7.87}$$

in return for

$$X_{1/4} = M \times I_0. \tag{7.88}$$

This means that the payoff we are after is equal to

$$V_{1/4} = M \times \text{Max}\,[0, I_0 - I_{1/4}]. \tag{7.89}$$

Since what the investment manager is really after is short-term portfolio insurance, this is simply the payoff of M **ordinary puts** with strike I_0. A 3-month ATM ordinary put will cost the investment manager 3.38%.

By buying puts the investment manager obtains the right to sell his portfolio for $M \times I_0$. If after three months his portfolio is worth more, he will let this right expire, i.e. cancel the contract, but if it is worth less he will exercise it. It may happen, however, that I_0 is not the highest index level reached and that implicitly selling at a later time would have produced more. Given our previous results, structuring insurance against a scenario like this is easy. We could for example replace I_0 by the stepwise maximum to produce a contract with a payoff equal to

$$V_{1/4} = M \times \text{Max} \left[0, S_{0,1/4}^+ - I_{1/4} \right]. \tag{7.90}$$

A contract like this is known as a **floating-strike ladder put**. It allows the investment manager to exchange the maturity value of his portfolio for the highest rung hit during the contract's life. Of course, a floating-strike ladder put will be more expensive than an ordinary put. Assuming we placed rungs at 102, 104 and 106 it would set the investment manager back 4.92%.

7.10.3 DIY Ladders

We already mentioned that technically the rungs in ladder options are not different from the barriers in knock-in and knock-out features. But there is more. When it comes to the pricing of ladder options it is helpful to know that the payoff of fixed-strike and floating-strike ladder puts and calls can be expressed as the sum of the payoffs of ordinary, knock-in and knock-out options. This means that **ladder options can be packaged by combining ordinary and barrier options**. We will discuss this below, concentrating on calls. Puts can be dealt with in exactly the same way.

Suppose we wanted to construct a **fixed-strike ladder call** with initial strike I_0 and two barriers H^1 and H^2 with $I_0 < H^1 < H^2$. Such an option pays its holder an amount equal to

$$V_T = \text{Max} \left[0, ES_{0,T}^+ - I_0 \right]. \tag{7.91}$$

The option locks in an amount $H^1 - I_0$ when the index reaches a level H^1 and a total amount $H^2 - I_0$ as soon as the index reaches H^2. The payoff of this option can also be obtained by (1) buying an ordinary call with strike I_0, (2) selling a knock-in put with strike I_0 with a barrier at H^1, (3) buying a knock-in put with strike H^1 and a barrier at H^1, (4) selling a knock-in put with strike H^1 and a barrier at H^2, and (5) buying a knock-in put with strike H^2 and a barrier at H^2. The first option is the initially required call with strike I_0. When the first barrier is reached, the second option comes into existence. Together with the call it forms a forward where one party pays the index value at maturity and the other pays a fixed amount I_0. The third option provides downside protection on this forward at a level of H^1. The same happens when the next barrier is hit. The fourth option neutralizes the third, while the fifth option locks in a total profit of $H^2 - I_0$ in case the index ends lower than H^2, while leaving the profit potential intact. This means that the time t price of the above fixed-strike ladder call can be written as

$$V_t = C_t[I_0] - IP_t[I_0, H^1] + IP_t[H^1, H^1] - IP_t[H^1, H^2] + IP_t[H^2, H^2], \tag{7.92}$$

where $IP_t[K, H]$ denotes the time t price of a knock-in put with strike K and barrier H.

Now suppose we wanted to construct a **floating-strike ladder call** with initial strike I_0 and two rungs at H^1 and H^2 with $I_0 > H^1 > H^2$. Such an option pays its holder an amount equal to

$$V_T = \text{Max} \left[0, I_5 - S_{0,T}^- \right]. \tag{7.93}$$

This option permanently adjusts the strike downwards from I_0 to H^1 if the index reaches a level of H^1 and again adjusts the strike to H^2 as soon as the index reaches H^2. We can package such an option by (1) buying a knock-out call with strike I_0 and barrier H^1, (2) buying a knock-in call with strike H^1 and barrier H^1, (3) writing a knock-in call with strike H^1 and barrier H^2, and (4) buying a knock-in call with strike H^2 and barrier H^2. The first option makes sure we start out with an option with strike I_0. If the reference index reaches H^1, this call disappears and is replaced by the second option with strike H^1. If subsequently the index reaches H^2, the second option is neutralized by the third option and is replaced by the last option with strike H^2. This means that the time t price of the above ladder option can be written as

$$V_t = OC_t[I_0, H^1] + IC_t[H^1, H^1] - IC_t[H^1, H^2] + IC_t[H^2, H^2], \qquad (7.94)$$

where $OC_t[K, H]$ ($IC_t[K, H]$) denotes the time t price of a knock-out (knock-in) call with strike K and barrier H.

When packaging options to create new options it is important to look for a price for the whole package and not for prices for every individual option separately. Especially in cases like this, the expected hedging costs of the combination will often be significantly lower than the sum of the expected hedging costs of the component options.

7.11 CONCLUSION

In Chapter 6 we discussed how to structure derivatives that can substitute for cash market transactions. In this chapter we have taken things one step further and discussed the creation of payoff profiles that investors will not be able to easily create themselves. We left the realm of forwards and swaps for the world of options, because many applications require a counterparty to be able to cancel the contract in question if so desired. Amongst others, our analysis yielded three different ways to protect an equity portfolio against a drop in the market: buy puts, sell calls or do both. Whatever strategy is followed, however, one always pays for the protection in the form of reduced upside potential. This confirms the general rule that **a better payoff in one area can only be obtained by accepting a worse payoff in another**.

We also looked at two other applications. It was shown that equity derivatives can be structured such that the foreign exchange risk on foreign equity investments is eliminated. Since the contracts that we structured are specifically designed to hedge an amount of foreign currency that only becomes known in the future, this is a great achievement. More traditional currency hedging techniques can only hope to accomplish such a result. Equity derivatives, in the form of lookback and ladder options, may also solve timing problems. Since timing errors have a profound influence on performance, it is not really surprising that lookback and ladder options are relatively expensive. In the next chapter we therefore discuss a number of ways to make options cheaper.

8
Reducing the Costs of Buying Options

8.1 INTRODUCTION

It often happens that one structures a contract to solve a certain problem and the client rejects it because he thinks it is too expensive. Forwards and swaps do not provide many problems, but as soon as the option right is introduced complaints start coming in. This is not completely unjustified. Paying an upfront premium of 5.57% for a 1-year ATM ordinary put or 8.85% for a 6-month ATM fixed-strike lookback put indeed looks a bit steep, no matter how much these options improve the overall payoff profile. The importance of being able to make options cheaper becomes especially clear if we realize that the difference in performance between first decile and last decile ranked mutual funds is generally less than the price of an ordinary put.

Given the above, derivatives structurers are always thinking of ways to make options cheaper. This is much easier said than done, however. Derivatives are solutions to problems. Derivatives contracts are therefore not to be tampered with arbitrarily, as this may cause them to lose their economic relevance. The set of possible paths that the index may take to reach its maturity value can be divided into two subsets. The primary set contains all paths the investor holds highly likely. The secondary set includes all others. To make a contract cheaper while retaining its basic characteristics we must provide the investor with a similar payoff as before if the reference index ends up in the primary set, but with a less favorable payoff if it ends up in the secondary set. Basically, we look for something that the derivatives firm considers to be of value but the investment manager does not.

Over time derivatives structurers have come up with an impressive number of tricks. In this chapter we will look at the following.

- Changing the contract parameters
- Changing the reference index
- Buying less
- Piecewise linear segmentation
- Knock-in and knock-out options
- Changing exchange rate risk
- Pay-later and money-back options
- Instalment options
- Callable options
- Asian options
- Revised monitoring for path-dependent options

Although **these techniques can easily be combined**, we will discuss each technique separately. For brevity, we concentrate on ordinary calls as the option contracts in question, but most techniques work equally well for ordinary puts as well as other types of options.

8.2   CHANGING THE CONTRACT PARAMETERS

The most obvious way to reduce the price of an option is to change one or more contract parameters. In the previous chapter we saw how shortening the **time to maturity** of ordinary call and put options reduces these options' prices. In the same chapter we saw that raising the **strike** on an ordinary call or lowering the strike on an ordinary put has the same effect. Figure 8.1 shows the payoff of an ATM ordinary call as well as an OTM ordinary call with strike $1.1I_0$. From the graph we clearly see that if we increase the strike, the option payoff for every index value higher than the original strike comes down. The further away the new strike is from the old strike, the further the payoff profile will move out to the right.

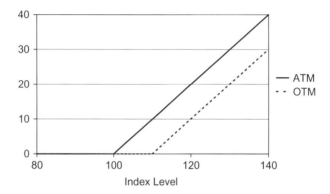

Figure 8.1   Payoff profile for ATM and OTM ordinary call

8.3   CHANGING THE REFERENCE INDEX

Apart from simply changing one or more contract parameters, we may sometimes also be able to lower the option price by changing the reference index. In most applications this is not a viable alternative, because the problem in question evolves around a specific index or set of indices. Sometimes, however, the choice of index is only of secondary importance. If it is, the following two tricks may bring some relief.

8.3.1   A Higher Dividend Yield

One reason why it may be helpful to change to another reference index is dividends. We already touched upon this in Chapter 7. Because it makes a company worth less, the payment of dividends puts a brake on the upward trend in a company's stock price. The higher the dividends paid, the weaker the upward trend and the lower the expected payoff of calls and the higher the expected payoff of puts. We can use this to our advantage by using indices that pay a relatively high dividend as reference indices for calls, and indices that pay little or no dividends as reference indices for puts. Figure 7.5 gives an example of how the price of ATM ordinary calls and puts with one year to maturity changes with the dividend yield of the reference index. This graph makes it clear that **it does not take a large change in dividends to significantly move the prices of these options**.

8.3.2 Basket Options

One of the determinants of the price of an option is the volatility of the reference index. Assuming a convex payoff profile, the lower the volatility of the index, the cheaper the contract. We discussed this in Chapter 5. We can reduce volatility in two ways. First, we can change to an index with a lower volatility. Instead of working with a country-specific index, like the DAX or the CAC 40 for example, we could work with a more global index like the Eurotop 100 or the Eurostoxx 50. Partly for this reason the Eurostoxx 50 has become the dominant index for equity-linked notes (see Chapters 9–12) in Europe. Second, instead of with one reference index, we could work with a **basket of indices**. A basket is typically less volatile than its components because of the imperfect correlation between the returns on the latter. When two indices are perfectly correlated there is no use in combining them into a basket because if one goes up (down) the other will go up (down) as well. However, if they are not perfectly correlated there is a chance that one will go up while the other goes down, leaving the value of the basket more or less unchanged.

After replacing the single index in the option payoff by a basket of N indices the payoff of an ordinary call with strike K is equal to

$$V_T = \text{Max}\left[0, \sum_{i=1}^{N}(M^i \times I_T^i) - K\right],\tag{8.1}$$

where M^i denotes the number of shares of index i included in the basket and I_T^i denotes the time T value of index i. To calculate the above option payoff we have to decide on the individual index multipliers M^i. This is not the most common way to think about baskets, however. Most people think in terms of an initial basket value and a set of **basket weights** that say how the initial basket value is divided over the component indices. With an **equally-weighted** basket the basket value is divided equally over all indices. With a **value-weighted** basket on the other hand the basket value is divided in accordance with the value of the individual indices.

We can accommodate this way of thinking by **redefining the basket value as an index number** as follows

$$I_0 = 100,\tag{8.2}$$

$$I_t = 100 \times \sum_{i=1}^{N}\left[x_i \times \left(\frac{I_t^i}{I_0^i}\right)\right],\tag{8.3}$$

where x_i denotes the basket weight of index i and N denotes the number of indices in the basket. This makes the basket value an index number with a $t = 0$ value of 100. We discussed this in Chapter 4. Having turned the basket value into a single reference index, the payoff of an **ordinary basket call** can be expressed in exactly the same way as before except that now the reference index is not taken directly from the market but created by ourselves, i.e.

$$V_T = \frac{B_0}{100} \times \text{Max}\,[0, I_T - K],\tag{8.4}$$

where B_0 denotes the initial basket value. Taking the basket value as the relevant reference index means there is no need to determine the individual index multipliers. **We can**

Table 8.1 Estimates of index correlation coefficients for 1997–1999

	S&P 500	FTE 100	DAX	CAC 40	Nikkei 225
S&P 500	1.00				
FTSE 100	0.64	1.00			
DAX	0.61	0.65	1.00		
CAC 40	0.62	0.69	0.75	1.00	
Nikkei 225	0.19	0.34	0.31	0.34	1.00

determine the option payoff from the basket weights, the initial value of the basket and the individual index returns. Note that it may look as if we have no need for the initial values of the component indices, but that is not the case. Instead of using the latter to determine the individual index multipliers we now need them to calculate the individual index returns.

When selecting a basket, correlation is the key. In the mid-1980s correlation coefficients between the returns on the various European equity markets hardly ever rose above 0.25. Nowadays things are quite different though. **Equity markets have become more and more correlated over the past decennium**, reflecting the increasing integration of equity markets across the world and especially within Europe. Table 8.1 gives an indication of the degree of correlation between various major market indices as observed over the period 1997–1999. This shows the high correlation within Europe as well as between the European indices and the S&P 500. The Nikkei 225, however, appears to be only loosely correlated with the other indices. Correlations between stock and index returns also tend to increase substantially during periods of high volatility. During the last quarter of 1998, for example, the correlation between the FTSE 100 and the DAX went up from a typical 0.65 to more than 0.80. This means that in a crisis situation the volatility of a basket of indices will not be much lower than the volatility of its components.

To calculate the volatility of a basket of indices we can use the following results. First, we express the basket return as a function of the returns on the component indices. This yields

$$BR_{0,T} = \sum_{i=1}^{N} x_i \times R_{0,T}^i, \tag{8.5}$$

where $R_{0,T}^i$ denotes the vanilla return on index i over the period from $t = 0$ until $t = T$. Given this expression we can calculate the volatility of the basket return as

$$\sigma_{\mathrm{B}} = \sqrt{\sum_{i=1}^{N}\sum_{j=1}^{N} x_i \times x_j \times \mathrm{Cov}\left[R_{0,T}^i, R_{0,T}^j\right]}, \tag{8.6}$$

which can also be expressed as

$$\sigma_{\mathrm{B}} = \sqrt{\sum_{i=1}^{N} x_i^2 \sigma_i^2 + \sum_{i=1,i\neq j}^{N}\sum_{j=1,j\neq i}^{N} x_i \times x_j \times \mathrm{Cov}\left[R_{0,T}^i, R_{0,T}^j\right]}, \tag{8.7}$$

where

$$\mathrm{Cov}\left[R_{0,T}^i, R_{0,T}^j\right] = \sigma_i \times \sigma_j \times \rho_{ij}, \tag{8.8}$$

σ_i is the volatility of index i and ρ_{ij} denotes the correlation coefficient between the return on index i and the return on index j. Suppose we had three indices, each with an annualized volatility of 20%. If the correlation between the returns on these indices was 0.70, an equally-weighted basket ($x_i = 1/3$) would have a volatility of 17.89%. However, if the correlation was 0.30 the same basket would have a volatility of only 14.61%.

8.4   BUYING LESS

Another way to lower the price of an option is simply to buy less, i.e. reduce the contract multiplier. Figure 8.2 shows the payoff of 1m ATM ordinary calls, 0.5m ATM ordinary calls, and 0.25m ATM ordinary calls. Assuming one year to maturity, the price of the first payoff is 10.45%, of the second 5.22%, and of the third 2.61%. Although the advice 'buy less' may seem rather silly at first, it is quite a popular solution as often it is not the price of the individual option but the total amount to be invested in options which is the problem. As can be seen in the graph, buying less reduces the total price to be paid by reducing the degree of participation in the market. The less we buy, the flatter the non-flat part of the payoff profile becomes.

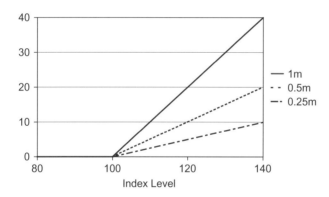

Figure 8.2   Payoff profile for different numbers of ATM ordinary calls

8.5   PIECEWISE LINEAR SEGMENTATION

As can be seen in Figures 8.1 and 8.2, changing the strike or buying less does not change the general form of the payoff function. We can, however, also come up with alternatives that make more substantial changes to the payoff function. One of them is to introduce a second strike and only buy exposure up to that strike. When bought for profit this limits the profit potential. When bought for protection this limits the degree of protection offered. Whatever the case, the option becomes cheaper as its expected payoff drops.

Let's look at an ordinary call with strike I^1. Limiting the exposure beyond $I^2 > I^1$ means the investment manager is now looking for a payoff equal to

$$V_{1/2} = M \times \text{Max}\,[0, \text{Min}\,[I^2, I_{1/2}] - I^1], \tag{8.9}$$

which can also be expressed as

$$V_{1/2} = M \times \left(\text{Max}\left[0, I_{1/2} - I^1\right] - \text{Max}\left[0, I_{1/2} - I^2\right]\right). \tag{8.10}$$

This payoff allows the investment manager to participate in a market rise from I^1 upwards, but only up to an index level of I^2. Looking at (8.10) more closely, we see that it is nothing more than the difference between the payoff of an ordinary call with strike I^1 and an ordinary call with strike I^2, i.e. a **call spread** with lower strike I^1 and upper strike I^2. In other words, instead of an ordinary call, the investment manager now buys an ordinary call spread.

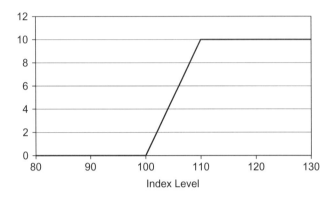

Figure 8.3 Payoff profile for call spread

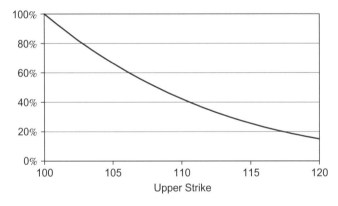

Figure 8.4 Price difference between ATM ordinary call and equivalent call spread as a function of the call spread's upper strike

Figure 8.3 shows the payoff profile of a call spread with lower strike I_0 and upper strike $1.1I_0$. The graph clearly shows that instead of two linear segments the payoff is now made up of three linear segments; hence the term piecewise linear segmentation. Figure 8.4 gives an indication of the price difference (as a percentage of the price of the ordinary call) between a 6-month ATM ordinary call and a 6-month call spread with an ATM lower strike as a function of the call spread's upper strike. When the call spread's upper strike equals the lower strike, the call spread is worthless and the price difference therefore is 100%. When the upper strike goes up, the call spread gains value and the price difference drops. Note that if we were working with a basket of indices instead of a single reference index additional savings might be obtained by, instead of capping the value of the basket as a whole, capping the value of every component index separately.

The above call spread does not allow for any participation beyond the second strike I^2. Although this may save quite a lot of money, it may also conflict with the reason why the investment manager was buying the option in the first place. We can easily adjust this by structuring a contract with a payoff equal to

$$V_{1/2} = M \times \text{Max} \left[0, I_{1/2} - I^1\right] - M^* \times \text{Max} \left[0, I_{1/2} - I^2\right], \quad 0 \leqslant M^* \leqslant M. \quad (8.11)$$

This payoff allows the investment manager to participate in an upgoing market at a multiple M, but when the index reaches I^2 the multiplier comes down to $M - M^*$. Instead of M call spreads the investment manager now buys M^* call spreads plus $M - M^*$ ordinary calls with strike I^1. In other words, the investment manager buys M calls with strike I^1 and simultaneously sells M^* calls with strike I^2. Compared to the previous case he thus simply **sells less calls with strike I^2**. Assuming $I^1 = I_0, I^2 = 1.1I_0$ and $M^* = 0.7M$, Figure 8.5 shows the payoff profile of such a **partial call spread**. The higher M^* the flatter the last segment of the payoff profile will be. Choosing $M^* = M$ produces the previous case where the last segment is completely flat. Choosing $M^* = 0$ on the other hand takes us back to the straightforward purchase of ordinary calls.

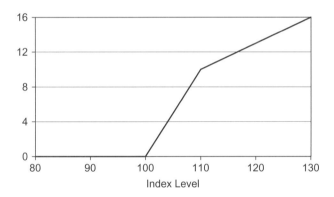

Figure 8.5 Payoff profile for partial call spread

We can take the process of piecewise linear segmentation a lot further. Instead of three we could work with four, five or more segments. When doing so, however, one should always keep in mind why the investment manager is buying the options. **Making options cheaper is about selling off exposure to scenarios the option holder considers unlikely** while retaining the exposure to scenarios he considers more likely. If an investment manager thought the index was about to show an exceptionally strong rise, it would be wrong to reduce the contract payoff for high index values. In that case, however, we might be able to save money by reducing the payoff for lower index values.

8.6 KNOCK-IN AND KNOCK-OUT OPTIONS

Another way to make a contract cheaper is to throw in a knock-in or knock-out feature. Since it forms an additional constraint on the contract payoff, knock-in and knock-out features reduce the expected payoff. As discussed in Chapter 3, with a knock-in condition the contract pays off **only if** some predefined event occurs. If not, the contract is cancelled. A knock-out condition is the mirror image and makes the contract pay off **unless** some prespecified event occurs. If it does, the contract is cancelled. The event that triggers a knock-in or knock-out can be anything, but the most popular solution is to make a contract knock-in or out when some barrier variable hits a prefixed barrier level. Many people refer to options with a knock-in or knock-out feature as **barrier options**, despite the fact that barrier options are merely a subset. We continue with a discussion of the price effects of adding American inside and outside barriers to ordinary calls and puts. As always, we concentrate on intuition rather than formal results. For the latter the reader is referred to the bibliography.

8.6.1   Inside Barrier Options

Since a barrier condition introduces an additional constraint on the contract payoff, it makes options cheaper. How much cheaper depends on the barrier level chosen. Suppose we were thinking of adding a knock-out barrier. If we set the barrier equal to spot, the option would knock out the moment the contract was signed. The option would therefore be worthless. If we moved the barrier away from spot we would introduce a non-zero probability that the option would not knock out, which would give the option value. The further away the barrier is from spot, the lower the probability of a knock-out and therefore the more valuable the option. If the barrier was extremely far away, the probability of a hit would go to zero and the option would turn into an ordinary option. Of course, the reverse is true for a knock-in option.

Fixing the barrier level we have to make a trade-off between price reduction and the risk of hitting or not hitting the barrier. Figure 8.6 shows, as a function of the barrier level, the price difference (as a percentage of the price of the ordinary call) between a 6-month ATM ordinary call and an equivalent knock-out and knock-in call, both with a barrier which is monitored continuously during the full life of the option. From the graph we clearly see that for the knock-out call the price difference is higher the closer the barrier is to spot, reflecting the higher probability that the option knocks out. With a barrier at 100 the difference is 100% because the knock-out option is worthless. The reverse is true for the knock-in call. Figure 8.6 also shows that a knock-in call and an equivalent knock-out call always sum to an ordinary call. If one knocks in, the other knocks out and the other way around.

Although the results in Figure 8.6 are in line with what we discussed, there is something unexpected about these graphs. The price of the **knock-out call** changes more if we move the barrier downwards. With a barrier at 85 the price difference with an ordinary call is almost zero, while with a barrier at 115 the knock-out call is still 80% cheaper than the ordinary call. To understand the option price better we have to look at the joint probability that (a) the option is alive at maturity and (b) it produces a positive payoff. With a barrier below spot the option will only knock out if the index goes down. Since we are talking about a call, for the option to end ITM the index will need to go up. This means that for the option to pay off all the index needs to do is not go down. With the index (assumed to be) drifting upwards, this is not an unlikely scenario. The expected payoff is therefore quite high and so is the option price. With a barrier above spot things are different. To make the option end ITM the index needs to go up. However, this will also cause the

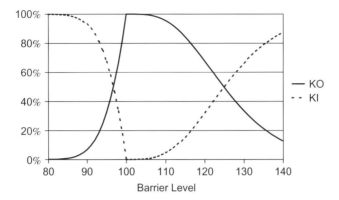

Figure 8.6   Price difference between ATM ordinary call and equivalent inside barrier call as a function of barrier level

option to knock out. To produce a positive payoff the index has to go up but never further than the barrier level. Since the probability of this happening is low and it only allows for relatively small payoffs, the expected payoff and therefore the option price are low as well. Only if we move the barrier sufficiently far away does the option gain some value.

If we look at the **knock-in call** we observe a similar phenomenon. For the option to end ITM the index needs to go up. However, if we place the barrier below spot, the index needs to go down first to make the contract knock in. Since the probability of this happening is low, the option price drops quickly if we lower the barrier level. If the barrier is above spot things are a lot easier. The index has to go the same way to make the option knock in as well as end ITM. The probability of a positive payoff is therefore much higher, which translates into a higher option price.

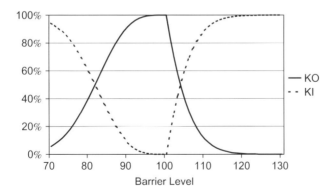

Figure 8.7   Price difference between ATM ordinary put and equivalent inside barrier put as a function of barrier level

We can perform the same analysis for **put options**. The results are shown in Figure 8.7. To make a put end ITM the index has to go down. This means that if we place the barrier above spot there is a relatively high probability for a knock-out put to produce a positive payoff and for a knock-in put to produce a zero payoff. The knock-out put will therefore still be quite expensive while the knock-in put will be relatively cheap. If we fix the barrier below spot, the index has to go in the same direction as the barrier to produce a payoff. This is good for knock-in options but not for knock-out options. The knock-out put is therefore slow to gain value while the knock-in put is slow to lose value. Again we see that a knock-in put and a knock-out put sum to an ordinary put.

We can also look at this in another way. Instead of looking where the index needs to go to generate a non-zero payoff at maturity, and how likely that is, we can simply look at what we gain or lose if the barrier is hit. A knock-out call with a barrier below spot is relatively expensive because if the barrier is hit we lose an option that is unlikely to pay off anyway. In other words, adding such a barrier does not do much damage to the option payoff. With a knock-out barrier above spot this is different. If the barrier is hit we lose an option which is likely to provide its holder with a positive payoff. Adding such a barrier therefore does a lot of damage. This is reflected in a much lower price. We can do the same for a knock-in call. With a barrier below spot a knock-in will yield an option that is unlikely to generate a positive payoff. The price is therefore low. If the barrier was above spot on the other hand we would gain an option which is much more likely to pay off, resulting in a higher price.

Looking at Figures 8.6 and 8.7 it is clear what we need to do to save money on call options: buy calls with a knock-in barrier below spot or calls with a knock-out barrier above spot. There is a problem with this strategy though. These options are cheap for a reason. It is quite unlikely that they will provide the option holder with a significant payoff. **When choosing the location of the barrier we do not want to interfere too much with the reasoning behind the purchase of the option**. The barrier should be located such that the investment manager obtains the same payoff as with an ordinary option if his view is correct, but less if it is wrong. This means that an investment manager buying ordinary calls because he is bullish should fix the barrier such that the options knock in if the market goes up or knock out if the market goes down. This allows him to benefit from a market rise but with the additional restriction that if the market does not rise enough or shows a decline instead, the option does not pay off. Likewise, puts bought to capitalize on a bearish view should be made to knock out when the market goes up or knock in when the market goes down.

In practice barrier options are often named depending on the location of the barrier relative to spot. A knock-out option with a barrier below spot is called a **down-and-out** option, while a knock-out option with a barrier above spot is referred to as an **up-and-out** option. Likewise, a knock-in option with a barrier below spot is called a **down-and-in** option, and a knock-in option with a barrier above spot is an **up-and-in** option. Options with a knock-out barrier in the ITM region and options with a knock-in barrier in the OTM region are known as **reverse barrier** options. With these options the barrier is at the 'wrong' side of spot. As we saw earlier, **reverse barrier options are cheaper than normal barrier options but tend to make less sense**.

8.6.2 Outside Barrier Options

Instead of an inside barrier we can also equip our options with an outside barrier, i.e. let another index decide on the knocking in or out of the contract. We could for example structure an ordinary call that knocked in if the interest rate went down. Likewise, we could structure a put that knocked out if the exchange rate went up. Outside barriers allow us to tailor the option not only to the view which the investment manager has on the payoff variable, but also to his view on the barrier variable. It may be that the investor sees the barrier variable as a determinant of the payoff variable, but this is not necessary. Having a separate barrier variable available makes things easier, as we can now split up tasks. The barrier variable decides the life and death of the option and, if alive, the payoff variable decides the size of the payoff. With an inside barrier things are more complicated because one and the same index has to perform both tasks at the same time.

Since the barrier feature is an additional restriction on the option payoff, outside barrier options are cheaper than ordinary options. As with an inside barrier, the difference in price depends heavily on the barrier level chosen. In addition, we also have to take account of the degree of correlation between the payoff and the barrier variable. Let's look at the influence of the barrier level first, assuming that the payoff and the barrier variable are **uncorrelated**. Figure 8.8 shows the price difference (as a percentage of the price of the ordinary option) between a 6-month ATM ordinary call and an equivalent call with an outside knock-out or knock-in barrier as a function of the barrier level. The graphs are similar to the ones we saw before in Figure 8.6. With a barrier at spot the knock-out call is worthless and the knock-in call identical to an ordinary call. If we move the barrier away from spot the knock-out call gains value and the knock-in call loses value. There is one difference though. Unlike with inside barriers, the price of the outside barrier option reacts in more or less the same way irrespective of whether we move the barrier upwards or downwards. This is due to the fact that the life-and-death decision is now taken separately from the payoff decision, by a variable that is uncorrelated with the payoff variable. We are now purely looking at the probability of a barrier hit. The slight asymmetry in both graphs is the result of the upward drift in the index.

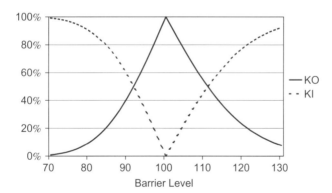

Figure 8.8   Price difference between ATM ordinary call and equivalent outside barrier call as a function of barrier level

The next step is to introduce non-zero correlation. In this case we can find the effect of a change in the barrier level in the same way as with inside barrier options: we look at the probability that the option will pay off at maturity. Suppose we choose a new barrier variable which was **negatively correlated** with the payoff variable. This means that the payoff variable and the barrier variable tend to go opposite ways. Let's look at a knock-out call. For the option to end ITM the payoff variable has to go up. If this happens, however, the barrier variable is likely to go down. This means that, compared with the case of zero correlation, the probability of a positive payoff increases for options with a barrier above spot and decreases for options with a barrier below spot. Options with a barrier above spot become more and options with a barrier below spot become less expensive. A similar reasoning holds if we change to a barrier variable which is **positively correlated** with the payoff variable. Now the payoff variable and the barrier variable tend to go the same way. For the knock-out call this means that if the option moves ITM the barrier variable is likely to go up as well. Therefore, the probability of a positive payoff increases for options with a barrier below spot and decreases for options with a barrier above spot. Options with a barrier below spot become more and options with a barrier above spot become less expensive.

Figure 8.9 shows the price difference (as a percentage of the price of the ordinary call) between a 6-month ATM ordinary call and an equivalent call with an outside knock-out barrier as a function of the barrier level for correlation coefficients of 0.8 and −0.8. The graph clearly shows that if the correlation coefficient increases the price of knock-out calls with a barrier below spot goes up and the price of calls with a barrier above spot goes down. If we compare the graph for a correlation coefficient of 0.8 with the graph for an inside knock-out call in Figure 8.6 we see that they are very similar. This is no coincidence, as with a correlation coefficient of 1 the payoff variable and the barrier variable effectively become one. In other words, **with a correlation coefficient of 1 there is no difference between an inside or an outside barrier**.

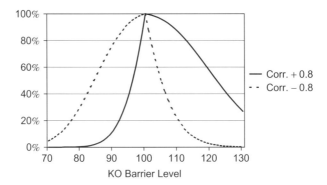

Figure 8.9   Price difference between ATM ordinary call and equivalent outside knock-out call as a function of barrier level

Of course, we can tell a similar story for knock-in calls and outside barrier puts. For example, if the correlation between the barrier and the payoff variable increases, the probability of receiving a positive payoff from a knock-in call with a barrier above spot increases because the option will tend to knock in while it moves ITM. With a knock-in barrier below spot the reverse is true. In that case the probability of a positive payoff decreases because the option will tend not to knock in if the index goes up.

8.6.3   Inside versus Outside Barriers

With perfect positive correlation between the payoff variable and the barrier variable, an outside barrier option will cost as much as an otherwise identical inside barrier option.

Since we know how the correlation between the payoff variable and the barrier variable influences the price of outside barrier options, the difference in price between inside and outside barrier options when the correlation is less than perfect can easily be determined. For example, given that the price of an outside knock-out call with a barrier located below spot is a positive function of the correlation between the payoff and the barrier variable, we know that the option is most expensive with perfect positive correlation. Combined with the fact that with perfect positive correlation inside and outside barrier options are identical, it follows that with less than perfect correlation the outside barrier option must be cheaper than the inside barrier option, with the difference increasing as the correlation declines.

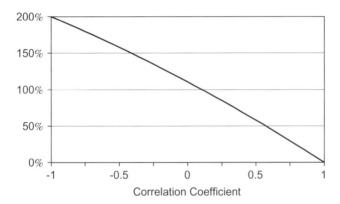

Figure 8.10 Price difference between inside and outside knock-in call as a function of correlation coefficient

Figure 8.10 shows the price difference (as a percentage of the price of the inside barrier call) between a 6-month ATM inside knock-in call with a barrier at 95% of spot and a 6-month ATM outside knock-in call with a barrier also at 95% of spot as a function of the correlation coefficient. The price of a call with an outside knock-in barrier located below spot is lowest with perfect positive correlation. With less than perfect correlation the inside barrier option must therefore be less expensive than the outside barrier option, with the difference increasing as the correlation coefficient falls. This is exactly what we see in Figure 8.10. With perfect positive correlation the inside and outside barrier options are identical. If the correlation coefficient drops the price of the outside barrier option goes up. With perfect negative correlation the outside barrier option is three times as expensive as the inside barrier option.

Since perfect positive correlation is something that only happens in extreme crisis situations, the above means that both an outside knock-out call with a barrier below spot and an outside knock-in call with a barrier above spot will be cheaper than an equivalent inside barrier call. Likewise, an outside knock-out put with a barrier above spot and an outside knock-in put with a barrier below spot will both be cheaper than an equivalent inside barrier put. As such, **these options make an interesting alternative for reverse inside barrier options**. As discussed, the latter are cheap but typically do not make much sense.

8.7   CHANGING EXCHANGE RATE RISK

In case the reference index is denominated in a foreign currency we may be able to make the option cheaper by **eliminating all or part of the exchange rate risk**. Let's look at an example. Suppose an investment manager was bullish on some foreign index. Having read Chapter 7 of this book he is thinking of going abroad to buy a 6-month ATM ordinary call on the foreign index to capitalize on this view. At maturity such a **foreign call struck in foreign currency**, or **foreign call** for short, pays off a domestic currency amount equal to

$$V_{1/2} = M \times E_{1/2} \times \text{Max} \left[0, I_{1/2} - I_0 \right] = M \times \text{Max} \left[0, E_{1/2} I_{1/2} - E_{1/2} I_0 \right]. \quad (8.12)$$

This is not the only possibility though. Instead of at the exchange rate at maturity we could convert the option payoff at the exchange rate at $t = 0$. This would yield a payoff equal to

$$V_{1/2} = M \times E_0 \times \text{Max} \left[0, I_{1/2} - I_0 \right] = M \times \text{Max} \left[0, E_0 I_{1/2} - E_0 I_0 \right]. \quad (8.13)$$

The payoff to the investment manager now only depends on the foreign equity index and no longer on the exchange rate. An option like this is known as a **quanto call**. Another possibility would be to convert the index value at the exchange rate at maturity but convert the strike at the $t = 0$ exchange rate. This yields a payoff equal to

$$V_{1/2} = M \times \text{Max} \left[0, E_{1/2} I_{1/2} - E_0 I_0 \right]. \quad (8.14)$$

An option with a payoff like this is known as a **foreign call struck in domestic currency**, or more simply as a **composite call**.

Whether the quanto and the composite call will be more or less expensive than the foreign call depends, as always, on the derivatives firm's expected hedging costs. The pricing shortcut we discussed in Chapter 5 can help out here. According to our shortcut, if domestic interest rates are higher than foreign rates we must assume that the foreign currency is about to appreciate, i.e. that the exchange rate is about to rise above E_0. On the other hand, if domestic interest rates are lower than foreign rates we must assume that the foreign currency is about to depreciate, i.e. the exchange rate is about to fall below E_0. This means that if the foreign interest rate is relatively low, the quanto call will be less expensive than the foreign call because it does not allow the investment manager to benefit from the expected appreciation. The composite call will in that case be more expensive than the foreign call because it allows the investment manager to capture more of the expected appreciation. The reverse is true if the foreign interest rate is higher than the domestic rate.

Because the above reasoning revolves around the interest rate differential, it works better the longer the maturity of the contract in question. For 6-month calls the interest rate differential needs to be quite substantial before we see any significant price difference. For a 5-year call, however, the price difference can be very significant even with a relatively small interest rate differential. Figure 8.11 shows the price difference (as a percentage of the price of the foreign call) between a 5-year ATM foreign call on the one hand and an equivalent quanto call and composite call on the other as a function of the foreign interest rate. The graph confirms that if the foreign interest rate is lower than the domestic rate

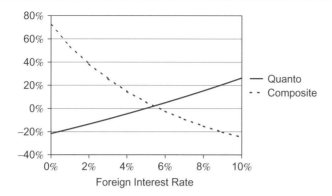

Figure 8.11 Price difference between foreign call and (a) quanto call and (b) composite call as a function of foreign interest rate

the quanto call is less and the composite call is more expensive than the foreign call. The opposite is true in case the foreign rate is higher than the domestic rate.

The cost savings that can be obtained by modified currency conversion are not necessarily a free lunch. If the foreign currency appreciates, the payoff to the investment manager from a quanto call will be lower than what he would have received if he had bought the foreign option. Likewise, if the foreign currency depreciates the payoff of a composite call will be less than that of a foreign call. Fortunately, research has shown that there is no good reason why one should expect the exchange rate to actually do what is implied by the interest rate differential, especially in the short run. Over the period 1998–2000, for example, the British pound showed a remarkable rise vis-á-vis the euro, despite relatively high interest rates in the UK. **When the investment manager's view is that the exchange rate will move against the interest rate differential, a quanto call or a composite call makes an extremely interesting alternative**.

8.8 PAY-LATER AND MONEY-BACK OPTIONS

The techniques discussed so far reduce the option premium with certainty by selling off exposure to scenarios that the investor thinks unlikely. One can, however, also think of alternatives which reduce the option premium only when certain conditions are met. In that case we speak of **contingent premium options**. The most popular contingent premium options are options with so-called money-back and pay-later features. With a **money-back** feature the initial option premium is paid back at maturity when the reference index exhibits some prespecified behavior. The possibility of receiving one's money back means that whether the buyer will really have to pay for the option only becomes clear at maturity. We can also formulate this directly in the form of a **pay-later** feature, which says that the initial option premium is zero but that the option has to be paid for in the future when the index exhibits some prespecified behavior. Pay-later and money-back features come in two types; path-independent and path-dependent. In the first case the amount to be exchanged depends solely on the index value at maturity, while in the second case it is a function of the path taken by the index to arrive at its maturity value. We discuss path-independent money-backs and pay-laters first.

8.8.1 Path-Independent Money-Backs and Pay-Laters

A path-independent **money-back option** is an option which, apart from its normal payoff, pays back the initial option premium when at expiration the index is within a predetermined range. Because of the possibility of getting the option premium back at maturity, i.e. the higher expected payoff, a money-back option will be more expensive than an otherwise identical standard option. However, as long as one gets one's money back this is not a problem.

Suppose an investment manager intended to buy a 6-month ATM ordinary call. We could turn the latter option into a money-back option that pays the initial premium back when the index at maturity is higher than I_0 by changing the option payoff into

$$V_{1/2} = M \times \text{Max} \left[0, I_{1/2} - I_0 \right] + D \times V_0, \tag{8.15}$$

where

$$D = 0, \quad \text{if } I_{1/2} < I_0,$$
$$= 1, \quad \text{if } I_{1/2} \geqslant I_0.$$

From this expression we see that the payoff of such a money-back call consists of two parts. The first part is the payoff of M ordinary calls. The second part is the **money-back feature**: if the index at maturity is equal to or higher than I_0 the payoff to the investment manager is V_0, i.e. he gets back what he initially paid. If the index is lower than I_0 the payoff is zero. Note that apart from its time to maturity and initial price, **the money-back feature requires no information about the option it is added to**.

The money-back feature provides a payoff identical to the payoff of a **digital call**. This means that pricing the above money-back call boils down to finding the value of V_0 that solves the budget equation given by

$$V_0 = M \times C_0^{\text{a}}[I_0, 0.5] + V_0 \times DC_0^{\text{a}}[I_0, 0.5], \tag{8.16}$$

where $DC_0^{\text{a}}[H, T]$ is the derivatives firm's offer for a digital call that pays off 1.00 at time T if the index is equal to or higher than H. Under the usual assumptions the derivatives firm quotes an offer price of 0.53% for the digital call. Taking $M = 1$ this yields

$$V_0 = 6.86 + 0.53V_0, \tag{8.17}$$

meaning that V_0 must be 14.60%. Compared to the price of an ordinary call of 6.86%, this means the money-back call is more than twice as expensive. However, if the investment manager's view is correct, he will get the full option premium returned at maturity and the option will not have cost him anything.

It is not necessary to put the money-back boundary above which the option premium is refunded equal to the option's strike. The boundary can be set higher or lower. Of course, this will influence the price of the money-back feature, i.e. the price of the digital call. The lower the boundary, the higher the probability that the index finishes above the boundary level, the more likely it is that the digital will pay off, and therefore the more expensive the money-back option will be. This is also illustrated in Figure 8.12, which shows the price of a 6-month ATM money-back call as a function of the money-back boundary.

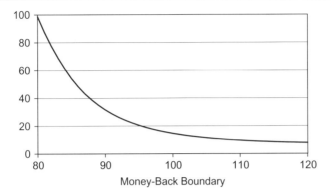

Figure 8.12   Price of money-back call as a function of money-back boundary

Instead of paying the investment manager his money back when his view is correct, we can also do the reverse and pay him when he is wrong. To do so we have to offer him a contract with a payoff equal to (8.15) but with

$$D = 1, \quad \text{if } I_{1/2} < I_0,$$
$$= 0, \quad \text{if } I_{1/2} \geq I_0.$$

Although a contract like this protects the investment manager against being wrong, the result if he is right is not very appealing as the premium he will have to pay will be substantially higher than that for an ordinary option. The budget equation for the above money-back call would be

$$V_0 = 6.86 + 0.45 V_0, \tag{8.18}$$

where the 0.45 is simply the derivatives firm's offer for a **digital put** that pays off 1.00 at time T if the index is lower than I_0. From this it follows that the option would cost the investment manager 12.47%, i.e. 82% more than an ordinary call would cost him.

The money-back feature can be extended by introducing additional segments. Such options are called **complex money-backs**. When the segment boundaries are chosen such that the probability that the option premium will be returned is reduced, a complex money-back will be cheaper than a simple money-back and the other way around. In general terms, a complex ATM money-back call will provide the investment manager with a payoff equal to

$$V_{1/2} = M \times \text{Max} [0, I_{1/2} - I_0] + \sum_{i=1}^{n} D^i \times X_i, \tag{8.19}$$

where

$$D^i = 1, \quad \text{if } a_i \leqslant I_{1/2} < a_{i+1},$$
$$= 0, \quad \text{if } a_i < I_{1/2} \text{ or } I_{1/2} \geqslant a_{i+1}.$$

The parameters a_i and a_{i+1} denote the lower and upper boundary of the ith segment of the outcome space of $I_{1/2}$. Segments are numbered in ascending order with the upper boundary a_{i+1} not being included in the ith segment. n is the total number of segments and X_i denotes the amount to be received by the investment manager when the index finishes in segment i. Since the money-back feature must span the complete outcome space, $a_1 \equiv 0$ and $a_{n+1} \equiv \infty$. To get to the simple money-back call we discussed earlier we would only have to set $n = 2$ and $a_2 = I_0$, i.e. we would have two segments: one between zero and I_0 and the other between I_0 and infinity. In addition, we would have $X_1 = 0$ and $X_2 = V_0$.

The pricing of complex money-back options is analogous to the pricing of a simple money-back. The relevant budget equation is given by

$$V_0 = M \times C_0^a[I_0, 0.5] + \sum_{i=1}^{n} X_i \times DS_0^a[a_i, a_{i+1}, 0.5], \tag{8.20}$$

where $DS_0^a[H^1, H^2, T]$ denotes the derivatives firm's offer for a **digital spread** that pays off 1.00 at time T if the index is equal to or higher than H^1 but lower than H^2. As always, when getting a price from the derivatives firm we do not ask for prices on the individual digital spreads, but we have to let the firm know that we plan to trade them all simultaneously. It should be noted that a digital spread is nothing special and can easily be packaged from digital calls. A digital spread pays off if at the monitoring date the index is between H^1 and H^2. A digital call pays off if the index is above a certain value. This means that the payoff of a digital spread can also be obtained by buying a digital call which pays off above H^1 while simultaneously selling a digital call which pays off above H^2.

The above equation can be used to calculate the option price for given values of X_i, but may also be used to calculate the value of X_i implied by a given option price and the other $(n-1)$ values of X_i. Suppose we had three segments with $a_1 = 0$, $a_2 = 1.1I_0$ and $a_3 = 1.2I_0$. The budget equation would in that case be equal to

$$V_0 = 6.86 + 0.70X_1 + 0.16X_2 + 0.12X_3. \tag{8.21}$$

If our investment manager thought that the index was going to rise over the next six months by 10% to 20%, he might consider putting $X_1 = 0$, $X_2 = V_0$ and $X_3 = 0$. The resulting complex money-back call would pay the investment manager's money back if the underlying price rose by 10% to 20%. If the underlying price were to fall, rise by less than 10% or by 20% or more, there would be no payback. As can be calculated from (8.21), the price of such an option would be equal to $V_0 = 6.86/(1 - 0.16) = 8.17\%$. Although this is 31% more than the price of an otherwise identical ordinary call, this premium would only have to be paid when the option finished OTM, less than 10% ITM or 20% or more ITM.

Pay-later options are the mirror image of money-back options. A path-independent pay-later option is an option with an initial price of zero which only has to be paid for if at maturity the index is within a predetermined range. Since there is a possibility that the pay-later option does not have to be paid for at all, the amount to be paid when the pay-later option does have to be paid for (what we might refer to as the pay-later option's 'price') will exceed the price of an otherwise identical standard option. Again, this need not be disadvantageous. An investor with a bullish view might consider buying a pay-later call which would only have to be paid for if the option finished OTM. Formally, the option payoff would in this case be equal to

$$V_{1/2} = M \times \text{Max}\left[0, I_{1/2} - I_0\right] - D \times L_{1/2}, \tag{8.22}$$

where

$$D = 1, \quad \text{if } I_{1/2} < I_0,$$
$$ = 0, \quad \text{if } I_{1/2} \geqslant I_0.$$

The second part of the above expression is the **pay-later feature**. If at maturity the index was lower than I_0, the investment manager would have to pay $L_{1/2}$. If the investment manager's view proved correct, however, there would be no payment required and the option would have been obtained for free.

The price of the pay-later call, $L_{1/2}$, can be solved from the budget equation

$$0 = M \times C_0^a[I_0] - L_{1/2} \times DP_0^a[I_0, 0.5], \tag{8.23}$$

where $DP_0^a[H, T]$ is the derivatives firm's offer for a **digital put** that pays off 1.00 at time T if the index is lower than H. Under the assumptions made this yields

$$0 = 6.86 - 0.45L_{1/2}, \tag{8.24}$$

producing a value for $L_{1/2}$ of 15.24%. Compared to the price of an equivalent ordinary call of 6.86%, this means the pay-later call is 122% more expensive. However, if the investment manager's view is correct, the option will not cost him anything. The pay-later call looks more expensive than an equivalent money-back call (112%), but that is due to the timing of the premium payment. With a money-back call the investment manager pays upfront while with a pay-later he pays at maturity.

If we compare the budget equation for the above pay-later call with that for the money-back call that pays back when the investment manager's view turns out to be wrong, i.e. (8.18), we see that they are more or less identical. This is the result of the fact that in both options the contingent premium feature pays off when the index ends below its initial value. If it does, the money-back feature pays off V_0 and the pay-later feature pays off $-L_{1/2}$, but in the end that is just semantics.

As with money-back options, we can place the pay-later boundary anywhere we want. The lower the boundary the more expensive the pay-later call will become, because the probability that the option will have to be paid for, i.e. that the derivatives firm is going to get paid, will fall. This is also illustrated in Figure 8.13. We can also turn the contract around and make the investment manager pay when he is right. Although this protects him against being wrong, it substantially reduces his profits when he is right. In the above example, instead of 6.86% he would end up paying 12.94% when the index ended above I_0. Finally, we can create **complex pay-laters** by making the payment scheme more elaborate. The payoff of a complex ATM pay-later call is given by

$$V_{1/2} = M \times \text{Max}\,[0, I_{1/2} - I_0] - \sum_{i=1}^{n} D^i \times X_i, \tag{8.25}$$

where D^i is the same as in the case of a complex money-back call. This means the relevant budget equation is equal to

$$0 = M \times C_0^a[I_0, 0.5] - \sum_{i=1}^{n} X_i \times DS_0^a[a_i, a_{i+1}, 0.5]. \tag{8.26}$$

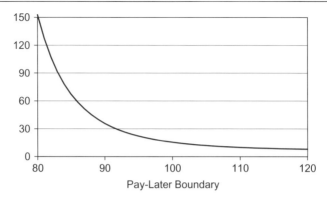

Figure 8.13 Price of pay-later call as a function of pay-later boundary

The simple pay-later call we discussed before can be seen as a special case with $n = 2$, $a_2 = I_0$, $X_1 = L_{1/2}$ and $X_2 = 0$. Note again that (8.26) is not really different from the budget equation we had before for the complex money-back call, i.e. (8.20).

Suppose the investment manager expected the index to rise by 10% to 15% over the next six months. To fit the latter expectation, we could construct a complex pay-later which does not have to be paid for when the index indeed rises by 10% to 15%, by segmenting the outcome space at 10% and 15% above the current index level and choosing $X_2 = 0$ and $X_1 = X_3$. If the investment manager is right, the option comes for free, while otherwise he has to pay $X_1 = X_3$. The segments where the option has to be paid for may be stratified further to make the investment manager pay more the further away the index at maturity is from the targeted range. In this way the investment manager is rewarded when he is right and punished when he is wrong, with the punishment being more severe the more he is wrong. Suppose we divided the outcome space into seven segments, starting at I_0 and moving upwards by 5% until 25%. The budget equation is then given by

$$0 = 6.86 - 0.45X_1 - 0.13X_2 - 0.12X_3 - 0.09X_4 - 0.07X_5 - 0.05X_6 - 0.07X_7. \quad (8.27)$$

X_4 should be fixed at zero to make the option come for free when the investment manager's expectation proves correct. Additionally, we might put $X_1 = X_7 = 0.5X$, $X_2 = X_6 = 0.3X$ and $X_3 = X_5 = 0.2X$, to make the amounts payable evolve symmetrically around the expected outcome range. The value of X can now be solved from (8.27), which yields $X = 19.49$.

Comparing simple and complex money-backs and simple and complex pay-laters it becomes clear that **in essence there is very little difference** between them. Simple money-backs and pay-laters are special cases of complex money-backs and pay-laters. Moreover, complex pay-laters are nothing more than complex money-backs where the payback amounts are negative and the initial price is set equal to zero. This means we can use the same framework to structure contracts where in some cases the buyer of the option pays the seller and in other cases the seller pays the buyer. Having chosen the basic option to which the feature is to be added, we (1) divide the outcome range of the index into a number of segments, (2) determine the relevant budget equation, and (3) decide on the amounts receivable/payable. Only in the latter step do we fix the exact nature of the feature, i.e. money-back, pay-later or a mix of the two. **These features can be added to**

any type of contract. In the above we concentrated on ordinary calls, but we could have taken any other type of option (or forward).

8.8.2   Path-Dependent Money-Backs and Pay-Laters

With path-dependent money-back and pay-later options the amounts to be exchanged depend on the path taken by the index to reach its maturity value. The most popular way to do so is using a **barrier structure**, where the amounts to be exchanged depend on whether during (part of) the life of the option the index hits one or more prefixed barrier levels. When there is more than one barrier, payment is due at each barrier level. This means that we can construct money-back options where the full premium is paid back when the barrier is hit, but also options which pay the initial premium back in a more gradual stepwise fashion. Barrier-driven pay-laters can be structured in the same way.

Structuring barrier-driven money-back and pay-later options is similar to the path-independent case. Suppose we wanted to create a 6-month ATM money-back call which at maturity paid back the initial premium if during the life of the option the index was up by 10% or more. Such an option would pay off

$$V_{1/2} = M \times \text{Max} \left[0, I_{1/2} - I_0 \right] + D \times V_0, \tag{8.28}$$

where

$$D = 0, \quad \text{if } \forall j \ I_j < 1.1I_0,$$
$$= 1, \quad \text{if } \exists j \ I_j \geqslant 1.1I_0.$$

The budget equation that goes with this payoff is given by

$$V_0 = M \times C_0^a[I_0, 0.5] + V_0 \times AID_0^a[1.1I_0, 0, 0.5, 0.5], \tag{8.29}$$

where $AID_0^a[H, t_1, t_2, T]$ is the derivatives firm's offer for an **American knock-in digital** that pays off 1.00 at $t = T$ if at any of the monitoring points between $t = t_1$ and $t = t_2$ the index is equal to or higher than H. Assuming we monitor the index continuously for a barrier hit, this yields a budget equation of

$$V_0 = 6.86 + 0.52V_0. \tag{8.30}$$

The option price is therefore $V_0 = 6.86/(1 - 0.52) = 14.29\%$. Although this is twice the price of an otherwise identical ordinary call, this price only has to be paid when the underlying price does not hit the barrier.

As mentioned, we could also work with **multiple barriers** to pay the initial premium back in a stepwise fashion. Suppose we worked with three barriers, i.e. three American knock-in digitals instead of one. The budget equation for an ATM money-back call with barriers at 5%, 10% and 15% above the initial index level is given by

$$V_0 = 6.86 + 0.74X_1 + 0.52X_2 + 0.35X_3, \tag{8.31}$$

where the three coefficients are simply the prices of the three digitals involved. If we put $X_1 = 0.2V_0$, $X_2 = 0.3V_0$ and $X_3 = 0.5V_0$, we would obtain a complex money-back call which paid back 20% of the initial premium at the first barrier, 30% at the second and the final 50% at the third. As is easily calculated, such an option would cost the investment manager 13.17%.

Barrier-driven pay-laters can be created in the same way as before, i.e. by setting $V_0 = 0$ in the budget equation. Doing so in (8.30), we obtain a pay-later call which will have to be paid for if the underlying price rose from its present level by 10% or more. Likewise, we can use (8.31) to create a complex pay-later call which requires its holder to pay 0.2 times the maximum premium amount to be paid at the first barrier, 0.3 times the maximum premium at the second and 0.5 times the maximum premium at the third barrier. To do so, we have to put $V_0 = 0$ and $X_1 = 0.2X$, $X_2 = 0.3X$ and $X_3 = 0.5X$, where X is the maximum amount of premium to be paid (when all three barriers are hit).

To find out the effect on the option price of a change in the location of the barriers we have to consider the amounts to be exchanged at the barriers and the probability that this exchange will indeed take place, i.e. how far away the barriers are from the current index value. With money-back options the higher the amount to be paid back and the closer the barrier to spot, the higher the option's expected payoff and therefore its price. The reverse is true for pay-later options. The more likely it is that the investment manager will pay, the lower the expected payoff and the cheaper the option will be.

8.9   INSTALMENT OPTIONS

Another way for our investment manager to manipulate the costs of buying options is not to buy the desired option directly, but to enter into a contract where he pays for the option in two or more instalments. The first instalment needs to be paid with certainty, but the remaining instalments do not. With such an **instalment option** every time an instalment comes up for payment the investment manager has to decide whether he wants to proceed or not. If he does, he pays. If he does not, he simply does not pay and loses his claim to a payoff. Options like this are sometimes also referred to as **pay-as-you-go options**. The advantage of an instalment option is straightforward. If the investment manager's view proves wrong he can stop paying and thereby limit his losses. On the other hand, if his view proves correct he would have been better off with a standard option as the instalment route, which offers **additional flexibility**, i.e. a higher expected payoff, will in that case be more expensive.

Let's look at a simple example. Suppose an investment manager thought the market was likely to go up over the next six months. Instead of paying for a 6-month ATM ordinary call upfront he could also enter into a contract where he paid the derivatives firm in two instalments; one upon entering the contract and one two months later. After two months there are two possible outcomes depending on the value of a 4-month call with strike I_0. If the latter option is worth more than the instalment to be paid the investor will pay and thereby obtain a claim to the option payoff. However, if after two months the price of the 4-month call is lower than the instalment to be paid the investment manager will not pay and thus forego his claim to a payoff.

The advantage of the instalment call is that if after two months the investment manager's view proves wrong and the index goes down instead of up, he only loses the first instalment and not the full premium for a 6-month call. Since the option is paid for in two instalments, when structuring the option we are free to choose one instalment ourselves. Figure 8.14 shows the trade-off between the first instalment and the second instalment of a 6-month ATM instalment call with the second instalment to be paid after two months. From the

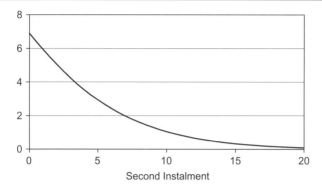

Figure 8.14   Trade-off between first and second instalment of an ATM instalment call

graph we see that when the second instalment is zero, the first instalment is equal to the price of a 6-month ATM ordinary call. This makes sense since in that case the instalment feature is trivial. When the second instalment rises, the first instalment drops quickly. If we wanted **to minimize the cost of being wrong, we should choose a relatively high second instalment**.

If the investment manager's view proved correct he would have been better off if he had bought the 6-month ATM ordinary call directly instead of buying an instalment call. From Figure 8.14 we can calculate how much more expensive the instalment route is by adding the first and second instalments and comparing this with the price of a 6-month ATM ordinary call, which is equal to 6.86%. The difference (as a percentage of the price of the ordinary call) is shown in Figure 8.15. When the second instalment is zero the difference is equal to zero because in that case the first instalment and the ordinary call price are equal. However, when the second instalment rises, the additional costs of the instalment route increase. If we wanted **to minimize the cost of being right, we should keep the second instalment relatively low**.

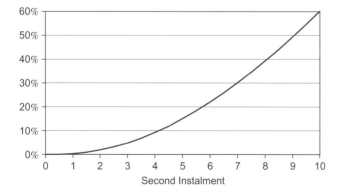

Figure 8.15   Additional costs of an ATM call paid in two instalments as a function of second instalment

The above implies that when it comes to choosing the instalments there is a trade-off to be made. To keep the cost of being wrong down, one should choose a high second instalment. To keep the cost of being right down, one should choose a low second instalment. Given that the typical clientele for an instalment option are people who think the market will go up but who at the same time are afraid it will go down, a good solution might be to set the second instalment equal to what the underlying option would be worth if the index did not change. In our case that means setting the second instalment equal to 5.41%, implying a first instalment of 2.68%. If the investment manager was right the 6-month call would cost him 8.09% instead of 6.86%. If he was wrong, however, it would only cost him 2.68% instead of 6.86%.

So far we have only looked at the case of two instalments. There is no reason why we could not expand the idea to three or more instalments. More instalments allow for more flexibility and will therefore make the option more expensive if all instalments are paid for. Assuming equal instalments and equally spaced instalment dates, Figure 8.16 shows the difference between the price of a 6-month ATM ordinary call and the total cost of an instalment option, i.e. the sum of all instalments, as a function of the number of instalments. As in Figure 8.15, the difference is expressed as a percentage of the price of the ordinary call.

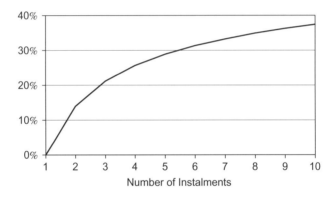

Figure 8.16   Additional costs of an ATM call paid in instalments as a function of number of instalments

Another way to interpret instalment options is in terms of so-called **compound options** or options on options. The instalment option in the above example can also be interpreted as a contract where in two months time the derivatives firm gives the investment manager a 4-month ordinary call, the investment manager pays a fixed amount and also has the right to cancel the contract at maturity. This is known as a **call on a call** or a **compound call**. If after two months the value of the 4-month ordinary call exceeds the fixed amount to be paid by the investment manager he will proceed with the exchange. If not he will cancel the deal. This shows that generally speaking an instalment option is the same as a multiple compound call where every instalment date is a maturity date and every instalment is a strike.

8.10   CALLABLE OPTIONS

Another way to make an option cheaper is to give the writer of the option the right to cancel the option contract at a prefixed time and price. This yields a so-called **callable**

option. Although it may look like a big thing, making an option callable is not difficult. All the buyer of the option needs to do is enter into a second contract with the same counterparty which calls for the buyer to give up the option and for the seller to pay a fixed amount, and which in addition gives the seller the right to cancel that deal when it matures. If the option value drops, the seller will cancel but if it goes up he will let the contract mature and take back the option in return for a fixed amount. This is no different from an ordinary call, except that in this case we are not talking about exchanging a fixed amount for the index value but about exchanging a fixed amount for an option. As discussed in the previous section, this is known as a **compound call**. The buyer of the option underlying the compound option pays a premium to the seller for the first option, but at the same time receives a premium for selling the compound call. On balance this makes the option which he buys cheaper.

Buying a callable option means buying an option while simultaneously selling a compound call on that option. Depending on whether the compound call can be exercised early or not we can distinguish between European, Bermudan and American callable options. With a **European** callable option the writer of the option can buy the option back at only one point in the future; the compound call's maturity date. With a **Bermudan** callable option he can do so at a fixed number of points in time, and with an **American** callable option the writer can buy the option back at any time during the so-called **call period**. Of course, this call period is simply the period during which the option writer can exercise his compound call early.

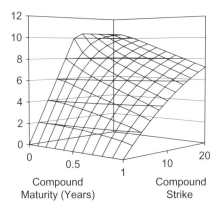

Figure 8.17 Price of a European callable ATM ordinary call as a function of compound call strike and compound call time to maturity

By giving the writer of an option the opportunity to buy it back at a prefixed price, the option buyer implicitly sells off his profit potential. If the option moves ITM the option writer becomes more likely to call the option. The decision to call depends of course also on the amount he will have to pay when he does, i.e. the compound call's strike. The lower this amount, the more likely he is to call and therefore the cheaper the callable option should be. Figure 8.17 shows the price of a 1-year European callable ATM ordinary call as a function of the compound call's strike and its time to maturity. The ordinary call is worth 10.45%. When the strike is zero, a compound call is no different from an ordinary call. Therefore, for a zero compound call strike the callable option is worthless. When the compound call strike goes up, the price of the callable call goes up as well. On the other hand, it is a negative function of the compound call's time to maturity, because the value of the compound call rises with maturity.

8.11   ASIAN OPTIONS

Another way to save money is to calculate the contract payoff not from the index value at maturity, but from the average index value observed during the life of the option. Since the average moves slower than the index itself, it is less likely to make big swings. In other words, the volatility of the average is lower than that of the index. If the index goes up (down), the average goes up (down) as well, but less. This means that replacing the index value at maturity by the average index value will lower the expected payoff and thereby the price of the option.

The average will be calculated over a number of monitoring points which are typically assumed to be equally spaced. The more monitoring points, the lower the volatility of the average will be. For various index volatilities σ Table 8.2 provides some insight into the behavior of the volatility of the average as the number of monitoring points n increases. We assume the average is calculated over a one year period. From the table we see that if there is only one monitoring point the volatility of the average is equal to that of the index. If the number of monitoring points increases, the volatility of the average comes down quickly. Monitoring the index once a day ($n = 260$) is enough to make the volatility drop by almost 50%. If we increase the number of monitoring points further, the volatility of the average stabilizes at 0.582 times the volatility of the index.

Now suppose we were dealing with a 6-month ATM ordinary call and we replaced the index value in the payoff function by the average. The resulting contract would offer a payoff equal to

$$V_{1/2} = M \times \text{Max} \left[0, A_{0,1/2} - I_0\right], \tag{8.32}$$

where A_{t_1,t_2} denotes the average index value over the period from $t = t_1$ up to $t = t_2$. An option with a payoff like this is known as a **fixed-strike Asian call**. Assuming we monitored the index daily, such an option would cost 3.83%. In line with the almost 50% drop in volatility, this is almost half the 6.86% one would have to pay for an ordinary call.

The expected hedging costs of the Asian option are substantially lower than for an ordinary option. This becomes clear if we look at how one can hedge a payoff equal to the average. We start by buying the index. As time passes, we gradually sell off the shares we own and take the proceeds to the bank. At maturity the value of our bank deposit

Table 8.2 Volatility of the average as a function of number of monitoring points and index volatility

n	$\sigma = 0.1$	$\sigma = 0.2$	$\sigma = 0.3$	$\sigma = 0.4$
1	0.1000	0.2000	0.3000	0.4000
2	0.0793	0.1587	0.2383	0.3182
12	0.0618	0.1237	0.1858	0.2484
260	0.0584	0.1169	0.1757	0.2349
1000	0.0582	0.1166	0.1753	0.2344
10,000	0.0582	0.1165	0.1752	0.2342
100,000	0.0582	0.1165	0.1752	0.2342

will have grown to an amount equal to the average and our stock holdings will have depleted. This strategy is extremely simple and does not require any assumptions about the volatility of the index. Another interesting fact is that since we get paid interest on our bank deposit, at inception we can buy less than one share of the index. In other words, to obtain the average index value at maturity we do not have to pay the full index value. We can of course also interpret this in terms of expected payoffs. The average may offer a lower expected payoff than the index, but according to our pricing shortcut it should offer the same expected return. Therefore, it should be cheaper.

Another way to make an ordinary call cheaper is to replace the option's strike, instead of the index-linked cash flow, by the average. This produces a contract payoff equal to

$$V_{1/2} = M \times \text{Max} \left[0, I_{1/2} - A_{0,1/2} \right].\qquad(8.33)$$

An option with a payoff like this is known as a **floating-strike Asian call**. It will be substantially cheaper than an equivalent ordinary option, because if the index goes up, so does the average. The Asian call therefore offers a lower expected payoff than the ordinary call. Assuming daily monitoring the above Asian call will cost 3.88%.

8.12 REVISED MONITORING OF THE INDEX

For contracts with payoffs that depend on the path taken by the index to reach its value at maturity, we have to specify a number of monitoring points at which the index will be monitored. **A change of monitoring points can sometimes significantly change an option's price**. There are two things we can do. We can either make the **monitoring period**, i.e. the period between the first and the last monitoring point, longer or shorter, or we can change the **monitoring frequency** within the monitoring period. The effect of changing the monitoring period and/or frequency depends of course on the type of contract we are dealing with. Since derivatives prices can be interpreted as discounted expected payoffs, however, a little probabilistic intuition is enough to figure these effects out. Remember that when the monitoring period covers only part of a contract's life we speak of **partial** instead of **full** monitoring. This gives rise to options like partial lookback options, partial barrier options or partial Asian options.

8.12.1 Lookback and Ladder Options

To unveil the effect of partial monitoring on lookback and ladder options we first have to look at these options' payoffs. Fixed-strike lookback or ladder calls are call options where instead of the index at maturity the seller pays the (stepwise) maximum index value observed at the monitoring points. Likewise, floating-strike lookback or ladder calls are calls where the buyer pays the (stepwise) minimum. Fixed-strike lookback or ladder puts are puts where instead of the index the buyer pays the (stepwise) minimum, while floating-strike lookback or ladder puts are puts where the seller pays the (stepwise) maximum. Because it lowers the probability of observing a new maximum or minimum, it will be clear that **a shorter monitoring period reduces the price of all the above types of lookback and ladder options**.

How the option price drops if we reduce the monitoring period depends on the exact location of the monitoring period. We could have a monitoring period which starts at inception but ends before maturity, but we could also have it start after inception and end

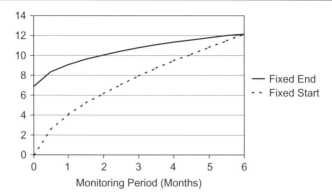

Figure 8.18   Price of an ATM partial fixed-strike lookback call as a function of monitoring period

at maturity, or have it start after inception as well as end before maturity. Figure 8.18 shows the price of a 6-month ATM partial **fixed-strike lookback call** as a function of the length of the monitoring period. One graph assumes the monitoring period always starts at inception and the other assumes the monitoring period always ends at maturity. During the monitoring period the index is monitored continuously. The graphs show that when the monitoring period gets shorter, both option prices drop. However, there are significant differences.

We can understand these differences if we look at the extreme case of one monitoring point. If we only monitored at the start of the option's life we would end up with a maximum equal to I_0. In that case the option would be worthless. If we only monitored at maturity the maximum would be equal to the index value at maturity, in which case the lookback call would be identical to an ordinary call. If we increase the monitoring period the price of both options rises because this introduces the probability of finding a maximum higher than I_0 or I_T, respectively. However, the price of the option with monitoring starting at inception will increase more than that of the other option, because we are more likely to find an index value higher than I_0 during the first week of monitoring than we are to find an index value higher than I_T during the last week of monitoring. With full monitoring both options are identical.

Figure 8.19 shows the price of a 6-month ATM partial **floating-strike lookback call** as a function of the length of the monitoring period. As before, one graph assumes the monitoring period always starts at inception and the other assumes the monitoring period always ends at maturity. During the monitoring period the index is monitored continuously. In the graphs we see similar effects as with the fixed-strike call. If we were to monitor only once, the option with monitoring starting at inception would be identical to an ordinary call and the option with monitoring ending at maturity would be worthless. By increasing the monitoring period we introduce the probability of finding a minimum lower than I_0 or I_T, respectively and both option prices will rise. The price of the option with monitoring ending at maturity has to rise much more than that of the other option, however, because eventually both options become one and the same.

Turning to the monitoring frequency we see similar effects. Monitoring the index less frequently means we have a lower chance of detecting a new maximum or minimum. This reduces the options' expected payoff and thereby their price. Figure 8.20 shows the prices of a 6-month ATM fixed-strike and floating-strike lookback call as a function of the

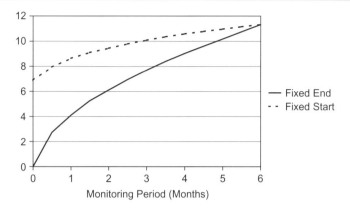

Figure 8.19 Price of a partial floating-strike lookback call as a function of monitoring period

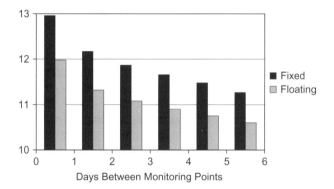

Figure 8.20 Price of an ATM fixed-strike and floating-strike lookback call as a function of monitoring frequency

number of days between monitoring points, assuming full monitoring. The graph shows clearly that **the price of both types of lookback calls drops significantly when the monitoring frequency comes down**. The same is true for ladder options.

When changing the monitoring period on lookbacks and ladders (or any other contract parameter for that matter) it is important to keep a close eye on the reason why someone is buying or selling the option in question. The main reason for the existence of fixed-strike lookback and ladder options is to help investors with the timing of their market exit. We discussed this in Chapter 7. To actually do so the monitoring period needs to end at or at least close to maturity. A similar reasoning goes for the floating-strike varieties. These are used to improve market entry. The monitoring period should therefore start at inception. Unfortunately, for both of these types of options the first weeks of monitoring are also the most expensive as we are most likely to find a new extremum during those weeks.

8.12.2 Barrier Options

With lookbacks and ladders the effect of partial and less frequent monitoring is fairly straightforward. With knock-in and knock-out barriers things are more complicated as we also have to take the location of the barrier into account. By itself, a longer monitoring period or a higher monitoring frequency implies a higher probability of hitting the barrier. It therefore makes it more likely that an option with a knock-out barrier will knock out or that an option with a knock-in barrier will knock in. **A longer monitoring period or higher monitoring frequency makes knock-out options less and knock-in options more expensive**.

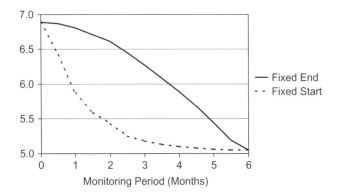

Figure 8.21   Price of an ATM 95% partial knock-out call as a function of monitoring period

With no monitoring at all, a knock-out option is identical to a standard option and a knock-in option will be worthless. This means that if the monitoring period becomes shorter, the price of a knock-out option will rise towards the price of an equivalent standard option and the price of a knock-in option will drop to zero. How this happens depends on where we put the monitoring period. Figure 8.21 shows the effect of changing the monitoring period on the price of a continuously monitored ATM knock-out call with six months to maturity and a barrier at 95% of spot. One graph assumes the monitoring period always starts at inception; the other assumes the monitoring period always ends at maturity. If we fix the monitoring period at inception the option price drops much quicker when the monitoring period is increased. This reflects the fact that the probability of the index reaching a level of 95 is much higher at inception than at maturity. The effect of a change in the monitoring frequency on the same option with full monitoring can be found in Figure 8.22. The graph shows clearly how the option price drops if the monitoring frequency increases. With weekly monitoring the option is worth 5.44%, while with continuous monitoring it is worth only 4.64%.

How strong the effect of a change in the monitoring period and/or frequency is also depends on the **location of the barrier**. This becomes clear if we look at reverse barrier options, i.e. options that knock out if they become ITM or that knock in if they become OTM. Since the location of the barrier is such that it is unlikely the option will pay off, adding a reverse barrier has a much stronger impact than adding a normal barrier. The effect of a change in the monitoring period will therefore be stronger for reverse barriers as well. The opposite is true for the monitoring frequency though. Because the introduction of a reverse barrier has such a large impact on the option price, changing the monitoring frequency does not make much difference any more.

Figure 8.23 shows the effect of a change in the monitoring period on the price of a continuously monitored ATM knock-out call with six months to maturity and a barrier at

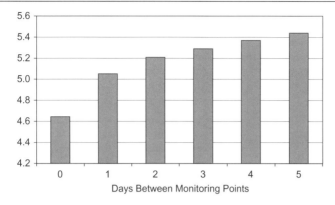

Figure 8.22   Price of an ATM 95% knock-out call as a function of monitoring frequency

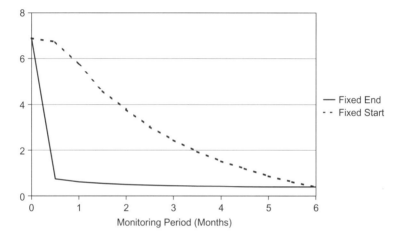

Figure 8.23   Price of an ATM 110% partial knock-out call as a function of monitoring period

110%. As before, one graph assumes the monitoring period always starts at inception; the other assumes the monitoring period always ends at maturity. Since the barrier is at the other side of spot now, our previous results are reversed. Fixing the monitoring period at inception makes the option price drop much less than fixing it at the end, reflecting the fact that the probability of a barrier hit is much higher at maturity than it is at inception. Figure 8.24 shows the effect of increasing the monitoring frequency on the above option with full monitoring. The option price drops, but in absolute terms the drop is only small.

8.12.3 Asian Options

Not surprisingly, the prices of Asian options also vary with the monitoring period and the monitoring frequency. As with lookbacks and ladders, there are four versions. Fixed-strike Asian calls are calls where instead of the index at maturity the seller pays the average of the index values observed at the monitoring points. Likewise, fixed-strike Asian puts are puts where the buyer pays the average. A floating-strike Asian call is a call where the buyer pays the average, while a floating-strike Asian put is a put where the seller pays the average. As before, we concentrate on calls.

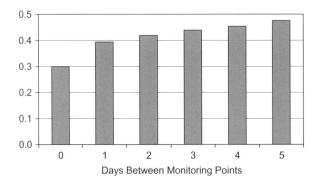

Figure 8.24 Price of an ATM 110% knock-out call as a function of monitoring frequency

Let's start with a **fixed-strike Asian call**. How the option price responds if we increase the monitoring period again depends very much on the location of the monitoring period. This becomes clear if we look at the extreme case of only one monitoring point. If we monitored at the start of the contract's life we would end up with an average equal to I_0. Assuming the option is ATM, this means the option will be worthless. On the other hand, if we only monitored at maturity the average would be equal to the index value at maturity, in which case the Asian call would be identical to an ordinary call. This means that if we increase the monitoring period the price of a fixed-strike Asian call with monitoring starting at inception will rise and the price of an equivalent Asian call with monitoring starting at maturity will drop. With full monitoring both prices will be equal. This is illustrated in Figure 8.25, which shows the price of a 6-month ATM fixed-strike Asian call option as a function of the monitoring period. The index is monitored daily.

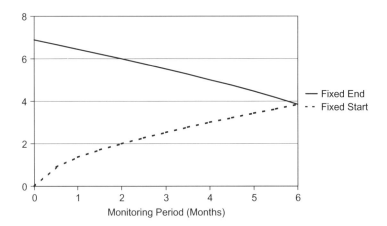

Figure 8.25 Price of an ATM partial fixed-strike Asian call as a function of monitoring period

As illustrated in Figure 8.26, a similar reasoning goes for **floating-strike Asian calls**. If we only monitored at the start of the contract's life we would end up with a strike equal to I_0. In that case the Asian call is identical to an ordinary call. If we only monitored at maturity the strike would be equal to the index value at maturity and the option would be worthless. This means that if we increase the monitoring period the price of a floating-strike Asian call with monitoring starting at inception will drop and the price of an equivalent Asian call with monitoring starting at maturity will rise.

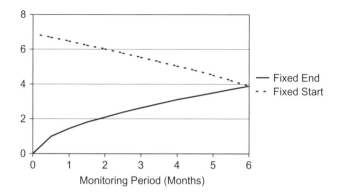

Figure 8.26   Price of a partial floating-strike Asian call as a function of monitoring period

The above analysis shows that in the case of an Asian option we do not have the same kind of general rule as for lookback, ladder or barrier options. We cannot simply say that if we increase the monitoring period Asian options will become cheaper. Prices only drop for fixed-strike calls with monitoring ending at maturity and floating-strike calls with monitoring starting at inception. With respect to the effect of the monitoring frequency it is helpful to go back to Table 8.2. As can be seen, given fairly frequent monitoring to start with, changing the monitoring frequency does not significantly change the volatility of the average. **The effect of a change in monitoring frequency will therefore not be very strong**. For example, with daily monitoring a 6-month fixed-strike ATM Asian call will cost 3.83%, while with weekly monitoring the same option will cost 3.85%.

8.13   A FINAL NOTE ON MONITORING

We have spent quite some time discussing all kinds of different options, but so far we have not specified when exactly the index will be monitored on the monitoring date(s) in question. We can do this on the opening, on the close or at any time in between. We could just pick a time, but both investors and derivatives firms tend to have their own preferences.

Investors typically prefer to monitor the index on the **official close of trading**. The advantage of this for the investor is that, since this information is readily available, he can easily check the calculation agent's calculations. Derivatives firms may sometimes have a problem with monitoring on the close as it may make it difficult for them to adjust their hedges. Consider the case of the average. To generate a cash flow equal to the average value of the index a derivatives firm will buy the index at inception and sell part of its holdings at every monitoring point. At maturity this leaves the firm with a cash position equal to the average index value. It is therefore important that the firm can sell at the same price used to calculate the average. Hedge maintenance is even more important when it comes to knock-out barrier options. If the barrier is hit, the derivatives firm will have to sell off its hedge portfolio as it is no longer needed. The models used for pricing barrier options assume this can be done at a price level equal to the barrier.

A second point concerns the **monitoring location**, i.e. the specific market where the reference index is monitored. In most cases this choice will be straightforward. However, it may happen that a stock trades on two or more markets at the same time. Although arbitrage will keep the prices on the different markets closely together, small differences may arise at times. In that case it has to be clear which price to use.

A derivatives contract needs to fully specify the dates, times and places where the index or indices in question are to be monitored. If not, this may cause serious problems down the line. Paying explicit attention to monitoring dates, times and locations is also of the utmost importance when entering into back-to-back deals, i.e. when buying from one party while at the same time selling to another. If the specifications of the contract bought do not exactly match those of the contract sold a derivatives firm may think it is fully hedged while it is not. There is a well published story[1] about a bank that in 1997 hedged a knock-out option on the dollar/yen exchange rate back-to-back, with one contract maturing in the Tokyo market and the other in New York. The Tokyo contract matured ITM while only a few hours later the New York contract knocked out. The bank supposedly lost USD 20m on the deal.

8.14 CONCLUSION

If we interpret derivatives prices as discounted expected payoffs, reducing the price of a derivatives contract boils down to finding ways to reduce its expected payoff. Expectations are a subjective matter though. When we talk about reducing the expected payoff we talk about the payoff which the derivatives firm expects. After all, it is derivatives firms that price derivatives. Derivatives firms tend to form their expectations in a much more objective and consistent manner than investors. As a result, we are sometimes able to find areas where there are significant differences between the investor's view and that of the derivatives firm. In those cases we can make derivatives cheaper for investors without losing economic relevance. The investor sells something which he considers to be of little or no value but gets paid handsomely for doing so.

We discussed quite a number of tricks, some of which are more popular than others. Changing parameters, buying less, piecewise linear segmentation and baskets are amongst the most popular. Pay-later, money-back, instalment and callable options on the other hand are less in vogue. The fact that these features are less straightforward is an important factor here. This makes them not only more difficult to explain to end-users, but also more difficult to price and hedge by derivatives firms. Many derivatives firms prefer to err on the safe side and therefore tend to quote relatively high prices for some of these more complex structures. Of course, this spoils much of the attraction of these products.

Our analysis has shown that it pays to be careful when setting the monitoring points for path-dependent options. When it comes to the choice of monitoring points, **end-users should always buy exactly what they need; not more, not less**. In Chapter 10 we will discuss how we can use what we discussed in this chapter to spice up the terms on so-called principal protected equity-linked notes. What these are is what we discuss next.

---

[1] See *Derivatives Week* (May 19th, 1997).

9

Equity-Linked Bull Notes

9.1 INTRODUCTION

Having seen some examples of what we can do for institutional investors, the next step is to investigate what we have to offer retail investors. We will not discuss how retail investors can use derivatives in the management of their own investment portfolios. This is no different from what we discussed before, except that the array of derivative instruments available to retail investors is typically limited to futures and listed ordinary puts and calls on the major stock market indices, and a limited number of individual stocks. Instead, we will concentrate on the structuring of investment products that can be sold to retail investors by banks, insurance companies, asset managers, etc.

9.2 STRUCTURING RETAIL PRODUCTS

When it comes to retail products, the first thing to note is that for most people the financial markets are very much a mystery. As a result, most retail investors do not shop around much, nor do they question the 'expert advice' which they get from their bank or financial advisor. As a result, **successfully selling retail products is very much a matter of distribution power**, i.e. the availability of a sufficiently large distribution network combined with the appropriate incentives for the sales force. This does not mean that product design is not important. It just means that a less interesting product which is marketed well is likely to do better than an interesting product that does not get sufficient marketing support.

With respect to investment products often a distinction is made between funds, notes, deposits, life insurance, pensions, etc. From a derivatives structuring perspective this distinction is not the most relevant, however, as it is more concerned with the formal structure of products than with the cash flows involved. From a structuring perspective it is more helpful to distinguish between products according to:

- **Payment.** Some products require investors to make an upfront payment while other products are designed for people who do not have money available but who (think they) are able to periodically put a certain amount aside. They pay as they go.
- **Maturity.** We can distinguish between products with a clear-cut maturity date and products with an undetermined maturity. The former cease to exist at some point in time, while the latter do not.
- **Number of payoffs.** Products with an undetermined maturity only provide a payoff when sold. Other investment products provide either one payoff or a stream of payoffs over time.
- **Type of payoff.** Sometimes investors are told exactly what index-linked payoff they will receive. With many investment products this is not the case, however. Some do aim for a specific type of payoff, but do not provide a guarantee.

Whether a product presents its issuer with an explicit hedging problem depends on whether the issuer commits to a particular exchange or not. Mutual fund participations are shares in a specific investment strategy. Because the holder participates fully in the ups and downs of the fund, the fund does not have an explicit hedging problem. Defined benefit pension plans aim to provide well-defined payoffs. This suggests the presence of a serious hedging problem. However, the premiums to be paid are typically not fixed in advance. This allows hedging errors to be corrected by changing the premiums. Now suppose we had a product which was paid for upfront and which at a prefixed future date provided investors with a predefined payoff linked to some stock market index. A product like this is commonly referred to as an **equity-linked note**, although there is little to prevent us from selling the same product as a fund participation, a deposit or even as life insurance. Since both the price and the payoff of an equity-linked note are clearly defined, equity-linked notes present their issuers with a serious hedging problem. In the next section we will discuss how this problem can be solved.

It should be noted that although a product may not present its issuer with an explicit hedging problem, competition introduces an implicit hedging problem. A mutual fund may not commit itself to providing a certain payoff, but it needs to do at least as well as its benchmark and its competitors if it does not want to lose business. Likewise, although technically a pension fund may be able to raise premiums, this will typically be considered a highly undesirable move.

In this chapter we will see that, apart from finding an acceptable hedging strategy, structuring retail investment products boils down to trading off (a) profit potential and (b) downside protection. Because both raise the expected payoff, both are valuable features. The trick therefore is to find the right combination. Doing so depends on:

- **Pricing environment.** Profit potential and downside protection both cost money. How much exactly depends on interest rates, dividends and implied volatilities. A significant change in interest rates and/or implied volatilities may open up interesting new opportunities, while at the same time eliminating others. Many innovations are the result of attempts to continue to offer attractive products in a deteriorating pricing environment.

- **Views and preferences.** It is the chemistry between investors' views and preferences which determines their behavior. However, investors do not always behave rationally, nor are their views always formed rationally. There are also significant **geographical differences** in retail investors' attitudes towards equity investment. In the US, retail investors have always had a strong desire to own a stake in corporate America. Retail investors in the US are therefore much more comfortable with direct equity investment and mutual funds than their European counterparts. As a result, there is less demand for downside protection in the US than there is in Europe.

- **Taxation.** When retail investors think about returns they think about after-tax returns. It is therefore important to study the fiscal system to see if there is any small print that might spoil the attraction of a product, or whether there are any loopholes that can be exploited.

- **Regulation.** Retail investors tend to be protected by a substantial chunk of regulation determining what can and cannot be sold to them and under what conditions. A similar reasoning goes for religion. The Koran contains strict stipulations for Islamic investors for example.

Apart from an appealing combination of profit potential and downside risk, retail investors tend to have some other matters on their wish list as well, such as (a) easy and fair entry and exit, (b) a known and trustworthy product provider, and (c) the ability to track the value of the product themselves. The latter is often accomplished by public listing.

When thinking of retail products we also have to consider what potential product providers are looking for. First of all, we have to realize that not all (potential) providers of retail products are equal. Some will already have an operation in place to deal with a large retail clientele while others do not. Potential product providers therefore want a product that (a) fits their organizational structure, (b) fits their tax, accounting and regulatory situation, (c) is easy to explain in a way which appeals to a large group of investors without an embedded risk of investor disappointment, i.e. reputational risk, and (d) offers a good profit margin. Since it reduces the risk of losing business, products with an undetermined maturity are often preferred over products with a prefixed maturity.

Although we will treat equity-linked notes as a retail product, this is not necessarily the case. There are various reasons why equity-linked notes make an attractive investment for institutional investors as well, such as:

- **Convenience.** In what follows we will see that equity-linked notes can be interpreted as packages of bonds, forwards and/or options. Assuming they knew which ones, institutional investors could of course buy these components in the market themselves. However, sometimes it might be easier and/or cheaper to buy them as a package.
- **Circumvent regulation.** In 1993 the National Association of Insurance Commissioners (NAIC) in the US raised risk-based capital requirements for common stock but not for investment grade bonds, including equity-linked notes. As a result, if an insurer buys common stock it is required to set aside much more capital than when buying the same equity exposure in the form of an equity-linked note.
- **Circumvent investment guidelines.** Sometimes an investment manager is confronted with a very conservative mandate which precludes him from investing in equity or making use of derivatives. By buying an equity-linked note the investment manager can stay within the investment guidelines and still obtain the type of equity exposure he desires.
- **Circumvent taxation.** Direct foreign investment subjects investors to foreign withholding taxes. Many institutional investors, however, are not able to reclaim these. By buying equity-linked notes this problem can be transferred to a party who is better suited to dealing with foreign withholding tax.

The above makes it clear that the risk of structured notes is not restricted to the risk of a defaulting issuer. **The market risks embedded in structured notes can be very substantial** and should always be evaluated very carefully.

Before we continue it has to be said that the wording in marketing advertisements and brochures for retail investment products is sometimes questionable to say the least. Brochures and advertisements tend to be written to create a strong something-for-nothing feeling, underlined by numerical examples based on highly optimistic scenarios. Unfortunately for potential participants, this is nothing more than an exercise in creative writing. As a rule, retail product providers take substantial profit margins; partly because they need to finance the relatively high cost of marketing and distribution of these products, and partly because the opportunity is simply there. Retail clients generally have no idea how a product is put together and therefore have no idea what a product is really worth.

Moreover, as long as nobody offers the same product at a significantly better price the only way they can acquire it is at the relatively high price at which it is offered. We will revisit these issues in Chapter 13.

9.3   THE GENERAL STRUCTURE OF A NOTE ISSUE

Before we delve into the details of equity-linked notes themselves, we first discuss the general structure of a structured note issue. Suppose a small private bank identified strong demand among its clientele for a note with a five year maturity that paid no coupons but instead gave its holder a fixed percentage of the rise (if any) of the equity market over the next five years. Since demand seems to be exceptionally strong, the bank thinks it should be able to make a nice profit if it could offer such a product. Although the bank could use the proceeds of the note for its own funding, issuing such a note itself would expose the bank to a lot of equity market risk. From a risk point of view, the bank would prefer to issue a standard floating rate note on which it pays a semi-annual coupon that is reset periodically based on the prevailing level of LIBOR. The bank therefore approaches a neighboring derivatives firm to see if it can enter into a **swap contract** under which the bank trades in a stream of cash flows equal to what it would have paid if it had issued a floating rate note against whatever it needs on top of the redemption of principal to redeem the equity-linked note. Obviously, the derivatives firm needs to have a **good credit rating** because the bank will still have to make all the payments, even if the derivatives firm defaults.

Let's look at the timing of the cash flows and the amounts payable under the desired swap. At $t = 0$ the collective of investors pays the bank the amount they want to invest, say 100 million, and after five years the bank pays them their 100m back plus an additional amount V_5 to compensate them for parting with their money for five years. This means that over a period of five years these investors make a return on their money of $(V_5/100\text{m}) \times 100\%$. The bank pays the derivatives firm 10 LIBOR-based coupons C_i, $i = 1, 2, \ldots, 10$, and the firm pays the bank whatever it needs to pay the investors for the use of their money, i.e. V_5. Figure 9.1 depicts these cash flows schematically.

The benefits of the scheme for the derivatives firm and the investors are obvious. The derivatives firm gets to take a profit on the swap and the investors get the product they

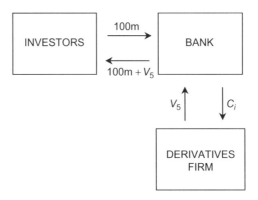

Figure 9.1   Cash flow profile for structured note swap deal (I)

want. But what about the bank? The bank can realize its profit in a number of ways. First, we could structure it as a **reduction of its funding rate**. Suppose that normally the bank would have been able to obtain funding at LIBOR flat. Under the swap agreement with the derivatives firm, however, there is no need to pay LIBOR flat. The bank can go to the derivatives firm and ask for a 'what-if' view on the swap, i.e. what conditions the firm can offer for what spread over LIBOR. The derivatives firm might for example say that if the bank paid LIBOR flat it could offer 95% participation in the equity market, but that if the bank paid LIBOR minus 100bp it could offer only 70% participation. Combining this information with an estimate of how price sensitive its clients are, it is then up to the bank to decide how much profit it wants to take. A second way for the bank to take out a profit is to simply pay the derivatives firm LIBOR flat but ask the latter not only to make the swap payment at maturity, but also to **pay the bank an amount upfront**. This is not really different from the first alternative, except that the bank now receives its profit upfront instead of as a stream of payments over a five year period.

So far we have assumed the bank issues as well as distributes the equity-linked note. This is not necessary though. Suppose that the bank did not want to issue the note itself. How could it get its hands on the product its clients are looking for? Again, it is the derivatives firm that comes to the rescue. The latter will typically not be willing to issue the note itself, but it will know a number of possible issuers with varying credit ratings that will be interested in a way to reduce their funding rate. Like the bank, the new issuer will not be willing to issue the note without hedging the equity market risk. The derivatives firm will therefore offer the issuer the possibility to hedge himself in exactly the same way as it did before when the bank issued the note. The issuer issues the note and the bank distributes it to its clients (in return for a fee).

The beauty of the above deal structure is that, being able to hedge all unwanted risks, the issuer will be indifferent as to what he issues. The details of the structure can therefore be driven by the demand side. Again, the reason why everybody wants to participate in this deal is simple. The derivatives firm gets to take a profit on the swap, the issuer is able to negotiate a reduction in its funding rate as well as further diversify its funding base, and the bank gets paid a distribution fee. This fee can be paid by either the derivatives firm or the issuer. If paid by the derivatives firm, the latter will price the fee into the swap together with its own margin. If paid by the issuer, the latter will want to reduce its funding rate further to make up for the fee to be paid. Assuming the bank is paid by the derivatives firm, Figure 9.2 depicts the cash flows involved in this deal.

If the bank issues the note itself it is taking the risk that the derivatives firm defaults. It will therefore require a highly rated swap counterparty. If the bank only distributes the note, the bank's clients take all the risk. Although the bank will protect its clients against taking excessive risk, it may be tempted to take a somewhat less strict stance on credit risk if it helps to improve the conditions of the note and/or generate a higher fee. Derivatives firms with a low credit rating capitalize on this by issuing their own equity-linked notes. Since these firms fund at a relatively high rate, they are able to offer better terms and/or higher distribution fees than higher rated issuers. Actually, for these firms this is often the only way to get into the equity-linked note business as they will be unable to successfully compete for the swap due to their low rating. It is important to

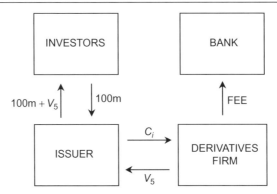

Figure 9.2 Cash flow profile for structured note swap deal (II)

understand, however, that the **better terms on notes issued by low rated issuers simply reflect the higher credit risk**.

9.4   THE STRUCTURING PROCESS

Structuring equity-linked notes is a matter of having a good feel for what investors are looking for and being creative. In our capacity of consultants to the bank, this is how we go about it.

- **Step 1.** Identification of (the bank's understanding of) investors' basic view. Do investors think the market will go up, down, up or down, or stay more or less unchanged?
- **Step 2.** Incorporation of the above view into a simple note structure. We do not expect the bank to actually buy this note right away, but it provides a starting point for step 3.
- **Step 3.** Amendment of the vanilla structure to take account of the bank's objections. Typically, the bank will want a higher payoff in case the investors' view proves correct, as well as more solid protection against adverse market movements. As this does not go together we will need to study different alternatives and the trade-offs involved.
- **Step 4.** Presentation of our findings to the bank and conclusion. This is a crucial stage since when left to its own devices the bank may not come to a rational decision within an acceptable period of time. We therefore need to be careful to present our findings in an easily understandable and logical manner, and we may have to push matters forward a little to 'help' the bank make up its mind.

The technical aspects of the structuring process emerge during steps 2 and 3. It is important not to structure notes in the way typically advocated in other books on derivatives, i.e. by combining forwards and options with zero-coupon bonds. In what follows we will see that many notes can indeed be interpreted in this way, but **it is an unnatural approach that unnecessarily restricts the outcome of the structuring process**. We will follow the following procedure.

- **Step 1.** We ask ourselves what type of return the investor would like to receive on his investment. Having thought of something, we write down the desired note payoff formally.

- **Step 2.** We derive the payment the derivatives firm will have to make to the issuer and try to express the latter in terms of the payoffs of contracts the firm already knows how to price. If this is possible, the firm can use the pricing models for the **embedded contracts** to price the note. If not, the firm's financial engineers will have to develop a new pricing model especially for this note, which may require significant effort.
- **Step 3.** We formulate a budget equation that equates the present value (to the derivatives firm) of the interest payments to be made by the issuer to the present value (again to the derivatives firm) of the payments to be made by the derivatives firm.
- **Step 4.** We price the note for a number of likely parameter choices. This will help us to answer the questions the bank will undoubtedly fire at us if we present the note.

It is important to emphasize that although in step 2 we try to split the note payoff into familiar components, **the note payoff is not conceived by combining existing products**. It is the result of a combination of experience and imagination. Much of the necessary experience can be obtained by continuing reading this book and trying out the many different cases for oneself. Unfortunately for many, the imagination is there or it is not.

As discussed in Chapter 5, when thinking about derivatives it is important to concentrate on contracts' expected payoffs. Since we can interpret prices as discounted expected payoffs, to find the consequences of a change in a contract parameter we have to find out what that change means for the contract's expected payoff. A higher expected payoff means a higher price and the other way around. With notes there is one special twist though. Since the amount investors want to invest is given, the issue price of the note is fixed. A change in a parameter that affects the note's expected payoff will therefore have to be compensated by an offsetting change in another parameter to keep the expected payoff from changing. The same is true when adding special contract features. The many examples that follow will clarify this further.

It has become quite fashionable to look at the probability distribution of the return on equity-linked notes. Merrill Lynch for example has a semi-annual publication that does so for notes issued in Europe.[1] Unfortunately, the information which this type of analysis provides is limited because it is based on one particular index return distribution/process. As a result, the analysis only tells us how somebody with that particular view on the index would see the note in question. An investor with a different view on the index might obtain a completely different result. A similar reasoning goes for comparisons between notes. Since different investors will have different preferences, a note that makes good sense for one investor may not do so for another. What all this boils down to is the fact that **there is not one single note that is optimal for all investors at the same time**. Investors with different views and different preferences will be drawn to different note structures.

ASSUMPTIONS & NOTATION (CHAPTERS 9–12)

In Chapters 9–12 we will discuss a large number of equity-linked notes. Although we discuss a lot of them, the discussion is by no means complete. What we have tried to do is provide some insight into the trial and error process that typically leads up to a deal. Because he does not know exactly what he wants, the distributor of the note will generally want to see a variety of ideas priced up before a final choice is made. For simplicity we will assume the distributor and the issuer of the note are one and the same, and refer

---

[1] See Merrill Lynch, Structured Retail Products; Semi-Annual Review of the European Market.

to the latter as 'the bank'. Note, however, that in practice it is not just banks that issue and distribute equity-linked notes, neither do distributors always issue the notes they sell themselves.

We will assume that the collective of investors has 100m to invest and that the bank takes out a spread of 40bp per annum. All reference indices are assumed to be at 100 and pay no dividends. The issue size/notional amount of a note is denoted N. The number of shares in the reference index that an amount N buys is denoted M, i.e. $M = N/I_0$. Under the above assumptions $N = 100$m and $M = 1$m. Except where mentioned, all notes are assumed to be issued at par, i.e. the issue price equals the notional amount used to calculate the note payoff at maturity. Not doing so makes it more difficult to evaluate the note payoff in terms of return on investment.

For pricing purposes we stick to the assumptions made before in Chapter 7. The term structure of continuously compounded interest rates is flat and constant at 5%. The derivatives firm's trading desk is willing to price any of the option contracts listed in the glossary in **Appendix B**. Since the payoffs of the notes we are about to discuss can all be expressed in terms of the payoffs of these options, the derivatives firm can price these notes without having to develop new pricing models. For simplicity, we ignore the derivatives firm's profit margin and assume bid and ask prices to be equal to the theoretical price. The latter is obtained from a pricing model calibrated to a term structure of implied volatility which is flat and constant at 20% without any skew. In the text, offers are indicated by the superscript 'a' (for ask) and bids by the superscript 'b' (for bid). The notation used to denote the prices of the various options is summarized in **Appendix C**.

SOFTWARE (CHAPTERS 9 AND 10)

As mentioned in the Preface, much of the programming necessary for the chapters that follow was done by others. Michalis Ioannides, a Ph.D. student at the ISMA Centre at the time this book was written, did the programming for Chapters 9 and 10. Michalis has turned his part of the code into a user-friendly calculator which allows the user to easily study the effects of a change in one or more note parameters as well as pricing inputs. He can be contacted at Michalis_Ioannides@hotmail.com.[2]

9.5 UNPROTECTED BULL NOTES

With the above deal structure in mind we can now proceed with the discussion of a number of investment ideas. We concentrate on structured notes suitable for investors with a bullish view. This is by far the most common situation. In Chapter 11 we discuss notes suitable for investors with bearish, mixed and neutral views.

9.5.1 Vanilla Bull Note

Suppose the bank was looking for a note which allowed investors to participate in the expected rise of some specific stock market index. What could we come up with? Thinking back to what we discussed in Chapter 4, a simple solution would be to make V_5 equal

---

[2] Of course, neither the author nor the publisher accept any liability for the software itself or any possible losses due to its use.

to a multiplier times the value of the reference index at maturity. This would mean that investors would receive the interest on the money they lend to the bank in the form of stocks. The disadvantage of this solution is that it does not give investors a lot of exposure to the index. With an interest rate of 5% the present value of the interest to be received on a 100m 5-year investment is only 22.12m.

An alternative is to set V_5 equal to a fraction of the return on the index over the note's life. Formally, this means that at maturity investors receive an amount X_5 equal to

$$X_5 = N \times \left(1 + \alpha \left(\frac{I_5 - I_0}{I_0} \right) \right), \tag{9.1}$$

where N equals the note principal, i.e. the total amount invested. Writing the note payoff in this way shows that at maturity investors will be paid a return on their investment equal to a fraction α of the index return. The fraction α is known as the note's **participation rate**.

There is nothing special about this note. In fact, it is very much like an **index participation** which pays investors as if they had bought the index themselves. This becomes clear if we rewrite the above expression as

$$X_5 = (1 - \alpha)N + \alpha M \times I_5. \tag{9.2}$$

This shows that the note payoff is equal to a fixed amount $(1 - \alpha)N$ plus the payoff of αM index participations. However, instead of index participations the investors are now buying a structured note. In some cases this distinction is important as there may be significant differences in the tax, accounting and/or regulatory treatment of equity-linked notes and index participations.

The value of the participation rate at which the deal can get done depends on the bank's funding target and the way the derivatives firm prices the swap. We can get insight into the latter if we write the amount the derivatives firm has to pay in terms of the payoff of a more familiar contract. In doing so, we end up with the following expression

$$V_5 = X_5 - N = \alpha M \times (I_5 - I_0). \tag{9.3}$$

This shows that what the derivatives firm really does is sell the bank αM contracts where at maturity the derivatives firm pays the bank the value of the index and the bank pays the derivatives firm the value of the reference index at inception. Obviously, such a contract is nothing more than a **vanilla forward** with forward price I_0.

What we need to do next is equate the present value (to the derivatives firm) of the coupons which the bank pays with the value of the above forwards. In other words, the participation rate can be derived from the following budget equation

$$PVC = \alpha M \times F_0^a[I_0, 5], \tag{9.4}$$

where PVC denotes the present value (to the derivatives firm) of the coupons which the bank pays and $F_0^a[K, T]$ is the derivatives firm's offer for a vanilla forward with forward price K and T years to maturity. For simplicity, assuming that the bank pays the derivatives firm one large coupon at maturity, PVC can be calculated as

$$PVC = e^{-5r_5} \times \left(e^{5(r_5 - S)} - 1 \right) N = \left(e^{-5S} - e^{-5r_5} \right) N = 20.14\text{m}, \tag{9.5}$$

where S denotes the spread taken by the bank.

The price which the derivatives firm will quote for the forward depends on the expected hedging costs of the contract. Fortunately, as discussed in Chapter 6, the hedging strategy for the above forward is simple: the firm borrows money and buys the index. In five years this returns I_5 at a cost of $e^{5r_5}I_0$. Under the forward contract, however, the firm only gets paid I_0. To make up for the difference the firm will therefore require an upfront payment of

$$F_0^a[I_0, 5] = e^{-5r_5} \times \left(e^{5r_5} - 1\right) I_0 = (1 - e^{-5r_5})I_0 = 22.12 \tag{9.6}$$

to enter into the forward contract. Note that if the index paid a dividend yield of δ the required upfront payment would have been $(e^{-5\delta} - e^{-5r_5})I_0$. In that case the required payment would be lower as the derivatives firm would get to keep the dividends that it received during the life of the contract. With the bank paying 20.14m it is entitled to $20.14\text{m}/22.12 = 910{,}000$ forwards. With 100m to invest and an index value of 100 the participation rate must therefore be equal to 0.91. **The only reason why the participation rate is not equal to 1.00 is the spread taken out by the bank**. If the spread was zero, PVC would be equal to 22.12m and the particiption rate would be 1.00.

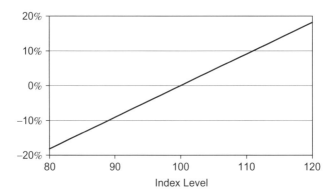

Figure 9.3   Return profile for vanilla bull note

What do investors get with a participation rate of 0.91? Figure 9.3 shows the note's return profile as a function of the index value at maturity. Because the return is calculated from a base value of 100, investors make money if the index ends higher than 100 and lose money if it ends lower than 100. With the interest rate at 5% a zero-coupon bond would pay off 28.4% after five years. To beat a fixed income investment the index therefore has to rise to at least 131.

Discussing this note idea with the bank, the bank expresses some concern that investors will not do much better than with a fixed income investment unless the index shows a substantial rise. Is it possible to offer investors a better return for relatively low index returns?

9.5.2   Vanilla Bull Note with a Reduced Base

One way to solve the above problem is to lower the index base level used to calculate the index return, i.e. **lower the value of I_5 which yields a zero return**. If we were to modify payoff (9.1) as follows

$$X_5 = N \times \left(1 + \alpha \left(\frac{I_5 - bI_0}{I_0}\right)\right), \quad b < 1, \tag{9.7}$$

we would give investors a head start as they would make $\alpha N \times (1 - b)$ even if the index did not move. Their return on investment would be zero if the index at maturity was equal to bI_0 instead of I_0 as before. This sound very attractive but, as we will see, there is a catch.

The above note can be hedged in exactly the same way as before. The derivatives firm borrows money and buys the index. After five years this returns I_5 at a cost of $e^{5r_5}I_0$. Under the forward contract, however, the firm gets paid only bI_0. To make up for the difference the firm will therefore require a higher upfront payment equal to $(1 - be^{-5r_5})I_0$. If we assume a **base rate** of 0.9 this means the forward now costs 29.90 instead of 22.12. With the bank still paying 20.14m it is therefore entitled to 20.14m/29.90 = 670,000 forwards, implying a participation rate of only 0.67.

Figure 9.4 shows the note's return profile as a function of the index value at maturity for $b = 0.9$. For comparison we also included the return of a note with $b = 1$. The graph shows that, since investors now start making money when the index ends above 90 instead of 100, for relatively low index returns the note with $b = 0.9$ outperforms the note with $b = 1$. However, since the participation rate is lower with $b = 0.9$, they make less for every per cent rise in the index. As a result, the note with $b = 0.9$ does not outperform the other note over the whole range of possible outcomes. When the index ends above 128 the note with $b = 1$ shows better performance. Intuitively, this makes perfect sense. **Improved potential in one area can only come at the cost of reduced potential in another**.

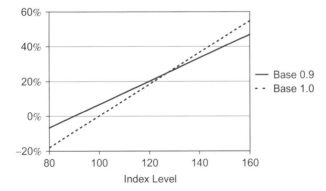

Figure 9.4   Return profile for a vanilla bull note with reduced base

The next step is to investigate what participation rate we get if we choose other values for b. Figure 9.5 shows the trade-off between the **base rate** and the participation rate. We assume that we set the base rate ourselves and solve for the participation rate. When desired, however, one may of course also set the participation rate and solve for the base rate. From Figure 9.5 we see that if the base rate goes up, the participation rate goes up

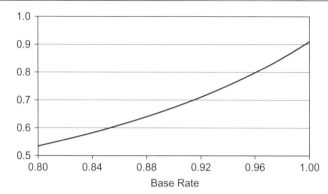

Figure 9.5 Trade-off between base rate and participation rate for a vanilla bull note with reduced base

as well. With a base rate of 0.8 the participation rate is only 0.53, while with $b = 1$ we have a participation rate of 0.91.

To understand the change in the participation rate resulting from a higher or lower base rate we can either fall back on our pricing shortcut and look at what happens to the note's expected payoff or revert to the note's budget equation and see how it changes the various terms in the equation.

- **Expected note payoff.** If we raise the base rate, the expected payoff of the note drops because the payoff for every possible index value falls. Normally, this would make the contract in question cheaper. Since the issue price of the note is fixed, however, this cannot be the case here. Because under our pricing shortcut all financial assets offer an expected return equal to the interest rate, by fixing the issue price we have fixed the expected payoff as well. The participation rate therefore has to rise to compensate for the drop in the expected payoff. In other words, **with the issue price of the note fixed, fixing one parameter also fixes the other**.
- **Budget equation.** With the price of the forward being equal to $(1 - be^{-5r_5})I_0$, it is clear that when the base rate goes up, the price of the forward goes down. Since PVC is given, however, this translates directly into a higher value for the participation rate.

Since the pricing shortcut not only applies to notes but also to all individual assets in the budget equation, going through the budget equation is not really different from looking at the expected note payoff directly. However, often the budget equation is too complex to quickly draw a conclusion about how a change in one parameter will influence another parameter.

9.5.3 Capped Bull Note

Reducing the base level reduces the participation rate. If we wanted to get the participation rate back to its original level we could consider preventing the note return from rising above some preset level. Since this eliminates the most desirable outcomes it reduces the expected payoff of the note. With the issue price of the note and the expected return fixed, however, this means that the participation rate has to go up. With a **cap** on payoff (9.7) the note payoff to the investors can be written as

$$X_5 = N \times \left(1 + \text{Min} \left[H, \alpha \left(\frac{I_5 - bI_0}{I_0} \right) \right] \right). \tag{9.8}$$

At maturity investors now receive their money back plus a return on investment equal to the lowest of the **cap rate** H and a fraction α of the index return. If the participation rate times the index return exceeds the cap rate the investors will receive a return equal to H.

Since now we have to set (1) the base rate, (2) the cap rate, as well as (3) the participation rate, pricing this note can mean three different things.

- We can fix the base rate and the cap rate and solve for the participation rate.
- We can set the base rate and the participation rate and solve for the cap rate.
- We can set the cap rate and the participation rate and solve for the base rate.

Since we introduced the cap to get the participation rate on the note with reduced base level back to where it was with the vanilla bull note, we will assume that the base rate and the participation rate are given and that we need to determine the cap rate.

The first thing to do then is to see if we can rewrite the amount payable by the derivatives firm in terms of the payoffs of more familiar contracts. In this case this is easy since the amount payable by the derivatives firm can be expressed as

$$V_5 = N \times \left(H + \text{Min} \left[0, \alpha \left(\frac{I_5 - bI_0}{I_0} \right) - H \right] \right), \tag{9.9}$$

which, using the fact that $\text{Min}\,[0, a] = - \text{Max}\,[0, -a]$, can also be expressed as

$$V_5 = N \times H - \alpha M \times \text{Max} \left[0, I_0 \left(b + \frac{H}{\alpha} \right) - I_5 \right]. \tag{9.10}$$

This shows that the payment to be made by the derivatives firm can be split into two parts. The first part is a fixed amount which can be interpreted as the redemption of a loan which the bank provides to the derivatives firm. The second part is an index-linked cash flow which is either zero if the cap is reached or negative, i.e. the derivatives firm receives money, if the cap is not reached. This cash flow is identical to the payoff of αM **ordinary puts** with strike $I_0(b + H/\alpha)$. In other words, the derivatives firm buys αM ordinary puts from the bank. If the index at maturity exceeds the strike, the derivatives firm will cancel the options. If not, the derivatives firm receives on balance $I_0(b + H/\alpha) - I_5$ on every option it has bought, which compensates part of the fixed payment of $N \times H$.

Expression (9.10) is not the only way to write the amount payable by the derivatives firm. We can also write the amount payable by the derivatives firm as

$$V_5 = \alpha M \times (I_5 - bI_0) - \alpha M \times \text{Max} \left[0, I_5 - I_0 \left(b + \frac{H}{\alpha} \right) \right]. \tag{9.11}$$

According to this expression the derivatives firm pays the bank the same amount it would have paid if it had sold the bank αM **forwards** with forward price bI_0 and at the same time bought from the bank αM **ordinary calls** with strike $I_0(b + H/\alpha)$. We can see this result as an application of **put–call parity**, which says that ordinary calls can be statically hedged with forwards and ordinary puts.

The cap rate must be set such that the present value of V_5 equals the present value of the coupons which the bank pays. Building on (9.10), this means the cap rate has to be such that is satisfies the following budget equation

$$PVC = e^{-5r_5}(N \times H) - \alpha M \times P_0^b \left[I_0 \left(b + \frac{H}{\alpha}\right), 5\right].$$ (9.12)

Alternatively, we can derive a budget equation from (9.11). This yields

$$PVC = \alpha M \times \left(F_0^a[bI_0, 5] - C_0^b \left[I_0 \left(b + \frac{H}{\alpha}\right), 5\right]\right).$$ (9.13)

When the derivatives firm prices puts, calls and forwards consistently, both approaches should produce the same value for the cap rate. It never hurts to check though.

Suppose we set $b = 0.9$ (as in Section 9.5.2) and $\alpha = 0.91$ (as in Section 9.5.1). This creates a note with the upside capture of the vanilla bull note with a base rate of 1.0 but with a better payoff for lower index returns. With the derivatives firm receiving a stream of coupons with a present value of 20.14m, this yields a cap rate equal to 75%. In other words, under the assumptions made the note can be structured such that, calculated from a base of $0.9I_0$, investors receive 0.91 times the index return up to a maximum payout of 75%. The cap rate of 75% still allows investors to make an average return of 11.3% per annum, which is definitely not bad given that interest rates are at 5%. Note that it is not the index return that is capped but the note return. In terms of the index level the cap is at

$$I_5 = I_0 \times \left(b + \frac{H}{\alpha}\right) = 172.$$ (9.14)

In other words, the cap becomes active at an index level equal to the strike of the options embedded in the note payoff.

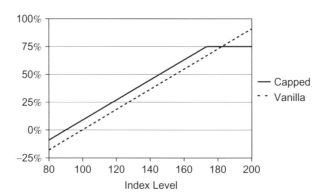

Figure 9.6   Return profile for a capped bull note

If we look at the return profile of the capped bull note in Figure 9.6 and compare it with that of a vanilla bull note with a base rate of 1.0 we see clearly that, thanks to its lower base rate, up to an index level of 182 the capped bull note provides investors with a higher return than the vanilla bull note. Unlike what we saw in Figure 9.4, both graphs do not grow closer together as the index rises because we set an equal participation rate of 0.91 for both notes. Because the extra return on the capped bull note has to come from somewhere, however, the return on the capped bull note never gets higher than 75%.

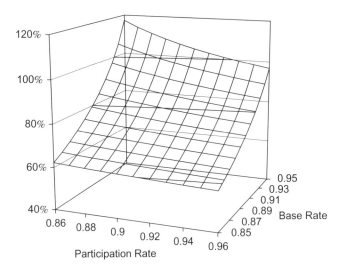

Figure 9.7   Trade-off between base rate, participation rate and cap rate for a capped bull note

It is interesting to take a closer look at the trade-off between the **base rate**, the **participation rate** and the cap rate. Figure 9.7 depicts this trade-off. From the graph we see that the cap rate increases when the base rate goes up and the participation rate goes down. With $b = 0.85$ and $\alpha = 0.96$ the cap rate is 58%, but with $b = 0.95$ and $\alpha = 0.86$ it is 117%. Looking at this in terms of the expected note payoff, this makes perfect sense. If the base rate goes up or the participation rate drops, the expected payoff of the note goes down. With the issue price and the expected return fixed, however, this means the cap rate has to go up to compensate for this. Although it is more difficult to see, the budget equation of course leads to the same conclusion.

The Marketer's View

In (9.8) we expressed the note payoff as the principal amount plus an additional amount which depends on the value of the index at maturity. If the market goes up the index-linked part of the payoff will be positive. We are saying that investors will get their money back and that if their view proves correct, we will pay them extra up to a maximum of the cap level. Since **successful marketing is not about inspiring hope but about creating greed**, this is not the most appealing description of the note. With a cap present we can also describe the note payoff in another way that puts less emphasis on the fact that investors might not make money, or even lose part of their principal. We can do so by rewriting (9.8) as

$$X_5 = N \times \left((1+H) - \text{Max}\left[0, H - \alpha \left(\frac{I_5 - bI_0}{I_0} \right) \right] \right), \qquad (9.15)$$

which translates as 'we will pay you an exceptionally high return of $H\%$ but if your view that the index will rise substantially is not correct you may have to pay some of it back'. Marketers at derivatives firms, banks and insurance companies prefer the latter description of the note payoff because it makes the note sound much more secure. It explains the note as a bond instead of as equity.

For the above story to have the desired impact, it is of course important that the pricing environment is right. From the budget equation we see that much depends on the prices at which the bank can write the embedded puts or calls (depending on what version of the budget equation we look at). **High option prices produce a high cap rate**. If put prices rise, the left-hand side of (9.12) will come to exceed the right-hand side. To keep both sides equal, the cap rate will therefore have to rise. From the budget equation it also follows that **the higher the interest rate, the higher the cap rate**. If interest rates were at 7% the cap rate would be 103%. With an interest rate of 10% the cap rate would be 156%. On the other hand, interest rates should not be too high either. An investor who can make a riskless 10% by simply putting his money in the bank will be a lot less open to the idea of buying a capped bull note than when interest rates are at 5%.

Buy-Writes

Since the capped bull note has three parameters that we can vary, it offers some interesting special cases. Suppose we set $b = 1$ and $\alpha = 1$. This would yield a payoff to the investors equal to

$$X_5 = N \times \left(1 + \text{Min} \left[H, \left(\frac{I_5 - I_0}{I_0} \right) \right] \right), \tag{9.16}$$

which can also be expressed as

$$X_5 = M \times I_5 - M \times \text{Max} \left[0, I_5 - I_0 (1 + H) \right]. \tag{9.17}$$

This is the same payoff investors would have obtained if they had bought M **index participations** and at the same time had written M **ordinary calls** with strike $I_0(1 + H)$. The above structure is therefore referred to as a **buy-write**. Fixing $b = 1$ and $\alpha = 1$ again makes the cap rate the variable to solve for. This yields a cap rate of 146%. Checking with (9.14), this means that the cap becomes active at an index level of 246, which is unusually high. This is understandable, however, if we realize that the 100m which the investors pay for the note also buys 1m index participations. This means that **all the written calls need to do is make up for the spread that the bank is taking out**.

Because solving for the cap rate is a fairly trivial exercise when $b = 1$ and $\alpha = 1$, in practice it is common to fix the cap rate in advance as well and instead calculate by how much this would allow the bank to discount the issue price of the note. In other words, instead of issuing a note with an unknown cap rate at par the bank now issues a note with a prefixed cap rate at a discount. This explains why these structures are referred to as **discount rights**. The issue price is now the variable to solve for. Suppose we wanted to offer investors a cap rate of 60%. In that case the payoff to be priced would be

$$X_5 = M \times I_5 - M \times \text{Max} \left[0, I_5 - 1.6I_0 \right], \tag{9.18}$$

which is equal to the payoff of M index participations minus the payoff of M ordinary calls with strike $1.6I_0$.

To find the issue price we need to look at the hedge the bank will put on. From the above expressions it is clear that the bank could hedge itself by buying M index participations while simultaneously selling M calls. The index participations would cost 100m but the calls would bring in 9.87m. If the bank took out 1.98m in profits, this would imply an issue price of 92.11m. The problem with this hedge is that it leaves nothing for the bank's funding. This would not be a problem if the bank was issuing the note just to make a profit, but it would be if it intended to use the proceeds of the note for its own funding.

The bank might prefer to enter into a swap with the derivatives firm where it paid the derivatives firm LIBOR over 100m and at maturity the derivatives firm paid the bank

$$V_5 = M \times (I_5 - I_0) - M \times \text{Max}\,[0, I_5 - 1.6I_0]\,. \tag{9.19}$$

The first term in the above expression is equal to the payoff of M forwards with forward price I_0. The second term is equal to the payoff of a short position of M ordinary calls with strike $1.6I_0$. Because the note is to be issued below par, the bank will not receive 100m while under the swap it does have to pay LIBOR on 100m. To solve this, the derivatives firm can pay the value of the call options, for which it quotes a bid of 9.87%, to the bank upfront. To determine the issue price all we need to do then is check the derivatives firm's quote for the forward and compare that with the value of the coupons paid by the bank. For the forwards the derivatives firm quotes an upfront offer of 22.12m. It values the coupons to be paid by the bank at exactly the same amount. This means the bank can obtain the above payoff without making further payments. If we assume the bank took out an upfront profit of 1.98m, this means the issue price has to be $100 - 9.87 + 1.98 = 92.11$m. At inception the bank receives 92.11m from the investors and 9.87m from the derivatives firm; 101.98m in total. During the contract's life the bank pays the firm coupons with a present value of 22.12m. At maturity the derivatives firm pays the bank an amount equal to (9.19), which the bank passes on to the investors together with 100m of its own.

The above example shows that for the bank there are **two ways to make money**. The bank can decide to issue a note at par and then determine the exact details of the note payoff, or it can first decide on the payoff that it wants to offer and then determine the issue price. In the first case the bank's profit comes from offering a less advantageous payoff. In the second case it comes from raising the issue price.

Reverse Convertibles

If we look back at (9.8) again, we see that in case the index does not rise enough to make the note payoff reach the cap level, the payoff to the investors will be equal to

$$X_5 = (1 - \alpha b) \times N + \alpha M \times I_5. \tag{9.20}$$

This means that if we set the participation rate and the base rate such that $\alpha \times b = 1$, the note payoff will be equal to the value of αM shares in the index. So far we have assumed that the capped bull note pays off in cash. This is not necessary though. With the above choice of parameters we could say that investors will **physically receive the (stocks in the) index** if at maturity it ends such that the note produces a return lower than the cap rate. If the index ends higher, they get paid in cash.

Notes like this are known as **reverse convertibles**. This name is inspired by the fact that contrary to a convertible bond the note holder receives stocks when the stock price goes down instead of up. In the terminology of Chapter 3 it would be better to refer to reverse convertibles as being 'exchangeable', as it is the issuer who has the right to exchange the note for stocks and not the holder of the note. If we set $b = 0.8$ and $\alpha = 1.25$ we would obtain a cap rate of 47%, which becomes active at an index level of 118. A cap rate of 47% over five years translates into an annual rate of 8%. This means the bank can present the note to its investors by saying that the bank will pay them an exceptionally high rate of return of 8% per annum, but that if the index at maturity is lower than 118, instead of paying the 8% interest, the bank will physically deliver 1.25 shares of the index for every 100 invested in the note. Even if the index is unchanged the stocks will be worth 125 and a real loss occurs only if the index drops below $bI_0 = 80$.

If we wanted to present the note like this it might be more convenient to **start by specifying the index level where the cap becomes active**, i.e. the index level below which investors will get paid in shares instead of cash. The latter is given by (9.14). Suppose we wanted the cap to become active at an index level of 100. This means we should write options with a strike of 100. This leaves us with three equations and three unknowns to solve for. The first equation is the budget equation. Going with (9.12) with a put price of 7.02%, this gives us a link between the cap rate and the participation rate. The second equation tells us that the product of the participation rate and the base rate must be equal to 1. This is required to make the note a reverse convertible. The third equation links the cap rate, the participation rate and the base rate, and says that (9.14) must be equal to 100. This yields a participation rate of 1.38, a cap rate of 38% and a base rate of 0.72. In marketing terms, the bank would pay investors an exceptional rate of return of 6.4% per annum, but if at maturity the index was lower than 100 the bank would, instead of paying interest, deliver 1.38 shares of the index for every 100 invested in the note. A real loss would only occur if the index dropped below $bI_0 = 72$.

Similar to buy-writes, reverse convertibles are sometimes **issued at a discount** instead of at par. This simplifies the structuring procedure considerably. If we wanted to redeem the note at par we should set the cap rate equal to zero. From (9.14) we then see that this makes the index level where the cap becomes active equal to bI_0. If we wanted the cap to become active at an index level of 100 we should thus set $b = 1$. For the note to be a reverse convertible we must have $\alpha \times b = 1$. This means we should set $\alpha = 1$. The resulting payoff is therefore equal to

$$X_5 = N \times \left(1 + \text{Min}\left[0, \left(\frac{I_5 - I_0}{I_0}\right)\right]\right) = N - M \times \text{Max}\,[0, I_0 - I_5]. \qquad (9.21)$$

To find the issue price we have to look at the hedge the bank will put on. Suppose the bank did not really need additional funding and issued the note purely to make a profit. In that case it could simply buy zeros paying off an amount N at maturity and sell M put options with strike I_0. The zeros would cost 77.88m and the puts would yield 7.02m. This means the above payoff would cost the bank 70.86m. This price does not include the bank's profit margin, however. On a note issued at par it makes 1.98%, i.e. an issue price of 100m includes a profit of 1.98m. To make a comparable margin the bank should therefore take an upfront profit of 1.43m, making the issue price equal to 72.29m.

We now have two notes where the cap kicks in when the index ends higher than 100. The first is issued at par with a participation rate of 1.38, a cap rate of 38% and a base rate of 0.72. The second is issued at a 28% discount and has a participation rate of 1, a cap rate of 0% and a base rate of 1. These notes look completely different, but on closer inspection we see that they are not. This becomes clear if we look at the payoffs of both notes and the investment required to obtain those payoffs. The first note yields a payoff equal to

$$X_5 = N \times \left(1 + \text{Min}\left[0.38, 1.38\left(\frac{I_5 - 0.72I_0}{I_0}\right)\right]\right) \tag{9.22}$$

in return for paying 100m now. The second note pays off

$$X_5 = N \times \left(1 + \text{Min}\left[0, \left(\frac{I_5 - I_0}{I_0}\right)\right]\right) \tag{9.23}$$

in return for paying 72.29m. If we invested 100m in the second note as well, we would be able to buy 1.38 units of the note and would therefore obtain a total payoff equal to

$$X_5 = 1.38 \times N \times \left(1 + \text{Min}\left[0, \left(\frac{I_5 - I_0}{I_0}\right)\right]\right), \tag{9.24}$$

which is the same as (9.22).

The fact that the two notes are identical means that we can also find the parameters of a reverse convertible which is issued at par by means of a simple iterative process. The first step would be to invest 100m minus 1.98m profit in a traditional zero. With interest rates at 5% this would yield 125.9m at maturity. The next step is to write ordinary puts with a strike equal to the index level where we wanted the cap to become active. The number of puts would have to be such that when multiplied by the options' strike we would get 125.9m again. With a strike equal to 100 this means we should write 1.259m put options. Doing so would bring in 8.84m, which is equivalent to 11.35m at maturity. This therefore allows us to sell another 0.1135m put options with strike 100. This brings in 0.8m, which is equivalent to 1.03m at maturity. Using this we can write an additional 0.0103m puts, etc. Repeating this routine leave us with a total of 1.38m puts written. This is αM, implying that $\alpha = 1.38$. Since the product of the participation rate and the base rate must be 1, this means the base rate must be 0.72. With the cap kicking in at 100 this in turn implies a cap rate of 38%.

Reverse convertibles were first launched in 1993 to solve the problem of an investment manager who, confronted with substantial cash inflows, did not want to put the money on deposit because of low interest rates but also did not want to invest it in equity because he thought the market was overvalued. The reverse convertible pays an exceptionally high return if the index goes up and delivers the stocks that the investment manager would have bought otherwise if the market goes down. Although a reverse convertible is just a capped bull note, this type of clever marketing has led many investors to think the reverse convertible is a deal without downside. One commentator put it as follows:[3] '... combining an investment grade bond from a favored name with a mouth-watering coupon and, as a worst case scenario, the chance of picking up shares at (or below) the current market price in another favored name almost necessitates a mop and bucket'. Reverse convertibles, typically with maturities of around two years, have become very popular with retail investors. Over the period 1998–1999 more than $50 billion of reverse convertibles

---

[3] A. Webb, Reverse Convertibles: Drive-By Deals, *IFR Financial Products* (September 10th, 1998, p. 18).

were issued in Europe alone. With investors extremely eager to get their hands on these notes, the parties involved in these issues managed to make very healthy profit margins.

Buying puts or calls from the issuers of reverse convertibles is quite popular amongst derivatives firms. Due to the popularity of principal protected bull notes (see later) most derivatives firms find themselves confronted with very large short positions in longer dated call options. The hedging of these positions easily becomes problematic. The options implicitly or explicitly written by the issuers of reverse convertibles, however, provide an attractive hedge for these short positions. Derivatives firms therefore tend to show sharp bid quotes for the options embedded in reverse convertibles. A similar argument goes for other structures where options are written instead of bought, such as buy-writes for example.

9.5.4   Capped Bull Note with Knock-In/Knock-Out Downside Risk

Going over our results with the bank again, it now starts to express some concern about the downside risk on the notes; something which we have not given much attention to so far. One way to deal with this is to introduce a **knock-in** feature on the note's downside risk. We could for example say that the investors receive a return equal to the cap rate except when during the life of the note the index drops below some prefixed barrier level $L < I_0$. In that case they receive the lowest of the cap rate and a fraction α of the index return. Formally, this means we are now talking about a payoff equal to

$$X_5 = N \times (1 + \mathrm{Min}\,[H, D]), \tag{9.25}$$

where

$$D = \alpha \left(\frac{I_5 - bI_0}{I_0} \right), \quad \text{if } \exists j \; I_j \leqslant L,$$

$$= \infty, \quad \text{if } \forall j \; I_j > L.$$

The subscript j counts the monitoring points. D only takes on two values. In case a knock-in is triggered D is equal to α times the index return. If not, D is equal to infinity, which effectively takes it out of the equation. Without the knock-in feature D would simply be equal to α times the index return, which would take us back to the capped bull note discussed earlier.

We can express the amount payable by the derivatives firm in a similar way as before, except that we now have a knock-in feature to deal with as well. This yields

$$V_5 = N \times H - \alpha M \times D \times \mathrm{Max} \left[0, I_0 \left(b + \frac{H}{\alpha} \right) - I_5 \right], \tag{9.26}$$

where now

$$D = 1, \quad \text{if } \exists j \; I_j \leqslant L,$$

$$= 0, \quad \text{if } \forall j \; I_j > L.$$

This shows that the derivatives firm is still buying puts from the bank, but instead of ordinary puts these are now **knock-in puts**. In other words, ordinary puts which are nullified if during the life of the contract the index does not hit the barrier. This means the cap rate must be set such that it satisfies the following budget equation

$$PVC = e^{-5r_5}(N \times H) - \alpha M \times IP_0^b \left[I_0 \left(b + \frac{H}{\alpha} \right), L, 0, 5, 5 \right],$$ (9.27)

where $IP_0^b[K, B, t_1, t_2, T]$ denotes the derivatives firm's bid for an American knock-in put with a strike equal to K, a barrier at B, monitoring between t_1 and t_2, and time to maturity T.

Because the knock-in feature is an additional restriction on the option payoff, knock-in puts will be cheaper than ordinary puts. Selling them to the derivatives firm will therefore not bring in as much money as selling ordinary puts, meaning that the cap rate will go down. How much the cap rate will drop depends on the barrier level chosen. Suppose we set $b = 0.9$, $\alpha = 0.91$, $L = 85$ and monitor the index continuously during the full life of the note. This would yield a cap rate of 56%, becoming active at an index level of 152. Assuming a knock-in occurs, the resulting return profile of the note is given in Figure 9.8. If we compare this with the return profile of the capped bull note without the knock-in feature we see a very substantial drop in the upside participation. With the capped bull note the note return reaches its maximum of 75% at an index value of 172. With the capped knock-in bull note the maximum is 56%, and it is already reached at an index value of 152.

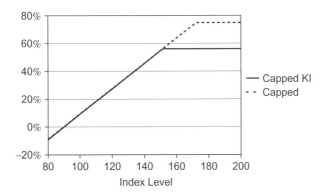

Figure 9.8   Return profile for capped knock-in bull note

It is interesting to take a closer look at the trade-off between the **barrier level** and the cap rate, and especially at what happens if we set the barrier above the current index level instead of below. Figure 9.9 depicts this trade-off assuming $b = 0.9$ and $\alpha = 0.91$. The thing to keep an eye on here is the probability that the index ends relatively low while hitting the barrier in the process. Only in that case will the note return be lower than the cap rate. From the graph we see that the cap rate is highest if we set the barrier equal to 100. If we do, the downside risk knocks in the moment the contract is signed and the knock-in note is identical to an ordinary capped bull note. If we move the barrier away from 100 the expected payoff of the note goes up because the downside risk may not knock in. The cap rate comes down to compensate for this.

Despite the fact that the probability of a barrier hit is high, **even a small move in the barrier reduces the cap rate significantly**. This is understandable if we realize what the cap means for the note's expected payoff. Introducing a cap means that we obtain a

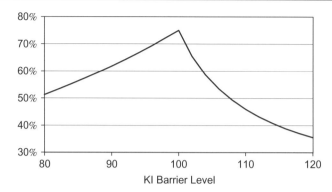

Figure 9.9 Trade-off between barrier level and cap rate for a capped knock-in bull note

relatively high probability of a note return equal to the cap rate and a zero probability of a return higher than that. In the calculation of the expected payoff all returns exceeding the cap rate are replaced by the cap rate itself. As a result, the expected payoff comes down. Given that the index return is normally distributed (see Figure 5.2), the intensity of this phenomenon is stronger the lower the cap rate. If we start with a relatively low cap rate we need to move it down only a little to significantly change the expected payoff. On the other hand, if we start with a relatively high cap rate it will take quite a drop to change the note's expected payoff. This is exactly what happens in our example. The 75% cap becomes active if the index ends higher than 172. However, despite the 5-year maturity, the probability of the index ending that high is quite low. This means that to have a significant impact on the note's expected payoff the cap rate will have to come down substantially.

Starting at spot, **the cap rate drops quicker if we move the barrier upwards than if we move it downwards**. To understand this we have to realize that to change the payoff of the note it is not enough for the downside risk to knock in. The index also needs to end sufficiently low to actually produce a return lower than the cap rate. Suppose we set the barrier above spot. Since the probability of the index going up first to cause a knock-in and then going down again to produce a low return is small, the expected payoff of the note goes up quite a bit, which can only be undone by a substantially lower cap rate. With the barrier below spot it is more likely that the downside risk will knock in and damage the note return because both require the index to drop. The rise in the note's expected payoff and the required drop in the cap rate are therefore smaller.

With the knock-in feature there is downside risk **only if** the barrier is hit. We can of course also turn this around and say that there will always be downside risk **unless** the barrier is hit. This means adding a **knock-out feature** to the note's downside risk. Still assuming a barrier at $L < I_0$, this means the payoff to the investors is given by

$$X_5 = N \times (1 + \text{Min}\,[H, D])\,, \tag{9.28}$$

where

$$D = \infty, \quad \text{if } \exists j\ I_j \leqslant L,$$

$$= \alpha \left(\frac{I_5 - bI_0}{I_0} \right), \quad \text{if } \forall j\ I_j > L.$$

This is the same payoff as before, except that we have switched the terms in D. To generate this payoff the bank has to sell the derivatives firm **knock-out puts**, i.e. ordinary puts which are nullified if during the life of the contract the index hits the barrier. This means the cap rate must be set such that it satisfies the budget equation given by

$$PVC = e^{-5r_5}(N \times H) - \alpha M \times OP_0^b \left[I_0 \left(b + \frac{H}{\alpha} \right), L, 0, 5, 5 \right], \qquad (9.29)$$

where $OP_0^b[K, B, t_1, t_2, T]$ denotes the derivatives firm's bid for an American knock-out put with a strike equal to K, a barrier at B, monitoring between t_1 and t_2, and time to maturity T.

Since knock-out puts are cheaper than ordinary puts, selling them to the derivatives firm will bring in less money for the bank. This means that the cap rate on the note will have to come down again. If we set $b = 0.9$, $\alpha = 0.91$ and $L = 85$ we would get a cap rate of 27%, which would become active at an index level of 120. This is very low indeed, especially if we realize that the lowest cap rate we can get, which can be calculated by setting the put price in the budget equation equal to zero, is 25.9%. Figure 9.10 shows the trade-off between the **barrier level** and the cap rate, assuming $b = 0.9$ and $\alpha = 0.91$. The crucial thing here is the probability that the index ends relatively low without hitting the barrier. Only in that case will the note pay less than the cap rate. The graph shows that the cap rate is at its lowest if we set the barrier equal to 100. In that case the downside risk knocks out immediately and the note becomes a traditional zero coupon bond paying 5% interest per year. If we move the barrier up or down the cap rate goes up because it introduces the probability that the index ends down without the downside risk knocking out.

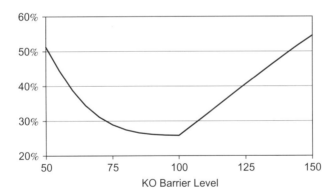

Figure 9.10   Trade-off between barrier level and cap rate for a capped knock-out bull note

From the graph we see that **we have to move the barrier far away from spot to make a difference**. There are two reasons for this. First, there is the high probability of a barrier hit. Because the downside risk remains quite likely to knock out, the expected payoff of the note does not deteriorate much if we move the barrier. The cap rate therefore does not need to go up much. Second, a cap at 25.9% corresponds to an index level of 118. Since it is highly probable that the index will end higher than that, the cap rate only has to rise a little to produce a significant increase in the note's expected payoff. The

graph also shows that **moving the barrier downwards has less effect than moving it
upwards**. This results from the fact that to produce a return lower than the cap rate the
index has to go down. However, with the barrier below spot this causes the downside risk
to knock out as well. The joint probability that the index ends relatively low and does
not hit the barrier is therefore small. Only if the barrier is set far below spot is there a
real possibility of getting paid less than the cap rate without knocking out first.

Before we move on, it is important to note that the knock-in and knock-out structures
provide protection on a very high level. **Instead of protecting against a real loss, they
protect against a return lower than the cap rate**. In the next section we will discuss a
structure that offers a more modest form of protection.

9.6 PRINCIPAL PROTECTED BULL NOTES

During our discussions the bank's attention has shifted more and more from the note's
upside potential to the note's downside risk. The knock-in feature we added is considered
insufficient as it does not provide protection against a large drop in the index. In sum, **we
have arrived at a point where solid downside protection is considered a first priority**.
Fear has conquered greed. Our next step is therefore to structure a note which offers such
protection. We start by installing the required downside protection on a vanilla bull note.
In the next chapter we then study a number of ways to improve the upside participation.

What the bank wants is a floor on the payoff of the note, i.e. it wants to know in
advance that at maturity investors are never going to get less than a prefixed amount.
Formally, this means we should offer investors a note payoff equal to

$$X_5 = N \times \left(1 + \text{Max} \left[F, \alpha \left(\frac{I_5 - I_0}{I_0} \right) \right] \right), \tag{9.30}$$

where F denotes the **floor rate**, i.e. the guaranteed minimum return offered on the note.
The above payoff formula tells us that at maturity investors will receive their money back
plus a return on investment equal to the highest of the floor rate and a fraction α of the
index return. A note like this is known as a **principal protected bull note**. Principal
protected bull notes have become very popular with retail investors in Europe, with an
estimated total issuance from 1997 until 2000 of around $100 billion.

Taking the floor rate as given, to find the participation rate on this principal protected
note we go through the same procedure as before. First, we formalize the amount payable
by the derivatives firm and rewrite it in terms of the payoffs of more familiar contracts
that the derivatives firm already knows how to price. This gives us

$$V_5 = N \times \left(F + \text{Max} \left[0, \alpha \left(\frac{I_5 - I_0}{I_0} \right) - F \right] \right), \tag{9.31}$$

which in turn can be expressed as

$$V_5 = N \times F + \alpha M \times \text{Max} \left[0, I_5 - I_0 \left(1 + \frac{F}{\alpha} \right) \right]. \tag{9.32}$$

This payment is made up of a fixed amount and an index-linked amount. The latter is
equal to the payoff of αM **ordinary calls** with a strike of $I_0(1 + F/\alpha)$. In other words,
implicitly the derivatives firm borrows money from the bank (assuming F is positive)

and simultaneously sells the bank αM ordinary calls. If the index at maturity is below the strike, the bank will cancel the options. If not, the derivatives firm will on balance have to pay $I_5 - I_0(1 + F/\alpha)$ per option, which comes on top of the fixed payment of $N \times F$.

We can also follow another route (or, which is the same, let put–call parity loose on the previous expression) and write the amount payable by the derivatives firm as

$$V_5 = \alpha M \times (I_5 - I_0) + \alpha M \times \text{Max}\left[0, I_0\left(1 + \frac{F}{\alpha}\right) - I_5\right]. \tag{9.33}$$

This shows we can see the payment by the derivatives firm also as the payoff of αM **forwards contracts** with forward price I_0 plus αM **ordinary puts** with strike $I_0(1 + F/\alpha)$.

With the derivatives firm receiving coupons which it values at 20.14m, we can find the participation rate from either one of the following two budget equations. We can use

$$PVC = e^{-5r_5}(N \times F) + \alpha M \times C_0^a\left[I_0\left(1 + \frac{F}{\alpha}\right), 5\right], \tag{9.34}$$

or we can use

$$PVC = \alpha M \times \left(F_0^a[I_0, 5] + P_0^a\left[I_0\left(1 + \frac{F}{\alpha}\right), 5\right]\right). \tag{9.35}$$

Suppose we offered investors a floor return of -5% over five years. Going with (9.34), this would yield a fixed payment of $-5m$, which to the derivatives firm has a present value of $-3.89m$. With 20.14m coming in and $-3.89m$ going out, the derivatives firm will therefore set the participation rate on the deal such that the calls are worth 24.03m. This yields a participation rate of 0.74, meaning that the floor becomes active at an index level of 93. In other words, the note can be structured such that at maturity investors receive a return on investment of 0.74 times the return on the index with a minimum of -5%. It is interesting to note that if the bank did not take out a spread, the participation rate would be 0.80 instead of 0.74. This substantial difference is caused by the fact that, although low in absolute terms, the bank's spread is quite high compared to the prevailing interest rate.

Figure 9.11 shows the return profile of the principal protected bull note as well as that of an equivalent vanilla bull note. The graph clearly shows the floor provided by the principal protected note as well as the lower participation rate. Both graphs cross at an index value of 100 because both notes calculate the index return from a base value of 100. For index values below 100 the principal protected note provides a higher return than the vanilla bull note, with a minimum of -5%. However, due to the higher participation rate, for index values higher than 100 the vanilla bull note outperforms the principal protected note.

Figure 9.12 shows the trade-off between the **floor rate** and the participation rate. From the graph we see that lowering the floor raises the participation rate. This is no surprise as lowering the floor lowers the expected payoff on the note. Since the issue price and the expected return are fixed, however, this means that the participation rate has to go up. Raising the floor lowers the participation rate. There is a definite limit to this though as the derivatives firm cannot guarantee a minimum return higher than the interest which it gets paid. Therefore, the participation rate will be zero if the floor equals the interest which the derivatives firm receives over the five year period. In our example this happens when the floor rate is 25.9%.

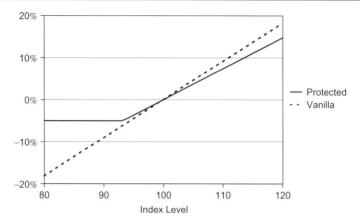

Figure 9.11   Return profile for principal protected bull note

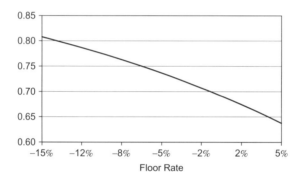

Figure 9.12   Trade-off between floor rate and participation rate for a principal protected bull note

When choosing the floor rate one should take a broader view than just the attainable participation rate. Since the floor turns a risky investment into a riskless investment, a floor that is set too high may have undesirable **tax and/or regulatory consequences**. In The Netherlands for example until recently tax regulation required investors to put at least 7% of their capital at risk. If they did, the return on the note would be tax-free. If they did not, the note return would be taxed as income. To escape this kind of problem we can of course also **issue the product somewhere else or call it by a different name**. Because German investment law does not allow funds to formally guarantee full principal protection, most German principal protected notes are issued in the form of Luxembourg based closed-end funds. Reverse convertibles in Belgium are typically structured as Eurobonds issued by a Luxembourg based entity, while reverse convertibles in Portugal are structured as bank deposits to avoid having to register a prospectus.

Protected Equity

With the bank taking out a significant profit and investors protected against a loss, the principal protected bull note can only offer a participation rate of 0.74. As we will see in the next chapter, derivatives structurers have come up with a variety of ways to raise the participation rate given the issue price of the note. We can, however, also approach the problem from another angle and simply raise the issue price of the note while leaving the notional amount N unchanged. Let's look at the previous principal protected bull note which provides a payoff of

$$X_5 = 100\text{m} \times \left(1 + \text{Max}\left[-0.05, 0.74\left(\frac{I_5 - I_0}{I_0}\right)\right]\right). \tag{9.36}$$

We determined the above parameters assuming the note was going to be issued at par. Now suppose we issued the note at 7.65% above par but kept the notional at 100m. In that case we would have 107.65m available and we could have a note payoff equal to

$$X_5 = 100\text{m} \times \left(1 + \text{Max}\left[-0.05, \left(\frac{I_5 - I_0}{I_0}\right)\right]\right). \tag{9.37}$$

The note now offers a participation rate of 1.0. This does not come for free, however. The floor rate and the index return are still applied to a notional of 100m and not 107.65m, i.e. the note still offers the old guaranteed minimum payoff of 95m. Related to the initial investment of 107.65m this represents a floor of -11.75% instead of -5% as before. In other words, **issuance above par means investors trade in downside protection for upside participation**.

Taking the participation rate up to 1.0 allows marketers to explain the principal protected bull note to the investing public in a very appealing way. Instead of selling the note as a note it can now be sold as so-called **protected equity**. By paying 107.65 investors get one share of the index protected at a level of 95 for five years. If after five years the index is higher than 95 investors receive the index value. If the index is lower than 95 they receive 95.

9.7   THE MARKET FOR PRINCIPAL PROTECTED BULL NOTES

Taking another look at (9.34) we see that the participation rate that can be offered depends heavily on interest rates and the market price of calls. The lower the interest rate, the less money there is to buy calls with. Also, the more expensive the options the less we can buy. When interest rates fall and options become more expensive at the same time, the participation rate comes down very quickly. This is exactly what has happened over time.

Starting in Switzerland in the early 1990s, principal protected bull notes have become a very familiar sight, especially in Europe. In the early nineties interest rates were relatively high and implied volatilities relatively low, allowing for relatively high participation rates as well as excellent profit margins. In July 1992 for example Midland offered one of the first principal protected bull notes in the UK. The 5-year note was linked to the FTSE 100 index and had a participation rate of 1.0. Since interest rates were around 10% at the time, and FTSE implied volatility was about 18.5%, Midland was able to take an upfront profit of over 15% on the note. Not surprisingly, competitors were quick to enter the market and offer notes with more attractive participation rates. Given the extremely advantageous pricing environment, however, even a participation rate of 1.33 allowed for more than 8% profit in those days. The party did not last long, as UK interest rates started to drop. As a result, issuers were forced to lower participation rates as well as profit margins.

By the end of 1995 participation rates on all major indices started a downward trend that lasted for almost four years. Especially during the Asian, Russian and LTCM (see later) crises in 1997–1998, implied volatilities rose strongly. At the same time world interest rates declined. Euro participants saw their longer term rates converge to 4.0%, with especially Spain and Italy showing accelerated rate cuts during 1998. From the second quarter of 1999 participation rates picked up again due to falling longer dated implied volatility and a rise in longer term interest rates. The latter drop in implied volatility can partly be attributed to a change in supply and demand conditions due to institutional option writing and the popularity of reverse convertibles, and partly to cash market volatility returning to normal levels after the Asian, Russian and LTCM (see later) crises.

For various European market indices, Table 9.1 gives an indication of the end-of-second-quarter participation rates on a 5-year principal protected vanilla bull note with a zero floor as seen over the period 1994–1999. Some of the entries in the table are higher than one. This is the result of a relatively high dividend yield. As we will discuss in the next chapter, the higher the dividend yield, the cheaper the calls options embedded in these notes and therefore the higher the participation rate. Obviously, in the absence of dividends (like with the DAX) the participation rate cannot be higher than one. Looking at the participation rates for the FTSE 100, we clearly see the effect of GBP rates being substantially above euro rates.

With participation rates coming down, principal protected notes have become less interesting. This is reflected in note issuance activity. According to estimates from Warburg Dillon Read,[4] average issuance of longer dated principal protected structures in Europe in 1997 (including the structures we will encounter in later chapters) was about $10 billion per quarter. Although partly due to changes in the tax and regulatory environment, in 1998 this dropped to $7.7b, while in 1999 it dropped further to $4.6b. Although pricing conditions have improved since, issuance has not. This is thought to be partly the result of the popularity of reverse convertibles and partly due to European retail investors becoming more accustomed to direct equity investment. The declining participation rate has also led derivatives structurers to investigate ways to make principal protected notes look more sexy. We look at this in the next chapter.

With implied volatility rising, in 1997–1998 most banks became reluctant to sell any more longer dated calls, which caused implieds to rise even further. Around this time several hedge funds stepped in to supply the much needed liquidity, selling longer dated calls while delta hedging them in the cash market. The idea behind this strategy is that

Table 9.1 Participation rates on 5-year principal protected bull note with a 0% floor rate over 1994–1999

Index	1994	1995	1996	1997	1998	1999
AEX	1.32	1.47	1.31	0.95	0.70	0.52
DAX	0.84	0.83	0.80	0.72	0.61	0.43
FTSE 100	1.41	1.42	1.30	1.22	0.93	0.73
IBEX	1.30	1.38	1.23	0.91	0.61	0.51
MIB 30	1.00	1.02	1.06	0.85	0.62	0.48
SMI	0.93	0.91	0.84	0.59	0.46	0.39

---

[4] A. Ineichen, Structured Equity Products, Warburg Dillon Read Index Derivatives Research, 1999.

as long as cash market volatility is below implied volatility this will on average produce positive hedging errors. One of those hedge funds was Long Term Capital Management (LTCM), co-founded by Myron Scholes and Robert Merton. LTCM started writing longer dated options late in 1997, with an eagerness that surprised everybody in the market. LTCM not only supplied new options to the market but also absorbed parts of major banks' existing positions. Dunbar[5] for example reports that by January 1998 LTCM had taken over a quarter of J.P. Morgan's longer dated equity exposure. Although LTCM's newly built equity derivatives position was not the only factor behind its demise, it played a very important role. In September 1998 the crisis in Russia caused longer dated implieds to rise to new highs, requiring LTCM to put up more and more capital as security for the options it had written. With growing doubts about LTCM's future, the market started to quote against LTCM, requiring LTCM to put up even more capital. When it ran out of collateral, LTCM was forced to restructure.

9.8 SOME PRACTICAL CONSIDERATIONS

Implicitly, we have made a few simplifying assumptions during the above discussion. In this last section we will correct this.

9.8.1 Dealing with a Marketing Period

When issuing an equity-linked note the bank may require a couple of weeks to introduce and sell the note to its clientele. Fixing all the relevant note parameters at the beginning of such a marketing period creates a risk. Consider a bank issuing a 5-year principal protected bull note with a 0% floor. The bank will hedge the market risk on the note with a derivatives firm by implicitly buying $\alpha N / I_0$ ATM ordinary calls. With a marketing period there is a problem, however. The notional N only becomes known at the end of the marketing period. If the bank postpones entering into the swap until the end of the marketing period, it would be confronted with a dangerous short position. If the index went up during the marketing period the swap would become more expensive. Because all the note parameters are fixed, this would mean the bank's profit margin would have to come down.

There are various ways the bank can deal with this problem. The two most obvious ones are:

- **Buy at beginning.** Instead of waiting until the end of the marketing period, the bank could make an estimate of the size of the issue and enter into a swap for that amount at the beginning of the marketing period. However, this leaves the risk that the bank under- or overestimates the demand for the note. If its estimate was incorrect it would be forced to buy more or sell part of the swap at the price prevailing at the end of the marketing period.
- **Buy-as-you-go.** The bank could also follow a middle-of-the-road strategy and enter into the swap stepwise during the marketing period. With such a buy-as-you-go scheme the bank does not have an estimation problem because it only buys after having sold. However, unless a large part of the note is sold at the beginning of the market period there is substantial price risk remaining.

---

[5] N. Dunbar, *Inventing Money*, Wiley, 2000, p. 178.

A more effective way to solve the problem of price risk during a marketing period is to **leave one parameter to be fixed at the end of the marketing period**. This allows the bank to postpone setting the full terms of the note until after the sale, thereby creating an outlet for whatever type of price pressure might arise during the marketing period. The bank can wait until the end of the marketing period to buy its hedge and set the parameter in question such that it balances the budget on that date. Although any parameter will do, one alternative is to delay the setting of the base level used for the calculation of the index return until the end of the monitoring period. The idea here is that since investors will not pay the bank until the end of the monitoring period, there is no reason why the calculation of the index return should start before that. The payoff of the note would in that case be given by

$$X_5 = N \times \left(1 + \text{Max} \left[0, \alpha \left(\frac{I_5 - S_{t^*}}{S_{t^*}} \right) \right] \right),$$ (9.38)

where S_{t^*} denotes the base level set at the end of the marketing period.

Although the above does the job, the bank might prefer to give investors a more accurate indication of the terms of the note. If so, the bank could **specify in advance how the base level of the index was going to be set**. The bank could for example say than it was going to use the index value at the end of the marketing period to calculate the index return. Although this would be more restrictive than leaving things completely open, it would still provide a good hedge against index movements. If the index went up, the calls which the bank needed to buy would become more expensive (in absolute terms). On the other hand, the bank would need less of them. On balance, the effect of the higher index would therefore be minimal. This is not true for changes in implied volatility, however. If implied volatility went up, the calls which the bank needed would become more expensive and the bank's profit margin would suffer.

To hedge itself against changes in implied volatility the bank could fall back on the buy-at-the-beginning scheme. The bank could estimate the size of the issue and at the start of the marketing period enter into a swap where at maturity the derivatives firm paid

$$V_5 = N \times F + \frac{\alpha N}{I_{t^*}} \times \text{Max} \left[0, I_5 - I_{t^*} \left(1 + \frac{F}{\alpha} \right) \right],$$ (9.39)

with I_{t^*} denoting the index value at the end of the marketing period. The bank would still buy calls but these calls now have two special features. First, the strike is not set at $t = 0$ but at the end of the monitoring period. This is known as a **forward-starting strike**. Second, the multiplier is index-linked. This means the options are **quantity-adjusting**. With quantity-adjusting options the number of options adjusts to changes in the index. This is exactly what we need since, given the expected notional, the bank can do with fewer options if the index goes up but needs more options if the index goes down. Buying quantity-adjusting options guarantees that by the end of the monitoring period the bank has exactly enough options to cover the expected notional.

9.8.2 Avoiding Surprises

When the payoff of a note (or any other contract for that matter) is critically dependent on the index value on one or two particular dates it may be a good idea to replace these values by short-term averages. With a 5-year principal protected vanilla bull note the note payoff depends completely on I_0 and I_5. As a result, a **short-lived disturbance** in the market could make a significant difference in the note payoff. To avoid this, we could replace I_0 and I_5 in the payoff function by, for example, the hourly average index value over the relevant day or the daily average index value over the relevant week. In that case the payoff of the principal protected bull note would become

$$X_5 = N \times \left(1 + \text{Max} \left[F, \alpha \left(\frac{A_T - A_0}{A_0} \right) \right] \right), \tag{9.40}$$

where A_T denotes the average index value over the last week of the note's life and A_0 denotes the average over the first week of the note's life. In this case we can no longer express the payment to be made by the derivatives firm in terms of ordinary calls where the firm pays I_5 and the bank pays I_0. We now have to price calls where the derivatives firm pays A_T and the bank pays A_0. This is a little more involved, but with today's pricing technology does not present any problem.

Using short-term averages not only protects against short-lived random disturbances but also against **deliberate manipulation**. Building in protection against deliberate manipulation is an important consideration when structuring derivatives, especially when knock-in or knock-out barriers are involved. We would not want the investor to become the victim of a trader who would prefer to give the index a little swing himself instead of living with the pressure of having to hedge a contract which was on the verge of knocking out. We could solve this problem by, instead of with standard barriers, working with lazy barriers or barriers based on a moving average. These types of barriers would require the trader to keep the barrier variable at the other side of the barrier for a longer period of time. The costs of doing so will typically be high enough to make the trader reject the option of manipulation.

9.9 CONCLUSION

The arrival of the OTC derivatives market has opened up a whole new world for retail investors. Apart from the linear payoff profiles offered by stocks and mutual funds, retail investors nowadays have access to much more complex payoff profiles in the form of equity-linked notes. **It was this product line which put structured equity derivatives on the map**. Structuring equity-linked notes is all about mixing upside potential and downside protection. How much of both we can afford depends on the pricing environment, i.e. interest rates, dividends and implied volatilities. Given the latter, the decision how to mix them and the exact form we want to give them depends on investors' views and preferences as well as tax and regulatory considerations.

In this chapter we followed the typical trial-and-error process leading up to a note issue. Given investors' desire to participate in an expected bull market we started off with a note offering straightforward equity exposure, i.e. upside as well as downside exposure. When the proposed note met with some objections concerning the upside offered we first played around with the upside while leaving the downside more or less intact. Eventually, however, it turned out that the bank thought downside protection was much more important than initially indicated. Going back to the drawing board we created a note with solid downside protection; a principal protected bull note. We will continue the discussion of this type of note in the next chapters.

Raising the Participation Rate

10.1 INTRODUCTION

Even with a 5% deductible, the cost of protection is so high that the participation rate on the principal protected bull note is only 0.74. Since this does not look too interesting, we have to think of ways to raise the participation rate again. Ideally, this means giving up something that is worth a lot to the derivatives firm, but not to the investors. Although this sounds easy, it is typically very hard to think of something. It sometimes pays to keep track of derivatives firms' books. When a certain type of product is in vogue derivatives firms' books tend to fill up with specific types of risk. When this is the case, firms are happy to enter into contracts which reduce these risks again. Generally, however, the best thing to do is to simply try out a number of different solutions and see what the derivatives firm's and the bank's response is. Another reason for this trial and error approach is pricing. In this book we assume that the term structures of interest rates and volatility are flat and that there is no volatility skew. In reality this is not the case, however. **(Changes in) the shape of these term structures as well as the volatility skew can have a significant and sometimes quite unexpected impact on the actual pricing of derivatives**.

In this chapter we look at a number of ways to improve the participation rate on principal protected bull notes. In the previous chapter we saw that the payoff of a principal protected bull note can be decomposed into a fixed amount plus the payoff of a number of ordinary calls. Given the desired floor rate, to raise the participation rate on a principal protected bull note we therefore have to make the embedded call options cheaper. This in turn means we can fall back on what we discussed earlier in Chapter 8. We will look at the following:

- Changing the note parameters
- Changing the reference index
- Buying less principal protection
- Piecewise linear segmentation of principal protection
- Piecewise linear segmentation of upside participation
- A floating cap on the upside participation
- Knock-in and knock-out principal protection
- Knock-in and knock-out upside participation
- Changing exchange rate risk
- Addition of an Asian tail
- Revised monitoring for path-dependent notes
- Introduction of additional risks

Although we discuss these features one by one, it is important to keep in mind that whenever so desired **we can always combine two or more of them into a single note**. Another important point is that the possibilities are not limited to just the ones we discuss here. Successful structuring of derivatives is first and foremost about being creative and responsive. **There are as many solutions as you can think of**. We use the same assumptions and notation as in Chapter 9.

10.2   CHANGING THE NOTE PARAMETERS

Since the price of the note is fixed in advance, the participation rate on the principal protected bull note is determined by fixing the other parameters of the note. One way to raise the participation rate is therefore to change one of the note parameters. Reducing the floor rate is of course the most obvious choice, but that would change the note payoff too much. We will keep the latter fixed at -5% throughout.

10.2.1   A Higher Base

Previously we saw how reducing the base level used for the calculation of the index return reduced the participation rate. Of course, it also works the other way around. By increasing the base level we increase the participation rate. We could for example calculate the return from a level of bI_0 with $b > 1$. This would make the note payoff equal to

$$X_5 = N \times \left(1 + \text{Max} \left[F, \alpha \left(\frac{I_5 - bI_0}{I_0} \right) \right] \right), \quad b > 1. \tag{10.1}$$

This payoff is identical to that of the principal protected bull note we discussed in the previous chapter, except that instead of calculating the index return as the change from I_0 we now calculate it as the change from bI_0. The amount payable by the derivatives firm can in this case be written as

$$V_5 = N \times F + \alpha M \times \text{Max} \left[0, I_5 - I_0 \left(b + \frac{F}{\alpha} \right) \right], \tag{10.2}$$

meaning we can solve the participation rate from the budget equation given by

$$PVC = e^{-5r_5}(N \times F) + \alpha M \times C_0^a \left[I_0 \left(b + \frac{F}{\alpha} \right), 5 \right]. \tag{10.3}$$

This is exactly the same equation as (9.34), except that the calls have a slightly higher strike. Assuming we set $b = 1.1$ this yields a participation rate of 0.89, implying that the floor becomes active at an index level of 104.

Figure 10.1 shows the return profile of the note with a base rate of 1.1 as well as that of a similar note with a base rate of 1. From the graph we see that both notes offer the same level of downside protection, but not the same upside potential. With $b = 1$ the floor becomes active at an index level of 93, while with $b = 1.1$ it becomes active at 104. When the index goes up, the note with $b = 1.1$ picks up more of the change in the index than the note with $b = 1$. This reflects the higher participation rate. Both payoffs are equal at an index level of 159. Above that the note with $b = 1.1$ pays off more than the note with $b = 1$. Figure 10.2 shows the trade-off between the **base rate** and the participation rate. The higher the base rate, the lower the payoff for a given index value and therefore the lower the expected payoff. To compensate for this the participation rate has to go up. The same conclusion can be drawn from the budget equation. A higher base rate means a higher strike for the embedded calls, which will make them cheaper. Since PVC is

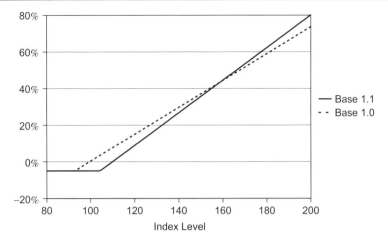

Figure 10.1   Return profile for a principal protected bull note with raised base

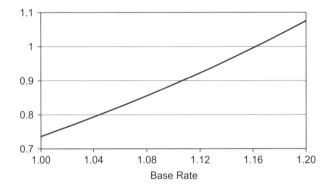

Figure 10.2   Trade-off between base rate and participation rate for a principal protected bull note with raised base

fixed, this means that the participation rate has to go up to balance both sides of the equation.

10.2.2   A Longer Time to Maturity

Changing a principal protected bull note's time to maturity may also raise the participation rate. Of course, this is only viable in cases where investors have no specific preferences concerning the note's maturity. It works as follows. The interest received by the derivatives firm increases with maturity. This means that the longer the maturity, the more money there is to spend. Theoretically, increasing the time to maturity will also raise the price of call options. As we saw in Figure 7.2, however, call prices increase less than proportionally with time to maturity. This means that **theoretically a principal protected bull note with a longer maturity will offer its holder a higher participation rate**. Figure 10.3 shows the trade-off between the time to maturity and the participation rate on a principal protected bull note with a −5% floor rate. From the graph we see clearly how the participation rate rises with time to maturity. With one year to maturity

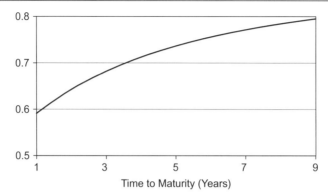

Figure 10.3 Trade-off between time to maturity and participation rate for a principal protected bull note

the participation rate is 0.58, with five years it is 0.74 and with nine years to maturity it is 0.79.

Unlike what we assumed when making Figure 10.3, in practice the term structure of implied volatility will often not be flat. If the slope of the term structure is negative, option prices will increase slower than in theory. If the slope is positive they will increase faster. In the latter case, the participation rate may go down instead of up if we increase a note's time to maturity. In other words, **with principal protected bull notes a steep volatility term structure favors shorter maturities**. In 1998–1999 the term structure of implied volatilities became extremely steep for some indices. This led to a significant shortening of maturities of the notes issued. In 1998 41% of the principal protected notes issued in Europe had a maturity of six years or longer. In the first half of 1999 this dropped to 24%.

It is interesting to note that capped bull notes respond to a change in maturity in exactly the opposite way. With a capped bull note the bank writes options. Increasing the time to maturity will raise the price of these options but, as shown in Figure 7.2, the increase will be less than proportional. This means that on a per annum basis it pays better to write short dated than longer dated options, implying that we can raise the cap rate by reducing the lifetime of the note. If we drop the assumption of a flat term structure of implied volatility we see that **with capped bull notes a steep volatility term structure favors longer maturities**. With the term structure steepening in 1998–1999, the market also saw a significant rise in the maturity of the capped bull notes issued.

The steepening of the volatility term structure in 1998–1999 can partly be attributed to the unwillingness of derivatives firms to expand their longer dated books and partly to the success of reverse convertibles. With reverse convertibles having shorter maturities than principal protected notes, the selling of puts by the issuers of reverse convertibles causes significant pressure on the short end of the market. In a way the success of the reverse convertible contributed to restoring a normal two-way flow in the short end of the options market, with lower implieds being the result. This contrasts with the market for longer dated options, which is very much one-sided. Although derivatives firms use short-term options to hedge themselves, prices in the latter market are primarily driven by the demand for principal protected notes.

10.3   CHANGING THE REFERENCE INDEX

Sometimes the choice of reference index is only of secondary importance. Most retail investors are much more interested in obtaining general stock market exposure than in obtaining exposure to specific company names. If that is the case, we may be able to raise the participation rate by switching to another reference index. This is what we discuss next.

10.3.1   A Higher Dividend Yield

Dividends reduce the upward trend in stock prices by making stock prices drop on the ex-dividend dates. As a result, a higher dividend will make call options cheaper and put options more expensive. This means that we may be able to raise the participation rate on a principal protected bull note by changing to a reference index which pays a higher dividend yield. It also explains why the DAX, which does not pay dividends, is less popular as a reference index for equity-linked notes.

Figure 10.4 shows the relationship between the participation rate of a 5-year principal protected bull note with a floor rate of −5% and the dividend yield on the reference index. From the graph we see clearly how the participation rate rises with the dividend yield. With zero dividends the participation rate is 0.74. With a 2% dividend yield the same note offers a participation rate of 1. If we were able to find a reference index that paid 4% dividends, the note could even offer a participation rate of more than 1.3. **A small increase in dividend yield is enough to raise the participation rate significantly**.

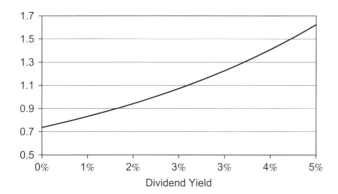

Figure 10.4   Participation rate for a principal protected bull note as a function of dividend yield reference index

10.3.2   A Basket of Indices

So far we have assumed that the reference index is a single stock price or a single stock market index. However, we can structure the same payoffs based on the return on a basket of stocks or a basket of stock market indices. A basket of indices tends to be less volatile than an individual index due to the imperfect correlation between the component indices. Since lower volatility means cheaper calls, this will improve the participation rate.

How well this works depends on the degree of **correlation** between the indices used. Correlation between individual stock returns can be quite low. On the other hand, as we saw in Table 8.1, stock market indices in Europe and the US tend to be highly correlated. Far Eastern indices, are much less correlated with Western indices, which explains why many index baskets used in the market include the Nikkei 225. A word of caution is in order here though. In theory the savings that can be achieved by working with baskets are significant. However, given the increased popularity of basket products, derivatives firms are adjusting their pricing upwards. In part this is a reflection of the fact that these firms' books are filling up, and partly it is simple demand and supply economics.

Suppose we made an equally-weighted basket consisting of three domestic stocks. In that case we would have three reference indices: I_t^1, I_t^2 and I_t^3. From Chapter 4 we know that the return on a basket of reference indices, can be written as the weighted sum of the returns on the individual indices, with the weights being the basket weights. The payoff for the principal protected bull note would therefore become equal to

$$X_5 = N \times \left(1 + \text{Max}\left[F, \alpha\left(1/3R_{0,5}^1 + 1/3R_{0,5}^2 + 1/3R_{0,5}^3\right)\right]\right), \tag{10.4}$$

where $R_{0,5}^i$ denotes the individual index return. We can simplify things further if we **turn the basket value into an index number** by defining

$$I_0 = 100, \tag{10.5}$$

$$I_t = 100 \times \frac{1}{3} \times \left[\left(\frac{I_t^1}{I_0^1}\right) + \left(\frac{I_t^2}{I_0^2}\right) + \left(\frac{I_t^3}{I_0^3}\right)\right]. \tag{10.6}$$

This makes the basket value an index number with a $t = 0$ value of 100. With the basket value turned into a reference index, the payoff of the principal protected bull note can be expressed as in (9.30). This shows that implicitly the bank buys αM **ordinary basket calls** which call for the exchange of the strike in return for an amount equal to I_5 calculated according to (10.6).

The above example also shows that when working with a basket of indices instead of a single index **the payoff expressions do not need to change**. The only thing that changes is that we no longer work with a reference index that is taken directly from the market, but with an index that we created ourselves. Suppose we had a 5-year principal protected bull note with a -5% floor rate where the payoff depended on an equally-weighted basket of three reference indices. All three indices have an annualized volatility of 20%. Figure 10.5 shows the relationship between the participation rate of this note and the **average correlation** between the indices in the basket. From the graph we see clearly how the participation rate rises when the correlation coefficient falls.

10.3.3 A Foreign Reference Index

As a shortcut, we can say that derivatives firms price derivatives contracts as if (a) every reference index has an upward drift equal to the interest rate and (b) exchange rates trend upwards or downwards at a rate equal to the interest rate differential. This means that we might be able to improve the participation rate on a principal protected bull note by replacing the domestic reference index with a foreign index denominated in a currency with an interest rate lower than that of the domestic currency. Because the interest rate is lower, the foreign index's upward trend will be lower as well. This lowers the note's expected payoff and thereby allows for a higher participation rate. Of course, the exchange

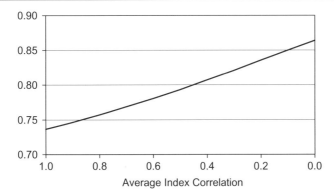

Figure 10.5 Participation rate for a principal protected bull note as a function of average correlation coefficient

rate will (be assumed to) be drifting upwards. As long as we only convert the rise in the index and not the index itself, however, this will not neutralize the desired effect.

Probably the simplest way to incorporate the above idea into a note is to calculate the return on investment offered by the note as the best of a given floor rate and a fraction α of the foreign index return and convert that into a domestic return figure at the exchange rate at maturity, i.e. multiplying by E_5/E_0. Formally, this yields the following payoff

$$X_5 = N \times \left(1 + \frac{E_5}{E_0} \times \text{Max}\left[F, \alpha\left(\frac{I_5 - I_0}{I_0}\right)\right]\right), \quad (10.7)$$

where I_t denotes the time t value of the foreign index in foreign currency. This note gives investors floored exposure to the foreign index in the same way as before. However, due to the conversion factor E_5/E_0, investors are now also exposed to the exchange rate. They gain from an appreciation of the foreign currency and suffer in case of a depreciation. Note that the floor rate F floors the foreign index return. This means that the floor rate is denominated in the same foreign currency as the index return and therefore needs to be converted into domestic currency as well. Because this is done through multiplying by E_5/E_0, the floor rate in domestic currency is not completely fixed. This can easily be corrected by converting the floor rate using $E_0/E_0 = 1$ instead of E_5/E_0. We leave this case to the reader for further study.

The big question then is whether and how much we can improve the participation rate by moving to a foreign index. To find out we first write the payment to be made by the derivatives firm as

$$V_5 = N \times \frac{E_5}{E_0} \times F + \alpha M \times E_5 \times \text{Max}\left[0, I_5 - I_0\left(1 + \frac{F}{\alpha}\right)\right], \quad (10.8)$$

where because we are now working with a foreign index $M = N/E_0 I_0$. The above means we can solve the participation rate from the budget equation given by

$$PVC = e^{-5r_5^f}(N \times F) + \alpha M \times E_0 \times FC_0^a\left[I_0\left(1 + \frac{F}{\alpha}\right), 5\right], \quad (10.9)$$

where r^f is the foreign interest rate and $FC_0^a[K, T]$ denotes the derivatives firm's offer price (in foreign currency) for a call on the foreign index with a strike K (also in foreign

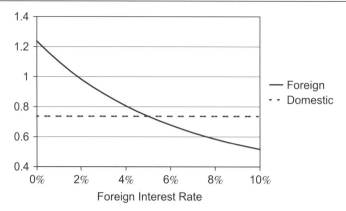

Figure 10.6   Participation rate for domestic and foreign principal protected bull notes as a function of foreign interest rate

currency) and time to maturity T. As discussed earlier in Section 8.7, such a call is referred to as a **foreign call struck in foreign currency**, or simply as a **foreign call**.

Assuming 20% volatility for the foreign index, Figure 10.6 shows the participation rate on the above note as well as a domestic principal protected bull note as a function of the **foreign interest rate**. From the figure we see that if the domestic and foreign interest rates are equal then so are the participation rates. **The foreign note offers a higher participation rate if the foreign interest rate is below and a lower participation rate if the foreign interest rate is above the domestic rate**. Even a small difference in interest rates makes a significant difference in participation rates. If we look at this result in the context of the budget equation it is perfectly clear why this happens. The price of a call depends quite heavily on the interest rate. The lower the interest rate, the cheaper the option. Since the interest paid by the bank does not change, this translates directly into a higher participation rate.

With a domestic interest rate three times as high as in Europe or the US, principal protected bull notes have become very popular with investors in South Africa. Notes linked to a basket of the Eurostoxx 50 and the Nikkei 225, which combines low volatility with a low foreign interest rate, have offered South African investors participation rates as high as 2.0, even with their issuers taking out very substantial profit margins. Of course, to sell a principal protected note in a high interest rate environment the bank will need to offer investors a very high participation rate. An investor who can easily get 15% interest on his savings account can be expected to be a lot less interested in alternatives than an investor who only gets 5%.

For simplicity we assumed that the implied volatility of the foreign index is equal to that of the domestic index. Of course, if it is higher, the trick will not work as well because a foreign call may not be much cheaper than a domestic call. In that case not all is lost though, because we might still be able to quanto the note, i.e. move to a foreign index but eliminate all currency risk. When the interest rate differential implies (according to our pricing shortcut) that the exchange rate is about to go up, giving up the exchange rate exposure will reduce the option price. We discussed this earlier in Section 8.7 and will do so again in Section 10.10.

10.4 BUYING LESS PROTECTION

The principal protected bull note provides investors with full protection. Investors know in advance they will never receive a return less than the floor rate. One way to get a better participation rate is to aim for a less strict form of protection by dividing the money available between a vanilla bull note with and without principal protection. Suppose that we invested a fraction f of the principal in a principal protected bull note and the remainder in a vanilla bull note. This would produce a payoff to the investors equal to

$$X_5 = (1 - f)N \times \left(1 + \alpha \left(\frac{I_5 - I_0}{I_0}\right)\right) + fN \times \left(1 + \text{Max}\left[F, \alpha \left(\frac{I_5 - I_0}{I_0}\right)\right]\right).$$
(10.10)

The derivatives firm will therefore have to pay an amount equal to

$$V_5 = \alpha(1 - f)M \times (I_5 - I_0) + fN \times F + \alpha fM \times \text{Max}\left[0, I_5 - I_0\left(1 + \frac{F}{\alpha}\right)\right].$$
(10.11)

In this case the derivatives firm's payment consists of the payoff of $\alpha(1 - f)M$ **vanilla forwards** plus a fixed amount plus the payoff of αfM **ordinary calls**. We can of course also express this as

$$V_5 = \alpha M \times (I_5 - I_0) + \alpha fM \times \text{Max}\left[0, I_0\left(1 + \frac{F}{\alpha}\right) - I_5\right],$$
(10.12)

which shows the payment by the derivatives firm can also be seen as the payoff of αM **vanilla forwards** plus the payoff of αfM **ordinary puts**.

We can calculate the participation rate either from the budget equation given by

$$PVC = \alpha(1 - f)M \times F_0^a[I_0, 5] + e^{-5r_5}(fN \times F) + \alpha fM \times C_0^a\left[I_0\left(1 + \frac{F}{\alpha}\right), 5\right]$$
(10.13)

or from

$$PVC = \alpha M \times F_0^a[I_0, 5] + \alpha fM \times P_0^a\left[I_0\left(1 + \frac{F}{\alpha}\right), 5\right].$$
(10.14)

Suppose we set $f = 0.5$. In that case the participation rate would be equal to 0.81. Figure 10.7 shows the return profile of such a note. From the graph we clearly see that the partially protected note provides less protection but also offers more upside participation than the principal protected note. If we wanted to trade in protection for participation we could simply lower f. This is also clear from Figure 10.8, which shows the trade-off between the **fraction invested in the protected note** and the participation rate. If we invested more in the principal protected note this would raise the expected payoff and the participation rate would come down. Depending on the fraction chosen the participation rate varies between that of a vanilla bull note and that of a principal protected bull note.

10.5 PIECEWISE LINEAR SEGMENTATION OF THE PROTECTION

With a principal protected bull note investors get the best of the floor return and a fraction of the index return. As soon as the product of the participation rate and the index return is less than the floor return the protection kicks in and the full difference is made good. One

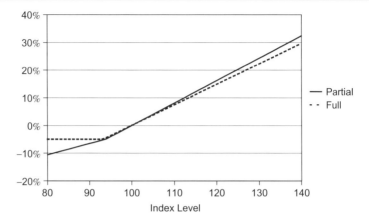

Figure 10.7   Return profile for a partially principal protected bull note

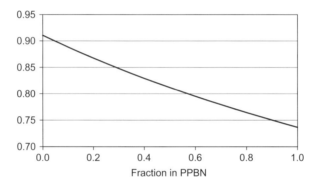

Figure 10.8   Trade-off between fraction in protected note and participation rate for partially principal protected bull note

way to raise the participation rate is to only make good losses up to a certain maximum amount. Suppose we said that the total amount of compensation paid would never be more than the notional amount N times a **compensation rate** E. Any loss exceeding the latter amount would have to be carried by the investors. This means providing investors with a payoff equal to

$$X_5 = N \times \left(1 + \text{Max}\left[\text{Min}\left[F, E + \alpha\left(\frac{I_5 - I_0}{I_0}\right)\right], \alpha\left(\frac{I_5 - I_0}{I_0}\right)\right]\right). \qquad (10.15)$$

With this note there are three possible outcomes. If the index rises above $I_0(1 + F/\alpha)$ investors receive α times the index return. If the index at maturity is between $I_0(1 + (F - E)/\alpha)$ and $I_0(1 + F/\alpha)$ investors make a return equal to F. Finally, and this is where this note differs from the principal protected bull note, if the index drops below $I_0(1 + (F - E)/\alpha)$ the note return is equal to α times the index return plus E.

Given (10.15) we can write the amount payable by the derivatives firm as

$$V_5 = N \times F + \alpha M \times \left(\text{Max}\left[0, I_5 - I_0\left(1 + \frac{F}{\alpha}\right)\right] - \text{Max}\left[0, I_0\left(1 + \frac{F - E}{\alpha}\right) - I_5\right]\right).$$
$$(10.16)$$

This shows that the amount which the derivatives firm pays at maturity can be seen as a fixed amount plus the payoff of αM **ordinary calls** minus the payoff of αM **ordinary puts**. The bank buys calls and sells puts in equal numbers but with different strikes. The fixed amount and the calls are the same as in the case of the principal protected bull note. The budget equation is given by

$$PVC = e^{-5r_5}(N \times F) + \alpha M \times \left(C_0^a \left[I_0 \left(1 + \frac{F}{\alpha} \right), 5 \right] - P_0^b \left[I_0 \left(1 + \frac{F - E}{\alpha} \right), 5 \right] \right).$$

(10.17)

The first two parts on the right-hand side are identical to what we already had for the principal protected bull note. The last part corresponds to the puts the bank is now implicitly selling. Writing puts generates the money required to raise the participation rate. However, at the same time it gives away part of the downside protection. If we set $E = 10\%$ we obtain a participation rate of 0.82.

Figure 10.9 shows the return profile of a limited and an ordinary principal protected bull note with the same floor rate. From the graph we clearly see that the increased upside potential is obtained at the cost of reduced downside protection. If the index drops below 82, the investors have to pick up the tab again. Figure 10.10 shows the trade-off between the **compensation rate** and the participation rate. With a compensation

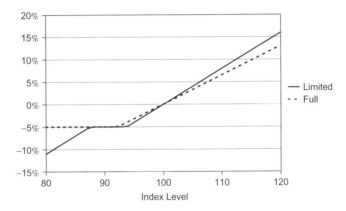

Figure 10.9   Return profile for a limited principal protected bull note

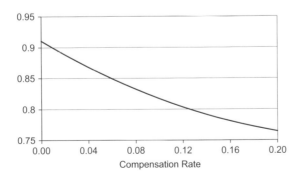

Figure 10.10   Trade-off between compensation rate and participation rate for a limited principal protected bull note

rate of 0 there is no downside protection. The participation rate is therefore equal to that of a vanilla bull note. If we raise the compensation rate, the expected payoff of the note goes up and the participation rate has to come down to compensate. If the compensation rate increases, the participation rate approaches that of a principal protected bull note.

10.6 PIECEWISE LINEAR SEGMENTATION OF THE UPSIDE

If the bank insisted on full protection we would be forced to work on the note's upside to save the money needed to raise the note's participation rate. An obvious alternative is to sell off some upside potential in the form of a **cap**. We already saw how this works in the case of a capped bull note. Combining principal protection with a cap creates a **collar** on the note return as it cannot go lower than the floor rate or higher than the cap rate. Denoting the cap rate as H, this turns the note payoff into

$$X_5 = N \times \left(1 + \text{Min}\left[H, \text{Max}\left[F, \alpha\left(\frac{I_5 - I_0}{I_0}\right)\right]\right]\right). \qquad (10.18)$$

At maturity investors are paid a return on investment equal to a fraction of the index return, but never less than F or more than H.

We now have three parameters to work with: (1) the floor rate, (2) the cap rate and (3) the participation rate. Choosing two of them fixes the third. Let's assume that we set the floor rate and the cap rate and solve for the participation rate. To find the participation rate we again have to concentrate on the amount payable by the derivatives firm. This can be expressed as

$$V_5 = N \times F + \alpha M \times \left(\text{Max}\left[0, I_5 - I_0\left(1 + \frac{F}{\alpha}\right)\right] - \text{Max}\left[0, I_5 - I_0\left(1 + \frac{H}{\alpha}\right)\right]\right).$$
$$(10.19)$$

This shows that this time the amount to be paid by the derivatives firm is made up of the usual fixed amount corresponding to the guaranteed minimum return and two index-linked amounts. Looking at the index-linked part more closely we see that the derivatives firm sells the bank αM **ordinary calls** with strike $I_0(1 + F/\alpha)$ and at the same time buys from the bank αM **ordinary calls** with strike $I_0(1 + H/\alpha)$. Given that this is nothing more than an **ordinary call spread**, we can solve the participation rate from the budget equation given by

$$PVC = e^{-5r_5}(N \times F) + \alpha M \times CS_0^a\left[I_0\left(1 + \frac{F}{\alpha}\right), I_0\left(1 + \frac{H}{\alpha}\right), 5\right]. \qquad (10.20)$$

If we fixed the cap rate at 60% and the floor rate at -5% this would yield a participation rate of 1.34. Remember that for pricing purposes we must **look for a price on the call spread** and not for two separate call prices.

Figure 10.11 shows the return profile of a principal protected bull note with and without cap. The graph shows that with the capped note investors buy increased upside participation for lower index values at the cost of participation for higher index values. The capped note's payoff reaches its maximum at an index level of 145. Figure 10.12 shows the trade-off between the **cap rate** and the participation rate. If we raise the cap rate, the participation rate comes down very quickly. This reflects the fact that a low cap rate

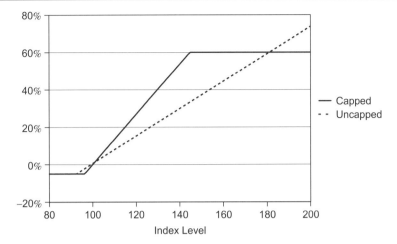

Figure 10.11 Return profile for a capped principal protected bull note

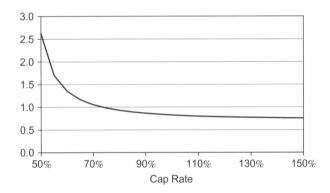

Figure 10.12 Trade-off between cap rate and participation rate for a capped principal protected bull note

reduces the note's expected payoff a lot more than a higher cap rate. As a result, a low cap rate produces a substantially higher participation rate.

Just as with the capped bull note, thanks to the presence of the cap we can describe the note payoff in quite attractive terms. Instead of saying that investors will never get a return higher than $H\%$, we can also say that they will be paid an exceptionally high return of $H\%$, but that if the market does not rise as much as expected they may have to pay some of it back. They will never have to pay back more than $(H - F)\%$ though, which means their principal is (more or less) safe.

With a cap we split the note's upside into two segments: one with participation rate α and another with participation rate equal to zero. A less aggressive cut in upside capture can be obtained by allowing for the second participation rate to be higher than zero or by splitting the upside into more than two segments, each with its own participation rate. If we allowed for **three participation rates** this would lead to a note payoff that formally could be expressed as

$$X_5 = N \times \left(1 + \text{Max}\left[F, PLR_{0,5}\right]\right),$$

(10.21)

where $PLR_{0,5}$ stands for the **piecewise linear return** over the period from $t = 0$ to $t = 5$. The latter is equal to

$$PLR_{0,5} = \alpha_1 \, \text{Min} \left[0.2, \frac{I_5 - I_0}{I_0} \right] + \alpha_2 \, \text{Min} \left[0.2, \text{Max} \left[0, \frac{I_5 - 1.2I_0}{I_0} \right] \right]$$

$$+ \alpha_3 \, \text{Max} \left[0, \frac{I_5 - 1.4I_0}{I_0} \right]. \tag{10.22}$$

We have split the outcome space into three segments. If the index return is 20% or less, the participation rate is equal to α_1. If the index return is between 20% and 40% we have two participation rates: α_1 and α_2. The first applies to the first 20% of the rise and the second to the remainder. If the index return is higher than 40% we have three participation rates: α_1, α_2 and α_3. The first applies to the first 20% of the rise, the second to the next 20% and the third to the remainder.

With three different participation rates around we can choose two of them ourselves and the third will then follow automatically. However, we first need to come up with a budget equation from which we can solve this third participation rate. Rewriting the amount payable by the derivatives firm yields

$$V_5 = N \times F + \alpha_1 M \times \left(\text{Max} \left[0, I_5 - I_0 \left(1 + \frac{F}{\alpha_1} \right) \right] - \text{Max} \left[0, I_5 - I_0 \left(1.2 + \frac{F}{\alpha_1} \right) \right] \right)$$

$$+ \alpha_2 M \times \left(\text{Max} \left[0, I_5 - I_0 \left(1.2 + \frac{F}{\alpha_2} \right) \right] - \text{Max} \left[0, I_5 - I_0 \left(1.4 + \frac{F}{\alpha_2} \right) \right] \right)$$

$$+ \alpha_3 M \times \text{Max} \left[0, I_5 - I_0 \left(1.4 + \frac{F}{\alpha_3} \right) \right]. \tag{10.23}$$

This looks complicated but it is not. Expression (10.23) simply tells us that, apart from a fixed amount, the amount payable by the derivatives firm can be expressed in terms of the payoffs of five **ordinary calls**. Just as before, the first one gives the investors an upside participation of α_1. However, we do not want this to continue until infinity. At some point we want to fix $\alpha_1 \times 20\%$ and move on to the next participation rate α_2. This is accomplished by the second and third call payoffs. The second call locks in $\alpha_1 \times 20\%$ and the third call switches the participation rate to α_2. The fourth and fifth calls do exactly the same. The fourth call locks in $\alpha_2 \times 20\%$ and the last call switches the participation rate from α_2 to α_3.

Given the above expression we can solve the missing participation rate from the budget equation given by

$$PVC = e^{-5r_5}(N \times F) + \alpha_1 M \times CS_0^a \left[I_0 \left(1 + \frac{F}{\alpha_1} \right), I_0 \left(1.2 + \frac{F}{\alpha_1} \right), 5 \right]$$

$$+ \alpha_2 M \times CS_0^a \left[I_0 \left(1.2 + \frac{F}{\alpha_2} \right), I_0 \left(1.4 + \frac{F}{\alpha_2} \right), 5 \right]$$

$$+ \alpha_3 M \times C_0^a \left[I_0 \left(1.4 + \frac{F}{\alpha_3} \right), 5 \right]. \tag{10.24}$$

Assuming we fixed $\alpha_1 = 0.3$ and $\alpha_2 = 1.5$ this yields $\alpha_3 = 0.66$. Remember again that although we can see the amount payable by the derivatives firm made up of the payoffs

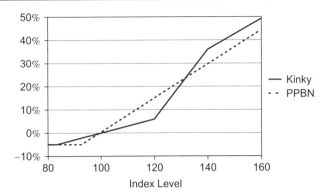

Figure 10.13   Return profile for a kinky principal protected bull note

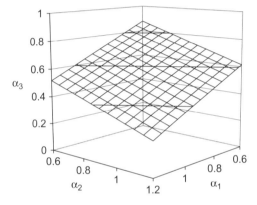

Figure 10.14   Trade-off between three participation rates for a kinky principal protected bull note

of two call spreads and an ordinary call, for pricing purposes we have to treat all of these as one single contract.

Figure 10.13 shows the return profile of the kinky and an ordinary principal protected bull note. From the graph we clearly see the difference between both notes. The ordinary note offers constant upside potential, while the kinky note's upside varies with the index level. For index values at maturity between 83 and 100, as well as between 131 and 220, the kinky note pays off more than the standard note. However, for index values between 100 and 131 and above 220 it pays off less. The graph in Figure 10.14 shows the trade-off between the three **participation rates** on the kinky bull note. It shows clearly that since the issue price of the note is fixed, a rise in one of the participation rates has to be compensated for by a drop in one or both of the others. Note that setting $\alpha_1 = 0.6$ and $\alpha_2 = 1.2$ yields a higher value of α_3 than setting $\alpha_1 = 1.2$ and $\alpha_2 = 0.6$. This reflects the fact that the index is more likely to end above I_0 than it is to end above $1.2I_0$.

10.7   A FLOATING CAP ON THE UPSIDE

Putting a cap on the note payoff raises the participation rate. There is no reason why the cap should always be a fixed amount though. We can also use index-linked cash flows as caps. Suppose we choose a second reference index I^2 and use the return on that index as the cap rate on the return on our original reference index I^1. This would produce a note that is sometimes referred to as a principal protected **worst-of-two note**. Formally, the note payoff would in that case become

$$X_5 = N \times \left(1 + \text{Max} \left[F, \text{Min} \left[\alpha \left(\frac{I_5^1 - I_0^1}{I_0^1} \right), \alpha \left(\frac{I_5^2 - I_0^2}{I_0^2} \right) \right] \right] \right). \tag{10.25}$$

On top of their principal investors would receive a return on investment equal to a fraction α of the lowest of both index returns, but never less than the floor rate F.

The attraction of an index-linked cap is that when the returns on both indices are positively correlated the cap level will tend to go up with the original reference index. As a result, the cap might never kick in despite the first index rising steadily. This sounds too good to be true and indeed it is. A fixed cap raises the participation rate because it lowers the expected payoff of the note. Since it is fixed, the cap rate has zero correlation with the reference index. If we opt for a variable cap rate that is positively correlated with the index, the cap tends to move with the index and therefore does not lower the note's expected payoff as much as a fixed cap does. The higher the correlation between both indices, the lower the participation rate will be. On the other hand, as long as there is no perfect correlation we should still be able to achieve a somewhat higher participation rate than with an ordinary principal protected bull note.

To find out how much we can save we first need to price the worst-of-two note. Assuming that $I_0^1 = I_0^2 = I_0$ we can rewrite the derivatives firm's payment to the bank as

$$V_5 = N \times F + \alpha M \times \text{Max} \left[0, \text{Min} [I_5^1, I_5^2] - I_0 \left(1 + \frac{F}{\alpha} \right) \right], \tag{10.26}$$

which is the same expression as for a principal protected bull note but with I_5 replaced by $\text{Min} [I_5^1, I_5^2]$. The index-linked part of (10.26) equals αM times the payoff of a contract where the derivatives firm pays the lowest of both index values, the bank pays a fixed amount $I_0(1 + F/\alpha)$ and also has the right to cancel the deal at maturity. Such a contract is known as a **call on the worst-of-two** with strike $I_0(1 + F/\alpha)$. This means that we can find the participation rate from the following budget equation

$$PVC = e^{-5r_5}(N \times F) + \alpha M \times CW_0^a \left[I_0 \left(1 + \frac{F}{\alpha} \right), 5 \right], \tag{10.27}$$

where $CW_0^a[K, T]$ is the derivatives firm's offer for a call on the worst-of-two with strike K and time to maturity T. Assuming a correlation coefficient between the returns on both indices of 0.3, this yields a participation rate of 1.74.

Figure 10.15 shows the return profile of the above note. The graph clearly shows that the note will only pay off more than the floor rate if neither of the indices drops. How likely this is depends heavily on the degree of correlation (as perceived by the derivatives firm) between both indices. Figure 10.16 shows the relationship between the **correlation coefficient** and the note's participation rate. With perfect positive correlation both indices are effectively identical. In that case the worst-of-two note offers the same participation rate as an ordinary principal protected bull note. If the correlation coefficient drops, one index may go up while the other goes down. The resulting reduction in the note's expected payoff is compensated by a higher participation rate.

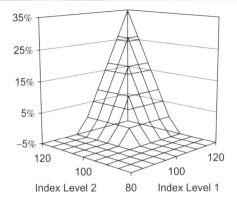

Figure 10.15   Return profile for a principal protected worst-of-two bull note

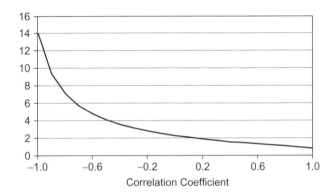

Figure 10.16   Participation rate for a principal protected worst-of-two bull note as a function of correlation coefficient

10.8   KNOCK-IN AND KNOCK-OUT PROTECTION

In Chapter 9 we discussed the addition of a knock-in or knock-out feature to the downside risk of a capped bull note. Of course, this is the same as adding a knock-out or knock-in feature to the relevant downside protection. We can do the same with the principal protected bull note. This means the protection will be there only if (for knock-in protection) or unless (for knock-out protection) the index hits a prefixed barrier level. Suppose we went for a **knock-in** feature. In that case we could say that the investors will receive a return on investment equal to α times the index return except when during the life of the note the index drops below some prefixed barrier level L. In that case they receive the highest of the floor rate and α times the index return. This means a payoff equal to

$$X_5 = N \times \left(1 + \mathrm{Max}\left[D, \alpha \left(\frac{I_5 - I_0}{I_0} \right) \right] \right), \qquad (10.28)$$

where

$$D = F, \quad \text{if } \exists j \; I_j \leqslant L,$$
$$= -\infty, \quad \text{if } \forall j \; I_j > L.$$

The subscript j counts the monitoring points. D takes on two values: F in case a knock-in is triggered and $-\infty$ if not. In the first case the note pays off as a principal protected bull note and in the second case as a vanilla bull note. This makes the amount payable by the derivatives firm equal to

$$V_5 = \alpha M \times (I_5 - I_0) + \alpha M \times D \times \text{Max}\left[0, I_0\left(1 + \frac{F}{\alpha}\right) - I_5\right], \qquad (10.29)$$

where now

$$D = 1, \quad \text{if } \exists j \; I_j \leqslant L,$$
$$= 0, \quad \text{if } \forall j \; I_j > L.$$

This payment consists of two parts. The first part equals the payoff of αM **forwards** with forward price I_0. The second part equals the payoff of αM **knock-in puts**. Given the above expression, the participation rate must be set such that it satisfies the budget equation

$$PVC = \alpha M \times F_0^a[I_0, 5] + \alpha M \times IP_0^a\left[I_0\left(1 + \frac{F}{\alpha}\right), L, 0, 5, 5\right]. \qquad (10.30)$$

With a barrier at 60 and continuous monitoring for a barrier hit this yields a participation rate of 0.78. We are not held to place the barrier below spot of course. We can put it wherever we want. With a barrier at 110 the participation rate would be 0.80 for example.

Buying knock-in puts is cheaper than buying ordinary options. The money saved can be spent on upside participation. However, the fact that even with a barrier as low as 60 we are only able to raise the participation rate by 0.04 is quite disappointing. Figure 10.17 provides a more complete insight into the trade-off between the **barrier level** and the participation rate. With a barrier at spot the note is identical to an ordinary principal protected bull note. The participation rate is therefore 0.74. If we move the barrier downwards, the participation rate does not really change until we get to a barrier level of around 75. This reflects the fact that the probability that the protection will knock in and pay off does not drop significantly unless the barrier is sufficiently far below spot. We

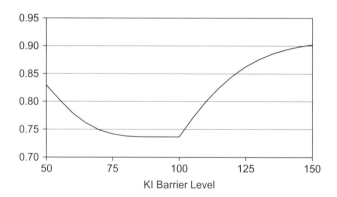

Figure 10.17 Trade-off between barrier level and participation rate for a bull note with knock-in principal protection

encountered the same phenomenon when we discussed the effect of barriers on option prices in Section 8.6. If we move the barrier upwards, the participation rate rises quickly as it quickly becomes less likely that the protection will knock in and pay off. With a barrier at 120 the participation rate is already up to 0.85, while at 145 it is 0.90. In sum, **a knock-in barrier above spot raises the participation rate more than a barrier below spot**.

We can turn the above structure around and say that the downside protection will always be there unless the barrier is hit. This means adding a **knock-out feature** to the note's downside protection by buying **knock-out puts** instead of knock-in puts. The result is shown in Figure 10.18. With a barrier at spot the participation rate is 0.91. In that case the note is identical to a vanilla bull note. If we move the barrier downwards the probability that the protection does not knock out and pays off does not drop much until we get to fairly low barrier levels. If we move the barrier upwards, however, the participation rate comes down quickly as the probability that the protection does not knock out and pays off goes up. With a barrier at 115 the participation rate is down to only 0.80, while at 135 it is down to 0.75. **A knock-out barrier below spot raises the participation rate more than a barrier above spot**.

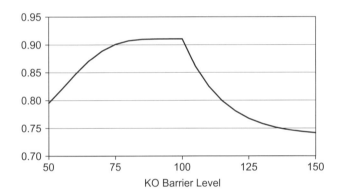

Figure 10.18   Trade-off between barrier level and participation rate for a bull note with knock-out principal protection

10.9   KNOCK-IN AND KNOCK-OUT UPSIDE

We added knock-in and knock-out features to the principal protected bull note's downside protection but we can do the same with the note's upside. We could for example introduce a **knock-out** feature and say that investors will receive a fraction of the index return unless the index falls below $L < I_0$. If the index falls below L they only make the floor return. This yields a note payoff of

$$X_5 = N \times (1 + \text{Max}\,[F, D]),\tag{10.31}$$

where

$$D = -\infty, \quad \text{if } \exists j\ I_j \leqslant L,$$

$$= \alpha \left(\frac{I_5 - I_0}{I_0} \right), \quad \text{if } \forall j\ I_j > L.$$

In case a knock-out is triggered D is equal to $-\infty$, which effectively takes it out of the equation. If not, D equals α times the index return.

The additional constraint introduced by the knock-out feature reduces the note's expected payoff and thereby allows for a higher participation rate. Writing the amount payable by the derivatives firm as a fixed amount plus the payoff of a number of calls, we end up with the same result as for the principal protected bull note except that the derivatives firm now sells the bank **knock-out calls** instead of ordinary calls. If the options do not knock out the derivatives firm's payment is the same as in the vanilla case. If the options knock out the option part of the derivatives firm's payment is nullified and it only pays the bank the guaranteed minimum.

As before, the participation rate depends heavily on the barrier level chosen. If the barrier is equal to spot the knock-out calls will be worthless, yielding an infinite participation rate. If we move the barrier away from spot we introduce the possibility that the note's upside will not knock-out. This raises the note's expected payoff which in turn requires the participation rate to come down. Figure 10.19 shows the trade-off between the **barrier level** and the participation rate for barriers below as well as above spot. Obviously, with a barrier close to spot we get extremely high participation rates as in that case it is extremely unlikely that the note's upside will not knock out. If we move the barrier downwards, the participation rate comes down quickly. With a barrier at 95 the participation rate is 2.65, while with a barrier at 75 it is 0.83. If we lower the barrier further the participation rate approaches that of an ordinary principal protected bull note. If we put the barrier above spot we see the same effect: the further the barrier is away from spot, the lower the participation rate. There is an important difference though. A barrier 50% below spot produces a participation rate of 0.74. A barrier 50% above spot yields a participation rate of 9.91. Even with a barrier at 270 the participation rate is still higher than 1. This makes sense as for the note to pay off more than the floor rate the index needs to go up, but that is also where the knock-out barrier is. Therefore **a knock-out barrier above spot raises the participation rate more than a barrier below spot**.

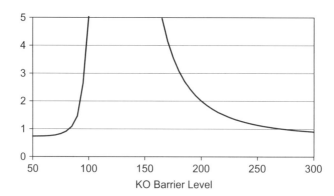

Figure 10.19 Trade-off between barrier level and participation rate for a bull note with knock-out upside participation

The case of **knock-in** upside participation, where the bank buys **knock-in calls** instead of knock-out calls, is shown in Figure 10.20. With a barrier at spot the note is identical

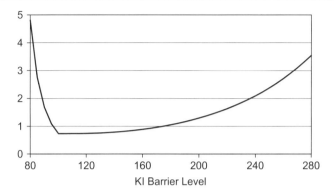

Figure 10.20 Trade-off between barrier level and participation rate for a bull note with knock-in upside participation

to an ordinary principal protected bull note with a participation rate of 0.74. If we lower the barrier, the participation rate rises quickly as the probability that the note's upside will knock in and pay off drops. If we raise the barrier the same happens, but it takes a lot longer. At a barrier level of 125 the participation rate is still only 0.75. At 145 it is 0.81 and at 165 it is 0.92. **A knock-in barrier below spot raises the participation rate more than a barrier above spot**.

In practice we do not encounter structures like these very often because the knock-in or knock-out conditions are generally thought to be too aggressive. As discussed in Chapter 3, there are several ways around this problem. We can take a **moving average** of the reference index and use that as the relevant barrier variable. Since a moving average moves slower than the index itself this will only trigger a knock-in or knock-out if the index stays at the other side of the barrier long enough to also pull its moving average to the other side. A second possibility is to use **lazy barriers** requiring at least a number of observations to be on the other side of the barrier before action is triggered. A third solution is to split the note's upside into several **tranches** and give each tranche its own barrier. This makes the note's upside knock in or knock out tranche by tranche. Unfortunately, all the above measures to sweeten up the note have the same effect: they raise the expected payoff of the note and thereby lower the participation rate.

Another way to make a knock-in or knock-out note more attractive is by offering investors a **rebate** in case the note knocks out or does not knock in. Typically, the rebate is a fixed amount which is paid when the note knocks out or does not knock in. Such a feature can easily be created by adding a knock-in or knock-out digital to the note payoff. Unfortunately, adding a rebate has the same problem as other ways to soften the knock-in or knock-out: since the rebate is a valuable addition to the note payoff, its inclusion reduces the participation rate.

10.10   CHANGING EXCHANGE RATE RISK

A different way of currency conversion can sometimes improve the participation rate as well. Suppose the investors wanted to take a view on a foreign index. One way to do so is by buying a note like the one we discussed before in Section 10.3, i.e. a note with a

foreign payoff equal to

$$X_5 = N \times \left(1 + \frac{E_5}{E_0} \times \text{Max}\left[F, \alpha\left(\frac{I_5 - I_0}{I_0}\right)\right]\right). \tag{10.32}$$

This note gives investors exposure to the foreign index as well as the exchange rate. Instead of converting with a factor E_5/E_0, we could also convert with a factor $E_0/E_0 = 1$. This would yield a note with a **quanto payoff** equal to

$$X_5 = N \times \left(1 + \frac{E_0}{E_0} \times \text{Max}\left[F, \alpha\left(\frac{I_5 - I_0}{I_0}\right)\right]\right) = N \times \left(1 + \text{Max}\left[F, \alpha\left(\frac{I_5 - I_0}{I_0}\right)\right]\right). \tag{10.33}$$

Since the exchange rate is not in there, this note's payoff is immune to exchange rate movements. Of course, investors could also go for something in between and for example buy a note with a **composite payoff** such as

$$X_5 = N \times \left(1 + \text{Max}\left[F, \alpha\left(\frac{E_5 I_5 - E_0 I_0}{E_0 I_0}\right)\right]\right). \tag{10.34}$$

The composite payoff is similar to the quanto payoff except that this time the index value at maturity is converted at the exchange rate at maturity instead of the exchange rate at inception.

The budget equations for these three notes are similar to (9.34). As shown earlier in Section 10.3, the budget equation for the first note is given by

$$PVC = e^{-5r_5^f}(N \times F) + \alpha M \times E_0 \times FC_0^a\left[I_0\left(1 + \frac{F}{\alpha}\right), 5\right], \tag{10.35}$$

where $M = N/E_0 I_0$. Likewise, for the quanto note we have a budget equation equal to

$$PVC = e^{-5r_5}(N \times F) + \alpha M \times QC_0^a\left[E_0 I_0\left(1 + \frac{F}{\alpha}\right), 5\right], \tag{10.36}$$

where $QC_0^a[K, T]$ is the derivatives firm's offer (in domestic currency) for a **quanto call** with domestic strike K and maturity T. Finally, for the composite note we have

$$PVC = e^{-5r_5}(N \times F) + \alpha M \times CC_0^a\left[E_0 I_0\left(1 + \frac{F}{\alpha}\right), 5\right], \tag{10.37}$$

where $CC_0^a[K, T]$ is the derivatives firm's offer (also in domestic currency) for a **composite call** with domestic strike K and maturity T.

Whether the quanto or the composite note can offer a higher participation rate than the foreign note depends on the interest rate differential between both currencies. Suppose domestic interest rates were higher than foreign rates. In that case our pricing shortcut tells us that the foreign currency is about to appreciate relative to the domestic currency. Given that with the quanto note investors do not benefit from an appreciation, this means that if they had the same participation rate the quanto note would offer a lower expected payoff than the foreign note. The reverse is true for the composite note. The quanto note should therefore offer a higher and the composite note a lower participation rate than the foreign note. If domestic interest rates were lower than foreign rates the opposite would happen.

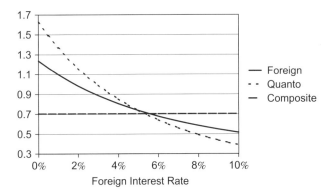

Figure 10.21 Participation rate for foreign, quanto and composite principal protected bull notes as a function of foreign interest rate

The quanto (composite) note would have a lower (higher) participation rate because it would (not) offer protection against the expected depreciation of the foreign currency.

Assuming exchange rate volatility to be at 10%, Figure 10.21 shows the participation rate on a 5-year foreign, quanto and composite principal protected bull note as a function of the **foreign interest rate**. The first thing to notice is that the participation rate of the composite note is independent of the foreign interest rate. We can understand this if we realize that a composite call is nothing more than an ordinary call on a self-made reference index with time t value $E_t I_t$. The derivatives firm can hedge such an option in the usual way, i.e. by borrowing domestic currency and buying the index. If the index goes up it borrows and buys more and if it goes down the firm does the reverse. Because the firm does all of its borrowing in domestic currency, however, the foreign interest rate is irrelevant. At 0.70, the participation rate offered by the composite note is slightly lower than that offered by an equivalent purely domestic note (0.74). This is due to the fact that, being the product of the foreign index and the exchange rate, the self-made reference index in the composite note is slightly more volatile (22.4%) than the reference index in the domestic note (20%).

10.11   AN ASIAN TAIL

Another way to save some money is to calculate the index return not from the index value at maturity but from the average index value over some period ending at maturity. This is known as an **Asian tail**. Since the average moves slower than the index itself it is less likely to make big swings over the monitoring period. When the index goes up, the average goes up as well but less. The result is that by replacing the index value at maturity by the average the expected payoff of the note falls and the participation rate can go up. It is interesting to note that working with **an average also provides protection against a drop in the index towards the end of the note's life**. This is sometimes used as a marketing pitch. It turns a necessity into a desirable feature and thereby increases the chances of the note being sold.

How much participation do investors gain if we replace the value of the index at maturity by the average index value over the last year of the note's life? First, we have to write things down formally, which yields the following payoff

$$X_5 = N \times \left(1 + \text{Max} \left[F, \alpha \left(\frac{A_{4,5} - I_0}{I_0} \right) \right] \right), \tag{10.38}$$

where $A_{4,5}$ denotes the average over the period from $t = 4$ up to the note's maturity date $t = 5$. This payment is identical to that of a principal protected bull note except that the index at maturity is replaced by the average. As a result, instead of ordinary calls, the bank is now buying **fixed-strike Asian calls** where the derivatives firm pays the average and the bank pays a fixed amount $I_0(1 + F/\alpha)$. If we denote the derivatives firm's offer for an Asian call with strike K, monitoring from $t = t_1$ to $t = t_2$ and time to maturity T as $AC_0^a[K, t_1, t_2, T]$, this means we can solve the participation rate from the budget equation

$$PVC = e^{-5r_5}(N \times F) + \alpha M \times AC_0^a \left[I_0 \left(1 + \frac{F}{\alpha} \right), 4, 5, 5 \right]. \tag{10.39}$$

Under the assumption that we monitor the index daily this yields a participation rate of 0.82.

Although with a participation rate of 0.82 the note looks a lot more attractive than a standard principal protected bull note, one has to keep in mind that we are now talking about participation in the average index return. Figure 10.22 shows the return profile of the principal protected bull note with Asian tail, assuming that the index moves to its value at maturity in a straight line. If we compare this return profile with that of an ordinary principal protected bull note as given by Figure 9.11, we see there is no difference. Of course, this is due to the assumption that the index moves in a straight line. If the index behaved significantly differently, we might see a significant difference between the payoff of the principal protected bull note with Asian tail and without.

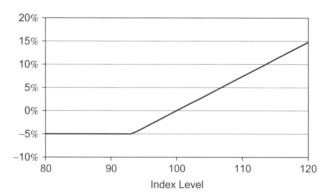

Figure 10.22   Return profile for a principal protected bull note with Asian tail

With an Asian tail we have to decide on the monitoring points and the participation rate. We plotted the trade-off between the **start date of the monitoring period** and the participation rate in Figure 10.23, assuming the index is monitored daily. The monitoring period always ends at maturity. From the graph we clearly see that the participation

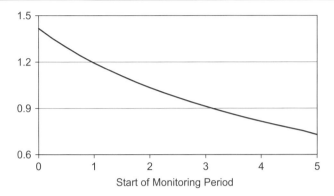

Figure 10.23 Trade-off between start of monitoring period and participation rate for a principal protected bull note with Asian tail

rate is higher the earlier we start monitoring. Obviously, when the start date equals the maturity date the Asian note is identical to an ordinary principal protected bull note, yielding a participation rate of 0.74. If we were to monitor the index during the note's full life the participation rate would be 1.42, which is almost twice the participation rate on the standard principal protected bull note. This reflects the fact that in such a case the embedded fixed-strike Asian call is worth about half as much as an equivalent ordinary call. We discussed this in Section 8.11.

10.12 REVISED MONITORING OF THE INDEX

In Chapter 8 we discussed how we can make path-dependent options cheaper by revising their monitoring frequency and/or monitoring period. We showed amongst others that increased monitoring of the barrier variable will make knock-in options more and knock-out options less expensive. Since the payoffs of equity-linked notes can be expressed in terms of option payoffs, we can use this to influence the participation rates on notes with path-dependent payoffs. To improve the participation rate on a bull note with knock-in principal protection for example we could reduce the monitoring frequency and/or the monitoring period. This will reduce the probability of the protection knocking in and thereby raise the participation rate. We can do the same to raise the participation rate on a bull note with knock-in upside participation. Changing the monitoring points may also raise the participation rate on notes with other path-dependent payoffs, such as notes which incorporate lookback or ladder features for example. We will discuss some of these in the next chapter.

10.13 ADDITIONAL RISKS

We can also introduce additional risks to raise the participation rate on a note. We could for example introduce some explicit **credit risk** in the note payoff. Suppose we had a principal protected bull note linked to the Eurostoxx 50 index. We could introduce credit risk in this note by saying that as long as none of the companies in the index defaults the note would pay off like an ordinary principal protected bull note. However, if one company defaulted the note return would be lowered by 2%, if two companies defaulted it would be lowered by 4%, etc. With a feature like this, the principal of the note would no longer be protected. There are various ways to solve this. We could reduce the costs of default or we could put a cap on the costs of default so the total loss would never be more than a prefixed amount. We could also say that there needed to be at least three defaults before the feature would knock in. How much the introduction of explicit credit risk raises the participation rate depends of course on the exact details of the structure as well as conditions in the market for credit derivatives. Concerning the latter it is important to note that premiums in the credit derivatives market may sometimes be a lot higher than one would expect. Even providing insurance against the default of a highly rated company or country may at times yield a not insignificant premium.

10.14   ONE LAST TRICK

With retail investors sometimes being extremely focused on a note's participation rate, several cosmetic tricks can be used to make a note look more attractive than it really is. Issuance above par is one of them. We discussed this in Chapter 9. Another trick that is sometimes used is to calculate the index return differently. Throughout our discussions we have calculated the index return as

$$\frac{I_5 - I_0}{I_0},$$

(10.40)

which is the standard way of calculating a return figure. Sometimes, however, one sees the index return being calculated as

$$\frac{I_5 - I_0}{1.1 I_0}.$$

(10.41)

Since we are now dividing by a higher number, this yields a lower return. The participation rate can therefore be higher. Because there is no reason to use a denominator different from I_0, the above trick is typically hidden by applying a similar rise to the base level. In that case the index return is calculated as

$$\frac{I_5 - 1.1 I_0}{1.1 I_0},$$

(10.42)

which will of course raise the participation rate even further. Although similar at first sight, the two changes made are very different. Changing the base value used for the return calculation has a clear economic interpretation. Using a denominator other than I_0 on the other hand has no obvious economic interpretation. Why would anyone want to relate the change in the value of the index to anything other than the index value at the beginning of the relevant period?

10.15   CONCLUSION

In this chapter we discussed a variety of ways to raise the participation rate on a principal protected bull note. There are two ways to look at this; either through the budget equation or the note's expected payoff. Since the payoff of a principal protected bull note can be rewritten as a fixed amount plus the payoff of a number of ordinary calls, to raise the participation rate we have to make the embedded call options cheaper. This frees up money which can then be spent on additional upside participation. Alternatively, we could say that since every note has to offer an expected return equal to the interest rate and the initial investment is fixed in advance, what we are really looking for is ways to reduce the note's expected payoff. With the initial investment fixed, a drop in the expected payoff will call for the participation rate to rise to compensate. Working to raise the participation rate, however, it is important to keep an eye on the reason why investors are interested in principal protected bull notes. **Cutting too deep into a note's downside protection or upside potential may create a note that has little attraction left**.

11
Market Timing and Non-Bullish Views

11.1 INTRODUCTION

We have spent quite some time on equity-linked notes already, but there is a lot more to discuss. One issue concerns **timing**. In most cases discussed so far the note payoff only depends on the index value at maturity. None of these notes therefore offers any protection against a scenario where the index rises first but unexpectedly drops later. The market could go up four out of five years, but that still would not mean investors would get paid because the index might drop significantly in the last year. Apart from market exit, market entry may also cause a problem. Consider a principal protected bull note where the index return is calculated from a base level equal to the value of the reference index at inception. If after entering into the note the index drops first only to rise later, the note will not pay off as expected despite the fact that the investors' view was largely correct.

Apart from timing there are two other issues that require attention. First, we have assumed investors are bullish. Although this covers most cases of interest, sometimes a structurer will be asked to structure **notes for investors with different views**. The investors in question could hold any of a number of views, which we will classify as (a) bearish, (b) mixed, or (c) neutral. Bearish investors expect the index to go down. Mixed investors expect the index to either go up or down, and neutral investors expect the index to go nowhere, i.e. stay within some range. Second, some investors may not feel certain enough to choose one particular reference index. They will be looking for a note which helps them with their **asset allocation** decision; for example a note which provides a return on investment equal to that of the best of two or more different asset classes.

In this chapter we discuss how to structure principal protected notes which tackle the above problems. We start with the timing of market exit and entry, followed by some examples of notes that cater to investors with non-bullish views. We conclude with two examples of asset allocation notes. Although some of these notes are quite different from the ones we discussed in the two previous chapters, the structuring process itself is unchanged. Moreover, as we will see, the budget equations for most of these notes are of the same form as for an ordinary principal protected bull note. **It is only the embedded option contract that changes**. We use the same assumptions and notation as in Chapter 9.

11.2 TIMING MARKET EXIT

It is fairly easy to improve the timing of market exit in a principal protected note. If we do, however, the note becomes more likely to provide investors with a significant payoff. As a result, there will be an additional charge which will show up in the form of a lower participation rate. In practice, structurers will try to keep the participation rate at an acceptable level by including one or more of the cost saving measures we discussed in

Chapter 10. We will not do so, however, as this unnecessarily complicates the discussion. The reader is invited to do some experimenting of his own in this area.

11.2.1 Principal Protected Lookback and Ladder Bull Notes

To protect investors against an unexpected drop in the index we need to replace I_5 in the payoff formula for a principal protected bull note by a cash flow that locks in intermediate profits in some way. One obvious candidate is a cash flow equal to the highest index value recorded over, for example, the last year of the note's life. Denoting the latter as $M_{4,5}^+$, the note payoff would in that case be equal to

$$X_5 = N \times \left(1 + \text{Max} \left[F, \alpha \left(\frac{M_{4,5}^+ - I_0}{I_0} \right) \right] \right). \tag{11.1}$$

Apart from protecting investors' principal, this note also protects investors against a drop in the index over the last year as the return is not calculated from the index value at maturity but from the highest index level reached during year 5. When the index value at maturity is also the highest value over the year the note pays off like an ordinary principal protected bull note. In all other cases, however, it pays off more.

Of course, we do not get something for nothing here. Offering a more attractive payoff, the note will be more expensive, i.e. the participation rate will be lower than that of an ordinary principal protected bull note. To see how much lower, we first rewrite the amount payable by the derivatives firm as

$$V_5 = N \times F + \alpha M \times \text{Max} \left[0, M_{4,5}^+ - I_0 \left(1 + \frac{F}{\alpha} \right) \right]. \tag{11.2}$$

This shows that apart from the usual fixed amount the derivatives firm implicitly sells the bank αM **partial fixed-strike lookback calls** with strike $I_0(1 + F/\alpha)$. We can therefore solve the participation rate from the following budget equation

$$PVC = e^{-5r_5}(N \times F) + \alpha M \times LC_0^a \left[I_0 \left(1 + \frac{F}{\alpha} \right), 4, 5, 5 \right], \tag{11.3}$$

where $LC_0^a[K, t_1, t_2, T]$ is the derivatives firm's offer for a lookback call with strike K, maturity T and monitoring starting at time t_1 and ending at time t_2. If we compare the above expression with the budget equation for an ordinary principal protected bull note we see that **the difference lies in the option used**. One requires an ordinary call and the other a partial fixed-strike lookback call. Under the assumption that the index is monitored continuously for a new high and a -5% floor rate, this yields a participation rate of 0.52. The difference with the 0.74 participation rate of the principal protected bull note is the price of the newly added lock-in feature.

The principal protected lookback note provides investors with exactly the protection they want. Even with a fairly short monitoring period, however, the participation rate is extremely low. The closest thing to the outright maximum is the **stepwise maximum**. We could replace I_5 in the principal protected bull note payoff by the stepwise maximum index value over the period from $t = 4$ to $t = 5$. This means that at maturity the investors will get paid based on the highest rung of the ladder that was hit during the last year of the note's life. This structure has one major drawback though. Suppose we had a ladder with rungs at 120, 140 and 160. If during the monitoring period the index reached a level of 120 an index return of 20% would be locked in, i.e. at maturity investors would receive a return on investment of at least $\alpha \times 20\%$. The same would happen at 140 and 160. Now suppose the index ended at 158 without ever touching 160. In that case investors would get paid based on an index value of 140, not 158. The same would happen if the index ended higher than 160, say at 176. In that case the investors would get paid based on an index value of 160, not 176.

To correct this, we can use the **extended stepwise maximum** instead of the standard stepwise maximum. This yields a note payoff equal to

$$X_5 = N \times \left(1 + \text{Max} \left[F, \alpha \left(\frac{ES_{4,5}^+ - I_0}{I_0} \right) \right] \right). \tag{11.4}$$

We simply replaced I_5 in the principal protected bull note payoff by the extended stepwise maximum index value over the period from $t = 4$ to $t = 5$. We can rewrite this payoff in terms of the stepwise maximum as follows

$$X_5 = N \times \left(1 + \text{Max} \left[F, \alpha \left(\frac{S_{4,5}^+ - I_0}{I_0} \right), \alpha \left(\frac{I_5 - I_0}{I_0} \right) \right] \right). \tag{11.5}$$

This clearly shows that what we are doing here is using the stepwise maximum as a floor on the payoff of the principal protected bull note. Investors get paid the highest of three return alternatives. The first is the floor rate. The second is the return calculated from the stepwise maximum and the third alternative is the return calculated from the index value at maturity. If the index goes down, the floor rate kicks in and if the index goes up first but down later the stepwise maximum provides the desired protection.

Knowing the desired note payoff we can go the usual route to arrive at the budget equation. Not surprisingly, the latter is the same as for an ordinary principal protected bull note except that we are now confronted with an embedded **partial fixed-strike ladder call**. This means that before we can solve for the participation rate we have to decide on the level of the rungs. We could just pick some numbers but a more practical way to proceed is to make them a function of the participation rate. This allows us to choose the first rung such that it locks in the 25% interest investors would have received if they had bought a fixed income instrument instead of the note in question. To do so, we need to set $H^1 = I_0(1 + 0.25/\alpha)$. Assuming we have two rungs, we can fix the second rung such that it locks in a return of 50% by setting $H^2 = I_0(1 + 0.5/\alpha)$. Assuming that the index is monitored continuously and the floor rate is -5%, this yields a participation rate of 0.68, implying rungs at 136.9 and 173.8.

The lookback and ladder note respond to changes in the **floor rate** in much the same way as an ordinary principal protected bull note. If we raise the floor rate, the participation rate comes down because there is less money available to buy upside potential. Alternatively, we could of course say that the lower participation rate compensates the increase in the note's expected return resulting from a higher floor rate. Figure 11.1, which shows the trade-off between the floor rate and the participation rate on the lookback and ladder note, clearly shows the substantial difference in the level of participation offered by both notes. As intended, the participation rates on the ladder note are much closer to those on an ordinary principal protected bull note than the participation rates on the lookback note.

Since we are now dealing with an embedded lookback or ladder call, we also have a set of monitoring points to set. Figuring out how the choice of **monitoring points**

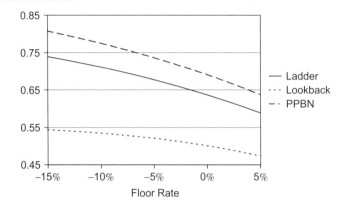

Figure 11.1 Trade-off between floor rate and participation rate for a principal protected lookback and ladder bull note

influences the participation rate is easy if we think back to our discussion of lookback and ladder options in Chapter 8. We saw there that a longer monitoring period and/or a higher monitoring frequency will make lookback and ladder options more expensive. This means that if we increase the monitoring period and/or monitoring frequency the participation rate will drop. Figure 11.2 shows the participation rate on the lookback and ladder note as a function of the start date of the monitoring period. The monitoring period always ends at the maturity date and monitoring is done continuously. When the start date equals the note's maturity date both notes are identical to an ordinary principal protected bull note. The participation rate is therefore 0.74. If we place the start date before the maturity date this opens up the possibility of finding a (stepwise) maximum higher than I_5. The earlier the monitoring period starts, the more likely we are to find such a value and therefore the lower the participation rate.

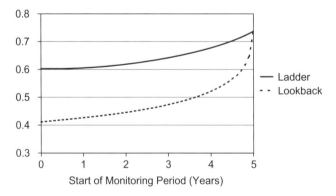

Figure 11.2 Trade-off between start of monitoring period and participation rate for a principal protected lookback and ladder bull note

Especially for the lookback note, the drop in the participation rate is stronger for relatively short monitoring periods. In other words, **an extra week of monitoring at the end of the note's life does a lot more damage to the participation rate than an extra**

week at the beginning. This reflects the fact that we are much more likely to find a new maximum close to maturity than close to inception. A similar reasoning goes for the ladder note. We see hardly any change in the participation rate as the start date comes into year 1 because a barrier hit that close to inception is not very likely.

Apart from the floor rate and the monitoring points, the participation rate on the ladder note also depends on the number of **rungs** and the location of those rungs. Similar to what we saw in Chapter 7, increasing the number of rungs will raise the expected payoff of the note and therefore reduce the participation rate. The budget equation leads to the same conclusion as more rungs will make the ladder option more expensive. As far as the location of the rungs is concerned, there are two opposite forces at work again. As a rung is chosen further away from the current level of the index, the probability that it is actually going to get hit will drop. By itself this raises the participation rate to compensate the drop in the expected payoff of the note. On the other hand, as the rung is further away, the return that is locked in when it is hit will be larger. This lowers the participation rate.

With both the lookback and the ladder notes we have to set a date where the lookback or ladder feature becomes active. This means there is still some timing left to be decided upon. If the index drops shortly before the start of the monitoring period the lookback or ladder feature will not pay off as planned. Monitoring right from inception, i.e. over the full life of the note, would capture every upward move of the index and provide the ultimate in exit timing. However, this would be extremely expensive in terms of loss of participation. The lookback note would have a participation rate of 0.41 and the ladder note a participation rate of 0.60. We might be able to cheapen things somewhat by substantially reducing the monitoring frequency to once a year for example. Since in that case we would check for a new (stepwise) maximum only once a year, the lookback or ladder feature would hardly be noticeable any more. Many will therefore no longer refer to these notes as lookback or ladder notes, although technically they definitely still are.

11.2.2 Principal Protected Asian Bull Note

Thinking back to the index-linked cash flows we discussed in Chapter 4, it could be argued that replacing the vanilla index return by the average index return provides a timing service since if the index drops at the end of the note's life this will not affect the average index value so much as most of it was determined in the years before. This means we are now talking about an Asian note payoff similar to the one we discussed before in Section 10.11. Such an Asian note will offer a higher participation rate than a principal protected bull note, but this is not a free lunch. With an Asian note structure investors participate in the average index return and not the vanilla index return.

11.2.3 Principal Protected Cliquet Bull Note

Another way to capture more of the index's ups over the note's life derives from the fact that the index return over the note's five year life is (roughly) equal to the sum of the five subsequent 1-year returns. Instead of concentrating on the 5-year return we could shift attention to the five 1-year returns that make up the 5-year return. With every single 1-year return we can do everything we have done before with the 5-year return. Instead of putting a floor on the 5-year return we could floor every one of the individual 1-year returns separately. This yields a so-called **cliquet note** or **ratchet note**. Formally, the payoff of such a note can be written as

$$X_5 = N \times \left(1 + \sum_{i=1}^{5} \text{Max} \left[F, \alpha \left(\frac{I_i - I_{i-1}}{I_{i-1}} \right) \right] \right), \tag{11.6}$$

where F now denotes the floor placed on the 1-year return and the subscript i counts the years from $t = 0$.

The above expression tells us that at maturity investors receive a return equal to the sum of five individually floored 1-year returns. By itself this provides extremely solid protection against unexpected drops in the index. Suppose that the participation rate was equal to 1 and that we registered the following 1-year returns: 14%, 23%, −12%, 11%, −17%. With each year individually floored at −5% the sum of the floored 1-year returns would be $14 + 23 - 5 + 11 - 5 = 38\%$. The 5-year return on the other hand would only have been half of that. There is one major catch though. Because flooring every year separately raises the note's expected payoff, unlike what we assumed, **the participation rate on the cliquet note will be significantly lower than on a principal protected bull note**.

To see what the difference is we first need to find a smart way to price the cliquet note. We can express the amount payable by the derivatives firm as

$$V_5 = N \times 5F + \alpha N \times \sum_{i=1}^{5} \frac{1}{I_{i-1}} \text{Max} \left[0, I_i - I_{i-1} \left(1 + \frac{F}{\alpha} \right) \right]. \tag{11.7}$$

The first part is the usual fixed amount associated with the floor rate. On top of that we have five index-linked amounts. The first is equal to αM times the payoff of what looks like an ordinary call. There is one new feature though: on the maturity date the derivatives firm pays the index value as observed at $t = 1$ and not $t = 5$. This means that what we have here is an ordinary 1-year call with **settlement delayed** until $t = 5$. The next four index-linked amounts also look very much like 1-year ordinary call payoffs, but on closer inspection they are a bit more complicated than that. Settlement is again delayed by $5 - i$ years. In addition, the strike as well as the number of contracts is not fixed from the start but set at some future date $t = i - 1$. As mentioned in Chapter 9, options with a strike that is determined at a later date are referred to as **forward-starting**. Options where the contract size is fixed at a later date are said to be **quantity-adjusting**. In sum, the derivatives firm's payment to the bank consists of a fixed amount plus an amount equal to what the firm would have paid if it had sold the bank a number of ordinary and forward-starting quantity-adjusting calls, all with settlement delayed until the note's maturity date.

Knowing what the derivatives firm needs to pay to the bank we can solve the participation rate from the budget equation

$$PVC = e^{-5r_5}(N \times 5F) + \alpha M \times C_0^a \left[I_0 \left(1 + \frac{F}{\alpha} \right), 1, 5 \right]$$

$$+ \alpha N \times \sum_{i=2}^{5} QAFC_0^a \left[\frac{1}{I_{i-1}}, I_{i-1} \left(1 + \frac{F}{\alpha} \right), i, 5 \right], \tag{11.8}$$

where $C_0^a[K, t, T]$ is the derivatives firm's offer for an ordinary call with strike K, payoff determination at $t = t$ and settlement at $t = T$. Likewise, $QAFC_0^a[M, K, t, T]$ is the offer for a quantity-adjusting forward-starting call with multiplier M, strike K, payoff determination at time t and settlement at time T. Note again the important rule that despite the fact we can express the payment to be made by the derivatives firm in terms of the payoffs of a number of different option contracts we should concentrate on **pricing the package** and not the individual options. Dissecting the derivatives firm's payment as we do is only meant to speed up the pricing process not change the price. Suppose we choose a floor rate of -1%. This means that investors cannot loose more than 5% over five years. In that case the participation rate would be equal to 0.53.

Figure 11.3 shows the trade-off between the **floor rate** and the participation rate in the cliquet note. As always, a higher floor rate leads to a lower participation rate. To raise the participation rate we can use all the tricks we discussed earlier. In practice, capping the yearly index returns is the most popular. Apart from it being an effective solution, there sometimes is another reason for this. In the US principal protected cliquet bull notes tend to be sold aggressively by insurance companies, who refer to them as **equity-indexed annuities**. By calling them annuities instead of notes and by keeping the exposure embedded in these notes low, insurance companies escape having to register them with the SEC while investors may gain a tax advantage.

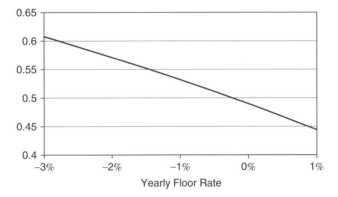

Figure 11.3 Trade-off between floor rate and participation rate for a principal protected cliquet bull note

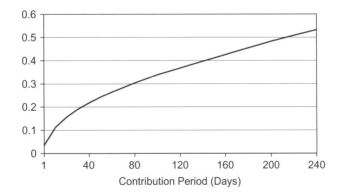

Figure 11.4 Trade-off between length of contribution period and participation rate for a principal protected cliquet bull note

Of course, we do not necessarily have to go for an annual cliquet. We can choose any contribution period we see fit. Doing so, however, we have to keep in mind that changing the length of the **contribution period** may have a significant effect on the participation rate. This is also shown in Figure 11.4. The graph shows that the participation rate rises with the length of the contribution period. With daily contributions the participation rate is only 0.04. With semi-annual contributions the participation rate is 10 times as high at 0.4. The rise of the participation rate reflects the drop in the note's expected payoff that results from a longer contribution period. In the extreme case of only one contribution period the cliquet note is identical to an ordinary principal protected bull note and therefore offers a participation rate of 0.74.

11.3 TIMING MARKET ENTRY

Market entry is not without problems either. If right after buying a principal protected bull note the index drops and only starts to rise later, the note will not pay off as expected despite the fact that, apart from the initial drop, the investors' view was correct. In this section we look at two principal protected notes that solve this problem using the lookback and ladder concepts we discussed earlier.

What we want is that if the index drops shortly after buying the note the index return is no longer calculated from its starting value but from a lower value. This means we have to replace the usual index base level by some index-linked cash flow. One candidate is a cash flow equal to the lowest index value recorded over, for example, the first year of the note's life. Denoting the latter by $M_{0,1}^-$ the note payoff would in that case be equal to

$$X_5 = N \times \left(1 + \text{Max} \left[F, \alpha \left(\frac{I_5 - M_{0,1}^-}{I_0} \right) \right] \right). \tag{11.9}$$

Apart from protecting investors' principal, this note also protects investors against a drop in the index over the first year of the note's life.

If over the first year the index never gets below its starting value, the index return is the same as for an ordinary principal protected bull note. However, if the index drops below its starting value the index return will be higher. Whether the note payoff will also be higher depends of course on what happens to the participation rate if we introduce this lookback feature. By itself the feature raises the expected payoff of the note and will therefore lower the participation rate. Given the desired note payoff, the amount payable by the derivatives firm can be written as

$$V_5 = N \times F + \alpha M \times \text{Max} \left[0, I_5 - \left(M_{0,1}^- + \frac{F \times I_0}{\alpha} \right) \right]. \tag{11.10}$$

This shows that implicitly the bank is buying αM **partial floating-strike lookback calls**. From here we can solve the participation rate from the budget equation

$$PVC = e^{-5r_5}(N \times F) + \alpha M \times LC_0^a \left[M_{0,1}^- + \frac{F \times I_0}{\alpha}, 0, 1, 5 \right]. \tag{11.11}$$

It will not come as a surprise to learn that this note suffers from the same handicap as the lookback bull note: because the lookback option is so expensive, it offers a very low participation rate.

There are several ways to obtain a better participation rate. One alternative is to reduce the **monitoring frequency**. This will make it less likely that we find a new minimum. The expected payoff will drop and the participation rate will rise. With quarterly monitoring the participation rate would be 0.64, with semi-annual monitoring it would be 0.65 and in the extreme case of annual monitoring the participation rate would be 0.67. Although a participation rate of 0.67 does not look bad compared to the 0.74 offered by an ordinary principal protected bull note, it comes at quite a high price. With annual monitoring there is little left of the timing feature we initially envisaged as with a monitoring period of one year there would only be one monitoring point, one year from inception.

A second route to a higher participation rate is to replace the actual minimum by the **stepwise minimum**. Similar to what we did before this means creating a ladder, comparing the observed index values with the ladder's rungs and rounding them upwards to the nearest rung. This means that at maturity the investors get paid based on the lowest rung of the ladder that was hit during the monitoring period. Formally, the note payoff to the investors would be equal to

$$X_5 = N \times \left(1 + \text{Max} \left[F, \alpha \left(\frac{I_5 - S_{0,1}^-}{I_0} \right) \right] \right). \tag{11.12}$$

The stepwise minimum starts off at I_0, i.e. the index return is initially calculated from a base of I_0. However, if the index goes down and hits a rung the base level is set equal to the level of the rung that was hit. The amount payable by the derivatives firm and the resulting budget equation can be expressed in the same way as before, except that in this case the note contains an embedded **partial floating-strike ladder call**. Assuming that we set the first rung at 95 and the second at 90 and that the index is monitored continuously, this yields a participation rate of 0.69.

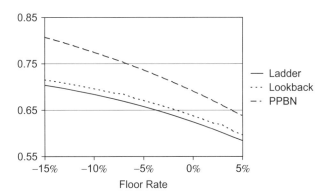

Figure 11.5 Trade-off between floor rate and participation rate for a principal protected bull note with lookback and ladder base

As with the lookback and ladder bull notes discussed earlier, the participation rate of the above notes depends strongly on the floor rate and the choice of the monitoring points. The trade-off between the **floor rate** and the participation rate can be found in Figure 11.5. The note with a lookback base has annual monitoring and the note with a ladder base has continuous monitoring with rungs at 95 and 90. Although still significantly lower, both notes' participation rates come fairly close to that of a standard principal protected bull note. It is interesting to note that the lookback note offers a higher participation rate than the ladder note. This emphasizes the meagre timing services offered by the lookback note with annual monitoring. It also makes it clear that **ladder options are not always cheaper than lookback options**. This is only true if they share the same monitoring points.

Figure 11.6 shows the trade-off between the **end of the monitoring period** and the participation rate. The monitoring period always starts at $t = 0$. When monitoring also ends at $t = 0$ both notes are identical to an ordinary principal protected bull note. When the monitoring period is extended, the participation rates on both notes drop. However, after about one year the participation rate on the ladder note shows little response any more. This reflects the fact that the probability of a barrier hit at 95 and/or 90 is highest close to inception and does not change much after one or two years. A similar reasoning goes for the note with a lookback base, except that the effect is less pronounced because the probability of finding a new minimum keeps increasing when the monitoring period grows longer. Figure 11.6 also shows that which note offers a better participation rate depends heavily on the length of the monitoring period. For short monitoring periods the lookback note beats the ladder note, while for longer monitoring periods the ladder note offers the highest participation rate. Of course, this would not be the case if both notes had the same monitoring frequency. In that case the embedded ladder option would always be cheaper than the lookback option, resulting in a higher participation rate for the ladder note.

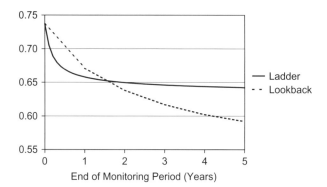

Figure 11.6 Trade-off between end of monitoring period and participation rate for a principal protected bull note with lookback and ladder base

11.4 NOTES FOR NON-BULLISH VIEWS

So far we have assumed investors to be bullish but we can follow exactly the same procedure to structure notes for investors with bearish, mixed or neutral views. However, for longer horizons such views are uncommon. Starting with Edgar Smith's book *Common Stocks as Long-Term Investments* which was published in 1925, a large body of literature and the long bull market have convinced modern day investors that in the long run investing in equity cannot go wrong. In an extensive study of US stocks from 1802 onwards, Siegel[1] showed that over any 30-year investment horizon stocks never produced

---

[1] J. Siegel, *Stocks for the Long Run*, McGraw-Hill, 1998.

an annualized inflation corrected total return lower than 2.6% or higher than 10.6%. Over shorter periods of time things are of course different. Over 1-year horizons his returns are between -38.6% and 66.6%. Over 5-year horizons, however, things already start to clear as the lowest annualized 5-year return recorded is -11% and the highest 26.7%. Siegel not only studied the performance of equity investments but also looked at bonds and T-bills. His results showed that over a 5-year horizon stocks outperformed bonds and T-bills about 70% of the time. Over a 30-year horizon stocks beat bonds and T-bills 100% of the time. Motivated by results like these, many pension funds have increased their equity allocations over the years and nowadays work with actuarial assumptions of investment returns as high as 10%.

The above means that it will be hard to find investors interested in products that take a longer term bearish, mixed or neutral view. Sometimes, however, some investors may be willing to take a short-term non-bullish view. In what follows we will discuss a number of principal guaranteed notes that might be suitable in that case, assuming a note **maturity of two years**. Sticking to the assumption that the bank takes out 40 bp profit per annum, this brings the present value of the coupons received by the derivatives firm (PVC) down to 8.72m.

11.4.1   Principal Protected Bear Note

The simplest way to structure a note which pays investors if the market goes down is to turn the principal protected bull note upside down. We can do so by saying that the payoff at maturity will be equal to the initial investment plus a floored fraction of the drop in the reference index. Formally, this yields a payoff equal to

$$X_2 = N \times \left(1 + \mathrm{Max} \left[F, \alpha \left(\frac{I_0 - I_2}{I_0} \right) \right] \right). \tag{11.13}$$

At maturity the investors get their money back plus a return on investment equal to the best of the floor rate and $-\alpha$ times the index return. If the index goes up investors receive the floor rate and if it goes down they are paid a fraction of the negative of the index return. Pricing this bear note follows exactly the same lines as before. First, we express the amount payable by the derivatives firm in terms of the payoffs of contracts that it already knows how to price. As shown by the following expression, this time the derivatives firm can be thought of as selling the bank αM **ordinary puts** with strike $I_0(1 - F/\alpha)$

$$V_2 = N \times F + \alpha M \times \mathrm{Max} \left[0, I_0 \left(1 - \frac{F}{\alpha} \right) - I_2 \right]. \tag{11.14}$$

The participation rate must therefore follow from the budget equation

$$PVC = e^{-2r_2}(N \times F) + \alpha M \times P_0^a \left[I_0 \left(1 - \frac{F}{\alpha} \right), 2 \right]. \tag{11.15}$$

Assuming a floor rate of -2% this yields a participation rate of 1.48.

A 2-year principal protected bull note with a floor rate of -2% would offer a participation rate of only 0.58. This means **the bear note offers a participation rate that is almost three times as high as that of a similar bull note**. This reflects the fact that, because over time stock prices tend to drift upwards, with the same participation rate the expected payoff of the bull note is higher than that of the bear note. However, since the initial investment is equal, both notes should offer the same expected payoff. This is accomplished by the higher participation rate for the bear note. Instead of the expected note payoff, we can of course also turn to the budget equation to explain the difference in participation rate between the bull and the bear note. With the bull note investors implicitly buy calls, while with the bear note they buy puts. As we saw in Chapter 7, for longer maturities puts tend to be a lot less expensive than calls, which allows for a higher participation rate on the bear note.

Figure 11.7 shows the return profile of the bear note. For comparison we also included the return profile for an equivalent bull note. Both notes offer the same floor rate but the graph also clearly shows that the bear note offers a much higher participation rate. The trade-off between the **floor rate** and the participation rate can be found in Figure 11.8. Apart from the fact that the participation rates are higher this graph is very similar to what we saw before for the bull note. A higher floor increases the expected payoff which is compensated by a lower participation rate.

It is interesting to see how the dividend yield on the index influences the above results. In Chapter 10 we saw that a higher dividend yield produces a significantly higher participation rate for a principal protected bull note. The opposite is true for a bear note.

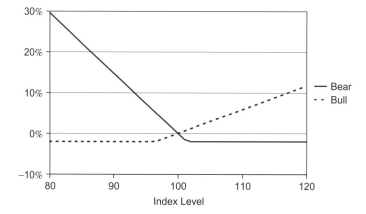

Figure 11.7   Return profile for a principal protected bear note

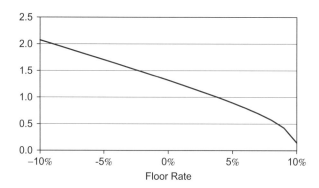

Figure 11.8   Trade-off between floor rate and participation rate for a principal protected bear note

A higher dividend yield reduces the participation rate on a principal protected bear note. This results from the fact that the higher the dividend, the more the stock price will drop on the ex-dividend date. This raises the expected note payoff, which has to be compensated by a lower participation rate.

From this point onwards we could proceed in exactly the same way as before. To improve the participation rate we could introduce a cap, lower the index return base level, introduce multiple participation rates, Asian tails, knock-in/knock-out features, a second reference index, or switch to another currency. Likewise, to solve doubts concerning the timing of exit and entry we could create lookback, ladder, cliquet or Asian structures. We will not go into this because the results would be virtually identical to those for the bull note. After all, all that it takes to turn a bullish structure into a bearish structure is to put a minus sign in front of the index return in the payoff formula.

11.4.2   Principal Protected Mixed and Chooser Notes

Sometimes, for example shortly before an election, one encounters investors who have little idea what direction the market will take but know that it will either go up or down. In that case we can offer them a note that pays off either way. The most obvious thing to do is to combine a bull note with a bear note. This produces a note payoff equal to

$$X_2 = N \times \left(1 + \text{Max} \left[F, \alpha \, \text{Max} \left[\frac{I_2 - I_0}{I_0}, \frac{I_0 - I_2}{I_0} \right] \right] \right). \tag{11.16}$$

This time investors receive a return on investment equal to the highest of the floor rate and the absolute value of the index return. Positive index returns stay unchanged but negative index returns are multiplied by -1. If the index goes up by 20% the investors get paid based on an index return of 20%, but if the index goes down by 20% they get paid the same amount. The index return used to calculate the note payoff is therefore always positive. This also means that **it is no use to choose the floor rate lower than zero**.

From the payoff formula we can derive the amount payable by the derivatives firm as

$$V_2 = N \times F + \alpha M \times \left(\text{Max} \left[0, I_2 - I_0 \left(1 + \frac{F}{\alpha} \right) \right] + \text{Max} \left[0, I_0 \left(1 - \frac{F}{\alpha} \right) - I_2 \right] \right). \tag{11.17}$$

This shows that implicitly the derivatives firm is simultaneously selling the bank **ordinary calls** with strike $I_0(1 + F/\alpha)$ and **ordinary puts** with strike $I_0(1 - F/\alpha)$. If the index goes up the bank will cancel the puts and if the index goes down it will cancel the calls. We can solve the note's participation rate from the budget equation given by

$$PVC = e^{-2r_2}(N \times F) + \alpha M \times \left(C_0^a \left[I_0 \left(1 + \frac{F}{\alpha} \right), 2 \right] + P_0^a \left[I_0 \left(1 - \frac{F}{\alpha} \right), 2 \right] \right). \tag{11.18}$$

Under the assumptions of a 0% floor rate this yields a participation rate of 0.38. Compared to the 0.54 and 1.32 we would have obtained for a 2-year bull note and a 2-year bear note, respectively, this does not look very good. It also does not look good when compared with an interest rate of 5%. For the note to pay off more than a fixed income investment the absolute index return over the note's lifetime must be at least 13.2%. Figure 11.9 shows the return profile of the principal protected mixed note.

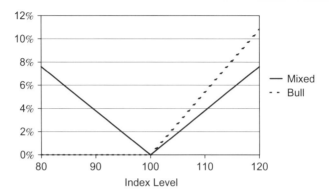

Figure 11.9   Return profile for a principal protected mixed note

The principal protected mixed note offers an extremely low participation rate because it pays off in bull as well as bear markets. One way to think about this note is as a contract that at maturity allows investors to choose whether the note is a bull note or a bear note. If the market has gone up they will make it a bull note and if the market has gone down they will opt for a bear note. Looking at the mixed note in this way makes it clear why the participation rate is so low. Investors can wait until the note's maturity date before they decide. This points us to a way to raise the participation rate. If we make investors **choose between bull and bear some time before maturity** we introduce the risk that they choose wrong which reduces the note's expected payoff and thereby allows for a higher participation rate. Formally, this yields a note payoff given by

$$X_2 = N \times \left(1 + \text{Max} \left[F, D \times \alpha \left(\frac{I_2 - I_0}{I_0} \right) \right] \right), \tag{11.19}$$

where

$$D = +1, \quad \text{if the investor chooses } \textbf{bull},$$
$$= -1, \quad \text{if the investor chooses } \textbf{bear}.$$

If the investor chooses a bull note ($D = 1$), the note pays off the same as a principal protected bull note. However, if he prefers it to be a bear note ($D = -1$) it pays off as a principal protected bear note. One problem with this so-called **chooser note** is that the bank has to ask every individual investor for his particular choice. This is not a problem when the number of investors is only small, but it can be quite problematic when dealing with a large number of investors. From an operational point of view **the chooser note is therefore not suited for retail distribution**. The same is true for other structures that require active investor participation of some sort.

To find the participation rate on the chooser note we can rewrite the derivatives firm's payment to the bank as

$$V_2 = N \times F + \alpha M \times \text{Max} \left[0, D \times \left(I_2 - I_0 \left(1 + D \times \frac{F}{\alpha} \right) \right) \right]. \tag{11.20}$$

This expression shows that apart from paying the guaranteed minimum the derivatives firm also enters into a special type of contract with the bank where the bank not only has the right to cancel the deal at maturity but also has the right to decide who is going to pay the index value at maturity and who is going to pay the fixed amount. If the bank decides the derivatives firm is to pay the index at maturity the contract turns into an ordinary call. If on the other hand the bank decides to pay the index value at maturity itself the contract turns into an ordinary put. A contract like this is known as a **chooser option**.

If we assume that the investors have to make a choice one year from now, we can solve the participation rate from the budget equation

$$PVC = e^{-2r_2}(N \times F) + \alpha M \times CH_0^a \left[I_0 \left(1 + \frac{F}{\alpha} \right), I_0 \left(1 - \frac{F}{\alpha} \right), 1, 2 \right], \qquad (11.21)$$

where $CH_0^a[K^1, K^2, t, T]$ is the derivatives firm's offer for a chooser option with call strike K^1, put strike K^2, **choice date** t and maturity T. Assuming a 0% floor rate this produces a participation rate of 0.44, which is a significant improvement over the 0.38 we found for the mixed note.

The trade-off between the **floor rate** and the participation rate on both the mixed and the chooser note can be found in Figure 11.10. The graphs show that the participation rate on both notes behaves in very much the same way, except that it is slightly higher for the chooser note for lower floor rates. For floor rates over 7%, however, the difference is negligible, which reflects the fact that with floor rates like that there is hardly any money left to buy upside with, irrespective of the type of note. Figure 11.11 shows the trade-off between the **choice date** and the participation rate, again assuming a 0% floor rate. If we allow investors to postpone their choice between bull and bear until maturity, the chooser note is identical to a mixed note and offers a participation rate of 0.38. If we force them to make a choice sooner the participation rate will rise to compensate the falling expected note payoff. If the choice has to be made at $t = 0$ the note is the same as a 2-year principal protected bull note (which is the rational choice) and offers a participation rate of 0.54.

11.4.3 Principal Protected Neutral Note

We have discussed bullish, bearish and mixed views on the market. This leaves us with investors who think that on balance the market will neither go up nor down, i.e. stay

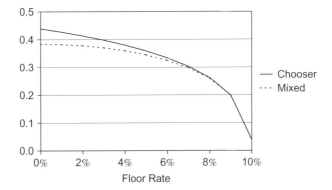

Figure 11.10 Trade-off between floor rate and participation rate for a principal protected mixed and chooser note

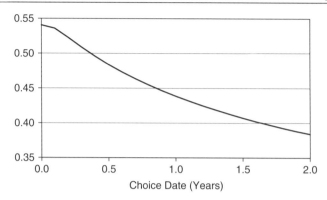

Figure 11.11 Trade-off between choice date and participation rate for a principal protected chooser note

within a fairly narrow range around its present level. When confronted with a neutral view, we can structure a principal protected note which pays investors a return that is higher the closer the index at maturity is to its value at inception. This means offering them a payoff equal to

$$X_2 = N \times \left(1 + \text{Max} \left[F, R^{\text{M}} - \alpha \, \text{Max} \left[\frac{I_2 - I_0}{I_0}, \frac{I_0 - I_2}{I_0} \right] \right] \right), \tag{11.22}$$

where R^{M} is the maximum return achievable. It is paid if the index return is zero, i.e. the index at maturity equals the index at inception. If the index return is higher or lower than zero a fraction of that index return is deducted from the maximum return. We can easily calculate the levels of the index at maturity where the floor kicks in. Doing so shows us that if the index at maturity rises above $H^2 = I_0(R^{\text{M}} + \alpha - F)/\alpha$ or falls below $H^1 = I_0(F + \alpha - R^{\text{M}})/\alpha$ investors will be paid the floor rate. If the index ends up in the range between H^1 and H^2 they will receive more. Note that the range is symmetrical around I_0, i.e. $H^2 = 2I_0 - H^1$.

Since the market is expected to be without direction, it is no longer the participation rate that is of prime interest. That role now goes to the maximum return. Given the range boundaries H^1 and H^2 and the floor rate, we want to know what the maximum return is going to be. To calculate this we first write the amount payable by the derivatives firm as

$$V_2 = N \times R^{\text{M}} - \alpha M \times (\text{Max} [0, I_2 - I_0] - \text{Max} [0, I_2 - H^2] + \text{Max} [0, I_0 - I_2]$$
$$- \text{Max} [0, H^1 - I_2]). \tag{11.23}$$

This shows that the derivatives firm commits itself to pay the bank the maximum return and simultaneously buys from the bank (a) an **ordinary call spread** with strikes I_0 and H^2 as well as (b) an **ordinary put spread** with strikes I_0 and H^1.

If we select a floor rate and two range boundaries a complication arises. Looking at (11.23) it looks as if it is going to be impossible to solve for the maximum return because given the floor rate and the range boundaries we still have two unknown parameters: the maximum return and the participation rate. However, we do have expressions for the range boundaries in terms of the maximum return, the floor rate and the participation rate. After having chosen the range we can turn one of these expressions around to express the participation rate in terms of the maximum return, the floor rate and the relevant range boundary. We can therefore calculate the maximum return from the budget equation given by

$$PVC = e^{-2r_2}(N \times R^M) - N \times \frac{F - R}{H^1 - I_0} \times (CS_0^b[I_0, H^2, 2] + PS_0^b[I_0, H^1, 2]), \quad (11.24)$$

where $PS_0^b[K^1, K^2, T]$ is the derivatives firm's bid for a put spread with upper strike K^1, lower strike K^2 and maturity T. Assuming a lower range boundary of 90, an upper range boundary of 110 and a floor rate of -2%, this yields a maximum return of 83.2%.

Figure 11.12 shows the return profile of the principal protected neutral note for a range between 90 and 110 as well as a range between 85 and 115. For index values outside the range the note pays a return on investment equal to the floor rate of -2%. If the index at maturity is within the range the note return exceeds the floor rate. The closer the index is to 100, the higher the return. The maximum return is paid at an index value of 100. The trade-off between the **floor rate** and the maximum return is shown in Figure 11.13. As always, a higher floor rate leads to less upside, this time in the form of a lower maximum return. Figure 11.14 shows how the maximum return varies with the **range width** $H^2 - H^1$. A wider range raises the note's expected payoff. With everything else being given, however, the only way to compensate for this is to lower the maximum return. Note that the drop in the maximum return comes to an end at some point. This reflects the fact that at some point the range becomes so wide that widening it any further does not change the note's expected payoff any more.

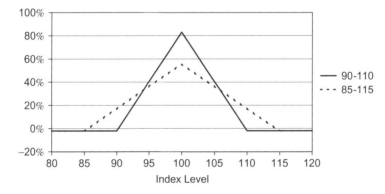

Figure 11.12   Return profile for a principal protected neutral note

11.4.4   Principal Protected Range Accrual Note

The principal protected neutral note has one serious problem: its payoff depends exclusively on the value of the index at maturity. The index may be within the chosen range for most of the note's life, but if it is not in there at maturity the investors make nothing more on their investment than the floor rate. To solve this problem we have to structure a note which accumulates its payoff over time depending on whether the index is inside or outside the range. One way to do this is to structure a note with an index-linked payoff equal to the

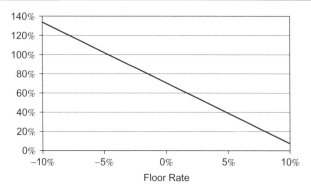

Figure 11.13 Trade-off between floor rate and maximum return for a principal protected neutral note

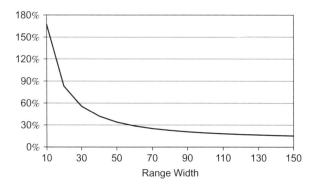

Figure 11.14 Trade-off between range width and maximum return for a principal protected neutral note

sum of the index-linked payoffs of a strip of neutral notes with increasing times to maturity. This is similar to what we did earlier to arrive at the principal protected cliquet note.

Most investors, institutional as well as retail, focus on predicting the direction of future stock price movements, not their volatility. Our classification into bull, bear, mixed and neutral market views reflects this. One reason for investors' lack of interest in predicting future volatility is that there are not many ways to capitalize on these predictions. The type of notes we discuss here can also be interpreted as instruments that allow investors to take a view on market volatility. As such they form a welcome addition to the instruments available to investors to fully capitalize on their views.

Suppose we split our 2-year neutral note into 24 identical parts, one maturing every month, but all with settlement delayed until the note's maturity date. Formally, this would mean that at maturity the note would pay investors an amount equal to

$$X_2 = N \times \left(1 + \sum_{i=1}^{24} \mathrm{Max} \left[F, R^{\mathrm{M}} - \alpha\, \mathrm{Max} \left[\frac{I_{i/12} - I_0}{I_0}, \frac{I_0 - I_{i/12}}{I_0} \right] \right] \right), \qquad (11.25)$$

where F and R^{M} now denote the floor rate and the maximum return per month. Note that, instead of flooring the note payoff at maturity, we have floored every month's contribution individually. This also puts a floor under the total payoff but it is not the same as flooring the total directly. Flooring every individual month is more in line with the idea behind the note.

Given the note's payoff formula, we can write the derivatives firm's payment to the bank as

$$V_2 = N \times 24R^{\mathrm{M}} - \alpha M \times \sum_{i=1}^{24} (\mathrm{Max}\,[0, I_i - I_0] - \mathrm{Max}\,[0, I_i - H^2] + \mathrm{Max}\,[0, I_0 - I_i]$$

$$- \mathrm{Max}\,[0, H^1 - I_i]), \tag{11.26}$$

where as before H^1 is the lower range boundary and H^2 is the upper range boundary. This shows that the derivatives firm's payment to the bank consists of two parts: a fixed amount covering the maximum return minus an amount equal to what the bank would have paid if it had sold the derivatives firm 48 **ordinary call and put spreads**, all with settlement delayed until the note's maturity date.

Before we can calculate the maximum monthly return we need to eliminate the participation rate from the above expression again. We can do this in exactly the same way as before since we still have $H^2 = I_0(R^{\mathrm{M}} + \alpha - F)/\alpha$ and $H^1 = I_0(F + \alpha - R^{\mathrm{M}})/\alpha$. This means that the maximum monthly return can be calculated from the budget equation given by

$$PVC = e^{-2r_2}(N \times 24R^{\mathrm{M}})$$

$$- N \times \frac{F - R^{\mathrm{M}}}{H^1 - I_0} \times \sum_{i=1}^{24} (CS_0^{\mathrm{b}}[I_0, H^2, i/12, 2] + PS_0^{\mathrm{b}}[I_0, H^1, i/12, 2]), \tag{11.27}$$

where $CS_0^{\mathrm{b}}[K^1, K^2, t, T]$ is the derivatives firm's bid for a call spread with lower strike K^1, upper strike K^2, payoff determination at time t and settlement at time T. Likewise, $PS_0^{\mathrm{b}}[K^1, K^2, t, T]$ is the derivatives firm's bid for a put spread with upper strike K^1, lower strike K^2, payoff determination at time t and settlement at time T.

With a lower range boundary of 90, an upper range boundary of 110 and a monthly floor rate of $-2/24\%$, the note offers a maximum monthly return of 2.05%. This means that if the index were right in the middle of the range at the end of every subsequent month, investors would make a 2-year return on investment equal to 49.2%. This is substantially lower than the maximum return of 83.2% offered by the neutral note, but this simply reflects the fundamentally different structure of the range accrual note. The range accrual note's payoff builds up slowly over 24 different points in time. If one month does not pay then maybe the next month will. The neutral note on the other hand is an all-or-nothing structure with a payoff which fully depends on the index at maturity. Assuming a range between 90 and 110, Figure 11.15 shows the negative trade-off between the monthly **floor rate** and the maximum monthly return. The trade-off between the **range width** and the maximum monthly return can be found in Figure 11.16. Similar to what we saw for the neutral note, the graphs shows that if the range gets very wide, the maximum return more or less stabilizes. With a range width of 100 the maximum monthly return is 0.63%, while with a range width of 150 it is not too much lower at 0.54%.

We still have not completely eliminated the timing problem, as what happens to the index in between the monthly contributions is still irrelevant for the note's payoff. To solve this we could split up the note further, i.e. allow for more frequent contributions

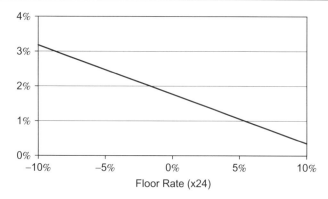

Figure 11.15 Trade-off between monthly floor rate and maximum monthly return for a principal protected range accrual note

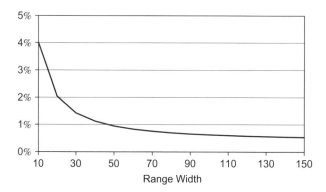

Figure 11.16 Trade-off between range width and maximum monthly return for a principal protected range accrual note

to the note's payoff at maturity. Figure 11.17 shows the trade-off between the length of the **contribution period** and the maximum lifetime return on a principal protected range accrual note with a lower range boundary of 90, an upper range boundary of 110 and a lifetime floor rate of -2%. As we saw before, with monthly contributions (20 days) the maximum return achievable over the note's life is 49.2%. Because making more frequent contributions raises the note's expected payoff, it reduces the maximum lifetime return. With daily contributions the latter comes down to 46.4%.

11.4.5 Principal Protected Knock-Out Range Accrual Note

It pays to give some more thought to ways to raise the maximum return. Since a higher maximum return raises the note's expected payoff we need to find a way to relieve the pressure that raising the maximum return will cause. We could fiddle around with the existing parameters, but we could also introduce one or more new parameters. We could for example equip all periodic contributions with a **double knock-out barrier** feature with barriers equal to the lower and upper range boundaries H^1 and H^2. This would mean that the payoff accumulation process would stop if at any of the monitoring points

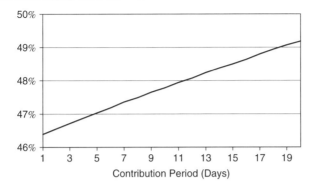

Figure 11.17 Trade-off between length of contribution period and maximum lifetime return for a principal protected range accrual note

the index hit one of the range boundaries. Sticking with the 2-year monthly structure, this would mean offering investors a payoff equal to

$$X_2 = N \times \left(1 + \sum_{i=1}^{24} \text{Max}\,[F, D_i]\right), \tag{11.28}$$

where

$$D_i = -\infty, \quad \text{if } \exists j\ I_j \leqslant H^1 \text{ or } I_j \geqslant H^2,$$

$$= R^{\text{M}} - \alpha\,\text{Max}\left[\frac{I_{i/12} - I_0}{I_0}, \frac{I_0 - I_{i/12}}{I_0}\right], \quad \text{if } \forall j\ H^1 < I_j < H^2$$

The subscript j counts the monitoring points from $t = 0$ until $t = i/12$. As long as the index is within the range, the knock-out range accrual note accumulates its payoff in exactly the same way as the standard range accrual note. However, as soon as the index hits one of the range boundaries the contribution of that month as well as all months that follow is fixed at the floor rate.

To price this note, i.e. to find the maximum monthly return the bank can offer to investors, we can write the derivatives firm's payment to the bank as

$$V_2 = N \times 24F + N \times \sum_{i=1}^{24} D_i \times \left((R^{\text{M}} - F) - \frac{\alpha}{I_0}(\text{Max}\,[0, I_i - I_0] - \text{Max}\,[0, I_i - H^2]\right.$$

$$\left. + \text{Max}\,[0, I_0 - I_i] - \text{Max}\,[0, H^1 - I_i])\right), \tag{11.29}$$

where now

$$D_i = 0, \quad \text{if } \exists j\ I_j \leqslant H^1 \text{ or } I_j \geqslant H^2,$$

$$= 1, \quad \text{if } \forall j\ H^1 < I_j < H^2$$

This is pretty much the same expression as before, except that this time we have separated the floor rate from the part of the payment that is controlled by the knock-out feature. Every month's contribution to the note payoff at $t = 2$ now consists of three parts.

- The first part is a fixed amount corresponding to the floor rate. We can single this part out because the floor rate gets paid irrespective of whether a knock-out occurs or not.
- The second part is a fixed amount equal to $R^{M} - F$, which comes with a knock-out condition: it is paid unless a barrier is hit. This is the payoff of a **double barrier knock-out digital**.
- The third part of the monthly return contribution is made up of the payoffs of a short **double barrier knock-out call spread** and a short **double barrier knock-out put spread**, both with settlement delayed until $t = 2$. This part is nullified after a barrier hit as well.

If neither of the barriers is hit the first two parts contribute R^{M} to the note return at maturity, with the third part acting as a correction term. In case of a knock-out, both the second and the third parts are nullified and the contribution drops to F.

Knowing what the derivatives firm will have to pay at maturity, we can calculate the maximum monthly return from the budget equation given by

$$PVC = e^{-2r_2}(N \times 24F) + N \times \sum_{i=1}^{24}(AOD_0^a[H^1, H^2, 0, i/12, 2] \times (R^M - F)$$

$$- \frac{F - R^M}{H^1 - I_0} \times (OCS_0^a[I_0, H^2, H^1, H^2, 0, i/12, i, 2]$$

$$+ OPS_0^a[I_0, H^1, H^1, H^2, 0, i/12, i, 2])), \tag{11.30}$$

where $AOD_0^a[H^1, H^2, t_1, t_2, T]$ is the derivatives firm's offer for an American double barrier knock-out digital paying 1.00 at time T, with two barriers at H^1 and H^2 which are active between time t_1 and time t_2. $OCS_0^a[K^1, K^2, H^1, H^2, t_1, t_2, t, T]$ and $OPS_0^a[K^1, K^2, H^1, H^2, t_1, t_2, t, T]$ denote the derivatives firm's prices for American double barrier knock-out call and put spreads with strikes K^1 and K^2, barriers at H^1 and H^2, monitoring from $t = t_1$ to $t = t_2$, payoff determination at time t and settlement at time T. With a lower range boundary of 80, an upper range boundary of 120 and a $-2/24\%$ monthly floor rate this yields a maximum monthly return of 1.61%. This compares very favorably with the 1.12% we would have obtained for an equivalent standard range accrual note. However, it is certainly not a free lunch as with the knock-out note a single barrier hit will eliminate all further upside potential.

It is interesting to note that although we said that the options embedded in the knock-out range accrual note are double barrier call and put spreads, this is not really the case. The second option in each spread has a strike which is equal to a knock-out barrier. This means that these options will always knock out before they come ITM. **The second option in each spread is therefore worthless**.

Figure 11.18 shows the trade-off between the monthly **floor rate** and the maximum monthly return. For comparison we also included the results for an equivalent standard range accrual note. The graph shows that for low floor rates the knock-out note compares very favorably with the standard note. For higher floor rates, however, the difference becomes smaller. The trade-off between the **range width** and the maximum monthly return can be found in Figure 11.19. For range widths up to around 60 the knock-out note offers a significantly higher maximum return than the standard range accrual note. For a range width of 40 the knock-out note pays a maximum monthly return of 1.61%,

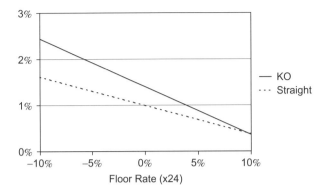

Figure 11.18 Trade-off between monthly floor rate and maximum monthly return for a principal protected knock-out range accrual note

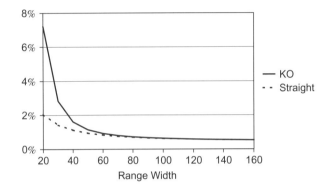

Figure 11.19 Trade-off between range width and maximum monthly return for a principal protected knock-out range accrual note

while the standard note pays only 1.12%. For a range width of 60 these numbers are 0.92% and 0.83%, respectively and for a range width of 100 the knock-out note pays a maximum of 0.63% while the standard note pays 0.62%. This reflects the drop in the knock-out probability that occurs when the range is widened. With respect to the knock-out probability it should be noted, however, that it is not just the occurrence but also the timing of the knock-out which is important here. The note payoff will accumulate as long as the index does not move outside the range. This means that **the real danger lies in an early knock-out**. A knock-out close to maturity can do little harm any more.

Figure 11.20 shows the trade-off between the length of the **contribution period** and the maximum lifetime return on a knock-out range accrual note with a lower range boundary of 80, an upper range boundary of 120 and a −2% lifetime floor rate. Since the range is fairly narrow, the maximum return offered by the knock-out note is substantially higher than that offered by the standard note. From the graph we see that if we increase the number of contribution periods, i.e. decrease the length of a contribution period, the maximum return drops slightly for both notes. The difference between them, however, is more or less constant at around 11%.

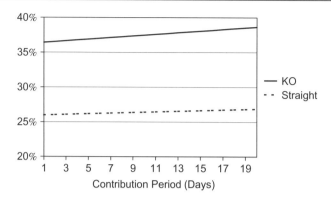

Figure 11.20 Trade-off between length of contribution period and maximum lifetime return for a principal protected knock-out range accrual note

Allowing all future contributions to knock out if the index hits one of the range boundaries will often be considered a bit extreme. There are various ways in which we can **soften the knock-out feature**. First, the knock-out barriers need not be equal to the range boundaries. We could place the barriers (but not the range boundaries) further away from spot. This will reduce the probability of a knock-out. Second, instead of letting all future contributions knock out we could restrict the knock-out to the contribution of the month in which the barrier hit occurs. If during a month the index hit one of the barriers, the contribution for that month would be fixed at the floor rate, irrespective of the value of the index at the end of the month. The following months would not be affected though. Doing so would hardly change the above expressions. The only difference would be that this time we would be confronted with digitals and call and put options where both knock-out barriers were only active during the month before the payoff determination instead of from inception. Of course, all of this will lower the maximum return that can be paid on the note.

11.5 NOTES OFFERING IMPROVED ASSET ALLOCATION

Until now we have concentrated on the case of investors who have a view on a specific reference index and who want to capitalize on that view without risking (much of) their principal. Some investors may not feel certain enough to choose one particular reference index, however. They could simply spread their money evenly over a number of indices, but there is another alternative as well. We could structure a note which takes the asset allocation decision for them. This is what we discuss next.

Suppose investors had to decide between two different reference indices I^1 and I^2. Both are expected to go up but they simply cannot make up their minds which one will go up more. In that case we can offer them a note which pays a return on investment derived from the best performing of the two. Formally, this yields a payoff equal to

$$X_2 = N \times \left(1 + \text{Max} \left[F, \alpha \left(\frac{I_2^1 - I_0^1}{I_0^1} \right), \alpha \left(\frac{I_2^2 - I_0^2}{I_0^2} \right) \right] \right). \qquad (11.31)$$

If the first index shows the best performance, the note pays off like a principal protected bull note with I^1 as reference index. However, if the second index produces the highest return it pays off like a principal protected bull note with I^2 as reference index. Two things about the above payoff are worth noting. First, it is identical to the best-of-equity, bonds-and-cash payoff we discussed earlier in Section 7.4.3. Second, it is very straightforward to extend the concept to three or more reference indices. All this would require is placing more returns within the Max operator. For simplicity, however, we will stick to the case of two indices.

If we assume that $I_0^1 = I_0^2 = I_0$, the amount payable by the derivatives firm can be expressed as

$$V_2 = N \times F + \alpha M \times \text{Max}\left[0, \text{Max}\,[I_2^1, I_2^2] - I_0\left(1 + \frac{F}{\alpha}\right)\right]. \qquad (11.32)$$

The index-linked amount equals αM times the payoff of a contract where the derivatives firm pays the highest index value at maturity, the bank pays a fixed amount $I_0(1 + F/\alpha)$ and also has the right to cancel the deal at maturity. This is known as a **call on the best-of-two** with a strike of $I_0(1 + F/\alpha)$. From here it follows directly that we can find the participation rate from the budget equation given by

$$PVC = e^{-2r_2}(N \times F) + \alpha M \times CB_0^a\left[I_0\left(1 + \frac{F}{\alpha}\right), 2\right], \qquad (11.33)$$

where $CB_0^a[K, T]$ is the derivatives firm's offer for a call on the best-of-two with a strike of K and time to maturity T. To price the embedded option we need to make an assumption about the correlation between both index returns. Under the assumption of a 0.40 correlation between the returns on both indices and a -2% floor rate this yields a participation rate of 0.37. Obviously, this is much lower than the 0.58 we would have obtained if there was only one reference index. The difference can be interpreted as the price of the perfect asset allocation service which the note provides.

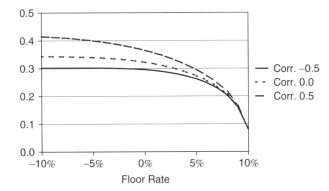

Figure 11.21 Trade-off between floor rate and participation rate for a principal protected best-of-two bull note

Figure 11.21 shows the trade-off between the **floor rate** and the participation rate on the principal protected best-of-two bull note for correlation coefficients of -0.5, 0 and

0.5. From the graph we see that the lower the correlation between both index returns, the lower the participation rate for a given floor rate. This reflects the fact that the lower the correlation, the more likely the note is to pay off. As always, the lower the floor rate, the higher the participation rate. There is a definite end to this, however, when the floor rate drops further. With a correlation coefficient of -0.5 the participation rate for floor rates below -2% shows hardly any improvement. For a correlation coefficient of 0 this point comes at a floor rate of around -5% and for a correlation coefficient of 0.5 at a floor rate of around -10%. We encountered this phenomenon before in Chapter 7. It means that **the bank can offer investors a fairly high floor rate without doing any significant damage to the participation rate**.

To improve the best-of-two note's participation rate we can use our old bag of tricks again, but there is also a new trick to be learned. The best-of-two note provides investors with perfect asset allocation services. This explains the low participation rate. If we make the service a little less perfect the participation rate would rise. The bank could for example pay investors a return on investment equal to the weighted average of the return on the best performing index and the return on the worst performing index. This would produce a payoff equal to

$$X_2 = N \times \left(1 + \text{Max} \left[F, \alpha \left(\beta \, \text{Max} \left[\frac{I_2^1 - I_0^1}{I_0^1}, \frac{I_2^2 - I_0^2}{I_0^2} \right] \right. \right. \right.$$

$$\left. \left. \left. + (1 - \beta) \, \text{Min} \left[\frac{I_2^1 - I_0^1}{I_0^1}, \frac{I_2^2 - I_0^2}{I_0^2} \right] \right) \right] \right). \tag{11.34}$$

Proceeding with the pricing of the note, we see that, assuming $I_0^1 = I_0^2 = I_0$, the derivatives firm's payment to the bank is given by

$$V_2 = N \times F + \alpha M \times \left(\beta \, \text{Max} \left[0, \text{Max} \left[I_2^1, I_2^2 \right] - I_0 \left(1 + \frac{F}{\alpha} \right) \right] \right.$$

$$\left. + (1 - \beta) \, \text{Max} \left[0, \text{Min} \left[I_2^1, I_2^2 \right] - I_0 \left(1 + \frac{F}{\alpha} \right) \right] \right). \tag{11.35}$$

This shows that instead of simply buying a call on the best-of-two, the bank now buys two different option contracts: a **call on the best-of-two** and a **call on the worst-of-two**. We encountered the latter before in Chapter 10. This means that we can find the participation rate from the budget equation given by

$$PVC = e^{-2r_2} (N \times F) + \alpha M \times \left(\beta C B_0^a \left[I_0 \left(1 + \frac{F}{\alpha} \right), 2 \right] \right.$$

$$\left. + (1 - \beta) C W_0^a \left[I_0 \left(1 + \frac{F}{\alpha} \right), 2 \right] \right). \tag{11.36}$$

Assuming a floor rate of -2%, a correlation coefficient between the returns on both indices of 0.40 and a weighting factor of 0.5, this yields a participation rate of 0.58.

If there were three or more reference indices involved, results would be similar except that the number of options would increase. Suppose there were three reference indices and we wanted to pay the weighted average of the return on the best performer, the second best and the worst performing index. In that case we could split the payment to be made to the bank into the payoff of a call on the best-of-three, a call on the second-best-of-three and a call on the worst-of-three.

The trade-off between the **floor rate** and the participation rate is shown in Figure 11.22. The graph clearly shows how much higher the participation rate on the mixed best-of/worst-of bull note is, especially for lower floor rates. Figure 11.23 shows the trade-off between the **weighting factor** β and the participation rate on a principal protected mixed best-of/worst-of bull note with a floor rate of -2% for correlation coefficients of -0.5, 0 and 0.5. Not surprisingly, the more weight is put on the best-of-two part, the lower the participation rate. When $\beta = 1$ the note is the same as the best-of-two bull note discussed in the previous subsection. On the other hand, with $\beta = 0$ it is the same as the principal protected worst-of-two note we discussed earlier in Chapter 10.

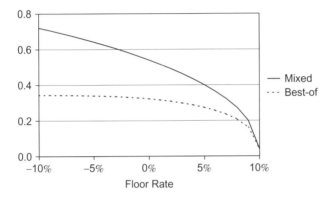

Figure 11.22 Trade-off between floor rate and participation rate for a principal protected mixed best-of/worst-of bull note

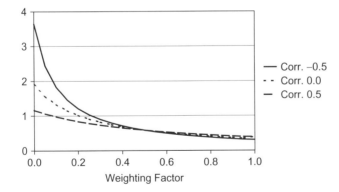

Figure 11.23 Trade-off between weighting factor and participation rate for a principal protected mixed best-of/worst-of bull note

Since the participation rate on the worst-of-two note is a negative function (see Figure 10.16) and the participation rate on the best-of-two note is a positive function of the correlation coefficient (see Figure 11.23), the influence of the correlation coefficient on the participation rate depends heavily on the weighting factor. For $\beta < 0.5$ the participation rate drops when the correlation coefficient increases, while, although much less pronounced, for $\beta > 0.5$ the opposite happens. For $\beta = 0.5$ the participation rate is independent of the correlation coefficient. Actually, for $\beta = 0.5$ the participation rate is equal to that of a 2-year standard principal protected note, irrespective of the correlation between both indices.

11.6 CONCLUSION

In this chapter we presented a number of notes suitable for investors with non-bullish views. We also discussed a number of note ideas that offer investors help with their market timing or asset allocation. Although we discussed these features in isolation, technically there is nothing to prevent us from combining two or even more of them into one single note. However, given that timing features tend to come at a high price in practice, this hardly ever happens. To compensate the drop in the participation rate resulting from the addition of a timing feature we can introduce one or more of the tricks we discussed in Chapter 10. Especially in a less favorable pricing environment, the market does not see many notes with lookback, ladder or best-of features that do not include one or more cost cutting measures. In this context it is important to emphasize that what we showed here is only a fraction of what is possible. Derivatives structuring is about being creative. It is more art than science. If you can think of it, it might be something worthwhile.

A final remark concerns the fact that since (a) the bulk of the more exotic equity derivatives deals done by derivatives firms are to support equity-linked note issues and (b) the majority of these notes find their way to retail investors, **the bulk of the exotic equity derivatives traded eventually ends up in the hands of retail investors**. This contrasts with popular belief, which says that, since they are the only ones to really understand their workings, the use of exotic equity derivatives is limited to only the most sophisticated institutional investors. On the other hand, it is not that surprising either. The typical retail investor lacks the sophistication to reverse engineer even the simplest product and even if he could, he would not be able to create it himself at a better price. As a result, the retail market has become product providers' favorite hunting ground. We will see another example of this in Chapter 13.

12

Digital and Coupon Bearing Notes

12.1 INTRODUCTION

All notes discussed so far pay investors a return on investment which depends heavily on the index value at maturity and sometimes also on the path taken by the index to get there. The index decides not only whether the note will actually pay a return above the floor rate, but also how much if it does. Sometimes investors may prefer to have a better insight into what exactly they are going to get paid in case their view proves correct. To accommodate this objective we can **digitalize** the notes that we structured before. Instead of paying investors a higher return the more the index moves in the direction they predicted, we simply pay them a prefixed amount. As a result, we no longer have return profile graphs with upward and downward sloping lines, but only with horizontal lines.

Another objection against the notes we have dealt with so far could be that none of them pays any **intermediate coupons**. Sometimes investors do not want to buy zero-coupon notes. It may not fit in with their cash flow or tax planning, or they simply may not be allowed to buy zeros. To accommodate this we can either introduce a fixed coupon or simply break up the payment that the zero makes on top of the redemption of principal and spread it over a number of coupons that are paid during the life of the note. We will first discuss some examples of digital(ized) notes, followed by a few notes that pay either fixed or index-linked coupons. We use the same assumptions and notation as in Chapter 9.

12.2 DIGITALIZED NOTES

In this section we digitalize some of the notes which we discussed earlier in Chapters 9–11. We will see that because the resulting payoff formulas are very straightforward, pricing these notes boils down to pricing one or more European or American single or double barrier digitals.

12.2.1 Digital Principal Protected Bull Note

A principal protected bull note pays investors an amount which depends on the value of the reference index at the end of the note's life relative to its value at the beginning. If the index drops investors receive the floor rate and if the index goes up they get a fraction of the actual index return. Although by itself this is not too complicated, we can make things even simpler by instead of an amount equal to a fraction of the index return simply paying a prefixed amount when the index at maturity is equal to or higher than some critical value. This means there are only two outcomes: either we pay the floor rate or we pay the prefixed amount. Let's look at the resulting note's payoff more formally. It is given by

$$X_5 = N \times (1 + F + D \times B), \tag{12.1}$$

where

$$D = 0, \quad \text{if } I_5 < \gamma I_0,$$
$$ = 1, \quad \text{if } I_5 \geqslant \gamma I_0.$$

This shows that investors automatically lock in a return of at least F. If at maturity the index is equal to or higher than a constant **digital factor** γ times the index value at the beginning of the note's life they receive a **bonus rate** of B on top of that, bringing the note return to $F + B$.

To complete the structuring of the note we need to decide on (1) a floor rate, (2) a bonus rate and (3) a digital factor γ. If we fix the floor rate at -5% and the digital factor at 1.0, this leaves the bonus rate to be solved for. To do so we first look at the amount payable by the derivatives firm at maturity which can simply be expressed as

$$V_5 = N \times F + N \times B \times D. \tag{12.2}$$

This shows that the derivatives firm's payment consists of the usual fixed amount associated with the guaranteed minimum return plus an index-linked amount. Unlike with the principal protected bull note, this index-linked amount is extremely straightforward. It is equal to either 0 when the index return is lower than 0% or $N \times B$ when the index return is equal to or higher than 0%. This is nothing more than the payoff of $N \times B$ **digital calls** paying off 1.00 at $t = 5$ when on that same date the index is equal to or higher than 100. We can therefore calculate the bonus rate from the following budget equation

$$PVC = e^{-5r_5}(N \times F) + N \times B \times DC_0^a[I_0, 5]. \tag{12.3}$$

Under the assumptions made this yields a bonus rate of 48.9%, meaning that if the index at maturity is higher than 100 investors are paid a return on investment equal to 43.9%. If not, they make a return of -5%.

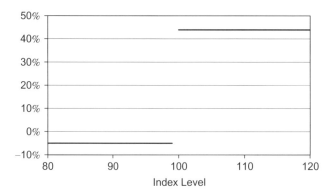

Figure 12.1 Return profile for a digital principal protected bull note

Figure 12.1 shows the return profile of the digital principal protected bull note. The graph clearly shows the digital nature of the note's payoff. For index levels below 100 investors realize a return on investment of -5%, while for index levels of 100 and higher

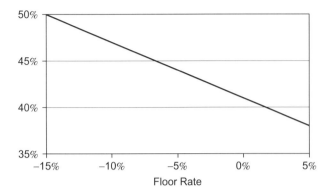

Figure 12.2 Trade-off between floor rate and payoff rate for a digital principal protected bull note

the return jumps to 43.9%. Of course, the bonus rate depends heavily on the floor rate and the digital factor we choose. With a digital factor of 1.0, Figure 12.2 shows the trade-off between the **floor rate** and the **payoff rate**, i.e. the sum of the floor rate and the bonus rate. The payoff rate is the actual return on investment investors will make if at maturity the index is higher than 100. From the graph we see that the payoff rate drops if the floor rate is increased. This makes perfect sense if we look at the note's expected payoff. The floor rate is the rate which investors make if the index goes down. The payoff rate is the rate they make if the index goes up. Raising the floor rate means investors get paid more when the index goes down. Because the expected payoff cannot change, however, this means they must get paid less when the index goes up. The same conclusion can be drawn from the budget equation. With *PVC* and the price of the digitals fixed, the only outlet for a higher floor rate is a lower bonus rate.

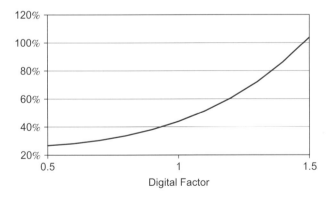

Figure 12.3 Trade-off between digital factor and payoff rate for a digital principal protected bull note

Figure 12.3 shows the trade-off between the **digital factor** and the payoff rate, assuming a floor rate of −5%. The graph shows that the higher the digital factor, the higher the payoff rate. This reflects the decreasing probability that investors will get paid a bonus, i.e. the increasing probability they will make the floor rate. For really low values of the digital factor, a change in the digital factor has no significant effect on the payoff rate. This is in line with the fact that with a very low digital factor the probability that the holder of the note does not get paid a bonus, i.e. only gets paid the floor rate, is very low as well.

Since the note payoff is digital we are confronted with an implicit cap on the note payoff. This means that **we can tell the same story in two different ways**, one of which may make the note payoff sound more interesting than the other. So far we have said 'if the index goes up, the bank will pay you a return on investment of 43.9% but if the index goes down you will lose 5%'. This is not the most appealing description of the note payoff, as it emphasizes too much that it is not at all sure that investors will make the 43.9% return on investment. Alternatively, describing the note payoff as 'the bank will pay you an exceptionally high return on your investment of 43.9% but in (the unlikely) case the index does not go up this will be reduced to -5%' makes it sound as if they already have the 43.9% in their pocket. From a marketing perspective the latter description is therefore generally preferred. A similar reasoning goes for the digital notes that follow.

12.2.2 Digital Principal Protected Cliquet Bull Note

In the previous chapter we saw that for every year within the note's life a principal protected cliquet bull note pays an amount the size of which depends on the value of the reference index at the end of that year relative to its value at the beginning of the year. We can simplify this by instead of paying an amount equal to a fraction of the index return simply paying a prefixed amount when the index at the end of the year is equal to or higher than some critical value. Again, this puts a cap on the note payoff as we know in advance that in total the bank will never have to pay more than the sum of these prefixed amounts. The resulting note's payoff would be equal to

$$X_5 = N \times \left(1 + 5F + \sum_{i=1}^{5} D_i \times B\right),$$ (12.4)

where

$$D_i = 0, \quad \text{if } I_i < \gamma I_{i-1},$$
$$= 1, \quad \text{if } I_i \geqslant \gamma I_{i-1}.$$

Again, this payoff formula is extremely straightforward. Every year investors automatically lock in a return of F. If at the end of the year the index is equal to or higher than a constant γ times the index value at the beginning of the year, they receive a bonus of B on top of that, bringing that year's contribution to the note return to $F + B$. At maturity all five years' contributions are summed and paid out.

To determine the bonus rate we have to look at the amount payable by the derivatives firm again. Similar to the digital principal protected bull note we have

$$V_5 = N \times 5F + N \times B \times \sum_{i=1}^{5} D_i.$$ (12.5)

From this we see that apart from the floor, every year contributes to the note payoff an amount equal to either 0 if the index return over the year is lower than $\gamma - 1$ or $N \times B$

if the index return is equal to or higher than $\gamma - 1$. All five bonuses equal the payoffs of **digital calls**. However, there are two unusual features.

- **Delayed settlement.** In four out of five cases the index is monitored for a barrier hit one or more years before the maturity date. Instead of at maturity, the first year's bonus is determined at $t = 1$, the second year's bonus at $t = 2$, etc. Only the fifth year's bonus is determined on the maturity date.

- **Forward-starting barrier.** In four out of five cases the barrier level is fixed one or more years after inception. The first year's barrier is fixed at $t = 0$. However, the second year's barrier is fixed at $t = 1$, the third year's barrier at $t = 2$, etc.

Knowing that the bank can obtain the required bonus payments by buying **digital calls** we can solve the bonus rate from the budget equation given by

$$PVC = e^{-5r_5}(N \times 5F) + N \times B \times \sum_{i=1}^{5} DC_0^a[\gamma I_{i-1}, i, 5], \qquad (12.6)$$

where $DC_0^a[H, t, T]$ denotes the derivatives firm's offer for a digital call which pays off 1.00 at time T if at time t the index is equal to or higher than H. With a yearly floor rate of -1% and a digital factor of 1.0 this yields a yearly bonus rate of 10%. In other words, under the assumptions made, the note can be structured such that the note return increases by 9% for every year that the index goes up.

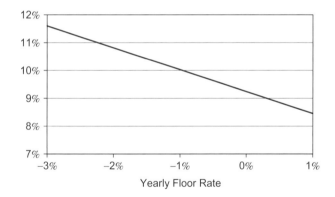

Figure 12.4 Trade-off between yearly floor rate and yearly payoff rate for a digital principal protected cliquet bull note

Figure 12.4 shows the trade-off between the yearly **floor rate** and the yearly payoff rate for the digital cliquet note, assuming a digital factor of 1.0. Of course, the trade-off is very similar to what we saw before for the digital principal protected bull note. The payoff rate drops when the floor rate rises. The trade-off between the **digital factor** and the yearly payoff rate can be found in Figure 12.5. The yearly floor rate is -1%. Figure 12.5 is similar to Figure 12.3, except that it is a lot steeper for higher values of γ. This reflects the fact that this time everything is done on a yearly basis instead of on a 5-year basis. With a digital factor of 1.1 the index has to rise 10% in one year to secure the bonus. With the digital principal protected bull note on the other hand, the index has five years to do so.

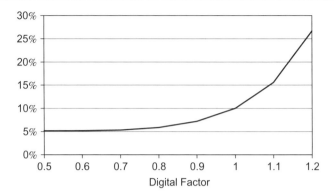

Figure 12.5 Trade-off between digital factor and yearly payoff rate for a digital principal protected cliquet bull note

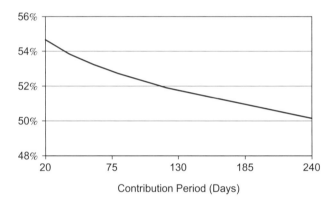

Figure 12.6 Trade-off between length of contribution period and lifetime payoff rate for a digital principal protected cliquet bull note

Figure 12.6 shows the trade-off between the length of the **contribution period** and the lifetime payoff rate, i.e. the periodic payoff rate times the number of contribution periods, assuming a yearly floor rate of -1% and a digital factor of 1.0. The graph shows that **the lifetime payoff rate drops when the contribution period gets longer**. This reflects the way in which the payoff at maturity builds up. The longer the contribution periods, the more likely each period is to generate a bonus, i.e. the more likely the index is to go up. In the extreme case of only one contribution period, the digital principal protected cliquet note would be identical to a digital principal protected bull note and offer a payoff rate of only 43.9%. Conversely, the shorter the contribution period, the higher the probability that some periods do not generate a bonus. To compensate for this, the lifetime payoff rate for short contribution periods has to be higher than for longer contribution periods.

12.2.3 Bivariate Digital Principal Protected Cliquet Bull Note

Digital principal protected cliquet notes have been quite popular with retail investors in the UK, where they are sometimes referred to as **escalator bonds**. The popularity of these notes is not surprising since the payoff principle is extremely easy to explain and understand. There is no reason why the concept should remain limited to just one reference index. We can very easily copy it to the case of two reference indices by saying that investors will receive their bonus only if both reference indices go up by more than a given percentage. If one of them or both of them go down investors only receive the floor rate. In this case the note payoff would be equal to

$$X_5 = N \times \left(1 + 5F + \sum_{i=1}^{5} D_i \times B \right), \tag{12.7}$$

where

$$D_i = 0, \quad \text{if } I_i^1 < \gamma_1 I_{i-1}^1 \text{ and/or } I_i^2 < \gamma_2 I_{i-1}^2,$$
$$= 1, \quad \text{if } I_i^1 \geqslant \gamma_1 I_{i-1}^1 \text{ and } I_i^2 \geqslant \gamma_2 I_{i-1}^2.$$

This is identical to the case with only one reference index except that the bonus is now triggered by two indices instead of one. Because of this the probability of receiving a bonus decreases, which allows for an increase of the bonus rate. We can express the amount to be paid by the derivatives firm and the resulting budget equation in exactly the same way as before, except that we are now talking about **bivariate digital calls**. Under the same assumptions as before and assuming the correlation coefficient between the returns on the two indices is 0.5, this yields a yearly bonus rate of 15.6% and thus a yearly payoff rate of 14.6%.

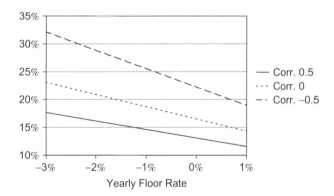

Figure 12.7 Trade-off between yearly floor rate and yearly payoff rate for a bivariate digital principal protected cliquet bull note

Assuming a digital factor of 1.0, Figure 12.7 shows the trade-off between the yearly **floor rate** and the yearly payoff rate for correlation coefficients between the returns on both indices of 0.5, 0 and −0.5. Apart from the fact that a higher floor rate implies a lower payoff rate, Figure 12.7 also makes it clear that much depends on the degree of correlation between the returns on both indices. With a correlation coefficient of 1, both indices are effectively the same and the bivariate cliquet note is identical to the univariate cliquet note discussed earlier. However, with imperfect correlation the probability of receiving a bonus decreases as both indices may not move in the same direction. As a result, the expected payoff falls and the bonus rate rises. Given the floor rate, **the lower the correlation, the higher the payoff rate**.

Figure 12.8 shows the trade-off between the **digital factor** and the yearly payoff rate, assuming a yearly floor rate of −1%. As with the univariate cliquet note, the payoff rate increases with the digital factor, with little happening if the digital factor moves below 0.8. However, as we get to higher digital factors the payoff rate on the bivariate cliquet note appears to increase much faster than on the univariate cliquet note. How much faster depends again on the correlation between both index returns. The lower the correlation, the higher the increase. This reflects the fact that for low levels of correlation it is quite unlikely that investors will receive their bonus. Figure 12.9 shows the trade-off between the length of the **contribution period** and the lifetime payoff rate, again assuming correlation coefficients of 0.5, 0 and −0.5. The yearly floor rate is −1% and the digital factor 1.0. As with the univariate cliquet note, the payoff rate drops when the contribution period grows longer.

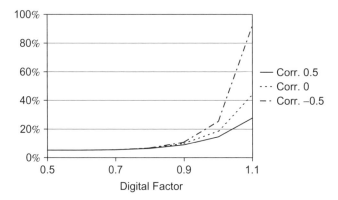

Figure 12.8 Trade-off between digital factor and yearly payoff rate for a bivariate digital principal protected cliquet bull note

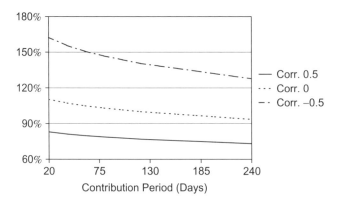

Figure 12.9 Trade-off between length of contribution period and lifetime payoff rate for a bivariate digital principal protected cliquet bull note

12.2.4   Digital Principal Protected Range Accrual Note

With the principal protected range accrual note discussed in Chapter 11 the contribution of every month depends on the value of the reference index at the end of that month. The closer the index is to its value at the beginning of the note's life, the higher that month's contribution to the payoff at maturity. Some might argue that this is not right. The only thing that should matter is whether the index ends the month within the range. If it does, the note should pay a bonus equal to a prefixed amount. If not, investors should make the floor rate. This means digitalizing the note to produce a payoff equal to

$$X_2 = N \times \left(1 + 24F + \sum_{i=1}^{24} D_i \times B \right), \tag{12.8}$$

where B denotes the monthly bonus rate and

$$D_i = 0, \quad \text{if } I_{i/12} \leqslant H^1 \text{ or } I_{i/12} \geqslant H^2,$$
$$= 1, \quad \text{if } H_1 < I_{i/12} < H^2.$$

If at the end of month i the index is not between the two range boundaries that month only contributes F to the note's return. If on the other hand the index is within the range, the month contributes $F + B$. In other words, if the index ends in the range investors receives a bonus of B on top of the floor rate of F. All payable on the note's maturity date of course. Note that the bonus part of (12.8) is nothing more than what in Chapter 4 we referred to as a **hamster**.

By digitalizing the principal protected range accrual note things become a lot simpler as we no longer need to produce the pyramid shaped monthly payoff we saw before in Figure 11.12. As a result, we can do without all the call and put payoffs that made pricing the note so complicated. It is all digitals now, as is also clear from the expression for the amount payable by the derivatives firm, which is given by

$$V_2 = N \times 24F + N \times B \times \sum_{i=1}^{24} D_i. \tag{12.9}$$

Apart from the fixed amount corresponding to the guaranteed minimum return, the derivatives firm pays the bank an index-linked amount equal to $N \times B$ times the sum of the payoffs of 24 **digital spreads**. The budget equation for the digital principal protected range accrual note is therefore given by

$$PVC = e^{-2r_2}(N \times 24F) + N \times B \times \sum_{i=1}^{24} DS_0^a[H^1, H^2, i/12, 2], \tag{12.10}$$

where $DS_0^a[H^1, H^2, t, T]$ is the derivatives firm's offer for a digital spread paying 1.00 at time T if at time t the index is between H^1 and H^2. Assuming a monthly floor rate of $-2/24\%$ and range width 20, this yields a monthly bonus rate of 1.12% and therefore a monthly payoff rate of 1.04%. Note that there is nothing fancy about the above digital spread. It is nothing more than a **European double barrier knock-out digital**. If at the time of monitoring the index is found outside the range defined by the barriers, the cash flow knocks out. As mentioned before, a payoff like this can easily be packaged from digital calls or puts.

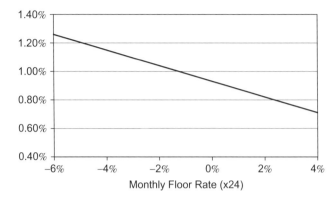

Figure 12.10 Trade-off between monthly floor rate and monthly payoff rate for a digital principal protected range accrual note

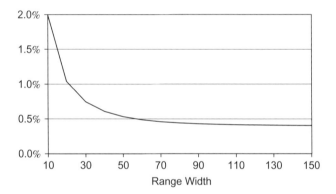

Figure 12.11 Trade-off between range width and monthly payoff rate for a digital principal protected range accrual note

For a range width of 20, Figure 12.10 shows the trade-off between the monthly **floor rate** and the monthly payoff rate. As usual, the payoff rate drops when the floor rate increases. The trade-off between the **range width** and the monthly payoff rate can be found in Figure 12.11. For a relatively narrow range the payoff rate is quite high because it needs to compensate the low probability of finding the index within that range. As the range widens, the probability of a bonus increases. This requires the payoff rate to come down. Figure 12.12 shows the trade-off between the length of the **contribution period** and the lifetime payoff rate, assuming the range is between 90 and 110. Contrary to the cliquet notes, **the payoff rate increases with the length of the contribution period**. This reflects the probability of receiving a bonus, i.e. finding the index within the range, decreasing when the contribution period becomes longer.

12.2.5 Digital Principal Protected Knock-Out Range Accrual Note

We can digitalize principal protected knock-out range accrual notes in exactly the same way. The resulting payoff formula would be the same as before, except that the digital

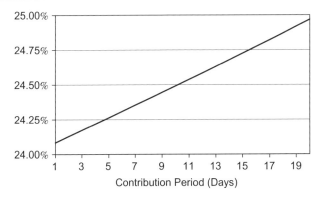

Figure 12.12 Trade-off between length of contribution period and lifetime payoff rate for a digital principal protected range accrual note

D_i would now be given by

$$D_i = 0, \quad \text{if } \exists j \ I_j \leqslant H^1 \text{ or } I_j \geqslant H^2,$$
$$= 1, \quad \text{if } \forall j \ H^1 < I_j < H^2$$

where j counts the monitoring points between $t = 0$ and $t = i/12$. As long as the index stays within the range investors get a bonus equal to a prefixed amount. However, as soon as the index comes out of the range, all future bonuses are set to zero. In other words, if the index hits a range boundary the note return is fixed at a rate equal to the return accumulated so far plus the floor rate times the number of full months left to maturity plus one.

The amount payable by the derivatives firm in this case is given by the same expression as before, except that this time the derivatives firm pays the bank an index-linked amount equal to $N \times B$ times the sum of the payoffs of 24 **American double barrier knock-out digitals**. The budget equation for the digital principal protected range accrual note is therefore given by

$$PVC = e^{-2r_2}(N \times 24F) + N \times B \times \sum_{i=1}^{24} AOD_0^a[H^1, H^2, 0, i/12, 2]. \qquad (12.11)$$

With a monthly floor rate of $-2/24\%$ and range boundaries at 80 and 120 this yields a monthly bonus rate of 1.11% and therefore a payoff rate of 1.03%.

For a range between 80 and 120 Figure 12.13 shows the trade-off between the monthly **floor rate** and the monthly payoff rate. We also included the results one would have obtained for an equivalent standard range accrual note with range width 40. The graph clearly shows the effect of the knock-out feature. It should be noted that, as with the knock-out range accrual note discussed in Chapter 11, it is not only the occurrence but also the timing of the knock-out that is important here. Since the note payoff accumulates as long as the index does not move outside the range, a knock-out close to maturity can do little harm any more. Reflecting the substantial probability of an early knock-out, Figure 12.13 shows that with a range between 80 and 120 the payoff rate on the knock-out note will be around twice as high as that on the standard note.

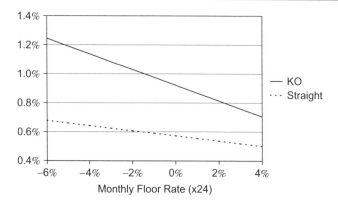

Figure 12.13 Trade-off between monthly floor rate and monthly payoff rate for a digital principal protected knock-out range accrual note

Figure 12.14 shows the trade-off between the **range width** and the monthly payoff rate. As before, the wider the range, the lower the payoff rate. The graph shows clearly that the difference between the knock-out note and the standard range accrual note becomes smaller when the range widens. From a range width of 100 onwards, i.e. range boundaries of 50 and 150, there is hardly any difference in the payoff rate any more. This reflects that for these ranges it is highly unlikely that the note will knock out relatively early. The effect of changing the length of the **contribution period**, again assuming a range width of 40, can be found in Figure 12.15. As with the standard range accrual note, the payoff rate tends to rise slightly when the contribution period grows longer because it becomes less likely for the index to stay in the range.

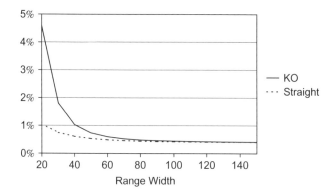

Figure 12.14 Trade-off between range width and monthly payoff rate for a digital principal protected knock-out range accrual note

Although the knock-out range accrual note offers a much higher bonus rate, the fact that once the index hits one of the boundaries the possibility of accumulating additional bonuses is lost could present a problem. We can solve this by saying that if during a month the index hits a barrier only that month's bonus is lost. All months to follow are

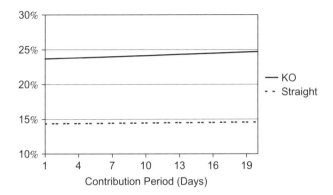

Figure 12.15   Trade-off between length of contribution period and lifetime payoff rate for a digital principal protected knock-out range accrual note

still able to generate bonuses. To price such a note all we have to do is prevent both barriers from becoming active right from inception. In other words, the budget equation for a note like this is given by

$$PVC = e^{-2r_2}(N \times 24F) + N \times B \times \sum_{i=1}^{24} AOD_0^a[H^1, H^2, (i-1)/12, i/12, 2]. \quad (12.12)$$

It is easy to think of other variations. In fact, since basically we are talking about hamsters, we already discussed a number of them in Chapter 4. We will therefore not do so again here but continue with the problem of providing investors with intermediate coupons.

12.3   NOTES WITH INTERMEDIATE COUPONS

Sometimes buying zero-coupon notes may not fit in with investors' cash flow or tax planning or simply not be allowed. In those cases we have to structure a note which pays intermediate coupons. Doing so, we can follow either one of two approaches. We can (a) add a fixed coupon to an existing zero-coupon note, or (b) spread the payment that the zero-coupon note makes on top of the redemption of principal over a number of coupons that are paid during the life of the note. We discuss fixed coupons first.

12.3.1   Fixed Coupons

Sometimes regulation requires a note to pay coupons. In that case adding a small fixed coupon is often the easiest solution. Suppose we had a standard 5-year principal protected bull note which we wanted to equip with a fixed annual coupon. This is easy to arrange. One way is to let the bank pay the coupons to the investor while deducting those payments from the coupons paid to the derivatives firm. Alternatively, the bank could pay the derivatives firm the usual coupons while in return the derivatives firm would not only pay the regular payment at maturity but also the desired intermediate coupons. The derivatives firm would pay the coupons to the bank and the bank would pass those coupons on to the holders of the note.

Let's take a closer look at the latter alternative. Of course, the derivatives firm is not going to do this for free. The coupons will have to come out of the PVC. In other words, the budget equation now becomes

$$PVC - \sum_{i=1}^{5} e^{-ir_i}(N \times C) = e^{-5r_5}(N \times F) + \alpha M \times C_0^a \left[I_0 \left(1 + \frac{F}{\alpha} \right), 5 \right], \quad (12.13)$$

where C denotes the **coupon rate**. The second term on the left-hand side equals the present value of the coupons which the derivatives firm now has to pay to the bank. Since the coupon rate is never negative and PVC is given, introducing intermediate coupons reduces the amount of money available to buy call options. As a result, the note's participation rate will drop. This is shown very clearly in Figure 12.16, which shows the trade-off between the coupon rate and the participation rate.

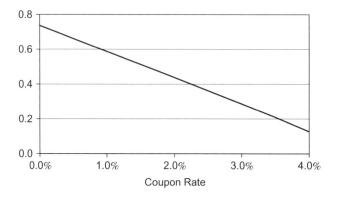

Figure 12.16 Trade-off between coupon rate and participation rate for a principal protected bull note

In a way, the introduction of coupons is similar to an increase of the floor rate. If we do not change the floor rate, investors get more protection from a coupon note than from a zero-coupon note. When adding a coupon we should therefore lower the floor rate to compensate for this. At maturity the coupons paid during the note's life are worth

$$C_T = \sum_{i=0}^{4} e^{ir_i}(N \times C). \quad (12.14)$$

The most obvious thing to do then is to reduce the floor rate by C_T/N. It should be noted that this will not take us back to the old participation rate of 0.74 though. If the index drops, the coupon note with the lower floor rate and the original zero-coupon note will provide the same payoff. If the index rises, however, investors still receive their coupons on top of the regular note payoff. The participation rate will therefore still be significantly lower. This is also shown in Figure 12.17, which shows the trade-off between the coupon rate and the participation rate assuming a floor rate equal to $-0.05 - C_T/N$. The graph shows that although we gain a little on the upside when the floor is lowered, on balance **the introduction of non-zero coupons causes a significant drop in the participation rate**.

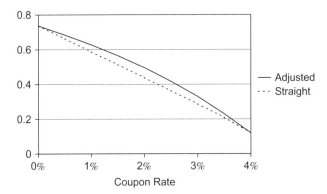

Figure 12.17 Trade-off between coupon rate and participation rate for a principal protected bull note with adjusted floor

12.3.2 Index-Linked Coupons

Another way to create intermediate coupons is to split the original payoff at maturity into a number of separate parts and spread those over the note's lifetime. Cliquet and range accrual notes are the easiest to break up as their payoff gradually accumulates over their life. Instead of accumulating every year's contribution until maturity, we can simply pay those contributions out as soon as they can be calculated. Compared to a zero coupon note this will again reduce the participation rate or the bonus rate because the derivatives firm can no longer hang on to the money until maturity. We discuss two examples to clarify the principle.

Let's look at a 5-year **digital principal protected cliquet bull note** with annual contributions. With this note the payment at maturity (on top of the return of the notional) is calculated by summing the payoff contributions of the five individual years that make up the note's time to maturity. If we pay out these contributions as soon as they arise, the derivatives firm would have to pay the bank an annual coupon equal to

$$C_i = N \times (F + D_i \times B), \quad i = 1, 2, 3, 4, 5, \tag{12.15}$$

where D_i has the same meaning as before. From this expression we see that every year the derivatives firm pays the bank an index-linked amount identical to the payoff of a **digital call**. Contrary to the zero-coupon note, however, these digitals now pay off on the same date the index is monitored for a barrier hit. We can therefore calculate the bonus rate from the budget equation given by

$$PVC = \sum_{i=1}^{5} (e^{-ir_i}(N \times F) + N \times B \times DC_0^a[\gamma I_{i-1}, i]). \tag{12.16}$$

This expression is very similar to the one we had before except that (a) the present value of the guaranteed minimum payments is higher because the money is paid out earlier, and (b) the first four digital calls will be more expensive because they now pay out on their respective monitoring dates instead of the note's maturity date. Under the assumptions made we therefore obtain a significantly lower yearly payoff rate of 9.3% (compared to 10.0% for the zero-coupon case).

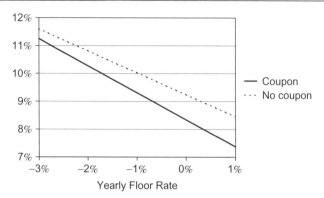

Figure 12.18 Trade-off between yearly floor rate and yearly payoff rate for a digital principal protected coupon cliquet bull note

Figure 12.18 shows the trade-off between the yearly **floor rate** and the yearly payoff rate for the digital cliquet note, assuming a digital factor of 1.0. The graph shows that **the coupon note replicates the behavior of the zero-coupon note but at a lower level**. Also, when the floor rate gets higher, the drop in the payoff rate of the coupon note accelerates. This reflects the fact that in the coupon note there is less money available to buy upside with, which becomes especially problematic when choosing a relatively high floor rate.

As a second example of turning a zero into a coupon note, let's look at a 2-year **digital principal protected range accrual note** with monthly contributions. Since the note pays the sum of 24 monthly contributions we can very easily turn this into a note with monthly index-linked coupons by instead of accumulating all contributions until maturity paying them out as soon as they are determined. In doing so, the derivatives firm would have to pay the bank a monthly coupon equal to

$$C_i = N \times (F + D_i \times B), \quad i = 1, 2, \ldots, 24, \tag{12.17}$$

where D_i has the same meaning as before. Again, this does not give rise to major changes in the budget equation, which in this case is given by the expression

$$PVC = \sum_{i=1}^{24} (e^{-i/12r_{i/12}} (N \times F) + N \times B \times DS_0^a[H^1, H^2, i/12]). \tag{12.18}$$

Under the same assumptions as before this yields a monthly payoff rate of 0.98% (compared to 1.04% for the zero-coupon case). Assuming range boundaries at 90 and 110, the trade-off between the monthly **floor rate** and the monthly payoff rate can be found in Figure 12.19. As we saw earlier with the cliquet note, the coupon range accrual note behaves very much like its zero-coupon counterpart but, because there is less money available to spend on upside participation, at a somewhat lower level.

12.4 CONCLUSION

In this final chapter on equity-linked notes we discussed how to digitalize notes and how to equip them with intermediate coupons. We saw that the payoffs of the digitalized versions

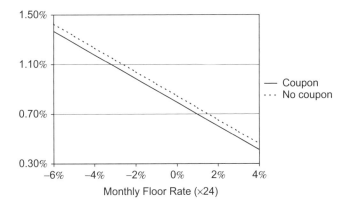

Figure 12.19   Trade-off between monthly floor rate and monthly payoff rate for a digital principal protected coupon range accrual note

of even quite sophisticated notes tend to be quite straightforward, which explains their popularity. Intermediate coupons, whether they be fixed or index-linked, tend to raise a note's expected payoff. As a result, a coupon paying note will offer a lower participation rate or bonus rate than an equivalent zero-coupon note. Looking at the budget equation leads to the same conclusion. Paying coupons reduces the amount of money available to buy upside with.

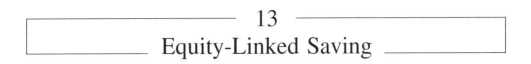

13
Equity-Linked Saving

13.1 INTRODUCTION

One problem with principal protected notes is that they are aimed at investors who already have money. This leaves a large group of people who might like to invest in equity but who simply do not have enough cash available (yet). Although the direct purchase of investment products is not an option, there is an alternative way for people like this to obtain the equity exposure they desire. They can enter into a swap contract with a product provider (typically a bank or insurance company) where over some period of time they pay the latter periodically, say monthly or quarterly, a fixed amount and in return receive an index-linked payment at maturity. In this way they obtain equity exposure without making an upfront payment. We refer to these type of products as **equity-linked savings products**.

ASSUMPTIONS & NOTATION

In this chapter we discuss a number of equity-linked savings products in more detail assuming that over a period of five years investors make 60 monthly payments of 100 to the product provider. As before, we will refer to the latter as 'the bank'. Otherwise we stick to the assumptions and notation introduced in Chapter 9.

13.2 UNPROTECTED EQUITY-LINKED SAVING

With investors making 60 monthly payments of 100, the question is what equity-linked payment at maturity the bank can offer them in return. The simplest solution is for the bank to take the investors' money every month and invest it in some stock or stock portfolio as soon as it comes in. At maturity the bank would liquidate the portfolio and pay the proceeds to the investors. One major problem with such a **buy-as-you-go scheme** is that neither the bank nor the investors know in advance what the payoff is going to be. If the index goes up, the bank can buy the investors less shares and if it goes down it can buy them more. Of course, the bank need not necessarily buy stocks. If it wanted a less risky product the bank could buy principal protected notes. If it wanted a more risky product the bank could buy forwards or ordinary call options. All these alternatives, however, suffer from the same deficiency: we cannot tell what the payoff is going to look like. Another problem with buy-as-you-go products is that the exposure builds up very slowly over time. For investors who want instant exposure, products like these are not very attractive. In this section we therefore discuss two products that solve these problems.

Suppose investors wanted to invest in a single reference index that paid no dividends. This index could be a single stock or a stock market index, but also a fund participation. In that case the bank could offer them a payment at maturity equal to

$$X_5 = M \times I_5,$$ (13.1)

where M is a constant. This payoff looks very much like the payoff of a buy-as-you-go scheme, but there is one important difference: the multiplier is fixed at $t = 0$. We will refer to this payoff as **product 1**. Since the investors pay only 100 every month, it is intuitively clear that the multiplier in (13.1) cannot be very large. If it was exposure investors were after we can do a lot better though. The bank could for example offer them a payoff equal to

$$X_5 = M \times I_5 - N_5, \tag{13.2}$$

where the **terminal lump sum** N_5 is a fixed amount. We will refer to this payoff as **product 2**.

Pricing

To be able to say more about the multiplier of product 1 or the multiplier and the terminal lump sum of product 2 we have to understand how the bank is going to hedge itself. One way is to do the same as with a structured note issue. The bank could approach a derivatives firm and enter into the same swap as the one with the investors and simply pass all payments through (after taking out a profit margin of course). The investors pay the bank 100 per month for five years. Suppose the latter took a profit of 5.62 out of every 100 and passed the remainder through to the derivatives firm. The derivatives firm would receive 60 monthly payments of 94.38, which it values at 5000. The multiplier and the terminal lump sum therefore have to be determined such that the index-linked payment to be made by the derivatives firm at maturity is worth 5000.

Taking a closer look at the payoff of **product 1** we see that it is identical to the payoff of M index participations. Assuming the derivatives firm hedges itself in the cash market and for simplicity abstracting from transaction costs, tracking error, profit margin, etc., to hedge one index participation the derivatives firm will need to invest an amount $I_0 = 100$ in the index. Since it has 5000 available, this means that the firm can offer a multiplier of 50. In other words, in return for 60 monthly payments of 100 investors will receive the value of 50 shares of the index five years from now.

We can do the same for **product 2**. At maturity, the derivatives firm has to pay an amount $M \times I_5 - N_5$. This amount consists of two parts. The first part is the payoff of M index participations. This can be hedged by purchasing M shares in the index, which currently trades at I_0. The second part can be hedged by borrowing an amount equal to $e^{-5r}N_5$, as this creates a debt of N_5 at maturity. The proceeds of the loan can be used to buy stocks. The budget equation for product 2 is therefore given by

$$5000 = M \times I_0 - e^{-5r_5}N_5. \tag{13.3}$$

The budget equation for product 2 leaves some freedom as to the values of the parameters involved. We can choose the terminal lump sum and use (13.3) to find the corresponding value of the multiplier, or we can choose the multiplier and solve for the terminal lump sum.

Figure 13.1 shows the terminal lump sum as a function of the multiplier. If we set $M = 50$ the terminal lump sum equals zero, taking us back to product 1. Since I_5 will always be equal to or larger than zero, the only risk the bank runs here is that the investors fail to make their monthly payments. This changes if we move on to higher multiplier values. **With a multiplier higher than 50, the terminal lump sum will be higher than**

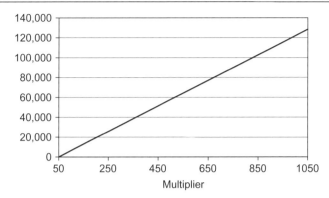

Figure 13.1   Terminal lump sum as a function of multiplier

zero. Since the value of the equity part of the payoff can theoretically drop to zero, the bank and the investors are now confronted with the risk of a negative payoff. Obviously, this risk increases with the multiplier. If we set $M = 500$ the terminal lump sum will be equal to 57,781. This means that product 2 provides investors with a negative payoff if at maturity the index is below 115.56. If we set $M = 1000$ the terminal lump sum will be equal to 121,983. This means that product 2 provides investors with a negative payoff if at maturity the index is below 121.98. How the index value below which the payoff of product 2 is negative varies with the multiplier is shown in Figure 13.2. Unlike what one might expect, if the multiplier increases, the index value below which the payoff of product 2 is negative converges to an index level of $e^{5r} \times I_0 = 128.4$.

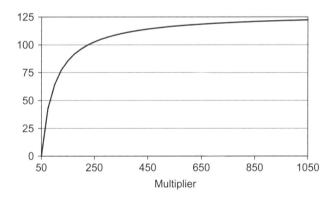

Figure 13.2   Index value below which payoff of product 2 is negative as a function of multiplier

We can set the multiplier of product 2 to any value we want, but a very interesting choice is to set the multiplier such that $N_5 = M \times I_0$. In that case investors receive a payoff at maturity equal to $M \times (I_5 - I_0)$, i.e. M times the change in the value of the index. Doing so yields a multiplier of 226. In other words, by making 60 monthly payments of 100 investors would acquire a payoff of 226 times the change in the value of the index over the next five years. We can calculate the investors' return as a function of the index value at maturity if we relate the product payoff to the present value of their monthly payments

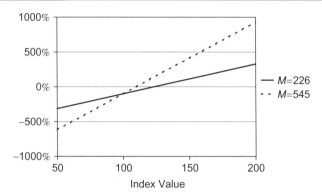

Figure 13.3   Investors' return as a function of index value at maturity

(which is 5298). The result is shown in Figure 13.3 (for $M = 226$). If the index rises by 60% investors receive an amount of 13,560. This represents a return of 156%. If the index goes up by 100% investors make 327%. Throughout the remainder of this chapter we will concentrate on the above version of product 2.

If the index dropped by 10% every investor would owe the bank an amount of 2260. The present value of 5.62 out of every 100, however, is only 298. This brings up the question of whether taking 5 out of every 100 is enough to compensate the bank for the credit risk it is taking. In answering this question two points have to be kept in mind. First, the probability that the index shows a drop over a 5-year period is relatively small. Assuming index returns are normally distributed with an expected annual return of 10% and an annual volatility of 20%, the probability of a 5-year return lower than zero is only about 13%. Second, we are talking about a retail product here. If successful, the product will be sold to tens of thousands of investors. Although they will all lose if the index drops, most of them will pay up, i.e. **the credit risk will be well diversified**.

In the context of credit risk it is also interesting to note that with the assumed flat and constant term structure of interest rates and $N_5 = M \times I_0$ the multiplier in product 2 is independent of the maturity of the product. With a 6-year maturity we would have ended up with a multiplier of 226 as well. This means that in case the index drops and the product payoff is negative the bank can offer investors an extension of the contract at no extra cost. Investors could continue to pay their monthly coupons of 100 and at the new maturity date they would still be paid 226 times the change in the index. The mirror image of the right to extend a contract is the right to make it mature prematurely. We could therefore also structure a long-dated contract and offer investors the possibility of exercising the contract early.

Dividends

So far we have assumed that the index does not pay any dividends. If it does, this changes the pricing of products 1 and 2 significantly. Since the product only pays the value of the index at maturity, dividends are left with the derivatives firm. This raises the amount received by the latter and therefore allows it to quote a higher multiplier. Suppose the index paid a fixed annual dividend of 3.00 per share. The present value to the derivatives firm of all dividends received on the index over the product's life would in that case be

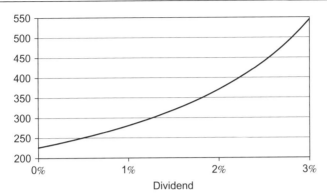

Figure 13.4 Multiplier as a function of annual dividend

equal to 12.95 per share of the index. This means that it can generate an amount of I_5 at a cost of $I_0 - 12.95 = 87.05$, which yields a multiplier of a little over 57; a significant improvement over the 50 we had before. We can do the same for product 2. This yields a multiplier equal to a staggering 545, compared to 226 before.

Figure 13.3 (for $M = 545$) shows the return on product 2 as a function of the index value at maturity. Comparing this graph with that for the zero dividend case ($M = 226$) makes it clear how serious the impact of dividends is. Figure 13.4 shows the multiplier of product 2 as a function of the annual dividend paid by the index. Many retail investors have little preference when it comes to stock selection other than that they want well-known names. Since **stocks that pay relatively high dividends allow for a high multiplier**, this allows us to beef up products 1 and 2 by using (a basket of) exactly those stocks as reference index.

Future dividends are not known with certainty. Since companies tend to be reluctant to reduce dividends, however, the assumption that future dividends will at least equal last year's dividend carries little downside risk. Another way to deal with dividend risk is to let investors absorb it themselves. In other words, if dividends do not turn out as expected at the time the product was priced investors will be asked to pay the difference. We discussed this before in Chapter 6. Instead of leaving the dividends with the derivatives firm we can of course also pass them on to the investors as they come in. Whether this makes for a better product is primarily a tax issue. Because the derivatives firm might be able to obtain certain tax advantages, it could be advantageous to leave them with the firm. On the other hand, in order to obtain a favorable tax treatment for the product at the investors' level it may be necessary to pass them on to the investors. We will come back to this later.

13.3 PROTECTED EQUITY-LINKED SAVING

An appealing level of equity exposure can only be obtained at the cost of higher downside risk for the investors. It is therefore worthwhile to look for ways to limit this risk. One way to do so is to give investors the right to cancel the contract at maturity. Since they will do so only if they have to pay, this means offering investors a payoff at maturity equal to

$$X_5 = M \times \text{Max}\,[0, I_5 - I_0]\,. \tag{13.4}$$

With a payoff like this investors receive an amount equal to a multiple of the change in the index value over the product's life, but only if the latter is positive. In return the investors make the usual 60 monthly payments of 100. We will refer to this payoff as **product 3**.

To be able to price the above product we need a budget equation. We can derive the latter in the same way as before. Under the swap agreement investors make 60 monthly payments of 100 to the bank. The latter takes a profit of 5.62 out of every 100 for himself and passes the remainder on to the derivatives firm that provides the required payoff. Since $\text{Max}[0, I_5 - I_0]$ is nothing more than the payoff of an ATM **ordinary call**, the budget equation is given by

$$5000 = M \times C_0[I_0, 5]. \tag{13.5}$$

The derivatives firm's offer for the call is 29.14%. The multiplier which the bank can offer investors is therefore equal to 172. As discussed in Chapter 7, ordinary calls become cheaper if the reference index pays dividends. This means that we can raise the participation rate of product 3 by selecting a reference index with a high dividend yield. With an annual dividend yield of 3% the option price comes down from 29.14% to 18.96%. As a result, the multiplier goes up from 172 to 264.

13.4 ALTERNATIVE HEDGES

So far we have assumed that the bank hedges itself by entering into a swap with a derivatives firm. This is not the only possibility though. Since hedging an index participation boils down to nothing more than buying the index, the bank could cut the derivatives firm out and easily hedge **product 1** itself. The bank could sell the stream of 60 monthly payments it will receive from the investors in the market and use the proceeds to buy the index. At maturity it would then liquidate the position and pay the investors. Although we speak of 'selling the 60 monthly payments in the market' this is of course nothing more than borrowing. The amount the bank borrows has to be such that the 60 monthly payments made by the investors are exactly enough to pay the interest on the loan as well as redeem it.

Product 2 can be hedged in the same way except that the size of the loan is larger now. With product 2 the monthly payments made by the investors are no longer enough to cover both interest and redemption, which is why the investors have to pay an additional lump sum at maturity. We might refer to this form of leverage as **aggressive leverage**, as opposed to the previous **conservative leverage** where the investors' monthly payments equal the combined payment of interest and redemption. Aggressive leverage can range from giving investors a little more exposure than with conservative leverage to giving them a lot more. Although the distinction between interest and redemption is artificial, we can think about it as follows. Starting with a conservatively leveraged position, if we increase the size of the loan, the redemption component in the investors' monthly payments shrinks and starts building up in the terminal lump sum. If we continue to increase the loan size we reach a point where the investors' monthly payments become pure interest payments. At this point the terminal lump sum equals the full size of the loan, i.e. $N_5 = M \times I_0$. Increasing the loan beyond this point means that apart from redemption, the terminal lump sum also contains an interest component.

If the multiplier in product 2 is chosen such that $N_5 = M \times I_0$ investors receive a payoff equal to $M \times (I_5 - I_0)$. Looking at this payoff more closely, we see that it is nothing

Table 13.1   Equity-linked savings products

Asset bought	Conservative leverage	Aggressive leverage
Stocks	Product 1	Product 2
Forwards	Product 2	
Calls	Product 3	

more than M times the amount investors would have received if they had entered into a forward contract where they paid the starting value of the index and received the index value at maturity. The bank can therefore hedge the issuance of product 2 not only by aggressively leveraging the purchase of the index, but also by conservatively leveraging the purchase of M off-market **forwards**. This shows that **conservative leverage is not necessarily less risky than aggressive leverage.** It all depends on how much implicit leverage there is in the assets that are purchased with the proceeds of the loan.

Product 3 can be interpreted in the same way. As we saw, the payoff of product 3 can be obtained by the conservatively leveraged purchase of **ordinary calls**. Table 13.1 summarizes the hedging alternatives for products 1, 2 and 3 using the concept of leveraged buying.

13.5   THE MARKETER'S PERSPECTIVE

The next question is how to present these products to the public. Let's look at **product 1** first. Irrespective of how the bank hedges itself, it acts as a swap provider to its investors. The investors periodically pay a fixed amount and in return the bank provides a payoff equal to the value of a certain number of stocks. Given what we discussed in the previous section, however, we can also present the bank as a financial intermediary that offers investors loans and at the same time arranges for the purchase of equity with the proceeds of those loans. We can explain product 1 by saying that investors borrow 5000 at $t = 0$ and invest the proceeds in equity. The loan is paid for and redeemed by 60 monthly payments of 100. At maturity the investors are free of debt and the stocks are theirs. The implied interest rate on the loan would be 7.4%.

A similar story can be told for **product 2**, where the investors effectively buy forwards. At $t = 0$ investors borrow 22,600 and invest the proceeds in equity. The interest on the loan is paid in the form of 60 monthly payments of 100. At maturity investors sell their stocks and redeem the loan. If the stocks are worth more than 22,600 they make a profit and otherwise they show a loss. The implied interest rate would be 5.3%. This is lower than for product 1 because the amount borrowed is higher while the bank's profit is unchanged.

We can present **product 3**, where the investors effectively buy ordinary calls, in a similar way. Investors borrow 17,200 and invest the proceeds in equity. This is identical to product 2. However, in the event that the stocks end up worth less than 17,200, the bank makes up for their loss. The implied interest rate would be 6.9%. This is higher than with product 2 for two reasons. First, the amount borrowed is lower. Second, investors have to pay for the guarantee. Apart from possible tax benefits, presenting product 3 in this way offers significant marketing opportunities. Who would not want to invest with a friendly financial intermediary that not only provides investors with loans at unbeatable rates and arranges for the purchase of equity at zero cost but which also guarantees that investors will never lose?!

Presenting products 1, 2 and 3 as leveraged equity purchases instead of as swaps may have significant tax consequences. Until recently, Dutch retail investors for example were allowed to deduct the interest paid on loans used to buy equity from their taxable income. With a 60% marginal income tax rate this made leveraged products where the interest paid is readily observable very attractive. With products 2 and 3 the monthly payment would be fully tax deductible. After tax a Dutch investor would therefore only pay 40 per month instead of 100. Note that to obtain favorable tax treatment it may be necessary for the bank to physically deliver stocks to the investors at maturity, instead of paying in cash. This emphasizes to the authorities that the investors are indeed buying stocks with borrowed money. For the same reason it may be necessary for the bank to pass all dividends on as well.

It is interesting to experiment a little more with different ways to present equity-linked savings products. Let's look at product 3 again. Instead of saying that investors will be paid a multiple times the positive change in the index, the bank can also express the payoff like that of an equity-linked note, i.e. in terms of a notional amount N, a participation rate α and the index return. This means rewriting (13.4) as

$$ X_5 = N \times \left(\text{Max} \left[0, \alpha \left(\frac{I_5 - I_0}{I_0} \right) \right] \right), \tag{13.6} $$

which is the same as

$$ X_5 = \frac{\alpha N}{I_0} \times \text{Max} \left[0, I_5 - I_0 \right]. \tag{13.7} $$

The bank now has two parameters to choose: α and N. Since nothing has changed the payoff which investors will receive at maturity, both parameters have to be set such that $\alpha N / I_0 = 172$. Making a choice, the bank has to keep in mind how investors will react. If it opts for a high notional amount and a low participation rate, investors may think they are getting a bad deal. From a marketing perspective it is therefore better to choose for a relatively low notional amount and a high participation rate. One alternative is to make the notional amount equal to the total amount paid by the investors over the product's life, i.e. 6000. This yields a participation rate of little over 2.87. In other words, the bank would pay investors 2.87 times the positive index return over a notional amount of 6000. Compared to the much lower levels of participation offered on principal protected notes this looks like a little miracle. Unfortunately, product 3 is not a principal protected note. Investing 6000 in a principal protected note with a 0% guaranteed minimum return will leave investors with at least 6000 at maturity. With product 3, however, all they are protected against is losing more than the 6000 that was put in.

13.6 THE INVESTOR'S PERSPECTIVE

So far we have first looked at what investors pay in, taken out some profit for the bank, and priced the deal up from there. This yields the best conditions the bank can offer investors given its desired profit margin and the derivatives firm's pricing. Looking back at products 1, 2 and 3 we could, however, ask ourselves whether at these prices the bank is not offering more than investors expect. If this is the case the bank can take more out of the deal without losing volume. Even if the bank lost some volume, since it makes more it can afford to do a little less.

What would investors consider a fair deal? There are several ways to answer this question. One way is to look at the **implied interest rate** and compare that with the interest rate investors could borrow at themselves. The implied interest rates for products 2 and 3 are shown in Figure 13.5 and are very interesting. With the bank taking out 5.62 of every 100 paid the implied interest rate is only 5.3% for product 2 and 6.9% for product 3, even when the interest is not tax deductible. From the graph we see that even if the bank took out 30 of every 100 the implied interest rate would not rise higher than 7.1% for product 2 and 9.4% for product 3. With non-zero dividends this will be even better. With wholesale rates at 5%, investors may not be able to borrow at these rates themselves, especially since they plan to use the proceeds to buy equity with. This strongly suggests that the bank could take out a lot more than 5.62. But there is more.

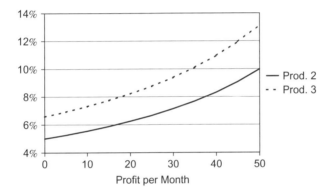

Figure 13.5 Implied interest rate as a function of monthly profit margin

We can also look at the product payoffs in **probabilistic terms**. Typically people think a gamble is fair if there is a 50–50 chance of winning and losing. So let's see what products 2 and 3 have to offer in these terms. Figure 13.6 shows the probability of a payoff lower than the present value of the payments made by the investors, assuming the index return is normally distributed with an expected annual return of 12% (a conservative estimate compared to those used in the typical marketing brochures for this type of product) and an annual volatility of 20%. Taking out 5.62 per month, the probability that the investors at least get their money back is 79% for product 2 and 74% for product 3. Figure 13.6 makes it clear, however, that if the bank took out 30 per month these probabilities would not drop very much; 74% for product 2 and 66% for product 3. It is easily calculated that if the product provider took out 30, the probability of at least doubling the money put in would be 47% for product 2 and 31% for product 3. The probability of at least tripling would be 22% for product 2 and 7% for product 3. In other words, **taking out 30 instead of 5.62 would still allow for a very impressive upside potential**. This again strongly suggests that the bank could take out a lot more than 5.62. If the bank took out a margin of 30 per month it would make an upfront profit of 1589.

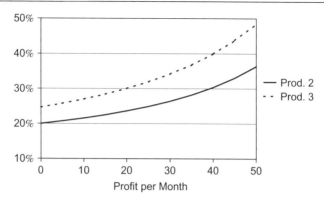

Figure 13.6   Probability payoff less than 5298 as a function of monthly profit margin

13.7   A REAL-LIFE EXAMPLE

Making 1589 by selling 127 ordinary call options worth only 3709 back-to-back may sound too fantastic to be true. Time therefore to look at a real-life example. One equity-linked savings product offered recently in The Netherlands required investors to pay 250 per month for three years. In return, the product provider would lend them 42,893 to be invested in a basket of three high yielding Dutch stocks. At maturity investors would receive the value of their stocks minus the 42,893 initially borrowed. Dividends were passed on to the investors at first but then paid back to the product provider in the form of an extra 'premium'. The way in which the product provider justified this premium is quite interesting. The product provider presented the purchase of the stocks in question as a three-step procedure. At $t = 0$ 14,298 worth of stocks was bought. At $t = 1$ another 14,298 worth of stocks was bought, and the same happened at $t = 2$. According to the product provider, the extra premium served to ensure that the stocks bought at $t = 1$ and $t = 2$ were, instead of at the prevailing prices, bought at $t = 0$ prices. Of course, in reality all stocks were bought at $t = 0$. The story of the three-step procedure just served to get the dividends back from the investors after first passing them on to emphasize that they were indeed buying equity.

Now let's see what the product provider took out of the deal. Taking the basket value as the relevant index, the payoff of the above product can be expressed as

$$X_3 = M \times I_3 - 42,893, \tag{13.8}$$

where $M = 42,893/I_0$. Let's assume the product provider hedged itself in the stock market. The first part of the above payoff can be hedged by buying M shares of the index. The cost of doing so is equal to $M \times I_0$ minus the present value of the dividends to be received on the stocks during the holding period. With a relatively high dividend yield of 2.8% and a funding rate of 4% (AA rated financial institution), the present value of the dividend is 3387. This means that to generate the first part of the above payoff the product provider needed 39,506. The second part of the payoff can be hedged by borrowing the present value of 42,893. With a 4% funding rate this is 38,043. This leaves a gap of 1463. However, at 4% the present value of the 36 monthly coupons is 8467, implying a **profit of 7004**. This may seem almost criminal, but in all fairness it should be emphasized that the marketing and operational costs of retail products can be very high.

Part of the above margin should therefore be seen as compensation for these costs and not as outright profit.

Over the last five years equity-linked savings products have become very popular in The Netherlands, with the notional outstanding now in the billions of euros. Initially, it was thought that the main reason why Dutch investors bought into equity-linked savings products was the tax advantage. When the authorities announced their plans to abolish the tax deductibility of interest, many therefore feared that the product would lose its appeal. Demand for equity-linked savings products continued to be strong, however. There are a number of possible explanations for this.

- Even with product providers taking out a very high margin, the expected payoffs are still quite fascinating, especially at the highly optimistic scenarios typically used to market these products.
- After missing out on a number of years of exceptionally strong equity market performance, retail investors simply want the exposure. Not only because they think markets will rise further, but also because they need to keep up with their neighbors. What is worse in today's society than to see your neighbor make money by doing something you could easily have done yourself as well?
- The product is acquired by paying relatively small amounts over a fairly long period of time. In many investors' minds it is therefore probably not more than an interesting gamble on the side instead of a serious investment.
- It has been argued that for many retail investors equity-linked savings products are the only way to acquire equity exposure. Although this is true for those who are not able to pay upfront, marketing research carried out by one of the main product providers suggests that many buyers do have sufficient cash available.
- Investors can easily replicate the payoffs of products 2 and 3 in the futures and listed options market. However, not many retail investors know enough about derivatives to figure this out and actually do so.

In sum, issuing equity-linked savings products is attractive because generally speaking **retail investors are short on sophistication as well as alternatives and do not always behave rationally**. Of course, this applies not only to equity-linked savings products but to a large variety of other financial products and services as well. In a way it is very much the raison d'être for a major part of the financial services industry.

13.8   VARIATIONS IN PROTECTED EQUITY-LINKED SAVING

Capitalizing on our newly acquired structuring skills we can take equity-linked savings products a lot further. Concentrating on product 3, we could allow for a guaranteed minimum return other than zero, we could introduce a cap as well as one or more other bells and whistles. After all, product 3 is no different from a conservatively leveraged call. In addition, we need not settle for one type of option. We can divide the money that comes in over two or even more different options. In what follows we look at some examples.

13.8.1   The Disappointment Bonus

One interesting possibility is to create a product that offers investors a payoff equal to

$$X_5 = M \times \left(\text{Max} \left[0, I_5 - I_0 \right] + \left(I_0 - M_{0,1}^- \right) \right), \tag{13.9}$$

where $M_{0,1}^-$ denotes the lowest value of the index over the first year of the product's life. This product pays investors a multiple of the positive change in the index plus a bonus equal to the same multiple times the difference between the initial index value and the lowest index value over the first year of the product's life. This bonus is obtained even if the index at maturity is below its starting value.

Looking more closely at the above payoff we see that the bank is doing nothing more than selling investors a combination of an **ordinary call** and a **fixed-strike lookback put**. The budget equation for the swap which would support a product like this is therefore given by

$$5000 = M \times \left(C_0^a[I_0, 5] + LP_0^a[I_0, 0, 1, 5] \right), \tag{13.10}$$

where $LP_0^a[K, t_1, t_2, T]$ is the derivatives firm's offer for a lookback put with strike K, monitoring from $t = t_1$ until $t = t_2$ and time to maturity T. The derivatives firm prices the options package at 47.15%, implying that the bank can offer investors a multiplier of 106.

If it wanted to disguise the true mechanics of the structure a little bit better, the bank could rewrite the above payoff as

$$X_5 = N \times \left(\text{Max} \left[0, \alpha \left(\frac{I_5 - I_0}{I_0} \right) \right] + \alpha \left(\frac{I_0 - M_{0,1}^-}{I_0} \right) \right). \tag{13.11}$$

The bank is free to choose the notional amount N and the participation rate α as it sees fit under the restriction that $\alpha N / I_0 = 106$. If the bank chooses a notional amount of 6000, the participation rate would be equal to 1.77. If the index went up, the product would therefore pay investors

$$X_5 = 6000 \times 1.77 \times \left(\left(\frac{I_5 - I_0}{I_0} \right) + \left(\frac{I_0 - M_{0,1}^-}{I_0} \right) \right). \tag{13.12}$$

In other words, over a notional amount of 6000, the product would pay investors 1.77 times the index return plus on top of that a bonus in case the index came below its starting value during the first year. This sounds too good to be true, but once again one has to realize that this is not a principal protected note. The only protection offered is that investors will not lose more than they put in.

With the above product the bonus has the same multiplier (or participation rate) as the part of the payoff related to the index return. This is not necessary though. We could for example structure a product that only paid investors half the above disappointment bonus. This would mean a payoff equal to

$$X_5 = M \times \left(\text{Max}[0, I_5 - I_0] + 0.5 \times \left(I_0 - M_{0,1}^- \right) \right). \tag{13.13}$$

The budget equation for this payoff is given by

$$5000 = M \times \left(C_0^a[I_0, 5] + 0.5 \times LP_0^a[I_0, 0, 1, 5] \right). \tag{13.14}$$

The derivatives firm prices the above options package at 38.14%. This means that in this case the bank can offer investors a multiplier of 131.

In our more general framework of notionals and participation rates the above product's payoff at maturity would be equal to

$$X_5 = N \times \left(\text{Max} \left[0, \alpha \left(\frac{I_5 - I_0}{I_0} \right) \right] + 0.5 \times \alpha \left(\frac{I_0 - M_{0,1}^-}{I_0} \right) \right), \qquad (13.15)$$

where the notional and the participation rate have to be set such that $\alpha N / I_0 = 131$. If we set the participation rate equal to 2 we could set the notional amount equal to 6550. If the index went up, this would leave investors with a payoff equal to

$$X_5 = 6550 \times \left(2 \times \left(\frac{I_5 - I_0}{I_0} \right) + \frac{I_0 - M_{0,1}^-}{I_0} \right). \qquad (13.16)$$

Over a notional amount of 6550, this product would pay investors 2 times the positive index return plus a bonus in case the index went down during the first year. The bonus, however, has an effective participation rate equal to 1 instead of 2.

Although this may seem a rather strange payoff to offer to retail investors, it allows for a very appealing story. The bank can explain this payoff to investors by saying that by paying 100 every month for five years they will get protected exposure to 6550 worth of equity and that if the index indeed goes up the bank will double their profits. In addition, if the index goes down in the first year, the bank will make up for their loss. Alternatively, the bank could of course say that investors will get protected exposure to 13,100 worth of equity and that if the index goes down in the first year the bank will make up half their loss.

13.8.2 The Partial Cap

Another interesting variation arises if we divide the money available over an ordinary call and a call spread. The bank could for example offer investors a payoff equal to

$$X_5 = N \times \left(\text{Max} \left[0, \alpha \left(\frac{I_5 - I_0}{I_0} \right) \right] + \text{Min} \left[H, \text{Max} \left[0, \alpha \left(\frac{I_5 - I_0}{I_0} \right) \right] \right] \right). \qquad (13.17)$$

The budget equation for the swap which would support such a product is given by

$$5000 = \frac{\alpha N}{I_0} \times \left(C_0^a [I_0, 5] + CS_0^a \left[I_0, I_0 \left(1 + \frac{H}{\alpha} \right), 5 \right] \right). \qquad (13.18)$$

Expression (13.18) shows clearly that by selling investors this product the bank is doing nothing more than selling them **ordinary calls** with strike I_0 as well as **call spreads** with lower strike I_0 and upper strike $I_0(1 + H/\alpha)$.

Before we can solve the budget equation we need to fix the cap rate H and either N or α. Suppose we fixed the cap rate at 60% and the participation rate at 1. For the call spread this implies an upper strike of $1.6I_0$. Knowing the strike, the derivatives firm prices the options package at 48.41%, meaning that the notional amount is going to be 10,328. The result is again quite interesting. By paying 100 every month during five years investors obtain protected equity exposure in the amount of 10,328 and if the index rises the bank doubles investors' profits up to a maximum of 6197 ($= 0.6 \times 10,328$).

13.8.3 Money-Back Structures

One thing people are always interested in is getting money back. We can very easily create a money-back structure by presenting the payoff of product 3 as consisting of two parts: (1) the regular payoff and (2) a money-back payment. With product 3 investors get paid 172 times the positive change in the index. The bank need not present the product in that way though. It could say that the actual product only paid off 112 times the change in the index and that the remaining 60 times the index change resulted from a special money-back feature that paid back part or even all of the money paid by the investors. With investors paying 6000 in total and the index initially at 100, the bank could say that investors get back 1% of what they pay for every 1% that the index goes up. If over the product's life the index went up from 100 to 140 the product would pay off $172 \times 40 = 6880$, of which $112 \times 40 = 4480$ would be considered ordinary payoff and $60 \times 40 = 2400$ would be considered money paid back. If the index went up to 200 the money-back part would be 6000. If it went above, the money-back payoff would be even higher. To prevent this, the money-back part will have to be capped at 6000. As we know from Chapter 8, this is easily done by writing 60 ordinary calls with strike 200. The premium received from doing so can be used to increase the multiplier on the standard part of the payoff again.

   The above money-back structure is created by simply splitting up the original product payoff into a standard part and a so-called money-back part. We can, however, also include more sophisticated types of money-back features like the ones we discussed in Chapter 8. Suppose we equipped product 3 with a single barrier money-back feature. With this money-back feature investors receive a prefixed amount B if during the life of the product the index goes up by $X\%$ or more from its value at inception. This yields a payoff function equal to

$$X_5 = M \times \text{Max}\,[0, I_5 - I_0] + D \times B, \tag{13.19}$$

where

$$D = 1, \quad \text{if } \exists j \; I_j \geqslant I_0(1 + X),$$
$$ = 0, \quad \text{if } \forall j \; I_j < I_0(1 + X).$$

The subscript j counts the monitoring points. With investors paying 6000 in total, we could set $B = 3000$, meaning investors would get half their money back if at any of the monitoring points the index was higher than $I_0(1 + X)$. If we set $X = 0.6$ the money-back feature itself would be worth 946, which in turn would yield a multiplier of 139.

13.8.4 Segmented Payoff Functions

In none of the above payoffs do we find a reference to the way investors pay for them. Instead of paying 60 monthly instalments of 100, investors might as well pay the bank the present value of that stream of cash flows upfront. If the bank wanted a product where the payoff relates directly to the 60 monthly payments which investors make, it could offer investors a payoff of

$$X_5 = 100 \times \left(\text{Max}\left[0, \alpha\left(\frac{I_5 - I_0}{I_0} \right) \right] + \text{Max}\left[0, \alpha\left(\frac{I_5 - I_{1/12}}{I_{1/12}} \right) \right] + \cdots \right.$$

$$\left. + \text{Max}\left[0, \alpha\left(\frac{I_5 - I_{59/12}}{I_{59/12}} \right) \right] \right) = 100\alpha \times \sum_{i=0}^{59} \text{Max}\left[0, \left(\frac{I_5 - I_{i/12}}{I_{i/12}} \right) \right]. \tag{13.20}$$

The above payoff is made up of 60 parts, each of which can be thought of as a $t = 5$ payoff bought with 100 at the end of month i. Every one of these monthly payoffs is equal to

$$X_5^i = 100\alpha \times \left(\frac{1}{I_{i/12}} \times \text{Max} \left[0, I_5 - I_{i/12}\right] \right), \quad i = 0, 1, \dots, 59, \quad (13.21)$$

which is the same as the payoff of 100α 5-year **quantity-adjusting forward-starting calls** with multiplier $1/I_{i/12}$ and strike price $I_{i/12}$. We can therefore find the participation rate that the bank can offer investors on the above product from the following budget equation

$$5000 = 100\alpha \times \sum_{i=0}^{59} QAFC_0^a \left[\frac{1}{I_{i/12}}, I_{i/12}, 5 \right], \quad (13.22)$$

where $QAFC_0^a[M, K, T]$ denotes the derivatives firm's offer price for a quantity-adjusting forward-starting call with multiplier M, strike K and time to maturity T. Of course, for $i = 0$ the quantity-adjusting forward-starting call is identical to an ordinary call. The derivatives firm quotes a price of 9.68% for the package. This yields a participation rate of 5.17. Compared to the participation rate of 2.87 that we found earlier (for product 3 with a notional of 6000) this may look high, but we should keep in mind that in this case investors only get paid the change in the index measured from the moment they make their payments and not from $t = 0$.

13.8.5   Variations in Investor Payment

Until now we have assumed investors pay 100 every month for the next five years. This is an obvious and straightforward choice. One can, however, arrange for payment in various other ways as well. We could vary the amounts paid deterministically, for example by instead of 100 only taking 25 during the summer holiday season and in December, or we could link them to another reference index. One interesting thought is to **attach knock-out conditions to the payments to be made by the investors**. The bank could say that if after three years the index was up by more than a certain percentage investors would not have to make any more payments. Clearly this means adding a European knock-out barrier to the payments to be made in years 4 and 5 so that if at $t = 3$ the index was higher than the barrier all year 4 and 5 payments would knock out. If this was thought too rigorous the bank might consider tranching the payments made by the investors and giving each tranche its own knock-out barrier. Suppose we split the 100 to be paid into five tranches of 20 each. If we then equipped all five tranches with a knock-out barrier at levels H^1 up to H^5, respectively we would have created a payment that knocked out stepwise. If no barrier was hit, the payments for years 4 and 5 would stay at 100. If only H^1 was hit, the monthly payment would drop to 80. If only H^1 and H^2 were hit, it would drop to 60, etc.

If we attach a knock-out condition we change the payments to be made by the investors from fixed cash flows to digital cash flows. The latter will be worth less than the fixed payments the investors used to make, and the multiplier will therefore have to come down. Let's look at product 3 again. Under the assumptions made, the present value of the investors' payments is 5298, the present value of the bank's margin is 298 and the present value of the payments to the derivatives firm is 5000. With the required call option costing 29.14% the multiplier is 172. Now suppose we added a European knock-out barrier to the payments to be made by the investors in years 4 and 5. If at $t = 3$ the index was higher than 140 all year 4 and 5 payments would knock out. Assuming the bank wanted to make the same profit as before, it will in this case be easier for the bank to simply pass all the investors' payments through to the derivatives firm and ask the latter to either make an upfront payment of 298 or provide a stream of 60 monthly payments of 5.62. The derivatives firm values the first three years of payments at 3336 and the second two years of digitals at 1495. Paying the bank 298 upfront this leaves 4533 for the call options. With one option worth 29.14%, this means the bank can now offer investors a multiplier of 155. In comparison with the standard product, which offers a multiplier of 172, many investors may consider this a very good deal.

13.9 CONCLUSION

In this chapter we showed how to structure, hedge, price and market equity-linked savings products. A typical equity-linked savings product is made up of two parts. The first part is a stream of periodic payments made by the investor. This is the savings part. The second part consists of a single payment at maturity which is linked to the behavior of the reference index or indices in question. This is the equity-linked part.

Equity-linked savings products are swaps. From a derivatives structuring perspective, however, it is helpful to think of these products as conservatively leveraged purchases of forwards or options. Another angle appears when marketing equity-linked savings products. Instead of presenting them as swaps, one may also present them as aggressively leveraged purchases of stocks (with additional bells and whistles). Apart from making the product a lot easier to explain, this could also bring significant tax advantages. **Telling the same story differently can sometimes make a big difference**. We saw this before when we discussed capped bull notes.

We also saw that when it comes to pricing we can follow either one of two routes. We can first decide on the desired profit margin and from there derive the conditions that can be offered, or we can first decide on the conditions to offer and then calculate the implied profit margin. Following the latter route, it appears that equity-linked savings products can offer product providers excellent margins. This confirms what bankers, (life) insurers and many others discovered many years ago: **it is hard to be too greedy in the retail business**.

Finally, it is interesting to note that equity-linked savings products can also be packaged with other products to make the latter 'equity-linked'. We could for example package a traditional mortgage together with product 3. Doing so would create an **equity-linked mortgage** which, at some future date, would provide the client with a reduction in the size of his mortgage, the size of which would depend on the value of the index on that date.

Appendix A

In this appendix we provide some information on a number of stock market indices. There is a lot more to these indices than we present here. However, things such as index composition, calculation period, dissemination frequency, stock selection criteria, review frequency, exchange traded options and futures, etc. are known to change significantly over time. We have therefore chosen not to discuss this in detail but instead to include a number of internet **websites** where this information can be obtained if required. Index publishers' websites typically contain one or more documents which explain in detail how the stocks in the index are selected and how the index is calculated. Often there is also an e-mail address for further enquiries.

Since it is of little use to know how an index is calculated without knowing where its most recent value can be observed, Table A.1 gives the Bloomberg and Reuters codes for the indices we discuss below.[1] Before taking prices from a screen, one should **always check whether those prices are indeed real-time**. Although capable of providing real-time data, a data provider may choose to do so only on certain subscriptions. On cheaper subscriptions prices may be refreshed only once every 10 minutes, or even less.

Table A.1 Bloomberg and Reuters codes for selected indices

Index name	Bloomberg code	Reuters code
S&P 500	SPX	.SPC
DJIA	INDU	.DJI
Eurotop 100	E100	.FTEU1
Eurostoxx 50	SX5E	.STOXX50E
FTSE 100	UKX	.FTSE
DAX	DAX	.GDAXI
AEX	AEX	.AEX
SMI	SMI	.SSMI
CAC 40	CAC	.FCHI
IBEX 35	IBEX	.IBEX
MIB 30	MIB30	.MIB30
Nikkei 225	NKY	.N225
Hang Seng	HSI	.HSI
ASX All Ord.	AS30	.AORD

---

[1] See also www.bloomberg.com

A.1   S&P 500

Publisher: Standard & Poor's

Component stocks: 500 stocks trading on the New York Stock Exchange, American Stock Exchange and the NASDAQ National Market System

Weighting: Value-weighted

Dividends: Not included

Useful websites:
www.spglobal.com = Standard & Poor's Index Services
www.cboe.com = Chicago Board Options Exchange
www.cme.com = Chicago Mercantile Exchange

A.2   DOW JONES INDUSTRIAL AVERAGE

Publisher: Dow Jones & Company

Component stocks: 30 stocks trading on the New York Stock Exchange and the NASDAQ National Market System

Weighting: Price-weighted

Dividends: Not included

Useful websites:
www.dowjones.com = Dow Jones
http://averages.dowjones.com = Dow Jones Indices
www.cbot.com = Chicago Board of Trade
www.cboe.com = Chicago Board Options Exchange

A.3   EUROTOP 100

Publisher: FTSE International Ltd

Component stocks: 100 stocks trading on the major stock markets of Europe (including the UK)

Weighting: Value-weighted

Dividends: Not included

Useful websites:
www.ftse.com = FTSE International
www.euronext.com = Euronext
www.liffe.com = London International Financial Futures and Options Exchange
www.nymex.com = New York Mercantile Exchange

A.4   EUROSTOXX 50

Publisher: Stoxx Ltd

Component stocks: 50 stocks trading on 10 European exchanges in the Eurozone

Weighting: Value-weighted

Dividends: Not included

Useful websites:
www.stoxx.com = Stoxx
www.matif.fr = MATIF
www.monep.fr = MONEP
www.eurexchange.com = Eurex

A.5   FTSE 100

Publisher: FTSE International Ltd

Component stocks: 100 stocks trading on the London Stock Exchange

Weighting: Value-weighted

Dividends: Not included

Useful websites:
www.ftse.com = FTSE International
www.liffe.com = London International Financial Futures and Options Exchange

A.6   DAX

Publisher: Deutsche Borse AG

Component stocks: 30 stocks trading on the Frankfurt Stock Exchange

Weighting: Value-weighted

Dividends: Included

Useful websites:
www.exchange.de = Deutsche Borse
www.xetra.de = XETRA (Exchange Electronic Trading System)
www.eurexchange.com = Eurex

A.7   AEX

Publisher: Amsterdam Exchanges NV

Component stocks: 25 stocks trading on the Amsterdam Stock Exchange

Weighting: Value-weighted

Dividends: Not included

Useful websites:
www.euronext.com = Euronext

A.8   SMI

Publisher: Schweizer Borse-SWX AG

Component stocks: 23 stocks trading on the stock exchanges of Zurich, Basel and Geneva

Weighting: Value-weighted

Dividends: Not included

Useful websites:
www.swx.com = Schweizer Borse
www.eurexchange.com = Eurex

A.9   CAC 40

Publisher: Paris Bourse-SBF SA

Component stocks: 40 stocks trading on the Premier Marche

Weighting: Value-weighted

Dividends: Not included

Useful websites:
www.euronext.com = Euronext
www.matif.fr = MATIF
www.monep.fr = MONEP

A.10   IBEX 35

Publisher: Sociedad de Bolsas SA

Component stocks: 35 stocks trading on the interconnected system of the exchanges of Madrid, Barcelona, Bilbao and Valencia

Weighting: Value-weighted

Dividends: Not included

Useful websites:
www.sbolsas.es = Sociedad de Bolsas
www.bolsamadrid.es = Madrid Stock Exchange
www.meffrv.es = Meff Renta Variable

A.11   MIB 30

Publisher: Borsa Italiana Spa

Component stocks: 30 stocks trading on the Italian Stock Exchange

Weighting: Value-weighted

Dividends: Not included

Useful websites:
www.borsaitalia.it = Borsa Italiana

A.12   NIKKEI 225

Publisher: Nihon Keizai Shimbun Inc.

Component stocks: 225 stocks trading in the first section of the Tokyo Stock Exchange

Weighting: Price-weighted

Dividends: Not included

Useful websites:
www.nni.nikkei.co.jp = Nikkei Net Interactive
www.tse.or.jp = Tokyo Stock Exchange
www.ose.or.jp = Osaka Securities Exchange
www.simex.com = Singapore International Monetary Exchange
www.cme.com = Chicago Mercantile Exchange

A.13   HANG SENG

Publisher: HSI Services Ltd

Component stocks: 33 stocks trading on the Stock Exchange of Hong Kong

Weighting: Value-weighted

Dividends: Not included

Useful websites:
www.hsi.com.hk = HSI Services
www.hkfe.com = Hong Kong Futures Exchange

A.14   ASX ALL ORDINARIES

Publisher: Standard & Poor's

Component stocks: 500 stocks trading on the Australian Stock Exchange

Weighting: Value-weighted

Dividends: Not included

Useful websites:
www.spglobal.com = Standard & Poor's Index Services
www.asx.com.au = Australian Stock Exchange
www.sfe.com.au = Sydney Futures Exchange

Appendix B

In this appendix we provide a brief glossary of the option contracts that we encountered in Chapters 6–13 as well as some others. As explained in Chapter 3, options are forwards where one of the counterparties is given the right to cancel the contract at maturity at no extra cost. Suppose we had a forward where counterparty A pays counterparty B and the other way around. If we give counterparty A the right to cancel the deal A would be **long** the option and B would be **short** the option. In terms of buying and selling, A has **bought** the option and B has **sold** the option. What kind of option we are talking about depends on what the owner of the option right is paying. If the counterparty who has bought the option pays an index-linked amount and the other party pays a fixed amount we speak of a **put option**. If on the other hand the counterparty who is long the option pays a fixed amount and the other party pays an index-linked amount we speak of a **call option**. In both cases the fixed amount is referred to as the option's **strike**. When both counterparties pay index-linked amounts the least volatile of the two is typically referred to as the so-called **floating strike**. References to technical papers and articles can be found in the bibliography.

Alternative Option. Option which pays the buyer the highest of the payoffs of two other option contracts. These can be two options of the same type with different reference indices but also two different options with the same reference index.

American Option. Option where the buyer has the right to let the contract mature immediately at any time during the life of the contract.

Barrier Option. Option with a knock-in or knock-out barrier feature.

Basket Option. Option where the index-linked cash flow to be exchanged depends on the value of a basket of reference indices.

Bermudan Option. Option where the buyer has the right to let the contract mature immediately at a limited number of times during the life of the contract. Middle ground between European and American option.

Callable Option. Option where the seller has the right to cancel the contract by paying the buyer a prefixed amount.

Chooser Option. Option where at some point before maturity the buyer has the right to decide who pays the fixed cash flow and who pays the index-linked cash flow.

Composite Option. Option where two counterparties exchange a fixed cash flow and an index-linked cash flow equal to the value of a foreign reference index converted to domestic currency at the exchange rate at maturity. Also known as a **foreign option struck in domestic currency**.

Compound Option. Option on an option, i.e. an option where two counterparties exchange a fixed cash flow and an index-linked cash flow equal to the price of an ordinary put or call. This gives rise to four cases: a call on a call, a call on a put, a put on a call, and a put on a put. The first two can also be seen as instalment options with only two instalments.

Contingent Premium Option. Option where the premium to be paid depends on the future behavior of some reference index.

Delayed Settlement Option. Option where the payoff is determined before the maturity date.

Double Barrier Option. Option with a double barrier knock-in or knock-out feature.

European Option. Option where neither counterparty has the right to let the contract mature immediately. All options that are not American or Bermudan are European.

Exchange Option. Option where two counterparties exchange two vanilla index-linked cash flows. Provides the same payoff as a spread option with a zero strike.

Expandible Option. Option where the buyer has the right to increase the multiplier of the contract by paying the seller a prefixed amount.

Extendible Option. Option where the buyer has the right to increase the time to maturity of the contract by paying the seller a prefixed amount.

Fixed-Strike Asian Option. Option where two counterparties exchange a fixed cash flow and an index-linked cash flow equal to the average of a number of subsequent index values.

Fixed-Strike Ladder Option. Option where two counterparties exchange a fixed cash flow and an index-linked cash flow equal to the extended stepwise extremum.

Fixed-Strike Lookback Option. Option where two counterparties exchange a fixed cash flow and an index-linked cash flow equal to the highest or lowest of a number of subsequent index values.

Floating-Strike Asian Option. Option where two counterparties exchange two index-linked cash flows, one equal to a vanilla index-linked cash flow and the other equal to the average of a number of subsequent index values.

Floating-Strike Ladder Option. Option where two counterparties exchange two index-linked cash flows, one equal to a vanilla index-linked cash flow and the other equal to the stepwise extremum.

Floating-Strike Lookback Option. Option where two counterparties exchange two index-linked cash flows, one equal to a vanilla index-linked cash flow and the other equal to the highest or lowest of a number of subsequent index values.

Foreign Option. Option where two counterparties exchange two index-linked cash flows, one equal to a fixed amount of foreign currency and the other equal to the value of a foreign reference index, both converted to domestic currency at the exchange rate at maturity. Also known as a **foreign option struck in foreign currency**.

Forward-Starting Barrier Option. Partial barrier option where the barrier level is equal to a fraction of the value of the barrier variable at some point before or on the first monitoring date.

Forward-Starting Strike Option. Option where two counterparties exchange two index-linked cash flows where one is a vanilla index-linked cash flow with delayed settlement.

FX Lock Option. Option where two counterparties exchange two index-linked cash flows, one equal to the value of a foreign reference index converted in domestic currency at the exchange rate at inception and the other equal to the value of the same index converted at the exchange rate at maturity. Also known as **equity-linked foreign exchange option** or simply **ELF-X**.

Inside Barrier Option. Option with a knock-in or knock-out barrier feature where the barrier variable is the same index as the reference index of the original contract.

Instalment Option. Option that is paid for in instalments. The option is alive as long as the buyer pays the instalments. If he misses an instalment, the option is nullified.

Knock-In Option. Option with a knock-in feature.

Knock-Out Option. Option with a knock-out feature.

Money-Back Option. Contingent premium option that offers the buyer the possibility to get paid (part of) the initial premium back at one or more later dates, depending on the value of the reference index.

Option on the Best-of-Two. Option where two counterparties exchange a fixed cash flow and an index-linked cash flow equal to the highest of two other index-linked cash flows.

Option on the Worst-of-Two. Option where two counterparties exchange a fixed cash flow and an index-linked cash flow equal to the lowest of two other index-linked cash flows.

Ordinary Option. Option where two counterparties exchange a fixed cash flow and a vanilla index-linked cash flow.

Outside Barrier Option. Option with a knock-in or knock-out barrier feature where the barrier variable is a different index than the reference index of the original contract.

Passport Option. Option where the reference index is the P&L on some trading account.

Pay-Later Option. Contingent premium option which does not have to be paid for in the present but which may have to be paid for at one or more later dates, depending on the value of the reference index.

Power Option. Option where two counterparties exchange a fixed cash flow and an index-linked cash flow equal to the square or higher power of the value of the reference index.

Puttable Option. Options where the buyer has the right to cancel the contract by requiring the seller to pay him a prefixed amount.

Quantity-Adjusting Option. Option with an index-linked multiplier.

Quanto Option. Option where two counterparties exchange a fixed cash flow and an index-linked cash flow equal to the value of a foreign reference index converted to domestic currency at the exchange rate at inception. Also known as a **fixed exchange rate foreign call**.

Shout Option. Option where two counterparties exchange a fixed cash flow and an index-linked cash flow equal to the shout extremum.

Spread Option. Option where two counterparties exchange a fixed cash flow and an index-linked cash flow equal to the difference between two vanilla index-linked cash flows with different reference indices.

Window Option. Option with a European double knock-out barrier which is monitored before maturity. For the option to pay off, the barrier variable has to move through the window created by both barriers.

Appendix C

This appendix provides an overview of the notation used for the prices of the different types of forwards and options mentioned in Chapters 9–13. We have tried to economize on notation by leaving out the monitoring frequency for path-dependent options. We do not explicitly distinguish between fixed and floating strike options. The difference between direct and delayed settlement will be evident from the number of parameters. The same is true for the difference between single and double barriers.

$AC[K, t_1, t_2, T]$ = Price of Asian call with strike K, monitoring between t_1 and t_2 with time to maturity T (fixed and floating strike).

$AID[H, t_1, t_2, T]$ = Price of American knock-in digital paying 1.00 at time T, with a barrier at H and monitoring between t_1 and t_2.

$AO[A, B, T]$ = Price of alternative option with time to maturity T paying the highest of payoff A and payoff B.

$AOD[H^1, H^2, t_1, t_2, T]$ = Price of American double barrier knock-out digital paying 1.00 at time T, with barriers at H^1 and H^2 and monitoring between t_1 and t_2.

$C[K, T]$ = Price of ordinary call with strike K and time to maturity T.

$C[K, t, T]$ = Price of ordinary call with strike K, payoff determination at time t and settlement at time T (delayed settlement).

$CB[K, T]$ = Price of call on the best-of-two with strike K and time to maturity T.

$CC[K, T]$ = Price of composite call with strike K and time to maturity T.

$CH[K^1, K^2, t, T]$ = Price of chooser option with call strike K^1, put strike K^2, choice date t and time to maturity T.

$CL[K^1, K^2, T]$ = Price of collar with lower strike K^1, upper strike K^2 and time to maturity T.

$CS[K^1, K^2, T]$ = Price of ordinary call spread with lower strike K^1, upper strike K^2 and time to maturity T.

$CS[K^1, K^2, t, T]$ = Price of ordinary call spread with lower strike K^1, upper strike K^2, payoff determination at time t and settlement at time T (delayed settlement).

$CW[K, T]$ = Price of call on the worst-of-two with strike K and time to maturity T.

$DC[H, T]$ = Price of digital call paying 1.00 at time T if the reference index is equal to or higher than H.

$DC[H, t, T]$ = Price of digital call paying 1.00 at time T if at time t the reference index is equal to or higher than H (delayed settlement).

$DP[H, T]$ = Price of digital put paying 1.00 at time T if the reference index is lower than H.

$DS[H^1, H^2, T]$ = Price of digital spread paying 1.00 at time T if the reference index is between H^1 and H^2.

$DS[H^1, H^2, t, T]$ = Price of digital spread paying 1.00 at time T if at time t the reference index is between H^1 and H^2 (delayed settlement).

$F[K, T]$ = Price of vanilla forward with forward price K and time to maturity T.

$FC[K, T]$ = Price of foreign call (in foreign currency) with strike K and time to maturity T.

$IC[K, H, t_1, t_2, T]$ = Price of American knock-in call with strike K, barrier H, monitoring from t_1 to t_2 with time to maturity T.

$IP[K, H, t_1, t_2, T]$ = Price of American knock-in put with strike K, barrier H, monitoring from t_1 to t_2 with time to maturity T.

$LC[K, t_1, t_2, T]$ = Price of lookback call with strike K, monitoring between t_1 and t_2 with time to maturity T (fixed and floating strike).

$LP[K, t_1, t_2, T]$ = Price of lookback put with strike K, monitoring between t_1 and t_2 with time to maturity T (fixed and floating strike).

$OC[K, H, t_1, t_2, T]$ = Price of American knock-out call with strike K, barrier H, monitoring from t_1 to t_2 with time to maturity T.

$OCS[K^1, K^2, H^1, H^2, t_1, t_2, t, T]$ = Price of American double barrier knock-out call spread with lower strike K^1, upper strike K^2, barriers at H^1 and H^2, monitoring between t_1 and t_2, with payoff determination at t and settlement at T (delayed settlement).

$OP[K, H, t_1, t_2, T]$ = Price of American knock-out put with strike K, barrier H, monitoring from t_1 to t_2 with time to maturity T.

$OPS[K^1, K^2, H^1, H^2, t_1, t_2, t, T]$ = Price of American double barrier knock-out put spread with upper strike K^1, lower strike K^2, barriers at H^1 and H^2, monitoring between t_1 and t_2, with payoff determination at t and settlement at T (delayed settlement).

$P[K, T]$ = Price of ordinary put with strike K and time to maturity T.

$PS[K^1, K^2, T]$ = Price of ordinary put spread with upper strike K^1, lower strike K^2 and time to maturity T.

$PS[K^1, K^2, t, T]$ = Price of ordinary put spread with upper strike K^1, lower strike K^2, payoff determination at t and settlement at T (delayed settlement).

$QAFC[M, K, T]$ = Price of quantity-adjusting forward-starting call with multiplier M, strike K and time to maturity T.

$QAFC[M, K, t, T]$ = Price of quantity-adjusting forward-starting call with multiplier M, strike K, payoff determination at time t and settlement at time T (delayed settlement).

$QC[K, T]$ = Price of quanto call with strike K and time to maturity T.

$SPC[K, a, b, T]$ = Price of spread call with strike K, weights a and b and time to maturity T.

Bibliography

This bibliography lists most of the literature on the pricing and hedging of equity derivatives. The list is fairly comprehensive but we have made one concession: we restrict ourselves to models where interest rates, volatility and dividend yields are deterministic and stock prices do not jump. Many researchers have tried to incorporate stochastic interest rates, stochastic volatility, stochastic dividends and jump processes in option pricing models. It is, however, still very much an open question whether this is worth the effort. The resulting models are typically a lot more complicated and especially a lot more difficult to estimate. It may well be that in these models modeling error is simply replaced by estimation error. In other words, they may look more realistic on the outside but may not yield significantly better hedges and prices that are a better indication of the actual expected hedging costs.

The bibliography consists of four parts. The first part concerns theoretical pricing formulas and procedures, the second part covers model calibration and implied volatility, and the third part concentrates on explicit hedging strategies. The final part is a list of books on equity derivatives. Given the vast amount of research that has been carried out in these areas over the years, and the way this research is scattered over an ever increasing number of academic journals, I have no illusion that I have actually been able to capture everything that is out there. If you know of a paper or article, written or published before October 2000, that should have been included, or if you think I misclassified a paper or article, please let me know at Comments@harrykat.com so this can be corrected in a possible next edition.

OPTION PRICING

American and Bermudan Options

Aitsahlia, F. and T. Roncalli (1999). A Canonical Optimal Stopping Problem for American Options and its Numerical Solution, *Journal of Computational Finance*, Winter, pp. 33–52.

Allegretto, W., G. Barone-Adesi and R. Elliot (1994). The Free Boundary of the American Put Option, Working Paper, University of Alberta.

Aparicio, S. and L. Clewlow (1997). American Featured Options, in: L. Clewlow and C. Strickland (eds.), *Exotic Options: The State of the Art*, International Thomson, pp. 35–63.

Barone-Adesi, G. and M. Chesney (1991). American Path-Dependent Options, Working Paper, University of Alberta.

Barone-Adesi, G. and R. Elliott (1991). Approximations for the Values of American Options, *Stochastic Analysis and Applications*, Vol. 9, pp. 115–131.

Barone-Adesi, G. and R. Whaley (1986). The Valuation of American Call Options and the Expected Ex-Dividend Stock Price Decline, *Journal of Financial Economics*, Vol. 17, pp. 91–111.

Barone-Adesi, G. and R. Whaley (1987). Efficient Analytical Approximation of American Option Values, *Journal of Finance*, Vol. 42, pp. 301–320.

Barone-Adesi, G. and R. Whaley (1988). On the Valuation of American Put Options on Dividend Paying Stocks, in: F. Fabozzi (ed.), *Advances in Futures and Options Research*, Vol. 3, Jai Press, pp. 1–14.

Barraquand, J. and T. Pudet (1996). Pricing of American Path-Dependent Contingent Claims, *Mathematical Finance*, Vol. 6, pp. 17–51.

Bjerksund, P. and G. Stensland (1993a). Closed-Form Approximations for American Options, *Scandinavian Journal of Management*, Vol. 9, pp. 87–99.

Bjerksund, P. and G. Stensland (1993b). American Exchange Options and a Put–Call Transformation: A Note, *Journal of Business Finance and Accounting*, Vol. 20, pp. 761–764.

Bjerksund, P. and G. Stensland (1994). An American Call on the Difference of Two Assets, *International Review of Economics and Finance*, Vol. 3, pp. 1–26.

Blomeyer, E. (1986). An Analytic Approximation for the American Put Price for Options on Stocks with Dividends, *Journal of Financial and Quantitative Analysis*, Vol. 21, pp. 229–233.

Bodurtha, J. and G. Courtadon (1995). Probabilities and Values of Early Exercise: Spot and Futures Foreign Currency Options, *Journal of Derivatives*, Fall, pp. 57–75.

Brennan, M. and E. Schwartz (1977). The Valuation of American Put Options, *Journal of Finance*, Vol. 32, pp. 449–462.

Brill, A. and R. Harriff (1986). Pricing American Options: Managing Risk with Early Exercise, *Financial Analysts Journal*, November–December, pp. 48–55.

Broadie, M. and J. Detemple (1994). The Valuation of American Options on Multiple Assets, Working Paper, Columbia University.

Broadie, M. and J. Detemple (1995). American Capped Call Options on Dividend Paying Assets, *Review of Financial Studies*, Vol. 8, pp. 161–191.

Broadie, M. and J. Detemple (1996). American Option Valuation: New Bounds, Approximations and a Comparison of Existing Methods, *Review of Financial Studies*, Vol. 9, pp. 1211–1250.

Broadie, M. and P. Glasserman (1997a). Pricing American-Style Securities Using Simulation, *Journal of Economic Dynamics and Control*, Vol. 21, pp. 1323–1352.

Broadie, M. and P. Glasserman (1997b). Monte Carlo Methods for Pricing High-Dimensional American Options: An Overview, *Net Exposure*, December.

Broadie, M., P. Glasserman and G. Jain (1997). Enhanced Monte Carlo Estimates for American Option Prices, *Journal of Derivatives*, Fall, pp. 25–44.

Broadie, M., J. Detemple, E. Ghysels and O. Torres (2000). Nonparametric Estimation of American Options' Exercise Boundaries and Call Prices, *Journal of Economic Dynamics & Control*, Vol. 24, pp. 1829–1857.

Buff, R. (2000). Worst-Case Scenarios for American Options, *International Journal of Theoretical and Applied Finance*, Vol. 3, pp. 25–58.

Bunch, D. and H. Johnson (1992). A Simple and Numerically Efficient Valuation Method for American Puts Using a Modified Geske–Johnson Approach, *Journal of Finance*, Vol. 47, pp. 809–816.

Bunch, D. and H. Johnson (1998). The First-Passage Approach to Valuing the American Put Option, Working Paper, University of California at Riverside.

Bunch, D. and H. Johnson (2000). The American Put Option and Its Critical Stock Price, *Journal of Finance*, Vol. 55, pp. 2333–2356.

Carr, P. (1994). The Valuation of American Exchange Options with Application to Real Options, Working Paper, Cornell University.

Carr, P. (1998). Randomization and the American Put, *Review of Financial Studies*, Vol. 11, pp. 597–626.

Carr, P. and D. Faguet (1994). Fast Accurate Valuation of American Options, Working Paper, Cornell University.

Carr, P., R. Jarrow and R. Myneni (1992). Alternative Characterizations of American Put Options, *Mathematical Finance*, Vol. 2, pp. 87–106.

Carriere, J. (1994). Valuation of the Early Exercise Price for Derivative Securities Using Simulations and Splines, Working Paper, University of Manitoba.

Chalasani, P., S. Jha, F. Egriboyun and A. Varikooty (1999). A Refined Binomial Lattice for Pricing American Asian Options, *Review of Derivatives Research*, Vol. 3, pp. 5–66.

Chen, D. and R. Welch (1993). The Relative Mispricing of American Calls under Alternative Dividend Models, in: D. Chance and R. Trippi (eds.), *Advances in Futures and Options Research*, Vol. 6, Jai Press, pp. 15–43.

Curran, M. (1995). Accelerating American Option Pricing in Lattices, *Journal of Derivatives*, Winter, pp. 8–18.

Dempster, M. and J. Hutton (1997a). Pricing American Stock Options by Linear Programming, Working Paper, University of Essex.

Dempster, M. and J. Hutton (1997b). Fast Numerical Valuation of American, Exotic and Complex Options, *Applied Mathematical Finance*, Vol. 4, pp. 1–20.

Dempster, M., J. Hutton and D. Richards (1998). LP Valuation of Exotic American Options Exploiting Structure, *Journal of Computational Finance*, Fall, pp. 61–84.

De Roon, F. and C. Veld (1996). Put–Call Parities and the Value of Early Exercise for Put Options on a Performance Index, *Journal of Futures Markets*, Vol. 16, pp. 71–80.

Dewynne, J. and P. Wilmott (1992). American Options as Variational Inequalities, Working Paper, Oxford University.

Dewynne, J., D. Howison, I. Rupf and P. Wilmott (1993). Some Mathematical Results in the Pricing of American Options, *European Journal of Applied Mathematics*, Vol. 4, pp. 381–398.

Eckardt, W. (1982). The American Put: Computational Issues and Value Comparisons, *Financial Management*, Autumn, pp. 42–52.

Fisher, E. (1993). Analytical Approximation for the Valuation of American Put Options on Stocks with Known Dividends, *International Review of Economics and Finance*, Vol. 2, pp. 115–127.

Gandhi, S., A. Kooros and G. Salkin (1993). American Option Pricing: An Analytic Approach, Working Paper, Imperial College.

Gao, B., J. Huang and M. Subrahmanyam (1996). An Analytical Approach to the Valuation of American Path-Dependent Options, Working Paper, New York University.

Gao, B., J. Huang and M. Subrahmanyam (2000). The Valuation of American Barrier Options Using the Decomposition Technique, *Journal of Economic Dynamics & Control*, Vol. 24, pp. 1783–1827.

Garman, M. (1989). Semper Tempus Fugit, *Risk*, May, pp. 34–35.

Geske, R. (1979). A Note on an Analytical Valuation Formula for Unprotected American Call Options on Stocks with Known Dividends, *Journal of Financial Economics*, Vol. 7, pp. 375–380.

Geske, R. (1981). Comments on Whaley's Note, *Journal of Financial Economics*, Vol. 9, pp. 213–215.

Geske, R. and H. Johnson (1984). The American Put Valued Analytically, *Journal of Finance*, Vol. 39, pp. 1511–1524.

Geske, R. and R. Roll (1984). On Valuing American Call Options with the Black–Scholes European Formula, *Journal of Finance*, Vol. 39, pp. 443–455.

Geske, R. and K. Shastri (1985). The Early Exercise of American Puts, *Journal of Banking and Finance*, Vol. 9, pp. 207–219.

Goldenberg, D. and R. Schmidt (1995). Estimating the Early Exercise Boundary and Pricing American Options, Working Paper, Rensselaer Polytechnic Institute.

Grant, D., G. Vora and D. Weeks (1996). Simulation and the Early Exercise Option Problem, *Journal of Financial Engineering*, Vol. 5, pp. 211–227.

Guth, M. (1992). Exercise by Numbers, *Risk*, February, pp. 33–37.

Haug, E. (1999). Closed Form Valuation of American Barrier Options, Working Paper, Tempus Financial Engineering.

Hilliard, J. (1994). Finite Horizon Hedge Ratios for American Options: A Minimum Variance Solution, *Journal of Financial Engineering*, Vol. 3, pp. 1–17.

Ho, T., R. Stapleton and M. Subrahmanyam (1994). A Simple Technique for the Valuation and Hedging of American Options, *Journal of Derivatives*, Fall, pp. 52–66.

Huang, J., M. Subrahmanyam and G. Yu (1996). Pricing and Hedging American Options: A Recursive Integration Method, *Review of Financial Studies*, Vol. 9, pp. 277–300.

Jacka, S. (1991). Optimal Stopping and the American Put, *Mathematical Finance*, Vol. 1, pp. 1–14.

Jamshidian, F. (1992). An Analysis of American Options, *Review of Futures Markets*, Vol. 11, pp. 73–80.

Johnson, H. (1983). An Analytical Approximation for the American Put Price, *Journal of Financial and Quantitative Analysis*, Vol. 18, pp. 141–148.

Ju, N. (1998). Pricing an American Option by Approximating its Early Exercise Boundary as a Multipiece Exponential Function, *Review of Financial Studies*, Vol. 11, pp. 627–646.

Ju, N. and R. Zhong (1999). An Approximate Formula for Pricing American Options, *Journal of Derivatives*, Winter, pp. 31–40.

Karatzas, I. (1988). On the Pricing of American Options, *Applied Mathematics and Optimization*, Vol. 17, pp. 37–60.

Kim, I. (1990). The Analytic Valuation of American Options, *Review of Financial Studies*, Vol. 3, pp. 547–572.

Kim, I. and S. Byun (1994). Optimal Exercise Boundary in a Binomial Option Pricing Model, *Journal of Financial Engineering*, Vol. 3, pp. 137–158.

Kim, I. and G. Yu (1996). An Alternative Approach to the Valuation of American Options and Applications, *Review of Derivatives Research*, Vol. 1, pp. 61–85.

Klemkosky, R. and B. Resnick (1992). A Note on the No Premature Exercise Condition of Dividend Payout Unprotected American Call Options: A Clarification, *Journal of Banking and Finance*, Vol. 16, pp. 373–379.

Kuske, R. and J. Keller (1998). Optimal Exercise Boundary for an American Put Option, *Applied Mathematical Finance*, Vol. 5, pp. 107–116.

Lai, T. (2000). Valuation and Exercise Boundaries of American Barrier and Lookback Options, Working Paper, Stanford University.

Lamberton, D. (1993). Convergence of the Critical Price in the Approximation of American Options, *Mathematical Finance*, Vol. 3, pp. 179–190.

Leisen, D. (1998). Pricing the American Put Option: A Detailed Convergence Analysis for Binomial Models, Working Paper, University of Bonn.

Little, T., V. Pant and C. Hou (2000). A New Integral Representation of the Early Exercise Boundary for American Put Options, *Journal of Computational Finance*, Spring, pp. 73–96.

Longstaff, F. and E. Schwartz (1998). Valuing American Options by Simulation, A Simple Least-Squares Approach, Working Paper, University of California at Los Angeles.

Macmillan, L. (1986). An Analytical Approximation for the American Put Price, in: F. Fabozzi (ed.), *Advances in Futures and Options Research*, Vol. 1, Jai Press, pp. 119–139.

Meyer, G. and J. van den Hoek (1997). The Evaluation of American Options with the Method of Lines, in: P. Boyle, G. Pennacchi and P. Ritchken (eds.), *Advances in Futures and Options Research*, Vol. 9, Jai Press, pp. 265–285.

Myneni, R. (1992). The Pricing of the American Option, *Annals of Applied Probability*, Vol. 2, pp. 1–23.

Omberg, E. (1987). The Valuation of American Puts with Exponential Exercise Policies, in: F. Fabozzi (ed.), *Advances in Futures and Options Research*, Vol. 2, Jai Press, pp. 117–142.

Parkinson, M. (1977). Option Pricing: The American Put, *Journal of Business*, Vol. 50, pp. 21–36.

Raymar, S. and A. Sheikh (1996). The Valuation of Compound Options and American Calls on Dividend Paying Stocks with Time Varying Volatility, *Journal of Financial Engineering*, Vol. 5, pp. 243–266.

Raymar, S. and M. Zwecher (1997). Monte Carlo Estimation of American Call Options on the Maximum of Several Stocks, *Journal of Derivatives*, Fall, pp. 7–23.

Roll, R. (1977). An Analytic Valuation Formula for Unprotected American Call Options on Stocks with Known Dividends, *Journal of Financial Economics*, Vol. 5, pp. 251–258.

Rubinstein, M. (1994). Return to Oz, *Risk*, November, pp. 67–71.

Stetson, C., S. Stokke, A. Spinner and R. Averill (1997). Markov Esteem, *Risk*, January, pp. 87–89.

Subrahmanyam, M. and G. Yu (1993). Pricing and Hedging American Options: A Unified Method and its Efficient Implementation, Working Paper, New York University.

Sullivan, M. (2000). Valuing American Put Options Using Gaussian Quadrature, *Review of Financial Studies*, Vol. 13, pp. 75–94.

Tan, K. and K. Vetzal (1995). Early Exercise Regions for Exotic Options, *Journal of Derivatives*, Fall, pp. 42–56.

Tilley, J. (1993). Valuing American Options in a Path Simulation Model, *Transactions of the Society of Actuaries*, Vol. 45, pp. 83–104.

Toft, K. and E. Reiner (1997). Currency Translated Foreign Equity Options: The American Case, in: P. Boyle, G. Pennacchi and P. Ritchken (eds.), *Advances in Futures and Options Research*, Vol. 9, Jai Press, pp. 233–264.

Villeneuve, S. (1999). Exercise Regions of American Options on Several Assets, *Finance and Stochastics*, Vol. 3, pp. 295–322.

Welch, R. and D. Chen (1991). Static Optimization of American Contingent Claims, in: F. Fabozzi (ed.), *Advances in Futures and Options Research*, Vol. 5, Jai Press, pp. 175–184.

Whaley, R. (1981). On the Valuation of American Call Options on Stocks with Known Dividends, *Journal of Financial Economics*, Vol. 9, pp. 207–211.

Wu, L. and Y. Kwok (1997). A Front-Fixing Finite Difference Method for the Valuation of American Options, *Journal of Financial Engineering*, Vol. 6, pp. 83–97.

Wu, L., Y. Kwok and H. Yu (1999). Asian Options with the American Early Exercise Feature, *International Journal of Theoretical and Applied Finance*, Vol. 2, pp. 101–112.

Asian Options

Andreasen, J. (1998). The Pricing of Discretely Sampled Asian and Lookback Options: A Change of Numeraire Approach, *Journal of Computational Finance*, Fall, pp. 5–30.

Angus, J. (1999). A Note on Pricing Asian Derivatives with Continuous Geometric Averaging, *Journal of Futures Markets*, Vol. 19, pp. 845–858.

Bergman, Y. (1985). Pricing Path Contingent Claims, in: H. Chen (ed.), *Research in Finance*, Vol. 5, Jai Press, pp. 229–241.

Bouaziz, L., E. Briys and M. Crouhy (1994). The Pricing of Forward-Starting Asian Options, *Journal of Banking and Finance*, Vol. 18, pp. 823–839.

Boyle, P. (1993). New Life Forms on the Option Landscape, *Journal of Financial Engineering*, Vol. 2, pp. 217–252.

Boyle, P. and D. Emanuel (1985). Mean Dependent Options, Working Paper, University of Waterloo.

Carverhill, A. and L. Clewlow (1990). Flexible Convolution, *Risk*, April, pp. 25–29.

Chalasani, P., S. Jha and A. Varikooty (1998). Accurate Approximations for European-Style Asian Options, *Journal of Computational Finance*, Summer, pp. 11–30.

Cho, H. and H. Lee (1997). A Lattice Model for Pricing Geometric and Arithmetic Average Options, *Journal of Financial Engineering*, Vol. 6, pp. 179–191.

Conze, A. and R. Viswanathan (1991). European Path Dependent Options: The Case of Geometric Averages, *Finance*, Vol. 12, pp. 7–22.

Curran, M. (1992). Beyond Average Intelligence, *Risk*, November, p. 60.

Curran, M. (1994). Valuing Asian and Portfolio Options by Conditioning on the Geometric Mean, *Management Science*, Vol. 40, pp. 1705–1711.

Dewynne, J. and P. Wilmott (1995a). A Note on Average Rate Options with Discrete Sampling, *SIAM Journal on Applied Mathematics*, Vol. 55, pp. 267–276.

Dewynne, J. and P. Wilmott (1995b). Asian Options as Linear Complementary Problems: Analysis and Finite Difference Solutions, in: P. Boyle, F. Longstaff and P. Ritchken (eds.), *Advances in Futures and Options Research*, Vol. 8, Jai Press, pp. 145–173.

Dufresne, D. (2000). Laguerre Series for Asian and Other Options, *Mathematical Finance*, Vol. 10, pp. 407–428.

Forsyth, P., K. Vetzal and R. Zvan (1999). Convergence of Lattice and PDE Methods for Pricing Asian Options, Working Paper, University of Waterloo.

Fu, M., D. Madan and T. Wong (1998). Pricing Continuous Asian Options: A Comparison of Monte Carlo and Laplace Transform Inversion Methods, *Journal of Computational Finance*, Winter, pp. 49–74.

Gandhi, S., A. Kooros and G. Salkin (1993). Average Price Option: An Analytic Approach, Working Paper, Imperial College.

Geman, H. and A. Eydeland (1995). Domino Effect, *Risk*, April, pp. 65–67.

Geman, H. and M. Yor (1993). Bessel Processes, Asian Options and Perpetuities, *Mathematical Finance*, Vol. 3, pp. 349–375.

Hansen, A. and P. Jorgensen (1998). Analytical Valuation of American Style Asian Options, Working Paper, University of Aarhus.

Haykov, J. (1993). A Better Control Variate for Pricing Standard Asian Options, *Journal of Financial Engineering*, Vol. 2, pp. 207–216.

Heenk, B., A. Kemna and T. Vorst (1990). Asian Options on Oil Spreads, *Review of Futures Markets*, Vol. 9, pp. 511–528.

Hull, J. and A. White (1993). Efficient Procedures for Valuing European and American Path-Dependent Options, *Journal of Derivatives*, Fall, pp. 21–31.

Iwaki, H., M. Kijima and T. Yoshida (1993). Approximate Valuation of Average Options, *Annals of Operations Research*, Vol. 45, pp. 131–145.

Kat, H. (1993). An Analytical Formula for Pricing Asian Options, Working Paper, MeesPierson.

Kemna, A. and T. Vorst (1990). A Pricing Method for Options Based on Average Asset Values, *Journal of Banking and Finance*, Vol. 14, pp. 113–129.

Levy, E. (1990). Asian Arithmetic, *Risk*, May, pp. 7–8.

Levy, E. (1992). Pricing European Average Rate Currency Options, *Journal of International Money and Finance*, Vol. 11, pp. 474–491.

Levy, E. (1997). Asian Options, in: L. Clewlow and C. Strickland (eds.), *Exotic Options: The State of the Art*, International Thomson, pp. 65–98.

Levy, E. and S. Turnbull (1992). Average Intelligence, *Risk*, February, pp. 53–59.

Milevsky, M. and S. Posner (1998). Asian Options, the Sum of Lognormals and the Reciprocal Gamma Distribution, *Journal of Financial and Quantitative Analysis*, Vol. 33, pp. 409–422.

Neave, E. (1991). Exact Solutions for Average Spot and Average Strike Price European Options on a Symmetric Random Walk, Working Paper, Queen's University.

Neave, E. (1994). A Frequency Distribution Method for Valuing Average Options, Working Paper, Queen's University.

Neave, E. and S. Turnbull (1994). Quick Solutions for Arithmetic Average Options on a Recombining Random Walk, Working Paper, Queen's University.

Posner, S. and M. Milevsky (1998). Valuing Exotic Options by Approximating the SPD with Higher Moments, *Journal of Financial Engineering*, Vol. 7, pp. 109–125.

Ritchken, P., L. Sankarasubramanian and A.M. Vijh (1990). Averaging Options for Capping Total Costs, *Financial Management*, Autumn, pp. 35–41.

Ritchken, P., L. Sankarasubramanian and A.M. Vijh (1993). The Valuation of Path Dependent Contracts on the Average, *Management Science*, Vol. 39, pp. 1202–1213.

Rogers, L. and Z. Shi (1995). The Value of an Asian Option, *Journal of Applied Probability*, Vol. 32, pp. 1077–1088.

Ruttiens, A. (1990). Classical Replica, *Risk*, February, pp. 33–36.

Turnbull, S. and L. Wakeman (1991). A Quick Algorithm for Pricing European Average Options, *Journal of Financial and Quantitative Analysis*, Vol. 26, pp. 377–389.

Vecer, J. (2000). A New PDE Approach for Pricing Arithmetic Average Asian Options, Working Paper, Carnegie Mellon University.

Vorst, T. (1992). Prices and Hedge Ratios of Average Exchange Rate Options, *International Review of Financial Analysis*, Vol. 1, pp. 179–193.

Vorst, T. (1996). Averaging Options, in: I. Nelken (ed.), *Handbook of Exotic Options*, Irwin, pp. 175–199.

Yor, M. (1993). From Planar Brownian Windings to Asian Options, *Insurance: Mathematics and Economics*, Vol. 13, pp. 23–34.

Zhang, P. (1994). Flexible Asian Options, *Journal of Financial Engineering*, Vol. 3, pp. 65–83.

Zhang, P. (1995). Flexible Arithmetic Asian Options, *Journal of Derivatives*, Spring, pp. 53–63.

Zhang, J. (1999). Arithmetic Asian Options with Continuous Sampling, Working Paper, City University Hong Kong.

Zvan, R., P. Forsyth and K. Vetzal (1997). Robust Numerical Methods for PDE Models of Asian Options, *Journal of Computational Finance*, Winter, pp. 39–78.

Basket Options

Curran, M. (1994). Valuing Asian and Portfolio Options by Conditioning on the Geometric Mean, *Management Science*, Vol. 40, pp. 1705–1711.
Dembo, R. and P. Patel (1990). Protective Basket, *Risk*, February, pp. 25–28.
Gentle, D. (1993). Basket Weaving, *Risk*, June, pp. 51–52.
Grannis, S. (1989). An Idea Whose Time Has Come, *Risk*, September, pp. 72–74.
Huynh, C. (1994). Back to Baskets, *Risk*, May, pp. 59–61.
Joy, C., P. Boyle and K. Seng (1996). Quasi Monte Carlo Methods in Numerical Finance, *Management Science*, Vol. 42, pp. 926–938.
Lamberton, D. and B. Lapeyre (1993). Hedging Options with Few Assets, *Mathematical Finance*, Vol. 3, pp. 25–41.
Milevsky, M. and S. Posner (1998). A Closed-Form Approximation for Valuing Basket Options, *Journal of Derivatives*, Summer, pp. 54–61.
Reiner, E. (1992). An Analysis of Premium Savings for Options on Asset Baskets and the USDX Index, Working Paper, Leland O'Brien Rubinstein Associates.

Chooser Options

Aparicio, S. and L. Clewlow (1997). American Featured Options, in: L. Clewlow and C. Strickland (eds.), *Exotic Options: The State of the Art*, International Thomson, pp. 35–63.
Nelken, I. (1993). Square Deals, *Risk*, April, pp. 56–59.
Nelken, I. (1996). Compound Options and Chooser Options, in: I. Nelken (ed.), *Handbook of Exotic Options*, Irwin, pp. 129–142.
Rubinstein, M. (1991). Options for the Undecided, *Risk*, April, p. 43.

Contingent Premium Options

Kat, H. (1994). Contingent Premium Options, *Journal of Derivatives*, Summer, pp. 44–54.
Turnbull, S. (1992). The Price is Right, *Risk*, April, pp. 56–57.

Delayed Settlement Options

Yu, G. (1994). Financial Instruments to Lock In Payoffs, *Journal of Derivatives*, Spring, pp. 77–85.

Digitals

Garman, M. (1978). The Pricing of Supershares, *Journal of Financial Economics*, Vol. 6, pp. 3–10.
Hakansson, N. (1976). The Purchasing Power Fund: A New Kind of Financial Intermediary, *Financial Analysts Journal*, November–December, pp. 49–59.
Hakansson, N. (1977). The Superfund: Efficient Paths Towards Efficient Capital Markets in Large and Small Countries, in: H. Levy and M. Sarnat, *Financial Decision Making under Uncertainty*, Academic Press, pp. 165–201.
Heynen, R. and H. Kat (1995). Partial Binary Barrier Options, Working Paper, First Chicago.
Heynen, R. and H. Kat (1996). Brick by Brick, *Risk*, June, pp. 58–61.
Hui, C. (1996). One Touch Double Barrier Binary Option Values, *Applied Financial Economics*, Vol. 6, pp. 343–346.
Ingersoll, J. (2000). Digital Contracts: Simple Tools for Pricing Complex Derivatives, *Journal of Business*, Vol. 73, pp. 67–88.
Liu, R. (1995). The Alchemy of Asian Exotics, *AsiaRisk*, November, pp. 50–52.
Pechtl, A. (1995). Classified Information, *Risk*, June, pp. 59–61.
Rubinstein, M. and E. Reiner (1991). Unscrambling the Binary Code, *Risk*, October, pp. 75–83. Erratum in *Risk*, December 1991–January 1992, p. 73.
Zhang, P. (1995). Correlation Digital Options, *Journal of Financial Engineering*, Vol. 4, pp. 75–96.

Exchange and Spread Options

Carr, P. (1988). The Valuation of Sequential Exchange Opportunities, *Journal of Finance*, Vol. 43, pp. 1235–1255.
Derman, E. (1996). Outperformance Options, in: I. Nelken (ed.), *Handbook of Exotic Options*, Irwin, pp. 244–250.
Derman, E. and I. Kani (1992). Valuing and Hedging Outperformance Options, Quantitative Strategies Research Note, Goldman Sachs.
Fischer, S. (1978). Call Option Pricing When the Exercise Price is Uncertain, and the Valuation of Index Bonds, *Journal of Finance*, Vol. 33, pp. 169–176.
Garman, M. (1992). Spread the Load, *Risk*, December, pp. 68–84.
Margrabe, W. (1978). The Value of an Option to Exchange One Asset for Another, *Journal of Finance*, Vol. 33, pp. 177–186.
Margrabe, W. (1993). Triangular Equilibrium and Arbitrage in the Market for Options to Exchange Two Assets, *Journal of Derivatives*, Fall, pp. 60–70.
McDonald, R. and D. Siegel (1986). The Value of Waiting to Invest, *Quarterly Journal of Economics*, Vol. 101, pp. 707–727.
Pearson, N. (1995). An Efficient Approach for Pricing Spread Options, *Journal of Derivatives*, Fall, pp. 76–91.
Poitras, G. (1998). Spread Options, Exchange Options and Arithmetic Brownian Motion, *Journal of Futures Markets*, Vol. 18, pp. 487–517.
Ravindran, K. (1993). Low-Fat Spreads, *Risk*, October, pp. 66–67.
Rubinstein, M. (1991). One for Another, *Risk*, July, pp. 30–32.
Shimko, D. (1994). Options on Futures Spreads: Hedging, Speculation and Valuation, *Journal of Futures Markets*, Vol. 14, pp. 183–213.

Forward-Starting Strike Options

Blazenko, G., P. Boyle, K. Newport (1990). Valuation of Tandem Options, in: F. Fabozzi (ed.), *Advances in Futures and Options Research*, Vol. 4, Jai Press, pp. 39–49.
Heynen, R. and H. Kat (1995). Quantity-Adjusting Options with Forward-Starting Strikes, Working Paper, First Chicago.
Rubinstein, M. (1991). Pay Now, Choose Later, *Risk*, February, p. 13.

Instalment, Compound and Extendible Options

Aparicio, S. and L. Clewlow (1997). American Featured Options, in: L. Clewlow and C. Strickland (eds.), *Exotic Options: The State of the Art*, International Thomson, pp. 35–63.
Carr, P. (1988). The Valuation of Sequential Exchange Opportunities, *Journal of Finance*, Vol. 43, pp. 1235–1255.
Chung, Y. and H. Johnson (1993). Extendible Options: The General Case, Working Paper, University of California at Riverside.
Davis, M., W. Schachermayer and R. Tompkins (2000). Pricing, No-Arbitrage Bounds and Robust Hedging of Instalment Options, Working Paper, Technical University, Vienna.
Geske, R. (1979). The Valuation of Compound Options, *Journal of Financial Economics*, Vol. 7, pp. 63–81.
Karsenty, F. and J. Sikorav (1993). Instalment Plan, *Risk*, October, pp. 36–40.
Longstaff, F. (1990). Pricing Options With Extendible Maturities: Analysis and Applications, *Journal of Finance*, Vol. 45, pp. 935–957.
Nelken, I. (1993). Square Deals, *Risk*, April, pp. 56–59.
Nelken, I. (1996). Compound Options and Chooser Options, in: I. Nelken (ed.), *Handbook of Exotic Options*, Irwin, pp. 129–142.
Omberg, E. (1987). A Note on the Convergence of the Binomial Pricing and Compound Option Models, *Journal of Finance*, Vol. 42, pp. 463–469.
Raymar, S. and A. Sheikh (1996). The Valuation of Compound Options and American Calls on Dividend Paying Stocks with Time Varying Volatility, *Journal of Financial Engineering*, Vol. 5, pp. 243–266.
Rubinstein, M. (1991). Double Trouble, *Risk*, December, p. 73.
Schroder, M. (1989). A Reduction Method Applicable to Compound Option Formulas, *Management Science*, Vol. 35, pp. 823–827.
Selby, M. and S. Hodges (1987). On the Evaluation of Compound Options, *Management Science*, Vol. 33, pp. 347–355.

Knock-In and Knock-Out Options

Ahn, D., S. Figlewski and B. Gao (1999). Pricing Discrete Barrier Options with an Adaptive Mesh Model, *Journal of Derivatives*, Summer, pp. 33–43.

Aitsahlia, F. and T. Lai (1997). Valuation of Discrete Barrier and Hindsight Options, *Journal of Financial Engineering*, Vol. 6, pp. 169–177.

Andersen, L. and R. Brotherton-Ratcliffe (1996). Exact Exotics, *Risk*, October, pp. 85–89.

Avellaneda, M. and L. Wu (1999). Pricing Parisian-Style Options with a Lattice Method, *International Journal of Theoretical and Applied Finance*, Vol. 2, pp. 1–16.

Beaglehole, D. (1992). Down and Out, Up and In Options, Working Paper, University of Iowa.

Benson, R. and N. Daniel (1991). Up, Over and Out, *Risk*, June, pp. 17–19.

Berger, E. (1996). Barrier Options, in: I. Nelken (ed.), *Handbook of Exotic Options*, Irwin, pp. 213–243.

Bermin, H. (1996a). Combining Lookback Options and Barrier Options: The Case of Look-Barrier Options, Working Paper, Lund University.

Bermin, H. (1996b). Time and Path Dependent Options: The Case of Time Dependent Inside and Outside Barrier Options, Working Paper, Lund University.

Bhagavatula, R. and P. Carr (1995). Valuing Double Barrier Options with Time-Dependent Parameters, Working Paper, Cornell University.

Boyle, P. and S. Lau (1994). Bumping Up Against the Barrier with the Binomial Method, *Journal of Derivatives*, Summer, pp. 6–14.

Boyle, P. and Y. Tian (1998). An Explicit Finite Difference Approach to the Pricing of Barrier Options, *Applied Mathematical Finance*, Vol. 5, pp. 17–43.

Broadie, M., P. Glasserman and S. Kou (1997a). A Continuity Correction for Discrete Barrier Options, *Mathematical Finance*, Vol. 7, pp. 325–349.

Broadie, M., P. Glasserman and S. Kou (1997b). Connecting Discrete and Continuous Path-Dependent Options, Working Paper, Columbia Business School.

Carr, P. (1995). Two Extensions to Barrier Option Valuation, *Applied Mathematical Finance*, Vol. 2, pp. 173–209.

Chance, D. (1994). The Pricing and Hedging of Limited Exercise Caps and Spreads, *Journal of Financial Research*, Vol. 17, pp. 561–584.

Chesney, M., J. Cornwall, M. Jeanblanc-Picque, G. Kentwell and M. Yor (1997). Parisian Pricing, *Risk*, January, pp. 77–79.

Cheuk, T. and T. Vorst (1996a). Breaking Down Barriers, *Risk*, April, pp. 64–67.

Cheuk, T. and T. Vorst (1996b). Complex Barrier Options, *Journal of Derivatives*, Fall, pp. 8–22.

Cornwall, J. and G. Kentwell (1995). A Quasi-Analytic Approach to the Occupation Time Barrier, Working Paper, Bankers Trust.

Cornwall, J., G. Kentwell and S. McDonald (1995). Computational and Discrete Time Results of the Occupation Time Barrier Option, Working Paper, Bankers Trust.

Davydov, D. and V. Linetsky (1998). Double Step Options, Working Paper, University of Michigan.

Derman, E. and I. Kani (1993). The Ins and Outs of Barrier Options, Quantitative Strategies Research Note, Goldman Sachs.

Derman, E., I. Kani, D. Ergener and I. Bardhan (1995). Enhanced Numerical Methods for Options with Barriers, *Financial Analysts Journal*, November–December, pp. 65–74.

Duanmu, Z. (1994). *First Passage Time Density Approach to Pricing Barrier Options and Monte Carlo Simulation of the HJM Interest Rate Model*, Ph.D. Thesis, Cornell University.

El Babsiri, M. and G. Noel (1998). Simulating Path-Dependent Options: A New Approach, *Journal of Derivatives*, Winter, pp. 65–83.

Figlewski, S. and B. Gao (1999). The Adaptive Mesh Model: A New Approach to Efficient Option Pricing, *Journal of Financial Economics*, Vol. 53, pp. 313–351.

Flesaker, B. (1992). The Design and Valuation of Capped Stock Index Options, Working Paper, University of Illinois at Urbana-Champaign.

Fusai, G. (1998a). Valuation of Corridor Derivatives, Working Paper, University Luigi Bocconi, Milan.

Fusai, G. (1998b). Generalizations of the Arc-Sine Law and Pricing of Corridor Derivatives, Working Paper, University di Firenze, Florence.

Geman, H. and M. Yor (1996). Pricing and Hedging Double Barrier Options: A Probabilistic Approach, *Mathematical Finance*, Vol. 6, pp. 365–378.

Haber, R., P. Schonbucher and P. Wilmott (1999). Pricing Parisian Options, *Journal of Derivatives*, Spring, pp. 71–79.

Hart, I. and M. Ross (1994). Striking Continuity, *Risk*, June, pp. 51–56.

Heynen, R. and H. Kat (1994a). Partial Barrier Options, *Journal of Financial Engineering*, Vol. 3, pp. 253–274.

Heynen, R. and H. Kat (1994b). Crossing Barriers, *Risk*, June, pp. 46–51.

Heynen, R. and H. Kat (1995). Window Options, Working Paper, First Chicago.

Heynen, R. and H. Kat (1996). Discrete Partial Barrier Options with a Moving Barrier, *Journal of Financial Engineering*, Vol. 5, pp. 199–209.

Heynen, R. and H. Kat (1997). Barrier Options, in: L. Clewlow and C. Strickland (eds.), *Exotic Options: The State of the Art*, International Thomson, pp. 125–157.

Hudson, M. (1991). The Value in Going Out, *Risk*, March, pp. 29–33.

Hugonnier, J. (1999). The Feynman–Kac Formula and Pricing Occupation Time Derivatives, *International Journal of Theoretical and Applied Finance*, Vol. 2, pp. 153–178.

Hui, C. (1997). Time Dependent Barrier Option Values, *Journal of Futures Markets*, Vol. 17, pp. 667–688.

Hui, C., C. Lo and P. Yuen (2000). Comment on 'Pricing Double Barrier Options Using Laplace Transforms' by Antoon Pelsser, *Finance and Stochastics*, Vol. 4, pp. 105–107.

Ikeda, M. and N. Kunitomo (1992). Pricing Options with Curved Boundaries, *Mathematical Finance*, Vol. 2, pp. 275–298. Correction in Vol. 10, pp. 459–460.

Jamshidian, F. (1997). A Note on the Analytical Valuation of Double Barrier Options, Working Paper.

Kat, H. and L. Verdonk (1995). Tree Surgery, *Risk*, February, pp. 53–56.

Kwok, Y., L. Wu and H. Yu (1998). Pricing Multi-Asset Options with an External Barrier, *International Journal of Theoretical and Applied Finance*, Vol. 1, pp. 523–541.

Levy, E. and F. Mantion (1997). Discrete by Nature, *Risk*, January, pp. 74–75.

Li, A. (1998). The Pricing of Double Barrier Options and Their Variations, in: P. Boyle, G. Pennaccni and P. Ritchken (eds.), *Advances in Futures and Options Research*, Vol. 10, Jai Press, pp. 17–41.

Li, A. and S. Liu (1995). Lattice Methods for Barrier Options, Working Paper, First Chicago.

Linetsky, V. (1998). Steps to the Barrier, *Risk*, April, pp. 62–65.

Linetsky, V. (1999). Step Options: The Feynman–Kac Approach to Occupation Time Derivatives, *Mathematical Finance*, Vol. 9, pp. 55–96.

Lyuu, Y. (1998). Very Fast Algorithms for Barrier Option Pricing and the Ballot Problem, *Journal of Derivatives*, Spring, pp. 68–79.

Owens, T. (1996). Constructing FX Options with Discrete Barriers—Using High Dimensional Number Integration Routines To Ensure Optimal Pricing and Hedging, Working Paper, Chase Manhattan.

Pelsser, A. (2000). Pricing Double Barrier Options Using Laplace Transforms, *Finance and Stochastics*, Vol. 4, pp. 95–104.

Pooley, D., P. Forsyth, K. Vetzal and R. Simpson (1999). Unstructured Meshing for Two Asset Barrier Options, Working Paper, University of Waterloo.

Ramanlal, P. (1997). Which Warrant, *Risk*, January, pp. 81–85.

Reimer, M. and K. Sandmann (1993). Down-and-Out Call, Working Paper, University of Bonn.

Reimer, M. and K. Sandmann (1995). A Discrete Time Approach for European and American Barrier Options, Working Paper, University of Bonn.

Rich, D. (1993). The Valuation and Application of Options with Stochastic Barriers, Working Paper, Virginia Polytechnic Institute.

Rich, D. (1994). The Mathematical Foundations of Barrier Option Pricing Theory, in: D.M. Chance and R.R. Trippi (eds.), *Advances in Futures and Options Research*, Vol. 7, Jai Press, pp. 267–311.

Ritchken, P. (1995). On Pricing Barrier Options, *Journal of Derivatives*, Vol. 3, pp. 19–28.

Roberts, G. and C. Shortland (1994). Pricing Barrier Options with Time Dependent Coefficients, Working Paper, University of Cambridge.

Rogers, L. and O. Zane (1997). Valuing Moving Barrier Options, *Journal of Computational Finance*, Fall, pp. 5–11.

Rubinstein, M. and E. Reiner (1991). Breaking Down the Barriers, *Risk*, August, pp. 28–35.

Schnabel, J. and J. Wei (1994). Valuing Takeover Contingent Foreign Exchange Call Options, in: D. Chance and R. Trippi (eds.), *Advances in Futures and Options Research*, Vol. 7, Jai Press, pp. 223–236.

Schroder, M. (2000). On the Valuation of Double Barrier Options: Computational Aspects, *Journal of Computational Finance*, Summer, pp. 5–34.

Sidenius, J. (1998). Double Barrier Options: Valuation by Path Counting, *Journal of Computational Finance*, Spring, pp. 63–79.

Steiner, M., M. Wallmeier and R. Hafner (1999a). Pricing Discrete Knock-Out Options with Tree Methods, *OR Spektrum*, Vol. 21, pp. 147–181.

Steiner, M., M. Wallmeier and R. Hafner (1999b). Pricing Near the Barrier: the Case of Discrete Knock-Out Options, *Journal of Computational Finance*, Fall, pp. 69–90.

Sullivan, M. (2000). Pricing Discretely Monitored Barrier Options, *Journal of Computational Finance*, Summer, pp. 35–52.

Tian, Y. (1996). Breaking the Barrier with a Two-Stage Binomial Model, Working Paper, University of Cincinnati.

Tian, Y. (1997). Pricing Options with Discontinuous Barriers, *Journal of Financial Engineering*, Vol. 6, pp. 193–216.

Trippi, R. and D. Chance (1993). Quick Valuation of the Bermuda Capped Option, *Journal of Portfolio Management*, Fall, pp. 93–99.

Vetzal, K. and P. Forsyth (1999). Discrete Parisian and Delayed Barrier Options: A General Numerical Approach, in: P. Boyle, G. Pennacchi and P. Ritchken (eds.), *Advances in Futures and Options Research*, Vol. 10, Jai Press, pp. 1–15.

Wei, J. (1998). Valuation of Discrete Barrier Options by Interpolations, *Journal of Derivatives*, Fall, pp. 51–73.

Yor, M., M. Chesney, H. Geman and M. Jeanblanc-Picque (1997). Some Combinations of Asian, Parisian and Barrier Options, in: M. Dempster and S. Pliska, *Mathematics of Derivative Securities*, Cambridge University Press, pp. 61–87.

Zhang, P. (1995). A Unified Formula for Outside Barrier Options, *Journal of Financial Engineering*, Vol. 4, pp. 335–349.

Zvan, R., P. Forsyth and K. Vetzal (1999). Discrete Asian Barrier Options, *Journal of Computational Finance*, Fall, pp. 41–67.

Zvan, R., P. Forsyth and K. Vetzal (2000). PDE Methods for Pricing Barrier Options, *Journal of Economic Dynamics and Control*, Vol. 24, pp. 1563–1590.

Ladder Options

Gastineau, G. (1994). Roll Up Puts, Roll Down Calls and Contingent Premium Options, *Journal of Derivatives*, Summer, pp. 40–43.

Kat, H. (1998). Improving Market Timing Using Exotic Options, *Derivatives: Tax, Regulation, Finance*, September–October, pp. 4–12.

Street, A. (1992). Stuck Up a Ladder?, *Risk*, May, pp. 43–44.

Lookback Options

Aitsahlia, F. and T. Lai (1997). Valuation of Discrete Barrier and Hindsight Options, *Journal of Financial Engineering*, Vol. 6, pp. 169–177.

Aitsahlia, F. and T. Lai (1998). Random Walk Duality and the Valuation of Discrete Lookback Options, *Applied Mathematical Finance*, Vol. 5, pp. 227–240.

Andreasen, J. (1998). The Pricing of Discretely Sampled Asian and Lookback Options: A Change of Numeraire Approach, *Journal of Computational Finance*, Fall, pp. 5–30.

Babbs, S. (2000). Binomial Valuation of Lookback Options, *Journal of Economic Dynamics & Control*, Vol. 24, pp. 1499–1525.

Bermin, H. (1996). Exotic Lookback Options: The Case of Extreme Spread Options, Working Paper, Lund University.

Cheuk, T.H.F. and A.C.F. Vorst (1997). Currency Lookback Options and the Observation Frequency: A Binomial Approach, *Journal of International Money and Finance*, Vol. 16, pp. 173–187.

Conze, A. and R. Viswanathan (1991). Path Dependent Options: The Case of Lookback Options, *Journal of Finance*, Vol. 46, pp. 1893–1907.

Garman, M. (1989). Recollection in Tranquillity, *Risk*, March, pp. 16–18.

Goldman, M., H. Sosin and M. Gatto (1979a). On Contingent Claims that Insure Ex-Post Optimal Stock Market Timing, *Journal of Finance*, Vol. 34, pp. 401–413.

Goldman, M., H. Sosin and M. Gatto (1979b). Path Dependent Options: 'Buy at the Low, Sell at the High', *Journal of Finance*, Vol. 34, pp. 1111–1127.

Gray, S. and R. Whaley (1997). Valuing S&P 500 Bear Market Warrants with a Periodic Reset, *Journal of Derivatives*, Fall, pp. 99–106.

He, H., W. Keirstead and J. Rebholz (1994). Double Lookbacks, Working Paper, University of California at Berkeley.

Heynen, R. and H. Kat (1994). Selective Memory, *Risk*, November, pp. 73–76.

Heynen, R. and H. Kat (1995). Lookback Options with Discrete and Partial Monitoring of the Underlying Price, *Applied Mathematical Finance*, Vol. 2, pp. 273–284.

Heynen, R. and H. Kat (1997). Lookback Options: Pricing and Applications, in: L. Clewlow and C. Strickland (eds.), *Exotic Options: The State of the Art*, International Thomson, pp. 99–123.

Heynen, R. and H. Kat (1998). Lookbacks with Barriers, Working Paper, Bank of America.

Hull, J. and A. White (1993). Efficient Procedures for Valuing European and American Path-Dependent Options, *Journal of Derivatives*, Fall, pp. 21–31.

Kat, H. (1995). Pricing Lookback Options Using Binomial Trees: An Evaluation, *Journal of Financial Engineering*, Vol. 4, pp. 375–397.

Levy, E. and F. Mantion (1997). Approximate Valuation of Discrete Lookback and Barrier Options, *Net Exposure*, November.

Options on the Best-of or Worst-of

Barone, E. and A. Bucci (1991). The Valuation of Multiple Options: An Application to the Exchange Rate Market of the Italian Lira, Working Paper, IMI Group.

Barraquand, J. (1995). Numerical Valuation of High Dimensional Multivariate European Securities, *Management Science*, Vol. 41, pp. 1882–1891.

Barraquand, J. and D. Martineau (1995). Numerical Valuation of High Dimensional Multivariate American Securities, *Journal of Financial and Quantitative Analysis*, Vol. 30, pp. 383–405.

Barrett, J., G. Moore and P. Wilmott (1992). Inelegant Efficiency, *Risk*, October, pp. 82–84.

Boyle, P. (1988). A Lattice Framework for Option Pricing with Two State Variables, *Journal of Financial and Quantitative Analysis*, Vol. 23, pp. 1–12.

Boyle, P. (1990). Valuation of Derivative Securities Involving Several Assets Using Discrete Time Methods, *Insurance: Mathematics and Economics*, Vol. 9, pp. 131–139.

Boyle, P. and X. Lin (1997). Bounds on Multiple Contingent Claims Based on Several Assets, *Journal of Financial Economics*, Vol. 46, pp. 383–400.

Boyle, P. and Y. Tse (1990). An Algorithm for Computing Values of Options on the Maximum or Minimum of Several Assets, *Journal of Financial and Quantitative Analysis*, Vol. 25, pp. 215–227.

Boyle, P., J. Evnine and S. Gibbs (1989). Numerical Evaluation of Multivariate Contingent Claims, *Review of Financial Studies*, Vol. 2, pp. 241–250.

Cheyette, O. (1990). Pricing Options on Multiple Assets, in: F. Fabozzi (ed.), *Advances in Futures and Options Research*, Vol. 4, Jai Press, pp. 69–81.

De Munnik, J. (1990). Options on Several Assets: A Multinomial Approach, Working Paper, Erasmus University, Rotterdam.

Engelmann, B. and P. Schwendner (1998). The Pricing of Multi-Asset Options Using a Fourier Grid Method, *Journal of Computational Finance*, Summer, pp. 53–61.

Hunziker, J. and P. Koch-Medina (1996). Two-Color Rainbow Options, in: I. Nelken (ed.), *Handbook of Exotic Options*, Irwin, pp. 143–174.

Johnson, H. (1984). The Pricing of Complex Options, Working Paper, University of California at Berkeley.

Johnson, H. (1987). Options on the Maximum or the Minimum of Several Assets, *Journal of Financial and Quantitative Analysis*, Vol. 22, pp. 277–283.

Kamrad, B. and P. Ritchken (1991). Multinomial Approximating Models for Options with k State Variables, *Management Science*, Vol. 37, pp. 1640–1652.

Rich, D. and D. Chance (1993). An Alternative Approach to the Pricing of Options on Multiple Assets, *Journal of Financial Engineering*, Vol. 2, pp. 271–285.

Romagnoli, S. and T. Vargiolu (2000). Robustness of the Black–Scholes Approach in the Case of Options on Several Assets, *Finance and Stochastics*, Vol. 4, pp. 325–341.

Ross, R. (1998). Good Point Methods for Computing Prices and Sensitivities of Multi-Asset European Style Options, *Applied Mathematical Finance*, Vol. 5, pp. 83–106.

Rubinstein, M. (1991). Somewhere Over the Rainbow, *Risk*, November, pp. 63–66.

Stulz, R. (1982). Options on the Minimum or the Maximum of Two Risky Assets, *Journal of Financial Economics*, Vol. 10, pp. 161–185.

Wu, X. and J. Zhang (2000). Options on the Minimum or the Maximum of Two Average Prices, *Review of Derivatives Research*, Vol. 3, pp. 183–204.

Ordinary Options

Andreasen, J., B. Jensen and R. Poulsen (1996). New Skin for the Old Ceremony: Eight Different Derivations of the Black–Scholes Formula, Working Paper, University of Aarhus.

Black, F. (1989). How We Came Up with the Option Formula, *Journal of Portfolio Management*, Winter, pp. 4–8.

Black, F. and M.S. Scholes (1973). The Pricing of Options and Corporate Liabilities, *Journal of Political Economy*, Vol. 3, pp. 637–654.

Brennan, M.J. (1979). The Pricing of Contingent Claims in Discrete Time Models, *Journal of Finance*, Vol. 34, pp. 53–68.

Geske, R., R. Roll and K. Shastri (1983). Over-The-Counter Option Market Dividend Protection and Biases in the Black–Scholes Model: A Note, *Journal of Finance*, Vol. 38, pp. 1271–1277.

Grinblatt, M. and H. Johnson (1988). A Put Option Paradox, *Journal of Financial and Quantitative Analysis*, Vol. 23, pp. 23–26.

Harpaz, G. (1988). The Non-Optimality of the Over-The-Counter Options Dividend Protection, *Economic Letters*, Vol. 27, pp. 55–59.

Merton, R. (1973). Theory of Rational Option Pricing, *Bell Journal of Economics and Management Science*, Spring, pp. 141–183.

Rubinstein, M. (1976). The Valuation of Uncertain Income Streams and the Pricing of Options, *Bell Journal of Economics and Management Science*, Autumn, pp. 407–425.

Passport Options

Ahn, H., A. Penaud and P. Wilmott (1998). Various Passport Options and Their Valuation, *Applied Mathematical Finance*, Vol. 6, pp. 275–292.
Anderson, L., J. Andreasen and R. Brotherton-Ratcliffe (1998). The Passport Option, *Journal of Computational Finance*, Spring, pp. 15–36.
Delbaen, F. and M. Yor (1999). Passport Options, Working Paper, ETH Zurich.
Henderson, V. (1999). Price Comparison Results and Super-Replication: An Application to Passport Options, Working Paper, University of Bath.
Henderson, V. and D. Hobson (2000). Local Time, Coupling and the Passport Option, *Finance and Stochastics*, Vol. 4, pp. 69–80.
Hyer, T. and D. Pugachevsky (1997). Valuation of Passport Options, Working Paper, Bankers Trust.
Hyer, T., A. Lipton and D. Pugachevsky (1997). Passport to Success, *Risk*, September, pp. 127–131.
Jamshidian, F. (1998). A Note on the Passport Option, Working Paper, Sakura Global Capital.
Lipton, A. (1996). Analytical Valuation of Passport Options, Working Paper, Bankers Trust.
Lipton, A. (1999). Similarities via Self-Similarities, *Risk*, September, pp. 101–105.
Nagayama, I. (1998). Pricing of Passport Options, *Journal of Mathematical Science of the University of Tokyo*, Vol. 5, pp. 747–785.
Penaud, A., H. Ahn and P. Wilmott (1998). Exotic Passport Options, Working Paper, Oxford University.
Shreve, S. and J. Vecer (1998). Passport Option: Probabilistic Approach for Solving the Symmetric Case, Working Paper, Carnegie Mellon University.
Shreve, S. and J. Vecer (2000). Options on a Traded Account: Vacation Calls, Vacation Puts and Passport Options, *Finance and Stochastics*, Vol. 4, pp. 255–274.
Vecer, J. and S. Shreve (2000). Upgrading Your Passport, *Risk*, July, pp. 81–83.

Power Options

Gheysen, K. (1995). Do You Know the Belgian Option?, Working Paper.
Heynen, R. and H. Kat (1995). Belgian Options: Some Comments, Working Paper, First Chicago.
Heynen, R. and H. Kat (1996). Pricing and Hedging Power Options, *Financial Engineering and the Japanese Markets*, Vol. 3, pp. 253–261.
Kreuser, J. and L. Seigel (1995). Derivative Securities: The Atomic Structure, Working Paper, World Bank.
Neuberger, A. (1994). The Log Contract, *Journal of Portfolio Management*, Winter, pp. 74–80.
Neuberger, A. (1996). The Log Contract and Other Power Contracts, in: I. Nelken (ed.), *Handbook of Exotic Options*, Irwin, pp. 200–212.
Tompkins, R. (1999). Power Options: Hedging Nonlinear Risks, *Journal of Risk*, Winter, pp. 29–45.

Quantity-Adjusting Options

Babbel, D. and L. Eisenberg (1993). Quantity-Adjusting Options and Forward Contracts, *Journal of Financial Engineering*, Vol. 2, pp. 89–126.
Heynen, R. and H. Kat (1995). Quantity-Adjusting Options with Forward-Starting Strikes, Working Paper, First Chicago.
Marcus, A. and D. Modest (1986). The Valuation of a Random Number of Put Options: An Application to Agricultural Price Supports, *Journal of Financial and Quantitative Analysis*, Vol. 21, pp. 73–86.

Quanto and Composite Options

Brooks, R. (1992). Multivariate Contingent Claims Analysis with Cross-Currency Options as an Illustration, *Journal of Financial Engineering*, Vol. 1, pp. 196–218.
Clyman, D. (1991). Anatomy of an Anomaly or What I Know About Fixed Exchange Rate Nikkei Put Warrants, Working Paper, Harvard Business School.
Clyman, D. (1992). Arbitrage and Fixed Exchange Rate Nikkei Put Warrants, Working Paper, Harvard Business School.
Cooper, M. (1997). Quanto Structures, in: L. Clewlow and C. Strickland (eds.), *Exotic Options: The State of the Art*, International Thomson, pp. 159–187.

Demeterfi, K. (1998). How to Value and Hedge Options on Foreign Indices, Goldman Sachs Quantitative Strategies Research Note.

Derman, E., P. Karasinski and J. Wecker (1990). Understanding Guaranteed Exchange Rate Contracts in Foreign Stock Investments, International Equity Strategies, Goldman Sachs.

Dravid, A., M. Richardson and T. Sun (1993). Pricing Foreign Index Contingent Claims: An Application to Nikkei Index Warrants, *Journal of Derivatives*, Fall, pp. 33–51.

Gruca, E. and P. Ritchken (1993). Exchange Traded Foreign Warrants, in: D. Chance and R. Trippi (eds.), *Advances in Futures and Options Research*, Vol. 6, Jai Press, pp. 53–66.

Jamshidian, F. (1994). Corralling Quantos, *Risk*, March, pp. 71–75.

Kat, H. and H. Roozen (1994). Pricing and Hedging International Equity Derivatives, *Journal of Derivatives*, Winter, pp. 7–19.

Kwok, Y. and H. Wong (2000). Currency-Translated Foreign Equity Options with Path Dependent Features and Their Multi-Asset Extensions, *International Journal of Theoretical and Applied Finance*, Vol. 3, pp. 257–278.

Reiner, E. (1992). Quanto Mechanics, *Risk*, March, pp. 59–63.

Wei, J. (1992). Pricing Nikkei Put Warrants, *Journal of Multinational Financial Management*, Vol. 2, pp. 45–75.

Wei, J. (1997). Valuing Derivatives Linked to Foreign Assets, in: A. Konishi and R. Dattatreya (eds.), *Frontiers in Derivatives*, Irwin, pp. 89–126.

Shout Options

Aparicio, S. and L. Clewlow (1997). American Featured Options, in: L. Clewlow and C. Strickland (eds.), *Exotic Options: The State of the Art*, International Thomson, pp. 35–63.

Cheuk, T. and T. Vorst (1997). Shout Floors, *Net Exposure*, November.

Thomas, B. (1993). Something to Shout About, *Risk*, May, pp. 56–58.

Windcliff, H., P. Forsyth and K. Vetzal (1999). Shout Options: A Framework for Pricing Contracts which Can Be Modified by the Investor, Working Paper, University of Waterloo.

Windcliff, H., K. Vetzal, P. Forsyth, A. Verma and T. Coleman (1999). An Object-Oriented Framework for Valuing Shout Options on High-Performance Computer Architectures, Working Paper, University of Waterloo.

MODEL CALIBRATION AND IMPLIED VOLATILITY

Abadir, K. and M. Rockinger (1997). Density-Embedding Functions, Working Paper, HEC.

Abken, P., D. Madan and S. Ramamurtie (1996a). Pricing S&P 500 Index Options Using a Hilbert Space Basis, Working Paper, Federal Reserve Bank of Atlanta.

Abken, P., D. Madan and S. Ramamurtie (1996b). Estimation of Risk-Neutral and Statistical Densities by Hermite Polynomial Approximation, Working Paper, Federal Reserve Bank of Atlanta.

Ait-Sahalia, Y. and A. Lo (1998). Nonparametric Estimation of State-Price Densities Implicit in Financial Asset Prices, *Journal of Finance*, Vol. 53, pp. 499–547.

Andersen, L. and J. Andreasen (1999a). Jumping Smiles, *Risk*, November, pp. 65–68.

Andersen, L. and J. Andreasen (1999b). Jump-Diffusion Processes: Volatility Smile Fitting and Numerical Methods for Pricing, Working Paper, Gen Re.

Andersen, L. and R. Brotherton-Ratcliffe (1997). The Equity Option Volatility Smile: An Implicit Finite-Difference Approach, *Journal of Computational Finance*, Winter, pp. 5–37.

Andreasen, J. (1996). Implied Modeling: Stable Implementation, Hedging and Duality, Working Paper, University of Aarhus.

Aparicio, S. and S. Hodges (1998). Implied Risk-Neutral Distribution: A Comparison of Estimation Methods, Working Paper, Financial Options Research Centre, University of Warwick.

Avellaneda, M., A. Carelli and F. Stella (2000). A Bayesian Approach for Constructing Implied Volatility Surfaces through Neural Networks, *Journal of Computational Finance*, Fall, pp. 83–107.

Avellaneda, M., C. Friedman, R. Holmes and D. Samperi (1997). Calibrating Volatility Surfaces via Relative Entropy Minimization, *Applied Mathematical Finance*, Vol. 4, pp. 37–64.

Bahra, B. (1996). Probability Distributions of Future Asset Prices Implied by Option Prices, *Bank of England Quarterly Bulletin*, August, pp. 299–311.

Bahra, B. (1997). Implied Risk-Neutral Probability Density Functions from Option Prices: Theory and Application, Working Paper, Bank of England.

Banz, R. and M. Miller (1978). Prices for State-Contingent Claims: Some Estimates and Applications, *Journal of Business*, Vol. 51, pp. 653–672.

Barle, S. and N. Cakici (1995). Growing a Smiling Tree, *Risk*, October, pp. 76–81.

Barle, S. and N. Cakici (1998). How to Grow a Smiling Tree, *Journal of Financial Engineering*, Vol. 7, pp. 127–146.

Bick, A. and H. Reisman (1994). Generalized Implied Volatility, Working Paper, Simon Fraser University.

Bliss, R. and N. Panigirtzolou (1999). Testing the Stability of Implied Probability Density Functions, Working Paper, Bank of England.

Bodurtha, J. and M. Jermakyan (1996). Regular Smiles, Working Paper, Georgetown University.

Bodurtha, J. and M. Jermakyan (1999). Non-Parametric Estimation of an Implied Volatility Surface, *Journal of Computational Finance*, Summer, pp. 29–60.

Bondarenko, O. (2000a). Recovering Risk-Neutral Densities: A Non-Parametric Approach, Working Paper, University of Illinois at Chicago.

Bondarenko, O. (2000b). Performance of Alternative Techniques for Estimating Risk Neutral Densities, Working Paper, University of Illinois at Chicago.

Breeden, D. and R. Litzenberger (1978). Prices of State-Contingent Claims Implicit in Option Prices, *Journal of Business*, Vol. 51, pp. 621–651.

Brenner, R. (1996). Volatility is Not Constant, in: I. Nelken (ed.), *Handbook of Exotic Options*, Irwin, pp. 293–315.

Brigo, D. and F. Mercurio (2000a). A Mixed-Up Smile, *Risk*, September, pp. 123–126.

Brigo, D. and F. Mercurio (2000b). Fitting Volatility Skews and Smiles with Analytically Tractable Asset Price Models, Working Paper, Banca IMI, Milan.

Britten-Jones, M. and A. Neuberger (2000). Option Prices, Implied Price Processes and Stochastic Volatility, *Journal of Finance*, Vol. 55, pp. 839–866.

Brogden, A. (2000). The Taming of the Skew, *Risk*, November, pp. 112–115.

Brown, G. and C. Randall (1999). If the Skew Fits, *Risk*, April, pp. 62–65.

Brown, G. and K. Toft (1999). Constructing Binomial Trees from Multiple Implied Probability Distributions, *Journal of Derivatives*, Winter, pp. 83–100.

Buchen, P. and M. Kelly (1996). The Maximum Entropy Distribution of an Asset Inferred from Option Prices, *Journal of Financial and Quantitative Analysis*, Vol. 31, pp. 143–159.

Campa, J., K. Chang and R. Reider (1998). Implied Exchange Rate Distributions: Evidence from OTC Option Markets, *Journal of International Money and Finance*, Vol. 17, pp. 117–160.

Carr, P. and D. Madan (1998). Determining Volatility Surfaces and Option Values from an Implied Volatility Smile, Working Paper, Morgan Stanley.

Carr, P., M. Tari and T. Zariphopoulou (1999). Closed Form Option Valuation with Smiles, Working Paper, Banc of America.

Chriss, N. (1996). Transatlantic Trees, *Risk*, July, pp. 45–48.

Clewlow, L. and R. Grimwood (2000). A Computational Framework for Contingent Claim Pricing and Hedging under Time Dependent Asset Processes, in: Y. Abu-Mostafa, B. LeBaron, A. Lo and A. Weigend, (eds.) *Computational Finance 1999*, MIT Press.

Clewlow, L., S. Hodges and G. Skiadopoulos (1998). The Dynamics of Implied Volatility Surfaces, Working Paper, Financial Options Research Centre, University of Warwick.

Coleman, T., Y. Li and A. Verma (1999). Reconstructing the Unknown Local Volatility Function, *Journal of Computational Finance*, Spring, pp. 77–102.

Cooper, N. (1999). Testing Techniques for Estimating Implied RNDs from the Prices of European and American-Style Options, Working Paper, Bank of England.

Corrado, C. and T. Su (1996). Skewness and Kurtosis in S&P 500 Index Returns Implied by Option Prices, *Journal of Financial Research*, Vol. 19, pp. 175–192.

Corrado, C. and T. Su (1997). Implied Volatility Skews and Stock Index Skewness and Kurtosis Implied by S&P 500 Index Option Prices, *Journal of Derivatives*, Summer, pp. 8–19.

Crouhy, M. and D. Galai (1995). Hedging with a Volatility Term Structure, *Journal of Derivatives*, Spring, pp. 45–52.

Das, S. and R. Sundaram (1999). Of Smiles and Smirks: A Term Structure Perspective, *Journal of Financial and Quantitative Analysis*, Vol. 34, pp. 211–239.

Dempster, M. and D. Richards (2000). Pricing American Options Fitting the Smile, *Mathematical Finance*, Vol. 10, pp. 157–178.

Derman, E. (1999). Regimes of Volatility, *Risk*, April, pp. 55–59.

Derman, E. and I. Kani (1994). Riding on a Smile, *Risk*, February, pp. 32–39.

Derman, E. and I. Kani (1998). Stochastic Implied Trees: Arbitrage Pricing with Stochastic Term and Strike Structure of Volatility, *International Journal of Theoretical and Applied Finance*, Vol. 1, pp. 7–22.

Derman, E. and J. Zou (1997). Predicting the Response of Implied Volatility to Large Index Moves, Goldman Sachs Quantitative Strategies Research Note.

Derman, E., I. Kani and N. Chriss (1996). Implied Trinomial Trees of the Volatility Smile, *Journal of Derivatives*, Summer, pp. 7–22.

Derman, E., I. Kani and M. Kamal (1997). Trading and Hedging Local Volatility, *Journal of Financial Engineering*, Vol. 6, pp. 233–268.

Derman, E., I. Kani and J. Zou (1996). The Local Volatility Surface: Unlocking the Information in Index Option Prices, *Financial Analysts Journal*, July–August, pp. 25–36.

Duan, J. (1996). Cracking the Smile, *Risk*, December, pp. 55–59.

Dumas, B., J. Fleming and R. Whaley (1998). Implied Volatility Functions: Empirical Tests, *Journal of Finance*, Vol. 53, pp. 2059–2106.

Dupire, B. (1994). Pricing with a Smile, *Risk*, January, pp. 18–20.

Flamouris, D. and D. Giamouridis (2000). Estimating Implied PDFs from American Options: A New Semi-Parametric Approach, Working Paper, City University, London.

Gemmill, G. and N. Kamiyama (1997). International Transmission of Option Volatility and Skewness, Working Paper, City University, London.

Gemmill, G. and A. Saflekos (1999). How Useful are Implied Distributions? Evidence from Stock-Index Options, Working Paper, City University, London.

Gentle, D. (1996). Mind the Curves, *IFR*, Issue 52, pp. 16–18.

Hartvig, N., J. Jensen and J. Pedersen (1999). Risk Neutral Densities of the 'Christmas Tree' Type, Working Paper, Aarhus University.

Hodges, H. (1996). Arbitrage Bounds on the Implied Volatility Strike and Term Structures of European-Style Options, *Journal of Derivatives*, Summer, pp. 23–35.

Huang, J. and J. Pang (2000). A Mathematical Programming with Equilibrium Constraints Approach to the Implied Volatility Surface of American Options, *Journal of Computational Finance*, Fall, pp. 21–56.

Hull, J. and W. Suo (2000). A Test of the Use of the Implied Volatility Function Model to Price Exotic Options, Working Paper, Queens University.

Jackson, N., E. Suli and S. Howison (1998). Computation of Deterministic Volatility Surfaces, *Journal of Computational Finance*, Winter, pp. 5–32.

Jackwerth, J. (1997). Generalized Binomial Trees, *Journal of Derivatives*, Winter, pp. 7–17.

Jackwerth, J. (1999). Option-Implied Risk Neutral Distributions and Implied Binomial Trees: A Literature Review, *Journal of Derivatives*, Winter, pp. 66–82.

Jackwerth, J. and M. Rubinstein (1996). Recovering Probability Distributions from Option Prices, *Journal of Finance*, Vol. 51, pp. 1611–1631.

Jackwerth, J. and M. Rubinstein (1998). Recovering Stochastic Processes from Option Prices, Working Paper, University of Wisconsin.

Jondeau, E. and M. Rockinger (1999). Reading the Smile: The Message Conveyed by Methods which Infer Risk Neutral Densities, Working Paper, HEC.

Kamal, M. and E. Derman (1997). The Patterns of Change in Implied Index Volatilities, Goldman Sachs Quantitative Strategies Research Note.

Kratka, M. (1998). No Mystery Behind the Smile, *Risk*, April, pp. 67–71.

Lagnado, R. and S. Osher (1997a). A Technique for Calibrating Derivative Security Pricing Models: Numerical Solutions of an Inverse Problem, *Journal of Computational Finance*, Fall, pp. 13–25.

Lagnado, R. and S. Osher (1997b). Reconciling Differences, *Risk*, April, pp. 79–83.

Laurent, J. and D. Leisen (1998). Building a Consistent Pricing Model from Observed Option Prices, Working Paper, University of Bonn.

Li, A. (1998). A One-Factor Volatility Smile Model with Closed-Form Solutions for European Options, Working Paper, ABN-AMRO.

Li, F. (2000). Option Pricing: How Flexible Should the SPD be?, *Journal of Derivatives*, Summer, pp. 49–66.

Malz, A. (1997). Estimating the Probability Distribution of the Future Exchange Rate from Option Prices, *Journal of Derivatives*, Winter, pp. 18–36.

Masson, J. and S. Perrakis (1997). A Jumping Smile, Working Paper, University of Ottawa.

Mayhew, S. (1995a). Implied Volatility, *Financial Analysts Journal*, July–August, pp. 8–20.

Mayhew, S. (1995b). On Estimating the Risk-Neutral Probability Distribution Implied by Option Prices, Working Paper, Purdue University.

Melick, W. and C. Thomas (1997). Recovering an Asset's Implied PDF from Option Prices: An Application to Crude Oil during the Gulf Crisis, *Journal of Financial and Quantitative Analysis*, Vol. 32, pp. 91–115.

Mirfendereski, D. and R. Rebonato (1999). Closed-Form Solutions for Option Pricing in the Presence of Volatility Smiles: A Density-Function Approach, Working Paper, NatWest.

Mixon, S. (2000). The Implied Volatility Term Structure of Stock Index Options, Working Paper, UBS Warburg.

Nagot, I. and R. Trommsdorff (1999). The Tree of Knowledge, *Risk*, August, pp. 99–102.

Nakamura, H. and S. Shiratsuka (1999). Extracting Market Expectations from Option Prices, Working Paper, Bank of Japan.

Pena, I., G. Rubio and G. Serna (1999). Why Do We Smile? On the Determinants of the Implied Volatility Function, *Journal of Banking and Finance*, Vol. 23, pp. 1151–1180.

Rosenberg, J. (1996). Pricing Multivariate Contingent Claims Using Estimated Risk-Neutral Density Functions, *Journal of International Money and Finance*, Vol. 17, pp. 229–247.

Rubinstein, M. (1994). Implied Binomial Trees, *Journal of Finance*, Vol. 49, pp. 771–818.

Rubinstein, M. (1995). As Simple as One, Two, Three, *Risk*, January, pp. 44–47.

Rubinstein, M. (1998). Edgeworth Binomial Trees, *Journal of Derivatives*, Spring, pp. 20–27.

Samperi, D. (1998). Implied Trees in Incomplete Markets, Working Paper, Decision Synergy.

Samperi, D. (2000). Model Calibration Using Entropy and Geometry, Working Paper, Decision Synergy.

Sherrick, B., P. Garcia and V. Tirupattur (1996). Recovering Probabilistic Information from Option Prices: Tests of Distributional Assumptions, *Journal of Futures Markets*, Vol. 16, pp. 545–560.

Shimko, D. (1991). Beyond Implied Volatility: Probability Distributions and Hedge Ratios Implied by Option Prices, Working Paper, University of Southern California.

Shimko, D. (1993). Bounds of Probability, *Risk*, April, pp. 33–37.

Shiratsuka, S. (1999). Information Content of Implied Probability Distributions: Empirical Studies of Japanese Stock Price Index Options, Working Paper, Bank of Japan.

Skiadopoulos, G., S. Hodges and L. Clewlow (2000). The Dynamics of the S&P 500 Implied Volatility Surface, *Review of Derivatives Research*, Vol. 3, pp. 263–282.

Soderlind, P. and L. Svensson (1996). New Techniques to Extract Market Expectations from Financial Instruments, Working Paper, Stockholm School of Economics.

Tompkins, R. (1999). Implied Volatility Surfaces: Uncovering Regularities for Options on Financial Futures, Working Paper, Financial Options Research Centre, University of Warwick.

Tompkins, R. (2000). Stock Index Futures Markets: Stochastic Volatility Models and Smiles, Working Paper, Vienna University of Technology.

Tsiveriotis, K. and N. Chriss (1998). Pricing with a Difference, *Risk*, February, pp. 80–83.

Zou, J. and E. Derman (1997). Monte Carlo Valuation of Path Dependent Options on Indexes with a Volatility Smile, *Journal of Financial Engineering*, Vol. 6, pp. 149–168.

OPTION HEDGING

Cash Market Hedging

Ahn, H., A. Muni and G. Swindle (1997). Misspecified Asset Price Models and Robust Hedging Strategies, *Applied Mathematical Finance*, Vol. 4, pp. 21–36.

Avellaneda, M. and A. Paras (1994). Dynamic Hedging Portfolios for Derivative Securities in the Presence of Large Transaction Costs, *Applied Mathematical Finance*, Vol. 1, pp. 165–193.

Bensaid, B., J. Lesne, H. Pagès and J. Scheinkman (1992). Derivative Asset Pricing with Transaction Costs, *Mathematical Finance*, Vol. 2, pp. 63–86.

Bergman, Y. (1981). A Characterization of Portfolio Strategies, Working Paper, University of California at Berkeley.

Bermin, H. (2000). Hedging Options: The Malliavin Calculus Approach versus the Delta Hedging Approach, Working Paper, Lund University.

Bertsimas, D., L. Kogan, A. Lo (1997). Pricing and Hedging Derivative Securities in Incomplete Markets: An ε-Arbitrage Approach, Working Paper, MIT.

Bertsimas, D., L. Kogan and A. Lo (2000). When is Time Continuous?, *Journal of Financial Economics*, Vol. 55, pp. 173–204.

Bossaerts, P. and P. Hillion (1994). Local Parametric Analysis of Hedging in Discrete Time, Working Paper, California Institute of Technology.

Boyle, P. and D. Emanuel (1980). Discretely Adjusted Option Hedges, *Journal of Financial Economics*, Vol. 8, pp. 259–282.

Boyle, P. and X. Lin (1997). Valuation of Options on Several Risky Assets when there are Transaction Costs, in: P. Boyle, G. Pennacchi and P. Ritchken (eds.), *Advances in Futures and Options Research*, Vol. 9, Jai Press, pp. 111–129.

Boyle, P. and K. Tan (1994). Lure of the Linear, *Risk*, April, pp. 43–46.

Boyle, P. and T. Vorst (1992). Option Replication in Discrete Time with Transaction Costs, *Journal of Finance*, Vol. 47, pp. 217–293.

Bhushan, R., A. Mello and H. Neuhaus (1991). A Portfolio Approach to Risk Reduction in Discretely Rebalanced Option Hedges, Working Paper, Massachusetts Institute of Technology.

Bouchaud, J., G. Lori and D. Sornette (1996). Real-World Options, *Risk*, March, pp. 61–65.

Carr, P. and R. Jarrow (1990). The Stop-Loss Start-Gain Paradox and Option Valuation: A New Decomposition into Intrinsic and Time Value, *Review of Financial Studies*, Vol. 3, pp. 469–492.

Chriss, N. and M. Ong (1995). Digitals Defused, *Risk*, December, pp. 56–59.

Crouhy, M. and D. Galai (1995). Hedging with a Volatility Term Structure, *Journal of Derivatives*, Spring, pp. 45–52.

Davis, M. and J. Clark (1995). A Note on Super-Replicating Strategies, in: S. Howison, F. Kelly and P. Wilmott, *Mathematical Models in Finance*, Chapman & Hall, pp. 35–44.

Davis, M., V. Panas and T. Zariphopoulou (1993). European Option Pricing with Transaction Costs, *SIAM Journal of Control and Optimization*, Vol. 31, pp. 470–493.

Dennis, P. and R. Rendleman (1995). An LP Approach to Synthetic Option Replication with Transaction Costs and Multiple Security Selection, in: P. Boyle, F. Longstaff and P. Ritchken (eds.), *Advances in Futures and Options Research*, Vol. 8, Jai Press, pp. 53–84.

Dewynne, J., A. Whalley and P. Wilmott (1995). Path-Dependent Options and Transaction Costs, in: S. Howison, F. Kelly and P. Wilmott, *Mathematical Models in Finance*, Chapman & Hall, pp. 67–79.

Dolbear, S. (1992). Hedging Lookback Options: An Empirical Analysis, in: S. Hodges (ed.), *Options: Recent Advances in Theory and Practice*, Vol. 2, Manchester University Press, pp. 3–12.

Dumas, B. and E. Luciano (1991). An Exact Solution to a Dynamic Portfolio Choice Problem Under Transaction Costs, *Journal of Finance*, Vol. 46, pp. 577–595.

Duque, J. and D. Paxson (1994). Implied Volatility and Dynamic Hedging, *Review of Futures Markets*, Vol. 13, pp. 381–421.

Edirisinghe, C., V. Naik and R. Uppal (1993). Optimal Replication of Options with Transaction Costs and Trading Restrictions, *Journal of Financial and Quantitative Analysis*, Vol. 28, pp. 117–138.

Esipov, S. and I. Vaysburd (1999). On the Profit and Loss Distribution of Dynamic Hedging Strategies, *International Journal of Theoretical and Applied Finance*, Vol. 2, pp. 131–152.

Figlewski, S. (1989). Options Arbitrage in Imperfect Markets, *Journal of Finance*, Vol. 44, pp. 1289–1311.

Figlewski, S. and T. Green (1999). Market Risk and Model Risk for a Financial Institution Writing Options, *Journal of Finance*, Vol. 54, pp. 1465–1499.

Flesaker, B. and L. Hughston (1994). Contingent Claim Replication in Continuous Time with Transaction Costs, Working Paper, Merrill Lynch.

French, D. and G. Henderson (1981). Substitute Hedged Option Portfolios: Theory and Evidence, *Journal of Financial Research*, Spring, pp. 21–31.

Gallus, C. (1999). Exploding Hedging Errors for Digital Options, *Finance and Stochastics*, Vol. 3, pp. 187–201.

Garman, M. (1992). Charm School, *Risk*, July–August, pp. 53–56.

Gatheral, J. (1997). Delta Hedging with Uncertain Volatility, in: I. Nelken (ed.), *Volatility in the Capital Markets*, Glenlake, pp. 95–112.

Gilster, J. (1990). The Systematic Risk of Discretely Rebalanced Option Hedges, *Journal of Financial and Quantitative Analysis*, Vol. 25, pp. 507–516.

Gilster, J. (1998). Discretely Rebalanced Option Hedges: Much Riskier Than We Thought, Working Paper, Michigan State University.

Gilster, J. and W. Lee (1984). The Effects of Transaction Costs and Different Borrowing and Lending Rates on the Option Pricing Model: A Note, *Journal of Finance*, Vol. 39, pp. 1215–1221.

Grannan, E. and G. Swindle (1996). Minimizing Transaction Costs of Option Hedging Strategies, *Mathematical Finance*, Vol. 6, pp. 341–364.

Gupta, A. (1997). On Neutral Ground, *Risk*, July, pp. 37–41.

Henrotte, P. (1993). Transaction Costs and Duplication Strategies, Working Paper, Stanford University.

Hodges, S. and L. Clewlow (1993). Optimal Delta Hedging Under Transaction Costs, Working Paper, Financial Options Research Centre, University of Warwick.

Hodges, S. and A. Neuberger (1989). Optimal Replication of Contingent Claims under Transaction Costs, *Review of Futures Markets*, Vol. 8, pp. 222–239.

Hoggard, T., E. Whalley and P. Wilmott (1994). Hedging Option Portfolios in the Presence of Transaction Costs, in: D. Chance and R. Trippi (eds.), *Advances in Futures and Options Research*, Vol. 7, Jai Press, pp. 21–35.

Hull, J. and A. White (1987). Hedging Through the Cap: Implications for Market Efficiency, Hedging and Option Pricing, *International Options Journal*, Vol. 4, pp. 17–22.

Kabanov, Y. and M. Safarian (1997). On Leland's Strategy of Option Pricing with Transaction Costs, *Finance and Stochastics*, Vol. 1, pp. 239–250.

Kamal, M. and E. Derman (1999). Correcting Black–Scholes, *Risk*, January, pp. 82–85.

Kat, H. (1992). *The Efficiency of Dynamic Trading Strategies in Imperfect Markets*, Ph.D. Thesis, University of Amsterdam.

Kat, H. (1996). Delta Hedging of S&P 500 Options: Cash versus Futures Market Execution, *Journal of Derivatives*, Spring, pp. 6–25.

Leland, H. (1985). Option Pricing and Replication with Transaction Costs, *Journal of Finance*, Vol. 40, pp. 1283–1301.

Levy, E. (1991). Capitalising on Correlation, *Risk*, May, pp. 30–33.

Mercurio, F. and T. Vorst (1995). Option Pricing and Hedging in Discrete Time with Transaction Costs and Incomplete Markets, Working Paper, Erasmus University, Rotterdam.

Mercurio, F. and T. Vorst (1996). Option Pricing with Hedging at Fixed Trading Dates, *Applied Mathematical Finance*, Vol. 3, pp. 135–158.

Mohamed, B. (1994). Simulations of Transaction Costs and Optimal Rehedging, *Applied Mathematical Finance*, Vol. 1, pp. 49–62.

Neuhaus, H. (1989). *Option Valuation and Hedging under Transaction Costs*, Ph.D. Thesis, London Business School.

Neuhaus, H. and Y. Kusuda (1997). Pricing and Hedging Equity Options: The Effect of Market Structure and Transaction Costs, in: Risk/Lehman Brothers, *Equity Derivatives*, Risk Publications, pp. 199–222.

Omberg, E. (1991). On the Theory of Perfect Hedging, in: F. Fabozzi (ed.), *Advances in Futures and Options Research*, Vol. 5, Jai Press, pp. 1–29.

Panas, V. (1993). *Option Pricing with Transaction Costs*, Ph.D. Thesis, Imperial College.

Perrakis, S. and J. Lefoll (2000). Option Pricing and Replication with Transaction Costs and Dividends, *Journal of Economic Dynamics & Control*, Vol. 24, pp. 1527–1561.

Reiss, A. (1999). Option Replication with Large Transaction Costs, *OR Spektrum*, Vol. 21, pp. 49–70.

Renault, E. and N. Touzi (1993). Option Hedging and Implicit Volatilities, Working Paper, University of Toulouse.

Robins, R. and B. Schachter (1994). Analysis of Risk in Discretely Rebalanced Option Hedges and Delta Based Techniques, *Management Science*, Vol. 40, pp. 798–808.

Robins, R., R. Sanders and B. Schachter (1996). An Empirical Investigation of Variance Reduction Through Non-Delta-Neutral Hedging, *Journal of Derivatives*, Winter, pp. 59–69.

Rubinstein, M. and H. Leland (1981). Replicating Options with Positions in Stock and Cash, *Financial Analysts Journal*, July–August, pp. 63–72.

Rumsey, J. (1991). An Optimum Rebalancing Schedule for Delta Hedging, Working Paper, University of Toronto.

Schachter, B. (1992). Breaking Up Is Hard to Do: The Risks in the Financial Engineering of Customized Options, *Journal of Financial Engineering*, Vol. 1, pp. 133–149.

Schaffer, S. (1989). Structuring An Option to Facilitate Replication With Transaction Costs, *Economic Letters*, Vol. 31, pp. 183–187.

Seidenverg, E. (1988). A Case of Confused Identity, *Financial Analysts Journal*, July–August, pp. 63–67.

Soner, H., S. Shreve and J. Cvitanic (1994). There is No Nontrivial Hedging Portfolio for Option Pricing with Transaction Costs, Working Paper, University of Minnesota.

Toft, K. (1996). On the Mean–Variance Tradeoff in Option Replication with Transaction Costs, *Journal of Financial and Quantitative Analysis*, Vol. 31, pp. 233–263.

Whalley, E. and P. Wilmott (1993a). A Comparison of Hedging Strategies, Working Paper, Oxford University.

Whalley, E. and P. Wilmott (1993b). Counting the Costs, *Risk*, October, pp. 59–66.

Whalley, E. and P. Wilmott (1993c). An Asymptotic Analysis of the Davis, Panas & Zariphopoulou Model for Option Pricing with Transaction Costs, Working Paper, Oxford University.

Whalley, E. and P. Wilmott (1994a). A Hedging Strategy and Option Valuation Model with Transaction Costs, Working Paper, Oxford University.

Whalley, E. and P. Wilmott (1994b). Hedge with an Edge, *Risk*, October, pp. 82–85.

Whalley, E. and P. Wilmott (1994c). Optimal Hedging of Options with Small but Arbitrary Transaction Cost Structure, Working Paper, Oxford University.

Whalley, E. and P. Wilmott (1997). Key Results in Discrete Hedging and Transaction Costs, in: A. Konishi and R. Dattatreya (eds.), *Frontiers in Derivatives*, Irwin, pp. 183–195.

Wilmott, P. (1994). Discrete Charms, *Risk*, March, pp. 48–51.

Parity and Symmetry Relationships

Babbel, D. and L. Eisenberg (1992). Generalized Put–Call Parity, *Journal of Financial Engineering*, Vol. 1, pp. 243–263.

Carr, P. (1994a). European Put Call Symmetry, Working Paper, Cornell University.

Carr, P. (1994b). European Put Call Symmetry with Smiles, Working Paper, Cornell University.

Carr, P. and M. Chesney (1997). American Put Call Symmetry, Working Paper, Cornell University.

Haug, E. (1999). Barrier Put–Call Transformations, Working Paper, Tempus Financial Engineering.

McDonald, R. and M. Schroder (1998). A Parity Result for American Options, *Journal of Computational Finance*, Spring, pp. 5–13.

Merton, R. (1973). The Relationship Between Put and Call Option Prices: Comment, *Journal of Finance*, Vol. 28, pp. 183–184.

Stoll, H. (1969). The Relationship Between Put and Call Option Prices, *Journal of Finance*, Vol. 24, pp. 802–824.

Stoll, H. (1973). The Relationship Between Put and Call Option Prices: Reply, *Journal of Finance*, Vol. 28, pp. 185–187.

(Semi-)Static Hedging

Andersen, L. and J. Andreasen (2000). Static Barriers, *Risk*, September, pp. 120–122.

Andersen, L., J. Andreasen and D. Eliezer (2000). Static Replication of Barrier Options: Some General Results, Working Paper, Gen Re.

Aparicio, S. and L. Clewlow (1997). A Comparison of Alternative Methods for Hedging Exotic Options, Working Paper, Financial Options Research Centre, University of Warwick.

Avellaneda, M. and A. Paras (1996). Managing the Volatility Risk of Portfolios of Derivative Securities: The Lagrangian Uncertain Volatility Model, *Applied Mathematical Finance*, Vol. 3, pp. 21–52.

Avellaneda, M., A. Levy and A. Paras (1995). Pricing and Hedging Derivative Securities in Markets with Uncertain Volatilities, *Applied Mathematical Finance*, Vol. 2, pp. 73–88.

Bowie, J. and P. Carr (1994). Static Simplicity, *Risk*, August, pp. 45–49.

Brown, H., D. Hobson and L. Rogers (1998). Robust Hedging of Barrier Options, Working Paper, University of Bath.

Carr, P. and A. Chou (1997a). Breaking Barriers, *Risk*, September, pp. 139–145.

Carr, P. and A. Chou (1997b). Hedging Complex Barrier Options, Working Paper, Morgan Stanley.

Carr, P. and J. Picron (1999). Static Hedging of Timing Risk, *Journal of Derivatives*, Spring, pp. 57–70.

Carr, P., K. Ellis and V. Gupta (1998). Static Hedging of Exotic Options, *Journal of Finance*, Vol. 53, pp. 1165–1191.

Carr, P., A. Lipton and D. Madan (2000). Going with the Flow, *Risk*, August, pp. 85–89.

Chou, A. and G. Georgiev (1998). A Uniform Approach to Static Replication, *Journal of Risk*, Fall, pp. 73–87.

Derman, E., D. Ergener and I. Kani (1994). Forever Hedged, *Risk*, September, pp. 139–145.

Derman, E., D. Ergener and I. Kani (1995). Static Options Replication, *Journal of Derivatives*, Summer, pp. 78–95.

El Karoui, N. and M. Jeanblanc-Picque (1997). Exotic Options Without Mathematics, Working Paper, Université Pierre et Marie Curie.

Hobson, D. (1998). Robust Hedging of the Lookback Option, *Finance and Stochastics*, Vol. 2, pp. 329–347.

Ingersoll, J. (1998). Approximating American Options and Other Financial Contracts Using Barrier Derivatives, *Journal of Computational Finance*, Fall, pp. 85–112.

Ingersoll, J. (2000). Valuation of Derivatives Contracts Using Payoff Event Approximation, Working Paper, Yale University.

Neuberger, A. and S. Hodges (1998). Rational Bounds on the Prices of Exotic Options, Working Paper, Financial Options Research Centre, University of Warwick.

Sbuelz, A. (1998). A General Treatment of Barrier Options, Working Paper, London Business School.

Thomsen, H. (1998). *Barrier Options: Evaluation and Hedging*, Ph.D. Thesis, University of Aarhus.

Toft, K. and C. Xuan (1998). How Well Can Barrier Options Be Hedged by a Static Portfolio of Standard Options, *Journal of Financial Engineering*, Vol. 7, pp. 147–175.

Tompkins, R. (1997). Static versus Dynamic Hedging of Exotic Options: An Evaluation of Hedge Performance via Simulation, *Net Exposure*, November.

Taylor Series Hedging

Alexander, G. and M. Stutzer (1996). A Graphical Note on European Put Thetas, *Journal of Futures Markets*, Vol. 16, pp. 201–209.

Ashraff, J., J. Tarczon and W. Wu (1995). Safe Crossing, *Risk*, July, pp. 56–57.

Bermin, H. and A. Kohatsu-Higa (1999). Local Volatility Changes in the Black–Scholes Model, Working Paper, Lund University.

Carr, P. (1993). Deriving Derivatives of Derivative Securities, Working Paper, Cornell University.

Chambers, D. and N. Lacey (1990). More Generalized Hedging Models for Options, in: F. Fabozzi, *Managing Institutional Assets*, Harper & Row, pp. 585–602.

Clewlow, L. and S. Hodges (1994). Gamma Hedging in Incomplete Markets with Transaction Costs, Working Paper, Financial Options Research Centre, University of Warwick.

Clewlow, L., S. Hodges, R. Martinez, M. Selby, C. Strickland and X. Xu (1993). Hedging Option Position Risk: An Empirical Examination, Working Paper, Financial Options Research Centre, University of Warwick.

Figlewski, S. (1987). Topics in Stock Index Futures and Options: Insuring Portfolio Insurance, First Boston Equity Research.

Frye, J. (1988). Greek Alphabet Soup: A Recipe for Success, *Risk*, March.

Garman, M. (1976). An Algebra for Evaluating Hedge Portfolios, *Journal of Financial Economics*, Vol. 3, pp. 403–427.

Haug, E. (1993). Opportunities and Perils of Using Option Sensitivities, *Journal of Financial Engineering*, Vol. 2, pp. 253–269.

Hull, J. and A. White (1987). Hedging the Risk from Writing Foreign Currency Options, *Journal of International Money and Finance*, Vol. 6, pp. 131–152.

Jones, E. (1984). Option Arbitrage and Strategy with Large Price Changes, *Journal of Financial Economics*, Vol. 13, pp. 91–113.

Malz, A. (2000). Vega Risk and the Smile, Working Paper, Riskmetrics Group.

Naik, V. (1991). Option Trading Strategies for Hedging Jumps in Asset Values and Return Volatility, Working Paper, University of British Columbia.

Rendleman, R. (1995). An LP Approach to Option Portfolio Selection, in: P. Boyle, F. Longstaff and P. Ritchken (eds.), *Advances in Futures and Options Research*, Vol. 8, Jai Press, pp. 31–52.

Rubinstein, M. (1978). A New Classification of Option Positions, Working Paper, University of California at Berkeley.

Taylor, J. and M. Smith (1987). Options Replication, *Intermarket*, December, pp. 16–55.

BOOKS ON (EQUITY) DERIVATIVES

Bhansali, V. (1998). *Pricing and Managing Exotic and Hybrid Options*, McGraw-Hill.

Brockhaus, O., A. Ferraris, C. Gallus, D. Long, R. Martin and M. Overhaus (1999). *Modelling and Hedging Equity Derivatives*, Risk Books.

Brockhaus, O., M. Farkas, A. Ferraris, D. Long and M. Overhaus (2000). *Equity Derivatives and Market Risk Models*, Risk Books.

Chriss, N. (1997). *Black–Scholes and Beyond: Option Pricing Models*, Irwin.

Clewlow, L. and C. Strickland (1998). *Implementing Derivatives Models*, Wiley.

Cox, J. and M. Rubinstein (1985). *Options Markets*, Prentice-Hall.

Haug, E. (1998). *The Complete Guide to Option Pricing Formulas*, McGraw-Hill.

Hull, J. (1999). *Options, Futures, and Other Derivative Securities*, Prentice-Hall.

Jarrow, R. and A. Rudd (1983). *Option Pricing*, Irwin.

Jarrow, R. and S. Turnbull (1996). *Derivative Securities*, South-Western.

Nelken, I. (2000). *Pricing, Hedging and Trading Exotic Options*, McGraw-Hill.

Ravindran, K. (1998). *Customized Derivatives*, McGraw-Hill.

Rubinstein, M. (1998). *Derivatives: A PowerPlus Picture Book*, In-The-Money (see www.in-the-money.com).

Taleb, N. (1997). *Dynamic Hedging: Managing Vanilla and Exotic Options*, Wiley.

Wilmott, P. (1998). *Derivatives*, Wiley.

Wilmott, P., J. Dewynne and S. Howison (1993). *Option Pricing; Mathematical Models and Computation*, Oxford Financial Press.

Zhang, P. (1997). *Exotic Options: A Guide to Second Generation Options*, World Scientific.

Index